Windows MFC Programming I

(3rd Edition)

Vic Broquard

Windows MFC Programming I
(3rd Edition)
Vic Broquard

Broquard eBooks
103 Timberlane
East Peoria, IL 61611
author@Broquard-eBooks.com
ISBN: 978-1-941415-57-3

Table of Contents

To all of my dedicated, persevering students,
and to L. Ron Hubbard, who taught me to "Simplify"

Preface

Learning to program Windows applications is most challenging; some call it a "black art." To master the material presented in this book, the industry typically allows a beginner four months of forty hour weeks. Don't panic just yet! I have been successfully teaching Windows programming at a junior college for some time now and we just do not have that kind of time available in a sixteen-week semester. This book greatly shortens that learning process!

The book begins with the very fundamentals and, in a step by step, gradient manner, develops most all of the basic Windows programming techniques. There are often many different ways to accomplish the same task. So as you move from example to example, expect to see alternative approaches illustrated. This book is not a reference manual; rather, expect to see the "whys" and "how comes" that lie behind many of the approaches and techniques. It is my opinion that if you have a feel for what is really going on, you can do a better job of programming and debugging.

I have included many of the easier to use, Windows features that can be handled easily at a beginning level.

Perhaps the most valuable aspect of this book are the sample programs which are designed to provide you with a usable shell or model to follow in your applications. The later chapter examples are not just snippets of coding that illustrate the topic at hand, but rather are more robust, real world examples. Two chapters illustrate how printing and print preview are done. In Chapter 7, you will see how to create various dialogs. In Chapter 9, one sample program shows you several methods of displaying a bmp image on the screen as well as numerous "special effects" to catch your user's attention. One Chapter 14 sample program shows you how to setup animated presentations for business use. Alternatively another Chapter 14 sample shows how to begin some game animation using the fast DIB Section. In Chapter 15, the complex document-view architecture is discussed in depth. Here splitter windows are used to present a left narrow window containing the editable company sales data while on the right side is a bar chart plot of that data which automatically redraws itself as the sales data are changed by the user.

There are a number of very important application design issues that are written this way.

Design Rule 1:

They highlight some of the potential traps and pitfalls that lie in waiting.

Perhaps the biggest barrier to learning Windows programming are the **enormous** number of identifiers, key values, the API (Application Programming Interface) and the MFC (Microsoft Foundation Classes) class member functions and variable names. The name-space pollution exceeds anything that I have ever come across, short of writing an operating system. For a beginner and more advanced reader, this proliferation of **must know** names and identifiers is nothing short of bewildering. In fact, I still remember my first session with Windows programming and the untold hours spent just trying to figure out what names had to be coded exactly as given and what were under my control! One of the **key** features of this book is that you will always have a greater **certainty** about what names must be coded as-is and what you have control over.

Typeface conventions are designed to aid you in knowing at a glance what names are yours and what are not. **All** variable names are in lowercase or begin with a lowercase letter; if it's lowercase, it's likely yours to name, unless it begins with **m_**. The two exceptions are **#define** names which by convention are always uppercase and class member function names which are capitalized. Even though you may use any convention desired in your coding, when you refer to this book, the guess work or hunting has been eliminated.

What do you already need to know to make effective use of this book? My assumption is that you know C and C++ and are comfortable with them. You do not need to be a C++ master. But you do need to know how to derive new classes from existing classes and how to allocate and use objects. Many introductory books spend several chapters on a "crash course" in C++. I do not.

On the other hand, the book **does not** use the famous or infamous "Application and Class Wizards" until the appropriate point in your learning. Microsoft provides two wizards that are supposed to enable one to rapidly create an application—button pushing style. There are many books on the market that are devoted to how to use the wizards. Some swear by them, others curse them. Since I am involved in both the teaching and the consulting industries, I have seen both viewpoints. It is my opinion and the opinion of many of my past students that the "wizards" are not the best beginning point for learning how to program Windows unless you prefer magic coding of which you have no idea what it really does. Rather the "wizards" should be considered an advanced topic, used by those who already are familiar with Windows programming.

Thus, when we get to the creation of dialogs in Chapter 7, the Class Wizard is introduced because at this point it is very useful to the programmer. Then, in Chapter 15 the AppWizard is introduced because it can create the basic shell program that we need for the document-view applications. When you have completed your study of this book, you will find yourself prepared to fully explore the "wizards" and, most importantly, you will be able to make good, effective use of them.

If you have any questions, problems, comments, want to report bugs, or just to chat, I can be reached at author@Broquard-eBooks.com.

Download your sample programs and test data that accompanies this book at: http://www.broquard-ebooks.com/pb/winmfci and take the appropriate link.

Chapter 1 The Basics of Windows Programming

Introduction to Windows Programming

For most of us, our programming background has been C++ text-based DOS programming. In text mode, the fundamental unit of I/O is a character and perhaps its screen color attribute byte. The DOS screen most frequently has 25 rows of 80 characters with each discrete position capable of holding one character. The location of a specific character on the screen is given by its column and row number, thought of as the x (column) and y (row) coordinates. Each character position occupies the same number of pixels both horizontally and vertically. Some characters use only a few horizontal pixels (the letter I) while others a maximum number (the letters w and m). The character nature of the text-based mode makes it relatively easy for a program to display a series of characters. And nearly all Business Data Processing programs follow the programming logic of: Input a record, Process the record, Output the record. This is the programming logic style with which non-Windows programmers are familiar and comfortable.

In contrast to the DOS text-based modes, Windows is a graphical operating environment. The graphics modes present new and huge complexities as compared to the text modes. The fundamental unit of I/O is now a single pixel. Access to a pixel is still by x and y coordinates, however, the resolution available varies widely along with the number of colors that can be simultaneously displayed on the screen.

The higher the resolution, the more pixels per inch, the finer the details, the better the resultant image. Perhaps the most commonly used graphics mode contains 1024x768 pixels with anywhere from 256-colors to true color mode. Each color mode has its own unique internal scheme for storing the pixel values. In the older 256-color mode, one pixel's color is stored in one byte. Thus, in 1024x786 256-color mode, 1024 times 768 or 786,432 bytes are required to store one screen image. A true color image contains four times that amount!

Windows owns the screen and provides the programmer with a standard method of sending data to the screen, providing device independence for the programmer. Output in graphics mode is pixel-based. Gone is the simple idea of displaying a single character, let alone a character string! A character is composed of a series of pixels that form a letter. The mapping of how to display characters is contained in a font. And there are numerous fonts available for a program's use.

Gone is the standard spacing or size that a text character occupies. The letter 'I', in some fonts, now occupies only a width of three pixels, off–on–off, whereas the letter 'w' has a larger width in pixels. The impact: in text mode, all characters have the same width; in graphics mode with these variable pitched fonts, characters have a variable width. Note one can force the usage of a fixed font if need be. In a variable pitch font, the two strings—cat and CAT—have completely different widths or lengths in pixels while in the older DOS in text mode, they have the same length! Therefore, in graphics mode, when displaying text in a variable pitched font, one must consider the "average character width" which is an imprecise amount. Columnar alignment of data becomes much more complex with these variable pitched fonts. Further, your display of information is compounded by the user who often wishes to choose both the font and the point size (the overall size of the letters).

For a programmer new to a graphical operating environment, Windows forces a new program design mode. Gone is the familiar Cycle of Data Processing—Input, Process, Output. The overall processing design of **every** Windows application is

```
get a message
while there is another message to process
 process the message
 get another message
end the program
```

This cycle of get and process a message is the highest level logic loop of **every** Windows application! In other words, a Windows application must be a "Message-Driven" application. One of your first hurdles will likely be learning how to write a program using these new message-driven techniques.

But there is more complexity. Imagine that the user has a WordPad session going, a Paintbrush image under construction, and a Solitary game in progress and the user has these all nicely tiled on the screen, moving from one to the other. Suppose you are writing an application that the user is also currently running. Your program no longer owns the screen; it must share it with all the other applications! Further, the user can resize your application window at any time. And, of course, any resizing of your application's window effects what text in your window is actually now visible!

It gets worse. From time to time, a Windows application is called upon to redraw its entire window, part of its window. For example, a dialog box closes, leaving a "black hole." All windows beneath the now gone dialog must re redisplayed. To do this, Windows sends each affected application a point message. Nearly all Windows applications have a function (often called Paint) that, when Windows (or even the application itself) requests it, can at any moment redisplay the application's entire screen! So here we have the idea that the Paint function must have all necessary data at hand to fully or in part redisplay the window's content. Contrast this with a typical DOS program that opens a file, inputs each record, performs the calculations, outputs the corresponding line and repeats this until the end of the file is reached. In a Windows application, the Paint function must have all of the "lines" available to it at any time so it can repaint the screen. Obviously, the data is likely stored in arrays for Paint's usage.

It gets still worse. Windows owns all the devices on the system, including the keyboard! When a key is pressed, Windows sends a message to the active application notifying it that a character has been entered. It is up to the application to figure out what, if anything, is to be done with that character. In DOS-based programs, we are used to using the **cin** stream to input fields of data. Such is forever gone in a Windows application. All such processing actions now take place in the message handler that processes a single character. To input a field, we must store the current character into a buffer and wait for the next character to be entered. Things are starting to get complicated rather quickly.

In a DOS application, one would open the file, read records, and close the file at the end of the job. In a Windows application, this is never done because of the inherent problems with crashes. When a Windows application needs a record (even just the next sequential record), it opens the file, positions to the desired record, reads the required record, and closes the file. Then it processes that record. A Windows application almost never leaves a file open any longer than is needed to retrieve the required record.

As you can see, the programming logic behind a Windows application is **totally** different from the logic of familiar DOS-based applications!

The Windows application programming interface, abbreviated API, consists of over thousands of confusing and sometimes overlapping function calls, hundreds of data structures used to pass the requisite information to these functions, and thousands of possible messages to which your application could be called upon to respond. Learning to write Windows applications is indeed a very daunting challenge and has been called by some a "black art."

Coding the Windows C API

To a programmer, the Windows API appears to be pure C. That is, the functions and methods are strictly C. (Realize that internally, Windows is object-oriented—written with a combination of C++, C, and Microassembler.) The external world interface is a C one.

When learning how Windows works and how to program the functions, one begins by using C. In fact, one could write all of your Windows applications in C alone. However, once the application goes beyond a simple window with perhaps a very, very few dialogs and minimal menu choices, the task of writing the application in C becomes a real nightmare. In the industry, the message processing loop in C is often called "the nightmare switch from Hell."

To preserve sanity, to get applications debugged quickly, to get applications written quickly, you will really want to wrap an object-oriented class library around the Windows API, coding in C++ using the class libraries. In fact, once you become comfortable with the C++ interface, you will **never ever** want to go back to the C nightmare. The wraparound class libraries are manufacturer dependent. At this point in time, the most prevalent library is the Microsoft Foundation Class library that comes with both Microsoft and Borland compiler packages.

The focus of this book is on the MFC. All sample programs are designed for use with the new Visual Studio .NET 2008 version, but both earlier and later versions of the MFC can be used.

The MFC is a shallow encapsulation of the Windows C API. This means that there is often a one-to-one correspondence between an MFC class member function and the corresponding C API function it is encapsulating. However, there are many C API functions that are not encapsulated by any MFC function. Hence, in larger applications, one, at times, does need to make straight API function calls. Additionally, to understand the MFC, one realistically does need to have some understanding of the C API in order to grasp what is being encapsulated and how to use such. There is, then, no escaping, really, a rudimentary knowledge of the underlying C API itself.

In this book, I show both the C API functions along with the MFC encapsulation of those functions. However, the first three chapters deal exclusively with the C API. One must learn first just how a message driven system operates and how to perform rudimentary programming tasks in such an environment. Then, in chapter 4, the actual MFC encapsulation is introduced. The remainder of the book covers the MFC encapsulation.

Common Windows Graphical Objects: a Review of Terms

To begin programming an application in Windows, a programmer must be thoroughly acquainted with the labels assigned to the many graphical elements. Our study of Windows programming begins with a quick review of these key graphical elements. Note the "official" names of these elements as they are often referred to in the literature.

All applications run in a **window** of some kind. Often the application has a border around the main window, facilitating window resizing; this is called a **frame window** and the area inside the frame window is known as the **client window**. Figure 1.1—Main Window Graphical Elements—identifies the major elements of the frame and client windows. All windows have a **title bar**—1—which contains the descriptive name of the application. Each application provides a character string to be used as the window's title; it may be changed while the application is running. For example, the WordPad program inserts the document name before the string " - WordPad". The **active application** or **task** has its title bar highlighted while all inactive applications are not.

Most title bars contain the **system menu icon**—5—used to pull down the **system menu**—6. The system menu normally contains choices for restoring the application, moving the window, resizing the window, minimizing and maximizing the window, closing the application, and task switching. Many of these are programmer-controlled so that it is possible to have a window that cannot be resized or that runs maximized, and so on. When a menu choice is not available, the menu item is **grayed out**. Windows automatically grays some items for you—if you notify Windows that a particular window cannot be resized, the "Size" menu item is grayed. Additionally, the programmer can request Windows to gray out other menu items and "enable" them—as occurs when using the usual cut and paste operations of any editing type application.

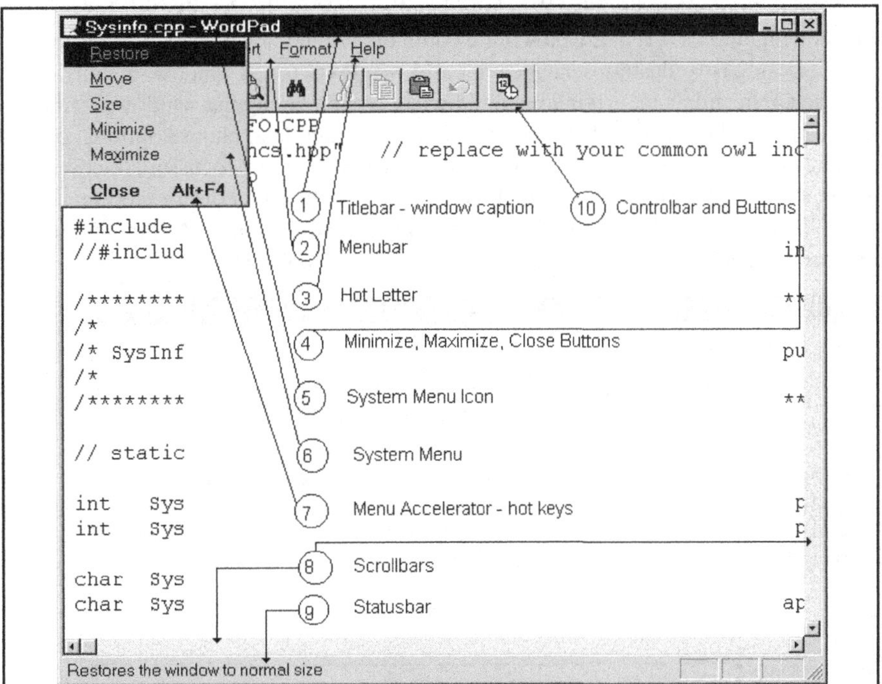

Figure 1.1 Main Windows Graphical Elements

An application may have one or more **menu accelerators**—7. These are hot keys for specific menu options. Here on the system menu, **Alt-F4** is the menu accelerator or hot key for closing the application. Additionally and far more commonly, menu items have an underlined letter, the **hot letter**—3. In the system menu, 'R' for restore; 'M' for move; 'S' for size, and so on. In non system menus, hot keys are programmer-defined; when you set up the menu, you can tell Windows what letter is the hot letter, if any.

Most applications also have a **menu bar**—2. Entries may be dynamically added and removed from the menu bar. Clicking on a menu choice can activate an option or pop up another submenu.

Design Rule 1: All Windows applications should follow the standard Windows look-and-feel design for ease of user operation and speed of user learning.

If you have not yet realized this fact, play around with the applications that you have installed on your system. Look at the way the various menu bars are constructed. For example, you will find that, if the application has anything to do with files, then the first menu item on the left is "Files." "Help" is **always** the last item on the right. If editing is an option, it follows Files. Even the hot keys and often the menu accelerators are the same. This common user interface is a major design advantage of Windows. Thus, well-behaved applications should follow the normal look-and-feel of Windows to greatly aid new users in learning how to use your application.

The title bar also may have one or more buttons on the left—the **minimize-maximize-normalize** buttons and the new close application or '**X**' button. These are application controlled. When your program begins execution, it notifies Windows which of these buttons, if any, are allowed. (You can dynamically alter these as well while the application is running.) Whenever the user activates one of these buttons, Windows sends the application a message telling the application to maximize itself, for example.

With all of the title bar buttons and with the system menu and any user menu bars, ALL of the details of pushing and releasing, selecting, mouse cursor movement, hot letter pressing, and accelerator keying is done by Windows itself. The application does not have to do anything other than tell Windows what title bar options are needed and how to construct the menu bar. Windows sends the program messages notifying the application whenever any of these have been activated by the user. In other words, you code only a minuscule amount to get a maximum amount of response!

Scrollbars—8—come in two types and two kinds. There are vertical and horizontal scrollbars; an application may have either or both or none. There can be **system scrollbars** that are provided and controlled by Windows itself. These scrollbars are always present, unless the application notifies Windows to remove them. Windows sends the application messages when the user is activating them. There are also **user scrollbars** that the applicaton controls totally. User scrollbars may dynamically appear and disappear as the application chooses; they are fully controlled by the application. Generally, system scrollbars are easier to program because Windows handles most of the details.

Control bars with buttons—10—are now quite common. Often they are called **tool bars** or **decorations**.

Figure 1.2 Open Modal Dialog Box illustrates the idea of **child windows**. Child windows are any subsequent windows that open over the top of the application's main window; child windows can be regular windows or dialogs.

A **dialog box** is a smaller window that permits the user to enter data, choose options, or similar actions. **Modal dialog boxes**, when launched (from menu choices most often), receive the input focus and the user is limited to completing actions in that dialog box only; the application's normal operations are halted until the user terminates the dialog box in some manner, at which time the dialog box disappears. **Modeless dialog boxes**, in contrast, can remain on the screen. The user can task-switch between the application and the dialog box. The Find-Replace Dialog Box is modeless.

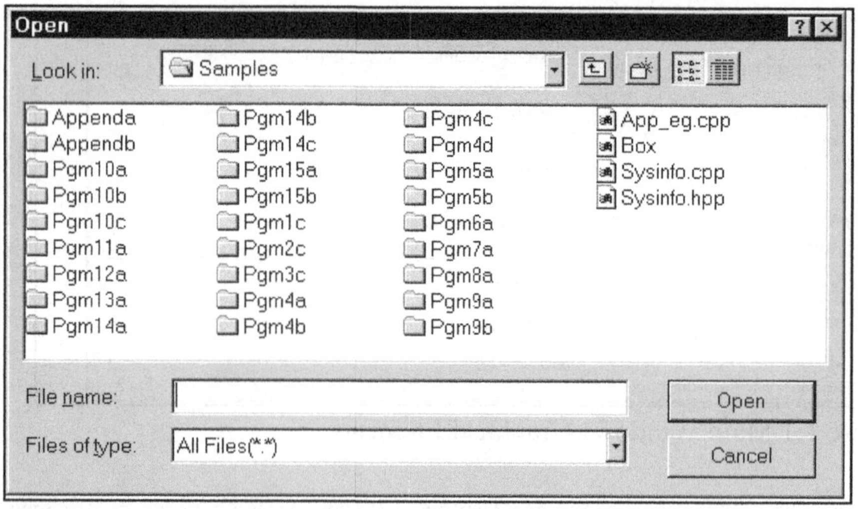

Figure 1.2 Open Modal Dialog Box

Further, Windows provides a series of standard dialog boxes for easy application use, known as the **common dialogs**. The Open File dialog is one of these. The application merely needs to request this dialog and Windows provides the box, handles all user entry, returns the filename chosen back to the calling program. There is a common dialog box for sending a document to the printer and one for choosing a font. Unless there is a compelling reason not to, all applications should utilize these common dialogs because the user instantly knows how to make the proper choices.

A dialog box can contain many different graphical elements, known as **controls**. **Push button controls**—"Open"—permit instant user responses. The **default push button** is differently highlighted and in Figure 1.2 is the "Open" button. Push buttons provide choices, such as "OK" or "Cancel," or to launch further dialogs or windows. Most often, their position is the upper left corner or bottom of a dialog box.

List Box Controls—the main window area shown here with folders and files—display a list of things for the user to see or choose. When the number of items in the list exceeds the list box size, scrollbars are used. **Combo Box Controls** combine a push button and a drop-down list box. Here the "Files of Type" is a combo box. The chosen entry from the list appears in the combobox window after a selection in the drop-down listbox portion is made.

An **Edit Control**—File name—allows the user to enter text data directly from the keyboard. An application can even add data editing features to edit boxes. While an edit box normally contains one line, they are not so limited. One could have an entire client window be one giant edit control.

Dialog boxes usually have many "titles" called **Static Text Controls**. Here the texts "Look in," "Files of type," and "File name" are static text controls. No user input can be made on these, but the application can change the string being shown as needed.

Figure 1.3 Find Modeless Dialog Box comes from the WordPad application. The Find modeless dialog box remains on the screen until you specifically cancel it or close the application that launched it. You can task-switch back to the original task at any time. This feature makes modeless dialogs useful in the right circumstances.

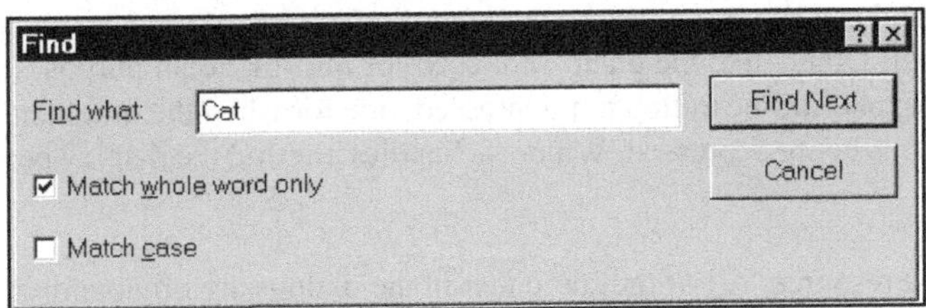

Figure 1.3 Find Modeless Dialog Box

Check Box Controls—Match whole word only—are commonly used as a toggle switch, enabling or disabling an option. For each check box, the application notifies Windows whether the box should be checkmarked or not; Windows takes care of the details.

Most dialogs have one or more **Group Box Controls,** which are static boxes that only serves to group items together. Figure 1.4 Fax Application's Properties with Radio Buttons and Slider Control illustrates three group boxes. They have a defined border; here, a simple line edge.

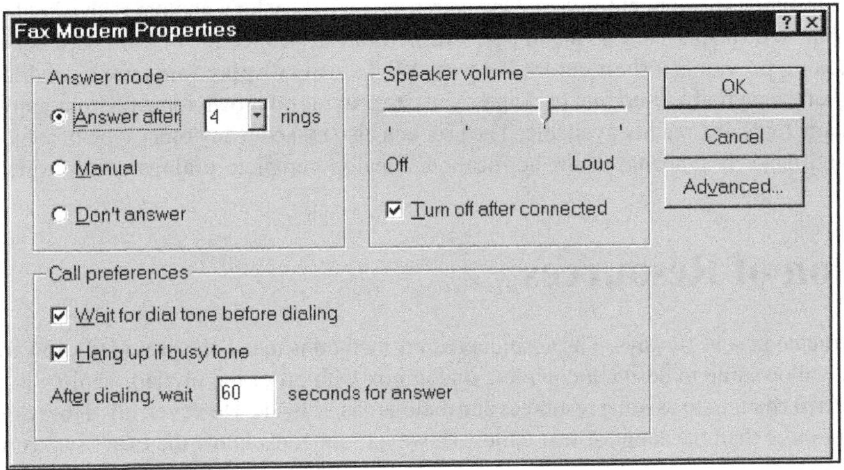

Figure 1.4 Fax Application's Properties with Radio Buttons and Slider Control

Radio Button Controls, contained in the "Answer mode" group in Figure 1.4, allow the user to select one option from a group. Notice the difference between check boxes and radio buttons. Each check box is a separate entity that can be checked or not. However, only one radio button in a group can be on at one time. This figure also shows one of the newer controls, the **slider**, which here controls the speaker volume.

Resources

These dialogs and windows are composed of a set of graphical elements known collectively as resources. Resources include the following

icons

cursors
bitmaps
character strings
menus
menu accelerators
fonts
complete dialog boxes
user-defined resources

An **icon** is a standard sized graphical image used to represent something. Commonly every application has an icon that Windows uses to represent that application when the user minimizes the program. A **cursor** is a small graphical image that represents the mouse cursor. The default is the standard arrow cursor. There are several other standard cursors that a program can use as replacements, such as the hourglass, finger pointers, and so on. Additionally, the application can provide its own cursors. **Bitmaps** come in all sizes and can represent nearly anything. Some bitmaps are very small, representing menu commands on the application's tool bar. Others like the giant ? are used for informational purposes only. Actually, push buttons are really a set of three bitmaps: one for the button not depressed, one for when the button has the focus and not depressed, and one for the button while it is being depressed. Windows handles altering the display between the three, yielding an action sequence.

Character strings are considered a resource. All of the static text in the dialogs are obviously character strings. Realize that Windows applications are often ported to foreign languages and in such cases, all messages must be converted into the appropriate foreign language. By collecting all text strings in the entire application into one set of resources found in one place, it is an easy task to translate the application into French, for example.

Thus, a major design consideration, often neglected for convenience by novice programmers, is to place **all** character stings into the application's resource file, including all strings normally found in say "**printf**'s!" An additional benefit of placing **every** string into the resource table is that the strings are removed from the code and data segments of the program, reducing the total memory footprint of the program. Only the strings that are currently needed are actually loaded into memory; all others are stored on disk.

Menus as a resource are straight forward. One enters the text of each menu item with a hot letter to be underlined and any accelerator hint to be displayed. The **menu accelerator table** is a collection of key board hot keys that correspond to specific menu choices, providing a short cut for the user. While many **display fonts** are available from the Windows system, including all of the myriad add-on font packages, you can provide your own fonts for your application. This is often not done, since so many fonts are readily available. The user can also make up any other type of object and call it a **user-defined resource** and make it available to the application. Finally, complete **dialogs** are considered as resources by Windows.

Construction of Resources

Resources are constructed in several ways. The absolute easiest method is to use the provided software **Resource Editor**. The Resource Editor allows one to design a complete dialog box with all of the myriad features in a graphical manner. Additionally, all kinds of changes to existing resources and dialogs can be made. However, all of the resources can be created by hand with nothing more than the simplest text editor. However, one must know the exact syntax and possible options available for each resource.

The resource file has the extension of .RC. When the compiler builds the program, it creates a binary version of the resource file called the .RES file. Then, the Linker program appends the res file onto the end of the application .EXE file. When an application needs a resource, Windows loads that resource into memory from res portion of the .EXE file. When the resource is no longer needed, it becomes "**discardable**." In other words, when the memory the no longer needed resources are occupying is needed, the resources are removed from memory. Should those resources be once again needed, Windows reloads them from disk. Hence, there is a vital role for the SMARTDRV cache mechanism.

Now you can see the benefit placing **all** character strings into the string resource table. Actually, Windows loads into memory groups of 16 strings at one time but only when a specific string is needed. Such strings do not then occupy space in the data segment of applications.

Resource Styles

The old Windows 3.1 graphical elements were rather plain. Microsoft next created what has become known as **3-D** replacements for all of the standard elements in an attempt to "dress up" dialogs and controls. Rather than drab, black and white dialogs, when the 3-D replacement package is selected, dialogs can have gray backgrounds, bumps and ridges for group box boundaries, and other effects. Under Windows, the dialogs and controls have been revised further and the 3-D look is now the default. Additionally, you can install replacement elements of your own design—**owner-draw controls**.

Windows Data Types and DEFINEs

The Windows API has defined many new data types and many new structure tags and classes to be used as data types for defining variables. Windows also defines many identifiers to represent specific values flags can have. Some of these differ from the Windows 3.1 API. Several common data types have different sizes depending upon which API is used. First, let's examine the common data types shown in Windows API Types, Table 1.

Table 1—Windows Data Types

Data Type	Win 95/98/ME/NT/2000	Win 3.1
int	32-bit signed number	16-bit signed number
unsigned	32-bit unsigned	16-bit unsigned
long	32-bit signed	32-bit signed
short	16-bit signed	16-bit signed
BOOL	an int whose values are TRUE or FALSE	
LPARAM	long value passed as a parameter	
WPARAM	unsigned int passed as a parameter	
LONG	long	
LPSTR	pointer to a string	
LPCSTR	pointer to a constant string	
UINT	unsigned int	
WORD	unsigned short int	
BYTE	unsigned char	
HANDLE	unsigned int used as index into a table	
HINSTANCE	handle to an instance of an app in memory—the exe file	
HWND	handle to a window	
HPEN	handle to a colored pen for drawing text and lines	
HBRUSH	handle to a brush for coloring areas, such as backgrounds	
HCURSOR	handle to a cursor, such as the arrow mouse cursor	
HFILE	handle to a file	
HGLOBAL	handle to a global memory area	

Data Type	Win 95/98/ME/NT/2000	Win 3.1
MSG	structure defining the information about a Windows message	
PAINTSTRUCT	structure defining the region of the client screen that needs to be updated	
POINT	structure defining a point, containing int x and int y	
RECT	structure defining a rectangle, containing four ints, called left, right, top, bottom	
SIZE	structure defining a size, containing two ints, cx and cy	
TEXTMETRIC	structure containing the basic information about a physical font, such as character heights and widths	
WNDCLASS	structure containing the window's class attributes, such as the window's style, icon to be used on minimizing, the cursor to be used, the background brush to color or paint the window's background, the main menu to be used	

All these are defined in the WINDOWS.H and WINUSER.H header files and other similar header files. They are fully documented in the on-line help system. Search on the specific identifier.

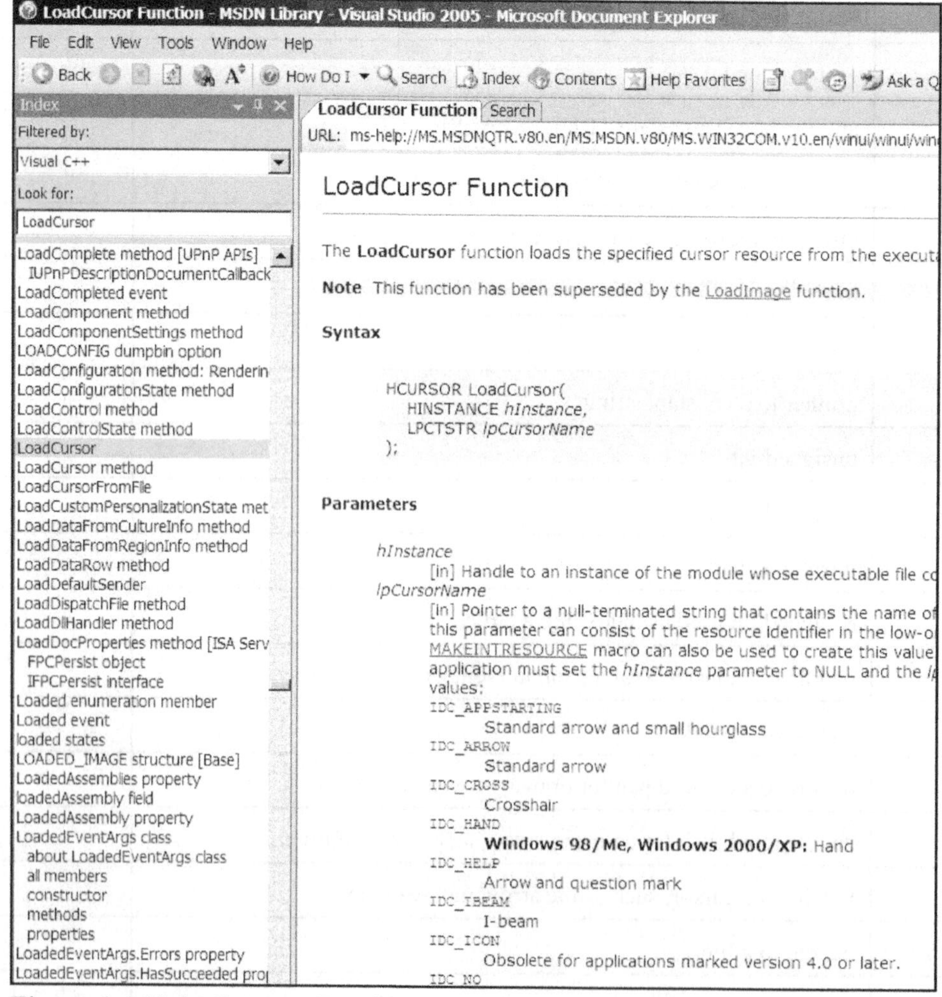

Figure 1.5 Help System: LoadCursor and IDC_ARROW

In addition, there are a huge number of numerical constants that identify various key or flag values. For example, **IDC_ARROW** identifies the standard arrow cursor. Such defined items are always in uppercase. Figure 1.5 shows the LoadCursor function in the MSDN Library Help system. The Help system is huge and it is well worth your time becoming familiar with it and how best to search for topics.

The #DEFINEs generally have a compound name, separated by the _ character. The name IDC refers to the IDentifier for a Cursor. Table 2 shows some of the other commonly used identifier prefixes.

Table 2—Some Common Identifier Prefixes

Id Prefix	Meaning
IDC	identifier for a cursor
IDI	identifier for an icon
IDS	identifier for a character string
IDM	identifier for a menu
CS	class style
CW	create window
WS	window style
WM	window message

There are identifiers for the standard colors, file attributes, error codes and many more. Again, they are in WINDOWS.H and WINUSER.H and similar files and in the on-line documentation.

Structure Alignment

When dealing with binary files, there is another architectural concern that must be understood and used. This is the principle of structure or data alignment in memory. Applications should align structure members and data values at addresses that are "natural" for the data type. A 4-byte type should be aligned on an address evenly divisible by four. An 8-byte type should be aligned on an address evenly divisible by eight. The reason for this is how the circuitry fetches data from memory. No matter how you have the data stored in memory, the circuitry will retrieve that data. It is a matter of how efficiently it gets that data.

When inputting data from disk, remember that DOS first inputs an entire cluster of data into its internal buffer in memory. Then, it extracts what has been requested from the buffer and moves it into the destination variable. Thus, a binary file on disk mirrors this structure alignment.

Suppose that we wished to access a **long** whose 4-byte value began at memory location 2 in the DOS buffer, which is an address not evenly divisible by four. The circuitry must fetch two 4-byte memory locations and then extract the desired 4-byte long from the two 4-byte locations. This is shown in Figure 1.6. This action causes a hardware fetch fault to occur. The hardware proceeds to get the two pieces from memory and join them into the 4-byte resulting **long** value. This faulting operation slows the memory accessing down significantly. But it guarantees that the requested data is retrieved. If the data is properly aligned, no fault occurs and the data is fetched normally and quickly.

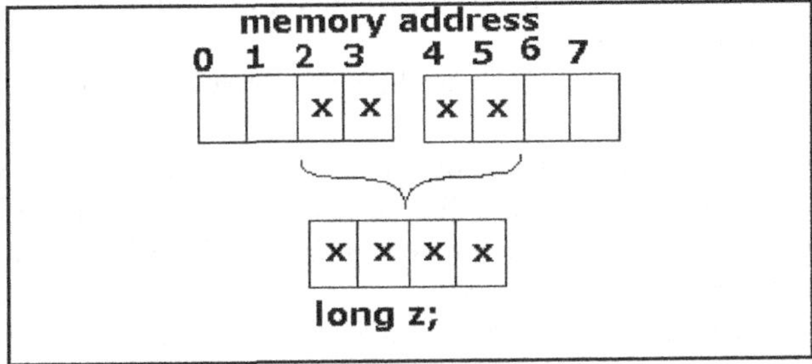

Figure 1.6 Fetching Unaligned Data

When you make a new project, Visual Studio sets the structure alignment to 8 bytes by default. The guideline is "a structure should begin on address boundaries of the worst type of data in the structure." In our case of **AccountRec** structure, the **double** is the worst type. Thus, each instance of the structure in memory should be aligned on 8-byte addresses.

However, how many bytes does our structure contain? It is 4 + 42 + 8 + 8 bytes or 62 bytes long. And this value is NOT evenly divisible by eight. If we look into the data file or the DOS internal buffer when that cluster containing the data has been input, successive records are not back to back in memory since 62 is not an even multiple of eight. If the structure alignment is 8 bytes, then the compiler adds some additional **gas** or **slack** or **pad** bytes to each structure instance so that the total size ends up a multiple of 8 bytes. That is, gas, pad, or slack bytes are added by the compiler to enforce the alignment.

On a computer with only 32-bit or 4-byte high speed registers, then the computer cannot fetch a 64-bit or 8-byte value directly from memory with one fetch: its registers are too small. In this case, 8-byte alignment becomes really 4-byte alignment. If however, you do have one of the new 64-bit PCs which has a 64-bit memory bus access, then the data will be aligned on an 8-byte boundary because the high speed work registers are indeed 8 bytes in size and can handle it.

Consider a binary file of Account Records that are defined as follows.

```
const int MaxNameLen = 42;
struct AccountRec {
 int     idNum;
 char    name[MaxNameLen];
 double creditBalance;
 double creditLimit;
};
```

I am using a 32-bit computer. Thus, the binary master file is aligned on 4-byte addresses. Since each structure instance that was written to disk contained only 62 bytes, the compiler automatically inserts two additional gas fill bytes. When you ask for the size of the **AccountRec**, the compiler returns 64 bytes not 62 bytes! When one looks at the actual data stored in the binary file, each record has an additional 2 bytes appended to it containing garbage.

When you are going to input a binary file, you **must** know what the structure alignment was in the program that wrote the binary file in the first place. Your program must match that structure alignment. If the original data was aligned on a byte boundary and your program inputs it aligned on a 4-byte boundary, then your program will input scrambled data! In the case of the **AccountRec** structure, each input would result in 64 bytes being input while the actual byte aligned data on disk had only 62 bytes.

Structure alignment is set through the project settings—Project Settings—C++ tab—Code Generation Category combo box choice—struct member alignment combo box—make your choice.

Rule: if the data was created with older DOS programs, the data is very likely to have been only byte aligned.

Corollary: if an older DOS program will be reading the data your program creates, then make sure that your project uses 1-byte alignment or the older DOS program will be inputting scrambled data.

To view a binary file, one needs an editor that can display the bytes in hex. Figure 1.7 shows the binary master file made using 8-byte structure alignment.

Each line in Figure 1.7 shows the precise contents of 16 bytes or 10 in hexadecimal. Each byte consists of two hexadecimal nibbles. Each line shows groups of 4 bytes separated by a blank column. On the far right side of each line are the corresponding ASCII equivalent characters if there are any. Notice that on the right side we can read the contents of the string name because those are ASCII characters. I also noted where the compiler inserted the two gas bytes, right after the end of the string in the structure. It added the gas bytes here so that the next two doubles would be aligned on an 8-byte boundary. I boxed in one record which occupies 64 bytes on disk.

In Figure 1.8, I rebuilt the project and binary master file using 1-byte alignment. Now each record is only 62 bytes long.

Here is one final detail about structure alignment. Suppose that your structure was 9 bytes long and you saved the data to a binary file. Suppose further that there were 100,000 records in that file. If we used 1-byte structure alignment, how many bytes would the file occupy on disk? 900,000. However, if we used 8-byte alignment on a computer that could handle 8-byte aligned data, how many bytes would the file size report? Since 9 is not evenly divisible by eight, the compiler would add an additional seven gas bytes to each structure instance. Now the file size on disk would be 1,600,000 bytes. This is a substantial difference in file size.

Hence, because of larger file sizes, many production applications that utilize large binary master files use 1-byte alignment to conserve disk space.

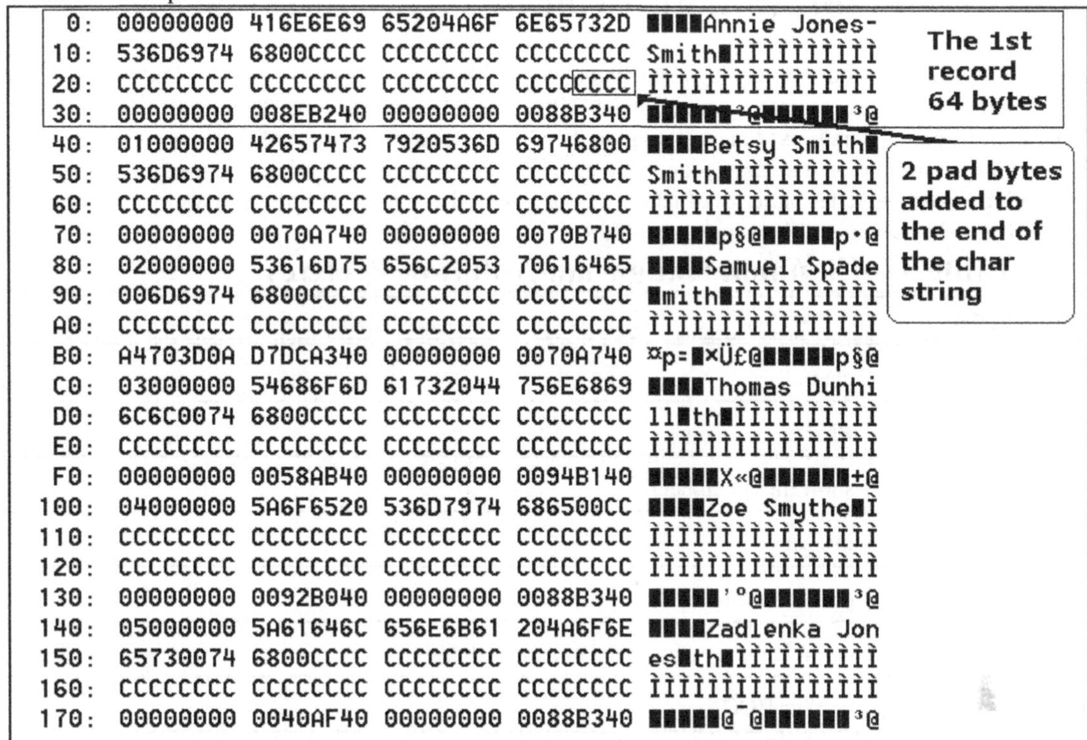

```
 0:  00000000 416E6E69 65204A6F 6E65732D ■■■■Annie Jones-
10:  536D6974 6800CCCC CCCCCCCC CCCCCCCC Smith■ÌÌÌÌÌÌÌÌÌÌ
20:  CCCCCCCC CCCCCCCC CCCCCCCC CCCCCCCC ÌÌÌÌÌÌÌÌÌÌÌÌÌÌÌÌ
30:  00000000 008EB240 00000000 0088B340 ■■■■■■²@■■■■■■³@
40:  01000000 42657473 7920536D 69746800 ■■■■Betsy Smith■
50:  536D6974 6800CCCC CCCCCCCC CCCCCCCC Smith■ÌÌÌÌÌÌÌÌÌÌ
60:  CCCCCCCC CCCCCCCC CCCCCCCC CCCCCCCC ÌÌÌÌÌÌÌÌÌÌÌÌÌÌÌÌ
70:  00000000 0070A740 00000000 0070B740 ■■■■■p§@■■■■■p·@
80:  02000000 53616D75 656C2053 70616465 ■■■■Samuel Spade
90:  006D6974 6800CCCC CCCCCCCC CCCCCCCC ■mith■ÌÌÌÌÌÌÌÌÌÌ
A0:  CCCCCCCC CCCCCCCC CCCCCCCC CCCCCCCC ÌÌÌÌÌÌÌÌÌÌÌÌÌÌÌÌ
B0:  A4703D0A D7DCA340 00000000 0070A740 ¤p=■×Ü£@■■■■■p§@
C0:  03000000 54686F6D 61732044 756E6869 ■■■■Thomas Dunhi
D0:  6C6C0074 6800CCCC CCCCCCCC CCCCCCCC ll■th■ÌÌÌÌÌÌÌÌÌÌ
E0:  CCCCCCCC CCCCCCCC CCCCCCCC CCCCCCCC ÌÌÌÌÌÌÌÌÌÌÌÌÌÌÌÌ
F0:  00000000 0058AB40 00000000 0094B140 ■■■■■X«@■■■■■■±@
100: 04000000 5A6F6520 536D7974 686500CC ■■■■Zoe Smythe■Ì
110: CCCCCCCC CCCCCCCC CCCCCCCC CCCCCCCC ÌÌÌÌÌÌÌÌÌÌÌÌÌÌÌÌ
120: CCCCCCCC CCCCCCCC CCCCCCCC CCCCCCCC ÌÌÌÌÌÌÌÌÌÌÌÌÌÌÌÌ
130: 00000000 0092B040 00000000 0088B340 ■■■■■'°@■■■■■■³@
140: 05000000 5A61646C 656E6B61 204A6F6E ■■■■Zadlenka Jon
150: 65730074 6800CCCC CCCCCCCC CCCCCCCC es■th■ÌÌÌÌÌÌÌÌÌÌ
160: CCCCCCCC CCCCCCCC CCCCCCCC CCCCCCCC ÌÌÌÌÌÌÌÌÌÌÌÌÌÌÌÌ
170: 00000000 0040AF40 00000000 0088B340 ■■■■■@¯@■■■■■■³@
```


Figure 1.7 The Binary File (values in hex) Using 8-Byte Structure Alignment

```
 0:  00000000 416E6E69 65204A6F 6E65732D ■■■■Annie Jones-
10:  536D6974 6800CCCC CCCCCCCC CCCCCCCC Smith■ÌÌÌÌÌÌÌÌÌÌ
20:  CCCCCCCC CCCCCCCC CCCCCCCC CCCC0000 ÌÌÌÌÌÌÌÌÌÌÌÌÌÌ■■
30:  0000008E B2400000 00000088 B3400100 ■■■■²@■■■■■■³@■■
40:  00004265 74737920 536D6974 6800536D ■■Betsy Smith■Sm
50:  69746800 CCCCCCCC CCCCCCCC CCCCCCCC ith■ÌÌÌÌÌÌÌÌÌÌÌÌ
60:  CCCCCCCC CCCCCCCC CCCCCCCC 00000000 ÌÌÌÌÌÌÌÌÌÌÌÌ■■■■
70:  0070A740 00000000 0070B740 02000000 ■p§@■■■■■p·@■■■■
80:  53616D75 656C2053 70616465 006D6974 Samuel Spade■mit
90:  6800CCCC CCCCCCCC CCCCCCCC CCCCCCCC h■ÌÌÌÌÌÌÌÌÌÌÌÌÌÌ
A0:  CCCCCCCC CCCCCCCC CCCCA470 3D0AD7DC ÌÌÌÌÌÌÌÌÌ¤p=■×Ü
B0:  A3400000 00000070 A7400300 00005468 £@■■■■■p§@■■■■Th
C0:  6F6D6173 2044756E 68696C6C 00746800 omas Dunhill■th■
D0:  CCCCCCCC CCCCCCCC CCCCCCCC CCCCCCCC ÌÌÌÌÌÌÌÌÌÌÌÌÌÌÌÌ
E0:  CCCCCCCC CCCCCCCC 00000000 0058AB40 ÌÌÌÌÌÌÌÌ■■■■■X«@
F0:  00000000 0094B140 04000000 5A6F6520 ■■■■■■±@■■■■Zoe
100: 536D7974 686500CC CCCCCCCC CCCCCCCC Smythe■ÌÌÌÌÌÌÌÌÌ
110: CCCCCCCC CCCCCCCC CCCCCCCC CCCCCCCC ÌÌÌÌÌÌÌÌÌÌÌÌÌÌÌÌ
120: CCCCCCCC CCCC0000 00000092 B0400000 ÌÌÌÌÌÌ■■■■■'°@■■
130: 00000088 B3400500 00005A61 646C656E ■■■■³@■■■■Zadlen
140: 6B61204A 6F6E6573 00746800 CCCCCCCC ka Jones■th■ÌÌÌÌ
150: CCCCCCCC CCCCCCCC CCCCCCCC CCCCCCCC ÌÌÌÌÌÌÌÌÌÌÌÌÌÌÌÌ
160: CCCCCCCC 00000000 0040AF40 00000000 ÌÌÌÌ■■■■■@¯@■■■■
170: 0088B340                            ■■³@
```

The 1st 62-byte record

Figure 1.8 The Binary Master File Using 1-Byte Structure Alignment

Hungarian Notation and Coding Conventions

Because of the critical nature of passing many parameters of the correct data type to the Windows API, when making up variable names, many programmers opt to use the Hungarian notational scheme. The Windows API does some data type checking of the parameters passed in an attempt to detect bad values in advance of their use.

Hungarian notation is named in honor of the Microsoft programmer Charles Simonyi. Simply put, all variable names begin with a lowercase letter or series of letters that represent the data type. This is followed by the capitalized variable name. Table 3 shows some of the common prefixes.

Table 3—Common Hungarian Notation Prefixes

Prefix	Meaning
c	char
by	BYTE
n	short int (a number)
I	integer
x, y	pixel coordinates
cx, cy	count lengths or sizes in the x and y directions
b	bool or BOOL
w	UINT or WORD or unsigned int
l	long
dw	DWORD or unsigned long
lp	long pointer or far pointer
lpsz	long pointer to a string
s	string
sz	null terminated string
h	handle

Thus, **lpszCmdParam** is long pointer to a null terminated string whose name is an abbreviation for command parameter. **hInstance** would be a handle to this instance of the application in memory. **hPrevInstance** is a handle to a previous instance or copy of the application in memory.

Similarly, when defining or referencing structures, the structures are often named the same only in lowercase. Often if the name is too long, it is abbreviated. For example

```
POINT       point;
RECT        rect;
PAINTSTRUCT ps;
```

Windows API Function Names

Windows API function names are all capitalized. For example

```
LoadIcon
LoadCursor
LoadString
CreateWindow
```

My Sample Program Coding Notation

The result of all these new names is **total confusion** for programmers just learning to program under Windows! As you look over the first few chapters, you may have an even more emphatic statement about all of this. It is not uncommon to be totally confused as to what must be coded exactly as is and what are **your** variable names. I still recall my first exposure to Windows programming; it was anything but pleasant! In fact, when you couple all of this complexity with the next layer—object-oriented classes—it becomes exceedingly difficult to decipher what is going on. Therefore, I am going to adopt "Vic's semi-understandable coding scheme."

In my beginning examples, when you see an identifier that has one or more capital letters in it, it is the name of a function or structure or message or #DEFINE and must be coded as is. The exceptions begin occurring when I start to create resources; at that point, I use uppercase defines as well. When we deal with the class libraries in Chapter 4, class names and functions are also capitalized and the scheme tends to break down. But by then you should have a good feel for names. All variables that are user-created names are in lowercase. I dislike Hungarian notation for many reasons. The only exception is that I will use the prefix h for handle fields.

In summary, in the initial examples, if an identifier has one or more capital letters in it, that identifier must be used **as is**; it is a Windows defined key item. If it has no capitals in it, it is a user nameable entity that can be called anything you desire. Hopefully, this will be of great assistance at the beginning trying to understand what is being coded.

When the class libraries are presented beginning in Chapter 4, I will capitalize member function names. However, class data members still follow the above lowercase style. Thus, from the name and capitalization, you can tell what it is. However, this is just a learning crutch. Feel free to use whatever stylistic approach you desire in your coding. I am just trying to make the learning process a bit easier for you.

Getting Started: The Software

All of the sample programs in this book are located under the subfolder **SamplePrograms** with each program in a separate project folder. To experiment with a specific sample program, either double click its .sln file or use the menu item File—Open Project and select the desired project.

When starting a new project, choose File—New Project and select under C++ **Win32** and then on the right, select Win32 Project. Next, enter the new name and select the folder. This is shown in the next figure, 1-9.

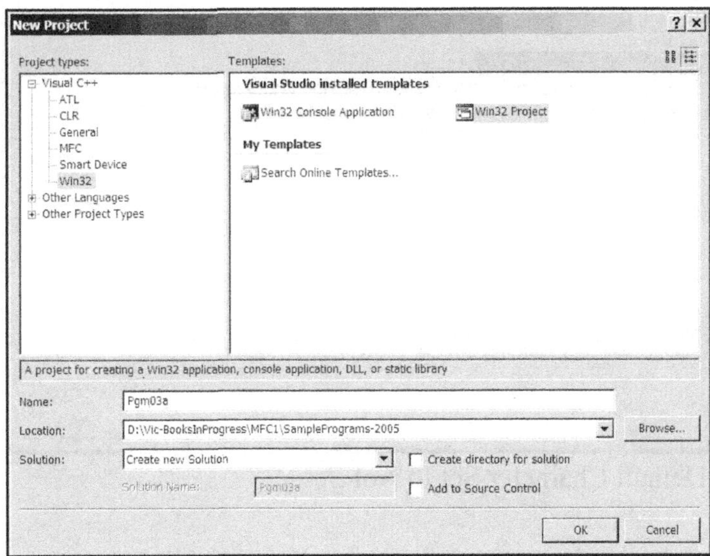

Figure 1-9 Making a New Win32 Windows Application

After clicking OK, in the next dialog, choose Application Settings and chose Empty Project. Make sure that the Windows Application radio button is selected. These settings are shown in the next figure, 1-10. After making these selections and clicking Finish, one Project setting must be made. Right click on the Project and choose Properties. Under the General Tab, go to Character Set. It defaults to Unicode. Change it to Not Set as shown in Figure 1-11 below.

When you add a new source file, for the pure C style programs of these first three chapters, the file extension can be either .c or .cpp.

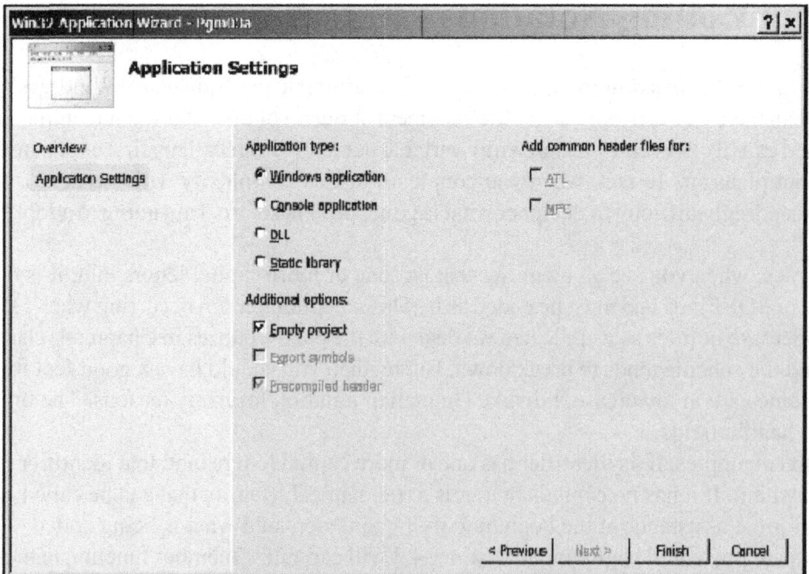

Figure 1.10 Choosing Empty Windows Application Settings

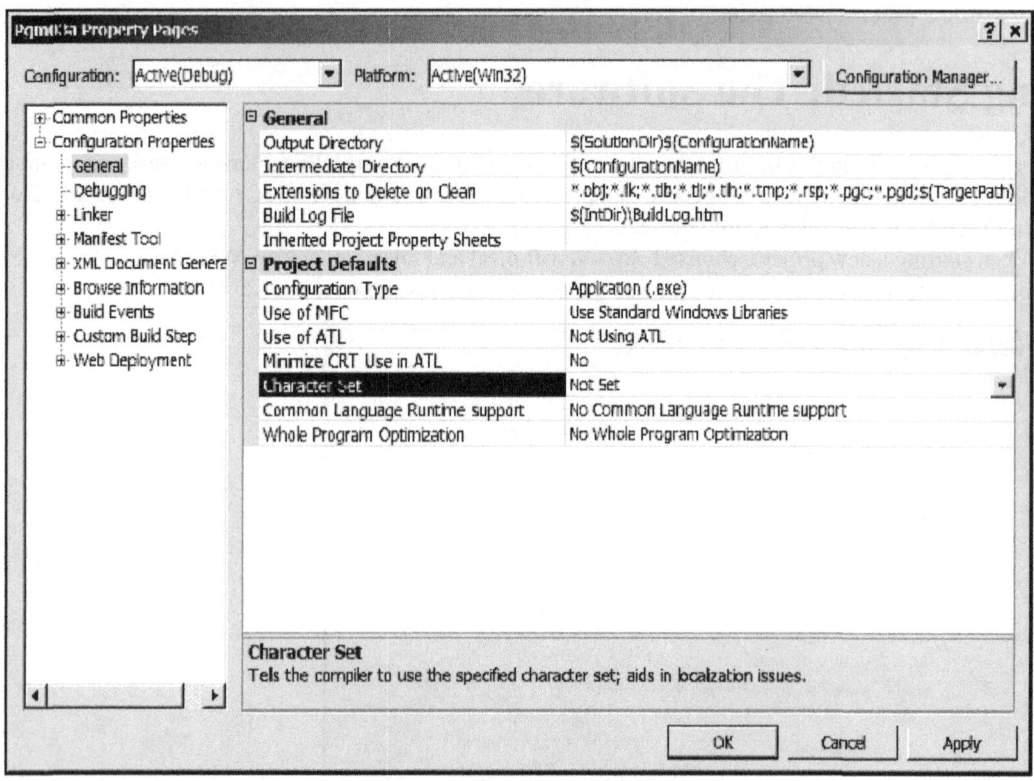

Figure 1-11 Changing the Default Character Set to Not Set

A Project's Files

A C style application contains a basic set of files. When the application is built, many additional files are created. The resultant .EXE file is the sole file needed for its execution. A C++ style application contains even more basic files, including a header file and code file for each class.

Let's begin with the normal "Hello World" type program. There are three files originally.

```
Pgm01a.c       - the C source file
Pgm01a.sln     - the desktop solution containing the project
Pgm01a.vcproj - the project file giving which files to use
```

The other files are used by Visual Studio to handle Intellisense and such matters. In later chapters, the resource files will be added.

```
.rc   - program's resource file defining dialogs, strings, etc.
resource.h    - a header file defining the resource ID numbers
```

When the build is done, many additional files are created. Now look at the Debug folder and find the exe file. Some of these include:

```
Pgm01a.exe  - the final product - the executable program
Pgm01a.obj  - the object file
Pgm01a.pch  - the pre-compiled header file
Pgm01a.res  - compiled resources in a form to be appended to
              the EXE file
```

Other additional files appear after debugging sessions—to remember your last set of breakpoints, for example. Notice that all of the object files, support files, and the EXE file are stored in the Debug folder.

Pre-compiled Headers: the .pch Files

The pre-compiled header file is an attempt to greatly speed up the compilation phase. The basic idea is that once each module's header files are compiled and saved on disk, then the next time the module is compiled, if there are no changes in the header files, the compiler merely inputs the pre-compiled header information, bypassing the including and compiling of the actual header files. This saves a great deal on time on larger projects. When using the MFC class libraries, without pre-compiled headers, the compile time is unbelievably slow.

However, the price you pay for indiscriminate use of pre-compiled headers is huge file size! On an 80K MFC program with ten cpp and h files, I have seen the pch (pre-compiled header file) exceed 10M! Therefore, some controls must be established when using pre-compiled headers to keep the pch file as small as possible.

Your own class header files are often subject to change until you get the application working. Any change to your headers also causes a complete redo of the pre-compiled headers file. Thus, only nonvolatile headers should be included. You must instruct the compiler to halt pre-compiling after the nonvolatile includes. The nonvolatile includes are: various window headers, normal C++ standard header files, and the MFC class library includes.

Thus, the best method is in **every** module (.C, .CPP, .H), place the nonvolatile headers first followed by the command to halt pre-compiling.

```
#pragma hdrstop
```

Further, to minimize the size of the pre-compiled headers file, the same set of files should be included in every file to be compiled. While this does require planning ahead to include all system header files that will be needed, doing so will drastically reduce the size of the pch file. When we get into the MFC style coding in chapter 4, this aspect will be automatically handled for us.

This was not done here in **Pgm01a.c** because there is only one file to compile. In subsequent sample programs, I will illustrate this optimum method of handling the precompiled headers.

Pgm01a: Hello World, a First Windows Program

Ok. We've put it off long enough or we've saved the best for last. Let's examine a C style program that displays a Hello message in a window. Be forewarned—it is **not** just three lines of code! Figure 1.7 shows what how the Hello Program appears when run. Examine Pgm01a.c.

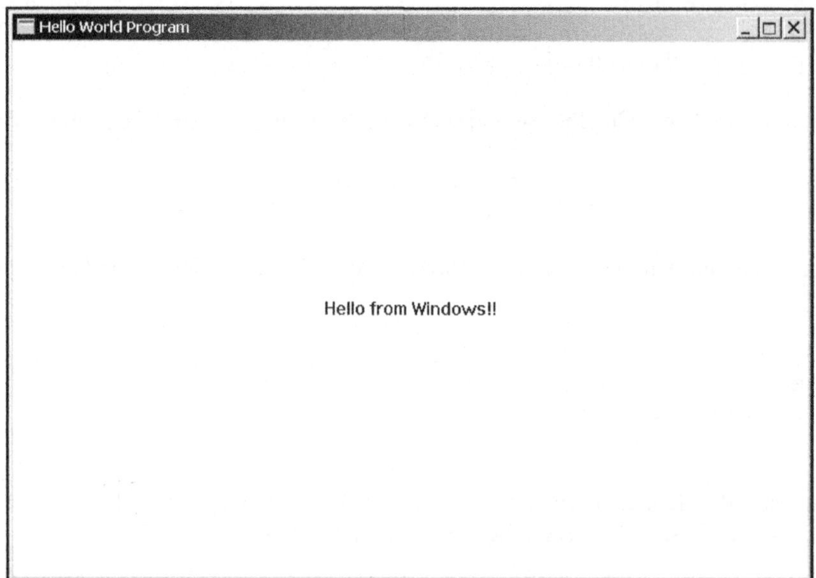

Figure 1.7 Pgm01a — The Hello World Program

Pgm01a - The Hello World Program

```
/***************************************************************/
/*                                                             */
/* Pgm01a - Hello in a window shell program by Vic Broquard    */
/*                                                             */
/* C style  basic model                                        */
/*                                                             */
/***************************************************************/

#include <windows.h>

/***************************************************************/
/*                                                             */
/* structure definitions, external/global data, and prototypes */
/*                                                             */
/***************************************************************/

// main window procedure - normally called WinProc
LRESULT CALLBACK winproc (HWND, UINT, WPARAM, LPARAM);

// make and register our window class
BOOL initapplication (HINSTANCE);

// construct an instance of our window
BOOL initinstance (HINSTANCE, int);

char appname[] = "HelloPgm"; // the name of our application


/***************************************************************/
```

```
/*                                                                 */
/* WinMain: windows equivalent to a "main" in C pgms               */
/*          it MUST always be coded                                */
/*                                                                 */
/*****************************************************************/

int APIENTRY WinMain (HINSTANCE hinstance,
                      HINSTANCE hprevinstance,
                      LPSTR  cmdline, int howshow) {
 MSG         msg;

 // under Windows 95 and NT, hprevinstance is now ALWAYS 0
 // invoke initapplication to construct the window's class
 //        parameters that tell Windows how to build the
 //        main window and register the window's class

 if (!initapplication (hinstance)) return FALSE;

 // create an instance of the main window, based upon the way
 // that the user desires the window to be shown
 // such as "launch minimized" for example

 if (!initinstance (hinstance, howshow)) return FALSE;

 // enter the main processing loop consisting of getting the
 // next message that Windows sends to this app, converting its
 // message into standard codes and sending that message to our
 // app's appropriate message handler
 // continue until Windows notifies us that there will never be
 // any further messages, because the app has requested
 //termination

 while ( GetMessage (&msg, NULL, 0, 0)) {
  TranslateMessage (&msg);
  DispatchMessage  (&msg);
 }

 // pass along the generated success/fail return code
 return (int) msg.wParam;
}


/*****************************************************************/
/*                                                                 */
/* initapplication:                                                */
/*   fill in the WNDCLASS structure about how to construct our    */
/*   main window and then register this window with Windows       */
/*                                                                 */
/* Note: better style is to call this function InitApplication    */
/*                                                                 */
/*****************************************************************/

BOOL initapplication (HINSTANCE hinstance) {

 WNDCLASS wndclass;

 // force repaint whenever the window size changes
 wndclass.style          = CS_HREDRAW | CS_VREDRAW;

 // name of our main window procedure
 wndclass.lpfnWndProc    = winproc;

 // advanced features - reserves extra space in windows class
 // and window structures
```

```
 wndclass.cbClsExtra     = 0;
 wndclass.cbWndExtra     = 0;

 // insert handle to this window's instance
 wndclass.hInstance      = hinstance;

 // load in the icon to be used whenever we are minimized
 // use the system provided default icon
 wndclass.hIcon          = LoadIcon (NULL, IDI_APPLICATION);

 // load the mouse cursor to be used - here it's the arrow cursor
 wndclass.hCursor        = LoadCursor (NULL, IDC_ARROW);

 // create the background colored brush
 wndclass.hbrBackground = GetStockObject (WHITE_BRUSH);

 // this will eventually be the id of our menu to be displayed
 wndclass.lpszMenuName  = NULL;

 // the char string name of the application
 wndclass.lpszClassName = appname;

 // registers this window so it can be shown
 return RegisterClass (&wndclass);
}


/*****************************************************************/
/*                                                               */
/* initinstance:                                                 */
/*   construct an instance of our main window using our just     */
/*   registered class                                            */
/*                                                               */
/* Note: a better style is to call this function InitInstance    */
/*                                                               */
/*****************************************************************/

BOOL initinstance (HINSTANCE hinstance, int howshow) {

 HWND hwnd;

 hwnd = CreateWindow (
        appname,                // char string ids the app
        "Hello World Program",// title bar caption
        WS_OVERLAPPEDWINDOW,    // window style
        CW_USEDEFAULT,          // window's initial x position
        CW_USEDEFAULT,          // window's initial y position
        CW_USEDEFAULT,          // window's initial x size - width
        CW_USEDEFAULT,          // window's initial y size- height
        NULL,                   // parent window's handle
        NULL,                   // handle to window's menu
        hinstance,              // handle of this instance
        NULL);                  // creation parameters - advanced

 if (!hwnd) return FALSE;       // window construction failed

 ShowWindow (hwnd, howshow);    // creates window on the screen
 return TRUE;
}


/*****************************************************************/
/*                                                               */
/* winproc: our main window procedure - normally called WinProc*/
```

```
/*                                                                */
/*****************************************************************/

LRESULT CALLBACK winproc (HWND hwnd, UINT msg, WPARAM wparam,
                          LPARAM lparam) {
 HDC         hdc;
 PAINTSTRUCT ps;
 RECT        rect;

 // our app's message processing section - given a message from
 // Windows, determine if the message is one that we wish to
 // respond to and do so or pass it on down to the Windows
 // provided default message handler to take the appropriate
 // Windows default handling
 // here is the tiniest "Nightmare Switch From Hell" - imagine
 // what it will look like when it processes hundreds of messages

 switch (msg) {

  // when a paint message is received, we are being asked to
  // redraw our window - either completely or in part

  case WM_PAINT:

    // acquire a device context upon which to draw
    hdc = BeginPaint (hwnd, &ps);

    // get the size of the client area that needs to be redrawn
    GetClientRect (hwnd, &rect);

    // printf a hello message
    DrawText (hdc, "Hello from Windows!!", -1, &rect,
              DT_SINGLELINE | DT_CENTER | DT_VCENTER);

    // notify Windows that we are done redrawing the window
    EndPaint (hwnd, &ps);

    // notify the message processor that we have successfully
    // handled the message
    return 0;


  // the user has selected the "Close Application" menu item
  // here we must handle any processing needed to terminate the
  // app - for now nothing

  case WM_DESTROY:

    // send ok to quit the app message back to Windows
    PostQuitMessage (0);

    // notify the message processor that we have handled
    return 0;
 }

 // all unhandled messages are passed on down to the default
 // Windows handler
 return DefWindowProc (hwnd, msg, wparam, lparam);
}
```

Using Comments

The first thing you should notice is the proliferation of comments! On this simple program since it is our first program, I have added many more instruction comments than are usually needed to make the program more understandable. In your programs, you **should** use appropriate instruction comments. Target your reader.

Design Rule 2: Use block comments to identify the major sections or functions of the program and instruction comments either just ahead or on the right of the instruction to identify what the instruction is to do.

Why? The three key reasons for the use of comments are as follows.

1. Comments will aid your understanding of both what and why, when you look at the code a month later.

2. Comments assist the person who performs program maintenance. If you do not fully document your program, other programmers will continually query you about the program code.

3. Commenting as you code helps you spot errors early before you compile and run.

The WinMain and Other Functions

In a DOS C/C++ program, the function **main** is automatically invoked by the C start up code. Similarly, in a Windows application, the start up code **always** invokes a function whose name is **WinMain**. Notice the capitalization.

Normally, this startup function has minimal coding and the coding is quite standard, program to program. Windows gives **WinMain** four parameters. Should you need to pick up values from the launching command line, the **LPSTR**, or long pointer to a string, that is, it is just a character string, points to the command line. Notice that the command line is not parsed into a variable number of character strings as it is in a DOS C/C++ program with its **argc** and **argv** parameters.

Two handles to program applications or exe files are passed. The first handle is the most important one; it is the handle to **this** instance of the application, us. Under Windows ever since Windows 95, the second handle, the handle to any previous instance currently running, is always 0 and is ignored.

The variable names usually assigned to these parameters are **hinstance** and **hprevinstance**. Some programmers capitalize these names for readability along with **CmdLine** or **nCmdLine**. The handle to this instance, **hinstance**, is used frequently in API function calls when we need items from the resource section; thus it will be used in later examples.

The fourth parameter determines how the application is to be shown onscreen. The default method that Windows uses is a window about ½ of the screen's dimensions. This variable usually has the value SW_SHOWNORMAL. Other often used possibilities include the following.

```
SW_SHOWNOACTIVE   - displays the window as an icon that is
                    minimized on start up
SW_SHOWMAXIMIZED  - displays the window in a maximized state
```

WinMain has three basic actions to perform. First, it must fill in a structure that defines how this application is to be run, including its style or class, and then register this definition with Windows. While the coding of these actions could be done directly in **WinMain**, I have placed this coding into an **initapplication** function. (Yes, I really want to call it **InitApplication**. However, it is lowercase here to assist you spotting what names are yours and what must be coded as-is.) Also, when we begin discussing the class libraries, this function will become a member function. Should the registration API function fail, **WinMain** terminates. Notice that this registration involves **not** a C++ "class" but rather a style and method of window display among other things. (In my opinion, **RegisterClass** is a misnomer.)

Second, **WinMain** must create an instance of the main window, based on the just registered style or class, and then show the window onscreen. Here, these steps are done in **initinstance**. Once more, it more likely would be called **InitInstance** and will also become a member function in the class libraries.

Third, **WinMain** runs the application through the message processing loop. Windows has a **MSG** structure that defines the hundreds of possible messages that could be sent to your application. The basic message processing code is simply: get a message, translate it, and send it to the appropriate function to handle it. The cycle continues until **GetMessage** returns 0, indicating there are no more messages and the application is done.

Windows dispatches messages to our main message processing function, which is here named **winproc**. In the industry, this function is usually called **WinProc**. It is within **winproc** that most of our application coding is found. Before we examine the coding details, examine the function prototype for **winproc** and the header for **WinMain**.

```
LRESULT CALLBACK  winproc (HWND, UINT, WPARAM, LPARAM);
int APIENTRY  WinMain (HINSTANCE hinstance,
                       HINSTANCE hprevinstance,
                       LPSTR  cmdline, int howshow) {
```

WinMain returns an integer success code, similar to a DOS C++ program and has an entry type or calling convention of **APIENTRY**. Alternatively one could use **WINAPI**. Both are equivalent. By default, C and C++ functions have the C calling convention.

There are several types of calling conventions or sequences: C, PASCAL, WINAPI. Many languages, except C, pass parameters in what is called the PASCAL style. The parameters are passed on the **stack**, which is a last in-first out save area (LIFO). In the PASCAL style, if one invoked a CALC function as:

```
CALC (a, b, c);
```

then the stack would contain parameters c, b, a in that order—last in-first out.

On the other hand, C style parameter passing stores the parameters in the order of appearance in the function call. In the above case, the parameters on the stack would be a, b, c. (C style places the parameters onto the stack in reverse order; LIFO then makes them appear in the forward order.) There are also some differences on stack cleanup after the function completes—does the caller or does the callee remove the parameters from the stack.

In general, the PASCAL style is more efficient, but the C style will handle a variable number of arguments. The WINAPI, among other things, combines the best of both, permitting speedy execution and variable number of arguments.

The prototype for **winproc** begins **LRESULT CALLBACK winproc**, signifying that it returns a long integer, LRESULT. The option **CALLBACK** indicates that this function is called from within the Windows API or that Windows will call back to this function. This is a common occurrence. Our application calls an API function that then calls back to one of our application's functions. This is parallel to the C **qsort** function in which **qsort** must call back to our comparison function. In a large application with many functions, very few functions must have this special option, **CALLBACK**.

Windows always passes **winproc** (**WinProc**) four parameters: a handle to the window that is receiving the message (yes, you can examine all messages), an **unsigned int** (**UINT**) representing the message id number, a **WPARAM** and an **LPARAM** that contain the various parameter values associated with this specific message. **winproc** always returns a **long** that contains either **TRUE** or **FALSE**, 0 or 1, showing whether we handled the message or not.

The global variable **appname** contains the character string name that we give to Windows to identify our application.

Next, examine the **initapplication** function. Two actions are performed: fill in the **WNDCLASS** structure members and then register that window class with Windows. Note that the use of the term "class" is not a true C++ class, rather just our window's style.

The variable **wndclass** is an instance of the structure **WNDCLASS**. The **WNDCLASS** structure defines many key elements about our window. The **style** member field determines many key features. This field is actually a bit string, whose individual bits represent the on/off status of the available possibilities. Often several options are needed. They are ORed together. Some possibilities include the following.

```
CS_DBLCLKS - send double clicks to the application
CS_HREDRAW - redraw the whole screen if the horizontal size
             changes
CS_VREDRAW - redraw the whole screen if the vertical size
             changes
```

The field **lpfnWndProc** is assigned the name of our message handling procedure—**winproc** (**WinProc**). It is through this field that Windows knows the name of our message processing function that it must call.

The field **hIcon** is assigned the icon that we wish to use to identify our application. The icon is used in many places to represent the application. Since we have not yet learned how to create icons, we use a default icon whose id is **IDI_APPLICATION**. However, that icon must be loaded into memory. The windows function **LoadIcon** is invoked. **LoadIcon** is passed the handle of this instance and the id number of the resource to load from our .EXE file. If we were loading our own icon, we might code it as follows.

```
LoadIcon (hinstance, IDI_OUR_ICON);
```

Table 4 shows other built-in icons. However, since we are loading a Windows-supplied icon, we use NULL for the application instance and the predefined identifier of the icon.

```
LoadIcon (NULL, IDI_APPLICATION);
```

Table 4 Standard Windows Icons

Icon Identifier	Meaning
IDI_APPLICATION	default application icon
IDI_ASTERISK	information icon
IDI_EXCLAMATION	exclamation point icon
IDI_HAND	hand or stop sign icon
IDI_QUESTION	question mark icon

A similar process sets the field **hCursor** to the desired default mouse cursor. (Note that we can change cursors any time later; this is just the default cursor.) Table 5 shows some of the standard cursors. The **LoadCursor** function expects parameters similar to the **LoadIcon**. Here we use the standard arrow cursor.

```
LoadCursor (NULL, IDC_ARROW);
```

Table 5 Some Standard Windows Cursors

Cursor Identifier	Meaning
IDC_ARROW	arrow cursor
IDC_CROSS	cross hair cursor
IDC_IBEAM	vertical I-beam cursor
IDC_WAIT	hourglass cursor
IDC_UPARROW	straight up arrow
IDC_SIZE	cursor used to resize a window
IDC_ICON	drag file icon
IDC_SIZENWSE	upper left to lower right two-headed arrow
IDC_SIZENESW	upper right to lower left two-headed arrow
IDC_SIZEWE	horizontal two-headed arrow
IDC_SIZENS	vertical two-headed arrow

Finally, Windows requires a colored brush for painting the background of our window. When our window is created or needs to be redrawn, say after an overlapping application is closed or moved, Windows repaints our corrupted background for us. Painting an area is done via **brushes**; painting lines (or text) is done with a **pen**. Makes sense doesn't it? Hence, we must create a colored brush for the background. Brushes may be created or "borrowed from" several stock, standard brushes provided by Windows. These are default, ready-made brushes, if you please. These are called "**Stock Objects**." Table 6 shows the stock brushes. Thus, we need to get a stock object, namely a colored brush, via the function **GetStockObject**.

```
GetStockObject (WHITE_BRUSH);
```

Table 6 Windows Stock Brushes

Brush Identifier
BLACK_BRUSH
WHITE_BRUSH

Brush Identifier
LTGRAY_BRUSH
DKGRAY_BRUSH

Notice the return values from **LoadIcon, LoadCursor,** and **GetStockObject**. All return handles to the appropriate graphical objects.

Once the **WNDCLASS** structure is filled, we invoke the **RegisterClass** function which registers our model of how we want our window to appear with Windows. Our window is then placed onto the potentially available queue of windows. No actual window has yet been made.

Examine function **initinstance** which actually constructs our visible window. Three steps are required. First, the actual memory instance of our window is created via the function **CreateWindow** which then returns a handle to our window in memory. We **must** save this handle; it will be used in subsequent functions. The **CreateWindow** function has many parameters that define specifically how the window is to be constructed and returns either a handle to the window or 0 if the function fails.

The first parameter is the **appname**, the same value used in the **WNDCLASS** structure before. Next comes the created window style—note that it is a different style field from the **WNDCLASS** style field. **CreateWindow**'s style offers many specific features for this window. When you look up this function in the documentation, you will see many different sets of possibilities. Realize that this function can be used not only to create a window, but also buttons, edit boxes, list boxes, combo boxes, and so on. For a main window, the options are prefixed with **WS_**.

As you examine some of the possibilities of **WS_** options in Table 7, notice that some imply others. This means that if you specify a certain option, you do not specifically need to mention the other associated options. For example, specifying **WS_CAPTION**, which creates a window with a title bar, automatically implies the **WS_BORDER**, which creates a window with a border. **WS_OVERLAPPEDWINDOW** is our choice and is a common one.

Table 7 Some Windows WS_ Style Identifiers

WS_ Identifier	Meaning
WS_MINIMIZEBOX	window has a minimize button on title bar
WS_MAXIMIZEBOX	window has a maximize button on the title bar
WS_BORDER	window with thin line border, no resizing
WS_CAPTION	window has a title bar, implies WS_BORDER
WS_THICKFRAME	window has a thick border for resizing
WS_SYSMENU	window has a System menu box on the title bar
WS_VSCROLL	window has a vertical scroll bar
WS_HSCROLL	window has a horizontal scroll bar
WS_OVERLAPPEDWINDOW	the usual main window type that implies WS_OVERLAPPED (the window can overlap others), WS_CAPTION, WS_SYSMENU, WS_MINIMIZEBOX, WS_MAXIMIZEBOX, and WS_THICKFRAME

The next four parameters are **int**s defining the starting x and y coordinates of the upper left corner of the window and the width (x size) and the height (y size) of the window. If you do not care how big or where the window will appear, you tell Windows to use its best judgment based upon what is currently on the screen by coding **CW_USEDEFAULT**.

Next come the handle of the parent window, if this is a child window followed by the menu handle. For now, these are NULL. Next to last is the handle of this application instance or **hinstance**. The last argument represents some advanced features and is NULL, meaning none.

Based upon these values, Windows creates our window in memory **only**—please note that the window is not displayed on the screen just yet. Two more steps are required. To actually display our window for the first time, we must call **ShowWindow**, passing our handle to the window and how we want the window to be currently displayed. Since this is the first time the window is to appear, the original how-to-show the window parameter that has been possibly passed down to us from Windows should be used, the **howshow**. For example, the user may want this application to begin in the minimized state. Normally, **howshow** has the default value indicating that the window is both active and visible.

ShowWindow draws the border, title bar, and similar items. However, Windows does **not** know how to draw what is inside our window, the client area. It just paints the background for us using the background brush we have already installed in the **WNDCLASS** structure. Finally, **ShowWindow** calls the **UpdateWindow** function which sends our application a message (**WM_PAINT**) saying that we need to paint our client area. The code to do that painting is found in our **winproc (WinProc)**. The **UpdateWindow** function forces an immediate repainting of a window. In this case, our window becomes visible for the first time. Note that any time you want to force an immediate repainting, you can call it too.

```
UpdateWindow (hwnd);
```

Now that the window is visible, the application enters the standard Windows processing cycle: get a message and then handle the message, until there are going to be no more messages.

Reviewing the **WinMain** function and its supporting functions, except for adjusting the various options for our windows, the coding is the same in every application.

Our message processing function, **winproc (WinProc)**, while here small, contains the rest of the entire application's processing. In real applications, this function becomes huge with many sub-functions added. Let's examine this minimal **winnproc** that processes Windows messages. It is called from within the Windows shell and is passed the handle of the window receiving the message, the **MSG** structure containing the message, and two message specific parameters. Its **entire** purpose is to process the messages that Windows passes it. A very different way to program indeed!

Examine the overall coding; there is one **switch** statement based upon the passed message number. There are predefined names for all the Windows message numbers. (Yes, we can create our own messages to send as well.) In the simplest case, we are checking for and handling just two messages: **WM_PAINT** sent anytime the client area of the window needs to be redrawn and **WM_DESTROY** sent after the user chooses "Close" from the system menu or the 'X' button.

The response to a **WM_PAINT** message nearly always begins with a call to the **BeginPaint** function, passing it the handle of our window and a reference to a paint structure. Windows fills the fields of the paint structure with information that we can use in the painting process of the client area. One step of the **BeginPaint** function is to erase the background of the client window. It does this by painting the background using the brush defined in the **WNDCLASS** passed on into the **RegisterClass** function. It then validates the client area (meaning that it has been successfully erased and painted), and then returns back a **handle to a device context**, an **HDC**. A **device context** defines an output device, here the screen, with all of its properties, such as its pen and brush. You **must** have a handle to a device context to display any graphics or text information on the screen!

When using this **HDC**, handle to a device context, Windows prevents any drawing outside of the client window specified in the HDC, even if you try to do so. The various functions that display text, draw graphics, circles, lines, fill solids and so on, all require a valid handle to a device context which defines the area of the screen upon which you can paint.

When the client area of the window has been completely painted as you desire, the **EndPaint** function is invoked. It is passed the handle of the window and a reference to the paint structure. Thus, **BeginPaint—EndPaint** functions **always** occur in **pairs**! When called, the pair validates the client area of the window, meaning that Windows may consider the window is displaying the currently correct information.

Whenever the window is resized, for example, Windows invalidates the client area and sends another **WM_PAINT** message to the application. The **BeginPaint / EndPaint** pair validates the client area again. Note: we can send ourselves an "Invalidate Window" message to force our paint routines to redraw the window. In fact, this becomes a prime method of operation. The paint code **must** know how to redraw the entire client area of the window at **any** time.

Within the paint code, the first step is to acquire the current dimensions of the client area, given in a **RECT**, **rectangle structure**, which contains the four **ints** known as: **left**, **top** (x, y coordinates of the upper left corner) and **right** and **bottom** (the width and height of the client area in pixels). The function **GetClientRect** is passed the handle of the window and a reference to a **RECT** (rectangle) structure that is to be filled.

There are many ways to display messages. A simple one is to use the function **DrawText**. It is passed the handle to the device context, the character string or message or text to be displayed, a -1 to show the text is a null-terminated string (or the number of bytes to be displayed if not null-terminated), a reference to the client rectangle in which to draw, and finally a series of bit flags that define how to draw the text. Here, we are displaying a single line of text that is to be centered in the client rectangle both horizontally and vertically. **DT_SINGLELINE** forces the text onto one line; **DT_CENTER** centers the text horizontally; **DT_VCENTER** centers the line vertically. Again, we code one function call and gain enormous functionality. Run the application and resize the window; watch how the text remains centered within the window. What happens to the text when the window becomes too narrow to display the whole message? Try it. Again, read about the

DrawText function in the on-line documentation and see the other possibilities. We will be discussing the **DrawText** further in the ensuing chapters.

Finally, the handling required in response to the **WM_DESTROY** message is to send Windows the "Okay to shut the application down" message. It's done with the **PostQuitMessage** function that places a **WM_QUIT** message into the message queue. This message is what causes **GetMessage** to return a 0 value and cause program termination.

Note that when each message has been processed, a 0 is returned, indicating our code has successfully handled that message.

All other messages that Windows passes our **winproc (WinProc)** drop out of the switch statement. Our coding returns back the results of taking the default Windows standard action by calling **DefWindowProc**, passing the message and the parameters on down to the default handlers. Here is where all of the other messages went, such as maximize, minimize, open the system menu, make a system menu selection, move the window, and so on.

When you run the application, notice all of the things that you can do to the window. Among these are moving the window, resizing, maximizing the window, minimizing it, activating the system menu, selection of system menu options. When maximizing, the maximize button on the title bar is replaced with the normalize button. Note Windows handles all of this functionality within **DefWindowProc**; our application only needs to respond to a redraw or paint message and to a close message—that's all!

Programming Problems

Program01-1—A Modified Hello Program

Using the sample program from this chapter, create a window that behaves as follows.

the background window color is light gray
a vertical scrollbar is present, but non-functional
has a titlebar
has a sizeable border
window appears with of width 400 pixels and height 200 pixels
has no maximize button (a grayed one is acceptable)
has a system menu or controlbar
has a minimize button

The titlebar should display the following text.

CS250 your name: Program 1

Top align in the window and horizontally center the following text.

This is my first Windows program.

Note: do not worry about the different background color behind the text. There is another function that we have not yet discussed that would set the text background color.

Chapter 2 Outputting Text and Using Scroll Bars

The Paint Process

Definition: The **Client Area** of a window is all of the space of the window except that space occupied by the thick borders, title bar, menu bar, and the scroll bars, if present. The dimensions of the client area are not necessarily constant; the user may resize the window at anytime. This gives rise to the following design rule.

Design Rule 3: Your paint routine must be able to accept whatever dimensions the current client area has and display what is appropriate in that client area at that time.

Besides resizing, many things can temporarily overlay the client area such as dialog boxes, message boxes, and other applications. The client area also needs repainting when the application is restored from a minimized state. Similarly, when the user activates a scroll bar, whatever is displayed in the client area needs to be adjusted.

Whenever your client area needs to be redrawn either completely or in part, Windows sends your application a **WM_PAINT** message. You can even send yourself a **WM_PAINT** message when you want to alter what is being displayed.

Design Rule 4: Structure your program so that it accumulates all of the data needed to display the client area and then force a repaint of the client area.

Part of the paint message is the rectangular dimension of the portion of the window that needs to be updated. Quite often, only a small portion of the entire client area needs to be updated. When dealing with graphical objects, rather than regenerating the whole image, the application can be structured so that it only updates that portion that needs to be repainted. We will do this in Chapter 9. However, when one is displaying text information, it is usually more convenient to just go ahead and repaint the whole client area.

Definition: The **Invalid Region or Update Region or Invalid Rectangle** is that portion of the client area that needs to be repainted; it is defined by a rectangle.

Thus, the presence of an invalid region in the client area is what prompts Windows to send the **WM_PAINT** message. **WM_PAINT** messages are "low priority" messages; others, such as resizing the window, are higher. Higher priority messages are sent first. Often, Windows simply accumulates your not yet sent **WM_PAINT** messages and consolidates these into one **WM_PAINT** message by adjusting the dimensions of the invalid rectangle.

A program can also force a repaint in order to get new information displayed. The function to invalidate your client area is **InvalidateRect**.

```
BOOL InvalidateRect (HWND, RECT*, BOOL eraseFlag);
```

If the **eraseFlag** is **TRUE**, Windows erases the background (that is, Windows paints the background with the background brush) and then processes the **WM_PAINT** message. The function returns **TRUE** if successful. If the **eraseFlag** is **FALSE**, the background is not erased. Typical usage is as follows.

```
InvalidateRect (hwnd, &rect, TRUE);
```

Within the paint code, one can get the invalid rectangle either directly from the **BeginPaint** function or by calling the **GetUpdateRect** function whose prototype is this.

```
BOOL GetUpdateRect (HWND, RECT*, BOOL eraseFlag);
```

Typical coding could be as shown.

```
RECT rect;
GetUpdateRect (hwnd, &rect, TRUE);
```

Since **TRUE** is passed, Windows sends a **WM_ERASEBKGND** message, but we normally just pass it onto the default handler which paints the background for us. Alternatively, we can gain access to the invalid portion by referencing member fields of the **PAINTSTRUCT** structure that are filled in by the **BeginPaint()** function. Typical coding is as shown.

```
PAINTSTRUCT ps;
hdc = BeginPaint (hwnd, &ps);
```

There are three fields of the paint structure intended for our use.

ps.hdc—the device context handle (**HDC**) that is returned by **BeginPaint**
ps.fErase—a **BOOL**—**TRUE** if Windows has erased the background already
ps.rcPaint—a **RECT** structure of the invalid portion of client area

The **RECT** structure members are **top, left, bottom, right**— all are **ints**. What do these integers contain? They are the coordinates (x, y) in pixels of the respective rectangle corners. Okay. But where exactly is the point (0, 0)?

The origin of the coordinate system of the client area is the upper left corner of the **client area**! How convenient—the GDI (Graphical Device Interface) coordinates with which we must deal are simply our working window area and **not** those of the full screen. Thus, we are not forever trying to adjust coordinates. (There are ways of obtaining a handle to the entire screen and displaying there, but realize that doing so may overlay other applications.)

Further, with GDI operations, Windows normally "**clips**" all display operations so that nothing is displayed outside of your client area. In fact, you do not even need to be concerned—just display the text, and, if the message is too long, Windows automatically clips. Rerun **Pgm01a** and resize the window way too narrow for the message and watch the clipping occur. Note that you can set up a smaller clipping region within your client area and force text/graphics to stay within that "clipping rectangle or region." Most likely, your processing of **WM_PAINT** messages appears like this.

```
case WM_PAINT:
  hdc = BeginPaint (hwnd, &ps);
  ... insert your paint code here
  EndPaint (hwnd, &ps);
  return 0;
```

Important note: if you do not process **WM_PAINT** messages, **pass** them on the default handler, which repaints the background. Failure to repaint the background results in a "black hole" along with an infinite loop of paint messages flooding your application as Windows desperately tries to get your window repainted. The minimal application painting coding is as follows.

```
case WM_PAINT: // minimal painting code
  BeginPaint (hwnd, &ps);
  EndPaint (hwnd, &ps);
  return 0;
```

If you want to create an infinite loop and lock up the application, just code this.

```
case WM_PAINT:
  return 0;      // forces infinite loop
```

Since the **BeginPaint/EndPaint** pair is not called, Windows does not mark the invalid region as now being valid. Thus, Windows immediately sends another **WM_PAINT** message, and another, and on and on and on!

Painting From Other Places

You can paint the screen from places other than in response to **WM_PAINT** messages. However, you must get a handle to a valid device context to do so. Think of the DC as being the link between Windows and the physical screen. There are several ways to get the DC; perhaps the simplest is to use the following function pair.

```
HDC  GetDC      (HWND);
     ReleaseDC (HWND, HDC);
```

Typical coding is done this way.

```
HDC hdc;
hdc = GetDC (hwnd);
... insert coding to paint
ReleaseDC (hwnd, hdc);
```

Design Rule 5: While processing some message, whenever you get a GDI object, such as a DC, you must release it before you end processing of that message (or before the automatic storage of the hdc is freed). Failure to do so results in a resource and memory leak.

Failure to release or delete resources causes the memory occupied by that GDI object to never get freed! And more importantly, there are a finite number of device contexts within Windows. Windows system resources just keep getting smaller and smaller with each debug run! This applies to nearly everything you allocate under Windows, from GDI objects you create, such as brushes and pens, to global memory allocations and fonts. If you fail repeatedly to free up or release or delete brushed and pens, Windows will eventually run out of its finite supply of them and crash.

Under Windows 3.1, this was a nightmare because there were only five device contexts available. Thus, if you asked for a DC to use and did not give it back when you were done with it, there were only four remaining to service all other windows and Windows itself. If this failure to release the DC was done in a paint section, after the fifth call, there would be no device contexts left. Windows 3.1 then could not even display a message box to notify you of its plight. A black screen of death resulted. Fortunately with Windows 95 and all later versions, the number of these system resources has been greatly expanded. However, all resources are finite in number. One could still run Window out of resources by never giving them back to Windows when you are done using them.

Often, memory and resource leaks are very hard to locate. Therefore, a tool like NuMega's Bounds Checker for Windows becomes invaluable, since it locates all such leaks. Visual C++, when in debugging mode, also notifies you of memory leaks.

A Better Way to Display Text: The TextOut Function

DrawText works well when a single line of text is all that is desired. However, often we need to display many lines and with many fields or columns within that line. The most commonly used method to display text is the **TextOut** function. Notice that you **must** have a valid DC in order to display text.

```
BOOL TextOut (HDC hdc, int x, int y,
              char *ptrstring, int length);
```

TextOut displays a string beginning at the coordinates (x, y) using the current pen stored in the DC. If the length parameter is -1 or omitted (the default if not coded is -1), it displays all characters up to the null-terminator. The upper left corner of the text string rectangle is aligned on the (x, y) coordinates. The (x, y) coordinates are based upon the client area.

Well, actually there are many coordinate schemes possible (see Chapter 11). These different schemes are based upon several forms called **mapping modes** which determine the type of coordinate system along with the actual units such as pixels, inches or millimeters. The default mapping mode is called **MM_TEXT** in which the upper left corner is (0, 0), the values increase downward and rightward, and the units of measurement are given in pixels. The other mapping modes are not frequently used.

When displaying text, what colors are used? Each time that one gets a DC, the device context contains a default pen and default background brush. These default objects are a black pen and a white brush. Another way of saying this is that the default color scheme is black text on a white background. However, we may have any color scheme that we desire.

The color scheme is a combination of four items. There is the default window background brush that Windows uses to erase the windows background. There is the default pen color that is used to paint the text. There is the default color to be used behind the text letters. The last item controls how the letters are displayed—transparent or opaque. When opaque is in effect, the text background color is used to paint the space not occupied by the pixels that compose the letter. When transparent is used, the window's background remains visible where no pixels of a letter occur. Chapter 4 addresses how to handle these effects.

The DC also provides a default clipping region that is the total size of the available client area. (Again, you could lessen this rectangle, if desired.) Note that the DC from **BeginPaint** has already inserted the invalid rectangular area that needs repainting and may be the entire client area or some smaller portion of it.

The DC also specifies what font is to be used. The default font when a DC is obtained is called **SYSTEM_FONT** and is that font that is used in the title bar. Fonts are fully covered in Chapters 8 and 10. However, some details must be fully understood right at the start. Many fonts, including the system font are called **variable-width fonts** because the letter 'I' has a smaller width than an 'm' or 'w'. In a **fixed-width font**, as used in DOS, all characters have the same width. There is also a **SYSTEM_FIXED_FONT** available which emulates the DOS style font in which all characters have the same dimensions. With variable-width fonts, spacing multiple lines in columnar alignment becomes much more difficult.

Acquiring Text Measurements

The text metrics or measurements of a font can be found by the function **GetTextMetrics** which retrieves those values from the passed handle to a DC. In other words, after some font has been selected into a DC (the system font by default), the function fills a structure with the relevant details about that font.

The function syntax is as follows.

```
BOOL GetTextMetrics (HDC, TEXTMETRICS*);
```

Coding would be similar to the following.

```
TEXTMETRIC tm;
HDC        hdc;
hdc = GetDC (hwnd);
GetTextMetrics (hdc, &tm);
ReleaseDC (hwnd, hdc);
```

Now where would this coding be placed? Not in the **WM_PAINT** handling! Normally, the metrics only need to be determined **once**, not over and over every time a paint is required. Unless you need to handle font changes, a better place to get these values would be in response to the **WM_CREATE** which is a message sent as the window is about to be created. Sample coding to get the text metrics of the default font could be done this way.

```
case WM_CREATE:
 hdc = GetDC (hwnd);
 GetTextMetrics (hdc, &tm);
 ... save values into global variables or static variables
 ReleaseDC (hwnd, hdc);
 return 0;
```

What character values are desired? Well, what we really need are the character's average width and height and the width of capital letters. The field in the **TEXTMETRICS** structure, **tmAveCharWidth,** contains the width. The height is given by **tmHeight**. However, there must be some whitespace separating the vertical lines of text which is given by adding in the value called **tmExternalLeading**. So that the total height would be given by the sum of **tmHeight** + **tmExternalLeading**. (See Chapter 10 for a complete discussion of this structure.)

Assume that we have defined three static variables to hold the average character dimensions.

```
static int avgCharWidth;  // average character width
static int avgCharHeight; // average character height
static int avgCapsWidth;  // caps average width
```

Capital letter widths in a variable width font are generally 150% of lowercase widths. In a fixed font, all letters have the same width. Since one does not know in advance what type of font the user may have installed, another **TEXTMETRICS** field is needed to identify which type of font, fixed or variable, is present. This member is the **tmPitchAndFamily**, which is 0 for fixed and 1 for variable fonts. The complete coding to capture these dimensions is as follows.

```
case WM_CREATE:
  hdc = GetDC (hwnd);
  GetTextMetrics (hdc, &tm);
  avgCharWidth  = tm.tmAveCharWidth;
  avgCharHeight = tm.tmHeight + tm.tmExternalLeading;
  avgCapsWidth  =
       (tm.tmPitchAndFamily & 1 ? 3 : 2)*avgCharWidth / 2;
  ReleaseDC (hwnd, hdc);
  return 0;
```

There is one additional subtle point that must be fully understood. Notice that the three variables are given their values in response to the **WM_CREATE** message and that their values are later used in response to a **WM_PAINT** message. Further, remember that we are dealing with pure C style coding, not C++ OOP. Consider the following coding of our **WinProc**.

```
LRESULT CALLBACK winproc (HWND hwnd, UINT msg, WPARAM, LPARAM) {
 HDC            hdc;
 PAINTSTRUCT ps;
 RECT           rect;
 int            avgCharHeight;
 int            avgCharWidth;

 switch (msg) {
  case WM_CREATE:
    // store values retrieved from a dc - for example:
    avgCharHeight = 42;
    avgCharWidth = 10;
    return 0;

  case WM_PAINT:
    hdc = BeginPaint (hwnd, &ps);
    // use avgCharHeight and avgCharWidth
    // what values are in these above two variables here?
    EndPaint (hwnd, &ps);
    return 0;

...
 return DefWindowProc (hwnd, msg, wparam, lparam);
}
```

The question for you is this: If in **WM_CREATE** processing I place the values of 42 and 10 into these two variables, what is in these two variables when the subsequent **WM_PAINT** message is sent and processed? The answer is core garbage! Both the two variables are automatic storage variables. Automatic storage is deleted when a function ends. Thus, when the function returns after processing the **WM_CREATE** message, the storage for the two variables is destroyed. When the function is recalled to handle painting, the storage for these two variables is recreated. Thus, in **WM_PAINT** they contain core garbage. Argh!

Design Rule 6: Any variable within WinProc that must retain its value from message to message must be defined to be static or made a global application variable.

Thus, we must code this way.

```
LRESULT CALLBACK winproc (HWND hwnd, UINT msg, WPARAM, LPARAM) {
 HDC            hdc;
 PAINTSTRUCT ps;
 RECT           rect;
 static int     avgCharHeight;
 static int     avgCharWidth;
...
```

Using the Text Measurements

Suppose that you are going to display several lines of text. The x coordinate for the start of each line is often at **avgCharWidth**, which leaves one character's worth of whitespace between the border of the window and the first letter. This greatly aids readability. However, the clever part is figuring out the y coordinate. The y coordinate of the ith line (i^{th} so that you can wrap a loop around the printing process) is given by

(i+1) * avgCharHeight

The +1 allows for one blank line at the top of the window so that the text is not placed against the menu or title bar.

Next, how do we replace our familiar **printf** or **cout** instructions? Suppose that **stud_id** is an array of **longs** and **grade** is an array of **ints**. To display the ith set of values, we are used to coding one of the following.

```
printf ("Student ID: %7ld  Grade: %3d", stud_id[i],
        grade[i]);
cout << "Student ID: " << setw(7) << stud_id[i]
     << " Grade: " << setw (3) << grade[i];
```

Design Rule 7: The Windows functions display only character strings.

I repeat—only character strings can be displayed by Windows functions. Thus, we need some method to convert the entire output of a line into one string. There are many ways of doing this. In C, we learned the trick of using **sprintf**.

```
char msg[70];
sprintf (msg, "Student ID: %7ld  Grade: %3d", stud_id[i],
        grade[i]);
```

In C++ we learned to use an **ostrstream**.

```
char msg[70];
ostrstream os (msg, sizeof (msg));
os << "Student ID: " << setw(7) << stud_id[i]
   << " Grade: " << setw (3) << grade[i] << ends;
```

Also, one could use the functions **itoa** and **ltoa** to convert the numerical values into two strings.

With the data nicely formatted into a text string, we can now pass the string **msg** to **TextOut** or **DrawText**. But there is an even better method. Windows provides a built-in function to replace **sprintf**. If we use the Windows replacement, **wsprintf**, then the **sprintf** library routine does not have to be included in our program, making a smaller final program. But there is one caveat—**wsprintf** does **not** support floating point numbers. Windows also supplies a replacement function for **strlen** called **lstrlen**.

Assuming that the field, **num_students**, contained the total number of students, the following would be TRY #1 for the paint operation. This method is doomed to failure if variable width fonts are used as we will see in the first program below, Pgm02a.

```
case WM_PAINT:
 hdc = BeginPaint (hwnd, &ps);
 for (i=0; i<num_students; i++) {
  wsprintf (msg, "Student ID: %7ld  Grade: %3d", stud_id[i],
            grade[i]);
  TextOut (hdc, avgCharWidth, (i+1) * avgCharHeight,
           msg, lstrlen(msg));
 }
 EndPaint (hwnd, &ps);
 return 0;
```

Suppose that there were 100 students and that the user maximized the window. How many student lines appear on the screen? About twenty-five lines, less one for the title bar, less one for the whitespace at the top would be shown. The first twenty-three or so students are displayed. Windows clips all the rest because they go off the bottom of the client window. (We need Scroll Bars!)

Setting the TextOut Alignment

Where is the text that we output positioned with respect to the (x, y) coordinates that we give **TextOut**? Consider the bounding rectangle that encloses the entire text string. **TextOut** defaults to aligning the top-left corner of the text string rectangle at the given (x, y) coordinates. Other alignments are possible via the function **SetTextAlign**.

```
UINT SetTextAlign (HDC, UINT alignflagbits);
```

The commonly used align bits can be one from each set ORed together.

x-direction:
```
TA_CENTER    - horizontal centering
TA_LEFT      - left side - the default
TA_RIGHT     - right side
```
y-direction:
```
TA_BASELINE - baseline or middle
TA_BOTTOM    - bottom edge
TA_TOP       - top edge - the default
```

The default alignment is given by coding the following. This is the default.

```
SetTextAlign (hdc, TA_LEFT | TA_TOP);
```

The following would right align all subsequent **TextOut**s.

```
SetTextAlign (hdc, TA_RIGHT | TA_TOP);
```

That is, the rectangle of text is positioned so that its upper right corner is located at the (x, y) coordinates. Be sure to include the length of the text when you calculate the (x, y) coordinates; that is, the x value is where the last character of the text string is located with the rest of the string flowing off to the left of that.

The function returns the previous alignment flags it is successful. For example, suppose that we wished to right align the previous student grade lines. We could code the following.

```
char msg[70];
int i;
...
case WM_PAINT:
 hdc = BeginPaint (hwnd, &ps);
 SetTextAlign (hdc, TA_RIGHT | TA_TOP);
 for (i=0; i<num_students; i++) {
  wsprintf (msg, "Student ID: %7ld  Grade: %3d", stud_id[i],
            grade[i]);
  TextOut (hdc, avgCharWidth * (1+70),
           (i+1) * avgCharHeight, msg, lstrlen(msg));
 }
 EndPaint (hwnd, &ps);
 return 0;
```

Notice that the x coordinate is given by the number of characters in the string plus one for the left space at the border times the average character width.

Obtaining the Current Size of the Client Area

Before scroll bar processing can be approached, the current size of the client area must be known. One would define a pair of **int**s to hold the (x, y) dimensions.

```
static int width, height;  // current client area size
```

When a window is being formed, both initially and after a resizing operation, the application is sent a **WM_SIZE** message with the new window dimensions stored in the **LPARAM**. The two short integers representing the new dimensions are stored in the one long parameter. Somehow, we must extract them. This idea of placing two 2-byte short integers into one 4-byte long is common place under Windows. Extracting the parameters from the message and placing them into usable fields is known as "**message cracking.**" (A major advantage of using the MFC is that it does all this message cracking for us.) Windows provide two macros to extract the two short integers from the long: **LOWORD** and **HIWORD**. The processing to obtain the window's new height and width is as follows.

```
case WM_SIZE:
  width  = LOWORD (lparam);
  height = HIWORD (lparam);
  return 0;
```

For any given client area dimensions, we have then the two formulae below.

```
int number_lines = height / avgCharHeight;
int number_chars = width / avgCharWidth;
```

What about division by 0? If **WM_CREATE** is not processed before the **WM_SIZE** message, then the character dimensions have not been determined and we could end up dividing by 0. When **WinMain** calls **CreateWindow**, the application is sent the **WM_CREATE** message; later during the **ShowWindow** call, the application is passed the **WM_SIZE** message. Thus, it is safe to insert the calculations in the **WM_SIZE** message processing; the average character dimensions are found in response to **WM_CREATE** before **WM_SIZE** is sent.

Be aware that it is possible for the number of lines determined from the above calculation to be 0! A very small window may show only part of a text line. Further, when an application is launched, it is passed a series of **WM_SIZE** messages, beginning with a size of (0, 0) or a point. Later in the construction sequence, it is sent additional **WM_SIZE** messages containing the actual dimensions the window is to have.

Scroll Bars: Theory of Operation

A scroll bar consists of two endpoint **arrow buttons**, a **thumb bar** that shows the relative position within the document, and a **slider track**. When the user clicks on either of the arrow buttons, you should scroll one unit. If text lines are shown, one unit would be one line or one column. If a graphical image is shown, usually the image is moved one pixel for smooth scrolling.

The thumb bar can be dragged by the user. Now you have two options. If you can repaint the client area quickly, you can immediately follow thumb bar motions on screen. However, if you cannot keep up, it is better to let the user reposition the thumb bar; when the button is released, then repaint the client area.

One game that every user tries when scrolling is to see if the application can keep up with their fast thumb bar movements. Your users will get an inordinate amount of satisfaction if your application cannot keep up with their actions. In graphics mode, even when you have complex images to reform, there are techniques you can use to give the user his "high" of seeing blazingly fast scrolls, keeping up with his every motion. This is covered in Chapter 9.

Finally, the user may click at some point within the slider area. Again you have two choices. You may scroll one page per click or you may position to the relative position that that position on the slider represents. I prefer the latter.

A window can have scroll bars placed automatically by Windows by using the **CreateWindow** styles of **WS_VSCROLL** and **WS_HSCROLL**. Note that Windows manages these graphical elements and that their dimensions are not included in the client area. They always appear on the right and bottom. (To get scroll bars to appear elsewhere, you must create your own bars as a resource.)

Four functions are used to manage scroll bars. Windows sends your application up to seven messages notifying you of user actions. Every scroll bar has an associated **range of travel** and the **current thumb bar position**. The four scroll bar functions include setting/getting the range and setting/getting the thumb bar position. The default range setting is from 0 to 100, where 0 is the top or left position and 100 represents the bottom or right position.

```
BOOL SetScrollRange (HWND, SB_VERT, min, max, BOOL redraw);
BOOL SetScrollRange (HWND, SB_HORZ, min, max, BOOL redraw);
```

Here, the integers **min** and **max** specify the new range. The **BOOL redraw** is **TRUE** if Windows is to redraw the scroll bar with the new range in effect. The second parameter is one of the two special identifiers that specify which scroll bar is being set.

The other three related functions include the following.

```
BOOL GetScrollRange (HWND, SB_VERT, int *min, int *max);
BOOL GetScrollRange (HWND, SB_HORZ, int *min, int *max);
```

The following sets the thumb bar position.

```
BOOL SetScrollPos (HWND, SB_VERT, int newpos, BOOL redraw);
BOOL SetScrollPos (HWND, SB_HORZ, int newpos, BOOL redraw);
```

The following gets the current thumb bar position.

```
int newpos GetScrollPos (HWND, SB_VERT);
int newpos GetScrollPos (HWND, SB_HORZ);
```

Here the **newpos** integer is a discrete position within the range including the endpoints. Thus, if a range of 0 to 100 were used, the thumb bar position could be from 0 to 100.

What causes a scroll bar to become visible? When a window specifies that it desires one or more scroll bars, Windows provides them and automatically sets the scrolling range to go from 0 to 100. Since this means that there is 100 units to scroll, the scroll bars must be visible. If you call the **SetScrollRange** function and specify the range to be from 0 to 0, then the scroll bar automatically disappears, since there is presumably nothing to scroll. If later on you recall the function and specify a non-zero range, the scroll bar reappears.

Windows takes care of handling the mouse actions, showing the reverse video flash on clicks, displaying the ghost box on thumb bar dragging, and sending your application appropriate messages concerning scroll bar events. Your responsibilities include initializing the range, processing the desired scroll bar messages, and updating the thumb bar's current position.

Each mouse action generates **two** messages—one when the button is pressed and one when it is released. The messages are **WM_VSCROLL** and **WM_HSCROLL**. The **LOWORD** of the **WPARAM** parameter that accompanies the message indicates what the mouse action was. The identifiers for these values, as you might guess by now, all begin with SB_. Obviously, we must respond to these messages and implement the scrolling operation.

Action	Pressed	Released
top or left button	SB_LINEUP	SB_ENDSCROLL
bottom or right button	SB_LINEDOWN	SB_ENDSCROLL
slider area top or left	SB_PAGEUP	SB_ENDSCROLL
slider area bot or right	SB_PAGEDOWN	SB_ENDSCROLL
thumb bar action	SB_THUMBTRACK	SB_THUMBPOSITION where the HIWORD (wparam) contains the current position of the thumb bar within the defined range

Note that while thumb bar action is going on, Windows sends the application a barrage of **SB_THUMBTRACK** messages. If you cannot keep up with them, then take action only on the **SB_THUMBPOSITION** message.

When we respond to these messages, how much do we scroll? The answer is that it is totally up to your application. However, the usual guidelines for a text display consists of the following. With **SB_LINEUP** or **SB_LINEDOWN**, one should move one line or one character if this is the horizontal scroll. With **SB_PAGEUP** or **SB_PAGEDOWN**, one should move one page's worth where a page is usually considered to be one window's worth of lines, less one. If there are 20 lines visible in the window, then I would scroll 19 lines up or down. This way, there is always one line remaining visible from the previous set of lines. If you scroll all 20 lines, the user tends to lose their sense of continuity. When scrolling a graphical image, I usually use one pixel or one screen's worth for the line/page amounts.

The New Style Scroll Bars

Beginning with Windows 95, there is a new style of scroll bar in which the dimension of the thumb bar indicates the amount of scrolling. If the scroll range is very small, the thumb bar becomes very big. If there is a huge amount to scroll, the thumb bar is very tiny in size. The size of the thumb bar is called the page size.

Windows provides one function to set the page size; it also sets the scroll range and thumb bar position. Hence, the preferred method of setting scroll ranges is the new function **SetScrollInfo**.

```
SetScrollInfo (hwnd, SB_VERT or SB_HORZ, &scroll_info, TRUE);
```

where the **TRUE** requests that the bar be repainted with the new settings. The address of a **SCROLLINFO** structure is passed which defines all of the information to set the range and page size.

The **SCROLLINFO** structure has the following members.

```
WORD fMask - ORed series specifying which of the following
             contain valid data in this structure instance
int cbSize - the size of this structure
int nMin   - the minimum scroll amount - usually 0
int nMax   - the maximum scroll amount - with text, the
             number of total lines in the collection
int nPage  - the size of a page - with text, the number of
             lines visible - height / avg char height
int nPos   - the current thumb bar position
int nTrackPos - the intermediate position of the thumb bar
                while the user is dragging it - we can
                access this value while processing scroll
                messages but not set it
```

The **fMask** flag contains one or more of the following values.

```
SIF_PAGE             - use the page amount to set page size
SIF_POS              - set the position, use nPos
SIF_RANGE            - set the range, use nMin and nMax
SIF_TRACKPOS         - track the thumb bar while scrolling
SIF_ALL              - sets all of the above flags
SIF_DISABLENOSCROLL  - disable the scroll bar
```

In the following example, the page size, scroll range, and thumb bar position are all set by one function call.

```
SCROLLINFO si;
si.cbSize = sizeof (si);
si.fMask = SIF_ALL;
si.nMin = 0;
si.nMax = TOTAL_LINE;
si.nPage = height / avgCharHeight;
si.nPos = 0;        // initial position at the start
SetScrollInfo (hwnd, SB_VERT, &si, TRUE);
```

Structuring a Program for Painting

It is true that you can get a DC to your client area and paint on it nearly anytime. Occasionally, this would be the optimum approach as we will see in the next chapter when we process key strokes. Another useful approach is to force a repainting by calling **InvalidateRect** which results in a paint message being sent. At other times, because **WM_PAINT** messages are low priority messages, you may force a repainting at once by invoking the **UpdateWindow** function.

```
UpdateWindow (hwnd);
```

However, the nature of Windows dictates that at some point Windows will be sending the application the **WM_PAINT** message and the application **must** at that point repaint the whole client area. (Task switching from an overlaying window is one example.) In other words, no matter what logical actions your application is doing, the **WM_PAINT** coding **must** be able to recreate the whole window.

Design Rule 8: It is best to structure the application so that all of the client area painting is done in response to the WM_PAINT message whenever possible.

This rule is **so** different from the normal processing logic with which programmers are comfortable that protests are not uncommon. Perhaps even curses. However, you will find that if you begin painting in multiple places, you end up duplicating code like mad. Let's examine how we might structure the text scrolling process so that the actual painting is done in response to **WM_PAINT**. We will concentrate on the vertical scrolling process.

The starting point is knowing the total possible number of lines that are to be displayed; let's call it **TOTAL_LINES**. When we receive the **WM_SIZE** message, we can retrieve the current size of the client area and save the dimensions in the static fields **width** and **height**. From this, we can calculate the number of lines per client window page as follows.

```
num_lines_per_page = height / avgCharHeight;
```

That is, the number of vertical pixels of the client area / the average height of a character in pixels gives the number of lines we can show on a page.

Now the total lines minus the number of lines per page plus one for the top blank line for readability gives the number of lines that are not yet on the screen, which is the number of lines to scroll. This would be the maximum scrolling range. However, if the total lines were fewer than could be shown or if the number of lines possible in the client area exceeds the total to be displayed, then the maximum number of lines to scroll would then be 0. Therefore, using the following, we can set the new vertical scroll range.

```
max_scroll_lines = max (0, TOTAL_LINES - num_lines_per_page + 1);
```

MFC provides a built-in pair of macros, **max** and **min**. These are handy when we need to find the minimum or maximum value of a pair of numbers.

The thumb bar's position is really the current line that is at the top of the client window; let's called it **current_top_line**. The thumb bar position is more complex. Consider the following situation. There are 50 lines to be shown; the client area can show 20; the user has scrolled such that line 10 is at the top of the window; the thumb bar would be setting at line 10; now the user resizes the window smaller. The **current_top_line** would still be 10. However, suppose that the user resized the window so that a potential of 60 lines could be shown. There are only 50 lines total. In this case, **max_scroll_lines** is reset to 0 by the above formula because the total lines minus the number of lines per page becomes negative. Also the **current_top_line** must also be lowered from 10 to 0. So after coding the following, we would then set the new current thumb position using this formula.

```
current_top_line = min (current_top_line, max_scroll_lines);
```

Now we can respond to scrolling messages by calculating the number of lines to scroll based upon the message; let's call this variable **num_lines_to_scroll**. When the **WM_VSCROLL** message is sent, the **LOWORD** of the **WPARAM** parameter contains the SB_ type of scroll that was requested. Usually, we switch on this value to separate the various scrolling cases. For line up/down requests, we set the number of lines to scroll to -1 for up, +1 for down. For page up/down requests, use the number of lines per page, forcing at least one line up or one line down. For the thumb bar motion, the **HIWORD** of the **WPARAM** parameter contains the current new position, so the new position minus **current_top_line** yields the amount to scroll.

Then to guard against variables out of range, we reassign the number of lines to scroll to be the larger of the current max number of lines we could go up and the requested number of lines to move, which itself is the smaller of the previously calculated number of lines to scroll and the difference between the current max lines and the current top line. This yields one of the nastiest formulas to grasp.

```
num_lines_to_scroll = max (-current_top_line,
                             // this is absolute max up
                          min (num_lines_to_scroll,
                             // this is the requested num lines
                          max_scroll_lines - current_top_line)
                             // is actual max num
                       );
```

Or just

```
num_lines_to_scroll = max (-current_top_line,
 min (num_lines_to_scroll, max_scroll_lines - current_top_line));
```

If there are lines to scroll, then three steps are needed. First, add the number of lines we are scrolling to the current top, giving the new current top line. Second, force the scroll by calling the **ScrollWindow** function. Third, reset the new thumb bar position.

The **ScrollWindow** function handles the scrolling details, like hiding the mouse cursor, sending the paint message, and restoring the cursor. As part of the process, a new paint message is sent.

```
BOOL ScrollWindow (hwnd,
                    int amount to horiz scroll,
                   int amount to vert scroll,
                    address of scrolling rectangle or NULL,
                    address of a clipping rectangle or NULL
                   );
```

The two null parameters are pointers to the actual scrolling rectangle within the client area and the clipping rectangle. Since we want the whole window, both can be null. In later chapters, we may desire some column headings to remain fixed while the actual report lines themselves scroll. In such a case, we can define a scrolling rectangle and pass its address for both the last two addresses. Then, any painting is forced to stay inside that rectangle leaving column headings alone. These last two parameters are both **RECT***.

When we call **ScrollWindow**, that function eventually sends us a **WM_PAINT** message. So in our paint section, we must repaint what is now on the screen.

Design Rule 9: When responding to WM_PAINT message during scrolling, to avoid massive flicker, only paint those lines that are in the invalid portion of the window.

This Design Rule is a crucial one, a vital one. Suppose that you have 1500 total lines that could be displayed and that only 20 lines can be shown in the window at one time. Do **not** just loop through all 1500 lines displaying them on successive lines! True, Windows clips all those whose coordinates are out of range for the current window size. However, the resultant time delay and massive flicker is terribly annoying and frustrating to the user.

It is a simple matter to determine with which line to start with and with which line to end the painting process. At first glance, it would seem that the current top line would be the beginning subscript into the array of 1500 lines with which to begin the paint. And the ending line subscript would be the current top line plus the number of lines per page or screen. If you use these values, you will achieve your objective of repainting the screen.

However, when the paint message is coming as a result of scrolling down one line, another aspect ought to be considered. And that is just how does **ScrollWindow** work. If you think of the display in the client window as being just a mass of colored pixels and if the scroll request is for one line down, then the vast majority of pixels currently on the screen remain on the screen only moved an average character height up. Only the very bottom line's worth of pixels will be different. Windows has a massive pixel copier function known as a **BitBlt**, bit block transfer, which copies pixels extremely fast. **ScrollWindow** actually uses a **BitBlt** function call to move all the pixels that will remain visible from their current location to their new location. It then determines that small rectangle that must be repainted with the new line that is to appear as a result of the scroll down one line message. So when **ScrollWindow** issues the **WM_PAINT** message, it sets the invalid rectangle for paint as being just that small rectangle at the bottom of the window.

So for very fast painting responses when scrolling, we should take advantage of this extra information. Instead of beginning our painting with the current top line, we should calculate a more accurate initial line to begin painting. The paint structure's rectangle's top coordinate divided by the **avgCharHeight** gives this offset from the current top line, should Windows request only part of the client area be repainted. Thus, the start line number is best calculated as follows. Note the -1 is to allow for the one average character height of whitespace we allow at the top.

```
start_line = max (0, current_top_line +
                     ps.rcPaint.top / avgCharHeight -1);
end_line = min (TOTAL_LINES, current_top_line +
                     ps.rcPaint.bottom / avgCharHeight);
for (i=start_line; i<end_line; i++) {
```

Within the display loop, all lines start at an x coordinate of **avgCharWidth** so there is some whitespace at the left border. The y coordinate would be **avgCharHeight** times the ith line less current top +1, where the +1 allows for the blank first line.

Using this scheme, your painting will always be as fast as it can be. Flicker is nearly nonexistent. And you have a professional scrolling application. Ok. So now we need some text to display to try all of this.

The SYSTEM METRICS Structure

The function **GetSystemMetrics** retrieves any one of the 40 system values, many of which are of keen interest to us as programmers. Among the metrics are the screen dimensions, the main window dimensions, whether a mouse is present and so on. The values are accessed by 40 special id number whose identifiers begin SM_ as you might suspect. The function returns the requested system value which is always an **int**.

```
int GetSystemMetrics (id_desired);
```

Pgm02a: a Wrong Way to Display with Variable Width Fonts

In **Pgm02a.cpp**, I adopted display logic that most of you are familiar with—create an array of 40 strings that contain the text including a %5d to be used as a control string. For each system metric value, I use a **wsprintf** to print into the text message both the control string text and the sysmetric's value. Under DOS, it works perfectly. Examine the coding in **Pgm02a.cpp** below. Notice how nicely formatted the strings in **sysmetrics_msg** appear. Also, notice there is an array of the special defined IDs, **sysmetrics_ids**.

Follow through the code and examine the implementation; then run the application and experiment with the scrolling. Notice that I took the liberty to use capitalization for **WinProc**, **InitApplication**, and **InitInstance** for greater readability. When you see the screen output, you will see why this is the wrong way to handle this. Figure 2-1 below shows how the screen appears when the application is maximized. Can you figure out **why** this has occurred?

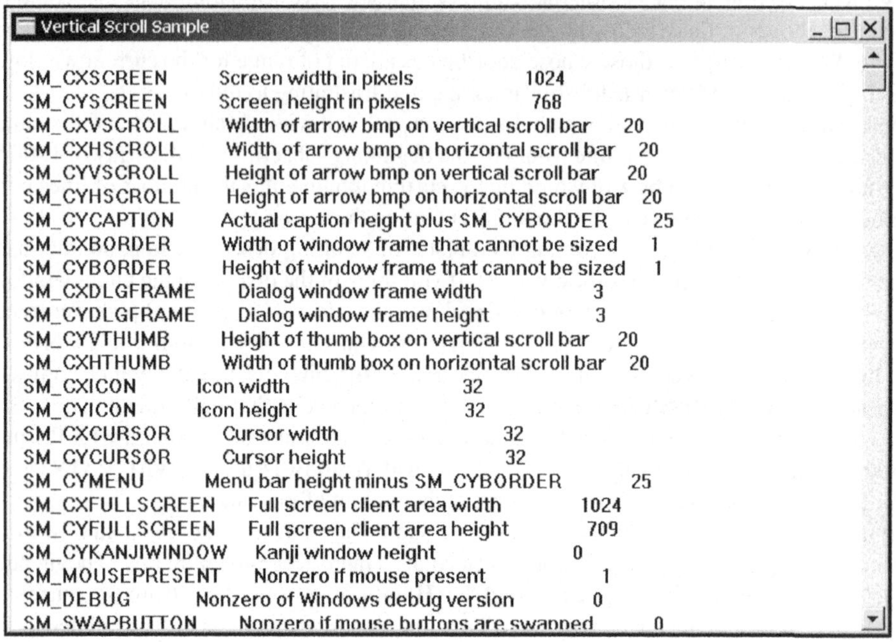

Vertical Scroll Sample

```
SM_CXSCREEN        Screen width in pixels                  1024
SM_CYSCREEN        Screen height in pixels                  768
SM_CXVSCROLL       Width of arrow bmp on vertical scroll bar    20
SM_CXHSCROLL       Width of arrow bmp on horizontal scroll bar    20
SM_CYVSCROLL       Height of arrow bmp on vertical scroll bar    20
SM_CYHSCROLL       Height of arrow bmp on horizontal scroll bar    20
SM_CYCAPTION       Actual caption height plus SM_CYBORDER      25
SM_CXBORDER        Width of window frame that cannot be sized     1
SM_CYBORDER        Height of window frame that cannot be sized     1
SM_CXDLGFRAME        Dialog window frame width               3
SM_CYDLGFRAME        Dialog window frame height              3
SM_CYVTHUMB        Height of thumb box on vertical scroll bar    20
SM_CXHTHUMB        Width of thumb box on horizontal scroll bar    20
SM_CXICON        Icon width                 32
SM_CYICON        Icon height                32
SM_CXCURSOR        Cursor width                 32
SM_CYCURSOR        Cursor height                32
SM_CYMENU        Menu bar height minus SM_CYBORDER              25
SM_CXFULLSCREEN     Full screen client area width          1024
SM_CYFULLSCREEN     Full screen client area height          709
SM_CYKANJIWINDOW     Kanji window height                0
SM_MOUSEPRESENT     Nonzero if mouse present                1
SM_DEBUG        Nonzero of Windows debug version           0
SM_SWAPBUTTON     Nonzero if mouse buttons are swapped          0
```

Figure 2.1 Pgm02a Scrolling System Metrics

Pgm02a Listing - Scrolling System Metrics - the Wrong Way

```
/**************************************************************/
/*                                                            */
/* Pgm02a Vertical Scrolling Shell            by Vic Broquard */
/*                                                            */
/* C style  basic model                                       */
/*                                                            */
/**************************************************************/

#include <windows.h>

/**************************************************************/
/*                                                            */
/* structure definitions, external/global data, and prototypes */
/*                                                            */
/**************************************************************/

LRESULT CALLBACK WinProc (HWND, UINT, WPARAM, LPARAM);
BOOL InitApplication (HINSTANCE);
BOOL InitInstance (HINSTANCE, int);

char appname[] = "ScrollPgm"; // the name of our application

```

```
// global constants facilitate processing SYSTEM METRICS display
const int TOTAL_LINES = 40;
const int TOTAL_CHAR_WIDTH = 71;  // width of message lines
const int NUM_WIDTH = 5;          // width of numerical values
const int LEN_CTL_SPEC = 3;       // length of %5d spec
const int TOTAL_WIDTH =
                 TOTAL_CHAR_WIDTH + NUM_WIDTH - LEN_CTL_SPEC + 1;

int sysmetrics_ids [TOTAL_LINES] = {
 SM_CXSCREEN,          SM_CYSCREEN,      SM_CXVSCROLL,
 SM_CXHSCROLL,         SM_CYVSCROLL,     SM_CYHSCROLL,
 SM_CYCAPTION,         SM_CXBORDER,      SM_CYBORDER,
 SM_CXDLGFRAME,        SM_CYDLGFRAME,    SM_CYVTHUMB,
 SM_CXHTHUMB,          SM_CXICON,        SM_CYICON,
 SM_CXCURSOR,          SM_CYCURSOR,      SM_CYMENU,
 SM_CXFULLSCREEN,      SM_CYFULLSCREEN,  SM_CYKANJIWINDOW,
 SM_MOUSEPRESENT,      SM_DEBUG,         SM_SWAPBUTTON,
 SM_CXMIN,             SM_CYMIN,         SM_CXSIZE,
 SM_CYSIZE,            SM_CXFRAME,       SM_CYFRAME,
 SM_CXMINTRACK,        SM_CYMINTRACK,    SM_CXDOUBLECLK,
 SM_CYDOUBLECLK,       SM_CXICONSPACING, SM_CYICONSPACING,
 SM_MENUDROPALIGNMENT, SM_PENWINDOWS,    SM_CMOUSEBUTTONS,
 SM_DBCSENABLED
};

char sysmetrics_msg [TOTAL_LINES] [TOTAL_CHAR_WIDTH] = {
"SM_CXSCREEN           Screen width in pixels                   "
     "    %5d",
"SM_CYSCREEN           Screen height in pixels                  "
     "    %5d",
"SM_CXVSCROLL          Width of arrow bmp on vertical scroll bar"
     "    %5d",
"SM_CXHSCROLL          Width of arrow bmp on horizontal scroll b"
     "ar  %5d",
"SM_CYVSCROLL          Height of arrow bmp on vertical scroll ba"
     "r   %5d",
"SM_CYHSCROLL          Height of arrow bmp on horizontal scroll "
     "bar %5d",
"SM_CYCAPTION          Actual caption height plus SM_CYBORDER   "
     "    %5d",
"SM_CXBORDER           Width of window frame that cannot be size"
     "d   %5d",
"SM_CYBORDER           Height of window frame that cannot be siz"
     "ed  %5d",
"SM_CXDLGFRAME         Dialog window frame width                "
     "    %5d",
"SM_CYDLGFRAME         Dialog window frame height               "
     "    %5d",
"SM_CYVTHUMB           Height of thumb box on vertical scroll ba"
     "r   %5d",
"SM_CXHTHUMB           Width of thumb box on horizontal scroll b"
     "ar  %5d",
"SM_CXICON             Icon width                               "
     "    %5d",
"SM_CYICON             Icon height                              "
     "    %5d",
"SM_CXCURSOR           Cursor width                             "
     "    %5d",
"SM_CYCURSOR           Cursor height                            "
     "    %5d",
"SM_CYMENU             Menu bar height minus SM_CYBORDER        "
     "    %5d",
"SM_CXFULLSCREEN       Full screen client area width            "
     "    %5d",
```

```
"SM_CYFULLSCREEN       Full screen client area height              "
        "     %5d",
"SM_CYKANJIWINDOW      Kanji window height                         "
        "     %5d",
"SM_MOUSEPRESENT       Nonzero if mouse present                    "
        "     %5d",
"SM_DEBUG              Nonzero of Windows debug version            "
        "     %5d",
"SM_SWAPBUTTON         Nonzero if mouse buttons are swapped        "
        "     %5d",
"SM_CXMIN              Minimum window width                        "
        "     %5d",
"SM_CYMIN              Minimum window height                       "
        "     %5d",
"SM_CXSIZE             Width of bmps contained in the title bar "
        "     %5d",
"SM_CYSIZE             Height of bmps contained in the title bar"
        "     %5d",
"SM_CXFRAME            Width of window frame that can be sized  "
        "     %5d",
"SM_CYFRAME            Height of window frame that can be sized "
        "     %5d",
"SM_CXMINTRACK         Minimum window tracking width               "
        "     %5d",
"SM_CYMINTRACK         Minimum window tracking height              "
        "     %5d",
"SM_CXDOUBLECLK        Double click x tolerance                    "
        "     %5d",
"SM_CYDOUBLECLK        Double click y tolerance                    "
        "     %5d",
"SM_CXICONSPACING      Horizontal icon spacing                     "
        "     %5d",
"SM_CYICONSPACING      Vertical icon spacing                       "
        "     %5d",
"SM_MENUDROPALIGNMENT  Alignment of pop up menu - if 0, left ali"
        "gn  %5d",
"SM_PENWINDOWS         Handle of Pen Windows DLL if installed   "
        "     %5d",
"SM_CMOUSEBUTTONS      Number of mouse buttons                     "
        "     %5d",
"SM_DBCSENABLED        Nonzero if double-byte character set enab"
        "led %5d"
};

/*******************************************************************/
/*                                                                 */
/* WinMain: windows equivalent to a "main" in C pgms               */
/*                                                                 */
/*******************************************************************/

int APIENTRY WinMain (HINSTANCE hinstance,
                      HINSTANCE hprevinstance,
                      LPSTR  cmdline, int howshow) {
 MSG          msg;

 // fill in WNDCLASS and register the app's window
 if (!InitApplication (hinstance)) return FALSE;

 // create an instance of the main window, based upon howshow
 if (!InitInstance (hinstance, howshow)) return FALSE;

 // enter the main processing loop consisting of getting the
 // next message, translating it and sending it to be handled
 while ( GetMessage (&msg, NULL, 0, 0)) {
```

```
  TranslateMessage (&msg);
  DispatchMessage  (&msg);
 }

 return (int) msg.wParam;  // pass along the return code
}


/*****************************************************************/
/*                                                               */
/* InitApplication:                                              */
/*   fill in the WNDCLASS structure about how to construct our   */
/*   main window and then register this window with Windows      */
/*                                                               */
/*****************************************************************/

BOOL InitApplication (HINSTANCE hinstance) {

 WNDCLASS wndclass;

 wndclass.style         = CS_HREDRAW | CS_VREDRAW;
 wndclass.lpfnWndProc   = WinProc;
 wndclass.cbClsExtra    = 0;
 wndclass.cbWndExtra    = 0;
 wndclass.hInstance     = hinstance;
 wndclass.hIcon         = LoadIcon (NULL, IDI_APPLICATION);
 wndclass.hCursor       = LoadCursor (NULL, IDC_ARROW);
 wndclass.hbrBackground = (HBRUSH) GetStockObject (WHITE_BRUSH);
 wndclass.lpszMenuName  = NULL;
 wndclass.lpszClassName = appname;

 // registers this window so it can be shown
 return RegisterClass (&wndclass);
}


/*****************************************************************/
/*                                                               */
/* InitInstance:                                                 */
/*   construct an instance of our main window using our just     */
/*   registered class                                            */
/*                                                               */
/*****************************************************************/

BOOL InitInstance (HINSTANCE hinstance, int howshow) {

 HWND hwnd;

 hwnd = CreateWindow (
        appname,                // char string that ids the app
        "Vertical Scroll Sample", // title bar caption
        WS_OVERLAPPEDWINDOW,    // window style
        CW_USEDEFAULT,          // window's initial x position
        CW_USEDEFAULT,          // window's initial y position
        CW_USEDEFAULT,          // window's initial x size - width
        CW_USEDEFAULT,          // window's initial y size- height
        NULL,                   // parent window's handle
        NULL,                   // handle to window's menu
        hinstance,              // handle of this instance
        NULL);                  // creation parameters - advanced

 if (!hwnd) return FALSE;       // window construction failed

 ShowWindow (hwnd, howshow);   // creates window on the screen
```

```
 return TRUE;
}



/********************************************************************/
/*                                                                  */
/* WinProc: our main window message processing function             */
/*                                                                  */
/********************************************************************/

LRESULT CALLBACK WinProc (HWND hwnd, UINT msg, WPARAM wparam,
                          LPARAM lparam) {

 static int numLinesPerPage;      // number of lines/page
 static int maxScrollLines;       // maximum vert scroll range
 static int currentTopLine = 0;   // current vert scroll pos
 static int numLinesToScroll = 0; // num lines to scroll

 static int avgCharHeight;   // average character height
 static int avgCharWidth;    // average character width
 static int avgCapsWidth;    // average capitals width
 static int height;          // current window height
 static int width;           // current  window width

 HDC         hdc;
 PAINTSTRUCT ps;
 TEXTMETRIC  tm;
 int    start_line;
 int    end_line;
 int    i, x, y;
 char   textbuffer [TOTAL_WIDTH];

 // our app's message processing section - given a message from
 // Windows, determine if the message is one that we wish to
 // respond to and do so or pass it on down to the Windows
 // provided default message handler

 switch (msg) {

/********************************************************************/
/*                                                                  */
/* WM_CREATE: window creation processing                            */
/*                                                                  */
/********************************************************************/

  case WM_CREATE:

   // acquire the system font's characteristics
   hdc = GetDC (hwnd);          // acquire a DC to get textmetrics
   GetTextMetrics (hdc, &tm); // get the information
   ReleaseDC (hwnd, hdc);     // free up the DC

   // calculate average character parameters
   avgCharWidth  = tm.tmAveCharWidth;
   avgCharHeight = tm.tmHeight + tm.tmExternalLeading;
   avgCapsWidth  = (tm.tmPitchAndFamily & 1 ? 3 : 2) *
                   avgCharWidth / 2;

   return 0;


/********************************************************************/
/*                                                                  */
```

```
/* WM_SIZE: resize the window processing                          */
/*                                                                */
/******************************************************************/

  case WM_SIZE:

   // get current client window size
   width = LOWORD (lparam);
   height = HIWORD (lparam);

   // calculate new max range based on current size
   numLinesPerPage = height / avgCharHeight;
   maxScrollLines = max (0, TOTAL_LINES - numLinesPerPage + 1);
   // note: if there is more screen than actual lines, set to 0

   // adjust thumb line position - could now exceed bottom pos
   currentTopLine = min (currentTopLine, maxScrollLines);

   // set up scroll range and position of thumb bar
   SetScrollRange (hwnd, SB_VERT, 0, maxScrollLines, FALSE);
   SetScrollPos   (hwnd, SB_VERT, currentTopLine, TRUE);

   return 0;


/******************************************************************/
/*                                                                */
/* WM_VSCROLL: process vertical scroll messages                   */
/*                                                                */
/******************************************************************/

  case WM_VSCROLL:

   switch (LOWORD(wparam)) {
    case SB_LINEUP:      // scroll up 1 line
      numLinesToScroll = -1;
      break;

    case SB_LINEDOWN:    // scroll down 1 line
      numLinesToScroll = +1;
      break;

    case SB_PAGEUP:      // scroll one screen up
      numLinesToScroll = min (-1, -numLinesPerPage);
      break;

    case SB_PAGEDOWN:    // scroll one screen down
      numLinesToScroll = max ( 1,  numLinesPerPage);
      break;

    case SB_THUMBTRACK: // follow thumb bar motion
                        // Win 3.1 used LOWORD(lparam)
      numLinesToScroll = HIWORD (wparam) - currentTopLine;
      break;

    case SB_TOP:         // goto top
      numLinesToScroll = -currentTopLine;
      break;

    case SB_BOTTOM:      // goto bottom
      numLinesToScroll = maxScrollLines - currentTopLine;
      break;

    default:
```

```
       numLinesToScroll = 0;
    }

   numLinesToScroll = max (-currentTopLine,
                              // this is absolute max up
                         min (numLinesToScroll,
                              // this is the requested num lines
                              maxScrollLines - currentTopLine)
                              // is actual max num
                       );

   if (numLinesToScroll !=0) { // any lines to really scroll?
    currentTopLine += numLinesToScroll;// increment thumb pos
    ScrollWindow (hwnd, 0, -avgCharHeight * numLinesToScroll,
                 NULL, NULL);
    // set new thumb bar position
    SetScrollPos (hwnd, SB_VERT, currentTopLine, TRUE);
   }
   return 0;


/*************************************************************/
/*                                                           */
/* WM_PAINT: display text upon the current client window     */
/*                                                           */
/*************************************************************/

   case WM_PAINT:

     hdc = BeginPaint (hwnd, &ps);

     // calculate start and ending lines to be displayed
     // start line num is the larger of 0 and the sum of the
     // current top line plus the number of lines from the top of
     // the window down to the invalid portion to be updated less
     // one for the blank line at the very top
     start_line = max (0, currentTopLine +
                       ps.rcPaint.top / avgCharHeight - 1);

     // end line num is the smaller of the total possible lines
     // and the sum of the current top line + the number of lines
     // that can fit in the invalid rectangle
     end_line = min (TOTAL_LINES, currentTopLine +
                             ps.rcPaint.bottom / avgCharHeight);

     // display only those lines that can be visible
     for (i=start_line; i<end_line; i++) {
      x = avgCharWidth;
      y = avgCharHeight * (1 - currentTopLine + i);
      TextOut (hdc, x, y, textbuffer,
               wsprintf (textbuffer, sysmetrics_msg[i],
                         GetSystemMetrics (sysmetrics_ids[i])));
     }

     EndPaint (hwnd, &ps);
     return 0;


/*************************************************************/
/*                                                           */
/* WM_DESTROY: close down the application processing         */
/*                                                           */
/*************************************************************/

```

```
  case WM_DESTROY:

    PostQuitMessage (0);
    return 0;
  }


/********************************************************************/
/*                                                                  */
/* Let Windows process all unhandled messages                       */
/*                                                                  */
/********************************************************************/

 return DefWindowProc (hwnd, msg, wparam, lparam);
}
```

Pgm02b: a Right Way to Display with Variable Width Fonts

The reason that the text columns did not align has to do with the variable width font. Letters have different widths between themselves and blanks. The first field contains all uppercase letters and had varying number of them. Thus, the total width of the capital letters' column varied from line to line. And so on throughout the lines.

The solution is to break the line down into three columns that are to be aligned. Specifically, the "metric id" is the first column; the description becomes the second; the integer value, the third. Further, the first two columns must be left aligned while the integer column must be right aligned.

Examine the included **SysMets.h** file that first defines the sysmetrics structure consisting of the three fields, allocates a global instance of it, and initializes that array.

SysMets.h - Definition of the System Metrics Display Structure

```
#pragma once

/********************************************************************/
/*                                                                  */
/* SysMetrics: defines system metrics arrays for display            */
/*                                                                  */
/********************************************************************/

const int TOTAL_LINES = 40;
const int COL_FIELD_2 = 22;
const int COL_FIELD_3 = 46;

struct {
 int  index;
 char *label;
 char *desc;
} SysMetrics [TOTAL_LINES] = {

{SM_CXSCREEN,            "SM_CXSCREEN",
                   "Screen width in pixels"},
{SM_CYSCREEN,            "SM_CYSCREEN",
                   "Screen height in pixels"},
{SM_CXVSCROLL,           "SM_CXVSCROLL",
                   "Width of arrow bmp on vertical scroll bar"},
{SM_CXHSCROLL,           "SM_CXHSCROLL",
                   "Width of arrow bmp on horizontal scroll bar"},
{SM_CYVSCROLL,           "SM_CYVSCROLL",
                   "Height of arrow bmp on vertical scroll bar"},
{SM_CYHSCROLL,           "SM_CYHSCROLL",
                   "Height of arrow bmp on horizontal scroll bar"},
{SM_CYCAPTION,           "SM_CYCAPTION",
```

```
                   "Actual caption height plus SM_CYBORDER"},
{SM_CXBORDER,           "SM_CXBORDER",
                   "Width of window frame that cannot be sized"},
{SM_CYBORDER,           "SM_CYBORDER",
                   "Height of window frame that cannot be sized"},
{SM_CXDLGFRAME,         "SM_CXDLGFRAME",
                   "Dialog window frame width"},
{SM_CYDLGFRAME,         "SM_CYDLGFRAME",
                   "Dialog window frame height"},
{SM_CYVTHUMB,           "SM_CYVTHUMB",
                   "Height of thumb box on vertical scroll bar"},
{SM_CXHTHUMB,           "SM_CXHTHUMB",
                   "Width of thumb box on horizontal scroll bar"},
{SM_CXICON,             "SM_CXICON",
                   "Icon width"},
{SM_CYICON,             "SM_CYICON",
                   "Icon height"},
{SM_CXCURSOR,           "SM_CXCURSOR",
                   "Cursor width"},
{SM_CYCURSOR,           "SM_CYCURSOR",
                   "Cursor height"},
{SM_CYMENU,             "SM_CYMENU",
                   "Menu bar height minus SM_CYBORDER"},
{SM_CXFULLSCREEN,       "SM_CXFULLSCREEN",
                   "Full screen client area width"},
{SM_CYFULLSCREEN,       "SM_CYFULLSCREEN",
                   "Full screen client area height"},
{SM_CYKANJIWINDOW,      "SM_CYKANJIWINDOW",
                   "Kanji window height"},
{SM_MOUSEPRESENT,       "SM_MOUSEPRESENT",
                   "Nonzero if mouse present"},
{SM_DEBUG,              "SM_DEBUG",
                   "Nonzero if Windows debug version"},
{SM_SWAPBUTTON,         "SM_SWAPBUTTON",
                   "Nonzero if mouse buttons are swapped"},
{SM_CXMIN,              "SM_CXMIN",
                   "Minimum window width"},
{SM_CYMIN,              "SM_CYMIN",
                   "Minimum window height"},
{SM_CXSIZE,             "SM_CXSIZE",
                   "Width of bmps contained in the title bar"},
{SM_CYSIZE,             "SM_CYSIZE",
                   "Height of bmps contained in the title bar"},
{SM_CXFRAME,            "SM_CXFRAME",
                   "Width of window frame that can be sized"},
{SM_CYFRAME,            "SM_CYFRAME",
                   "Height of window frame that can be sized"},
{SM_CXMINTRACK,         "SM_CXMINTRACK",
                   "Minimum window tracking width"},
{SM_CYMINTRACK,         "SM_CYMINTRACK",
                   "Minimum window tracking height"},
{SM_CXDOUBLECLK,        "SM_CXDOUBLECLK",
                   "Double click x tolerance"},
{SM_CYDOUBLECLK,        "SM_CYDOUBLECLK",
                   "Double click y tolerance"},
{SM_CXICONSPACING,      "SM_CXICONSPACING",
                   "Horizontal icon spacing"},
{SM_CYICONSPACING,      "SM_CYICONSPACING",
                   "Vertical icon spacing"},
{SM_MENUDROPALIGNMENT, "SM_MENUDROPALIGNMENT",
                   "Alignment of popup menu - if 0, left aligned"},
{SM_PENWINDOWS,         "SM_PENWINDOWS",
                   "Handle of Pen Windows DLL if installed"},
{SM_CMOUSEBUTTONS,      "SM_CMOUSEBUTTONS",
```

```
                       "Number of mouse buttons"},
{SM_DBCSENABLED,           "SM_DBCSENABLED",
                       "Nonzero if double-byte character set enabled"}
};
```

Next examine the revised **Pgm02b.cpp** program. Since I am now including a user header file, SysMets.h, I have included the **#pragma hdrstop** line to cause precompiled headers to not include the system metrics header file since it is subject to changes until I get it right. All changes are in bold face.

Pgm02b - Proper Scrolling of Sysmetrics Lines

```
/***************************************************************/
/*                                                             */
/* Pgm02b Vertical Scrolling Shell          by Vic Broquard    */
/*                                                             */
/* Proper way to handle scrolling columns of data              */
/*                                                             */
/***************************************************************/

#include <windows.h>
#pragma hdrstop

#include "SysMets.h"

/***************************************************************/
/*                                                             */
/* structure definitions, external/global data, and prototypes */
/*                                                             */
/***************************************************************/

LRESULT CALLBACK WinProc (HWND, UINT, WPARAM, LPARAM);
BOOL InitApplication (HINSTANCE);
BOOL InitInstance (HINSTANCE, int);

char appname[] = "BetterScroll"; // the name of our application


/***************************************************************/
/*                                                             */
/* WinMain: windows equivalent to a "main" in C pgms           */
/*                                                             */
/***************************************************************/

. . .
/***************************************************************/
/*                                                             */
/* WinProc: our main window message processing function        */
/*                                                             */
/***************************************************************/

LRESULT CALLBACK WinProc (HWND hwnd, UINT msg, WPARAM wparam,
                          LPARAM lparam) {

 static int numLinesPerPage;       // number of lines/page
 static int maxScrollLines;        // maximum vert scroll range
 static int currentTopLine = 0;    // current vert scroll pos
 static int numLinesToScroll = 0;  // num lines to scroll

 static int avgCharHeight;    // average character height
 static int avgCharWidth;     // average character width
 static int avgCapsWidth;     // average capitals width
 static int height;           // current window height
```

```
static int width;           // current  window width

HDC         hdc;
PAINTSTRUCT ps;
TEXTMETRIC  tm;
int   start_line;
int   end_line;
int   i, x, y;
char  textbuffer [10];

// our app's message processing section - given a message from
// Windows, determine if the message is one that we wish to
// respond to and do so or pass it on down to the Windows
// provided default message handler

switch (msg) {
```

. . .

```

 case WM_PAINT:

   hdc = BeginPaint (hwnd, &ps);

   // calculate start and ending lines to be displayed
   // start line num is the larger of 0 and the sum of the
   // current top line plus the number of lines from the top of
   // the window down to the invalid portion to be updated less
   // one for the blank line at the very top
   start_line = max (0, currentTopLine +
                     ps.rcPaint.top / avgCharHeight - 1);

   // end line num is the smaller of the total possible lines
   // and the sum of the current top line + the number of lines
   // that can fit in the invalid rectangle
   end_line = min (TOTAL_LINES, currentTopLine +
                         ps.rcPaint.bottom / avgCharHeight);

   // display only those lines that can be visible
   for (i=start_line; i<end_line; i++) {
    // calculate starting coords of this line
    x = avgCharWidth;
    y = avgCharHeight * (1 - currentTopLine + i);

    // display the capitalized string
    TextOut (hdc, x, y, SysMetrics[i].label,
             lstrlen (SysMetrics[i].label));

    // display the lowercase string, adjusting x for the length
    // of the capitalized field
    TextOut (hdc, x + COL_FIELD_2 * avgCapsWidth, y,
             SysMetrics[i].desc, lstrlen (SysMetrics[i].desc));

    // set for numbers right aligned
    SetTextAlign (hdc, TA_RIGHT | TA_TOP);

    // get the value, fill the textbuffer, and display text
    // adjusting x start to skip to end of msg column
    TextOut (hdc, x + COL_FIELD_2 * avgCapsWidth +
                  COL_FIELD_3 * avgCharWidth,
             y, textbuffer, wsprintf (textbuffer, "%5d",
                   GetSystemMetrics (SysMetrics[i].index))
            );

    // reset for normal left justification
```

```
        SetTextAlign (hdc, TA_LEFT | TA_TOP);
      }

      EndPaint (hwnd, &ps);
      return 0;

. . .
```

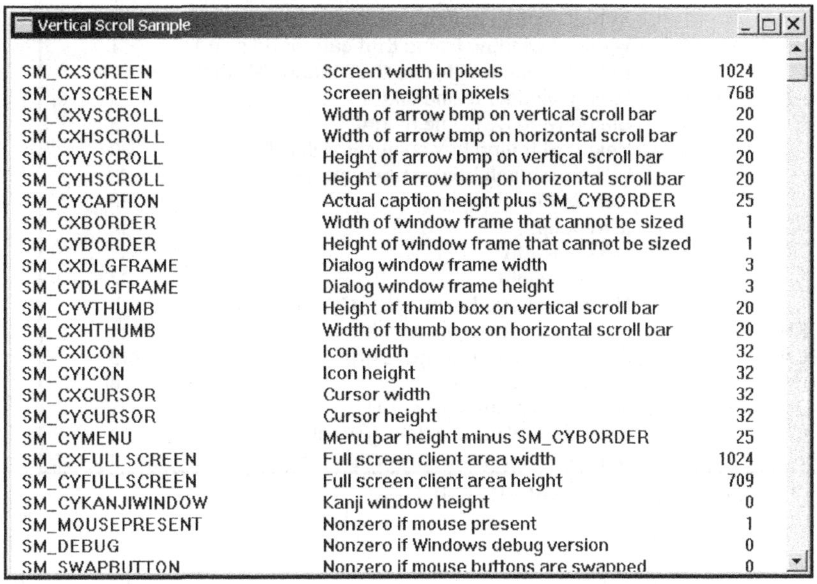

Vertical Scroll Sample

SM_CXSCREEN	Screen width in pixels	1024
SM_CYSCREEN	Screen height in pixels	768
SM_CXVSCROLL	Width of arrow bmp on vertical scroll bar	20
SM_CXHSCROLL	Width of arrow bmp on horizontal scroll bar	20
SM_CYVSCROLL	Height of arrow bmp on vertical scroll bar	20
SM_CYHSCROLL	Height of arrow bmp on horizontal scroll bar	20
SM_CYCAPTION	Actual caption height plus SM_CYBORDER	25
SM_CXBORDER	Width of window frame that cannot be sized	1
SM_CYBORDER	Height of window frame that cannot be sized	1
SM_CXDLGFRAME	Dialog window frame width	3
SM_CYDLGFRAME	Dialog window frame height	3
SM_CYVTHUMB	Height of thumb box on vertical scroll bar	20
SM_CXHTHUMB	Width of thumb box on horizontal scroll bar	20
SM_CXICON	Icon width	32
SM_CYICON	Icon height	32
SM_CXCURSOR	Cursor width	32
SM_CYCURSOR	Cursor height	32
SM_CYMENU	Menu bar height minus SM_CYBORDER	25
SM_CXFULLSCREEN	Full screen client area width	1024
SM_CYFULLSCREEN	Full screen client area height	709
SM_CYKANJIWINDOW	Kanji window height	0
SM_MOUSEPRESENT	Nonzero if mouse present	1
SM_DEBUG	Nonzero if Windows debug version	0
SM_SWAPBUTTON	Nonzero if mouse buttons are swapped	0

Figure 2.2 Pgm02b Proper Scrolling of the System Lines

The major changes are contained in the **WM_PAINT** section. They consist simply of doing three **TextOut** calls combined with **SetTextAlign** calls. Notice the calculations for the x coordinates of the second and third **TextOut** calls. The second display accounts for the width of the first field. The third display adjusts the x coordinate to the **ending** value of the third column since the numbers are to be right aligned. Figure 2.2 shows how the window appears.

Pgm02c: Using the New Style Scroll Bars

The new style scroll bars are easy to use. Recall that we must fill up an instance of the **SCROLLINFO** structure and pass it to the **SetScrollInfo** function. Thus, in the **WM_SIZE** processing section, remove these lines.

```
// set up scroll range and position of the thumb bar
SetScrollRange (hwnd, SB_VERT, 0, max_scroll_lines, FALSE);
SetScrollPos   (hwnd, SB_VERT, current_top_line, TRUE);
```

And then add in these lines.

```
// set up scroll range and position of the thumb bar
SCROLLINFO si;
si.cbSize = sizeof (si);
si.fMask = SIF_ALL;
si.nMin = 0;
si.nMax = TOTAL_LINES;
si.nPage = num_lines_per_page;
si.nPos = 0; // initial position at the start
SetScrollInfo (hwnd, SB_VERT, &si, TRUE);
```

Figure 2.3 shows what the window looks like using the new style scroll bars.

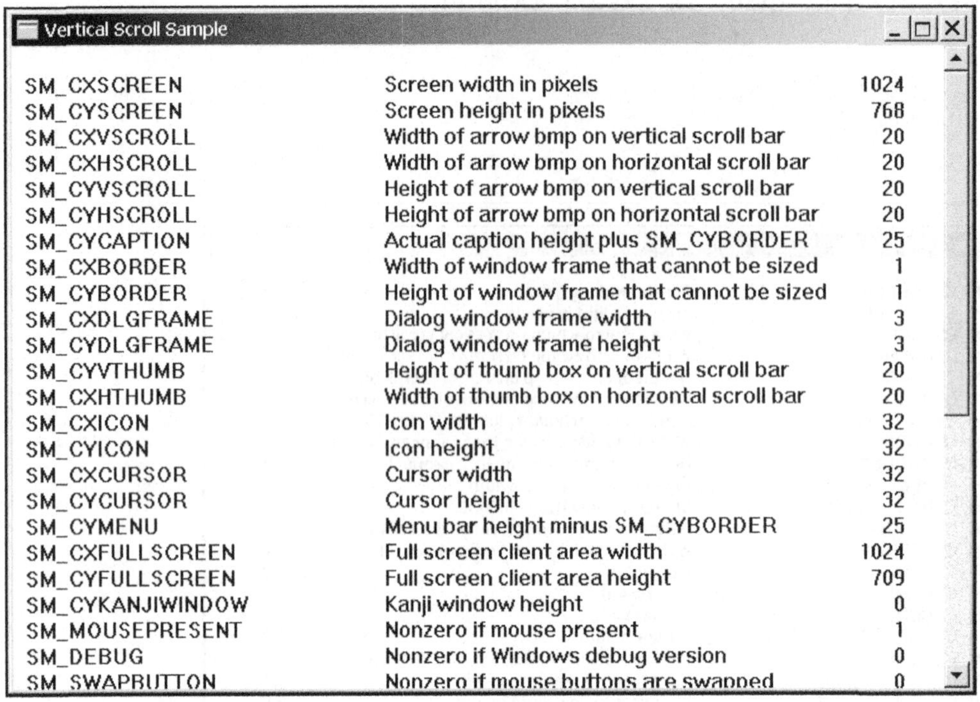

Vertical Scroll Sample

SM_CXSCREEN	Screen width in pixels	1024
SM_CYSCREEN	Screen height in pixels	768
SM_CXVSCROLL	Width of arrow bmp on vertical scroll bar	20
SM_CXHSCROLL	Width of arrow bmp on horizontal scroll bar	20
SM_CYVSCROLL	Height of arrow bmp on vertical scroll bar	20
SM_CYHSCROLL	Height of arrow bmp on horizontal scroll bar	20
SM_CYCAPTION	Actual caption height plus SM_CYBORDER	25
SM_CXBORDER	Width of window frame that cannot be sized	1
SM_CYBORDER	Height of window frame that cannot be sized	1
SM_CXDLGFRAME	Dialog window frame width	3
SM_CYDLGFRAME	Dialog window frame height	3
SM_CYVTHUMB	Height of thumb box on vertical scroll bar	20
SM_CXHTHUMB	Width of thumb box on horizontal scroll bar	20
SM_CXICON	Icon width	32
SM_CYICON	Icon height	32
SM_CXCURSOR	Cursor width	32
SM_CYCURSOR	Cursor height	32
SM_CYMENU	Menu bar height minus SM_CYBORDER	25
SM_CXFULLSCREEN	Full screen client area width	1024
SM_CYFULLSCREEN	Full screen client area height	709
SM_CYKANJIWINDOW	Kanji window height	0
SM_MOUSEPRESENT	Nonzero if mouse present	1
SM_DEBUG	Nonzero if Windows debug version	0
SM_SWAPBUTTON	Nonzero if mouse buttons are swapped	0

Figure 2.3 Pgm02c Using the New Style Scroll Bars

Another Way to Avoid the Complexities of Variable Width Fonts

Another way around the columnar alignment problem would be to switch to a fixed font. Windows provides a number of stock fonts. Several of these are fixed fonts. Their identifiers are **SYSTEM_FIXED_FONT** and **ANSI_FIXED_FONT**. We will examine their usage in greater detail in the next chapter. Briefly, to use a different stock font, you must select that font into the device context before you use that DC. The function is called **SelectObject**.

```
SelectObject (hdc, GetStockObject (ANSI_FIXED_FONT));
```

It is vitally important to remember to select in the desired font every time you acquire a new DC. In Pgm02, this means that we need to insert the above line after we get the DC in **WM_CREATE** and also in **WM_PAINT**. That way, the character dimensions are found for the font we wish to use in the paint section.

With a fixed font inserted into the DC, the text display appears just as it would under a DOS C++ window. If we had selected a fixed font in Pgm02a, then that program would have displayed the text nicely columnarly aligned because all characters have the same width.

Determining the Dimensions a Text String Would Occupy

There is a function that calculates the total length of a string in pixels, **GetTextExtentPoint32**. Whenever you need to know exactly the size of a particular string, this function is handy.

```
BOOL GetTextExtentPoint32 (HDC, char *, int len, SIZE* sz);
```

Pass the string and its length along with the address of your **SIZE** structure (which consists of two longs, **cx** and **cy**). The function calculates the pixel dimensions that the string would need based upon the font that is currently selected into the passed DC. A major use of this function is in handling line wrap problems which we explore in a later chapter.

Programming Problems

Pgm02-1—Horizontal Scrolling

Using the sample program, Pgm02b or Pgm02c, extend the scrolling of the system metrics display to include horizontal scrolling. Continue to allow 1 character's width of whitespace at the left edge initially; you do not need to maintain it when scrolled to the left.

Place your name and this problem number in the window's caption. For the additional fields you need, use a naming convention similar to what I have used to handle vertical scrolling.

You should use either the **SYSTEM_FIXED_FONT** or **ANSI_FIXED_FONT** since this greatly simplifies the horizontal scrolling process. To select in one of these fonts, code

```
SelectObject (hdc, GetStockObject (SYSTEM_FIXED_FONT) );
```

Thoroughly test your horizontal scrolling.

Pgm02-2—Horizontal Scrolling with Variable Pitched Font

Using the sample program, Pgm02b.cpp, extend the scrolling of the system metrics display to include horizontal scrolling. Continue to allow 1 character's width of whitespace at the left edge initially; you do not need to maintain it when scrolled to the left. If you prefer, you may use the new style scroll bars as shown in Pgm03c.

Place your name and this problem number in the window's caption. For the additional fields you need, use a naming convention similar to what I have used to handle vertical scrolling.

You must use the default variable-pitched font. That is, do not switch to any of the fixed fonts. Thoroughly test your horizontal scrolling.

Chapter 3 Handling the Keyboard and the Mouse

Keyboard Basics

A full treatment of the complete handling of the keyboard requires a thorough understanding of DOS keyboard operations and the microassembler language. (For a robust discussion of the keyboard, see the book by Charles Petzold, Programming Windows 95, Microsoft Press.) Fortunately, for most Windows programs, the process of obtaining keystrokes can be simplified. But first a bit of background.

The ASCII coding sequence stores characters in one byte; it is an arbitrary encoding scheme solidified in the early 1980's coming from the earlier CM/P 8-bit microcomputer era. For example, the 'A' character is stored as a hex 0x41 code or decimal 65; a 'B' is 0x42, 66. Commonly displayed special codes, such as !@#$%^&*(, are included. The control key + any letter, such as ^Z and ^C, are also stored along with some CRT control codes, such as carriage return \r, line feed \n, formfeed \f, and the ESC key, 0x1B. Two hundred fifty-six possibilities exist in one byte. The lower 127 bytes contain all of the above. The upper ASCII sequence holds the foreign language set, text codes that form boxes and text shading characters. These upper 127 values are seldom used in Windows applications and when needed are often entered by the Character Map applet.

The AT computer introduced the **extended key codes**, which provided support for the arrow keys, the function keys, ins, del, home, and end, and so on. Since the ASCII sequence was completely filled, more complexity entered. Special processing is required under DOS to get these extended 101 keystrokes. There are some possible keystrokes that DOS and BIOS do not interpret as anything, such as shift+right arrow, ALT+TAB, ALT+ESC. Under DOS, these are ignored; under Windows, some of these have meaning. More complexity enters when you consider that the keystroke could have the shift, alt, or control key being held down while the key was pressed, such as Alt-F4 for example.

Further, the keyboard sends two messages to the CPU: a key has been pressed down and a key is released. The CPU has to decide if the key was held down long enough to cause the auto repeat feature to begin; if so, it must generate multiple occurrences of that key. And the final complexity: the keyboard messages must be sent in real time, when they occur and not just when an application is requesting a keystroke. Windows allows an application to process keystrokes at any level of complexity desired.

Fortunately, unless your application is going to do exotic things with the keyboard, the process of getting keystrokes is nearly as simple as we are used to in C/C++. You only need to know whether the keystroke desired is a basic character/control code that is in the ASCII sequence or one of the 101+ special control codes. Bear in mind that **all** keystroke actions are passed along to your application, most of which your application simply passes along to the Windows default handler.

The Windows Keyboard Messages

Windows sends a series of keyboard messages. Assume that the letter A key is pressed. The following series of messages are sent.

```
WM_KEYDOWN - indicates which key is pressed
WM_CHAR    - indicates the key 'a' and a repeat count if any
WM_KEYUP   - indicates the key is released
```

If your application wishes to input normal characters and the ASCII control codes, only the **WM_CHAR** message is needed.

Assume that the left arrow key is pressed. The following series of messages are sent.

```
WM_KEYDOWN - indicates which key is pressed, the left arrow
WM_KEYUP   - indicates the key is released
```

Note that no **WM_CHAR** message is generated. If your application wishes to process any of the 101+ extended keys, only the **WM_KEYDOWN** message is normally needed.

If you use the Alt key in conjunction with a key press, then the following sequence is sent.

```
WM_SYSKEYDOWN - indicates which key is pressed
WM_SYSCHAR    - indicates the keystroke with Alt
WM_SYSKEYUP   - indicates the keys are released
```

Usually, Windows examines the sys key messages, looking for menu hot keys, task switch keys, and so on. There are several other possible keyboard messages and more complexity as well, but these are the basics. Looking these messages over, only two are commonly needed by applications: **WM_CHAR** and **WM_KEYDOWN**.

Design Rule 10: The WM_CHAR messages are processed to get normal characters and control codes.

Design Rule 11: The WM_KEYDOWN messages are processed for the 101 special key codes.

With both messages, **wparam** contains the keystroke code. When processing regular characters, filter out (and handle if desired) the control codes. When processing the 101 keys (arrow keys, PgUp, function keys), use the Windows key ID values listed in Table 1 or in WINUSER.H or in the Windows reference manuals.

Table 1 Windows Virtual Key Identifiers (wparam)

Identifier	hex value	Meaning
VK_CANCEL	0x03	Ctrl+Break Ctrl+C
VK_BACK	0x08	Backspace key
VK_TAB	0x09	Tab key
VK_CLEAR	0x0C	5 on numeric keypad with Numlock Off
VK_RETURN	0x0D	Enter key
VK_SHIFT	0x10	Shift
VK_CONTROL	0x11	Ctrl
VK_MENU	0x12	Alt
VK_PAUSE	0x13	Pause key or Ctrl+Numlock
VK_CAPITAL	0x14	Caps Lock
VK_ESCAPE	0x1B	Esc key
VK_SPACE	0x20	Spacebar
VK_PRIOR	0x21	Page Up key
VK_NEXT	0x22	Page Down key
VK_END	0x23	End key
VK_HOME	0x24	Home key
VK_LEFT	0x25	Left Arrow key
VK_UP	0x26	Up Arrow key
VK_RIGHT	0x27	Right Arrow key
VK_DOWN	0x28	Down Arrow key
VK_SNAPSHOT	0x2C	Print Screen key
VK_INSERT	0x2D	Ins key
VK_DELETE	0x2E	Del key
VK_0	0x30	ASCII '0'
....	....	
VK_9	0x39	ASCII '9'
VK_A	0x41	ASCII 'A'
....		
VK_Z	0x5A	ASCII 'Z'
With Numlock On		
VK_NUMPAD0	0x60	0
VK_NUMPAD1	0x61	1
VK_NUMPAD2	0x62	2
VK_NUMPAD3	0x63	3
VK_NUMPAD4	0x64	4
VK_NUMPAD5	0x65	5
VK_NUMPAD6	0x66	6
VK_NUMPAD7	0x67	7
VK_NUMPAD8	0x68	8
VK_NUMPAD9	0x69	9
VK_MULTIPLY	0x6A	*
VK_ADD	0x6B	+
VK_SUBTRACT	0x6D	-
VK_DECIMAL	0x6E	.
VK_DIVIDE	0x6F	/
VK_F1	0x70	F1 key

```
VK_F2               0x71     F2 key
VK_F3               0x72     F3 key
VK_F4               0x73     F4 key
VK_F5               0x74     F5 key
VK_F6               0x75     F6 key
VK_F7               0x76     F7 key
VK_F8               0x77     F8 key
VK_F9               0x78     F9 key
VK_F10              0x79     F10 key
VK_F11              0x7A     F11 key
VK_F12              0x7B     F12 key
```

Who Has the Input Focus?

The keyboard is a shared resource between the Windows system and all applications. When a key is pressed, the application with the **input focus** receives the keystroke messages. The **active window** or **active child window** normally has the input focus. Within a complex dialog box that has many controls, the control that has the input focus is shown by its altered image, often a dotted box around text within the button, for example. An application can trap **WM_SETFOCUS** and **WM_KILLFOCUS** messages as needed.

Responding to WM_KEYDOWN Messages

As an example of how to process **WM_KEYDOWN** messages, let us add a keyboard assist to the vertical scrolling sample program from Chapter 2. The up and down arrow keys should scroll one line; PgUp and PgDn keys should scroll up or down one client screen's worth of lines; Home and End go to the very top or very bottom. At first glance, one might decide to code this as follows.

```
case WM_KEYDOWN:
  switch (wparam) {
   case VK_HOME:   // same as SB_TOP
     num_lines_to_scroll = -current_top_line;
     break;
   case VK_END:    // same as SB_BOTTOM
     num_lines_to_scroll=max_scroll_lines-current_top_line;
     break;
   case VK_UP:     // same as SB_LINEUP
     num_lines_to_scroll = -1;
     break;
   case VK_DOWN:   // same as SB_LINEDOWN
     num_lines_to_scroll = +1;
     break;
   case VK_PRIOR: // same as SB_PAGEUP
     num_lines_to_scroll = min ( -1, -num_lines_per_page);
     break;
   case VK_NEXT:   // same as SB_PAGEDOWN
     num_lines_to_scroll = max ( 1, num_lines_per_page);
     break;
   default:
     break;
  }
  num_lines_to_scroll = max (-current_top_line,
      min (num_lines_to_scroll,
           max_scroll_lines - current_top_line));
  if (num_lines_to_scroll !=0) {
   current_top_line += num_lines_to_scroll;
   ScrollWindow (hwnd, 0, - avg_char_height *
                  num_lines_to_scroll, NULL, NULL);
   SetScrollPos (hwnd, SB_VERT, current_top_line, TRUE);
  }
 return 0;
```

However, we have just **duplicated** the scrolling code and this is a very bad practice! If you wanted to change the scrolling code, you would have to alter it in **two** separate places. The solution, and this is a commonplace solution, is to send our application the appropriate scroll message and let the existent scrolling code handle it.

Sending a Message to Your Own Application

Messages can be sent by using the **SendMessage** function whose signature appears as follows.

```
LRESULT SendMessage (HWND, UINT message, wparam, lparam);
```

where the **UINT** is the WM_ message id, **wparam** and **lparam** contain values appropriate for the message. In this instance, the message to send is **WM_VSCROLL**. The **wparam** contains an appropriate SB_nnnn code in the **LOWORD** and the thumb bar position in the **HIWORD**. The **lparam** handle of the scroll bar control is not needed. The thumb bar position can also be safely ignored. The keyboard processing now becomes the following.

```
case WM_KEYDOWN:
  switch (wparam) {
   case VK_HOME:  // same as SB_TOP
     SendMessage (hwnd, WM_VSCROLL, SB_TOP, 0L); break;
   case VK_END:   // same as SB_BOTTOM
     SendMessage (hwnd, WM_VSCROLL, SB_BOTTOM, 0L); break;
   case VK_UP:    // same as SB_LINEUP
     SendMessage (hwnd, WM_VSCROLL, SB_LINEUP, 0L); break;
   case VK_DOWN:  // same as SB_LINEDOWN
     SendMessage (hwnd, WM_VSCROLL, SB_LINEDOWN, 0L); break;
   case VK_PRIOR: // same as SB_PAGEUP
     SendMessage (hwnd, WM_VSCROLL, SB_PAGEUP, 0L); break;
   case VK_NEXT:  // same as SB_PAGEDOWN
     SendMessage (hwnd, WM_VSCROLL, SB_PAGEDOWN, 0L); break;
  }
  return 0;
```

The **SendMessage** function does not return back to the caller until the message that was sent has been fully processed. In contrast, the **PostMessage** function, which takes the same parameters, simply places the message into the message processing queue and then immediately returns to the caller without waiting for that message to actually get dispatched and handled.

```
LRESULT PostMessage (HWND, UINT message, wparam, lparam);
```

If you decide that based upon some keystroke that you wish to terminate the application, you must use

```
PostMessage (hwnd, WM_QUIT, 0, 0);
```

This is a very common error.

```
SendMessage (hwnd, WM_QUIT, 0, 0); // error
```

When **SendMessage** finally returns to the calling function, the application has terminated and been removed from memory. A crash often then occurs, because there is no function to return to!

Processing WM_CHAR Messages

When processing **WM_CHAR** messages, one first must filter out the control codes and perform any needed handlings of the control codes that are appropriate for the application to handle. For example, you may want to handle the CR LF keys or the backspace/rubout key. If the character is not a control code, then one proceeds to handle the character that was entered. One could choose to ignore invalid entries and so on. Also, the **LOWORD** of **lparam** contains the repeat count, if you wish to recognize the auto repeat feature.

As we embark on the processing steps required to input keystrokes, realize that there often can be an important simplification. Data entry is often done by using a dialog box which has one or more edit controls. With edit controls, Windows assumes total responsibility for processing all of the keystroke actions, returning back to the application the final complete string! These are discussed in Chapter 7.

When an application does need to trap **WM_CHAR** messages, the following represents a starting point.

```
case WM_CHAR:
 if (wparam<32) {   // all control codes are below a blank
  switch (wparam) {
   case '\b':    // backspace code
    ...
   case '\n':    // line feed code
    ...
   case '\r':    // carriage return code
    ...
   case '\f':    // formfeed code
    ...
```

or you can use their hex values

```
   case 0x08:
   case 0x0A:
   case 0x0D:
   case 0x0C:
 }
 else {
  ... ignore invalid data entries by doing nothing with them
  ... save or use character
 }
 return 0;
```

Inputting Text Lines: the Caret

When inputting text characters, normally the DOS cursor marks the current input location. Under Windows, terminology has changed. The **cursor** only refers to the mouse cursor. The **caret** only refers to the text insertion point—the old DOS cursor. The application is responsible for displaying a caret when needed. The main Windows functions for handling the caret include the following.

Function	Action Performed	Often Called From
CreateCaret	constructs a hidden caret	WM_SETFOCUS processing
DestroyCaret	destroys a caret	WM_KILLFOCUS processing
SetCaretPos	set caret position on the screen	WM_CHAR as chars are entered and used
HideCaret	hides the caret	WM_PAINT at the start before painting and WM_CHAR before displaying the entered character on the screen
ShowCaret	displays the caret	WM_PAINT at the end of all painting operation and WM_CHAR after displaying the entered character on the screen
SetCaretBlinkTime	sets the speed of caret blinking	WM_SETFOCUS processing after caret is created

The caret normally is a vertical line or sometimes a solid rectangle, but can even be a bitmap image. **SetCaretBlinkTime** can be used to force the caret to blink at its maximum for greater visibility.

Windows always sends an equal number of **WM_SETFOCUS** and **WM_KILLFOCUS** messages; that is, they always occur in pairs. During the processing of these messages, an application should create the caret and destroy the caret respectively. The **WM_SETFOCUS** message indicates that the application now has the input focus and is the active task. When the **WM_KILLFOCUS** message arrives, the application is no longer the active task and should either destroy or hide the caret.

The caret must be hidden before painting the window; if the caret is not hidden, it is painted over and leaves a residual area of strange looking pixels, often black in color. Thus, in response to a **WM_PAINT** message, the initial processing step should be to hide the caret and the last step would be to re-show the caret. Similarly, it is the application's responsibility to update the caret's position on the screen after a character has been inputted and displayed.

The different caret functions are coded as follows.

```
BOOL CreateCaret (HWND, HBITMAP, int width, int height);
```

If the **HBITMAP**, a handle to a bitmapped image is a real bitmap image, the width and height are ignored. If **HBITMAP** is NULL, the caret is a solid; if it is 1, the caret is gray. The function returns **TRUE** if successful. For now, the width and height are in pixels. Often the width is one or two pixels, while the height is **avg_char_height**, the average character height for that font.

All of the following functions return a **BOOL** which is **TRUE** if the function was successful. The return values are usually ignored.

```
DestroyCaret ();   // destroys and removes it from the screen
SetCaretPos  (int x, int y); // moves caret to x,y on screen
HideCaret    (hwnd);         // removes caret from screen
ShowCaret    (hwnd);         // redisplays caret on screen
```

Writing a Text Editor Or the Handling of Data Entry

Consider what steps are needed to enter a line of text with the caret always pointing to the next point for data entry. If this were a DOS application, one could set the caret to the initial entry column and get a character. Under DOS, you are used to coding just

```
cin >> quantity;
```

The user types in a series of digits and presses the enter key. As the user types, each keystroke appears on the screen and the DOS caret moves onward. If the user presses the backspace key, the character behind the caret is removed from the screen and the caret moves back one column. When the enter key is pressed, the character data is inputted and converted into the integer field.

Under Windows, you must perform each of these tiny details yourself, usually from within **WM_CHAR** processing. After displaying the character at the correct location on the screen, the caret must be advanced one column. With a variable-pitched font, just how much does one advance the caret's position? Yes, one can set the initial entry column and get the first character and display it, but exactly how many pixels does one advance the caret before showing it again? On a long line, just using the average character width can become so far off that the caret is several characters behind or ahead of the real insertion point! The easy way out is to always use a fixed system font—and that is just what the Notepad editor does. (Ever wondered why no font selection is possible under Notepad, yet font selection is possible in WordPad?) It gets worse. If you decide that the character that was entered is valid, you must have an array of char available in which to store that character along with a subscript. After storing the character, increment the subscript. And what about handling buffer overflow or the user entering more characters than the array can hold? Indeed, the processing of keystrokes under Windows is complex.

First, let's examine the fixed font issue which simplifies the location of the caret since all characters have the same width. Table 2 shows several of the Windows stock fonts which can be selected for use.

Table 1 Windows Stock Fonts

Stock Font IDs	Type of Font
ANSI_FIXED_FONT	Fixed-pitch font
OEM_FIXED_FONT	OEM-defined font
SYSTEM_FIXED_FONT	Font used by older versions of Windows
ANSI_VAR_FONT	Variable-pitch font
DEVICE_DEFAULT_FONT	Default device font
DEFAULT_GUI_FONT	Default GUI font
SYSTEM_FONT	Font used by Windows

By default, all DCs begin with the **SYSTEM_FONT** installed as the default. If a fixed font is desired, the **ANSI_FIXED_FONT** is recommended or alternatively the older **SYSTEM_FIXED_FONT**. To change fonts, one must have a valid DC. Until we examine dialog boxes, font changes are usually done at the beginning of **WM_PAINT** in order to install the required font before painting text and are done during the processing of **WM_CREATE** where the average character dimensions are currently acquired. The function **GetStockObject** retrieves the indicated stock object and the function **SelectObject** is used to install that new font or object into the DC. The two functions are often combined; the following installs a fixed font.

```
SelectObject (hdc, GetStockObject (ANSI_FIXED_FONT));
```

To restore the system proportional font, as the variable width fonts are known, code this.

```
SelectObject (hdc, GetStockObject (SYSTEM_FONT));
```

The two functions' prototypes are actually as follows.

```
HGDIOBJ SelectObject (HDC, HGDIOBJ);
HGDIOBJ GetStockObject (int object_id);
```

where **HGDIOBJ** is a handle to a GDI object, a generic handle that can be used not only for a font, but also for pens, brushes, color palettes and so on—any GDI object. Note that the function **SelectObject** returns the GDI object that was previously selected into this **HDC**. Later on when we begin to create our own GDI objects, such as brushes and pens, we will make use of the return values, specifically to delete no longer needed items.

Note that one could repair the **Pgm02a.cpp** sample program by switching to a fixed font; the application would then respond with proper columnar alignment as in DOS programs.

WM_SIZE messages are sent not only when the user resizes the window, but also when the application is about to become minimized or maximized. Hence, some care must be taken when processing **WM_SIZE** messages; some of these messages may force a repositioning of the caret. **WM_SIZE** caret processing must **only** occur **if** our application has the input focus. This can be checked by the function **GetFocus**. which returns the **hwnd** of the window with the input focus.

```
HWND GetFocus();
```

The following code illustrates where and how the various functions would be handled in a text processing application:

```
case WM_CREATE:
  hdc = GetDC (hwnd);
  SelectObject (hdc, GetStockObject (ANSI_FIXED_FONT) );
  ... // get average character dimensions
  ReleaseDC (hwnd, hdc);
  return 0;
case WM_SIZE:
  ... any handling for the size alterations such as the new
      caret position must be changed because where it was at
      is now not within the visible client area
      if so, hide the caret, set a new position, show caret
  if (hwnd == GetFocus()) SetCaretPos (xpos, ypos);
  ... note that if you are responding to the Set/Kill Focus
  ... messages, you might not need to do anything here
  return 0;
case WM_SETFOCUS:
  // create a block cursor
  CreateCaret (hwnd, NULL, avg_char_width, avg_char_height);
  SetCaretPos (xpos, ypos);
  ShowCaret (hwnd);
  return 0;
case WM_KILLFOCUS:
  HideCaret (hwnd);
  DestroyCaret ();
  return 0;
case WM_KEYDOWN:
  switch (wparam) {
   case VK_DELETE:
           // handle delete key processing
   case VK_INSERT:
           // handle insert key
   ... and other keys like arrows
  }
  return 0;
case WM_PAINT:
  hdc = BeginPaint (hwnd, &ps);
```

```
 SelectObject (hdc, GetStockObject (ANSI_FIXED_FONT) );
 HideCaret (hwnd);
 ... display all lines with TextOut
 ShowCaret (hwnd);
 EndPaint (hwnd, hdc);
 return 0;
case WM_CHAR:
 for (i=0; i< (int) LOWORD(lparam); i++) {
  // handle repeat count
  switch (wparam) {
   case '\b':
              // handle backspace
   case '\t':
              // handle tab
   case '\n':
              // handle linefeed
   case '\r':
              // handle carriage returns
   case 0x1b:
              // handle escape key
  }
  if (wparam) < 32)
   return 0; // all control codes done above
  Decide if this is an allowable char
  Handle any problems with buffer overflow
  Insert character into buffer and increment subscript
  Hide the caret
  Get a dc and install the font and colors, etc
  Textout this char
  Free up the dc
  Calc new caret position
  Set caret to the new position
  Show the caret
 }
 return 0;
```

Of course the details of how you handle each depends upon the application's needs. You may not want to handle all of the editing keys. Certainly processing character input can be challenging indeed. It is no wonder that dialogs are commonly used for user input operation because Windows does all these actions for us in the edit controls.

The Mouse Interface

To verify that a mouse is present, use **GetSystemMetrics (SM_MOUSEPRESENT)** which returns **TRUE** if a mouse is installed. This is a trivial point as it is nearly inconceivable that anyone seriously runs Windows with no mouse installed.

The mouse cursor is a small bit mapped graphical image that moves about the screen pointing out things. The "**hot spot**" is the precise pixel that the cursor is pointing to. The tip of the default arrow known as **IDC_ARROW** is that cursor's hot spot. The center of the hourglass known as **IDC_WAIT** is the hot spot for that cursor. The center of the cross hair known as **IDC_CROSS** is that cursor's hot spot. Later on in chapter 7, when we design our own cursors, we must notify Windows where our custom cursor's hot spot is located.

To install a cursor to be used as the default cursor for an application, load and assign it to **hCursor** in the **WNDCLASS** structure.

```
wndclass.hCursor = LoadCursor (NULL, IDC_ARROW);
```

In chapter 7, we will change cursors when needed, such as displaying the hour glass cursor when the application enters a time-consuming process.

A mouse has one or more buttons; most have two. They are identified as **LBUTTON**, **RBUTTON**, and **MBUTTON**. There are three mouse actions that occur with buttons and some additional complexity is introduced by holding the shift or control key down while pressing the button.

single click—press and release a button
double clicking—press and release twice sufficiently fast
dragging—moving the mouse while a button is pressed

While there are many possible mouse messages potentially available, an application usually only needs to respond to a few. There are twenty-four mouse messages; eleven are sent while the mouse is over the client area; these are called the **client messages**. Thirteen are sent when it is not, the **non-client messages**. Notice that, unlike keystroke messages that are queued and sent only when the application has the input focus, mouse messages are always sent, even when the application is not active or does not have the input focus. In fact, an application can **capture** all mouse actions whether or not they apply to your application. However, normally only those mouse events that occur over the client area are available for processing. In other words, Windows directs the mouse event messages to those applications that they pertain to or to those applications that request to see all events. Usually, an application only wants to see mouse event messages that occur over its client area and so it only responds to client mouse messages, passing all others to the default handler which handles the non-client mouse messages for us. The Windows default handler processes those events that occur on the frame window such as resizing and window moving, along with the actions involving clicking on the title bar, menus, and buttons.

Client Area Mouse Messages

Perhaps one of the more important messages is the **WM_MOUSEMOVE** message, which is sent anytime the mouse moves while over the client area. By processing these, you can know exactly where the cursor is within the client area. For example, in a window displaying a map of the world, this message could be used to continually update a message area that displays the current location—latitude and longitude. The **wparam** message parameter contains the status of the keys, such as shift or control being held down. One can test for the following keys being held down, using these identifiers.

```
MK_CONTROL for the control key
MK_SHIFT for the shift key
MK_LBUTTON, MK_MBUTTON, MK_RBUTTON for the buttons
```

The coding sequence to check for the presence of these could be as follows.

```
if (MK_SHIFT & wparam) {
 if (MK_CONTROL & wparam) {
   // here both are held down while moving
 }
 else {
   // here only the shift key
 }
}
else if (MK_CONTROL & wparam) {
  // here only the control key is held
}
else {
  // here none are held down
}
```

The current client area coordinates are found from **lparam** by extracting the two integer coordinates from the long value.

```
xpos = LOWORD (lparam);
ypos = HIWORD (lparam);
```

Button actions generate three possible messages for each available button on the mouse. For the left button, we have these.

```
WM_LBUTTONDOWN    when pressed
WM_LBUTTONUP      when released
WM_LBUTTONDBLCLK  when double clicked
```

Similar messages are sent for the middle and right buttons for a total of nine different messages. In these messages, **wparam** contains the status of the shift key while the client area coordinates are in **lparam**. If an application is **capturing** all mouse events, then the coordinates can be full screen coordinates; if not, they are client window based coordinates.

However, to receive the **double clicks**, the application **must** have requested Windows to send double clicks. This is done by adding **CS_DBLCLKS** to the **wndclass style**.

```
wndclass.style = CS_HREDRAW | CS_VREDRAW | CS_DBLCLKS;
```

Conveniently, for these messages, **lparam** contains the (x, y) coordinates of the hot spot at the time of the mouse action. The **LOWORD** contains the x coordinate, while **HIWORD**, the y coordinate. The **wparam** field contains the status of the buttons and the status of the shift and control keys at the time of the button press.

However, processing double clicks can get messy because a series of messages is sent. Assuming that one double clicks the left button over something in the client area, Windows sends the following series.

```
WM_LBUTTONDOWN, WM_LBUTTONUP, WM_LBUTTONDBLCLK, WM_LBUTTONUP
```

If a user double clicks several times, an entire volley of these messages are sent rapid fire. Notice that the **WM_LBUTTONDBLCLK** replaces a second **WM_LBUTTONDOWN**. Thus, if a single click means one thing and a double click means something totally disrelated, the application will have commenced processing actions when it receives the first click and then it must cancel that action upon detecting that it really is a double click! Therefore, we have the following rule.

Design Rule 12: Double Click messages are easier to handle if the first click of the sequence does the SAME action as a regular single click would have done. The ensuing double click then does something in addition to the simple single click.

Recall mouse actions upon filenames within the Explorer's List of Files list box. A single click selects (highlights) the filename. A double click also selects that filename and in addition, attempts to launch the associated application.

The Non-Client Area Mouse Messages

When the mouse is outside the client area window **but** still in the frame window area (such as on the frame border, the menu bar, or the title bar), Windows sends the same messages as given above but with a different message id number. The identifiers are prefixed with **NC** for non-client area. Thus, one would have messages such as these.

```
WM_NCMOUSEMOVE, WM_NCLBUTTONDOWN, WM_NCRBUTTONUP
```

where **wparam** contains a special id value that identifies which portion of the frame window is involved, such as **HTCAPTION** or **HTSYSMENU**. **lparam**'s (x, y) coordinates are total screen coordinates in which (0, 0) is the upper left corner of the screen.

Two functions convert between screen coordinates and client area coordinates. Both are passed a pointer to the **POINT** to be converted. Both convert the points within the structure, replacing the previous point values.

```
ScreenToClient (hwnd, &p);
ClientToScreen (hwnd, &p);
```

The next mouse message is the non-client area hit message, **WM_NCHITTEST**. This message precedes and accompanies **all** other mouse messages. With this message, **wparam** is not used but **lparam** does have the coordinates of the mouse. Applications usually pass this message onto the default handler who then uses it to generate all of the other mouse messages based upon where the mouse is actually located.

If an application has captured the mouse in response to a left button down in order to begin drawing a line, for example, a **WM_CAPTURECHANGED** message is sent when the window is going to losing mouse capture to another application that is suddenly activating. The **WM_MOUSEACTIVATE** message is sent when the cursor is in an inactive window and a button is pressed; here Windows default action is to reactivate that inactive application. Finally, a **WM_SETCURSOR** message is sent to a window when the mouse moves; it then generates the **WM_MOUSEMOVE** message.

Button Click Pairing

Usually one would think that if your application gets a button down message then it should get a corresponding button up message later on. But this is not always the case. If you click the left button over an inactive window, Windows changes the status to active and then passes **WM_LBUTTONDOWN** to the application. Thus, your application can safely assume that your window is active when processing **WM_LBUTTONDOWN** messages.

But if the user then holds the button down and drags the mouse into another application's window and then releases the button, no **WM_LBUTTONUP** is sent to your application. Similarly, if your application gets a **WM_LBUTTONUP** message, there may **not** have been a **WM_LBUTTONDOWN** sent—the user presses the mouse button while in one window, but then moves into your window and releases the button.

Other Mouse Functions

The mouse cursor can be hidden and re-shown by the function **ShowCursor** where **which** is **TRUE** for showing the cursor and **FALSE** for hiding the cursor.

```
ShowCursor (BOOL which);
```

The current mouse position can be found from **GetCursorPos** and the mouse position can be set to a specific location by **SetCursorPos**. Both return a **BOOL** if successful.

```
GetCursorPos (POINT *);
SetCursorPos (int x, int y);
```

Hit Testing

When one has a series of items from which the user may select, often the application, upon receiving the mouse click message, must determine which, if any, is the indicated item. This is known as **hit testing** or **hit checking**. Hit testing can be done many ways.

One fundamental method is to construct an array of valid object locations. One matches the (x, y) mouse position with each object's location. When the mouse position is within an object's location, the current index into the array is then used to reference the object. The array could contain two points: upper left corner and bottom right corner. Or the array could contain one bounding rectangle. From the standpoint of coding ease, points are preferred; from the standpoint of data names, rectangles are preferred.

When dealing with graphical objects, upper left and lower right points are directly used. When dealing with text lines, one either calculates and stores actual (x, y) points or converts the mouse position (x, y) into text row and column by dividing by the average character heights and widths.

In any event, hit testing can become a bit involved. Child windows can offer another easier approach, as we will shortly see. Using a special color palette with unique color indices is another method, see Chapter 9.

Working With Coordinates

Windows provides two structures that greatly aid the communication of coordinates: **POINT** and **RECT**. All fields are **int**s. The **POINT** fields are **x** and **y**, in that order, while the **RECT** contains **left, top, right, bottom**, in that order. The **SIZE** fields are **cx** and **cy**.

Often the **lparam** contains the (x, y) coordinates of some event. Windows provides a macro to convert the **lparam** coordinates into a **POINT** structure—**MAKEPOINT**.

```
POINT p = MAKEPOINT (lparam);
```

Notice that the **RECT** structure really is **two POINT** structures. Thus, one can convert from a **RECT** to **POINT**s this way.

```
POINT up_left = *((PPOINT) &rect.left);
POINT bot_rt  = *((PPOINT) &rect.right);
```

where **PPOINT** is a Windows defined type of a pointer to a **POINT** structure. An array of two points can be transferred into a **RECT** structure directly this way.

```
POINT p[2];
RECT  r = * (PRECT) p;
```

where **PRECT** is a type pointer to a **RECT**.

Messages Sent Upon Closing an Application

One very general idea found in repeatedly in Windows operations is that one basic message can beget a host of other messages in turn. One time that this happens is whenever the user attempts to close the application by any of the various methods, including the Alt-F4. The attempt generates a **WM_SYSCOMMAND** message into the system with **wparam** set to **SC_CLOSE**. This generates a **WM_CLOSE** message. **WM_CLOSE** then invokes the **DestroyWindow** function which generates a **WM_DESTROY** message which we have been responding to by invoking **PostQuitMessage(0);**. This then generates the **WM_QUIT** message that causes **GetMessage** to return 0 that cancels the message processing loop.

Very often, an application traps **WM_CLOSE** messages. Processing would include interrogating the user if he really wants to quit, asking about unsaved files, and doing other similar queries. In later chapters, I make heavy usage of these **WM_CLOSE** messages.

Some More Graphics Functions

Once a DC has been obtained, there are many graphics functions that can draw upon that canvas or can affect the drawing process. Although the default window background brush is selected when registering the class, when we get a default DC, only the black pen on white brush is provided. Before using the drawing functions, we can change from black on white by using the function **SelectObject**, which requires getting the required stock object by again using **GetStockObject**.

```
SelectObject (hdc, GetStockObject (LTGRAY_BRUSH));
```

Rectangles can be drawn using the **Rectangle** function.

```
Rectangle (hdc, left, top, right, bottom);
```

Ellipses and circles can be drawn with the **Ellipse** function.

```
Ellipse (hdc, left, top, right, bottom);
```

We can move the drawing pen to a position with the **MoveToEx** function.

```
MoveToEx (hdc, x, y, POINT*oldpt);
```

where **oldpt** is filled with the pen's previous coordinates.
We can draw a line from one position to another with the **LineTo** function.

```
LineTo (hdc, x, y);
```

And there are many, many more GDI functions that we will be discussing, particularly in Chapter 9.

MessageBeep and MessageBox Functions

There are two valuable Windows functions that are **very** useful for programmers: **MessageBeep** and **MessageBox**.

```
MessageBeep (type);
```

MessageBeep plays the sounds of the entries given in the WIN.INI [sounds] section or else a standard beep. The possibilities of the **type** integer are these.

```
0 the standard beep
MB_ICONASTERISK
MB_ICONEXCLAMATION
MB_ICONHAND
MB_ICONQUESTION
MB_OK
```

The **MessageBox** function fulfills a very important role—how to display something quickly and easily. When invoked, a window opens up over the top of everything, displaying an icon, a title bar message, a text message within the box, and buttons to press. The syntax is

```
MessageBox (hwnd, text string, titlebar string, box style);
```

The text strings can be literal strings or string variables. The box style is an ORed combination of one of each group of the following identifiers. (Note I am showing only the commonly used ones.)

button possibilities:

```
MB_ABORTRETRYIGNORE - 3 push buttons for Abort, Retry, Ignore
MB_OK               - 1 push button Ok
MB_OKCANCEL         - 2 push buttons Ok and Cancel
MB_RETRYCANCEL      - 2 push buttons Retry and Cancel
MB_YESNO            - 2 push buttons Yes and No
MB_YESNOCANCEL      - 3 push buttons Yes, No, and Cancel
```

informational icons to be displayed in the left area of the box:

```
MB_ICONASTERISK
MB_ICONEXCLAMATION
MB_ICONHAND
MB_ICONINFORMATION
MB_ICONQUESTION
MB_ICONSTOP
```

The **MessageBox** function returns the following ID depending upon which button was pressed.

```
IDABORT
IDCANCEL
IDIGNORE
IDOK
IDNO
IDRETRY
IDYES
```

I think that you can envision many uses for the simple message box. It is very handy and has widespread usage.

Using Child Windows

Often, the main window creates child windows to handle some additional processing steps. Normally, a child window appears over the top of the parent window's client area. For a child window to be used, it must have been registered with Windows before it can be created. The child window can be registered dynamically just before the application wishes to create it or perhaps more conveniently in the **WinMain** procedure just after the main window has been registered.

In other words, the construction of child windows parallels completely that of the main window. Namely, **wndclass** must be filled and **RegisterClass** called. The child window must have its own message processing function similar to **WinProc**. The child window is created by using the **CreateWindow** function.

If the child window properties are known and are not being dynamically determined in some fashion, the child windows are most often registered in **WinMain** just after registering the main window class. It is very convenient here since often the **wndclass** structure can have a few fields modified and then registered. The **wndclass.lpfnWndProc** must be assigned the name of the child window message processing function. If the child window does not have a frame and therefore max/min buttons and so on, the **wndclass.hIcon** is set to NULL. Then, the **wndclass.lpszClassName** is assigned a new string name of the class.

When it becomes appropriate to actually create the child windows, the **CreateWindow** function is used. The returned **HWND** must be saved. The create window style often includes **WS_CHILD | WS_VISIBLE**.

The tenth parameter to **CreateWindow** is either the handle to a menu or the **child window unique identifier**. It is important to note that if one is creating several instances of the same child window, each instance **must** be given a unique identifier when **CreateWindow** is invoked. Also, the parent's **HWND** and **HINSTANCE** are passed to the function.

Four functions can be used to acquire and set values contained in the **WNDCLASS** structure while the application is running.

```
DWORD GetClassLong (HWND, int id);
DWORD SetClassLong (HWND, int id, long newval);
```

For the **id** value, use the **GCL_** values given in Table 2.3 below. These access the **WNDCLASS** values. The next pair access this window's **WNDCLASS** values and any extra data allocated. These should use the ID values that begin with **GWL_**.

```
DWORD GetWindowLong (HWND, int id);
DWORD SetWindowLong (HWND, int id, long newval);
```

Table 2.3 The WNDCLASS and WINDOW Special IDs

Identifier	Action Taken
GCL_HCURSOR	get/set the cursor in use
GCL_HBRBACKGROUND	get/set the background brush
GCL_HICON	get/set the icon in use
GCL_CBCLSEXTRA	get/set extra bytes in WNDCLASS
GCL_CBWNDEXTRA	get/set extra bytes in window
GCL_MENUNAME	get/set the menu in use
GWL_HINSTANCE	get/set the hinstance
GWL_HWNDPARENT	get/set the parent window HWND
GWL_STYLE	get/set the window's style
GWL_ID	get/set the child window's id
GWL_USERDATA	get/set any userdata

The function call

```
GetWindowLong (hwnd, GWL_HINSTANCE);
```

is used to retrieve the parent's **HINSTANCE** value. For example, one could create a child window as follows.

```
hwndchild = CreateWindow (child_win_name, NULL,
      WS_CHILD | WS_VISIBLE,
      0, 0, 0, 0, hwnd, 1, // unique child window id
     (HINSTANCE) GetWindowLong (hwnd, GWL_HINSTANCE), NULL);
```

Now in **WinProc**, the main window message processor, we have access to the defined **hwndchild**. Thus it can communicate or send messages to the child window. But how about the child to its parent? Well, one could make the **hwnd** of the parent a global field, but a far better practice would be to have the child call the **GetParent** function.

```
hwndparent = GetParent (hwndchild);
```

where **hwndchild** is the **HWND** passed to the child window's message processing function. Messages can then easily be sent using **SendMessage**.

```
SendMessage (hwnd of receiver, message id,
             wparam for msg, lparam for msg);
```

With **SendMessage**, the sender does not get control back from the function until the receiver has finished processing the message. An alternative is the **PostMessage** function, in which control is returned to the sender as soon as Windows places the message in its message queue. Both functions have the same syntax and the same purpose.

Window Longs: an Advanced Feature

When working with child windows, frequently there is a need to have some kind of information readily available concerning a child window. Windows provides this capability. When registering any window class, one can request that Windows, when it allocates an instance of that class, to reserve some additional space in the class structure for user-defined fields. This is done with the **windclass.cbWndExtra** field. This extra storage is always allocated and referenced as **longs** or groups of 4-byte integer fields. Access to these **longs** is by their offset. The first reserved long is at offset 0; the second, at offset 1; and so on. For example to reserve a **long** of storage for our use, we could code this.

```
wndclass.cbWndExtra = sizeof (long); // 4 bytes for our use
```

Note that the meaning and use of these extra bytes is **totally** user defined. The memory is within the child window class instance. Next to access that data, we use the two functions below.

```
long GetWindowLong (hwndchild, offset);
SetWindowLong (hwndchild, offset, the new long value);
```

Note that the offset value is the offset from the start of the reserved longs, rather like a subscript. The Window long mechanism can be a very handy mechanism.

Finally, child windows can be moved by the application (not the user directly) by using the **MoveWindow** function.

```
MoveWindow (hwndchild, new x, new y, new width, new height,
            TRUE or FALSE to repaint or not);
```

Putting Keystrokes and Mouse Actions and Child Windows into Action: Tic Tac Toe

A Tic Tac Toe game illustrates all of the ideas covered here. Figure 3.1 shows our game in progress.

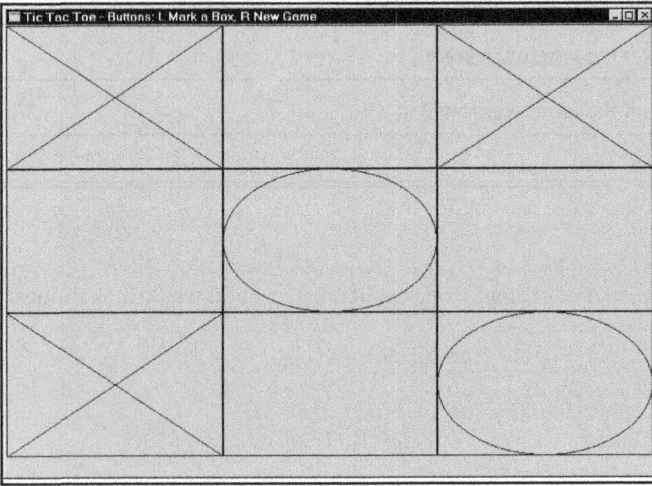

Figure 3.1 Pgm03a — Tic Tac Toe Game

The first implementation detail is how to handle the 3x3 grid of boxes. One approach would be to define a series of rectangles to represent the boxes. Displaying the grid would consist of drawing each box in turn. When the player presses the left button, we would place an X or O in the box. However, we must have smart code in the **WM_LBUTTONDOWN** message handler. It would first have to decide if the mouse cursor was over any box, then decide if the box was empty, and finally cause the X or O to be drawn. **WM_PAINT** must also be able to display the boxes and their contents. Suddenly, complexity is entering. There is a simpler method.

Let's have each "box" actually be a child window. Each child window can then draw its defining box as defined by the size of the child window's client rectangle. Now whenever the left button is pressed, if the cursor is within the client area of a box—the child window—then the child window's message processing function automatically passes the button message to the indicated child window. No coding is needed to decide where the mouse is at or to learn which, if any, "box" is selected. The parent window only needs to arrange the nine child windows into three rows of three columns by using the **MoveWindow** function.

While a global array could be used to contain the "box" or child window's current contents, namely empty, X or O, the class instance structure—the window long—could be easily used for this purpose. In other words, by requesting that Windows reserve one long of memory for each child instance, then each child instance contains that instance's contents (empty, an X, or an O) and is easily available for any needed accessing.

We can use the **Ellipse** function to draw O's and the pair **MoveToEx-LineTo** to draw the X's, where both the size of the O's and X's are based upon the current child window's client area dimensions. This allows the resizing operation of the main window to rearrange the nine child windows based upon the new main window's size and then each child window, in turn, redraws itself and its contents, the contained X's and O's! We are beginning to have an elegant solution.

How do we control the turns—whose turn it is—which also controls whether an X or O is drawn? If we have a global field, **whose_turn**, then, when a child window accepts and places an X or O, the child window can send the parent window a fake **WM_MBUTTONDOWN** message. The parent window's **WM_MBUTTONDOWN** can then toggle **whose_turn** between 1 and 2 for X and O. Of course, that coding also needs to check to see if the game has been won. When **whose_turn** is 0, no game is in progress and all messages can check for this before handling messages to prevent spurious actions. All actual drawing can now be done in the **WM_PAINT** sections.

What do we do with erroneous user actions, such as attempting to select an occupied box? How do we identify the winner to the user? On any invalid user action, we can do a **MessageBeep (0)**. A **MessageBox** can be used to announce the winner of the game.

So how about a new game? There ought to be a way that the user can request a new game at any point. The winner message box can ask if a new game is wanted. How can we allow the user to restart whenever he or she wishes? We can pick another unused mouse button, say the right button, which, when pressed, signals the start of a new game. Ok, but more than likely, the mouse cursor is over a child window that is receiving the right button down message, not the main window.

My solution is to use the keystroke CNTR-R (for Restart) as the actual message signal for a new game. (We can practice processing **WM_CHAR** messages.) Thus, a child window, upon detecting the right button down, can send the parent main window a **WM_CHAR** message with **wparam** set to the CNTR-R code. If the right button is pressed over the main window, it sends itself the CNTR-R code. This avoids the problems of the cursor being in the child window when the right button is pressed.

Figure 3.1 above, Tic Tac Toe Game In Progress, shows the main window and nine child windows in operation. Figure 3.2, Tic Tac Toe Game Over Display, shows the message box.

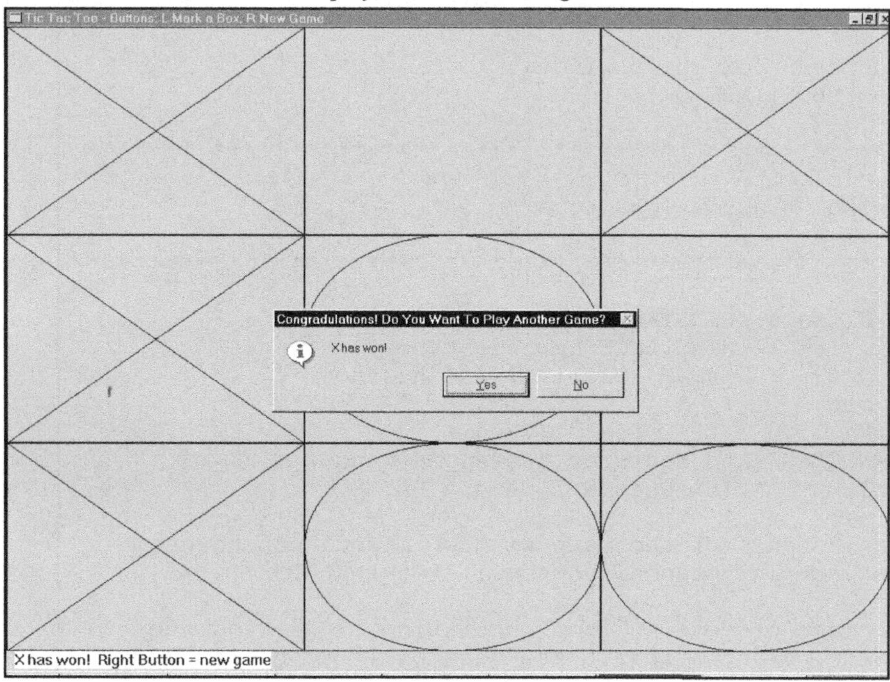

Figure 3.2 Tic Tac Toe Game Over Display

Notice the small message at the very bottom. Once the message box has closed, this text message reminds the players. Further, this is the only portion of the main client window that is visible. The nine child windows are hiding the rest of the main window's client area.

Note to compile this program, in the project settings, C++ tab, "Detect 64-bit Portability Issues" must be set to No.

Pgm03a - The Tic Tac Toe Game

```
/*****************************************************************/
/*                                                               */
/* Pgm03a Tic Tac Toe With Mouse, Keyboard, and Child Windows    */
/*                                                               */
/* C style  basic model                          by Vic Broquard */
/*                                                               */
/*****************************************************************/

#include <windows.h>
#pragma hdrstop
```

```
const int NUMBOX = 3;

/**************************************************************/
/*                                                            */
/* function prototypes - application wide global data         */
/*                                                            */
/**************************************************************/

BOOL InitApplication (HINSTANCE);
BOOL InitInstance (HINSTANCE, int);

LRESULT CALLBACK  WinProc (HWND, UINT, WPARAM, LPARAM);
LRESULT CALLBACK  BoxProc (HWND, UINT, WPARAM, LPARAM);

int IsWon (void); // checks on a possible winner

char appname[] = "TicTacToe";
char box_win_name[] = "box child window";

int  whose_turn; // 0, 1, 2 for none, X's, O's turn

// handles to the 9 box child windows
HWND hwndbox[NUMBOX][NUMBOX];

/**************************************************************/
/*                                                            */
/* WinMain: windows equivalent to a "main" in C pgms          */
/*                                                            */
/**************************************************************/

int APIENTRY WinMain (HINSTANCE hinstance,
                      HINSTANCE hprevinstance,
                      LPSTR  cmdline, int howshow) {
 MSG          msg;

 // fill in WNDCLASS and register the app's window
 if (!InitApplication (hinstance)) return FALSE;

 // create an instance of the main window, based upon howshow
 if (!InitInstance (hinstance, howshow)) return FALSE;

 // enter the main processing loop consisting of getting the
 // next message, translating it and sending it to be handled
 while ( GetMessage (&msg, NULL, 0, 0)) {
  TranslateMessage (&msg);
  DispatchMessage  (&msg);
 }

 return (int) msg.wParam; // pass along the return code
}


/**************************************************************/
/*                                                            */
/* InitApplication:                                           */
/*   fill in the WNDCLASS structure about how to construct our */
/*   main window and then register this window with Windows   */
/*   then alter WNDCLASS for the child windows and register   */
/*                                                            */
/**************************************************************/

BOOL InitApplication (HINSTANCE hInstance) {

```

```
 WNDCLASS wndclass;
 BOOL retcd1, retcd2;

 wndclass.style         = CS_HREDRAW | CS_VREDRAW;
 wndclass.lpfnWndProc   = (WNDPROC) WinProc;
 wndclass.cbClsExtra    = 0;
 wndclass.cbWndExtra    = 0;
 wndclass.hInstance     = hInstance;
 wndclass.hIcon         = LoadIcon (NULL, IDI_APPLICATION);
 wndclass.hCursor       = LoadCursor (NULL, IDC_ARROW);
 wndclass.hbrBackground = (HBRUSH) GetStockObject (LTGRAY_BRUSH);
 wndclass.lpszMenuName  = NULL;
 wndclass.lpszClassName = appname;

 retcd1 = RegisterClass (&wndclass); // registers main window

 wndclass.lpfnWndProc   = BoxProc; // msg processor for child win
 // 4 bytes for our x-o-empty id
 wndclass.cbWndExtra    = sizeof (long);
 wndclass.hIcon         = NULL;
 wndclass.lpszClassName = box_win_name;

 retcd2 = RegisterClass (&wndclass); // registers box window

 return retcd1 & retcd2;
}


/*****************************************************************/
/*                                                               */
/* InitInstance:                                                 */
/*   construct an instance of our main window using our just    */
/*   registered class                                            */
/*                                                               */
/*****************************************************************/

BOOL InitInstance (HINSTANCE hInstance, int howshow) {

 HWND hwnd;

 hwnd = CreateWindow (appname, // app's window class name
   "Tic Tac Toe - Buttons: L Mark a Box, R New Game",
    WS_OVERLAPPEDWINDOW,   // window style
    CW_USEDEFAULT,         // window's initial x position
    CW_USEDEFAULT,         // window's initial y position
    CW_USEDEFAULT,         // window's initial x size - width
    CW_USEDEFAULT,         // window's initial y size- height
    NULL,                  // parent window's handle
    NULL,                  // handle to window's menu
    hInstance,             // handle of this instance
    NULL);                 // no creation parameters

 if (!hwnd) return FALSE;  // window construction failed

 ShowWindow (hwnd, howshow); // creates window on the screen
 return TRUE;
}


/*****************************************************************/
/*                                                               */
/* WinProc: our main window message processing function         */
/*                                                               */
/*****************************************************************/
```

```

LRESULT CALLBACK WinProc (HWND hwnd, UINT msg, WPARAM wparam,
                          LPARAM lparam) {

 static int x_box_dim, y_box_dim; // box x,y dimensions
 static int y_msg;                // y coord for win message

 static int avg_char_height;      // average character height
 static int avg_char_width;       // average character width
 static int avg_caps_width;       // average capital chars width
 static int height;               // current client window height
 static int width;                // current client window width

 static int won; // indicates winner 1,2,3 are X, O, Cat or tie

 int         row, col;
 HDC         hdc;
 PAINTSTRUCT ps;
 TEXTMETRIC  tm;

 char win_msg1[] = " has won!";
 char win_msg2[] = "  Right Button = new game";
 char players[3][11] = {"The CAT", "X", "O"};
 char shortmsg[25];
 char textmsg[70];

/*****************************************************************/
/*                                                               */
/* Message Processing Loop:                                      */
/*                                                               */
/*****************************************************************/

 switch (msg) {

/*****************************************************************/
/*                                                               */
/* WM_CREATE: get text dimensions - build 9 child windows        */
/*                                                               */
/*****************************************************************/

  case WM_CREATE:

   // acquire the system font's characteristics
   hdc = GetDC (hwnd);
   GetTextMetrics (hdc, &tm);
   ReleaseDC (hwnd, hdc);

   // calculate average character parameters
   avg_char_width = tm.tmAveCharWidth;
   avg_char_height = tm.tmHeight + tm.tmExternalLeading;
   avg_caps_width = (tm.tmPitchAndFamily & 1 ? 3 : 2) *
                    avg_char_width / 2;

   // construct the child windows - for the 9 boxes - 3 X 3 grid
   for (row = 0; row<NUMBOX; row++) {
    for (col = 0; col<NUMBOX; col++) {
      hwndbox[row][col] = CreateWindow (box_win_name, NULL,
               WS_CHILD | WS_VISIBLE, 0, 0, 0, 0, hwnd,
               (HMENU)((col<<8) | row), // unique child window id
               (HINSTANCE) GetWindowLong (hwnd, GWL_HINSTANCE),
               (LPVOID) NULL);
    }
   }
   won = 0;          // set no one has won yet
```

```
    whose_turn = 1;  // set for start up game
    return 0;


/***************************************************************/
/*                                                             */
/* WM_SIZE: save window size and reposition child windows      */
/*                                                             */
/***************************************************************/

   case WM_SIZE:

    // get current client window size
    width  = LOWORD (lparam);
    height = HIWORD (lparam);

    // calculate new box sizes and y coord for winner msg based on
    // the current size of the main client window
    y_box_dim = (height - avg_char_height) / NUMBOX;
    x_box_dim = width / NUMBOX;
    y_msg     = y_box_dim * NUMBOX;

    // move child windows to their respective locations
    for (row = 0; row<NUMBOX; row++) {
     for (col = 0; col<NUMBOX; col++) {
      MoveWindow (hwndbox[row][col], col * x_box_dim,
                  row * y_box_dim, x_box_dim, y_box_dim, TRUE);
     }
    }
    return 0;


/***************************************************************/
/*                                                             */
/* WM_LBUTTONDOWN: main window left button presses = here error*/
/*                                                             */
/***************************************************************/

  case WM_LBUTTONDOWN:
   MessageBeep (0);      // sounds the beeper
   return 0;


/***************************************************************/
/*                                                             */
/* WM_RBUTTONDOWN: main window right button = start up new game*/
/*                                                             */
/***************************************************************/

  case WM_RBUTTONDOWN:
   // send CNTL-R code signaling new game
   SendMessage (hwnd, WM_CHAR, 18, 0L);
   return 0;


/***************************************************************/
/*                                                             */
/* WM_CHAR: normal keystrokes - CNTL-R = start a new game      */
/*                                                             */
/***************************************************************/

  case WM_CHAR:
   if (wparam==18) {  // is it CNTL-R?
    won = 0;          // set no winner
```

```
   // set no game yet so child windows can clear all boxes
   whose_turn = 0;

   for (row=0; row<NUMBOX; row++) {
     for (col=0; col<NUMBOX; col++) {
      // turn off X/O indicator
      SetWindowLong (hwndbox[row][col], 0, 0);
      // force box to be cleared
      InvalidateRect (hwndbox[row][col], NULL, TRUE);
     }
   }
   // force the erasing of the winner - new game message
   InvalidateRect (hwnd, NULL, TRUE);
  }
  whose_turn = 1; // activate game
  return 0;


/**************************************************************/
/*                                                            */
/* WM_MBUTTONDOWN: process main window middle button presses  */
/*                                                            */
/* child boxes signal that an X or O was placed               */
/*                                                            */
/**************************************************************/

 case WM_MBUTTONDOWN:
  // check for child's signal - both parameters being 0
  if (!wparam && !lparam) {
   won = IsWon(); // is there a winner now?
   if (won) {
    // if so, paint processing will show who
    InvalidateRect (hwnd, NULL, TRUE);
   }
   else
    whose_turn = whose_turn==1 ? 2 : 1; // no, so switch players
  }
  else MessageBeep (0); // beep on a real middle button press
  return 0;


/**************************************************************/
/*                                                            */
/* WM_PAINT: if winner, show who - otherwise clear window     */
/*                                                            */
/**************************************************************/

  case WM_PAINT:

   hdc = BeginPaint (hwnd, &ps);

   if (won) {                           // any winner yet?
    // construct short msg for message box and
    // the longer message for the main window bottom line
    if (won==3) {                        // is it a CAT game?
     // move in CAT as the winner
     strcpy_s (textmsg, sizeof(textmsg), players[0]);
     strcpy_s (shortmsg, sizeof(shortmsg), players[0]);
    }
    else {
     // no, a player won so move in player is the winner
     strcpy_s (textmsg, sizeof(textmsg), players[won]);
     strcpy_s (shortmsg, sizeof(shortmsg), players[won]);
    }
```

```
     // and add on the has won message
     strcat_s (textmsg, sizeof(textmsg), win_msg1);
     strcat_s (shortmsg, sizeof(shortmsg), win_msg1);
     strcat_s (textmsg, sizeof(textmsg), win_msg2);

     // show the winner on the bottom line of main window
     TextOut (hdc, avg_char_width, y_msg, textmsg,
              lstrlen(textmsg));

     // display message box and find out if another game is
     // desired but show congrats message box only once per game
     if (whose_turn) {
      whose_turn = 0;                        // halt game
      if (MessageBox (hwnd, shortmsg,
             "Congratulations! Do You Want To Play Another Game?",
             MB_ICONINFORMATION | MB_YESNO) == IDYES) {
       SendMessage (hwnd, WM_CHAR, 18, 0L); // send start new game
      }
     }
    }

    EndPaint (hwnd, &ps);
    return 0;


/*****************************************************************/
/*                                                               */
/* WM_DESTROY: close down the app processing                     */
/*                                                               */
/*****************************************************************/

   case WM_DESTROY:
    PostQuitMessage (0);
    return 0;
  }

 return DefWindowProc (hwnd, msg, wparam, lparam);
}



/*****************************************************************/
/*                                                               */
/* BoxProc: child window message processor                       */
/*                                                               */
/*****************************************************************/

LRESULT CALLBACK BoxProc (HWND hwnd, UINT msg, WPARAM wparam,
                          LPARAM lparam) {
 HDC         hdc;
 PAINTSTRUCT ps;
 RECT        rect;
 HWND        hwndparent;

 switch (msg) {

/*****************************************************************/
/*                                                               */
/* WM_CREATE: clear window long flag = box is empty              */
/*                                                               */
/*****************************************************************/

   case WM_CREATE:
    SetWindowLong (hwnd, 0, 0); // clear x-o flag
```

```
    return 0;


/*************************************************************/
/*                                                           */
/* WM_RBUTTONDOWN: right button = request for a new game     */
/*                                                           */
/*************************************************************/

  case WM_RBUTTONDOWN:
    // send parent window the start new game signal - a ctrl-R
    hwndparent = GetParent (hwnd);
    SendMessage (hwndparent, WM_CHAR, 18, 0L);
    return 0;


/*************************************************************/
/*                                                           */
/* WM_LBUTTONDOWN: left button = mark this box               */
/*                                                           */
/*************************************************************/

  case WM_LBUTTONDOWN:

    if (GetWindowLong (hwnd, 0) > 0){ // if box is in use, beep
     MessageBeep (0);
    }
    else {
     if (whose_turn > 0) {       // if X's or O's turn, then
      // mark an X or O in this box, based on whose_turn
      SetWindowLong (hwnd, 0, whose_turn);
      // force repaint to show X or O
      InvalidateRect (hwnd, NULL, TRUE);
      // notify parent a box has been chosen
      hwndparent = GetParent (hwnd);
      SendMessage (hwndparent, WM_MBUTTONDOWN, 0, 0L);
     }
      else MessageBeep (0);      // game not in progress-beep
    }
    return 0;


/*************************************************************/
/*                                                           */
/* WM_PAINT: draw box and insert X or O if needed            */
/*                                                           */
/*************************************************************/

  case WM_PAINT:
    hdc = BeginPaint (hwnd, &ps);

    GetClientRect (hwnd, &rect);              // get size of window
    SelectObject (hdc, GetStockObject (LTGRAY_BRUSH));
    // erase the contents of the window by drawing black/gray rect
    Rectangle (hdc, 0, 0, rect.right, rect.bottom);

    if (GetWindowLong (hwnd, 0) == 1) {       // draw an X case
     MoveToEx (hdc, 0, 0, NULL);
     LineTo (hdc, rect.right, rect.bottom);
     MoveToEx (hdc, 0, rect.bottom, NULL);
     LineTo (hdc, rect.right, 0);
    }
    else if (GetWindowLong (hwnd, 0) == 2) {  // draw an O case
     Ellipse (hdc, rect.left, rect.top, rect.right, rect.bottom);
```

```
   }
   EndPaint (hwnd, &ps);
   return 0;

 }
 return DefWindowProc (hwnd, msg, wparam, lparam);
}



/***************************************************************/
/*                                                             */
/* iswon: determines if there is yet a winner                  */
/*                                                             */
/* returns 0 = no winner, 1 = X, 2 = O, 3 = CAT                */
/*                                                             */
/***************************************************************/

int  IsWon (void) {

 int  row, col, i = 0, winner = 0;
 int  ans [NUMBOX*NUMBOX];
 BOOL notdone = FALSE;

 for (row=0; row<NUMBOX; row++) { // copy all box contents to ans
  for (col=0; col<NUMBOX; col++) { // for faster checking
   ans[i] = GetWindowLong (hwndbox[row][col], 0);
   if (ans[i++]==0)
    notdone = TRUE;
  }
 }

 // if blank boxes remain, then if there is no winner,
 // then the game is not done
 // check for winner
 if (ans[0]==ans[1] && ans[0]==ans[2] && ans[0]>0)
  winner = ans[0];
 else if (ans[3]==ans[4] && ans[3]==ans[5] && ans[3]>0)
  winner = ans[3];
 else if (ans[6]==ans[7] && ans[6]==ans[8] && ans[6]>0)
  winner = ans[6];
 else if (ans[0]==ans[3] && ans[0]==ans[6] && ans[0]>0)
  winner = ans[0];
 else if (ans[1]==ans[4] && ans[1]==ans[7] && ans[1]>0)
  winner = ans[1];
 else if (ans[2]==ans[5] && ans[2]==ans[8] && ans[2]>0)
  winner = ans[2];
 else if (ans[0]==ans[4] && ans[0]==ans[8] && ans[0]>0)
  winner = ans[0];
 else if (ans[2]==ans[4] && ans[2]==ans[6] && ans[2]>0)
  winner = ans[2];

 // if no winner yet and if no boxes remain empty, then
 // the CAT won the game - ie. a tie
 if (winner==0 && notdone==FALSE)
  winner = 3;

 return winner;
}
```

The two key global fields are **whose_turn** and **hwndbox** (a 3x3 array to store the nine child windows' HWNDs).

In **WinMain**, after the main window class is registered with a light gray background brush, the child window box class is also registered with **BoxProc** being the name of the child window message handler. Additionally, one extra long is reserved to store the box's contents.

In the main window's **WM_CREATE** section, the nine child windows are created. The unique child id becomes a combination of the 3x3 grid row/column index. Specifically I store the column index in the right most byte and the row index in the left byte (row << 8). The field **won** is set to 0 saying no winner yet and **whose_turn** is set to 1 for X goes first. Notice the int **id** is cast to **HMENU**.

In **WM_SIZE**, based upon the new main window client area, the child window sizes are calculated. However, space is left at the bottom of the main window for a winner message. This is in addition to the message box notification, which occurs only once per game. Why? If the user does not select a new game from the message box, then the game window appears as it last was. Thus, we need a message showing the winner and stating "press right button to restart." Finally, once the new dimensions are calculated, all child windows must be resized and/or moved and repainted.

The main window beeps if the left button is pressed while in the winner message at the very bottom of the window. If the right button is pressed here in the main window area which indicates starting a new game, a **WM_CHAR** with CNTR-R code is sent (a decimal 18 or 0x12).

In **WM_CHAR**, if the character entered is a CNTR-R or the faked sent CNTR-R, no winner is set and **whose_turn** becomes 0, implying that no game is in progress. Next, all child windows have their window long containing the box contents cleared and the child window is cleared. When no game is in progress, a child window only draws its box with nothing in it.

The **WM_MBUTTONDOWN** processes turns. It is invoked by messages sent from child windows after they have responded by placing an X or O in a box. I have used special values of **wparam** and **lparam**—0—to differentiate from real middle button presses from someone who actually has three mouse buttons. First, **iswon** is invoked to find out if the game is over or if it is time to switch players. If the game has been won, the main window is forced to be repainted which displays the bottom line status message.

The main window's paint process does nothing until there is a winner. Remember, all of the main window is hidden behind the nine child windows, except the results line at the bottom. When the game is won, two messages are constructed—one for the message box and one for the bottom of the window. The **whose_turn** coding keeps the message box from appearing more than once per game. If the user chooses "start new game," paint sends the CNTR-R message.

The child window message processor, **BoxProc**, is fairly short. In **WM_CREATE**, the reserved Window long is cleared. In response to **WM_RBUTTONDOWN**, the handle of the parent window is retrieved so that the CNTR-R or **WM_CHAR** message can be sent to the parent.

When the user presses the left button, if the window long is not zero, the box is already occupied and a beep results. If empty, the window long is set to the player number and the window invalidated so that paint draws the X or O. Finally, the next turn message, **WM_MBUTTONDOWN** is sent to the main window. The child **WM_PAINT** messages are processed by first installing a light gray background brush in the paint DC. Thus, the **Rectangle** function appears to outline the client area. Then, depending upon the child window's window long, either an X or O is drawn.

After each turn, the **iswon** function checks to see if there is a winner. If the boxes are all filled and neither X nor O has won, the CAT wins the game. Therefore, **iswon** must test the window longs of the child windows. This is why I made the array of handles global, so they can easily be referenced here. Perhaps you can come up with a better way to figure out a winner; my solution is rather crude.

Programming Problems

Pgm03-1—Mouse and Text Operations

This program combines mouse event and character processing techniques. Your main window should have a white background. When the child window becomes visible, it should have a gray background. When both windows are visible, it should appear as shown below.

The main window begins by displaying a message "Enter Text Here:" along with some mechanism for the user to know the maximum length of the possible text they can enter. In the above figure, I used a series of dashes located just below the location where the text that the user enters is to be displayed. Alternatively, you can use some kind of color scheme to so indicate this data entry area. It is suggested that the y coordinate be 3/4 of the window's height. Do not concern yourself about what happens if the user shrinks the window's width and cuts off all or part of the text entry area. As the window opens, the child window is not visible nor is **any** data entry possible; there is no caret as yet.

Data Entry Rules:
When the user left clicks on the "Enter text" message or anywhere in the available location where text can be entered as indicated by the dashes in the above figure, data entry can commence. Note that **on** the above message means clicking anywhere from the E of Enter through the last _ of the possible 50 characters.

1. If there is already text in the area, clear the area on the screen.
2. Clear out the character string in memory that is to hold the text.
3. Create a caret of your choice and position it at the beginning of the input area.
4. Accept any character except control codes and ignore any characters in the upper ASCII sequence—that is, those above 127.
5. Terminate data entry when any one of the following occurs:
   a) the enter key is pressed
   b) another mouse button press of **any** kind occurs
   c) 50 characters have been entered—ignore further characters
6. After terminating, there should be no caret visible and no additional characters are accepted or shown on the screen.

You do not need to handle any editing keys, such as the arrow keys, backspace, del, ins, and so on. If the user makes a typing error, he can re-click on the message and begin again.

Notice that the termination rule 5b is designed to greatly simplify your handling of the caret. Specifically, if the user tries to resize the window, **WM_SIZE** should end editing, for example. This also occurs should the user try to minimize or maximize the window because these all result in a new **WM_SIZE** message. To handle task switching, respond to **WM_KILLFOCUS** messages which also end any ongoing editing. It is suggested that you maintain a bool, isEditing, that can be tested and used from the many locations involved.

When the right button is pressed anywhere in the main client area, open or show a child window over the upper half of the main window as shown, using a light gray background. As long as the mouse cursor is **within** the child window, upon any mouse motion, display the cursor's position in the appropriate line. Calculate the actual full screen coordinates and display them as well. Just display the few characters representing the position; do not repaint the whole window because the jerkiness effect is very annoying.

Whenever the mouse moves out of the child window, the coordinates are no longer updated. Whenever the user presses the right button another time anywhere in the child window or main window, either destroy the child window or hide it.

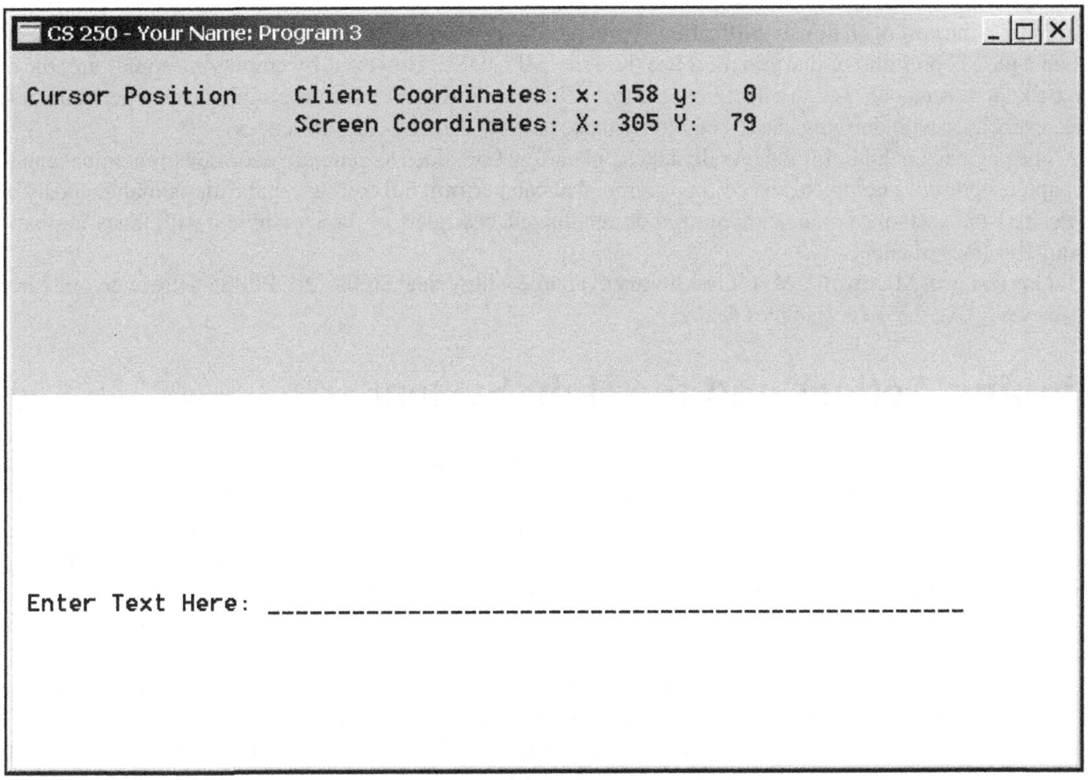

Pgm03-1 Main Window (in white) and Child Window (in gray)

Chapter 4 Controlling Windows From C++, the MFC (Microsoft Foundation Classes)

Introduction

Now that you have seen the basic C-style method of controlling Windows, you will certainly appreciate using a set of class libraries to simplify programming. The MFC offers many benefits over C-style Windows programming. Each actual window on the screen is associated with a single instance of a class. Thus, all coding for one class is located in one place, unlike the Tic Tac Toe game in the last chapter.

The giant message processing "switch" is replaced with class member function calls. Thus, **WM_PAINT** messages are routed to the MFC **OnPaint** member function of the window involved. The message "switch" logic is **totally** eliminated. (Actually, it is hidden deep within the class libraries.)

Furthermore, the class library performs all **message cracking**. This means that, when a member function that is to handle a message is invoked, the MFC environment presents that function with the parameters in a **usable** format. For example, when a window's paint function is invoked, **OnPaint**, you construct an instance of the **CPaintDC** class that encapsulates the invalid rectangle, the paint DC and so on. If the background also needs to be repainted, when **OnPaint** is invoked, the MFC has already done so for you.

Similarly, when the class libraries invoke the member function that handles **WM_MOUSEMOVE**, the first parameter is the status of the keys and the second is a point class object called **CPoint** that represents the cursor location. In other words, all parameters to the member functions are in a format easily used by that function.

If we were to rewrite the Tic Tac Toe game using the MFC, then the nine child windows would be controlled by nine instances of the child window class. MFC passes a hidden **this** pointer to the class instance. Additionally, the **this** parameter also simplifies and allows the removal of the static and global fields, since these can often be made class member fields and used only by the specific class instance.

What is the cost of all this simplification? Perhaps the single biggest complaint is that the size of the exe file is much larger than a pure C program or that you must use the 1M+ MFC DLL. However, by employing some care, the overall exe size can be kept reasonable. Yet, to effectively control Windows from MFC, the programmer must be well versed in C++ practices, especially with deriving classes and inheritance as well as using class instances.

The pay back is high, for it generally takes only a few C++ lines to generate enormous functional capabilities. In a later chapter, I present a complete text editor program that can perform full editing capabilities simultaneously on as many files as desired and each one could be minimized or maximized, cascaded, or tiled, complete with fancy toolbar—all done with about 100 lines of code!

This text uses Microsoft's MFC class library available with Visual Studio .NET 2005. However, one can use earlier versions as well. Use the older Samples folders.

Beginning Actions and the Help System

Where do you start? Okay, when you choose to make a new MFC project, two "wizards" take over. The first is called the Application Wizard. As you make your various project choices for the new project, it App Wizard is guiding you. Once you click Finish, the App Wizard then builds all of the needed files with proper coding such that if you actually built the program, its default window(s) with menus and the like appear. Of course, it is just like our Hello World window in that it doesn't really do any useful work. One then begins to modify these basic files to finish the application. While working on adding the functions and coding needed, it is the Class Wizard which performs much of the work for us, in terms of adding needed functions.

The only drawback of this powerful, advanced development platform is the "shell" applications that the App Wizard creates are way too complicated for very beginning applications. The wizard creates robust production style shells for you. Thus, in order to keep a proper learning gradient going, we will first manually create our simpler Windows applications. Once we get familiar with the basics, then the two wizards will be used.

Until we cover the wizards, to make a new MFC application, choose the normal Win32 application and empty project. Then copy and include as a part of your program files my basic shell files for this chapter in the folder Pgm04a. Of course, you can rename them as desired.

Based upon personal experience, I would strongly encourage you to browse the on-line MFC help system. The MFC

Help system provides an excellent help screen topic display for each MFC class.

Figures 1, 2 and 3 show screen snapshots of On-Line Help displaying information about the first of the class topics—**CWinApp**. Notice that all of the MFC classes all begin with the letter 'C'.

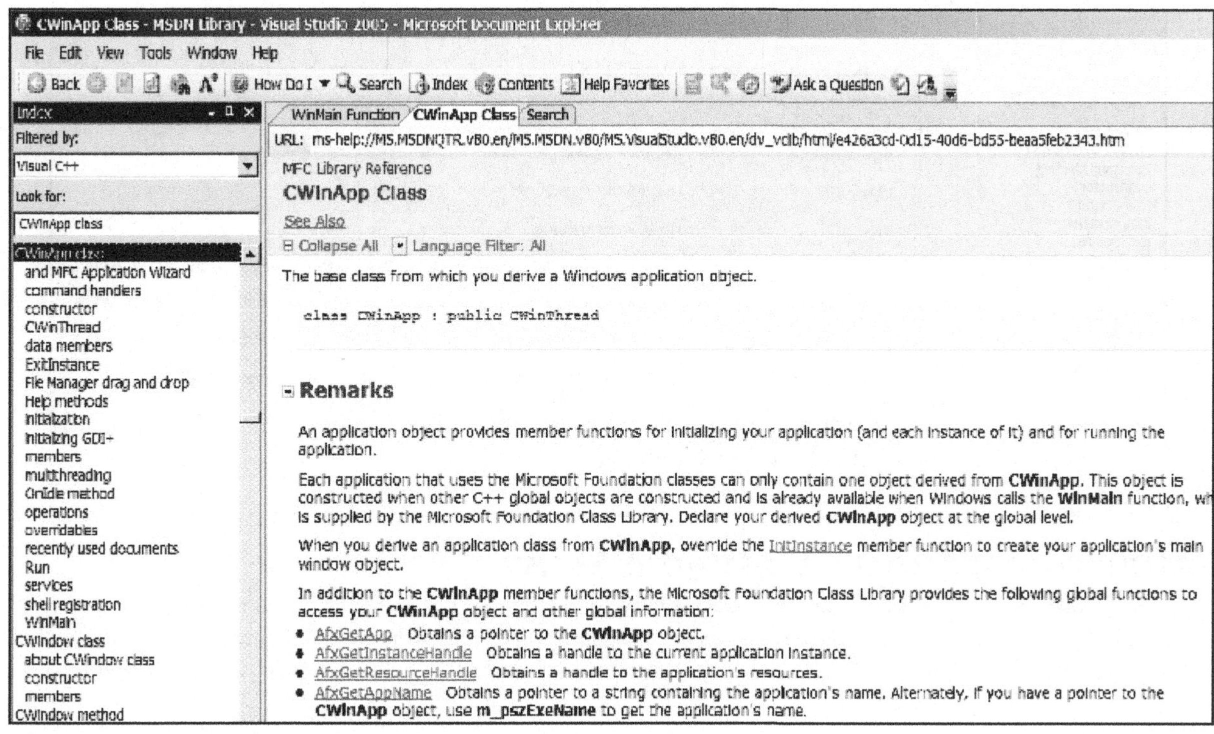

Figure 4.1 The CWinApp Overview

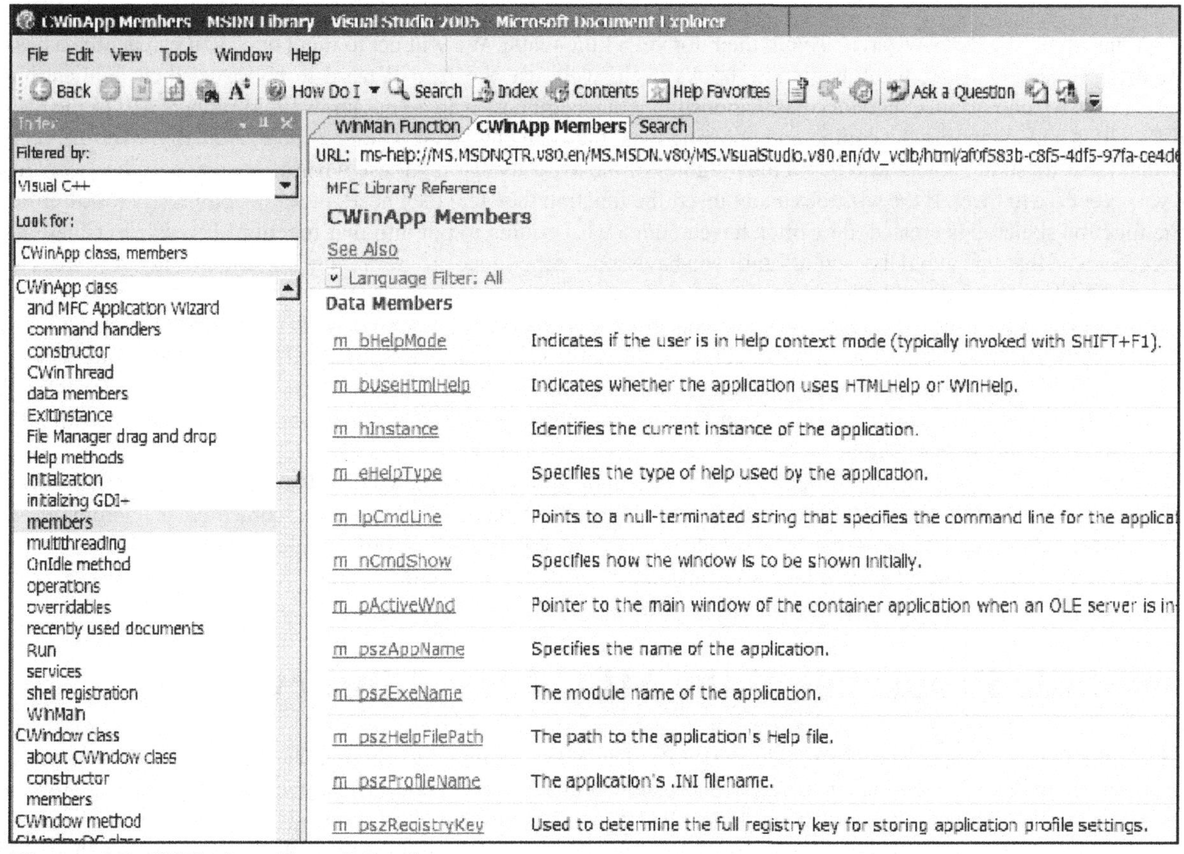

Figure 4.2 CWinApp Data Members

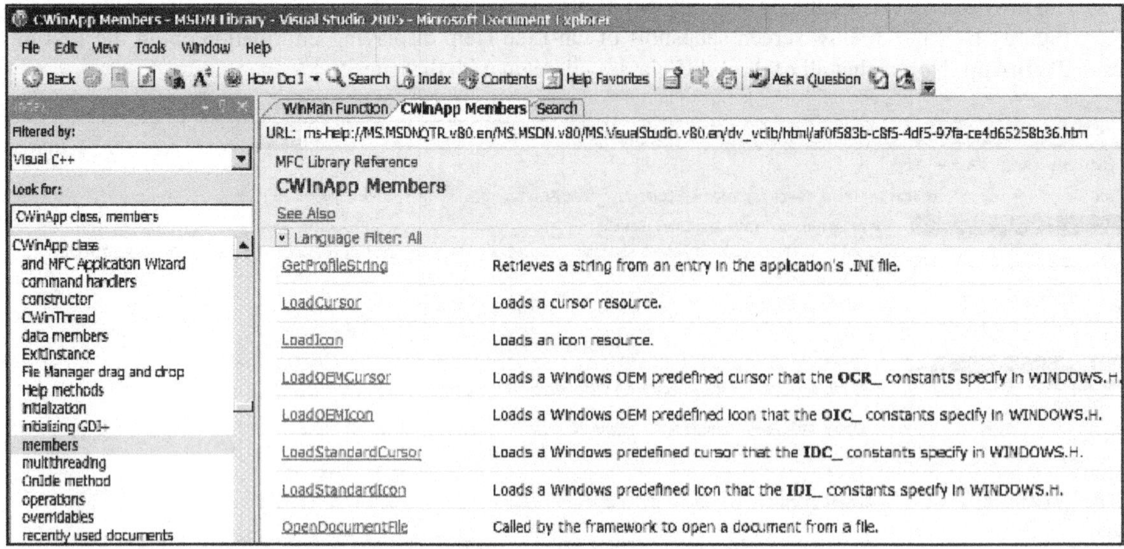

Figure 4.3 Some CWinApp Member Functions

Getting Started in an Optimum Way

In my many years of teaching windows programming, I have found that more students have had more trouble getting the appropriate basic shell to compile and successfully display the appropriate blank window on the screen than nearly anything else! Remember this when you get to the later chapters, especially when dealing with the fancy decorations or toolbars.

Design Rule 13: The first action when creating a new application, is to code only the basic shell required for that application and attempt to get the shell functioning.

What about the fancy wizards? Avoid them for yet a little while. We will get to them once you can handle a basic window using the MFC. True, many beginning books exclusively use the App Wizard to construct their applications. However, extensive classroom experience has demonstrated that beginners who do not know the Windows API or the MFC have difficulties understanding the coding and knowing what they can change, or where or how. Actually, over the years, I have found that those beginners who begin their studies of the MFC using only these wizards are some of the most "lost souls" you ever care to meet. If the wizards cannot insert the function they feel they need, they are completely lost. Further, once the function skeleton is created, they often have no idea what coding to put into that function! It is a grim situation. I highly recommend that you avoid the wizards until you have some experience programming Windows. When resources are introduced, the Class Wizard will be introduced.

When you survey the MFC texts and magazine articles, you may encounter a bewildering number of what appears to be totally different basic shells and models. This is a benefit of a good class library. There are numerous ways to accomplish the same task! But for very beginners who are even a little shaky on C++ coding, who are not intimate with Window C API programming, and who are not yet familiar with the names used and member fields contained within the classes, it can be awfully overwhelming.

Further, the exact sequence of initial function calls upon application and window launching can be both involved and confusing. What Windows options can be set, when, and where is perhaps not as well documented as it could be.

Hence, we are going to begin in a very simple manner and slowly add in more complexity. In this chapter, several basic shells are examined. Then, we examine the encapsulation of all of the functions that we have already discussed in the C API.

Some Basic Properties of the MFC Class Library

The MFC class library encapsulates the Windows C API. The MFC is limited to single inheritance. It is a thin wrapper. Further, there are many API functions that are not encapsulated in any class. Thus, it behooves one to know the C API as well. Roughly three-quarters of the member functions used by beginning programmers are merely a convenience "wraparound" of the C style interface. These member functions quite commonly have the same name as their API counterparts.

The MFC provides independence from the C-style giant message switch, message cracking, and overall simplification by use of the `this` parameter. For example, when dealing with a window class, there is no need of the HWND parameter; it is passed with the `this` parameter. For example, MFC encapsulates a Windows POINT structure in a CPoint class, storing the coordinates as integers: x and y. Note that the MFC classes begin with a 'C'.

Design Rule 14: Always compile with all messages on to get the best possible chance of having the compiler detect errors.

You can comment out the variable names in parameter lists to avoid warnings about variables not used in function headers.

```
void  Fun (int /*first_parm*/, char* /*title*/) {
```

Design Rule 15: There should be no errors or warnings when compiling any module in the program when the option to report all errors and warnings is enabled. Under MFC, use Level 4 warnings.

Building an MFC Project

The first step, as always, is to build the MFC project. Begin by choosing File—New Project and select Win32 just as you did for a C Project. Fill in the project path and the name of the project, but make sure it is a Windows Application and an Empty Project. Once the project solution is then built, right click and choose Properties. Now several settings must be made. One, on the C++ General Tab, Warning Level should be set to 4. On the General Tab, Character Set should be set to Not Set. For now, we will not be using pre-compiled headers. Note that these setting can be applied independently between the Debug version and the Release version of your program.

One setting is under your control: whether or not to use the MFC in a shared DLL or to use MFC in a static lib or use MFC in standard libraries. For now, we can use it in standard libraries, which is the default. When you make a release build intending the program to be run on other machines, if you use the DLL version, then the exe is smaller but you will have to install the runtime MFC DLLs on these other computers. To avoid doing that, use these other options which include the MFC classes as part of your exe file, making the exe larger.

When a project is using the MFC in a shared dll, the resultant exe file is much smaller. All of the MFC coding is contained in the 1M+ MFC dll which is loaded into memory when the application launches. Thus, one gets faster project linker runs during development because the exe is smaller and the linker does not have to include all of the MFC class functions. They are all contained in the huge MFC dll.

When a project is using the MFC in a static library, all of the MFC class coding is included as part of the resultant exe file. Thus, the exe file is larger and more linker time is required to build it. However, the final exe file does not need anything further to execute, save of course the actual Windows dlls.

Personally, I usually use MFC in a shared dll during the program development time. When I build the final release, I switch to using MFC in a static library. This keeps rebuild times as fast as possible during program development. When I issue a program into production, that exe is then totally self-contained. On the other hand, if you issue a program into production using the MFC in a shared dll, then you must provide an install program. The install program must search the machine on which your program is being installed to find if that machine already has a copy of the MFC release dll on it, and, if it does, is it the correct version of the MFC dll. If it is not the right version, you must install the proper release MFC dll in order for your application to be able to run on that machine.

MFC Basic Applications

All MFC programs begin by allocating an instance of their **CWinApp** derived class. **CAppWin** contains the **WinMain** function and provides application-wide activities. Thus, the first action in writing an MFC application is to create an application class, derived from **CWinApp**. The more often used public data members of **CWinApp** include the following.

```
CWnd*     m_pMainWnd        // pointer to app's main window
LPSTR     m_lpCmdLine       // the command line string
HINSTANCE m_hInstance;      // handle to this app instance
HINSTANCE m_hPrevInstance;  // handle to any prev instances
```

```
int        m_nCmdShow;       // how to display the window
LPSTR      m_pszAppName;     // char* - the app's string name
```

There are several global functions that the MFC provides for convenient access to application-wide information.

```
CWinApp* AfxGetApp (); // returns a pointer to the app object
HANDLE   AfxGetInstanceHandle (); // returns the handle to
                                  // this instance or exe file
HANDLE   AfxGetResourceHandle (); // returns a handle to the
                                  // app's resources
LPSTR    AfxGetAppName ();        // char* - the app's name
```

Design Rule 16: When you are not in your CWinApp derived class, these global member functions permit you to gain access to this application instance.

The handle to the application's resources is needed in order to load strings and dialogs from the resource file, for example. If you are inside of some child class and need to get access to a public function within the main window, one can always code the following to get a pointer to the main window class instance. This is very common coding.

```
AfxGetApp()->m_pMainWnd
```

So your very first step in creating a new MFC application is to derive your application class from **CWinApp**. A typical **CWinApp** derived class header is as follows.

```
class MyApp : public CWinApp {
public:
  MyApp () : CWinApp () {} // constructor of app
 ~MyApp () {}              // destructor of app
 virtual BOOL   InitInstance (); // create & install main window
 DECLARE_MESSAGE_MAP(); // reserve space for any message
                        // handlers required - currently none
};
```

For beginning applications, the constructor simply invokes the base class constructor; the destructor is not even needed if the application does not allocate items that need to be freed or destroyed, which is usually the case. All of the action occurs in the required **InitInstance** member function. Essentially, the **WinMain** framework function calls your **InitInstance** member which must be provided; then it calls the **Run** function; and finally calls your **ExitInstance** function, if you have provided one.

In **InitInstance**, one **must** allocate an instance of the main window class at least. Its coding closely parallels the C style interface; typical coding is as follows.

```
BOOL  MyApp::InitInstance () {
 // construct new frame window, storing it in m_pMainWnd
 m_pMainWnd = new FrameWin;
 // show window in the style passed from the Windows command line
 m_pMainWnd->ShowWindow (m_nCmdShow);
 return TRUE;
}
```

Finally, in the application cpp file, one constructs a global instance of the application class.

```
MyApp  myapp;  // constructs the app object and executes it
```

This simple line that creates a global instance of the MyApp class actually ends up executing the entire application! The **CWinApp** class constructor invokes **InitApplication**, **InitInstance**, **Run**; when the user quits the application, it calls **ExitInstance**. Notice how closely this parallels the C Stye API interface.

The four key functions of **CWinApp** are these.

InitApplication—perform application-wide initializations,
such as display a splash startup screen

InitInstance—allocate and show the main window class—this **must always** be coded

Run—execute the application (almost never overridden)

ExitInstance—any special termination processing (not often coded)

If there are any clean up actions that are required at the application level, such coding is placed in the **ExitInstance** function which is called as the application terminates.

The two fundamental actions you need to do within **InitInstance** are to
1. Create (via **new**) an instance of your main window class, storing the pointer returned by the **new** function in the class member **m_pMainWnd**.

2. Call **ShowWindow** to notify the framework how the window is to be displayed by passing along any parameter from the command line.

Run handles the main message processing loop. Whenever there are temporarily no more messages to be processed, **Run** invokes the **OnIdle** function, which we can override to perform idle-time processing. When the application terminates, **Run** invokes **ExitInstance**.

Deriving Your Main Window Class

The basic MFC window class is **CWnd,** from which many specialized window classes are derived. **CWnd** provides for a fully functional window class. However, it is rarely used as a main window because the main window must handle menus, toolbars, resizing and so on. Instead, another window class derived from **CWnd**, **CFrameWnd**, is a far better choice for the main window. **CFrameWnd** provides specialized operations for a window that is to be a main window. It conveniently handles borders, title bars, menu bars, menu operations, scroll bars, control bars, tool bars, and the status bar. These fancy items are easily handled through **CFrameWnd**.

A frame window can also support and manage a client window within its frame. And many fancier programs have a frame window class and a client window class that is derived from **CWnd**.

As we begin our first MFC examples, no use of any of the specialized member functions or members of the **CFrameWnd** class is needed. Hence, most items discussed in conjunction with **CFrameWnd** actually are inherited from the base **CWnd** class. Therefore, the following discussion applies to both classes.

Creating windows requires understanding of several interrelated **CWnd** member functions: the constructor, **PreCreateWindow**, **Create**, **OnCreate**, and **OnDestroy**. These five functions and their interrelationships are essential to understand of the window creation process along with the concept of the **Window Interface Element** versus the **Window Interface Object**.

The real window currently displayed on the screen is called a **Windows Interface Element** while the MFC C++ class instance is known as the **Windows Interface Object**. There is a specific pathway followed to get from instantiating an object of a class to having it appear on the screen. There are several steps involved in the process; you can intervene in many different places in this cycle to tailor the window creation process to your needs. The problem is knowing where and how to intervene to make the alteration you desire.

An interface object (that is, the class C++ instance) provides member functions for creating, initializing, managing, and destroying its associated Windows Interface Element and handling automatically many Windows details for you. These C++ classes encapsulate the data needed to handle communications such as window handles. Thus, the first step is to allocate (usually via **new**) a C++ instance of the class, the Windows Interface Object.

In the C++ constructor, the **CWnd Create** function is called to begin the Windows Interface Element construction. Then, at the point when the actual window is about to be physically constructed, the **CWnd** member functions, **PreCreateWindow** and **OnCreate**, are invoked. In **OnCreate** (which is really the **WM_CREATE** message handler) we should acquire those items that depend on the existence of a valid handle to a window, **HWND**.

If you have both a **CFrameWnd** and a client **CWnd**, then if the client window has installed itself as a child window of the parent frame window (the normal case), then when the MFC destroys the application, the **CFrameWnd** must remove the **CWnd** main client window by destroying the windows interface element and the C++ object. The best place for such coding would be in the **CFrameWnd** events response function that is invoked to process **WM_DESTROY** messages, **OnDestroy**. Here the frame window destroys the client child window and deletes the class object. No further actions on your part are required for proper application termination.

Actions to set up an Interface Object and its associated Interface Element

a) **CWinApp** constructor calls **InitApplication**, **InitInstance**, and then calls **Run** which eventually upon termination calls **ExitInstance**

b) The default **InitApplication** function is not normally overridden, unless splash screens are desired.

c) Your **InitInstance** function does the following steps.

1. allocate a new frame or window class which builds the Windows Interface Object
2. call **ShowWindow**—By altering **nCmdShow**, you can have the application appear minimized, maximized, or shown normally.

d) The **CFrameWnd** derived class calls the **AfxRegisterWndClass** and **Create** functions. Here you can specify all of the usual **WNDCLASS** items.

e) Note that **Create** then calls your window's **PreCreateWindow** function to allow you a last chance at altering the window's proposed style.

f) Next, **Create** sends the **WM_CREATE** message which is handled in the member function called **OnCreate**.

g) **After** invoking the **OnCreate** base class function, the real Windows Interface Element is built. The handle to the window is now **valid**. The window is now a point in size; the first of several **WM_SIZE** messages is sent. Now we can get the average character dimensions because a real **hwnd** exists.

h) The **ShowWindow CWnd** function call is now invoked by the application class. It sends the initial **WM_PAINT** message, which is handled in the **CWnd OnPaint** function.

i) While on screen, some items can be altered by **CWnd** member functions. Among these are the title caption, the current mouse cursor, and the window's position (**SetWindowPos** or **MoveWindow**).

j). Upon termination, the **WM_DESTROY** message is handled in the **CWnd OnDestroy** function.

Design Rule 17: With only a few exceptions, always invoke the base class version of the overridden function as your first action in the derived function. The exceptions are the destruction functions, such as OnDestroy; here you call the base class last.

Design Rule 18: If you need the HWND for some initialization steps, invoke the base class's OnCreate function first!

Design Rule 19: Always invoke the proper base class function from within the derived class.

Ignorance or carelessness with these three rules lead to the most common disasters of unrecoverable errors and crashes and totally weird behavior during program development!

Example 1. Crash.

```
MyFrameWinClass::OnCreate (...) {
  Get text metrics coding causes a crash
}
```

Why? Failure to code

```
CFrameWnd::OnCreate (...);
```

before getting text metrics.

Example 2. Weird behavior of menus and so on.

```
MyFrameWinClass::OnCreate (...) {
  CWnd::OnCreate (...);
  Get text metrics coding causes a crash
}
```

Why? Failure to call the proper base class!

Example 3. Crash.
```
MyFrameWinClass::OnDestroy (...) {
  CFrameWnd::OnDestroy (...);
  Now delete other class items = a crash
}
```
Why? The entire application is gone from memory when the base class function returns.

Example 4. Crash—a subtle error, but very commonly done.
```
MyFrameWinClass::MyFrameWinClass : CFrameWnd () {
  Create (...);
  myFont = new Cfont (...); // myFont is a pointer
}
MyFrameWinClass::OnCreate (...) {
  CFrameWnd::OnCreate (...);
  Insert myFont into the new DC
  Get text metrics - crash
}
```
Why? **myFont** pointer is core garbage inside of **OnCreate** because the new function call in the constructor has not yet been executed because the **Create** function has not yet returned to the constructor!

This sequence, then, provides a great flexibility in application design. For example, the class constructor could directly call the **Create** function dictating how the window is to appear. I take this approach in these beginning sample programs. However, there are circumstances in which the **Create** function must be called outside the constructor. This occurs when creating modeless dialogs and dynamically launching child windows, for example. The **Create** function could itself be overridden to provide special setup processing if needed. **OnCreate** is commonly overridden to provide for construction of tool bars and to construct needed objects that depend upon the existence of a real **HWND**, such as obtaining the character size.

CWnd and CFrameWnd Public Data Members

CWnd has a vital public data member that is frequently used, the handle to the real window, the HWND.
```
HANDLE  m_hWnd; // the handle of this window
```

However, due to some complexities, it is far safer to use a public member function to obtain the real handle to the window.
```
HWND GetSafeHwnd ();
```

The CFrameWnd and CWnd Constructors

Normally, both the **CFrameWnd** and the **CWnd** constructors need no parameters. However, since the constructors often invoke the **Create** function and therefore has access to the full **WNDCLASS** structure, if you wish the application derived class to pass such items as window style and placement, you can do so. With a frame window, for example, you might wish to pass the frame window constructor the caption title to be used and any potential child windows. Additionally, you might pass other application specific parameters.

If you are constructing a client window **CWnd** as the child window of a frame window, then to enable automatic destruction of the client window, you must pass a pointer to the parent frame window. The client **CWnd** then invokes the **Create** function, passing along the parent window pointer.

There is a reason that the **CWnd** and **CFrameWnd** constructors take no parameters—serialization. Serialization is a method by which a class can be dynamically constructed at run time from data stored on disk. In other words, a window could save its state (size and onscreen location) to disk; when the application starts, it can reload the window exactly as it was previously. Another term for this is a persistent data object. Nearly all of the entire MFC classes can be dynamically constructed. These topics are discussed at length in Chapter 15. Thus, when you decide to pass a parameter to your class constructors, realize that you are generally going to lose the built-in framework default ability to stream that class to and from disk. For now, this is of no importance, but it will become important in Chapter 15.

The CWnd Member Functions (and Inherited By CFrameWnd)

There are an enormous number of member functions in the **CWnd** class. Throughout the ensuing chapters, I will present many that are commonly used. Let's begin with all-important **Create**. The **Create** function is slightly different between the **CWnd** and **CFrameWnd** classes. For **CWnd** derived classes, the **Create** function prototype is this.

```
BOOL Create (LPCSTR classname, LPCSTR title, DWORD style,
             RECT &rect, CWnd *ptrparent, UINT childid);
```

while for **CFrameWnd** derived classes, the **Create** function is invoked as follows.

```
BOOL Create (LPCSTR classname, LPCSTR title, DWORD style,
             RECT &rect, CWnd *ptrparent, LPCSTR menu);
```

The **classname** is the null-terminated string name of a registered **WNDCLASS**, Windows class. Commonly, we use another global MFC function to first create a new **WNDCLASS** structure with our values installed and return the string name for **Create**'s use. It is called **AfxRegisterWndClass**.

```
LPCSTR AfxRegisterWndClass (UINT winstyle, HCURSOR cursor,
                            HBRUSH brush, HICON icon);
```

Typically, **winstyle** is the familiar **CS_VREDRAW | CS_HREDRAW** so that the window receives scroll messages. The **style** parameter of **Create** is often **WS_OVERLAPPEDWINDOW**. The **rect** contains the initial area to be occupied by the window. The special value, **rectDefault**, permits Windows to position and size the window as it chooses. For client windows, **ptrparent** should be a pointer to the parent frame window but for frame windows, it is 0. The **menu** parameter is the string name of the menu resource which is discussed in Chapter 6. Until a menu is used, it is also 0.

Notice in particular that you control the window style and placement and size. Additionally, you can provide the background brush or window background color, the default cursor, and the icon to be associated with the window. Specifically, the background brush is set by using the C API function.

```
::GetStockObject (WHITE_BRUSH);
```

Coding syntax note: the presence of :: before a function is used to denote that the pure Windows API function is being invoked. Many MFC functions have the same names as the C API function. Although the :: is purely optional (MFC determines which is which by the function's parameters), I use the :: in the examples to assist you in reading the code.

In the next chapter, we will see how to install all manner of background colors. The functions to install the cursor and icon depend upon whether or not the object is a Windows default stock object or one of our own creation. For the standard stock objects, use the following functions.

```
AfxGetApp()->LoadStandardCursor (IDC_ARROW);
AfxGetApp()->LoadStandardIcon (IDI_APPLICATION);
```

Notice that these functions belong to the **CWinApp** class and the global function **AfxGetApp** returns a pointer to the application class. Two other **CWinApp** functions can be used to load our own cursors and icons.

```
AfxGetApp()->LoadCursor (IDC_OURCURSOR);
AfxGetApp()->LoadIcon (IDI_OURAPP);
```

These are used in Chapter 7 when we learn how to create cursors and icons.

Another useful function not only moves the window to another location but can also alter its size is **SetWindowPos**.

```
BOOL SetWindowPos (CWnd* ptr_insert_after_window, int x, int y,
                   int width, int height, UINT flags);
```

The first parameter is a pointer to the window that will precede this one, and often is coded as 0 or NULL. (There are some other special values this parameter can have, but they are an advanced topic.) Next, come the location and dimensions of the window in pixels. The flags that are commonly used consist of these.

```
SWP_HIDEWINDOW   - to hide the window
SWP_SHOWWINDOW   - to display the window
```

The return value is nonzero if the window was previously visible or zero if it was previously hidden.

Contrast this function to the **MoveWindow** function which has two versions.

```
void MoveWindow (int x, int y, int nWidth, int nHeight,
                 BOOL bRepaint = TRUE);
void MoveWindow (LPCRECT lpRect, BOOL bRepaint = TRUE);
```

To destroy any child windows, the frame window must be able to acquire a pointer to its child. This is done using the **GetDescendantWindow** function whose prototype is this.

```
CWnd* GetDescendantWindow (int windowID);
```

This handy function returns a pointer to a specific child window. Recall that the child ID number is one of the parameters to the **Create** function. When a **CFrameWnd** wishes to destroy and delete a child or client **CWnd**, this function is invoked to obtain a pointer to the child window.

Another **CWin** function that can be sometimes used to setup the window's attributes is **PreCreateWindow** which is called by the framework before the actual **Create** process is launched. Its prototype is

```
BOOL PreCreateWindow (CREATESTRUCT&)
```

Here you have access to the same **CREATESTRUCT** as in the **Create** function whose members are these.

```
LPVOID lpCreateParams; // points to the data to create the
                       // window
HANDLE hInstance;      // the HINSTANCE of the owner, the
                      // .exe file
HMENU  hMenu;          // identifies the menu, if any
HWND   hwndParent;     // identifies the parent window
int    cy;             // these four specify the window's
int    cx;             // position and dimensions
int    y;
int    x;
LONG   style;          // the windows style flags
LPCSTR lpszName;       // window's name string
LPCSTR lpszClass;      // the WNDCLASS
DWORD  dwExStyle;      // any extended style flags
```

Here, one could also set the window's dimensions and initial position as well as any style types.

The **ShowWindow** function specifies how the window is to be shown.

```
BOOL ShowWindow (int nCmdShow);
```

The parameter **nCmdShow** commonly has one of the following values.

```
SW_HIDE
SW_SHOW
SW_SHOWMAXIMIZED
```

Functions that respond to events or messages are typically prefixed with **On**. Hence, the MFC member function that responds to **WM_PAINT** messages is **OnPaint**, which has no parameters. Instead of passing a DC ready for painting operations, the MFC provides another class, **CPaintDC** to encapsulate the paint DC. The first action upon entering **OnPaint** is often the following.

```
void  MyClass::OnPaint () {
 CPaintDC dc (this);
```

MFC provides several support classes that parallel exactly the Windows counterparts. The **CSize** class encapsulates a two-dimensional quantity such as the height and width of a rectangle.

CPoint class for **POINT** with **int** members: **x** and **y**.

CRect class for **RECT** with **int** members: **top**, **left**, **right**, and **bottom**.

CSize class for **SIZE** with **int** members: **cx** and **cy**.

To display our "Hello World" message centered, we need the size of the whole client area. The **CWnd** function **GetClientRect** returns the dimensions of the client area for us. The parameter **rect** must be an instance of the **CRect** class which also includes member functions for **Height ()** and **Width ()** of the rectangle. The **GetClientRect** function is passed a pointer to the **CRect** to be filled.

```
void  GetClientRect (CRect*);
void  GetClientRect (LPRECT);
```

Actually, **CPaintDC** is derived from the more general **CDC** class that encapsulates a C style **HDC**. The **CDC** class also has numerous functions for drawing and displaying, closely paralleling the **HDC**. One of the frequently used **CDC** functions sets the text alignment. The text alignment normally is left justified, but can be set under MFC by the **CDC** member function **SetTextAlign**.

```
SetTextAlign (typedesired);
```

where the **typedesired** could be **TA_CENTER**. Again, left justification is the default.

The **TextOut CDC** function is a bit different from the Windows counterpart; it now has four parameters.

```
TextOut (x, y, the text, length);
```

Often the length is omitted. If omitted, the default displays the whole null-terminated string. Notice all these **CDC** functions require the class instance, **dc**, for example.

```
dc.SetTextAlign (TA_CENTER);
dc.TextOut (x, y, "Hello");
```

Finally, the signature of the **OnDestroy** function of **CWnd** invoked as a window is terminating is this.

```
void OnDestroy ();
```

but for either **WM_PAINT** and **WM_DESTROY** messages to be passed to member functions, entries must be made in the message response table.

```
ON_WM_DESTROY()
ON_WM_PAINT()
```

MFC Message Response Tables and Windows WM_ Messages

The MFC event handler receives all Windows messages and routes each to the corresponding window instance. However, MFC must know which messages your derived windows class wishes to receive and what is the member function name that it is to invoke to handle that message. This is the purpose and contents of the **Message Response Table**. Note that if your derived class does not wish to respond to a message, the MFC framework then checks to see if your base class wishes to do so.

The Response Table contains a series of specially named functions that are invoked when the corresponding **WM_** messages are received. These specific functions begin with **ON_WM_** name of the message such as **ON_WM_MOUSEMOVE** and the MFC invokes a member function with the name **OnMouseMove**.

Design Rule 20: To determine the message identifier, take the normal Windows message ID and prefix it with ON_

Thus, the MFC response table message identifiers for the following:

```
ON_WM_SIZE          for the Windows message WM_SIZE
ON_WM_RBUTTONDOWN   for the Windows message WM_RBUTTONDOWN
ON_WM_LBUTTONDOWN   for the Windows message WM_LBUTTONDOWN
ON_WM_PAINT         for the Windows message WM_PAINT
```

Design Rule 21: To determine the event handler member function name:
a) remove the WM_ from the Windows message ID
b) prefix it with On
c) convert to a capitalized format

So for the above, the member functions would be these.

```
OnSize
OnRButtonDown
OnLButtonDown
OnPaint
```

If the **CWinApp** or **CWnd** derived class wishes to handle messages, the class definition header file must include a placeholder stating the fact that there will be such a table for that derived class. Additionally, the table itself must be defined in the cpp file, rather like a member function would be defined. Somewhere within the class definition or header file must be the following line.

```
DECLARE_MESSAGE_MAP();
```

The actual table is defined in the cpp file just like a member function. The basic syntax for an empty table is this.

```
BEGIN_MESSAGE_MAP(classname, baseclass)
END_MESSAGE_MAP();
```

Since there is no multiple inheritance in the MFC, there can only be one base class. In our simplest examples, we must respond to paint messages. Thus, the message map for our main window is this.

```
BEGIN_MESSAGE_MAP(FrameWin, CFrameWnd)
 ON_WM_PAINT()
END_MESSAGE_MAP();
```

Design Rule 22: Append a prefix of afx_msg to the event handler member function name in the class header, but do not use the prefix in the implementation cpp file.

In the **ClientWin** header file, the paint function must be declared as follows.

```
afx_msg  void  OnPaint ();
```

The prefix **afx_msg** must be present in the header. However, in the cpp implementation file, omit the prefix; it is just this.

```
void FrameWin::OnPaint () {
 CPaintDC dc (this);
}
```

You will see this AFX prefix through out the MFC. It has no meaning; it is just a made up symbol. However, you could call it "Application Framework." The **afx_msg** is the internal MFC mechanism that is roughly parallel to the C++ **virtual** keyword.

When you are creating a shell for your application, many functions are defined but no coding is yet placed in the member functions. For example, you might code the following.

```
void ClientWin::OnMouseMove () {
}
```

When the shell is operational, begin adding functional code step by step. This is an excellent approach, except with the **OnPaint** function.

Design Rule 23: In OnPaint functions, always at least get a CpaintDC.

A failure to get a paint dc in the **OnPaint** function may crash the application!

Predefined Headers: How to Make Them Work for You

The idea behind the use of predefined headers is to speed up the compilation cycle by compiling the headers and storing them on disk. The next time the program is compiled, if those headers have not changed, the compiler simply reads in the results from disk. Sounds simple.

When we get to MFC applications, the header files become huge and compilation time is very, very long, even on fast machines. (Notice how long it takes on your machine to build the first example **Pgm04a.**) Pre-compiled headers become a must **use** with the MFC. There are several approaches that one can take to effectively utilize pre-compiled headers. For simplicity in working with pre-compiled headers, I use the default MFC wizard's approach.

Construct a header file called **stdafx.h** and include all of the MFC headers required by the entire application. Secondly, create a one-liner cpp file called **stdafx.cpp** that includes this header file. Then, include **stdafx.h** in **every** cpp file as the very **first** header include. (It is not needed in the class header files, just the cpp files.) The default that the compiler uses is that only the includes contained in **stdafx.h** are included in the pre-compiled header file. The compiler creates the pch pre-compiled header file once and uses it for all of the other cpp files.

What are the header files that must be included? For now, the **stdafx.h** file appears as follows.

StdAfx.h Header File

```
/***************************************************************/
```

```
/*                                                          */
/* Major Includes For the Whole Application                 */
/*        done for best use of precompiled headers          */
/*        by default, only headers in this file are precompiled */
/*                                                          */
/************************************************************/
#define WINVER 0x0500   // Win2000 or better
#define _AFXDLL         // use the MFC
#pragma once
#include <afxwin.h>    // MFC core and standard components
#include <afxext.h>    // MFC extensions
#include <afxcmn.h>    // MFC support for Windows Common Controls
#define VC_EXTRALEAN
```

At the moment we are not using pre-compiled headers. The define for WINVER tells the compiler what version of Windows we are creating the program for, here Win2000 or higher. The _AFXDLL tells the compiler that we are using the MFC. There is a special define that can be used to reduce the size of the headers by not including rarely used portions from the headers.

```
#define VC_EXTRALEAN   // Exclude rarely-used stuff
```

The **StdAfx.cpp** file is trivial.

```
StdAfx.cpp File
```

```
#include "stdafx.h"
```

The Sample Hello World MFC Programs

If you look over the models used by several texts, magazine articles, bulletin board samples, and so on, you see a bewildering array of possibilities. That's the benefit of OOP. Which one do we use for our applications? Remember that in texts, magazines and BBS files, space is a premium; often the examples are extremely short, just illustrating some idea. Seldom are these examples a real world application! So while these are nice and compact for short examples, such an approach can lead to a humongous single source file in a real application.

Good C++ design has probably been forcing you to have an h and a cpp file for each class. This approach has many benefits and is the one that I recommend and follow myself. The only drawback, as far as I am concerned, is the rather large number of files that can be generated.

Sample Pgm04a: Your Model Shell

Pgm04a is your basic model to follow in your beginning MFC programs. There are six files that make up the project: the **StdAfx** pair, the **Pgm04a CWinApp** derived class pair, and the **FrameWin CFrameWnd** derived class pair. We've already examined the stdafx pair. So let's start with the application derived class.

```
Pgm04a CWinApp Definition File
```

```
#pragma once
/************************************************************/
/*                                                          */
/* Pgm04a Application Class Definition                      */
/*                                                          */
/************************************************************/
class Pgm04a : public CWinApp {
```

```
public:

      Pgm04a () : CWinApp () {} // ctor - no actions required
     ~Pgm04a () {}              // dtor - no actions required

BOOL  InitInstance ();       // constructs instance of framewindow

DECLARE_MESSAGE_MAP();       // future message response table
};
```

Pgm04a CWinApp Implementation File

```
#include "StdAfx.h"
#include "Pgm04a.h"
#include "FrameWin.h"

/*****************************************************************/
/*                                                               */
/* Message Response Table - currently none                       */
/*                                                               */
/*****************************************************************/

BEGIN_MESSAGE_MAP(Pgm04a, CWinApp)
END_MESSAGE_MAP ()

/*****************************************************************/
/*                                                               */
/* InitInstance: Allocate instances of our frame window          */
/*                                                               */
/*****************************************************************/

BOOL  Pgm04a::InitInstance () {

 // construct new main and frame windows
 m_pMainWnd = new FrameWin;

 // show window in the style passed from the Windows command line
 m_pMainWnd->ShowWindow (m_nCmdShow);
 return TRUE;
}

Pgm04a theApp;   // constructs the app object and executes it
```

Notice that I have included a message map definition and implementation in the **CWinApp** class. At the moment it is empty because there are no messages to which the application class should respond. However, later on when printing is covered, we discover that the **CWinApp** class encapsulates the printer. It also carries out some document opening activities in the document-view model. By coding the message map in the application derived class here, I am getting you used to seeing it here in the application class.

FrameWin CFrameWin Definition File

```
#pragma once

/*****************************************************************/
/*                                                               */
/* FrameWin Class Definition                                     */
/*                                                               */
/*****************************************************************/

class FrameWin : public CFrameWnd {

```

```
public:
              FrameWin ();    // constructor
             ~FrameWin () {}  // destructor
afx_msg void OnPaint ();      // paint the window - WM_PAINT msgs

DECLARE_MESSAGE_MAP();
};
```

FrameWin CFrameWin Implementation File

```
#include "stdafx.h"
#include "framewin.h"

/*****************************************************************/
/*                                                               */
/* FrameWin Message Response Table                               */
/*                                                               */
/*****************************************************************/

BEGIN_MESSAGE_MAP(FrameWin, CFrameWnd)
 ON_WM_PAINT ()
END_MESSAGE_MAP();

/*****************************************************************/
/*                                                               */
/* FrameWin: create the window by filling the WNDCLASS struct,   */
/*           registering the window, and creating an instance    */
/*                                                               */
/*****************************************************************/

FrameWin::FrameWin () : CFrameWnd () {

 Create (AfxRegisterWndClass (
          CS_VREDRAW | CS_HREDRAW,
          AfxGetApp()->LoadStandardCursor (IDC_ARROW),
          (HBRUSH) ::GetStockObject (LTGRAY_BRUSH),
          AfxGetApp()->LoadStandardIcon (IDI_APPLICATION)),
        "Hello From Windows - MFC Style", // window caption
        WS_OVERLAPPEDWINDOW,
        rectDefault, // CFrameWnd member = default rectangle
        0,           // the parent window, here none
        NULL);       // no menu
}

/*****************************************************************/
/*                                                               */
/* OnPaint: paint client window light gray and display "Hello"   */
/*                                                               */
/*****************************************************************/

void     FrameWin::OnPaint () {

 CPaintDC dc (this);             // create a paint dc
 CRect    rect;
 GetClientRect (&rect);          // get client size for scaling
 dc.SetTextAlign (TA_CENTER );   // set for centering text
 dc.TextOut (rect.right/2, rect.bottom/2, "Hello From Windows");
}
```

Notice how the call to the **AfxRegisterWndClass** function is nested within the call to the **Create** function. This is commonly done to avoid the necessity of defining a pointer to char to hold the returned registered application string. Again, use **Pgm04a** as your model to follow.

Pgm04b: Everything in One File for Magazine Articles

This example shows how everything can be condensed into one short file. It is only used for very short magazine-style articles, never a real program.

Pgm04b - Everything in One File - for Very Short Examples

```
#include "StdAfx.h"

/********************************************************************/
/*                                                                  */
/* Pgm04b Application Class Definition                              */
/*                                                                  */
/********************************************************************/

class Pgm04b : public CWinApp {

public:

      Pgm04b () : CWinApp () {} // ctor - no actions required
     ~Pgm04b () {}              // dtor - no actions required

BOOL  InitInstance ();       // constructs instance of framewindow

DECLARE_MESSAGE_MAP();       // future message response table

};

/********************************************************************/
/*                                                                  */
/* FrameWin Class Definition                                        */
/*                                                                  */
/********************************************************************/

class FrameWin : public CFrameWnd {

public:
             FrameWin ();     // constructor
            ~FrameWin () {}   // destructor
afx_msg void OnPaint ();      // paint the window - WM_PAINT msgs

DECLARE_MESSAGE_MAP();

};

/********************************************************************/
/*                                                                  */
/* Message Response Table - currently none                          */
/*                                                                  */
/********************************************************************/

BEGIN_MESSAGE_MAP(Pgm04b, CWinApp)
END_MESSAGE_MAP ()

/********************************************************************/
/*                                                                  */
/* InitInstance: Allocate instances of our frame window             */
/*                                                                  */
/********************************************************************/

BOOL  Pgm04b::InitInstance () {

 // construct new frame window
```

```
 m_pMainWnd = new FrameWin;

 // show window in the style passed from the Windows command line
 m_pMainWnd->ShowWindow (m_nCmdShow);
 return TRUE;
}

Pgm04b  theApp;  // constructs the app object and executes it


/***************************************************************/
/*                                                             */
/* FrameWin Message Response Table                             */
/*                                                             */
/***************************************************************/

BEGIN_MESSAGE_MAP(FrameWin, CFrameWnd)
 ON_WM_PAINT ()
END_MESSAGE_MAP();

/***************************************************************/
/*                                                             */
/* FrameWin: create the window by filling the WNDCLASS struct, */
/*          registering the window, and creating an instance   */
/*                                                             */
/***************************************************************/

FrameWin::FrameWin () : CFrameWnd () {

 Create (AfxRegisterWndClass (
          CS_VREDRAW | CS_HREDRAW,
          AfxGetApp()->LoadStandardCursor (IDC_ARROW),
          (HBRUSH) ::GetStockObject (LTGRAY_BRUSH),
          AfxGetApp()->LoadStandardIcon (IDI_APPLICATION)),
         "Hello From Windows - MFC Style", // window caption
         WS_OVERLAPPEDWINDOW,
         rectDefault, // CFrameWnd member = default rectangle
         0,           // the parent window, here none
         NULL);       // no menu
}

/***************************************************************/
/*                                                             */
/* OnPaint: paint client window light gray and display "Hello" */
/*                                                             */
/***************************************************************/

void     FrameWin::OnPaint () {

 CPaintDC dc (this);           // create a paint dc
 CRect    rect;
 GetClientRect (&rect);        // get client size for scaling
 dc.SetTextAlign (TA_CENTER ); // set for centering text
 dc.TextOut (rect.right/2, rect.bottom/2, "Hello From Windows");
}
```

Pgm04c: a Main Frame Window with a Child Client Window

Pgm04c is a much more complex shell. The **MainFrame** class is derived from **CFrameWnd** and it dynamically launches a **ChildView Cwnd** derived class as its client window. The idea here is to separate the frame window operations from the client screen activities. The frame window is responsible for menu operations, resizing, toolbar implementation and status bar operations. The client window is responsible for the actual application needed displaying of text and so on. This allows a separation of the total work load. Obviously, at this point, this is total overkill as there are no toolbars or a status bar or even a menu for the frame window to manage. But it does allow us to see a simple model implementation.

The stdafx files are identical to the other two versions. The **Pgm04c** application class is virtually the same as well.

```
Pgm04c.cpp - Application Class Implementation

#include "stdafx.h"
#include "Pgm04c.h"
#include "MainFrm.h"

/*****************************************************************/
/*                                                               */
/* Message Response Table - currently none                       */
/*                                                               */
/*****************************************************************/

BEGIN_MESSAGE_MAP(Pgm04cApp, CWinApp)
END_MESSAGE_MAP()

/*****************************************************************/
/*                                                               */
/* InitInstance: allocate and show the FrameWin main frame       */
/*                                                               */
/*****************************************************************/

BOOL Pgm04cApp::InitInstance() {
 m_pMainWnd = new MainFrame;
 m_pMainWnd->ShowWindow(SW_SHOW);
 return TRUE;
}


Pgm04cApp theApp; //the one and only instance of the app
```

The **MainFrame** class is quite different. First, an instance of the **ChildView** class is defined as a public data member, **m_wndView**. **OnCreate** is overridden so that the child view class can be created once the parent window is actually built. Notice that I am using the MFC way of naming member variables—using the **m_** prefix.

However, two other functions are needed. First, if the user clicks on the frame window portion to switch the focus back to this application, we should pass that signal on down to the client window who may respond by creating the caret, for example. Hence, we respond to **WM_SETFOCUS** messages with the function **OnSetFocus**.

```
void OnSetFocus(CWnd* pOldWnd);
```

It is passed the window that is losing the focus as this one is gaining the focus.

The second needed function is critical to proper message routing. Since we now have a client window, that window should get a crack at responding to any application messages that may be for it. This is an important function to understand, **OnCmdMsg**. The framework routes messages throughout the application. In this simple model, any messages are routed to the **CWinApp** and its derived class, to the **CFrameWnd** and its derived class, and later on, to any dialogs that are active. Since we have allocated a child window of the main frame class, we need to let that window also get a chance to be routed the messages so that it can respond to any that are directed or controlled by it. **OnCmdMsg** is the function that we can use to insert additional windows into the message processing loop.

```
BOOL OnCmdMsg (UINT nID, int nCode, void* pExtra,
               AFX_CMDHANDLERINFO* pHandlerInfo);
```

The implementation is simple. Route the message to our child window. If it handles it, we are done. If not, pass it along to out base class which is where it would have gone first if we had not intercepted it.

```
if (m_wndView.OnCmdMsg(nID, nCode, pExtra, pHandlerInfo))
  return TRUE;
return CFrameWnd::OnCmdMsg(nID, nCode, pExtra, pHandlerInfo);
```

Next, examine how the frame window is created. In the constructor, **Create** is called and as usual, it is passed the returned character string from **AfxRegisterWndClass** which is where we specify many of the construction details that our frame window should have. Specifically, notice that I am using a white background brush. The client window has a gray background brush. Thus, when you examine the display, any portion of the frame window's client area that is not occupied by the child client window is very visible. In this case, there isn't any because the child window is being forced to always occupy the entire client area of the frame window. That is done in the **OnCreate** function.

In **OnCreate**, after the call to the base class, the child window can be created. Remember, only after the call to the base class in **OnCreate** does this window actually exist, the interface element. We have defined an instance of the **ChildView CWnd** class as a public data member of our frame window class. Thus, its constructor has already been called, its default ctor. However, that child window constructor does not call its **Create** function. Rather, we explicitly call its **Create** function here in the parent window's **OnCreate** because only here do we have enough information to actually create it as a child window of the frame window.

This type of coding is widespread throughout the MFC classes. The default ctor only initializes the C++ wrapper. Then, at a later point in time, the **Create** function that actually builds the real interface element is explicitly invoked. In this case, the child window is created this way.

```
if (!m_wndView.Create (NULL, NULL, AFX_WS_DEFAULT_VIEW,
    CRect(0, 0, 0, 0), this, AFX_IDW_PANE_FIRST, NULL)) {
 return -1;
}
```

The special values, **AFX_WS_DEFAULT_VIEW** and **AFX_IDW_PANE_FIRST** provide first the style bits for a child window, such as **WS_CHILD**, and then the unique child id number. With this unique id, the framework handles its proper positioning. Try it, change the **AFX_IDW_PANE_FIRST** to some arbitrary number, such as 1 and rerun the program—the child window does not even appear because the framework does not realize that it is supposed to maintain this window. If we went this route, we would have to override **OnSize** and manually resize and position the child window using **MoveWindow** or **SetWindowPos**.

MainFrm.h - MainFrame Window Definition

```
#pragma once
#include "ChildView.h"

/*****************************************************************/
/*                                                               */
/* MainFrame class: allocates and manages a child CWnd client    */
/*                                                               */
/*****************************************************************/

class MainFrame : public CFrameWnd {
public:
 ChildView m_wndView;   // the child window

 MainFrame();           // create this window

 // routes all messages to the child window first
 BOOL OnCmdMsg(UINT nID, int nCode, void* pExtra,
               AFX_CMDHANDLERINFO* pHandlerInfo);

protected:
 // creates the child window
 afx_msg int OnCreate(LPCREATESTRUCT lpCreateStruct);

 // passes the focus on to the child window
 afx_msg void OnSetFocus(CWnd *pOldWnd);

 DECLARE_MESSAGE_MAP()
};
```

MainFrm.cpp - MainFrame Window Implementation

```
#include "stdafx.h"
#include "Pgm04c.h"
#include "MainFrm.h"

/********************************************************************/
/*                                                                  */
/* Message Response Table                                           */
/*                                                                  */
/********************************************************************/

BEGIN_MESSAGE_MAP(MainFrame, CFrameWnd)
 ON_WM_CREATE()
 ON_WM_SETFOCUS()
END_MESSAGE_MAP()

/********************************************************************/
/*                                                                  */
/* MainFrame: create the main frame window                          */
/*                                                                  */
/********************************************************************/

MainFrame::MainFrame() : CFrameWnd () {
 Create (AfxRegisterWndClass (
               CS_VREDRAW | CS_HREDRAW,
               AfxGetApp()->LoadStandardCursor (IDC_ARROW),
               (HBRUSH) ::GetStockObject (WHITE_BRUSH),
               AfxGetApp()->LoadStandardIcon (IDI_APPLICATION)),
   // note - white brush is used so we can see any difference
   // between this window's client area and child window
         "Hello From Windows - MFC Style",
         WS_OVERLAPPEDWINDOW,
         rectDefault,
         0,     // the parent window, here none
         NULL); // no main menu
}

/********************************************************************/
/*                                                                  */
/* OnCreate: Create the client window                               */
/*                                                                  */
/********************************************************************/

int MainFrame::OnCreate(LPCREATESTRUCT lpCreateStruct) {
 // vital: create the real frame win first!
 if (CFrameWnd::OnCreate(lpCreateStruct) == -1)
  return -1;

 // create a child view to occupy the client area of the frame
 if (!m_wndView.Create (NULL, NULL, AFX_WS_DEFAULT_VIEW,
  CRect(0, 0, 0, 0), this, AFX_IDW_PANE_FIRST, NULL)) {
  return -1;
 }

 return 0;
}

/********************************************************************/
/*                                                                  */
/* OnSetFocus: pass the focus on down to the child window           */
/*                                                                  */
/********************************************************************/

void MainFrame::OnSetFocus(CWnd* /*pOldWnd*/) {
```

```
 m_wndView.SetFocus();
}

/*************************************************************/
/*                                                           */
/* OnCmdMsg: pass all messages to the child window first     */
/*                                                           */
/*************************************************************/

BOOL MainFrame::OnCmdMsg (UINT nID, int nCode, void* pExtra,
                          AFX_CMDHANDLERINFO* pHandlerInfo) {
 // let the view have first crack at the command
 if (m_wndView.OnCmdMsg(nID, nCode, pExtra, pHandlerInfo))
  return TRUE;

 // otherwise, do default handling
 return CFrameWnd::OnCmdMsg(nID, nCode, pExtra, pHandlerInfo);
}
```

The child window is very simple. It is only concerned with the textual display. We can specify some of our desired window style characteristics in **PreCreateWindow**. After the call to the base class has filled the **CREATESTRUCT**, we can then modify it the way we like.

```
if (!Cwnd::PreCreateWindow(cs)) return FALSE;
cs.lpszClass = AfxRegisterWndClass (
                  CS_HREDRAW | CS_VREDRAW | CS_DBLCLKS,
                  ::LoadCursor(NULL, IDC_ARROW),
                  (HBRUSH) ::GetStockObject (LTGRAY_BRUSH),
                   NULL);
```

Here is where I set the light gray background brush and the arrow cursor.

ChildView.h - Child Window Definition

```
#pragma once

/*************************************************************/
/*                                                           */
/* ChildView: the CWnd that occupies whole framewin client area*/
/*                                                           */
/*************************************************************/

class ChildView : public CWnd {

public:
 ChildView() : CWnd () {} // ctor does nothing

protected:
 // virtual in case we derive from this child window
 virtual BOOL PreCreateWindow(CREATESTRUCT& cs);
 afx_msg void OnPaint();

 DECLARE_MESSAGE_MAP()
};
```

ChildView.cpp - Child Window Implementation

```
#include "stdafx.h"
#include "Pgm04c.h"
#include "ChildView.h"

```

```
/*************************************************************/
/*                                                           */
/* Message Response Table                                    */
/*                                                           */
/*************************************************************/

BEGIN_MESSAGE_MAP(ChildView,CWnd )
 ON_WM_PAINT()
END_MESSAGE_MAP()

/*************************************************************/
/*                                                           */
/* PreCreateWindow: alternative way to register this class   */
/*                                                           */
/*************************************************************/

BOOL ChildView::PreCreateWindow(CREATESTRUCT& cs) {
 if (!CWnd::PreCreateWindow(cs))
  return FALSE;

 // define how we want this window to appear
 // note: using a gray background brush to differentiate it from
 // the main frame client area which is white
 cs.lpszClass = AfxRegisterWndClass (
                  CS_HREDRAW | CS_VREDRAW | CS_DBLCLKS,
                  ::LoadCursor(NULL, IDC_ARROW),
                  (HBRUSH) ::GetStockObject (LTGRAY_BRUSH),
                  NULL);

 return TRUE;
}

/*************************************************************/
/*                                                           */
/* OnPaint: display the hello message                        */
/*                                                           */
/*************************************************************/

void ChildView::OnPaint() {
 CPaintDC dc(this);              // device context for painting
 CRect    rect;
 GetClientRect (&rect);          // get client size for scaling
 dc.SetTextAlign (TA_CENTER );   // set for centering text
 dc.TextOut (rect.right/2, rect.bottom/2, "Hello From Windows");
}
```

It is illustrative to examine what we would have had to code in the main frame class had we not made this client window be managed by the framework. The **CFrameWnd** has a useful function that returns a pointer to any child window, which are known as descendant windows, **GetDescendantWindow**. All that is required is the unique child id value.

```
CWnd*  GetDescendantWindow (child id number);
```

The function to destroy a window is **DestroyWindow**.

```
DestroyWindow ();
```

For example, suppose that the main frame window class wished to use an instance of a **CWnd** derived class called **ClientWnd**. In the construction portion of the main frame, we code the following and assign this client window an id of 1.

```
ClientWnd* ptrclient = new ClientWnd;
ptrclient->Create (...);
```

In **OnSize**, we reposition this window where we desire by using **GetDescendantWindow** to obtain a pointer to that window.

```
ClientWin *ptrclient = (ClientWin*) GetDescendantWindow (1);
if (ptrclient) ptrclient->MoveWindow (...);
```

Later, when the main frame window is being destroyed, we must manually delete our children that the framework does not know about. So in our function **OnDestroy** function, we code this.

```
ClientWin *ptrclient = (ClientWin*) GetDescendantWindow (1);
if (ptrclient) {     // if there is a client window, then
 ptrclient->DestroyWindow (); // destroy interface element
 delete ptrclient;            // delete the C++ object
}
CframeWnd::OnDestroy();
```

OnDestroy of the base class must be invoked **last**! Child windows are destroyed before their parents. Okay. It would have been simpler to just make a **ClientWnd** pointer be a data member of out main frame class; then we could avoid all of the **GetDescendantWindow** function calls.

One final note on the MFC typecasting. When a pointer is typecasted like this,

```
ClientWin *ptrclient = (ClientWin*) GetDescendantWindow (1);
```

it is not a **static type cast**, as the C syntax would suggest. It is actually a **dynamic cast**. In C, consider the effect of the following typecast.

```
void* ptrobject;
COSTREC* ptrrec = (COSTREC*) ptrobject;
```

This is a static cast. The compiler simply copies the address value being stored in **ptrobject** and places it into **ptrrec** ignoring totally whether or not **ptrobject** is actually pointing to a **COSTREC** structure or not! In C++ you learned how to do a dynamic cast.

```
COSTREC* ptrrec = dynamic_cast<COSTREC*>(ptrobject);
```

Here, if and only if **ptrobject** actually pointed to a **COSTREC** structure would the address be copied. If it did not point to one, a 0 or NULL value is placed into **ptrrec**.

Since the MFC coding is full of typecasts, because we are always deriving classes from the MFC base classes, the MFC treats these static looking type casts of pointers as if they were dynamic casts. We get a terrific simplification in coding!

Design Rule 24: When typecasting pointers in MFC coding, always check the resultant pointer. If it is 0, then the source pointer is not the desired type of object.

Handling Events: Pgm04d

Now that we can get a basic shell up and running, we need to actually do something useful. The next step in understanding the MFC is to get a feel for message handling, or action events. So using **Pgm04a** as our model, let's add some action events.

Only a very few Windows messages actually are directed automatically straight to a class's member function without specifying anything in the message map table; **PreCreateWindow** is one such example. The message map table is used to notify the MFC message handler which events or messages our instance wishes to explicitly handle.

If there is no message map entry for a specific message, then no member functions are ever called. For example, comment out the **ON_WM_PAINT()** entry in **Pgm04a**'s message map table and rerun **Pgm04a**. Even though the class defines and implements the **OnPaint** function, it is never called **unless** there is an entry for it in the message map!

By the way, this makes a very effective way to debug a larger program that is not working right. To remove a function temporarily from operations, just comment out its entry in the message map; that function is never called. So you don't have to comment out the function prototype in the class definition and comment out the function body in the cpp file. Just comment out its message map entry. Clever.

In general, messages come in two forms: those message that have a predefined corresponding function that is invoked and those messages which we must identify the name of the function that we wish to respond to that message. **OnPaint** is one such example of the first type. Merely by placing **ON_WM_PAINT()** in the message map, the framework always invokes **OnPaint**. Many other events or messages have no such ties to a specific function. In these cases we must also provide the name of the function to invoke when this message is found in the queue.

Let's begin with the simpler messages or events: mouse button presses. In addition, let's add in many MFC functions that correspond to those Windows functions that we have been using through Chapter 3. Figure 4.6 shows what **Pgm4d** looks like when launched and the left button pressed.

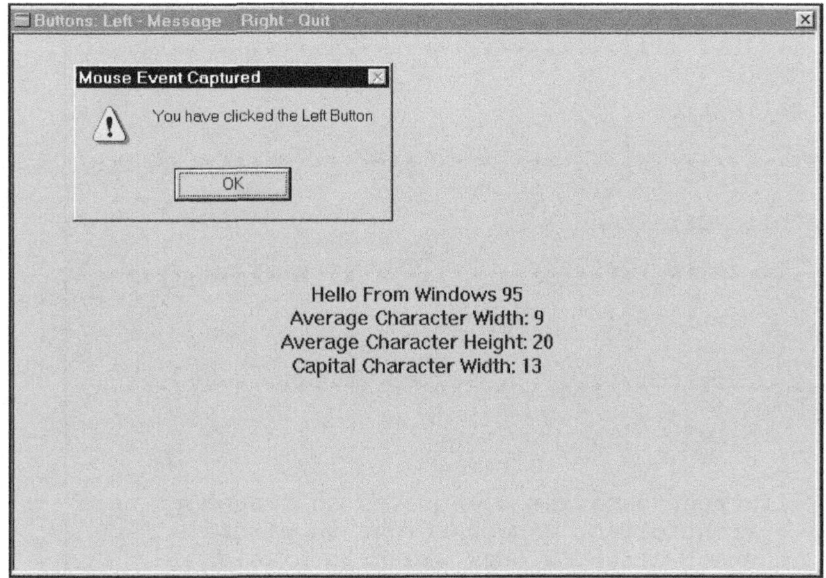

Figure 4.6 Pgm04d After a Left Button Click

Let's install a light gray background and adjust some of the window creation properties. Specifically, remove the maximize and minimize buttons from the title bar. Further, let's get the window resizing operation to really "center" the text properly by processing **WM_SIZE** messages. (If you run the previous programs, notice that they really do not handle the window resize operation by re-centering the text.)

Whenever the left button is pressed, display a message box notifying the user that the left button was pressed and set a **dataSaved** member to **false** to simulate a potential file save operation at application termination time. Normally, if a file has not been saved and a user attempts to close the application, a message box appears notifying the user of the situation and asking whether the file should be saved. The **OnClose** function responds to the **WM_CLOSE** messages. If no save is needed, **OnClose** destroys the window. If a save is needed, the application would carry out a save operation and then shut down. Here, however, I reset the **dataSaved** member to true. Figure 4.7 shows how the message appears on the screen.

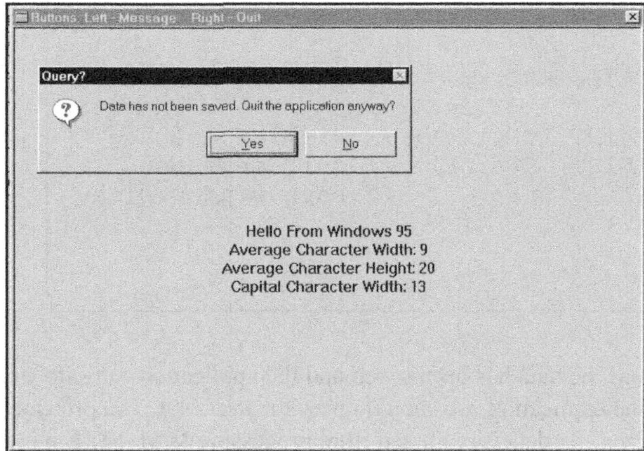

Figure 4.7 Pgm04d After a Close Request

With an **OnClose** function operational, let's have the right mouse button send an **OnClose** message just to see how to send ourselves a message. **Pgm04d** implements these actions. There are no significant changes to the **Pgm04d** application class coding from the previous examples. As a general rule, the **CWinApp** class remains unchanged for many chapters. Let's examine the **FrameWin** class definition in the **FrameWin.h** file.

FrameWin.h of Pgm04d Definition of FrameWin Class

```
#pragma once

/********************************************************************/
/*                                                                  */
/* FrameWin Class Definition                                        */
/*                                                                  */
/********************************************************************/

class FrameWin : public CFrameWnd {

 /*******************************************************************/
 /*                                                                 */
 /* Class Data Members                                              */
 /*                                                                 */
 /*******************************************************************/

protected:

bool dataSaved; // if true, data has been saved so tis ok to quit
int  height;    // current client window height in pixels
int  width;     // current client window width in pixels

int  avgCapsWidth;  // average capital letter width
int  avgCharWidth;  // average character width
int  avgCharHeight; // average character height

 /*******************************************************************/
 /*                                                                 */
 /* Class Functions:                                                */
 /*                                                                 */
 /*******************************************************************/

public:
              FrameWin ();         // construct the window
             ~FrameWin () {}       // destructor - no actions
afx_msg void  OnPaint ();          // respond to WM_PAINT msgs

protected:

afx_msg int   OnCreate (LPCREATESTRUCT);     // set avg char dims
afx_msg void  OnClose ();             // determines if app can quit
afx_msg void  OnLButtonDown (UINT, CPoint); // display message
afx_msg void  OnRButtonDown (UINT, CPoint); // quit message
afx_msg void  OnSize (UINT, int, int);      // save window size

DECLARE_MESSAGE_MAP();
};
```

The **dataSaved** protected member is **true** if the data has been saved and the application can safely close. When **dataSaved** is **false** and the user attempts to close the application, we should query the user first. The protected members, **height** and **width**, store the client area's current size. The data is extracted from processing **WM_SIZE** messages. Next, come the familiar three average character dimension fields. All member functions are overridden member functions of **CWnd**, the base class of **CFrameWnd**. The constructor, destructor, and **OnPaint** functions are defined exactly as before. What new functions and classes are needed? The following list shows the new MFC functions and classes we need to implement or use.

```
OnCreate
OnClose
OnLButtonDown
OnRButtonDown
```

```
OnSize
DestroyWindow
MessageBox
SendMessage
CclientDC
```

First, let's look at the signatures of these functions and then how they are used. Recall how the message map is constructed. If we wish to respond to the **WM_CREATE** message, in the message map the **ON_** prefix is added and the corresponding member function would be **OnCreate**, constructed be dropping the **WM_** and capitalizing the uppercase words. The signature of the overridden **OnCreate** function and the message map macro are as follows.

```
afxmsg int OnCreate (LPCREATESTRUCT lp);
ON_WM_CREATE()
```

Remember that you must invoke the base class's **OnCreate** before the **hwnd** becomes valid. Once the window element is constructed, the average character dimensions can be acquired using a **TEXTMETRIC** structure. However, the **GetTextMetrics** function required a DC. Whenever the handle to the window is valid, that is, the window interface element exists, a device context can be constructed using the **CClientDC** class whose constructor is passed the **this** parameter.

```
TEXTMETRIC  tm;
CClientDC *ptrdc = new CClientDC (this); // acquire a DC
ptrdc->GetTextMetrics (&tm);           // get the information
delete ptrdc;                          // delete the dc
```

or use

```
CClientDC dc (this);
dc.GetTextMetrics (&tm);
```

What is the difference between these two methods? When you dynamically allocate the DC, you can control when it is destroyed. If you use the automatic storage version, the **dc** item is only destroyed at block end. The average character dimensions are calculated exactly as before.

The **OnClose** function definition and message map macro are coded this way.

```
afx_msg void  OnClose ();
ON_WM_CLOSE()
```

In your **OnClose** the function, if the data needs to be saved, do so. In this example, I display a message box instead. When the application can terminate, then **OnClose** can either call the base class **OnClose** or can invoke **DestroyWindow** directly to complete the termination process. The **DestroyWindow** definition is as follows.

```
void  DestroyWindow();
```

The **OnSize** function responds to **WM_SIZE** messages; its prototype and message map macro are shown below.

```
afx_msg void OnSize (UINT type, int newwidth, int newheight);
ON_WM_SIZE()
```

The **type** field notifies you if the window is now maximized, minimized, or normal. Commonly used identifiers include **SIZE_MAXIMIZED**, **SIZE_MINIMIZED**, and **SIZE_RESTORED**. There are some other less frequently required choices that we will explore later on. In response to **WM_SIZE** messages, the size of the window's client area is acquired and saved in member variables for later use.

The **Invalidate** function forces a paint message to be sent, requesting that the entire window be repainted. It has one parameter, a **BOOL**, which when **TRUE** forces the background to be repainted as well. The **BOOL** defaults to **TRUE**. Normal usage is simply

```
Invalidate ();
```

In contrast, the **InvalidateRect** function can be used when only a portion of the window should be repainted. Its signature is this.

```
InvalidateRect (LPCRECT ptrrect, BOOL erasebkgrnd = TRUE);
```

WM_PAINT messages are one of the lowest priority messages Windows handles. They are processed and sent to windows only when there are no other higher priority messages in the system's queue. Sometimes an application must have an immediate screen repaint. In such situations, use the **UpdateWindow** function, which forces an immediate repainting of the window. The function takes no parameters.

```
UpdateWindow ();
```

This is precisely what goes on in the **CWinApp**'s **InitInstance** call to the **ShowWindow** function.

The mouse button down messages are sent via the message map to the functions: **OnLButtonDown, OnRButtonDown, and OnMButtonDown** which are defined this way.

```
afxmsg void  OnLButtonDown (UINT keys, CPoint at);
afxmsg void  OnRButtonDown (UINT keys, CPoint at);
ON_WM_LBUTTONDOWN ()
ON_WM_RBUTTONDOWN ()
```

Here **keys** could be a combination of one or more of the identifiers **MK_CONTROL**, **MK_SHIFT**, **MK_LBUTTON**, **MK_MBUTTON**, and/or **MK_RBUTTON**; the parameter **at** contains the coordinates of the point where the button was pressed down. Now examine the FrameWin implementation in the cpp listing.

FrameWin.cpp of Pgm04d Implementation of FrameWin Class

```
#include "stdafx.h"
#include "framewin.h"

/*****************************************************************/
/*                                                               */
/* FrameWin Message Response Table                               */
/*                                                               */
/*****************************************************************/

BEGIN_MESSAGE_MAP(FrameWin, CFrameWnd)
 ON_WM_PAINT ()
 ON_WM_LBUTTONDOWN ()
 ON_WM_RBUTTONDOWN ()
 ON_WM_SIZE ()
 ON_WM_CLOSE ()
 ON_WM_CREATE ()
END_MESSAGE_MAP();


/*****************************************************************/
/*                                                               */
/* FrameWin: create the window by filling the WNDCLASS struct    */
/*                                                               */
/*****************************************************************/

FrameWin::FrameWin () : CFrameWnd () {

 DWORD style = WS_OVERLAPPEDWINDOW; // set the basic window style
 // remove max/min buttons
 style &= ~(WS_MINIMIZEBOX | WS_MAXIMIZEBOX);

 CRect rect (100, 100, 500, 600);    // set initial pos and size

 Create (AfxRegisterWndClass (
               CS_VREDRAW | CS_HREDRAW,
               AfxGetApp()->LoadStandardCursor (IDC_ARROW),
               (HBRUSH) ::GetStockObject (LTGRAY_BRUSH),
               AfxGetApp()->LoadStandardIcon (IDI_APPLICATION)),
        "Buttons:  Left - Message   Right - Quit", // caption
         style,        // the modified style
         rect,         // initial size and location
         0,            // the parent window, here none
         NULL);        // no menu

 dataSaved = true;     // initialize control member
```

```
}


/**************************************************************/
/*                                                            */
/* OnCreate: get average character height and width          */
/*                                                            */
/**************************************************************/

int FrameWin::OnCreate (LPCREATESTRUCT lpCS) {

 if (CFrameWnd::OnCreate (lpCS) == -1) return -1;
 TEXTMETRIC  tm;

 // set the system font's characteristics in tm
 CClientDC *ptrdc = new CClientDC (this); // acquire a DC
 ptrdc->GetTextMetrics (&tm);             // get the information
 delete ptrdc;                            // delete the dc
 // or use
 // CClientDC dc (this);
 // dc.GetTextMetrics (&tm);

 // calculate average character parameters
 avgCharWidth  = tm.tmAveCharWidth;
 avgCharHeight = tm.tmHeight + tm.tmExternalLeading;
 avgCapsWidth  = (tm.tmPitchAndFamily & 1 ? 3 : 2) *
                     avgCharWidth / 2;
 return 0;
}


/**************************************************************/
/*                                                            */
/* OnSize: acquire the current dimensions of the client window */
/*                                                            */
/**************************************************************/

void FrameWin::OnSize (UINT, int cx, int cy) {

 height = cy;
 width = cx;

 // or do it this way
 // CRect rect;
 // GetClientRect (&rect);   // get the size of the client window
 // height = rect.Height();  // calc and save current height
 // width  = rect.Width();   // calc and save current width
}


/**************************************************************/
/*                                                            */
/* OnPaint: paint client window light gray and display "Hello" */
/*                                                            */
/**************************************************************/

void       FrameWin::OnPaint () {
 CPaintDC dc (this);          // create a paint dc
 CRect    rect;
 GetClientRect (&rect);       // get client area size for scaling
 // or use
 // CRect rect (0, 0, width, height);

 char msg [80];
```

```

 dc.SetTextAlign (TA_CENTER |TA_BASELINE );  // set centered text
 dc.SetBkMode (TRANSPARENT);             // background color visible

 dc.TextOut (width/2, height/2, "Hello From Windows 95");

 wsprintf (msg,"Average Character Width: %d", avgCharWidth);
 dc.TextOut (width/2, height/2 + avgCharHeight, msg);

 wsprintf (msg,"Average Character Height: %d", avgCharHeight);
 dc.TextOut (width/2, height/2 + avgCharHeight*2, msg);

 wsprintf (msg,"Capital Character Width: %d", avgCapsWidth);
 dc.TextOut (width/2, height/2 + avgCharHeight*3, msg);
}


/*************************************************************/
/*                                                           */
/* OnLButtonDown: display message box showing L Button received*/
/*                                                           */
/*************************************************************/

void FrameWin::OnLButtonDown (UINT, CPoint) {
 MessageBox ("You have clicked the Left Button",
             "Mouse Event Captured", MB_OK | MB_ICONEXCLAMATION);
 dataSaved = false;  // pretend that some data has been altered
}


/*************************************************************/
/*                                                           */
/* OnRButtonDown: send close msg and let CanClose do the work */
/*                                                           */
/*************************************************************/

void FrameWin::OnRButtonDown (UINT, CPoint) {
 SendMessage (WM_CLOSE); // send close signal
}


/*************************************************************/
/*                                                           */
/* OnClose: determine if the app can be shut down            */
/*                                                           */
/*************************************************************/

void FrameWin::OnClose () {
 if (!dataSaved) {
  if (MessageBox ("Data has not been saved."
             " Quit the application anyway?",
             "Query?", MB_YESNO | MB_ICONQUESTION) == IDYES) {
   CFrameWnd::OnClose ();
  }
  else {
   dataSaved = true;
   // one could save the data and exit by calling
   //    CFrameWnd::OnClose ()
   // just keep on running by not calling CFrameWnd::OnClose ()
  }
 }
 else
  CFrameWnd::OnClose ();
}
```

Notice in the constructor how window style options are added and removed. Use an **OR** operator to add additional style identifiers and **AND** the **NOT** value of an identifier to remove a style. Here, the style **WS_OVERLAPPEDWINDOW** implies that there are to be both maximize and minimize buttons. To remove them code this.

```
DWORD style = WS_OVERLAPPEDWINDOW;
style &= ~(WS_MINIMIZEBOX | WS_MAXIMIZEBOX);
```

We use the bit-wise NOT ~ and not the logical NOT ! operator. Please note that even though there are no resizing buttons, the user can still click on the title bar to maximize the application. Later on, I will show you how to remove the title bar clicking as well. (To force a window to specific dimensions the **WM_GETMINMAXINFO** message must be processed.) Next, we can force the window to initially be located at (x, y) coordinates (100, 100) and have an initial size of 500 by 600 pixels by constructing a rectangle with these values.

```
CRect rect (100, 100, 500, 600);
```

However, be careful of launching a window with such arbitrary dimensions. Depending upon the screen resolution (640x480, 800x600, 1024x768), the initial size can be very awkward indeed.

The OnSize Function

Whenever a window's dimensions change, Windows and MFC invoke that window's **OnSize** function to notify the application of the change. As the application launches, **OnSize** is invoked with a width and height of 0 pixels. Shortly thereafter during the construction steps, **OnSize** is called once more with the real dimensions desired. While the application is running, whenever the window is resized, maximized, or minimized, **OnSize** is again called. Notice that **OnSize** is strictly an informatory type of message. One does not need to call the base class function.

The **OnSize** function is passed the width and height of the actual client area. So we can copy these passed parameter values into our member variables **height** and **width**. Alternatively, the member function **GetClientRect** can be called to obtain the client area size. Observe that the only parameter needed is the rectangle—another class benefit is an overall reduction in the number of parameters needed. The **this** parameter is used by the class library to pass the "missing" **hwnd** argument.

The **CRect** class has member functions to retrieve the height and width fields from a rectangle class, creating more readable coding: **Height();** and **Width();** as shown below.

```
GetClientRect (&rect);
height = rect.Height();
width  = rect.Width();
```

The SetBkMode, SetBkColor, and SetTextColor Functions

Examine the **OnPaint** function. I added a new function, **SetBkMode**, that sets the background mode for **TextOut** operations to transparent. The DC has a default color scheme for **TextOut** operations—black on white. Did you notice that effect on the first three programs? If not, just run Pgm02 again. We set a window background color to light gray, but the text string was black on white—an interesting effect, but not often desirable. Two approaches may be used to create a more presentable screen.

First method: both foreground and background colors can be set for **TextOut** operations using the **CDC** functions. (More details on the use of color are found in the next chapter.)

```
SetBkColor (color);
SetTextColor (color);
```

Second method: when text is displayed, there is an option that toggles between displaying the actual selected (or default) background color—the **OPAQUE** option or allowing the window's background color to shine through—the **TRANSPARENT** option. The default is **OPAQUE**. The option is toggled by using the function **SetBkMode**. Notice the nice effect this option has on the text output in **Pgm04d** here.

```
SetBkMode (TRANSPARENT);
```

Since the **OnSize** function now sets the class members, **width** and **height**, the "Hello" message is now correctly centered whenever the window size is altered. Additionally, I also displayed the current values of the average character dimensions, in case you were curious about their actual values.

The OnLButtonDown Function

The mouse event message parameters are "cracked" by the MFC and our function is given the **unsigned int** flags identifying the status of the keys at the time of the button press (exactly as discussed in the previous chapter) and a **CPoint** reference of the cursor location. Later, as we work with the location of the cursor, having the (x, y) coordinates in a **CPoint** structure is a convenient feature.

In response to the left button press, a message box is displayed notifying the user of the event. Notice that there is one less parameter to the **MessageBox** function under MFC.

```
MessageBox (string to be displayed, string on titlebar,
            the flags);
```

Message boxes are extremely handy objects to display information, even debugging information! Frequently when I need to see the value of some data, I **wsprintf** the information into a string and display it in a message box. The only requisite item is you must have or find a valid handle to a window; however, if there is no window handle available, pass 0 and it works fine.

An alternate approach is to use the global macro **AfxMessageBox** which encapsulates the C style API **MessageBox** function.

```
int  AfxMessageBox (LPCSTR text, UINT type, UINT help = 0);
```

where the **type** is an ORed series of the normal **MessageBox** types, such as **MB_OK**. The return value is the button identifier that was pressed.

Just for fun, when the left button is pressed, I set the **dataSaved** member to **false** as if the data were somehow changed. In this manner, we can see the different operations of **OnClose** based on the **dataSaved** member.

Sending Messages

The user can close the application by ALT-F4 or by choosing "Close" from the system menu or by pressing the X button.

Additionally, when the right button is pressed, we will attempt to shut down the application. And once more, an all too frequent Windows programming design problem surfaces. Can you spot the design problem?

Whether or not it is safe to terminate the application is based upon the status of the **dataSaved bool**. Now both **OnClose** and **OnRButtonDown** can handle the termination request by interrogating **dataSaved**, displaying an appropriate "data not yet saved" message, and obtaining the user's response. This is a common design problem: the potential for multiple occurrences of the same coding.

Design Rule 25: Avoid multiple instances of the same coding. Code the action event once; then when similar circumstances arise elsewhere, simply send a fake message to the original event.

The MFC function is **SendMessage**. The first parameter is the message ID needed. Next, come the parameters to be sent based upon the type of message. Here, we wish to send the **WM_CLOSE** message, a message that requires no parameters. Therefore, code

```
SendMessage (WM_CLOSE);
```

This is all that is required. But what window gets the message? By default, the MFC passes the **this** parameter, which points to this window, **m_hWnd**. To force the message to go to say the parent window of this window, if one existed (which means that this is a child window as in the Tic Tac Toe game), one would use

```
GetParent()->SendMessage (WM_CLOSE);
```

Remember that when your application issues a **SendMessage**, processing is halted until that message is processed. Use **PostMessage** for asynchronous operations where it is not important that the message is fully handled before continuing operations.

Finally, notice one other feature in most of these On message response functions—there are no C style **return 0;** statements. Most **On** functions frequently have a void return. It is just another convenience of using class libraries.

The OnClose Function

If the **dataSaved** indicates data has been altered and not saved, a message box is displayed querying the user, who must select Yes or No. Until we learn about file processing, if the user does not want to quit, rather than saving the data and then proceeding with the close operation, we fail the **OnClose** operation simply by **not** invoking the base class; when the function ends, normal operations continue. Notice we call **CFrameWnd::OnClose**. What would occur if we coded just **OnClose**?

Using Fixed Fonts

One final detail, MFC provides an easy way to switch from the default variable width font, **SYSTEM_FONT**, to fixed pitch fonts, **SYSTEM_FIXED_FONT** or **ANSI_FIXED_FONT**. In the **OnPaint** function, use the **SelectStockObject** function.

```
dc.SelectStockObject (SYSTEM_FIXED_FONT);
```

One advantage of using a fixed font is that all characters have the same width. When handling text operations, this can be convenient. In a later chapter, we will examine how to work with variable width fonts.

Programming Problems

Problem Pgm04-1— The Tic Tac Toe Program

Rewrite the Tic Tac Toe program as an MFC application. Create a child window class that displays the bounding rectangle and the X's and/or O's. Define a 2-d array of them in the frame window parent class definition.

Chapter 5 Timers, Colors, Brushes, and Resource Files

Timers

Sometimes an application would like to use elapsed time intervals for special processing effects. Windows provides a number of interval timers for such usage. Each timer that is set needs a unique non-zero identifier that Windows uses when reporting to your application that the designated interval has elapsed.

A timer is basically software wrapped around a hardware clock and is rather involved. (See the Microsoft Press book by Charles Petzold book *Programming Windows 5th Edition* for a complete discussion of timers.) For many normal uses of the timer, only a few details are critical. The basic operation is quite simple. One sets the interval desired, such as 10 milliseconds (ms). Then, every 10ms Windows sends the application a **WM_TIMER** message until the application turns the timer off.

Perhaps the most significant detail is the fact that the **WM_TIMER** message sent to your application indicating that your indicated amount of time has elapsed is **not** an accurate timing event. Under DOS, timer intervals expiring are an asynchronous event; they occur in real time, or nearly so, and can be a fairly accurate measure of time. Under Windows, the **WM_TIMER** event is a low priority message, as is **WM_PAINT**, and is only sent and processed when the Windows system is in control during idle processing. If an application is tying up the CPU cycles, the timer messages are held back until that application releases control to Windows. Just like the **WM_PAINT** messages, several timer "dings" can be stacked up before the application is actually notified of the first timer "ding." There is no way to learn how many "dings" of the timer are actually represented by that one **WM_TIMER** "ding" message that you receive.

There are two basic functions needed to use timers, **SetTimer** and **KillTimer** and one message to respond to, **WM_TIMER**.

The C API syntax for these is as follows.

```
UINT SetTimer (hwnd, UINT uniqueID, UINT interval, NULL);
BOOL KillTimer (hwnd, UINT uniqueID);
case WM_TIMER:// wparam contains the ID of the expired timer
```

The interval is an **unsigned int** containing the number of milliseconds to count down. (1,000 milliseconds are in one second.) The last parameter is the address of any timer function to be notified, normally 0, in which case the **WM_TIMER** message is sent to the application.
If there are no more timers remaining, the **SetTimer** function returns 0. A well-behaved application should always check the return value and act appropriately upon the failure to set up a timer.

Once set, the timer keeps on "ticking" sending "dings" whenever the specified interval has elapsed. Therefore, before the application terminates, the timer **must** be turned off, or "killed." An application should have, therefore, a balanced number of **SetTimer/KillTimer** function calls. If a different interval is needed at some point, kill the existing timer and set a new timer.

When processing the **WM_TIMER** messages, if the application has set more than one timer, perform a switch on the **wparam**, which contains the timer's ID.

In the MFC, the timer is part of the **CWnd** class. The timer is often set in the **OnCreate** function and destroyed in the class destructor or in the **OnDestroy** member function. The **WM_TIMER** event is captured by using the message map event ID of **ON_WM_TIMER** and the corresponding member function that is invoked is **OnTimer**. The functions and message response or map are coded as follows.

```
UINT SetTimer (UINT uniqueID, UINT interval, NULL);
BOOL KillTimer (UINT uniqueID);
afx_msg void OnTimer (UINT); // message member function
BEGIN_MESSAGE_MAP(....       // and message map entry
  ON_WM_TIMER ()
END_MESSAGE_MAP();
```

What shall we do with a timer? As you look over the various texts on the market, you will see several interesting timer animation effects. Here, we will begin to create some animation effects of our own. One of the immediate questions you probably wondering about are the colors that Windows uses for various items. So let's start using them. Our animation effect is to cycle through all of the Windows **system colors** contained within the default color scheme you have installed via Control Panel—Set Colors.

How the System Colors Are Handled

The topic of colors under Windows is actually quite involved and the complete discussion must wait until the chapter devoted to the GDI interface and all of its details. The basic background color is set in the **WNDCLASS** member, **hbrBackground**. Should you alter the color scheme or even task switch to the Control Panel and use SetColors to change the system color scheme, you will notice an interesting effect. While the color chosen may appear in your window, it does not last long. When Windows sends a **WM_PAINT** message with erase the background, the **WNDCLASS** default once again determines the background color! Whenever you display text with **TextOut**, the default colors in the acquired DC are always black on white. Both problems can easily be solved.

Windows defines and maintains **twenty-one system colors** for painting the various parts of objects. You can get and change these colors by using the **GetSysColor** and **SetSysColor** functions. These colors can be altered from the Control Panel. The specific IDs of the twenty-one system colors are shown in Table 1; the most often used are in bold face.

Table 1 The Twenty-one System Color Identifiers

COLOR_APPWORKSPACE	**COLOR_BACKGROUND**
COLOR_SCROLLBAR	**COLOR_WINDOW**
COLOR_WINDOWTEXT	COLOR_WINDOWFRAME
COLOR_MENU	COLOR_MENUTEXT
COLOR_ACTIVECAPTION	COLOR_ACTIVEBORDER
COLOR_INACTIVECAPTION	COLOR_INACTIVEBORDER
COLOR_INACTIVECAPTIONTEXT	COLOR_BTNHIGHLIGHT
COLOR_BTNFACE	COLOR_BTNSHADOW
COLOR_BTNTEXT	COLOR_CAPTIONTEXT
COLOR_GRAYTEXT	COLOR_HIGHLIGHTTEXT
COLOR_HIGHLIGHT	

If you wish to have your window's background be the system default for consistency across all applications (though I do not know why anyone would want a Neon colored background), use the following C API style approach.

```
wndclass.hbrBackground = COLOR_WINDOW + 1;
```

Windows requires that you add 1 to these identifiers **only** when using them in the **WNDCLASS** background; it is done to avoid using a value of 0.

Next, whenever you are going to use display some text and have acquired a DC, the colors must be inserted into the DC. When displaying text, after the DC is obtained and before any **TextOut** usage, code the following in the C API style.

```
SetBkColor   (hdc, GetSysColor (COLOR_WINDOW));
SetTextColor (hdc, GetSysColor (COLOR_WINDOWTEXT));
```

Under MFC, the two **CDC** functions, **SetBkColor** and **SetTextColor**, are coded this way.

```
dc.SetBkColor   (::GetSysColor (COLOR_WINDOW) );
dc.SetTextColor (::GetSysColor (COLOR_WINDOWTEXT) );
```

To install an initial background brush into the **hbrBackground** of **WINDCLASS**, in the **CWnd** constructor's call to **Create** pass as the third parameter to **AfxRegisterWndClass** the following.

```
wndclass.hbrBackGround = ::CreateSolidBrush (
          ::GetSysColor (COLOR_WINDOW));
```

However, before we launch into brushes and pens, let us examine the colors further. The above procedure is the method to use if it is your desire to utilize the user's choice for the system colors. There is some benefit is so doing for if nothing else, it keeps the users happy.

Setting Colors

More often than not, we would like our own choices of color. Windows represents a specific color using the **RGB method**. That is, the color is formed from the combination of the three primary colors Red, Blue, and Green. The amount of each color is given by a single byte, an **unsigned char**, ranging from 0 to 255, where 0 implies none of that color and 255 represents the maximum of that color. Windows provides a handy macro to create the RGB combined color value.

```
RGB ( red amt, green amt, blue amt);
```

Try setting **wndclass.hbrBackground** to the following to have a wild background.

```
::CreateSolidBrush (RGB (255, 0, 0));   // red brush
```

Dynamic Alterations to WNDCLASS

Now suppose that one wishes to dynamically alter the background brush. There is a Windows function to allow access to the **WNDCLASS** structure while the application is running—the **SetClassLong** function that we saw in Chapter 3. However, if you wish to install a new background brush, the old brush must be deleted. So in keeping with cryptic C API style coding and in a generalized format, the background brush alterations could be done as follows.

```
DeleteObject (SetClassLong (hwnd, GCL_HBRBACKGROUND,
  (long) CreateSolidBrush (RGB (color[0], color[1], color[2]))));
```

The third parameter is the new replacement value. The function returns the old value so that you can delete it. Recall that the function **SetClassLong** allows changing several items based upon the identifiers:

```
GCL_HBRBACKGROUND    GCL_HCURSOR    GCL_HICON    GCL_STYLE
```

Incidentally, this would be the best method to dynamically alter the permanent cursor of the application as well. Always remember that if you cannot figure out how to do something within the MFC member functions, you can revert to pure C API coding at nearly any point.

In the MFC, unfortunately, the **CWnd** class does not encapsulate the **GetClassLong** or **SetClassLong** functions. Thus, **WNDCLASS** alterations are done C API style, using the public member **m_hWnd** or the **GetSafeHwnd** function for the handle to the window. The **RGB** macro is supported, though.

```
::DeleteObject ((HBRUSH)::SetClassLong (m_hWnd,GCL_HBRBACKGROUND,
(long)::CreateSolidBrush(::GetSysColor(colors[currentColor]))));
Invalidate ();
```

or

```
::DeleteObject ((HBRUSH)::SetClassLong (m_hWnd,GCL_HBRBACKGROUND,
(long) ::CreateSolidBrush (RGB (color[0], color[1], color[2]))));
Invalidate ();
```

The MFC does not have a color class. Thus, we use either **RGB** values or a **COLORREF** structure which is basically a 32-bit number whose format in hex is `0x00bbggrr` where each color is stored as a **BYTE** or **unsigned char**. The WIN32 macros **GetBValue, GetGValue** and **GetRValue** return the corresponding **BYTE** color value. The RGB macro takes the three color values and makes a **COLORREF** instance out of them.

Creating Brushes and Pens

There are several stock brushes available. What is more important, solid color brushes and hatch pattern brushes can be created. The C API style syntax is as follows.

```
HBRUSH hbrush = CreateSolidBrush (rgbcolor);
HBRUSH hbrush = CreateHatchBrush (hatch type, rgbcolor);
```

where hatch type can be one of these IDs.

```
HS_HORIZONTAL  HS_VERTICAL  HS_FDIAGONAL  HS_BDIAGONAL  HS_CROSS  HS_DIAGCROSS
```

Solid brushes are not necessarily a solid, pure color; when Windows selects the brush into a DC, it creates an 8X8 pixel bitmap of dithered colors. With the hatch style, the color you specify is the color of the lines of the pattern. More details are found in the GDI chapter.

The MFC has encapsulated brushes into the class **CBrush** with several different types of constructors.

```
CBrush br (RGB(...));
CBrush br (style, RGB(...));
```

For both, the **style** is one of the C API style hatch patterns given above. Alternatively, a **CBrush** member function can be used to create a new brush.

```
CBrush br;
br.CreateSolidBrush (RGB(...));
```

or

```
br.CreateSolidBrush (::GetSysColor(...));
```

Pens are similarly created. There are a few stock pens (**WHITE_PEN** and **BLACK_PEN**); more often, colored pens are used. C API style has two approaches.

```
HPEN pen = GetStockObject (WHITE_PEN);
```

or

```
HPEN pen = CreatePen (style, width, rgbcolor);
```

where **style** is one of these values.

```
PS_SOLID    PS_DASH    PS_DOT    PS_DASHDOT    PS_DASHDOTDOT
```

If the **width** is 0 or 1, the style can be any of these. However, if the **width** is greater than 1 and any style other than solid is used, the style is altered to **PS_SOLID** by Windows.

In the MFC, pens are similarly encapsulated by **Cpen**.

```
CPen pen (style, width, RGB(...));
```

Once the pen or brush is created, it must be selected into the dc for use. The C API style function **SelectObject** inserts this pen or brush into the **hdc** and returns the value of the old brush or pen as an **HGDIOBJECT** so you can delete it, if it is not a stock object.

```
HGDIOBJECT SelectObject (hdc, hpen or hbrush);
```

Under the MFC, a pen must be selected into the **dc** for use as well. The **CDC** member function **SelectObject** closely resembles the C API function.

```
CPen*   dc.SelectObject (CPen* ptrpen);
CBrush* dc.SelectObject (CBrush* ptrbrush);
```

This function inserts the pen or brush into the **dc** and returns a pointer to the old object that is deselected. Note that the returned pointer has been already typecasted to the correct GDI object type. Thus, if you wanted to insert a new pen for some action and then go back to the original pen, one might code the following.

```
CPen *ptroldpen;
CPen *ptrnewpen = ...
ptroldpen = dc.SelectObject (ptrnewpen);
... use it
dc.SelectObject (ptroldpen);
delete ptrnewpen;
```

All pens and brushes are GDI objects and they belong to the GDI itself. When a program terminates, Windows does not automatically delete the GDI objects you have created. You must specifically delete them. To avoid memory and resource leaks, adhere to the following design rules.

Design Rule 26: Delete all GDI objects that you create.

Design Rule 27: Do not delete GDI objects while they are selected into a DC!

Design Rule 28: Do not delete stock objects! (Windows ignores such a request.)

Creating pens and brushes does take time. If you find that you are continually creating pens and brushes in your **OnPaint** member, another approach can be used for faster operation. Make the pens and brushes members of your **CWnd** derived class and call their **Create** functions in the class constructor.

Other MFC Text Member Functions

Member functions and event responses exist for the other Windows text processing functions that we have covered. All work similar to their C API counterparts. For the MFC, the insertion point or text caret is handled by other **CWnd** member functions.

```
void CreateGrayCaret (int width, int height);
void CreateSolidCaret (int width, int height);
void CreateCaret (CBitmap* ptrbitmap);
void HideCaret ();
void ShowCaret ();
void SetCaretPos (CPoint);
CPoint GetCaretPos ();
```

Note that the member function **CreateCaret(CBitmap*)** must have a bitmap image to use as the caret; therefore, use **CreateGrayCaret** or **CreateSolidCaret**. There are no member function for **DestroyCaret** or for **SetCaretBlinkTime**; therefore, use the C API style versions.

Keyboard keystrokes are handled by the following events:

```
event id        event function
ON_WM_CHAR()    afx_msg void OnChar (UINT key, UINT repcnt,
                                     UINT flags);
ON_WM_KEYDOWN() afx_msg void OnKeyDown (UINT key, UINT repcnt,
                                        UINT flags);
```

Now let's put these to use in our first animation application.

Sample Program Pgm05a: Displaying the 21 System Colors

When program **Pgm05a** begins, it uses the standard system colors for the window's background. **OnPaint** displays the name of the system color in the client window. Whenever the down arrow key is pressed, the program installs the next system color in the background and displays its name. The up arrow key backs up one color. CTL-A toggles the animation effect on and off. When animation is active, the display cycles through all twenty-one system colors until another CTL-A key halts the animation. Figure 5.1 shows how the window appears.

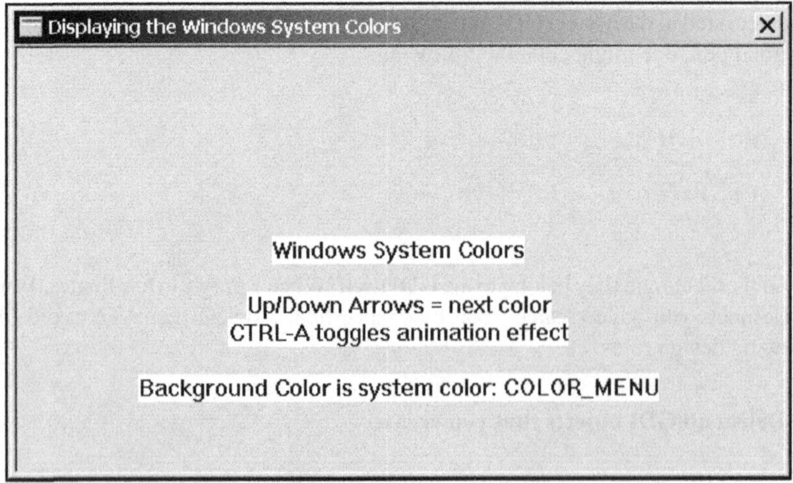

Figure 5.1 Pgm05a Displaying Window System Colors

There are no significant changes to the **CWinApp** derived class and it is not shown. All of the changes are in the **FrameWin** class and members. The **FrameWin** class definition contains the toggle switch called **animate** which controls the animation effects. When **animate** is true, the timer is active; **WM_TIMER** messages cause the next system color to be installed as the background color. The **current_color** member holds the index into the **colors** array that corresponds to the system color in use. New member functions now include the events: **OnChar**, **OnKeyDown**, and **OnTimer**. A pair of static data members, **colorMsg**, an array of twenty-one color name strings and **colors**, an array of the twenty-one system color IDs, remove the need of global values. By making these two arrays **static** members of the class, all functions can access them.

FrameWin.h Definition of FrameWin Class

```
#pragma once

const int MAX_COLORS = 21;      // 21 system colors
const int MAX_COLOR_LEN = 26;   // length of color names

/***************************************************************/
/*                                                             */
/* FrameWin Class Definition                                   */
/*                                                             */
/***************************************************************/

class FrameWin : public CFrameWnd {

 /**************************************************************/
 /*                                                            */
 /* Class Data Members                                         */
 /*                                                            */
 /**************************************************************/

protected:

// static members obviate the need for globals
static char colorMsgs[MAX_COLORS][MAX_COLOR_LEN]; //21 col names
static int  colors[MAX_COLORS];                  // 21 system color IDs

bool animate;        // when true, timer changes the bkgrnd color
int  currentColor;  // current idx of the system color in use
int  timerId;       // id of the timer
int  height;         // current client window height in pixels
int  width;          // current client window width in pixels

int  avgCapsWidth; // average capital letter width
int  avgCharWidth; // average character width
int  avgCharHeight;// average character height

 /**************************************************************/
 /*                                                            */
 /* Class Functions:                                           */
 /*                                                            */
 /**************************************************************/

public:
                FrameWin ();
               ~FrameWin () {}
afx_msg void   OnPaint ();                 // displays the results

protected:

afx_msg int  OnCreate (LPCREATESTRUCT); // gets avg char dims
afx_msg void OnClose ();                // can close app?
afx_msg void OnChar (UINT, UINT, UINT); // process CTL-A
afx_msg void OnSize (UINT, int, int);   // get window dimensions
afx_msg void OnKeyDown (UINT, UINT, UINT);// handle up/down arrow
afx_msg void OnTimer (UINT);            // switch bkgrnd color
afx_msg void OnDestroy ();              // kill any active timer
        void InstallBrush ();           // install new bkgrnd br

DECLARE_MESSAGE_MAP();

};
```

In the **FrameWin.cpp** file, the constructor sets **animate** to off, initializes the **timerId** field, and sets **currentColor** to 3, which is the subscript for **COLOR_WINDOW**. The **OnDestroy** function kills any timer still active. When the constructor invokes the **Create** function, installing the beginning background brush using **COLOR_WINDOW**.

In the **OnPaint** function, please note that the default text mode is **OPAQUE** which means the color choices for text background overlays any background color. This leaves the foreground text color always visible. I used the normal system colors for window text for the text foreground and background. This ensures that these messages are always visible independent of the window background color.

In the **OnKeyDown** function, the extended keys are detected; only up and down arrow are used. The process consists of incrementing or decrementing the **currentColor** index and forcing it into range should it go too high or low. Then, the previous background brush is deleted as the new brush is created and installed. Do not forget to call **Invalidate** to force a repaint of the window in order to make the changes visible at once. The **OnChar** function processes normal keystrokes. Here we want only the CTL-A key—for "animate." If it is pressed, then depending upon the setting of **animate**, the timer is killed or set to 1 second (1,000 milliseconds). The **OnTimer** coding duplicates the down arrow coding. In all cases, the helper function **InstallBrush** does the actual new background brush installation. Notice that the insertion of a new background brush involves four C API style functions.

```
::DeleteObject (
   (HBRUSH)::SetClassLong (m_hWnd, GCL_HBRBACKGROUND,
     (long) ::CreateSolidBrush (
         ::GetSysColor (colors[currentColor]))));
```

FrameWin.cpp Implementation of FrameWin Class

```
#include "stdafx.h"
#include "framewin.h"

/***************************************************************/
/*                                                             */
/* FrameWin Events Response Table                              */
/*                                                             */
/***************************************************************/

BEGIN_MESSAGE_MAP(FrameWin, CFrameWnd)
 ON_WM_KEYDOWN ()
 ON_WM_CHAR ()
 ON_WM_SIZE ()
 ON_WM_TIMER ()
 ON_WM_PAINT ()
 ON_WM_CREATE ()
 ON_WM_CLOSE ()
 ON_WM_DESTROY()
END_MESSAGE_MAP();

/***************************************************************/
/*                                                             */
/* Colors static arrays                                        */
/*                                                             */
/***************************************************************/

char FrameWin::colorMsgs[MAX_COLORS][MAX_COLOR_LEN] = {
  "COLOR_APPWORKSPACE", "COLOR_BACKGROUND",
  "COLOR_SCROLLBAR", "COLOR_WINDOW", "COLOR_WINDOWTEXT",
  "COLOR_WINDOWFRAME", "COLOR_MENU", "COLOR_MENUTEXT",
  "COLOR_ACTIVECAPTION", "COLOR_ACTIVEBORDER",
  "COLOR_INACTIVECAPTION", "COLOR_INACTIVEBORDER",
  "COLOR_INACTIVECAPTIONTEXT", "COLOR_BTNHIGHLIGHT",
  "COLOR_BTNFACE", "COLOR_BTNSHADOW", "COLOR_BTNTEXT",
  "COLOR_CAPTIONTEXT", "COLOR_GRAYTEXT", "COLOR_HIGHLIGHTTEXT",
  "COLOR_HIGHLIGHT"};
```

```
int FrameWin::colors[MAX_COLORS] = {
    COLOR_APPWORKSPACE, COLOR_BACKGROUND, COLOR_SCROLLBAR,
    COLOR_WINDOW, COLOR_WINDOWTEXT, COLOR_WINDOWFRAME,
    COLOR_MENU, COLOR_MENUTEXT, COLOR_ACTIVECAPTION,
    COLOR_ACTIVEBORDER, COLOR_INACTIVECAPTION,
    COLOR_INACTIVEBORDER, COLOR_INACTIVECAPTIONTEXT,
    COLOR_BTNHIGHLIGHT, COLOR_BTNFACE, COLOR_BTNSHADOW,
    COLOR_BTNTEXT, COLOR_CAPTIONTEXT, COLOR_GRAYTEXT,
    COLOR_HIGHLIGHTTEXT, COLOR_HIGHLIGHT};

/*************************************************************/
/*                                                           */
/* Framewin: Construct the window object                     */
/*                                                           */
/*************************************************************/

FrameWin::FrameWin () : CFrameWnd () {
 DWORD style = WS_OVERLAPPEDWINDOW;     // set basic window styles
 style &= ~(WS_MINIMIZEBOX | WS_MAXIMIZEBOX); // del max/min btns
 style |= WS_SYSMENU | WS_THICKFRAME;  // add menu and borders

 Create (AfxRegisterWndClass (
              CS_VREDRAW | CS_HREDRAW,
              AfxGetApp()->LoadStandardCursor (IDC_ARROW),
              ::CreateSolidBrush (GetSysColor (COLOR_WINDOW)),
              AfxGetApp()->LoadStandardIcon (IDI_APPLICATION)),
        "Displaying the Windows System Colors",
        style, rectDefault, 0, 0, NULL);
 animate = false;   // set animate feature off
 timerId = 1;       // assign a unique non-zero id for the timer
 currentColor = 3; // set the color idx in use
}

/*************************************************************/
/*                                                           */
/* OnDestroy: remove any timer still active                  */
/*                                                           */
/*************************************************************/

void FrameWin::OnDestroy () {
 if (animate) {
  KillTimer (timerId);
 }
 CFrameWnd::OnDestroy();
}

/*************************************************************/
/*                                                           */
/* OnCreate: get average character dimensions                */
/*                                                           */
/*************************************************************/

int FrameWin::OnCreate (LPCREATESTRUCT lpCS) {
 if (CFrameWnd::OnCreate (lpCS) == -1) return -1;

 TEXTMETRIC  tm;

 // get the system font's characteristics in tm
 CClientDC dc (this);          // acquire a DC
 dc.GetTextMetrics (&tm);      // get the information

 // calculate average character parameters
 avgCharWidth  = tm.tmAveCharWidth;
```

```
 avgCharHeight = tm.tmHeight + tm.tmExternalLeading;
 avgCapsWidth  = (tm.tmPitchAndFamily & 1 ? 3 : 2) *
                   avgCharWidth / 2;
 return 0;
}

/**************************************************************/
/*                                                            */
/* OnSize: acquire the current dimensions of the client window */
/*                                                            */
/**************************************************************/

void FrameWin::OnSize (UINT, int cx, int cy) {
 width = cx;  // save current height
 height  = cy;  // save current width
}

/**************************************************************/
/*                                                            */
/* OnPaint: displays instructions & the cur system color in use*/
/*                                                            */
/**************************************************************/

void FrameWin::OnPaint () {
 CPaintDC dc (this);  // create a paint dc
 char msg [80];

 dc.SetTextAlign (TA_CENTER |TA_BASELINE ); // for centered text

 // set specific colors - use default mode opaque so that
 // messages are always visible no matter what the background is
 dc.SetBkColor (::GetSysColor (COLOR_WINDOW));
 dc.SetTextColor (::GetSysColor (COLOR_WINDOWTEXT));

 // display the instructions
 dc.TextOut (width/2, height/2, "Windows System Colors");
 dc.TextOut (width/2, height/2 + avgCharHeight*2,
             "Up/Down Arrows = next color");
 dc.TextOut (width/2, height/2 + avgCharHeight*3,
             "CTRL-A toggles animation effect");

 // build and display current bkgrnd color message
 strcpy_s (msg, sizeof(msg),
           "Background Color is system color: ");
 strcat_s (msg, sizeof(msg), colorMsgs[currentColor]);
 dc.TextOut (width/2, height/2+avgCharHeight*5, msg);
}

/**************************************************************/
/*                                                            */
/* OnKeyDown: process up and down arrows to go to next color  */
/*                                                            */
/**************************************************************/

void FrameWin::OnKeyDown (UINT key, UINT, UINT) {
 if (!animate) {     // only effective when not in animation mode
  if (key==VK_UP) {  // get previous color
   currentColor--;  // back up one
   // force subscript back into range
   if (currentColor<0)
    currentColor = MAX_COLORS-1;
   InstallBrush (); // install new background color
  }
  else if (key==VK_DOWN) { // get next color
```

```
   currentColor++;
   if (currentColor>MAX_COLORS-1)  // force back into range
    currentColor = 0;
   InstallBrush (); // install new background color
  }
 }
}


/****************************************************************/
/*                                                              */
/* InstallBrush: installs a new background brush                */
/*                                                              */
/****************************************************************/

void FrameWin::InstallBrush () {
 // install new background color
 ::DeleteObject (
     (HBRUSH)::SetClassLong (m_hWnd, GCL_HBRBACKGROUND,
        (long) ::CreateSolidBrush (
           ::GetSysColor (colors[currentColor]))));
 Invalidate ();  // force window repaint
}


/****************************************************************/
/*                                                              */
/* OnChar: process CTL-A for animation toggle                   */
/*                                                              */
/****************************************************************/

void FrameWin::OnChar (UINT key, UINT, UINT) {
 if (key==0x1) {         // use only CTL-A code
  if (animate) {         // if animate is active
   KillTimer (timerId); // turn off timer
   animate = false;      // reset toggle switch
  }
  else {
   animate = true;          // turn on animation
   SetTimer (timerId, 1000, 0); // set for 1 second intervals
  }
 }
}

/****************************************************************/
/*                                                              */
/* OnTimer: process timer intervals - set the next system color*/
/*                                                              */
/****************************************************************/

void FrameWin::OnTimer (UINT) {
 currentColor++;  // get next color idx and force into range
 if (currentColor>MAX_COLORS-1) currentColor=0;
 InstallBrush (); // install new background color
}

/****************************************************************/
/*                                                              */
/* OnClose: determine if the app can be shut down               */
/*                                                              */
/****************************************************************/

void FrameWin::OnClose () {
 if (MessageBox ("Do you want to quit the application?",
```

```
        "Query?", MB_YESNO | MB_ICONQUESTION) == IDYES) {
  CFrameWnd::OnClose ();
 }
}
```

Resource Files: an Introduction

The next step is to begin to include **resource files** with our applications. Resource files have an extension of RC and contain various resources for an application. A resource file can contain character strings that are loaded when they are needed as well as menus, menu accelerators, bitmaps, icons, cursors, references to files that contain bitmaps, dialog boxes, and any user defined resources. That is a rather extensive list of things possibly found in the RC file. We will explore these one by one in the remainder of the text.

In order for these resources to be used by an application, they must be "compiled" by the Resource Compiler into their **binary format**. The binary format of the resource file has the extension RES. Once the RES file has been made, the linker then appends the resource file onto the end of the EXE file.

An application's resources are located at the end of the EXE file (or possibly in another DLL—dynamic link library). When the application requires a specific resource, Windows loads the requested item from the resource portion of the EXE file. When the application no longer needs that resource, the resource becomes **discardable**. If Windows needs the memory that the no longer needed resource occupies, it is discarded from memory. Should the application again need that same resource, Windows can reload it from the EXE file. Now you can see why SMARTDRV is really needed when running Windows. If one is lucky, the entire EXE file or at least the resource portion of it can remain in the extended memory buffer of SMARTDRV.

Memory is a precious commodity, even when running under the flat memory model. This scheme of discardable resources greatly reduces the total memory requirements of applications. Why waste memory retaining all these resources if they are not needed? Just bring them into memory when and for as long as they are required by an application.

The RC resource file is actually a simple text file that can be edited by any nearly any text editor, including the Developer Studio's editor. It can also be edited in a graphical manner by the Resource Editor. By default, when you open an RC file, Visual Studio opens it in a graphical editor. However, it can be opened in text editing mode just like a cpp file. There is a reason for this duality. While dialog boxes are best created in a graphical manner, sometimes it is much more convenient to edit the RC file in text mode. Thus, you should be comfortable modifying the RC file using either method. That way, you can choose the most optimum method to accomplish your editing task.

One of the sections of a resource file is the character strings section. It is here that the various strings are stored one after the other. Below is an excerpt from the string table from my WWII game.

```
STRINGTABLE
{
                           // hint messages
  CM_WW2_DSPLYMAP,         "Opens a new Map Window"
  CM_WW2_TOGGLEHINT,       "Toggles tool bar hint mode"
  CM_WW2_TOGGLEBAR,        "Toggles tool bar position"
                           // program messages
  IDS_WW2_NAME,            "World War II Game"
  IDS_WW2_FILE_OPEN_ERR,"Cannot Open File: %s"
  IDS_WW2_DRIVE_LET,       "C:\\"
  IDS_WW2_MAIN_PATH,       "WAR\\"
  IDS_WW2_MAP_PATH,        "MAPS\\"
  IDS_WW2_RES_PATH,        "RESOURCE\\"
  IDS_WW2_CLOSEAPP,        "Close down the whole game?"
  IDS_WW2_MAPFAILS,        "Map System Initialization Failure"
  IDS_WW2_MAPERROR,        "Cannot allocate another Map Object"
}
```

In a complex resource file, often the String Table is found near the end of the resource file. The String Table is identified by coding a begin-end block (many other sections have their own identifiers and begin/end block markers as well).

```
STRINGTABLE
{
}
```

or by

```
STRINGTABLE
BEGIN
```

```
END
```

A string in the table follows the following syntax.

```
unique ID, "string's contents"
```

Usually, string identifiers begin with the prefix IDS_ for ID for a String. Examine the significance of some of the strings above. Some look like drive and path specifications; others look like the hint messages that would appear as the cursor passes over the toolbar's icons; still others look like portions of error messages; and one even looks like a **printf** control string.

```
IDS_WW2_FILE_OPEN_ERR, "Cannot Open File: %s."
```

Design Rule 29: Any string can be stored in the resource file and loaded into memory when needed.

With character strings, this becomes valuable for several reasons. First, the overall memory requirements are lowered. Second, an application that has stored **all** of its character strings in the resource file can be easily converted into a foreign language. Imagine the problems attempting to search through a huge application trying to find the strings that need to be converted to say German. Thus, any application that has any possibility of overseas markets most definitely attempts to keep all of its strings in the resource file.

String Resources: a How To

A resource file always has an associated header file that defines all of the id numbers of the items contained in the RC file. Of course, the very first step is to add a resource file to a project that does not already have one.

Follow these steps to add a new resource file to a project. Right Click on the project icon in the Solution Explorer and choose Add New and then select Resource. A small dialog appears asking you to select what kind of resource to add, choose String Table.

The Graphical Resource Editor opens up. In Figure 5.2 you can see the entries I have made for this program. Three items make up a single entry: the ID, the corresponding numerical value, and the actual text to be associated with this ID.

To edit an existing item, just click on it and type away. To add a new one, scroll down to the bottom and click, a new entry will be automatically inserted. Now change the three values to what you desire. In this graphical mode, however, it takes time to enter a whole lot of strings. Here is one situation where it can be faster to edit the resource file as a text file and not in the graphical edit mode. To edit a resource file in text mode, right click on the .rc file and choose Open With and then choose Source Code Text Editor or even Notepad. Be sure to also open resource.h where the IDs are stored. Save both files when you are finished and then close their windows. Double clicking in the Resource pane on the resource file will once again open the graphical view of the resources.

Remember to keep these two files in synch with each other. The resource.h file contains all of the #defines of the ID values and their numerical values. The .rc file contains these ID symbolic values and the corresponding text strings.

Across all Windows programs, you will find that the numerical ID values for resource items do follow some guidelines. String Table entries always have the highest numerical values of anything in the resource file. Typically, the values are in the thousands or tens of thousands. If we change this initial ID value, then when you add additional strings, the Resource Editor automatically uses a new value one larger than this one.

In the case of **Pgm05a**, we wish to remove all of the constant character strings from the cpp files and place them into the RC file in the String Table. Looking over the program, we find the following strings.

From **FrameWin** ctor: "Pgm05b Displays the Windows System Colors"
from **OnPaint**: "Windows System Colors"
" Up/Down Arrows = next color"
" CTRL-A toggles animation effect"
" Background Color is system color: "
from **OnClose**: "Do you want to quit the application?"
" Query?"

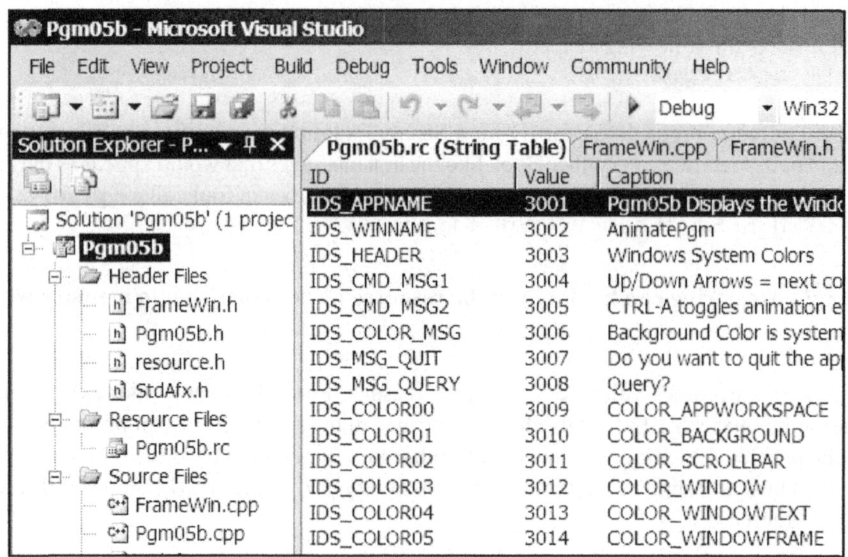

Figure 5-2 A New String Resource File

Finally, we can further reduce the storage requirements of the application by reworking the **colors_msg** array that occupied 21x26 or 546 bytes. Placing these strings into the String Table is again the best answer. To do so in this case requires the insertion of another **int** array that contains the corresponding string ID of the message. We cannot use the actual Windows ID names directly, so we make up names and tie them back to our **currentColor** index. Thus, we replace 546 bytes with 42 bytes for the **int** array, a good savings. Then in **OnPaint** when a specific color name is required, we load the one needed string into **msg2**.

Next, make up identifiers for these strings; it is common practice to prefix all strings in the String Table with IDS_ for ID of a String. Then, add a good descriptive name. The final String Table for **Pgm05b** is shown below.

```
STRINGTABLE DISCARDABLE
BEGIN
    IDS_APPNAME             "Pgm05b Displays the Windows System Colors"
    IDS_WINNAME              "AnimatePgm"
    IDS_HEADER               "Windows System Colors"
    IDS_CMD_MSG1             "Up/Down Arrows = next color"
    IDS_CMD_MSG2             "CTRL-A toggles animation effect"
    IDS_COLOR_MSG            "Background Color is system color: "
    IDS_MSG_QUIT             "Do you want to quit the application?"
END
STRINGTABLE DISCARDABLE
BEGIN
    IDS_MSG_QUERY            "Query?"
    IDS_COLOR00              "COLOR_APPWORKSPACE"
    IDS_COLOR01              "COLOR_BACKGROUND"
    IDS_COLOR02              "COLOR_SCROLLBAR"
    IDS_COLOR03              "COLOR_WINDOW"
    IDS_COLOR04              "COLOR_WINDOWTEXT"
    IDS_COLOR05              "COLOR_WINDOWFRAME"
    IDS_COLOR06              "COLOR_MENU"
    IDS_COLOR07              "COLOR_MENUTEXT"
    IDS_COLOR08              "COLOR_ACTIVECAPTION"
    IDS_COLOR09              "COLOR_ACTIVEBORDER"
    IDS_COLOR10              "COLOR_INACTIVECAPTION"
    IDS_COLOR11              "COLOR_INACTIVEBORDER"
    IDS_COLOR12              "COLOR_INACTIVECAPTIONTEXT"
    IDS_COLOR13              "COLOR_BTNHIGHLIGHT"
    IDS_COLOR14              "COLOR_BTNFACE"
END
STRINGTABLE DISCARDABLE
BEGIN
```

```
    IDS_COLOR15                 "COLOR_BTNSHADOW"
    IDS_COLOR16                 "COLOR_BTNTEXT"
    IDS_COLOR17                 "COLOR_CAPTIONTEXT"
    IDS_COLOR18                 "COLOR_GRAYTEXT"
    IDS_COLOR19                 "COLOR_HIGHLIGHTTEXT"
    IDS_COLOR20                 "COLOR_HIGHLIGHT"
END
```

The **resource.h** file defines section looks like this.

```
#define IDS_APPNAME                        3001
#define IDS_WINNAME                        3002
#define IDS_HEADER                         3003
#define IDS_CMD_MSG1                       3004
#define IDS_CMD_MSG2                       3005
#define IDS_COLOR_MSG                      3006
#define IDS_MSG_QUIT                       3007
#define IDS_MSG_QUERY                      3008
#define IDS_COLOR00                        3009
#define IDS_COLOR01                        3010
...
#define IDS_COLOR19                        3028
#define IDS_COLOR20                        3029
```

String Resource Coding Rules

The major coding rules are for string resources are as follows.

1. There is only one String Table per resource file (RC); however, if we have several, the compiler merges them into one automatically for us.
2. Strings can only be 1 line long with up to 255 characters.
3. Strings cannot contain any C style escape codes, such as '\n' except the tab code '\t'.
4. When retrieving one string, Windows actually loads a set of sixteen strings at one time; each string as stored in the string table is 255 bytes long.

When you request a string to be loaded, Windows does not just load in that single string. Windows organizes the string table into units of 16 strings, each of which is 255 bytes long, that is in 4k pages. When a request to load in a string is received, Windows loads in the entire unit of up to 16 strings or a 4k page. Thus, one should attempt to so organize the strings into "use blocks," keeping those that are likely to be needed together. This reduces the number of times units must be loaded from disk.

Normally, I would have liked to add a comment after each definition; when the file is viewed, the reader can more easily recall the significance of an ID. However, the Resource Editor removes all comments on every save operation.

Notice that the **resource.h** must be included in other cpp files where the resource IDs are needed.

Retrieving Strings at Runtime

To load a string from the resource file C API Style use the **LoadString** function

```
LoadString (HINSTANCE hInstance, UINT id, char *string, int len);
```

The C API Style **CanClose** function could be rewritten this way.

```
case WM_CLOSE:
 char mboxtitle[7];
 char mboxtext [38];
 LoadString (hinst, IDS_MSG_QUERY, mboxtitle,
             sizeof (mboxtitle));
 LoadString (hinst, IDS_MSG_QUIT,  mboxtext,
             sizeof (mboxtext));
 if (MessageBox (hwnd, mboxtext, mboxtitle,
                 MB_ICONQUESTION | MB_YESNO) == IDYES) {
 ...
```

You can load the strings into automatic storage fields that come and go as functions are invoked. Or you can reuse a static set of strings of a maximum length for the largest message to be used—which is a valuable approach in larger applications where memory is scarce.

The MFC offers two approaches; one is based upon the C API style function and the other uses a member function of the provided string class, **CString**. The C API style approach is useful if a **char*** version is handier. We use the global function **AfxGetApp** to retrieve the **hinstance**.

```
char msg[70];
::LoadString (AfxGetApp()->m_hInstance, IDS_ERRORMSG, msg,
              sizeof(msg));
```

The MFC version of **LoadString** is a member function of the **CString** class; also, the **CString** class has its own access to **HINSTANCE**. Further, all of the MFC functions that take a **char*** also may take a **CString** as well. The **CString** class has a large number of very useful string processing functions. Its signature is really simple.

```
BOOL LoadString (id);
```

To load in the window caption string, one would code the following.

```
CString title;
title.LoadString (IDS_APPNAME);
```

CStrings are powerful. You should spend a few minutes looking over this class in the on-line help to see what all you can do with one. For example, here are some of the things you can do with a **CString** instance.

```
CString s1;
CString s2 = "Hello";
s1 = s2;
s1 += " World";
s1 += s2;
int len = s1.GetLength ();
s1.Empty (); // forces the string to have 0 length
char c = s2.GetAt(2); // gets the letter l
c = s2[2]; also gets the letter l
if (s1.Compare (s2) == 0) // strings are equal
if (s1.CompareNoCase ("Hello") == 0)
const char* string = (LPCSTR) s1;
```

You can also directly manipulate the characters it is storing by getting a char* array.

```
char* str = s1.GetBuffer (s1.GetLength());
str[2] = 'a';
s1.ReleaseBuffer();
```

GetBuffer is passed the total number of bytes you desire to have in the array. **ReleaseBuffer** then cleans up the array by looking for the null terminator and restores the string.

The Improved Pgm05b Program

Rather than printing the entire **Pgm05b** set of modules, I have printed only the sections that have changed from **Pgm05a**, namely the **FrameWin** files; the new resource files are just above. Examine these changes. All changes are in bold face. The Graphical Resource Editor opens up. In Figure 5.2 you can see the entries I have made for this program. Three items make up a single entry: the ID, the corresponding numerical value, and the actual text to be associated with this ID.

To edit an existing item, just click on it and type away. To add a new one, scroll down to the bottom and click, a new entry will be automatically inserted. Now change the three values to what you desire. In this graphical mode, however, it takes time to enter a whole lot of strings. Here is one situation where it can be faster to edit the resource file as a text file and not in the graphical edit mode. To edit a resource file in text mode, right click on the .rc file and choose Open With and then choose Source Code Text Editor or even Notepad. Be sure to also open resource.h where the IDs are stored. Save both files when you are finished and then close their windows. Double clicking in the Resource pane on the resource file will once again open the graphical view of the resources.

Remember to keep these two files in synch with each other. The resource.h file contains all of the #defines of the ID values and their numerical values. The .rc file contains these ID symbolic values and the corresponding text strings.

Across all Windows programs, you will find that the numerical ID values for resource items do follow some guidelines. String Table entries always have the highest numerical values of anything in the resource file. Typically, the values are in the thousands or tens of thousands. If we change this initial ID value, then when you add additional strings, the Resource Editor automatically uses a new value one larger than this one.

```
FrameWin.h of Pgm05b FrameWin Definition
. . .
class FrameWin : public CFrameWnd {
. . .
protected:

// static members obviate the need for globals
static int colorsMsgIdx[MAX_COLORS]; // 21 IDS_ names
static int colors[MAX_COLORS];         // 21 system color IDs
...
```

```
FrameWin.cpp of Pgm05b Implementation
#include "stdafx.h"
#include "framewin.h"
#include "resource.h"

...
/***************************************************************/
/*                                                             */
/* Colors static arrays                                        */
/*                                                             */
/***************************************************************/

int FrameWin::colorsMsgIdx[MAX_COLORS] = {
    IDS_COLOR00, IDS_COLOR01, IDS_COLOR02, IDS_COLOR03,
    IDS_COLOR04, IDS_COLOR05, IDS_COLOR06, IDS_COLOR07,
    IDS_COLOR08, IDS_COLOR09, IDS_COLOR10, IDS_COLOR11,
    IDS_COLOR12, IDS_COLOR13, IDS_COLOR14, IDS_COLOR15,
    IDS_COLOR16, IDS_COLOR17, IDS_COLOR18, IDS_COLOR19,
    IDS_COLOR20};

int FrameWin::colors[MAX_COLORS] = {
     COLOR_APPWORKSPACE, COLOR_BACKGROUND, COLOR_SCROLLBAR,
...
/***************************************************************/
/*                                                             */
/* Framewin: Construct the window object                       */
/*                                                             */
/***************************************************************/

FrameWin::FrameWin () : CFrameWnd () {
 DWORD style = WS_OVERLAPPEDWINDOW;     // set basic window styles
 style &= !(WS_MINIMIZEBOX | WS_MAXIMIZEBOX); // del max/min btns
 style |= WS_SYSMENU | WS_THICKFRAME;  // add menu and borders

 CString title;
 title.LoadString (IDS_APPNAME);
 Create (AfxRegisterWndClass (
              CS_VREDRAW | CS_HREDRAW,
              AfxGetApp()->LoadStandardCursor (IDC_ARROW),
              ::CreateSolidBrush (GetSysColor (COLOR_WINDOW)),
              AfxGetApp()->LoadStandardIcon (IDI_APPLICATION)),
         title,
         style, rectDefault, 0, 0, NULL);
 animate = false;  // set animate feature off
```

```
 timerId = 1;       // assign a unique non-zero id for the timer
 currentColor = 3; // set the color idx in use
}
...
/********************************************************************/
/*                                                                  */
/* OnPaint: displays instructions & the cur system color in use*/
/*                                                                  */
/********************************************************************/

void FrameWin::OnPaint () {
 CPaintDC dc (this);  // create a paint dc
 CString msg;
 CString msg2;

 dc.SetTextAlign (TA_CENTER |TA_BASELINE ); // for centered text

 // set specific colors - use default mode opaque so that
 // messages are always visible no matter what the background is
 dc.SetBkColor (::GetSysColor (COLOR_WINDOW));
 dc.SetTextColor (::GetSysColor (COLOR_WINDOWTEXT));

 // display the instructions
 msg.LoadString (IDS_HEADER);
 dc.TextOut (width/2, height/2, msg);
 msg.LoadString (IDS_CMD_MSG1);
 dc.TextOut (width/2, height/2+avgCharHeight*2, msg);
 msg.LoadString (IDS_CMD_MSG2);
 dc.TextOut (width/2, height/2+avgCharHeight*3, msg);

 msg.LoadString (IDS_COLOR_MSG);
 msg2.LoadString (colorsMsgIdx[currentColor]);
 msg += msg2;
 // display current bkgrnd color message
 dc.TextOut (width/2, height/2+avgCharHeight*5, msg);
}
...
/********************************************************************/
/*                                                                  */
/* OnClose: determine if the app can be shut down                  */
/*                                                                  */
/********************************************************************/

void FrameWin::OnClose () {
 CString msgtitle;
 CString msgtext;
 msgtext.LoadString (IDS_MSG_QUIT);
 msgtitle.LoadString (IDS_MSG_QUERY);
 if (MessageBox (msgtext, msgtitle, MB_YESNO | MB_ICONQUESTION)
      == IDYES) {
  CFrameWnd::OnClose ();
 }
}
```

Programming Problems

Problem Pgm05-1—The Typing Tutor

Create an MFC application for a Typing Tutor. The main window should be maximized upon launching of the application and have a light gray background. Permit the user to be able to minimize the application, but do not permit window resizing; that is, no thick borders. The application always runs in full screen mode. The title bar should include "your name: Typing Tutor." (Use the default application icon and cursor.)

When the program starts, display a caret, accept normal characters as entered by the user, moving the caret as required and display the entered characters on the screen line by line. Use a maximum length of 80 characters per line; a maximum of 15 lines is permitted. Store the data in an array of 15 lines of 80 characters (or 81 if you want the null terminator). Display the entered character as you process **WM_CHAR** messages; do not force **OnPaint** to display the lines via an **Invalidate** call from **WM_CHAR** messages. However, **OnPaint** must be able to repaint all text that has been entered. (Consider what happens if the user minimizes the application and then restores it.)

The End of a line is signaled by the user pressing the enter key. You should move the start of the next line. When all lines have been entered, display a message box notifying the user of that fact and instructing him/her to enter a control code next.

Accept the following control codes **at any time**.

CTL-C—the user wants to quit the application
CTL-N—the user wants a New blank screen to start over

Across an unused portion of the bottom of the screen and using any desired color scheme of your choice, except the default color scheme, display the instructions to the user.

```
Enter CTL-C to quit
Enter CTL-N to get a new screen
```

There are no mouse events within the text window. You may change to the **SYSTEM_FIXED_FONT**.

When the application is about to close, if there is no text currently on the screen, just terminate the application. If there is text on the screen, display a message box asking if the user wishes to save the text. If the user **does** wish to save the text, return to normal editing operations. If the user does not wish to save the data, then terminate the application.

All text strings that are used in your coding should be stored in the resource file and loaded as needed. (But obviously not the text the user types, of course.) You can get an MFC application to launch maximized as follows.

```
pMainFrame->ShowWindow(SW_MAXIMIZE);
```

(Do not use a **CEdit** control or any such derived class.)
Extra Credit: get all 4 arrow keys working properly.
Extra Credit: get the insert key, delete key, and backspace working correctly.
Extra Credit: devise some method of caret location selection by using the mouse and clicking anywhere on the 15 lines.

Problem Pgm05-2—Balloon Busting Game

Write a "Balloon Busting" application. It should draw a balloon (a circle) on the screen and set the timer. The user has until the timer expires to position the mouse over the balloon and left click. **MessageBeep** if the user fails; use the "Ta-Da" sound if the user succeeds. Do it ten times and tally the user's score and display it. You could have the timer interval be user-adjustable. Use **GetSystemMetrics** to make the main window as large as possible.

Chapter 6 Menus

Menu Syntax

An application may have more than one menu, can have floating menus, and can have dynamically modified menus. A good place to begin is with the way a menu is defined in the resource file.

```
menuname MENU
{
 MENUITEM "your text1",   your ID number
}
```

or

```
menuname MENU
BEGIN
 MENUITEM "your text1",   your ID number
END
```

The following is vitally important!

The **menuname** can be either a defined ID number or a string. For example, if you call the menu by **MAINMENU**, then **MAINMENU** could be a #defined name or used as "**MAINMENU**".

```
MAINMENU MENU        // will be used as a string: "MAINMENU"
```

or

```
#define MainMenu 100 // in the resource.h file
MainMenu MENU      // will be used as an identifier: MAINMENU
```

When you ask for the menu resource, in the first case, you provide the string "**MAINMENU**" whereas in second case, you provide the identifier **MAINMENU** that is compiled to the resource number 100. Providing the wrong value is the source of many execution crashes.

Next, come the individual menu entries which can be either menu items as shown above or a pop-up menu. The **MENUITEM** has a fairly complex syntax.

```
MENUITEM "C&hoice\taccelerator info", ID number, other options
```

After the keyword **MENUITEM** comes the string that you want to be displayed for this item. If there is an '&' in the string, the character immediately **after** the '&' is underlined and is the **hot letter** which the user can press to activate this menu choice. In contrast, keyboard **accelerators** are hot keys that can be pressed when the menu is **not** activated to immediately perform the corresponding menu action as if the user had activated the menu and had chosen this item. If you use a keyboard accelerator for this menu item, then coding **\tacc** info displays your **acc**elerator information after the text of the choice and a tab character. If you use **\a**, the text after it is right justified in the column.

For normal menu items, the remaining options can be omitted and include the following.

```
CHECKED - displays a check mark to the left of the menu item
GRAYED  - displays an item greyed indicating it's not currently available
INACTIVE - shown normal, but does not do anything if selected
MENUBREAK - the item and the following items appear in a new column
MENUBARBREAK - the item and the following items appear in a new column with a
      vertical bar separating the columns
MENUITEM SEPARATOR - causes a horizontal line at this point in the list of menu
      items
```

The **ID numbers** are the numbers that Windows sends to your application when the item has been selected. These numbers must be unique. By convention, these ID numbers all begin **IDM_** for ID of a Menu item for Windows coding. Alternatively, use the prefix **CM_** for CoMmand . The App Wizard uses simply **ID_**. Personally, I prefer **CM_**.

In place of MENUITEM one can have a **pop-up** menu. The "File" menu choice is a pop-up menu that, when selected, pulls down another sub menu of choices. The syntax for pop-up menu items is this.

```
POPUP "menu &Choice"
 {
 MENUITEM ... etc
 }
```

Design Rule 30: Preserve the common look and feel of menus between Windows applications.

If you are going to have a "File" menu, it should be the leftmost menu entry. This is followed by the "Edit" group, if present. "Help" is always the rightmost menu entry. Further, the pop-up "File" menu from application to application commonly has similar sub menu items. Similarly, the pop-up "Edit" menu has standard sub menu items. Further, if in response to a menu item, the user must provide more information (typically retrieved from a dialog box), use the Windows ellipsis notation **(. . .)** to so indicate.

There is another reason for following the common look and feel. Later on, when our application has several different child windows and when the user switches between child windows, each child window's special menu modifications are made to the main menu dynamically by the framework. For example, if one child window is displaying a graphical image, then some very specific additions are likely to be desired in the main menu to provide support for changing line widths, colors, and brush effect. However, if the application supports a text editing child window, when that one is active, it does not have these additional menu items for changing colors, line widths, and so on. It may, instead, desire to have Find/Replace menu items available. By following the standard look and feel of Windows, these changes can easily be automated by the framework.

Definition: the relative position on the menu bar is called the **position** or often the **zero-position**. The first menu item, "Files" most often, is said to be identified as at position 0. "Edit," which is usually next, is position 1, and so on. The MFC makes use of the zero-position.

Let's examine a common menu definition for an application that would use files in some manner. We will include keyboard accelerator hints for the user.

```
MAINMENU MENU
BEGIN
    POPUP "&File"
    BEGIN
        MENUITEM "&New",                   CM_FILENEW
        MENUITEM "&Open...",               CM_FILEOPEN
        MENUITEM "&Close",                 CM_FILECLOSE, GRAYED
        MENUITEM SEPARATOR
        MENUITEM "&Save",                  CM_FILESAVE, GRAYED
        MENUITEM "Save &As...",            CM_FILESAVEAS, GRAYED
        MENUITEM SEPARATOR
        MENUITEM "&Print...",              CM_FILEPRINT, GRAYED
        MENUITEM "P&rint Setup...",     CM_FILEPRINTERSETUP, GRAYED
        MENUITEM SEPARATOR
        MENUITEM "E&xit\tAlt+F4",          CM_EXIT
    END
    POPUP "&Edit"
    BEGIN
        MENUITEM "&Undo\tAlt+BkSp",        CM_EDITUNDO, GRAYED
        MENUITEM SEPARATOR
        MENUITEM "Cu&t\tShift+Del",        CM_EDITCUT, GRAYED
        MENUITEM "&Copy\tCtrl+Ins",        CM_EDITCOPY, GRAYED
        MENUITEM "&Paste\tShift+Ins",      CM_EDITPASTE, GRAYED
        MENUITEM SEPARATOR
        MENUITEM "Clear &All\tCtrl+Del",   CM_EDITCLEAR, GRAYED
        MENUITEM "&Delete\tDel",           CM_EDITDELETE, GRAYED
    END

    POPUP "&Search"
    BEGIN
        MENUITEM "&Find...",               CM_EDITFIND, GRAYED
        MENUITEM "&Replace...",            CM_EDITREPLACE, GRAYED
        MENUITEM "&Next\aF3",              CM_EDITFINDNEXT, GRAYED
    END
    MENUITEM "&Display Map",               IDM_DISPLAYMAP
```

```
    POPUP "&Help"
    BEGIN
        MENUITEM "&About...",              CM_HELPABOUT
    END
END
```

Examining the **MAINMENU**, notice that several choices have the ... included, indicating that more information must be gathered from most likely a dialog box. Most accelerator hints are preceded by **\t**. Note that those menu selections that initially would not be active have been initialized to **GRAYED**—such as File Save. This is because these actions are not available under all circumstances. How can you close a file if no file is opened? How can you copy text if no text is selected?

Predefined MFC Menu ID Names and Numbers

The MFC has a number of built-in menu ID names and numbers that are used by the application framework. They all begin **ID_**. You do not have to use these predefined identifiers. However, it is most convenient to do so. The MFC provides an integrated set of commonly used identifiers and their associated resource items, such as menus, accelerators, tool bar hint strings, and tool bar bitmaps.

While you do not have to use them, the MFC's special IDs are closely tied to automatic framework commands. To avoid accidental triggering of framework menu command handlers, the use of the **ID_** prefix should be avoided when you are creating your own menu items. In a later chapter, these special **ID_** values are explored in depth. The best choice for our menus at this point is to use either **IDM_** or **CM_**. All of these special **ID_** identifiers are defined in one file, MFC\INCLUDE\AFXRES.H. So that it is quite clear, I have used either **IDM_** or **CM_** for menu items that are not using the MFC built-in command Ids. If you see an id that begins **ID_**, it is one of the built-in special MFC ids.

Technically, a user's menu item id numbers should lie between 0x8000 and 0xDFFF, while the internal MFC **ID_** numbers lie between 0xE000 and 0xEFFF. To assist us, the MFC provides the define **WM_USER** which is to be used as the base number for the user IDs. For example, one could code the following.

```
#define CM_MYMENU1      (WM_USER + 1)
#define CM_MYMENU2      (WM_USER + 2)
```

However, after you go to all this trouble to set up the #defines as above, as soon as the RC file is saved, the Resource Editor immediately turns these into the actual numerical values.

In fact, any small numerical value also works well. In practice, I often use small numbers for my MFC menu command ID numbers. By small, I mean in the hundred's range, but certainly a value that is less than 57344 or 0xE000.

```
#define CM_MYMENUITEM1    100
#define CM_MYMENUITEM2    101
```

The one thing that you want to avoid is to use the MFC built-in **ID_** names for some other purpose than for what they are defined to be used. These reserved IDs and numbers are processed internally by MFC and may yield different results than you intended when that menu item is selected.

Sample Menu for Pgm06a

Here is the relevant portion of the **resource.h** file for **Pgm06a**.

```
#define CM_DISPLAYMAP               101
#define CM_FILENEW                  102
#define CM_FILEOPEN                 103
#define CM_FILECLOSE                104
#define CM_FILESAVE                 105
#define CM_FILESAVEAS               106
#define CM_FILEPRINT                107
#define CM_FILEPRINTERSETUP         108
#define CM_EXIT                     109
#define CM_EDITUNDO                 110
#define CM_EDITCUT                  111
#define CM_EDITCOPY                 112
#define CM_EDITPASTE                113
```

```
#define CM_EDITDELETE          114
#define CM_EDITCLEAR           115
#define CM_EDITFIND            116
#define CM_EDITREPLACE         117
#define CM_EDITFINDNEXT        118
#define CM_HELPABOUT           119
#define IDS_MAINTITLE  200
#define IDS_WINNAME    201
#define IDS_MSG_QUIT   202
#define IDS_MSG_QUERY  203
```

And here is the relevant portion of the **Pgm06a.rc** file.

```
MAINMENU MENU DISCARDABLE
BEGIN
    POPUP "&File"
    BEGIN
        MENUITEM "&New",                CM_FILENEW
        MENUITEM "&Open...",            CM_FILEOPEN
        MENUITEM "&Close",              CM_FILECLOSE, GRAYED
        MENUITEM SEPARATOR
        MENUITEM "&Save",               CM_FILESAVE, GRAYED
        MENUITEM "Save &As...",         CM_FILESAVEAS, GRAYED
        MENUITEM SEPARATOR
        MENUITEM "&Print...",           CM_FILEPRINT, GRAYED
        MENUITEM "P&rint Setup...",     CM_FILEPRINTERSETUP, GRAYED
        MENUITEM SEPARATOR
        MENUITEM "E&xit\tAlt+F4",       CM_EXIT
    END
    POPUP "&Edit"
    BEGIN
        MENUITEM "&Undo\tAlt+BkSp",     CM_EDITUNDO, GRAYED
        MENUITEM SEPARATOR
        MENUITEM "Cu&t\tShift+Del",     CM_EDITCUT, GRAYED
        MENUITEM "&Copy\tCtrl+Ins",     CM_EDITCOPY, GRAYED
        MENUITEM "&Paste\tShift+Ins", CM_EDITPASTE, GRAYED
        MENUITEM SEPARATOR
        MENUITEM "Clear &All\tCtrl+Del", CM_EDITCLEAR, GRAYED
        MENUITEM "&Delete\tDel",        CM_EDITDELETE, GRAYED
    END
    POPUP "&Search"
    BEGIN
        MENUITEM "&Find...",            CM_EDITFIND, GRAYED
        MENUITEM "&Replace...",         CM_EDITREPLACE, GRAYED
        MENUITEM "&Next\aF3",           CM_EDITFINDNEXT, GRAYED
    END
    MENUITEM "&Display Map",            CM_DISPLAYMAP
    POPUP "&Help"
    BEGIN
        MENUITEM "&About...",           CM_HELPABOUT
    END
END
...
MAINMENU ACCELERATORS MOVEABLE PURE
BEGIN
    VK_DELETE,      CM_EDITCUT,             VIRTKEY, SHIFT
    VK_INSERT,      CM_EDITCOPY,            VIRTKEY, CONTROL
    VK_INSERT,      CM_EDITPASTE,           VIRTKEY, SHIFT
    VK_DELETE,      CM_EDITCLEAR,           VIRTKEY, CONTROL
    VK_BACK,        CM_EDITUNDO,            VIRTKEY, ALT
    VK_F3,          CM_EDITFINDNEXT,        VIRTKEY
END
...
STRINGTABLE DISCARDABLE
```

```
BEGIN
    IDS_MAINTITLE           "Menu Processing Program"
    IDS_WINNAME             "MenuPgm"
    IDS_MSG_QUIT            "Do you want to quit the application?"
    IDS_MSG_QUERY           "Query?"
END
...
```

Creation of a Menu Resource

Okay. So how does one create the menu in the first place? Once again, it can be done in graphical mode or in text mode. Let's examine both. I began by making a new empty project, setting the project settings to Character set: not set, Message Level: 4, Detect 64-bit incompatibilities: no. After adding in your usual cpp and h files into the project and then making the three needed project settings, right click on the project and choose Add New, choose resource, and then menu.
The graphical menu editor is then invoked as shown in Figure 6-1.

Here I added a new menu. Vitally important: note that it is shown as "MAINMENU" and not MAINMENU. The double quote marks around this menu identifier is your clue that this is a string name and not a #defined number. If there are no double quote marks around the menu name, then that name is actually a #defined name in the **resource.h** file—after compilation, it is just a numerical value. If there are double quote marks around the menu name, then there is **no** #define value—this menu must be referred to by the string "MAINMENU".

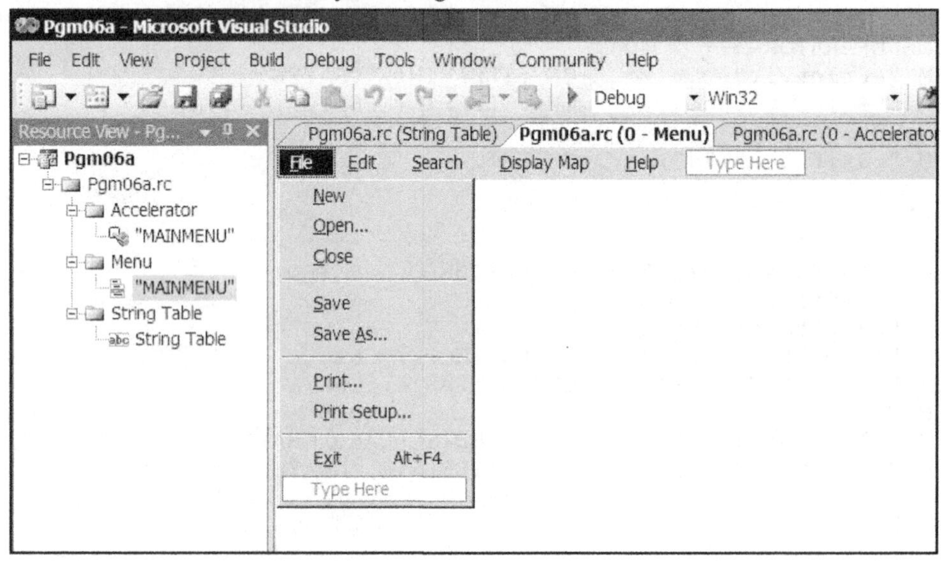

Figure 6-1 The Graphical Editor with Pgm06a Menu

You can change the name of the menu items and so on by selecting the name as is shown in the figure above and right clicking on it and choosing Properties. This is shown in Figure 6.2. You can enter any identifying name in the ID control as well as many other properties.

Notice that you provide an ID name, all uppercase letters, a Caption with an & before the hot letter of your choice. You may set other properties as well, such as enabled. However, another aspect of the MFC obviates the need to do much more than provide the ID and the caption as we will shortly see.

To get a new separator line, at the spot desired, right click and choose New Separator. If the empty slot is not where you wish the separator to be located, simply drag the empty slot up or drag the separator, if one already exists at the wrong location. This is a good graphical editor.

It is sometimes far faster to manually edit the menu. Again, to open the resource file as a text file, in the Solution Explorer, right click on the .rc file and choose Open With and select text editor or notepad. Don't forget to make any parallel changes in the resource.h file.

Now, with a menu made, how do we install it into our application? Again, I show how to do it C-style and the MFC methods. Many Direct-X games prefer to use the pure C-style interface and not the MFC.

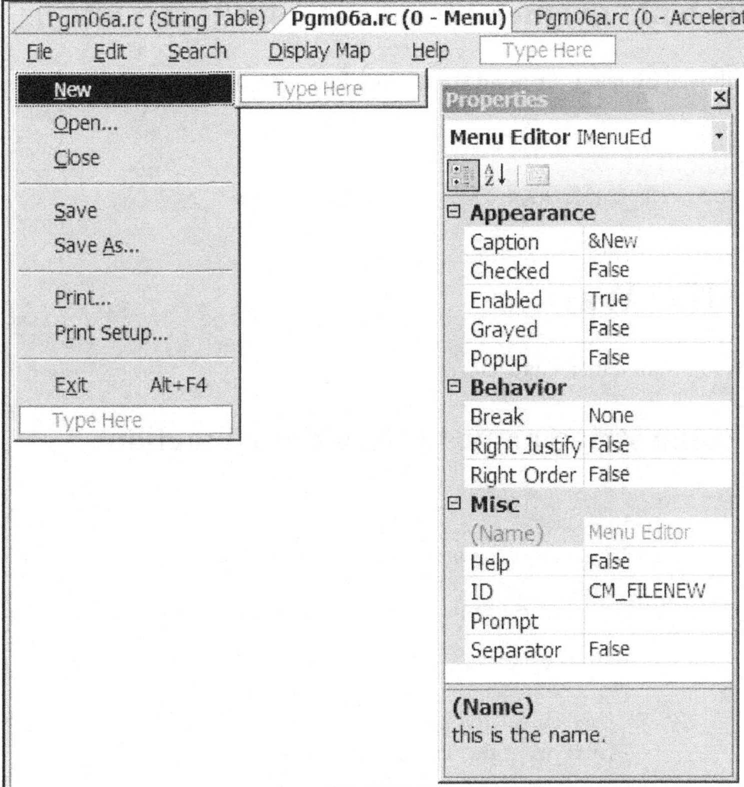

Figure 6-2 Editing the Properties of the New Menuitem

Installing a Menu C API Style

You must know whether your menu name is a string or a #defined symbol in order to properly install a menu. There are two methods of getting to the resource loaded—either by string name or by id. Constructing menus can be done several ways.

C API Method 1: assign the menu in the window class structure

If a string name is used, the main menu is often assigned in the **WNDCLASS** structure, using the **lpszMenuName** field.

```
wndclass.lpszMenuName = "MAINMENU";
```

If the menu id is a #defined symbol, then the resource id number must be converted into a resource using the **MAKEINTRESOURCE** macro.

```
wndclass.lpszMenuName = MAKEINTRESOURCE (IDM_MAINMENU);
```

or

```
wndclass.lpszMenuName = "#IDM_MAINMENU";
```

C API Method 2: dynamically load and install a menu

```
HMENU hMenu = LoadMenu (hinstance, "MAINMENU");
HMENU hMenu = LoadMenu (hinstance, MAKEINTRESOURCE (MAINMENU));
```

Then, specify **hMenu** as the ninth parameter to **CreateWindow**, if it is to be used at once. If the menu is to be used later, the menu can be installed later on by using the **SetMenu** function.

```
SetMenu (hwnd, hMenu);
```

Any menu attached to a window is destroyed when the window is destroyed; all others should be explicitly deleted.

C API Method 3: manually build the menu from component menuitems

By using the **CreateMenu** function followed by many **AppendMenu** functions, you can dynamically create new menus, but it is a tedious business.

```
hMenu = CreateMenu ();
hMenuPopup = CreateMenu();
AppendMenu (hMenuPopup, MF_STRING, IDM_NEW, "&New");
...
```

Installing a Menu the MFC Way

Under MFC, there are various methods to install a menu as well.

MFC Method 1: pass the menu string name to the Create function

```
Create ( AfxRegisterWndClass (
            CS_VREDRAW | CS_HREDRAW,
            AfxGetApp()->LoadStandardCursor (IDC_ARROW),
            (HBRUSH) GetStockObject (LTGRAY_BRUSH),
            AfxGetApp()->LoadStandardIcon (IDI_APPLICATION)),
        title,
        style,
        rect,
        ptrparent,
       "MAINMENU");          // assign the main menu
```

However, if the menu id is a #define name, use the following for the last parameter.

```
        MAKEINTRESOURCE (MAINMENU));
```

MFC Method 2: use the C API Method 2 or 3

This is done exactly the same way but now by using **CWnd** member functions **SetMenu**, **GetMenu**, **AppendMenu** and **LoadMenu**.

MFC Method 3: Use a CMenu class to construct menu objects

One can wrap a **CMenu** object around the real menu in use and then use that **CMenu** to perform many actions on that menu object. The key is to construct the menu object. If the application begins with a some initial main menu, go ahead and install it as normal. Then, in the **OnCreate** function, after passing control to the base classes, one can construct instances of the **CMenu** class in many ways, but the common way is from a resource. Here, **ptrmenu** is a protected **CMenu** data member.

```
CMenu menu;
menu.LoadMenu(resource id); // a new menu or use a string name
```

or

```
CMenu *ptrmenu = GetMenu(); // use the current window's menu
```

One can now make any number of changes to the menu. Where do we delete the allocated menus? The best place to remove items allocated in **OnCreate** is the **OnDestroy** function that is invoked just before the class destructor. If **ptrmenu** was really a protected **FrameWin** class member that was **new**ed in **OnCreate** or even **new**ed at another time during the running of the application, then we can destroy it as follows.

```
void  FrameWin::OnDestroy () {
 delete ptrmenu;
 CFrameWnd::OnDestroy();
}
```

With the menu installed, fancy actions can be dynamically done to the application's current menu. However, before we look at the more exciting effects including floating pop-up menus, let us see how the application is structured to respond to these menu choices.

Working with the Menu Choices of the User

Once the menu has been installed, Windows takes over total control of the menu and the user interactions with it via default frame window message processing. When the user makes a menu selection that is itself a pop-up menu, Windows pops up the submenu. The only action for which the application is responsible is to provide the coding to respond to the user selecting the menu choices.

When the user finally makes a menu selection that is currently enabled and not grayed and not a pop-up menu, Windows sends our program a **WM_COMMAND** message along with the menu ID number that the user selected. Note that many messages are sent concerning the menu events; but most are not of interest to the application, only the final user choice is normally wanted.

Thus, in the C API style coding, when processing the **WM_COMMAND** message, one immediately switches on the **wparam** using a case to process each of the menu possibilities. Here is where the message switch coding becomes lengthy, yielding the "nightmare switch from Hell." The MFC comes to our rescue.

MFC Style Menu Processing

Each possible menu selection that we wish to respond to has both a member function that performs the appropriate processing based upon the menu item selected and a corresponding entry in the Message Map Table. The table contains the **ON_COMMAND** macro as opposed to **ON_WM_COMMAND** as you might expect. **ON_COMMAND** message map macro has the following syntax.

```
ON_COMMAND(menu ID, member function),
```

You supply the menu ID number and the name of the member function that is to be invoked. The MFC traps the **WM_COMMAND** messages and deciphers which menu item is being requested and then invokes the correct member function to carry out that request based upon matching the id number with those in the message map table. The names of the functions that are to respond to the menu choices are totally user-defined. However, convention amongst programmers is to form these member function names based upon the menu ID number name.

I usually choose the menu id prefix **CM_** for all menu item identifiers. So I then must make the function member names follow some predictable pattern derived from the **CM_** identifier to avoid such confusions as these.

```
ON_COMMAND(CM_FILENEW, NewProcess),
```

because it is not immediately clear to the reader that **NewProcess** is invoked in response to the user selecting the menu item File—New.

The MFC response table for **Pgm06a** is as follows.

```
BEGIN_MESSAGE_MAP(FrameWin, CFrameWnd)
 ON_WM_SIZE ()
 ON_WM_PAINT ()
 ON_WM_CREATE ()
 ON_WM_CLOSE ()
 ON_WM_DESTROY ()
 ON_WM_RBUTTONDOWN ()
 ON_COMMAND(CM_DISPLAYMAP, CmDisplayMap)
 ON_COMMAND(CM_EXIT, CmExit)
 ON_COMMAND(CM_FILENEW,            CmFileNew)
 ON_COMMAND(CM_FILEOPEN,           CmFileOpen)
 ON_COMMAND(CM_FILECLOSE,          CmFileClose)
 ON_COMMAND(CM_FILESAVE,           CmFileSave)
 ON_COMMAND(CM_FILESAVEAS,         CmFileSaveAs)
 ON_COMMAND(CM_FILEPRINT,          CmFilePrint)
 ON_COMMAND(CM_FILEPRINTERSETUP, CmFilePrinterSetup)
 ON_COMMAND(CM_EDITUNDO,           CmEditUndo)
 ON_COMMAND(CM_EDITCUT,            CmEditCut)
 ON_COMMAND(CM_EDITCOPY,           CmEditCopy)
 ON_COMMAND(CM_EDITPASTE,          CmEditPaste)
 ON_COMMAND(CM_EDITCLEAR,          CmEditClear)
 ON_COMMAND(CM_EDITDELETE,         CmEditDelete)
 ON_COMMAND(CM_EDITFIND,           CmEditFind)
 ON_COMMAND(CM_EDITFINDNEXT,       CmEditFindNext)
```

```
 ON_COMMAND(CM_EDITREPLACE,       CmEditReplace)
 ON_COMMAND(CM_HELPABOUT,         CmHelpAbout)
END_MESSAGE_MAP()
```

The next coding step is the implementation of these myriad functions. For now, they all display a message box stating the function is not yet implemented.

Dynamically Check Marking, Graying/unGraying, Enabling/Disabling Menu Items

As you look over the menu items, a number were initialized to **GRAYED** because they currently have no meaning, such as the File Close menu item. Consider the File pop-up menu. File|Save and File|SaveAs are initially grayed because there is no file yet loaded. Whenever the user selects File|New or File|Open, then there is a file that could be saved. Now we would like to immediately have the menu item **UNGRAYED** to show that this choice is **now** available.

Note that the MFC **ignores** any **GRAYED** or **CHECKED** options in the menu proper. Instead, when the menu is constructed, the class library grays any menu item that has **no entry** in any window's response table anywhere in the application! It searches the frame window, the application class, and the client window (and a number of other classes) looking for one that would potentially respond to that command ID. If the MFC finds one that is going to respond to that command ID, the corresponding menu item is enabled. It grays out all those menu items for which it cannot find any message map entry that will respond to that command ID. The search is done using the message response tables and maps.

This behavior is perfect for such menu items as Choose Font, Bold, and File|New. It is not at all what we desire for menu items such as File|Save, Edit|Cut, and Edit|Paste. In these situations, if there is no file currently opened or no text selected or nothing on the clipboard to paste, having enabled active menu items is pointless as well as misleading to the user.

Similarly, some menu items, such as **BOLD FONT**, should be check marked when the user selects it, showing that that option is now in effect. Later, should the user again select **BOLD FONT** to turn it off, we would like the check mark to disappear.

With MFC, these kinds of minor alterations to existing menu items can be done in two entirely different ways: using **command enablers** functions or directly using **CMenu** member functions. Let's examine the command enablers first since their usage is widespread.

MFC Command Enablers

Under the MFC, any time that the user pulls down a pop-up menu or anytime that the main menu bar needs to be redrawn, the framework searches through all available message maps of the application looking for any command enablers for each of the menu items. If it finds a command enabler for a specific menu item, it invokes that enabler. The enabler function is allowed to set the various properties for that item, such as enabled, disabled, grayed, or checked. The message map macro for the command enabler is **ON_UPDATE_COMMAND_UI**.

Those menu items that have both an **ON_COMMAND** handler (which respond to those menu selections) and an **ON_UPDATE_COMMAND_UI** command enabler function (which enables and disables those menu items), are said to be following the MFC "command structure." Normally our menu items and commands would follow the MFC command structure.

For the GRAYING/UNGRAYING or the ENABLE/DISABLE operation, the command enabler function should return **TRUE** if enabled or **FALSE** if disabled or grayed. For each menu item that is to be controlled, you provide a member function defined as follows.

```
void   your_function_name (CCmdUI *ptrenabler);
```

Usually, the enabler's body is quite short, using the **CCmdUI** member function **Enable**. If **Enable** is passed **TRUE**, the menu item is enabled; **FALSE** disables or grays it. To avoid namespace pollution, choose function names that relate to the command that they are enabling. In the File|Save menu above, we would have the following function.

```
void MainFrame::CmEnableFileSave (CCmdUI *ptrenabler) {
 ptrenabler->Enable (haveFile);
}
```

where **haveFile** is likely a **bool** class data member.

There are two other enabler member functions.

```
SetText (new menu text string);
SetCheck (special id for check or no check);
```

For example, if the string, **menustr**, which is either a **char** array or a **CString**, contained the new text for this menu item, coding the following in the command enabler function installs this new text.

```
ptrenabler->SetText (menustr);
```

To use the check mark, call the **SetCheck** function passing it a 1 to show the check or 0 to remove the check.

```
ptrenabler->SetCheck (1); // shows check mark
```

Next, we must tie these enabler functions to the menu command to which they apply. Assume we have an enabler for the File|Save and File|SaveAs menu items. The coding in the response table to tie these functions to the menu ids is this.

```
ON_COMMAND(CM_FILESAVE, CmFileSave)
ON_COMMAND(CM_FILESAVEAS, CmFileSaveAs)
ON_UPDATE_COMMAND_UI(CM_FILESAVE, CmEnableFileSave)
ON_UPDATE_COMMAND_UI(CM_FILESAVEAS, CmEnableFileSaveAs)
```

Notice that the menu id is duplicated! **CM_FILESAVE** is used in both the **ON_COMMAND** and **ON_UPDATE_COMMAND_UI** macros. Again, by convention and for clarity, the enabler member functions use the same name as the actual command processing functions prefixed with **Enable**.

Design Rule 31: If you are going to both change the menu item's text and set a check mark, be sure that you set the text first, because the process overlays any previous check mark.

Using CMenu Member Functions

In many ways, the easiest method to gain total control of the menu system is by turning the main menu into a **CMenu** object and using the member functions to manipulate the menu. The **CMenu** member functions parallel to Windows API functions. The flags are a combination of one from one or more sets.

```
MF_STRING, MF_BITMAP, MF_OWNERDRAW,
MF_DISABLED, MF_ENABLED, MF_GRAYED
MF_CHECKED, MF_UNCHECKED
MF_MENUBREAK, MF_MENUBARBREAK, MF_SEPARATOR
MF_POPUP
MF_BYCOMMAND (item is an ID number), MF_BYPOSITION (is the item's zero-based
     position in the menu, where the left-most menu item is position 0, and
     so on.
```

The MFC functions include these.

```
AppendMenu (flags, ID, "menuchoice");
            // adds a menu item to the end of the menu
InsertMenu (ID current, flags, ID new, "menuchoice");
            // adds a menu item after the menu item of id
ModifyMenu (ID current, flags, ID new, "menuchoice");
            // changes the given menu item.
DeleteMenu (ID current, flags);
         // removes the menu item or pop-up item from a menu
EnableMenuItem (ID current, flags);
                // enables or disables the menu item,
                // usually check mark or grayed
CheckMenuItem (ID current, flag);
                // checks or unchecks the menu item,
                // use MF_CHECKED or MF_UNCHECKED
```

```
GetMenuState (ID current, flags to check status of);
                // returns the state of the indicated flags
                // of the menu item
```

and one **CWnd** member function:

```
DrawMenuBar();      // redraws the menu bar after alterations
```

To use these functions, set up a protected data member, often called **ptrmenu** which is a **CMenu***. Under the MFC, the **CMenu*** pointer is most often initialized in **OnCreate** and later deleted in **OnDestroy**.

```
int FrameWin::OnCreate (LPCREATESTRUCT lp) {
 int retcd = CFrameWnd::OnCreate (lp); // invoke base class
 ptrmenu = GetMenu (); // wraps ptrmenu around the main menu
 return retcd;
}
void FrameWin::OnDestroy () {
 delete ptrmenu;           // remove the CMenu
 CFrameWnd::OnDestroy(); // invoke base class last
}
```

Example 1: Add a new menu item to the menu bar

```
ptrmenu->AppendMenu (MF_STRING, IDM_NEWONE, "&NewItem");
```

Example 2: When we are processing the File|New or File|Open requests, after successfully creating a new file or opening an existing file, and before terminating the function, enable the Save menu item

```
ptrmenu->EnableMenuItem (CM_FILESAVE, MF_ENABLED);
```

or for a check mark

```
ptrmenu->CheckMenuItem (CM_FILESAVE, MF_CHECKED);
```

Remember, if you are in a function that is handling a part of the menu selection process, such as adding a new menu item, be sure to invoke **DrawMenuBar** after making the changes. This causes the changes to immediately appear on the screen. In other functions, such as in the **CmFileNew**, you do not need to redraw the menu bar, because it is not active because the user has already made a choice.

Free Floating Pop-up Menus

Floating or pop-up menus, which appear where the user right clicks, give a professional look to applications. Windows makes extensive use of floating pop-up menus which triggered by right mouse clicks. Floating menus are easily done under the MFC. Create a protected **CMenu** class member, called say **ptrmenu** that encapsulates the application's main menu. When the right button is pressed, in the **OnRButtonDown** function, handle the floating menu details.

If the floating menu is one of the existent pop-up menus from the menu bar, as often happens, one needs to get a handle to it. On the other hand, if the menu is a special one, you may need to load it from the resource file. Or one could painstakingly construct the entire menu from scratch. Let's assume that when the right button is pressed, we would like the Edit pop-up menu to appear. The key is to determine its zero-position number from the main menu bar. File is position 0, Edit is next at position 1. Thus, we code the following to handle the entire pop-up operation.

```
void      FrameWin::OnRButtonDown (UINT, CPoint point) {
 CMenu *ptrmenu  = GetMenu ();           // point to main menu
 CMenu *ptrpopup = ptrmenu->GetSubMenu (1); // point to edit
 ClientToScreen (&point);
 ptrpopup->TrackPopupMenu (0, point.x, point.y, this, 0);
}
```

The first and last parameters of **TrackPopupMenu** are normally 0; the second and third are the (x, y) coordinates at which to pop-up the menu; and the fourth is a handle to this window.

```
BOOL TrackPopupMenu (UINT flags, int x, int y, CWnd*, CRect*);
```

The flags can be an ORed value from each of two groups.

```
TPM_CENTERALIGN - centers the pop-up menu on x,y
TPM_LEFTALIGN   - position so left side is aligned on x
```

```
TPM_RIGHTALIGN   - position so right side is aligned on x
TPM_LEFTBUTTON   - pop-up tracks the left button
TPM_RIGHTBUTTON  - pop-up tracks the right button
```

The **CRect*** points to a **CRect** that contains the screen coordinates in which the user can click without dismissing the pop-up menu. If NULL, the pop-up is dismissed if the user clicks outside the menu. One slight detail arises.

The coordinates passed to the **OnRButtonDown** have their origin point the upper left edge of the client window. The pop-up function requires full screen coordinates. The function **ClientToScreen** converts a **Cpoint**.

```
ClientToScreen (&point);
```

Another **CWnd** function does the reverse.

```
ScreenToClient (&point);
```

The MFC framework and Windows work together to display the menu, get the user selection, remove the menu, repaint the overlaid windows, and invoke the command handler corresponding to the selected menu item.

Menu Accelerators

Keyboard menu accelerators are easy to set up. In the resource RC file, add an accelerators section.

```
identifier ACCELERATORS
{
}
```

The identifier is often the same name as the main menu. In our case, **MAINMENU**.

```
MAINMENU ACCELERATORS
BEGIN
END
```

The definition of an accelerator consists of the following values.

```
event, idvalue, type ALT SHIFT CONTROL VIRTKEY
```

Consider the following possible accelerator keys.

```
   "h", IDM_xxx                  ; the H key alone - DANGEROUS
   "H", IDM_xxx                  ; Shift + H key   - DANGEROUS
  "^H", IDM_xxx                        ; Control + H key
   "H", IDM_xxx, ALT                   ; Alt + H key
 VK_F7, IDM_xxx, VIRTKEY               ; F7 key
 VK_F7, IDM_xxx, SHIFT, VIRTKEY        ; Shift + F7 key
 VK_F7, IDM_xxx, CONTROL, VIRTKEY      ; Control + F7 key
 VK_F7, IDM_xxx, ALT, VIRTKEY          ; Alt + F7 key
 VK_F7, IDM_xxx, ALT, SHIFT, VIRTKEY ; Alt + Shift + F7 key
```

Careful! If you use a single letter or a letter and the shift key, these cannot then be enterable into a text stream. Instead they would trigger the command for which they are a shortcut.

For **Pgm06a**, the accelerator table is this.

```
MAINMENU ACCELERATORS
BEGIN
  VK_DELETE, CM_EDITCUT,        VIRTKEY, SHIFT
  VK_INSERT, CM_EDITCOPY,       VIRTKEY, CONTROL
  VK_INSERT, CM_EDITPASTE,      VIRTKEY, SHIFT
  VK_DELETE, CM_EDITCLEAR,      VIRTKEY, CONTROL
  VK_BACK,   CM_EDITUNDO,       VIRTKEY, ALT
  VK_F3,     CM_EDITFINDNEXT, VIRTKEY
END
```

The last step is to insert the accelerator table into the **FrameWin**. Under MFC, in the **FrameWin** constructor, code a call to **LoadAccelTable**.

```
LoadAccelTable ("MAINMENU"); // install keybd accelerators
```

There are also functions to access the system menu: adding, altering, and deleting system menu items. However, the user expects the system menu to be similar among all applications, so it is not wise to modify the system menu.

Pgm06a Menu Example Program

Figure 6.3 shows what the main menu looks like with the File pop-up group opened. Figure 6.4 shows the floating Edit pop-up menu activated by a right mouse click in the client area.

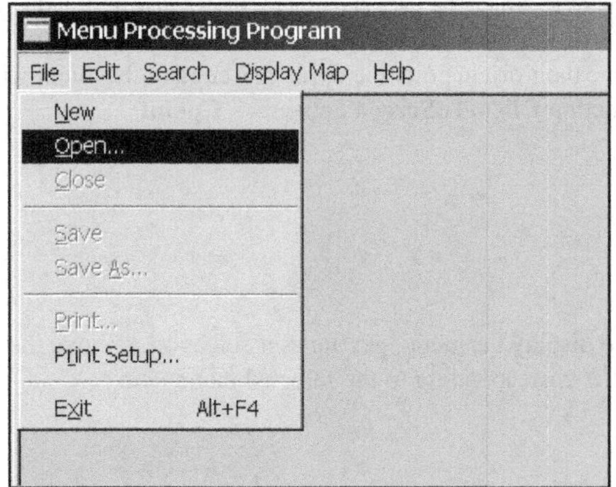

Figure 6.3 Pgm06a's File Pop-up Menu

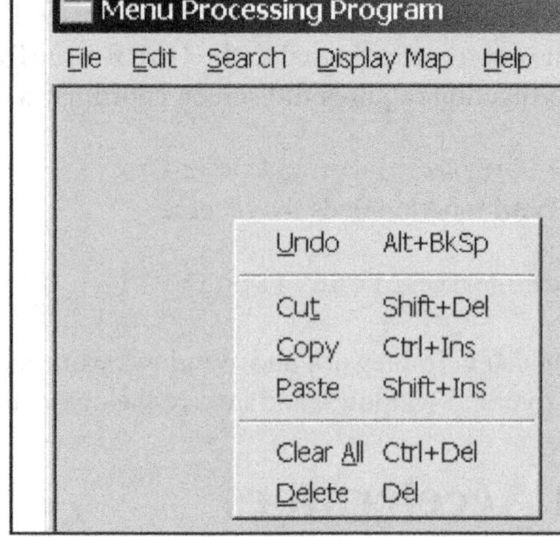

Figure 6.4 The Context Pop-up Menu

In Figure 6.4, notice that the MFC enables all of the Edit menu choices although they were GRAYED in the resource file. This occurs because MFC has found a corresponding command handler for these items but no command enabler functions.

Follow the **haveFile** and **haveSaved** logic through the various File menu choices. By having indicators such as these, the handling of menu enabling is easily done. Try out the floating pop-up edit menu. It is a nice effect. In the coding below, I have omitted the **CWinApp** derived class since it is essentially the same. Notice the extensive list of command handler member functions in the header file.

FrameWin Class Definition

```
#pragma once
/***************************************************************/
/*                                                             */
/* FrameWin Class Definition                                   */
/*                                                             */
/***************************************************************/
class FrameWin : public CFrameWnd {
 /**************************************************************/
 /*                                                            */
 /* Class Data Members                                         */
 /*                                                            */
 /**************************************************************/
protected:
int  height;        // current client window height in pixels
int  width;         // current client window width in pixels
int  avgCapsWidth; // average capital letter width
int  avgCharWidth; // average character width
int  avgCharHeight;// average character height
bool haveFile;      // when true, we opened or have a new file
bool haveSaved;     // when true, we have saved the existent file
 /**************************************************************/
 /*                                                            */
 /* Class Functions:                                           */
```

```
/*                                                              */
/****************************************************************/

public:
              FrameWin ();
             ~FrameWin () {}
afx_msg void  OnPaint ();                 // displays the results

protected:

afx_msg int  OnCreate (LPCREATESTRUCT); // gets avg char dims
afx_msg void OnClose ();                // can close app?
afx_msg void OnSize (UINT, int, int);   // get window dimensions
afx_msg void OnDestroy ();              // delete new things
afx_msg void OnRButtonDown (UINT, CPoint);  // pop up edit menu

afx_msg void CmExit ();
afx_msg void CmDisplayMap ();          // Display a map
afx_msg void CmFileNew ();             // start a new file
afx_msg void CmFileOpen ();            // open existing file
afx_msg void CmFileClose ();           // close the file
afx_msg void CmFileSave ();            // save the file
afx_msg void CmFileSaveAs ();          // save with new name
afx_msg void CmFilePrint ();           // print the file
afx_msg void CmFilePrinterSetup ();    // set up the printer
afx_msg void CmEditUndo ();            // undo last change
afx_msg void CmEditCut ();             // cut to clipboard
afx_msg void CmEditCopy ();            // copy to clipboard
afx_msg void CmEditPaste ();           // paste from clipboard
afx_msg void CmEditDelete ();          // delete text
afx_msg void CmEditClear ();           // clear text
afx_msg void CmEditFind ();            // find text
afx_msg void CmEditFindNext ();        // find next text
afx_msg void CmEditReplace ();         // find and replace
afx_msg void CmHelpAbout ();           // help about our app
afx_msg void CmEnableFileClose (CCmdUI*); // enable/disable Close
afx_msg void CmEnableFileSave (CCmdUI*);  // enable/disable Save
afx_msg void CmEnableFileSaveAs(CCmdUI*);// enable/disable SaveAs
afx_msg void CmEnableFilePrint (CCmdUI*); // enable/disable Print

DECLARE_MESSAGE_MAP();
};
```

FrameWin Class Implementation

```
#include "stdafx.h"
#include "framewin.h"
#include "resource.h"

/****************************************************************/
/*                                                              */
/* FrameWin Events Response Table                               */
/*                                                              */
/****************************************************************/

BEGIN_MESSAGE_MAP(FrameWin, CFrameWnd)
 ON_WM_SIZE ()
 ON_WM_PAINT ()
 ON_WM_CREATE ()
 ON_WM_CLOSE ()
 ON_WM_DESTROY ()
 ON_WM_RBUTTONDOWN ()
 ON_COMMAND(CM_DISPLAYMAP, CmDisplayMap)
```

```
 ON_COMMAND(CM_EXIT, CmExit)
 ON_COMMAND(CM_FILENEW, CmFileNew)
 ON_COMMAND(CM_FILEOPEN, CmFileOpen)
 ON_COMMAND(CM_FILECLOSE, CmFileClose)
 ON_COMMAND(CM_FILESAVE, CmFileSave)
 ON_COMMAND(CM_FILESAVEAS, CmFileSaveAs)
 ON_COMMAND(CM_FILEPRINT, CmFilePrint)
 ON_COMMAND(CM_FILEPRINTERSETUP, CmFilePrinterSetup)
 ON_COMMAND(CM_EDITUNDO, CmEditUndo)
 ON_COMMAND(CM_EDITCUT, CmEditCut)
 ON_COMMAND(CM_EDITCOPY, CmEditCopy)
 ON_COMMAND(CM_EDITPASTE, CmEditPaste)
 ON_COMMAND(CM_EDITCLEAR, CmEditClear)
 ON_COMMAND(CM_EDITDELETE, CmEditDelete)
 ON_COMMAND(CM_EDITFIND, CmEditFind)
 ON_COMMAND(CM_EDITFINDNEXT, CmEditFindNext)
 ON_COMMAND(CM_EDITREPLACE, CmEditReplace)
 ON_COMMAND(CM_HELPABOUT, CmHelpAbout)
 ON_UPDATE_COMMAND_UI(CM_FILECLOSE, CmEnableFileClose)
 ON_UPDATE_COMMAND_UI(CM_FILESAVE, CmEnableFileSave)
 ON_UPDATE_COMMAND_UI(CM_FILESAVEAS, CmEnableFileSaveAs)
 ON_UPDATE_COMMAND_UI(CM_FILEPRINT, CmEnableFilePrint)
END_MESSAGE_MAP();

/*************************************************************/
/*                                                           */
/* Framewin: Construct the window object                     */
/*                                                           */
/*************************************************************/

FrameWin::FrameWin () : CFrameWnd () {

 LoadAccelTable ("MAINMENU");        // install keybd accelerators

 DWORD style = WS_OVERLAPPEDWINDOW; // set basic window style
 CString title;
 title.LoadString (IDS_MAINTITLE);  // load caption of window

 Create ( AfxRegisterWndClass (
              CS_VREDRAW | CS_HREDRAW,
              AfxGetApp()->LoadStandardCursor (IDC_ARROW),
              (HBRUSH) GetStockObject (LTGRAY_BRUSH),
              AfxGetApp()->LoadStandardIcon (IDI_APPLICATION)),
         title,          // window caption
         style,          // wndclass DWORD style
         rectDefault,    // set initial window position
         0,              // the parent window, here none
         "MAINMENU");    // assign the main menu

 haveFile  = false;  // indicates no file loaded yet
 haveSaved = false;  // indicates file is not saved
}

/*************************************************************/
/*                                                           */
/* OnDestroy: remove dynamically allocated item - none       */
/*                                                           */
/*************************************************************/

void FrameWin::OnDestroy () {

}

/*************************************************************/
```

```
/*                                                              */
/* OnCreate: get average character dimensions                   */
/*                                                              */
/****************************************************************/

int FrameWin::OnCreate (LPCREATESTRUCT lpCS) {
 if (CFrameWnd::OnCreate (lpCS) == -1) return -1;

 TEXTMETRIC  tm;

 // get the system font's characteristics in tm
 CClientDC dc (this);         // acquire a DC
 dc.GetTextMetrics (&tm);     // get the information

 // calculate average character parameters
 avgCharWidth  = tm.tmAveCharWidth;
 avgCharHeight = tm.tmHeight + tm.tmExternalLeading;
 avgCapsWidth  = (tm.tmPitchAndFamily & 1 ? 3 : 2) *
                   avgCharWidth / 2;
 return 0;
}

/****************************************************************/
/*                                                              */
/* OnSize: acquire the current dimensions of the client window */
/*                                                              */
/****************************************************************/

void FrameWin::OnSize (UINT, int cx, int cy) {
 width = cx;  // save current height
 height = cy; // save current width
}

/****************************************************************/
/*                                                              */
/* OnPaint: a minimalist paint                                  */
/*                                                              */
/****************************************************************/

void FrameWin::OnPaint () {
 CPaintDC dc (this);  // create a paint dc
}


/****************************************************************/
/*                                                              */
/* OnClose: determine if the app can be shut down               */
/*                                                              */
/****************************************************************/

void FrameWin::OnClose () {
 CString msgtitle;
 CString msgtext;
 msgtext.LoadString (IDS_MSG_QUIT);
 msgtitle.LoadString (IDS_MSG_QUERY);
 if (MessageBox (msgtext, msgtitle, MB_YESNO | MB_ICONQUESTION)
     == IDYES) {
  CFrameWnd::OnClose ();
 }
}


/****************************************************************/
/*                                                              */
```

```
/* OnRButtonDown: popup edit menu as a floating menu            */
/*                                                              */
/****************************************************************/

void       FrameWin::OnRButtonDown (UINT, CPoint point) {
 CMenu *ptrmenu  = GetMenu ();                  // point to main menu
 CMenu *ptrpopup = ptrmenu->GetSubMenu (1);// point to edit popup
 ClientToScreen (&point);                       // convert coordinates
 ptrpopup->TrackPopupMenu (0, point.x, point.y, this, 0);
}

/****************************************************************/
/*                                                              */
/* CmDisplayMap: display our map                                */
/*                                                              */
/****************************************************************/

void       FrameWin::CmDisplayMap () {
 MessageBox ("DisplayMap is not yet implemented","Display Map",
             MB_ICONINFORMATION | MB_OK);
}

/****************************************************************/
/*                                                              */
/* CmExit:  determine if the app can be shut down               */
/*                                                              */
/****************************************************************/

void       FrameWin::CmExit () {
 SendMessage (WM_CLOSE);
}

/****************************************************************/
/*                                                              */
/* CmHelpAbout: shows who wrote this app                        */
/*                                                              */
/****************************************************************/

void       FrameWin::CmHelpAbout () {

 MessageBox (
   "Illustrates menu processing -"
   "try file menu items and right mouse button",
   "Help About PGM6A", MB_ICONINFORMATION | MB_OK);
}

/****************************************************************/
/*                                                              */
/* CmFileNew: open a new file                                   */
/*                                                              */
/****************************************************************/

void       FrameWin::CmFileNew () {
 if (haveFile && !haveSaved) {
  SendMessage (WM_COMMAND, ID_FILE_SAVE, 0L);
 }
 MessageBox ("File New is not yet implemented -"
             " will pretend have a new file",
             "File New", MB_ICONINFORMATION | MB_OK);
 haveFile  = true;
 haveSaved = false;
}

/****************************************************************/
```

```
/*                                                                  */
/* CmFileOpen: open an existent file                                */
/*                                                                  */
/********************************************************************/

void      FrameWin::CmFileOpen () {
 if (haveFile && !haveSaved)
  SendMessage (WM_COMMAND, ID_FILE_SAVE, 0L);
 MessageBox ("Open not implemented - pretend file is open",
             "File Open", MB_ICONINFORMATION | MB_OK);
 haveFile  = true;
 haveSaved = true;
}

/********************************************************************/
/*                                                                  */
/* CmFileClose: close an opened file                                */
/*                                                                  */
/********************************************************************/

void      FrameWin::CmFileClose () {
 if (haveFile && !haveSaved)
  SendMessage (WM_COMMAND, ID_FILE_SAVE, 0L);
 MessageBox ("Close not implemented - pretend file is closed",
             "File Close", MB_ICONINFORMATION | MB_OK);
 haveFile  = false;
 haveSaved = false;
}

/********************************************************************/
/*                                                                  */
/* CmEnableFileClose: enables/disables FileClose menu item          */
/*                                                                  */
/********************************************************************/

void      FrameWin::CmEnableFileClose (CCmdUI *ptrenabler) {
 ptrenabler->Enable (haveFile);
}

/********************************************************************/
/*                                                                  */
/* CmFileSave: save an existent file                                */
/*                                                                  */
/********************************************************************/

void      FrameWin::CmFileSave () {
 MessageBox ("Save not implemented -"
             " Pretending file has been saved",
             "File Save", MB_ICONINFORMATION | MB_OK);
 haveSaved = true;
}

/********************************************************************/
/*                                                                  */
/* CmEnableFileSave: enables/disables file save menu item           */
/*                                                                  */
/********************************************************************/

void      FrameWin::CmEnableFileSave (CCmdUI *ptrenabler) {
 ptrenabler->Enable (haveFile);
}

/********************************************************************/
/*                                                                  */
```

```
/* CmFileSaveAs: Save an existent file with a new name           */
/*                                                               */
/*****************************************************************/

void       FrameWin::CmFileSaveAs () {
 MessageBox ("SaveAs not implemented "
             "- Pretending file has been saved",
             "File SaveAs", MB_ICONINFORMATION | MB_OK);
 haveSaved = true;
}

/*****************************************************************/
/*                                                               */
/* CmEnableFileSaveAs: enables/disables file saveas menu item    */
/*                                                               */
/*****************************************************************/

void       FrameWin::CmEnableFileSaveAs (CCmdUI *ptrenabler) {
 ptrenabler->Enable (haveFile);
}

/*****************************************************************/
/*                                                               */
/* CmFilePrint: print an existing file                           */
/*                                                               */
/*****************************************************************/

void       FrameWin::CmFilePrint () {
 if (haveFile)
  MessageBox ("Print not implemented "
              "- Pretending file has been printed",
              "File Print", MB_ICONINFORMATION | MB_OK);
}

/*****************************************************************/
/*                                                               */
/* CmEnableFilePrint: enables/disables file print menu item      */
/*                                                               */
/*****************************************************************/

void       FrameWin::CmEnableFilePrint (CCmdUI *ptrenabler) {
 ptrenabler->Enable (haveFile);
}

/*****************************************************************/
/*                                                               */
/* CmFilePrinterSetup: set up the printer parameters             */
/*                                                               */
/*****************************************************************/

void       FrameWin::CmFilePrinterSetup () {
 MessageBox ("Printer Setup not implemented",
             "File PrinterSetup", MB_ICONINFORMATION | MB_OK);
}

/*****************************************************************/
/*                                                               */
/* CmEditUndo: undo last typing error                            */
/*                                                               */
/*****************************************************************/

void       FrameWin::CmEditUndo () {
}

```

```
/***************************************************************/
/*                                                             */
/* CmEditCut: cut selected text to clipboard                  */
/*                                                             */
/***************************************************************/

void      FrameWin::CmEditCut () {
}

/***************************************************************/
/*                                                             */
/* CmEditCopy: copy selected text to clipboard                */
/*                                                             */
/***************************************************************/

void      FrameWin::CmEditCopy () {
}

/***************************************************************/
/*                                                             */
/* CmEditPaste: paste from the clipboard to insertion point    */
/*                                                             */
/***************************************************************/

void      FrameWin::CmEditPaste () {
}

/***************************************************************/
/*                                                             */
/* CmEditClear: clear selected text                            */
/*                                                             */
/***************************************************************/

void      FrameWin::CmEditClear () {
}

/***************************************************************/
/*                                                             */
/* CmEditDelete: delete selected text                          */
/*                                                             */
/***************************************************************/

void      FrameWin::CmEditDelete () {
}

/***************************************************************/
/*                                                             */
/* CmEditFindNext: find next selected text                     */
/*                                                             */
/***************************************************************/

void      FrameWin::CmEditFindNext () {
}

/***************************************************************/
/*                                                             */
/* CmEditFind: find selected text                              */
/*                                                             */
/***************************************************************/

void      FrameWin::CmEditFind () {
}

/***************************************************************/
```

```
/*                                                                    */
/* CmEditReplace: replace text                                        */
/*                                                                    */
/**********************************************************************/

void      FrameWin::CmEditReplace () {
}
```

Stub Testing

As you examine this **FrameWin** implementation, I think that you can easily see stub testing effects. Here, I have got the basic shell of a file processing application up and running with all of the menu choices working. However, there is no functional coding in most all of the message handler functions. This is the way you bring up a Windows application. Get a shell working. Add in the menu and get the shell command handlers in operation. At this point one would begin to implement these myriad functions one at a time.

A Common Command Enabler Function

Notice that the four file command enabler functions are exactly the same. There is no reason for four different functions; one will do. Let's call it **CmEnableFileMenuItems**. In the Message Map, change the four lines to this.

```
ON_UPDATE_COMMAND_UI(CM_FILECLOSE, CmEnableFileMenuItems)
ON_UPDATE_COMMAND_UI(CM_FILESAVE, CmEnableFileMenuItems)
ON_UPDATE_COMMAND_UI(CM_FILESAVEAS, CmEnableFileMenuItems)
ON_UPDATE_COMMAND_UI(CM_FILEPRINT, CmEnableFileMenuItems)
```

Then, implement this single enabler function this way.

```
void  FrameWin::CmEnableFileMenuItems (CCmdUI *ptrenabler) {
 ptrenabler->Enable (haveFile);
}
```

With the Edit menu, Cut and Copy can share a common enabler based on whether a selection has been made or not. Edit Paste must have a different enabler based on whether or not there is information on the clipboard at the moment.

Programming Problems

Program Pgm06-1 Revised Tic Tac Toe Game

Revise the Tic Tac Toe game program from chapter 5 by adding a menu for the game. Under the File pop-up, include the items: New Game, Cancel Game, and Exit. Under the Help pop-up menu, include an item called Help About which, when selected, displays a simple message box identifying the program's author.

Chapter 7 Icons, Cursors, and Dialogs

Introduction

The Windows environment offers a wealth of graphical resources from simple items such as icons, cursors, and bitmaps, to more complex items such as list boxes, edit boxes, and buttons of all kinds (radio buttons, push buttons, and so on), several new controls such as the progress control, to complex items such as dialog boxes and property sheets or tabbed dialogs with many control elements. While this wide variety makes the Windows visually appealing for a user, this same wide variety offers a challenge to the Windows programmer.

This portion of Windows is so involved that an entire text could be written on using the controls, dialogs and property sheets. As you look over the books and their presentations of Windows resources, one can easily be overwhelmed by its complexity. There are many different approaches to resource construction to say nothing about the mechanical and artistic styles involved. Construction and use of Windows resources in an application range from the tedious bit by bit, manual construction from the "ground up" approach to the almost "one coding line" approach using a previously created resource built in the Workshop.

Resources can be used all by themselves within part of the main window area, such as a push button off to one side in the window. Such are known as **child window controls**. Often, the resources are organized into a package presented to the user upon demand, in other words, a **dialog box**. An application can even have these resources, especially a dialog box, as its main window! Windows provides several **Common Dialog Boxes** to simplify several universal situations: selecting a file to open, choosing a color, choosing a font, and printing a file, for example.

If we were to discuss all aspects of resource creation and usage from the C API style and the MFC styles and the various methods of construction via resource editors, we would consume all the remaining pages of this text. Thus, it is at this point that some restrictions on our coverage must be made.

1. Whenever possible, resources are created using the Visual Studio graphical editor.
2. Because of Restriction 1, only the basic syntax involved in manual construction of resources is discussed and then only as it applies to using resources already constructed.
3. The major coding discussions illustrate the MFC approach to using resources. C API style is not covered.
4. Only the basics of how to use these resources is covered. This is likely one area that you will continually be learning new and fancier ways of doing things.

Realize that in the creation of a real application, a great deal of time is spent designing the optimum visual resources and their intended methods of use. Do not be surprised to discover that you are spending nearly 1/3 of your program development time on this task.

Using Developer Studio to Browse Existing Resources

An excellent place to begin your study of resources is to examine the resources of known applications. Their resources are stored in their EXE files. Bring up the Visual Studio and Choose File|Open File; browse for your favorite Windows application and choose Open. The workshop then de-compiles the resources and displays the resources in the window. Now select the different dialogs and icons and cursors to view. Notice that it is possible to extract a resource from an application and copy it into your own resource file. Browse until you get a feel of what different resources look like and the various styles and the look and feel of Windows dialogs. Then, make a play project and Insert a New Resource and experiment creating some resources.

Creation of Icons, Bitmaps, and Cursors

Let's begin with the simpler resources: icons, cursors, and bitmaps. What does the application require? Normally, one icon represents the application in all of the various locations, not only when it is minimized. If the standard mouse cursors are not sufficient, then perhaps you will need a cursor or two. Bitmaps are often small pictures that represent something. For now, we have almost no use for them. However, when we add tool bars (control bars) and tool boxes to our frame windows in a later chapter, bitmaps play a vital role. When we discuss the graphics interface in a later chapter, bitmaps become crucial.

See if you can create an icon and a cursor. Figure 7.1 and 7.2 show what the pair that I created for this sample program look like.

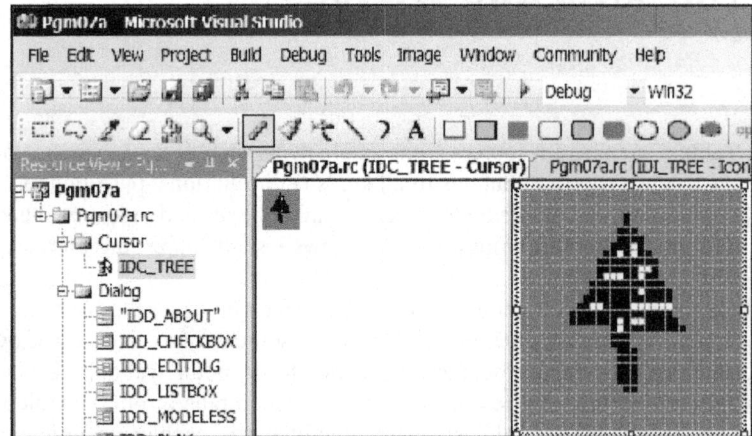

Figure 7-1 Tree Cursor

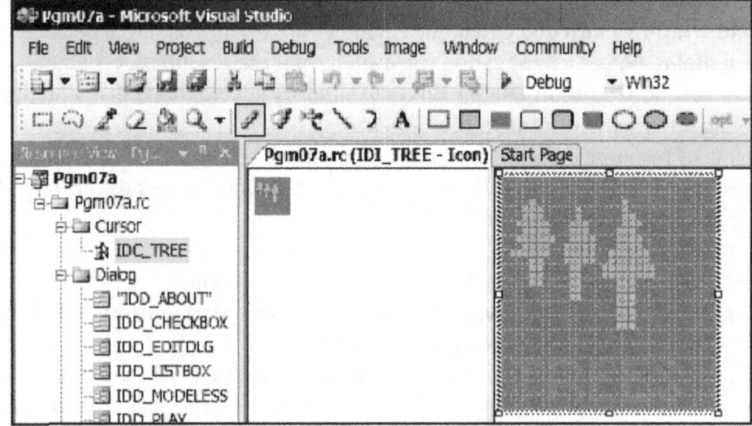

Figure 7-2 Tree Icon

In the RC file, they are defined as separate files to be included. The ID numbers are given in the **resource.h** file.

```
IDI_TREE   ICON    "trees.ico"
IDC_TREE   CURSOR "tree.cur"
```

Observe the convention: the prefix **IDI_** identifies icons; the prefix **IDC_** identifies cursors. (It is only a convention.) As with the name of a menu, the identifiers, **IDI_TREE** and **IDC_TREE**, can be used as shown—in other words, as string identifiers—or one could define these names in the **resource.h** file, in which case they become resource ID numbers. I chose the latter, actual numbers.

The numbering scheme: Within a dialog, menu, string table, and so on, the ID numbers must be different. However, the same numbers can be reused on different type objects. That is, the one menu, icon, bitmap, and cursor can all have the same number, say 100, and still be independent items.

When the resource compiler is run as part of the Build program option, it includes the above two resource files. You can also code a partial or full path to these files. For example, if the files were in a resource subdirectory, one could code the following

```
IDI_TREE   ICON    "resource\trees.ico"
```

or

```
IDI_TREE   ICON    "d:\learnwin\vc\pgm07a\resource\trees.ico"
```

However, supplying the full path makes the program development non-portable; it now is tied to a specific drive and set of subdirectories. I recommend using only the first method.

Using Icons and Cursors

We already know how to install the application icon by using the **LoadIcon** function on the assignment to the **wndclass.hIcon** member using the C style approach. Under the MFC, the icon would be loaded in the **FrameWin** constructor's invocation of the **Create** function as the fourth parameter to **AfxRegisterWndClass** as has been done in all examples thus far.

```
AfxGetApp()->LoadIcon (IDI_TREE)),// set min icon
```

After the invocation of **Create**, the cursor can be loaded by using the **LoadCursor** function and installed by using the **SetClassLong** function.

```
hcursor = LoadCursor (AfxGetApp()->m_hInstance,
                      MAKEINTRESOURCE (IDC_TREE));
SetClassLong (m_hWnd, GCL_HCURSOR, (long) hcursor);
```

However, let's examine some possible dynamic uses of a cursor. Assume that the arrow cursor is the default. Whenever an application enters a relatively long processing process, it is common to change the cursor to the hourglass. When the process is finished, the arrow cursor is returned. Since this is so frequently desired, the MFC has provided an extremely easy method to perform this switching. The **CWnd** class is derived from the **CCmdTarget** class. It is this base class that provides the wait cursor capabilities. To switch cursors, use the following.

```
BeginWaitCursor ();    // installs the hourglass cursor
EndWaitCursor ();      // restores the previous cursor
RestoreWaitCursor ();  // restores wait cursor after an
                       // interruption such as a MessageBox
                       // or dialog box operations are done
                       // during a wait sequence
```

These functions are best utilized within the processing sequences of a single message. When Windows is allowed to process other messages during the long wait period, the cursor can be altered by other framework actions we are about to see.

Another common use of changing cursors is to provide a special cursor while within a particular window. For example, in my WWII game, the arrow cursor is the normal cursor. However, when the cursor is over a map window, a special location cross hair cursor appears. When the mouse moves out of the map window, the arrow cursor reappears. This behavior comes about because of the default behavior of the **CWnd** message handler **OnSetCursor**.

If the mouse is not captured and mouse movement is within a window, the framework calls the window's **OnSetCursor** handler. The default implementation calls the parent window's handler before it calls the child window's handler. It uses the arrow cursor if the mouse in not in the client area of the window. If the mouse is in the client area, then the registered class cursor is used. Thus, if the application is using a **CFrameWnd** only and has installed a special cursor, then when the mouse is over the client area, the special cursor is automatically used; when the mouse is over the frame window elements, such as the menu bar, the arrow cursor appears.

This behavior is implemented in the sample programs in this chapter. The sample programs install a special cursor for use while within the client area; the arrow cursor appears automatically when the mouse moves outside the client window area. Simply by changing the cursor registered to the **CWnd** class, our applications can make use of this behavior. In case you wish to refine the process further, the signature of the **OnSetCursor** function is this.

```
afxmsg  BOOL  OnSetCursor (CWnd* ptrwin, UINT hittest, UNIT msg);
```

The **msg** parameter is one of the various mouse messages, while the **hittest** parameter is one of the many mouse hit identifiers, such as **HTCLIENT,** meaning it is within the client area. See the documentation given in **CWnd::OnNcHitTest** for the rather long list of hit codes.

The new cursor must be loaded. If the cursor is not going to change, one can install it directly into the **WNDCLASS** structure. If the cursor is being loaded once only, it makes sense to install it directly into the **WNDCLASS** structure as the window is being registered at creation time.

Method 1: Using the C API Functions

The **LoadCursor** function requires the **m_hInstance** value and the cursor identifier which can be given in one of two ways depending upon whether the cursor identifier is a string or an ID number. If the identifier is a number, use the macro **MAKEINTRESOURCE** to convert it into a string.

```
HCURSOR  hcursor;
hcursor = LoadCursor (AfxGetApp()->m_hInstance,
```

```
                        MAKEINTRESOURCE (IDC_TREE)); // id is numeric
```
or
```
hcursor = LoadCursor (AfxGetApp()->m_hInstance, IDC_TREE);
```

If you have access to **WNDCLASS**, code it this way.
```
wndclass.hCursor = hcursor;
wndclass.hCursor = LoadCursor (AfxGetApp()->m_hInstance,
                               MAKEINTRESOURCE (IDC_TREE));
```
or
```
::SetCursor (hcursor);
```

Method 2: Use the CWinApp functions to load the cursor

```
HCURSOR  LoadCursor (stringid);
HCURSOR  LoadCursor (UINT id);
```
where **stringid** is a **char*** or **LPCTSTR**. In the above example, one could code it this way.
```
wndclass.hCursor = AfxGetApp()->LoadCursor (IDC_TREE);
```

If the cursor is one of the Windows supplied cursors (there are a lot of them—use Explorer and look in the \WINDOWS\CURSORS folder), then use the following **CWinApp** function.
```
HCURSOR LoadStandardCursor (LPCTSTR lpszCursorName) const;
```

The identifiers are defined in **windows.h** and include the following.
```
IDC_ARROW     Standard arrow cursor
IDC_IBEAM     Standard text-insertion cursor
IDC_WAIT      Hourglass cursor used when Windows performs
              time-consuming task
IDC_CROSS     Cross-hair cursor for selection
IDC_UPARROW   Arrow that points straight up
IDC_SIZE      Cursor to use to resize a window
IDC_ICON      Cursor to use to drag a file
IDC_SIZENWSE  Two-headed arrow with ends at upperleft & lowerright
IDC_SIZENESW  Two-headed arrow with ends at upperright & lowerleft
IDC_SIZEWE    Horizontal two-headed arrow
IDC_SIZENS    Vertical two-headed arrow
```

Method 3: the SetClassLong

This method is best used when you wish to dynamically alter the cursor while the application is running.
```
SetClassLong (type id, (long) cursor object);
```

The type id can be any one of the following identifiers.
```
GCL_HCURSOR      - changes cursor
GCL_HICON        - changes the minimize icon
GCL_HBACKGROUND  - changes the background brush
GCL_STYLE        - changes window styles
```

To permanently alter the cursor, code this call.
```
SetClassLong (GCL_HCURSOR, (long) HCURSOR);
```

These approaches are used in **Pgm07a**; experiment with the mouse cursor. Notice that when it is over the client window area, the "tree" cursor is visible. When the cursor passes over the menu bar or out of the window all together, the standard arrow cursor reappears.

Controls and Dialog Boxes

The basic controls that communicate user-entered information include: push buttons, list boxes, edit boxes, check boxes, radio button groups, combo boxes, and scroll bars. Windows 95 added some new controls: progress bars, spin bars (up/down control), track bars, and tree views. Also, property sheets or tabbed dialog boxes were new with Windows 95. Note that any needed scroll bars within list and combo boxes are automatically handled by Windows; we examine general scroll bars later. For now, concentrate on the others.

The basic procedure to create a new dialog begins with right clicking on the rc file and choosing Add New and then selecting dialog. Note, do not select any of the specialized sub-dialog menu items. A new, mostly empty, dialog is created which has two buttons: Ok and Cancel. Position the cursor in some empty space in the dialog and right click, choosing Properties. In the Properties dialog, enter the name you wish to call the dialog. Figure 7.3 shows the new dialog and I undocked the toolbox and moved it close to the dialog for handy reference. Let's name this one IDD_PLAY.

By convention, all dialog Ids begin with **IDD_**.

In the Properties of the Dialog window, you can set an enormous number of properties, including its IDD name and caption. Experiment with changing many of these and see the visual impact upon the dialog's appearance. Try setting the 3D-Look and Centered. These two options give the dialog a three-dimensional appearance and cause the dialog to be centered when it is launched. Figure 7-4 shows the Dialog Properties in action.

From the Format menu, select the last item, Test. This action runs the dialog in a preview mode. You can play with it to see how it is working and appearing. When you click on Ok or Cancel, the test is terminated. This is shown in Figure 7.5.

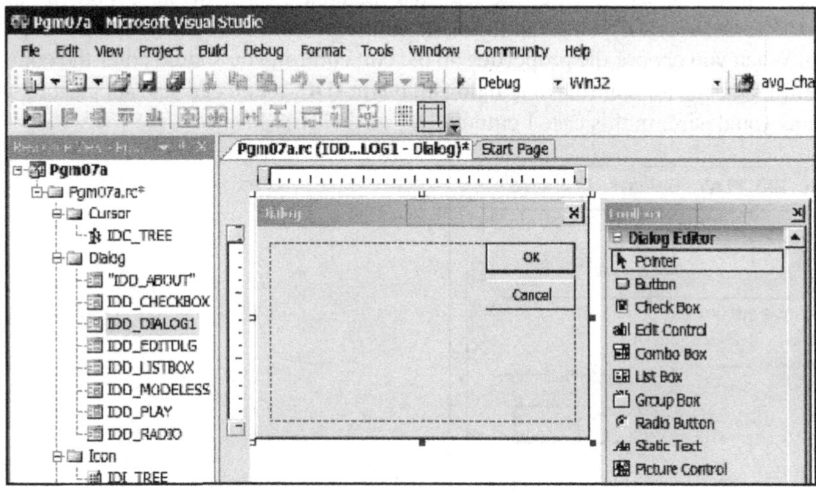

Figure 7-3 Creating a New Dialog

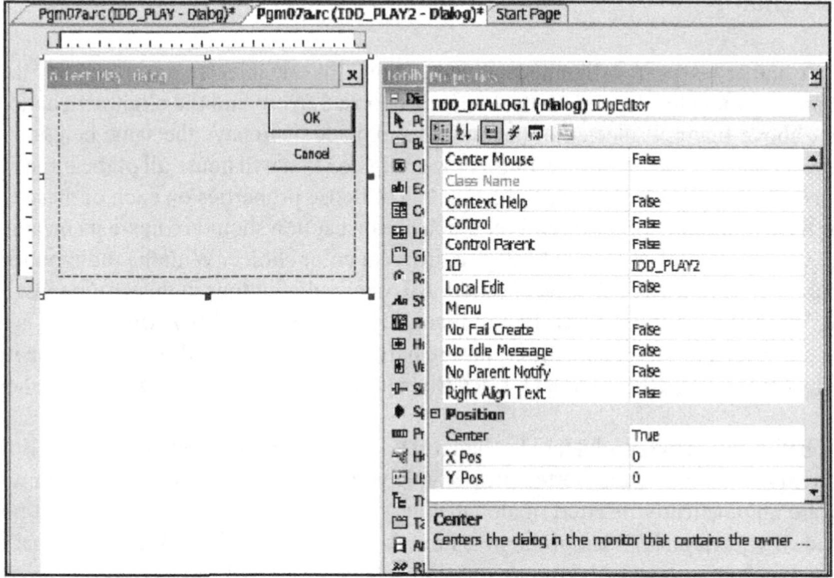

Figure 7-4 Dialog's Properties with ID Set

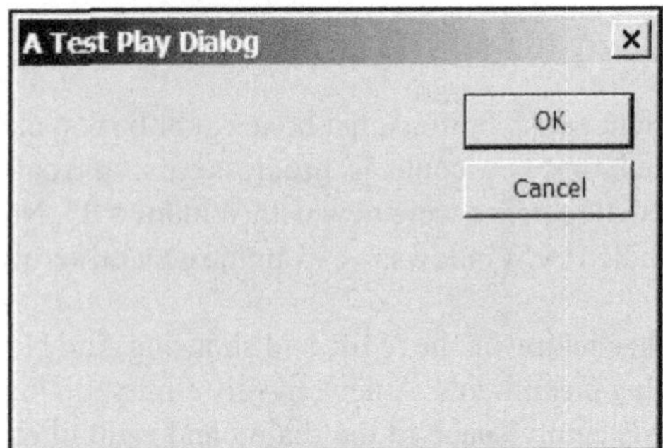

Figure 7-5 Testing the Dialog

Next, experiment with some of the other many style options. After selecting an option, use Layout-Test to see how that choice will appear when the dialog actually runs.

Now notice the buttons on the Controls tool box on the right side. This box contains icons representing many of the controls that can be placed within the dialog. To insert one, click on the desired control in the Control box, drag it to the dialog, and release it. Then, resize and reposition the new control as desired. Try adding a static control and an edit control similar to Figure 7.6. When the controls are where you want them, select each control in turn and right click and choose properties. With the static text control, you should enter the text that the control is to display. You can also adjust the appearance of the control with the various style options. On the static control, I used the Sunken option. Experiment to see what looks best for your dialog. When you choose the properties on the edit control, you should enter the control id number that you wish to use. By convention, the ids for controls of a dialog all begin **IDC_**. You can also set various styles to make the edit control appear and act as you desire. In this case I entered IDC_EDITNAME.

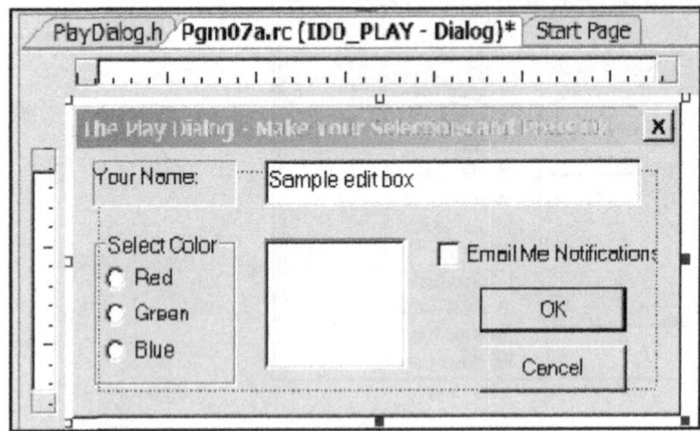

Figure 7-6 The Play Dialog

On the Layout menu are numerous control alignment choices. Typically, one selects a group of controls by left-click and drag, placing a focus rectangle around the desired controls. Then, choose Layout and the alignment action to perform on the group of controls. In the above figure, I selected both controls and made them have the same height.

Next, let's add three radio buttons. Begin by inserting a new group box that will house all of the three radio buttons. Then, insert three radio button controls positioned inside the group box. Choose properties on each of these four controls. The group box should provide the overall title for the button set. Each button caption should indicate its meaning. Here, the group box says "Select Color" while each of the buttons displays a different color choice. With the radio button properties, the first button in the group must have Group and Tab Stop checked. All other radio buttons in this group must have the Tab Stop checked. This is **crucial**. Windows uses the **Group flag** to recognize that **this specific radio button** is the **first** of a group of radio buttons and that the radio buttons coming after this are part of this group of radio buttons. The ids that I used for these buttons were **IDC_RADIO_RED**, **IDC_RADIO_GREEN**, and **IDC_RADIO_BLUE**. This is shown above in Figure 7.6.

Next, add in a list box below the edit control. Here I called it **IDC_LIST_CITY**. I added the Client Edge and Static Edge styles. The one crucial item to examine is the Sorted property. If you leave this item checked, then when you add strings into the list box, they are automatically inserted in alphabetical order. While this is convenient, it poses a major problem when the user has made a selection. And that problem is how do you correlate that selection to what it is that you are to do with it. If the list box is selecting a record from an array to subsequently edit, how do you determine what the subscript of the selected item is if the list box items are in a different order than the array of records is in? Sometimes, unsorted is more convenient. Figure 7.7 shows the list box.

Finally, add in a check box to the right of the list box. I called this one **IDC_CHECK_EMAIL**. The final dialog view is shown in Figure 7.6.

The final step is to get the tab order set properly. When the dialog is in operation, users often tab from control to control as they make their selections. The tab order is adjustable by choosing Format—Tab Order. When you select this option, large numbers appear beside each control. You change the order by sequential clicking on each control in the order you wish them to be. Figure 7.7 shows the final settings of my tab order. To end the tab order selection, choose Layout—Tab Order once again. Note that this menu item is actually a checked menu item.

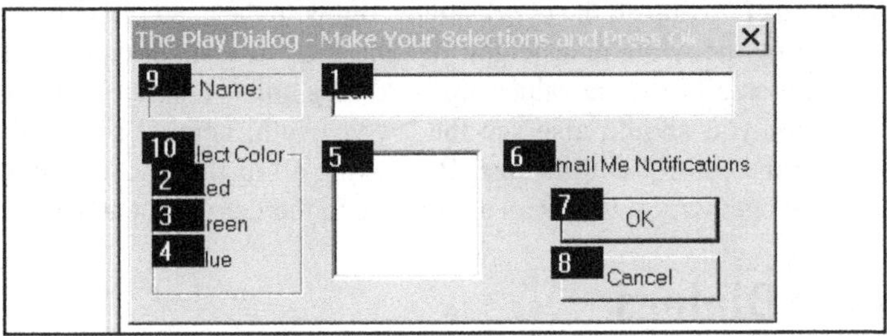

Figure 7.7 Setting the Tab Order of the Play Dialog

After you save everything, let's see what is actually stored in the text RC file. Open the RC file as text. Scroll down to the new dialog. Here is what my RC file now contains.

```
IDD_PLAY DIALOGEX 0, 0, 203, 81
STYLE DS_MODALFRAME | DS_3DLOOK | DS_CENTER | WS_POPUP | WS_CAPTION |
    WS_SYSMENU
CAPTION "The Play Dialog - Make Your Selections and Press Ok"
FONT 8, "MS Sans Serif"
BEGIN
    EDITTEXT        IDC_EDITNAME,63,4,128,14,ES_AUTOHSCROLL
    CONTROL         "Red",IDC_RADIO_RED,"Button",BS_AUTORADIOBUTTON |
                    WS_GROUP | WS_TABSTOP,9,35,29,10
    CONTROL         "Green",IDC_RADIO_GREEN,"Button",BS_AUTORADIOBUTTON |
                    WS_TABSTOP,9,46,35,10
    CONTROL         "Blue",IDC_RADIO_BLUE,"Button",BS_AUTORADIOBUTTON |
                    WS_TABSTOP,9,57,30,10
    LISTBOX         IDC_LIST_CITY,63,28,48,40,LBS_NOINTEGRALHEIGHT |
                    WS_VSCROLL | WS_TABSTOP,WS_EX_CLIENTEDGE |
                    WS_EX_STATICEDGE
    CONTROL         "Email Me Notifications",IDC_CHECK_EMAIL,"Button",
                    BS_AUTOCHECKBOX | WS_TABSTOP,121,28,75,10
    DEFPUSHBUTTON   "OK",IDOK,136,43,50,14
    PUSHBUTTON      "Cancel",IDCANCEL,136,61,50,14
    LTEXT           "Your Name:",IDC_STATIC,5,4,49,14,SS_SUNKEN
    GROUPBOX        "Select Color",IDC_STATIC,6,25,48,48
END
```

From this listing, notice that the tab order is given by the sequential placement of the control definition lines. The **EDITTEXT** control is the first entry in the dialog and first in the tab stop order. The Red radio button comes next. Thus, you can manually cut and paste these control definitions into a different order to change the tab stop order. Also notice the vitally important styles of the radio buttons, highlighted in bold face above. The first radio button in a group of radio buttons must have the **WS_GROUP** as well as **WS_TABSTOP**. All other radio buttons in the group just have **WS_TABSTOP**.

The Text Syntax of Dialogs and Controls

The dialog box definition syntax is as follows.

```
Id of dialog DIALOGEX x, y, width, height
STYLE    ORed string of WS_ DS_ styles
CAPTION  "caption for the title bar"
FONT     points, "name"
BEGIN or {
```

One can easily reset the coordinates that the dialog box pops-up at, the (x, y) values. But with the centered option, these are not actually used. However, be careful about resetting the width and height; making these too small can result in some controls being truncated or not appearing at all! Further, all of these values are in "dialog units" and not in pixels.

As you examine the syntax of the controls, you should also see the "x, y, width, height" series of numbers representing the location of the upper left corner of the control and its size. By making all of the x values of a series of controls have the same value, you are aligning them together. So this is an alternative to the Layout menu choices.

General Design Guidelines for Dialogs

There are two major dialog types: **modal** and **modeless**. A **modal** dialog is the most common. When activated, the user is only allowed to make entries in the dialog box; the rest of the application is locked out from receiving any messages until the dialog box has completed and disappears. The **MessageBox** is modal, for example. **Modeless** dialog boxes appear and stay visible on the screen until the user terminates them. Unlike a modal dialog, a modeless dialog allows the application to continue receiving and processing events. The title bar highlighting notifies the user which window has the input focus or is currently active. The Find-Replace dialogs are a familiar example. One very common usage of modeless boxes is to display some additional information often as informational boxes.

There are some dialog design guidelines that should be followed. Expect to spend some time getting your dialogs just the way that you want them to look.

Design Rule 32: Dialog Box Design Guidelines

1. Group all radio button items of which the user is to select one into a visible group box.

2. Buttons are usually on the right or bottom.

3. User entry Edit boxes and other control items should have some form of static text prompt or descriptive label.

4. If there are many entries or groups for the user to enter, the TAB key should proceed in an orderly manner from one to the next—top down, left to right.

5. Follow the industry guidelines for good screen data entry design—if in doubt, consult relevant texts on good screen design layouts.

If you discover that the Tab feature is not moving through the controls in a reasonable manner, top-down and left-right, you can use a text editor on the dialog in the RC file and cut and paste the controls into the correct order. Even better, use Layout|Tab Order. The Tab feature begins on the first control in the dialog given in the resource file and moves on down the sequence.

Programming Tip: When developing a new application with dialogs and controls, first create a basic shell and construct the shell **resource.h** and RC file, perhaps with a menu. Get this shell running. Next, construct the dialogs with the Developer Studio and adjust them with a text editor, if needed. Finally, compile the basic shell with the RC file and remove any accidental resource file errors. Only then go on to code the actual usage of the dialogs. Use a building block approach; it is easier to debug.

Implementing Dialogs: a Myriad of Choices

With the dialog resource built, the next step is to implement it in the application. And here in lies all of the complexity for there are many different MFC ways to actually handle the dialog operations. In order to grasp what and how you are going to actually implement a dialog, let's examine the fundamentals of dialog operations. To begin our discussion, assume that the dialog contains four edit controls that make up a cost record: the **itemNumber**, **quantity**, **cost**, and **description**. Further, assume that the **FrameWin** has an array of **COSTREC** structures called **costRecDataBase**. The dialog class is called **AddCostRec** and is derived from **CDialog**.

In response to a menu item, Add a Cost Record, the function **CmAddCostRecord** is called via the Message Map. To launch and execute an instance of a dialog, we code the following.

```
void FrameWin::CmAddCostRecord () {
 AddCostRec dlg (this);
 if (dlg.DoModal () == IDOK) {
 }
}
```

The **CDialog** function **DoModal** launches and executes a dialog instance returning **IDOK** if the Ok button was pressed or **IDCANCEL** if Cancel was chosen. Normally, one wishes to do further actions only if the user clicked Ok in the dialog. The above is, therefore, a very standard handling.

The **CDialog** class, while it is derived from **CWnd**, operates very differently. Instead of **OnCreate**, it uses another function to actually build the real **hwnd** of the dialog, **OnInitDialog**. In other words, the real dialog window does not exist until the call to **CDialog::OnInitDialog** returns to our derived class's **OnInitDialog**. And herein lies the major task of dialog operations—how is the necessary information or data passed back and forth between the real dialog's controls and the C++ dialog wrapper and the invoker of the dialog, **FrameWin**? Further, what if this dialog were going to update an existing record in the array. How does the caller **FrameWin** get the current record's information into the C++ wrapper and then on down into the actual real dialog controls? This mechanism is known as **data transfer** and is accomplished via one or more **transfer buffers**. Illustration 7.1 shows the complexity that must be examined.

The **FrameWin** has an area in which the new data is to be placed (Add and Update) or from which the initial values to be shown in the controls are to come (Update). Perhaps, it is the ith element of an array of **COSTREC** structures. Our dialog class has member fields to store that data, very often they are **CStrings**. The real edit controls show only character strings in them. So numerical values must somehow be converted into strings before they can be inserted into the controls. When the user clicks Ok, the strings in the real edit controls must be retrieved and moved into the dialog's fields before the base class **CDialog::OnOk** is called because when that function returns, the real dialog and controls have been destroyed.

When an Update type of dialog is to be launched, the data in the ith element of **FrameWin**'s array of **COSTREC** structures must be passed into our C++ dialog class. However, the real edit controls do not exist until later on, when **CDialog::OnInitDialog** is called. Thus, these initial values are often stored in data members of our C++ wrapper class. Then, when the real edit controls do exist, that data must be moved into the edit controls. Illustration 2 shows this process.

This transfer of data can be done in many different ways! Let's examine three of these many different approaches. One can do it manually at each step of the process, which yields maximum flexibility and control. One can do it using the MFC's built-in dynamic data transfer as implemented by the Class Wizard. One can do it the way that the Windows Common Dialogs do it. Windows provides a few common dialogs for application handling of very common actions. These common dialogs are the File-Open-Save dialog, Choose Font dialog, Find-Replace dialog, Choose Color dialog and those for File-Print and Print Setup.

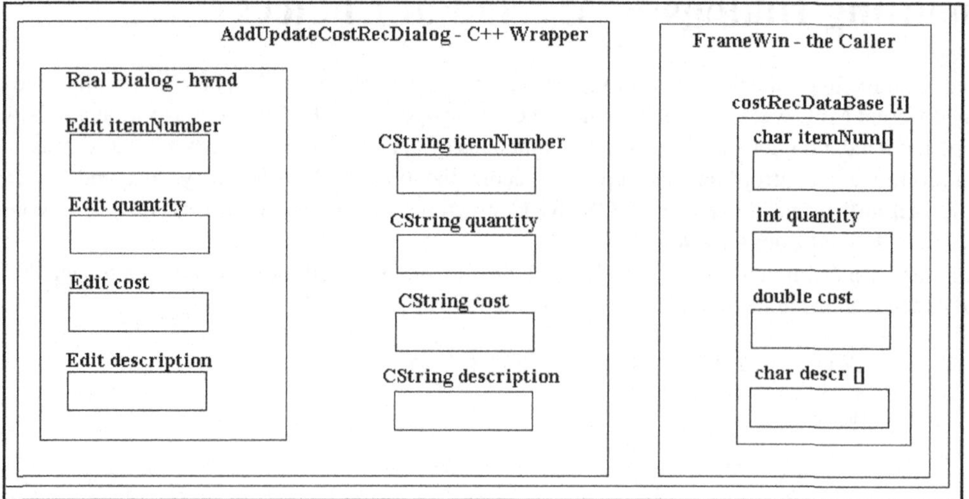

Illustration 1 The Dialog General Situation

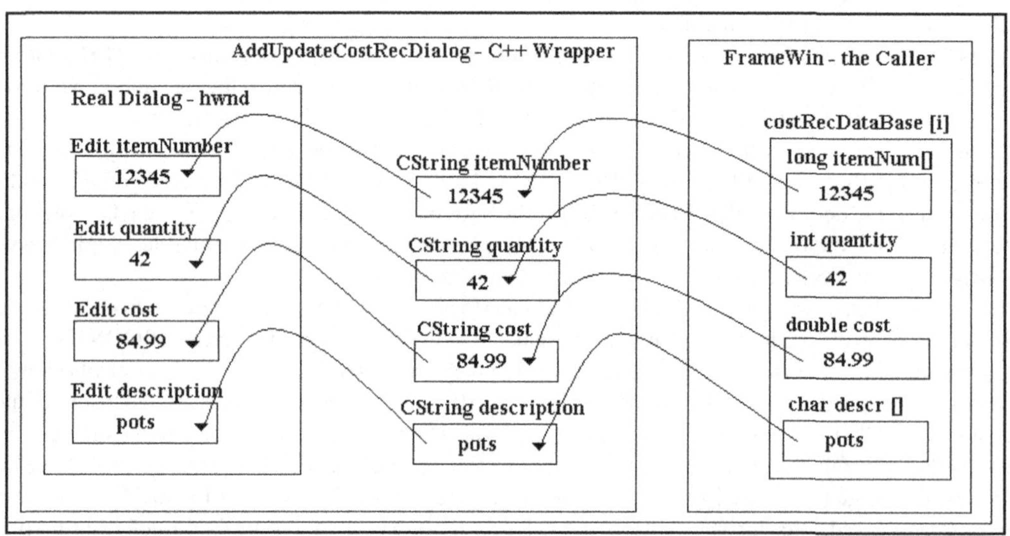

Illustration 7.2 Transferring the FrameWin's Initial Data into the Edit Controls

The First Approach is called the manual approach. It invokes the appropriate Get/Set functions for each type of control. For an Edit control, the functions are **GetDlgItemText** and **SetDlgItemText**.

```
SetDlgItemText (control's id, char* newstring);
GetDlgItemText (control's id, char* string to be filled,
                max length of string);
```

With these two functions, one can place new data into a control or retrieve a control's contents at any time that control is in existence. This method is very handy when the dialog has a couple additional buttons: Clear and Reset. Typically, the Clear button causes the entire contents of the edit controls to be cleared out. The Reset button typically resets the contents of the edit controls back to the original contents that they initially contained when the dialog was launched. When performing data entry, these are handy. If one is updating the contents of the edit controls and one has made too many goofs, pressing reset puts all the data values back to the beginning values so one can start over. Other times, it is easier to just wipe out all of the contents and type in the new values. So these are two handy buttons users like to see in dialogs.

Illustrations 7.1 and 7.2 above are not set up to handle the Reset operation. Another set of four dialog members would likely have to be defined. These would hold the original contents with which the four fields began when the dialog was launched. Either that or provide some mechanism for the dialog member functions to get access back to the **FrameWin**'s original data to be updated.

The Second Approach is to use the Class Wizard method which uses the MFC's built-in automatic data transfer method. The **CDialog** class has member functions that can transfer data from dialog member fields to and from the actual edit controls on the screen. This method, however, does not handle in any way the transfer of the data into or out of the dialog C++ class itself. We must provide means to do that step so that when the user clicks Ok, the data ends up automatically back in the **FrameWin**'s appropriate data areas.

The Third Approach that is followed by the Windows Common Dialog classes is to totally ignore the transfer of data to and from the dialog and the caller, **FrameWin**. Instead, all the data are stored in the dialog C++ wrapper in public access data areas. When **FrameWin** wishes to launch a dialog of this type, it first allocates an instance of the dialog. The **FrameWin** must copy the necessary data into the dialog's public data members and then invoke **DoModal**. When the dialog is finished, while the real edit controls are long gone, the C++ instance of the dialog class is not. So the **FrameWin** now copies the data from the public dialog members back into **FrameWin** data areas.

The Third Approach often uses the Second Approach to actually transfer the data from the dialog data members into the real edit controls and from the controls back to the data members. Realize that there are still other methods.

The beginning point centers around the MFC's method of automatic data transfer of data to the actual edit controls from the C++ data members and vice versa. The MFC **CWnd** class, from which **CDialog** is descended has a function called **DoDataExchange** that is called to handle the data transfer. It is coded like this.

```
virtual void DoDataExchange (CDataExchange *ptrdata);
void MyDlg::DoDataExchange (CDataExchange *ptrdata) {
 CDialog::DoDataExchange (ptrdata);
 ... place the macros to transfer the data here
}
```

After the call to the base class, the instance of **CDataExchange** is initialized and ready for operations. A **BOOL** data member of this class keeps track of the intended direction of data flow—from the controls to the data member (**TRUE**)or from the data members to the controls (**FALSE**). We merely pass this instance of **CDataExchange** onto the actual macros that perform the data transfer. These macros are called **DDX**es short for dynamic data exchange. Each type of control has its own particular **DDX** macro.

Text operations

```
DDX_Text (CDataExchange* pDX, int nIDC, BYTE& value);
DDX_Text (CDataExchange* pDX, int nIDC, int& value);
DDX_Text (CDataExchange* pDX, int nIDC, UINT& value);
DDX_Text (CDataExchange* pDX, int nIDC, long& value);
DDX_Text (CDataExchange* pDX, int nIDC, DWORD& value);
DDX_Text (CDataExchange* pDX, int nIDC, CString& value);
DDX_Text (CDataExchange* pDX, int nIDC, float& value);
DDX_Text (CDataExchange* pDX, int nIDC, double& value);
```

Special control types—check box, radio button, list and combo box

```
DDX_Check (CDataExchange* pDX, int nIDC, int& value);
DDX_Radio (CDataExchange* pDX, int nIDC, int& value);
DDX_LBString (CDataExchange* pDX, int nIDC, CString& value);
DDX_CBString (CDataExchange* pDX, int nIDC, CString& value);
DDX_LBIndex (CDataExchange* pDX, int nIDC, int& index);
DDX_CBIndex (CDataExchange* pDX, int nIDC, int& index);
DDX_LBStringExact (CDataExchange* pDX, int nIDC,
                   CString& value);
DDX_CBStringExact (CDataExchange* pDX, int nIDC,
                   CString& value);
DDX_Scroll (CDataExchange* pDX, int nIDC, int& value);
```

Getting a pointer to the actual control's window

```
DDX_Control (CDataExchange* pDX, int nIDC, CWnd& rControl);
```

For edit controls, we may use any of the Text **DDX** versions. The most common one is the **CString** one. Remember that all text in the real edit control is character string data. So it makes sense for the transfer buffer in the dialog class to be a **CString**.

```
DDX_Text (CDataExchange* pDX, int nIDC, CString& value);
```

Here, the **nIDC** is the id for the specific edit control in question and the **value** is our dialog's data member. Based upon whether it is saving the control's values into the data members (**TRUE**) or whether it is updating the control's contents from the data members (**FALSE**), the **DDX** does the data transfer.

Another **CWnd** function calls **DoDataExchange** passing it the current request. That function is called **UpdateData**. It takes a **BOOL** indicating the direction of the data transfer which defaults to **TRUE**, meaning to transfer the data from the controls into the class member fields.

```
BOOL UpdateData (BOOL saveAndValidate = TRUE);
```

We may call this function anytime that we wish to transfer the data.

However, **CDialog** calls **UpdateData** from two locations. When the user clicks on the Ok button, **OnOk** is called. One of the steps within the default implementation of **OnOk** is to call **UpdateData (TRUE)**. Further, in **CDialog::OnInitDialog**, once the real dialog controls have been created, **UpdateData (FALSE)** is called.

So what must we code in our **CDialog** derived class in order for this mechanism to function properly? We must define member fields of the correct data type to match what the control's **DDX** macro expects, such as a **CString** for an edit control. We must override the **DoDataExchange** function in our class and insert the correct **DDX** macros that tie each edit control to its corresponding data member in our class. Additionally, in the constructor, these data members must be initialized to their starting values. The starting values can be null strings for an Add Record dialog or the existing data that we wish to present in an Update Record dialog.

These steps are indeed fairly simple to implement manually. However, the Class Wizard does a terrific job of setting all this up for us. So it is now time to learn how to use the Class Wizard with our dialogs.

Using Class Wizard to Create and Maintain Our CDialog Classes

Go ahead and make yourself a play dialog similar to the one I did above in Figure 7.6. Then you can follow along with this discussion step by step.

With the new dialog completed in the resource editor and with your screen appearing as shown in Figure 7.6, launch the Class Wizard by double clicking in the dialog, but not on a control. You should see the Welcome to the MFC Class Wizard dialog as shown in Figure 7-7.

Our objective is to have the Class Wizard build us a shell dialog class wrapped around our new dialog. The Class Wizard makes a derived class from **CDialog**.

We can pick what base class is desired, but with a dialog, there is only one real choice, naturally.

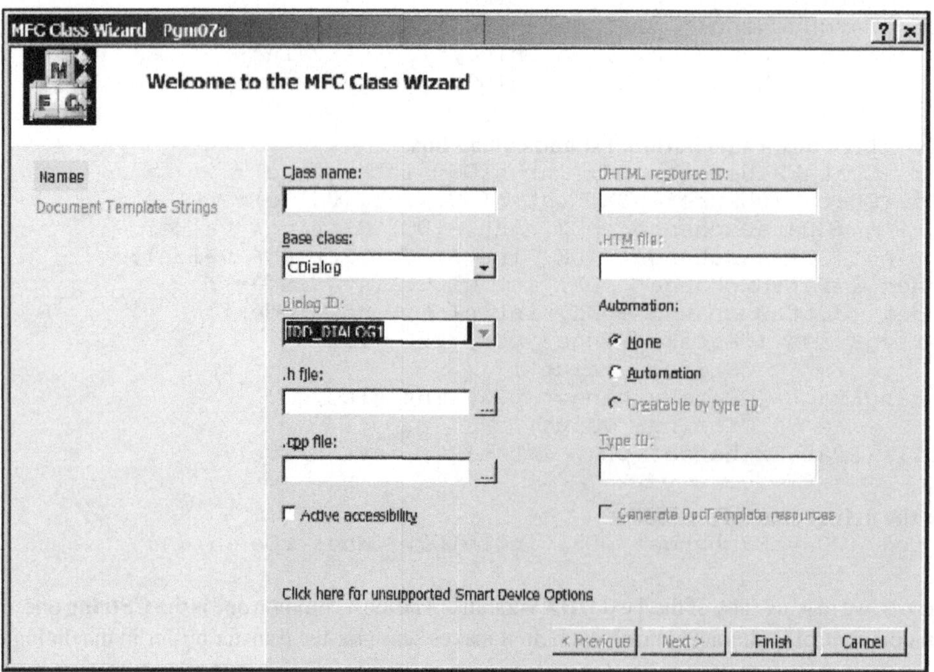

Figure 7-7 The Class Wizard Opening Dialog for Our New Dialog

Notice that the Class Wizard immediately discovers that this dialog we just double clicked upon and it does not yet have a C++ class wrapped around it and asks you to fill in the details for the new **CDialog** derived class. Enter a Class name and alter the names of the h and cpp files, if desired. In the above figure, I had to make another dummy dialog because Play already existed in this project. You should see **IDD_PLAY** as yours, if you are re-creating this example. Notice that the Class Wizard has already preselected **CDialog** as the base class and has also tied this new class to the dialog by using its id **IDD_PLAY**. I entered **PlayDialog** for the new class name. When all is as you desire, click Finish. The new class header and cpp file are built. Now we need to tie the dialog controls to data members of our new class.

In the dialog window, right click on the specific control that needs to be tied into our class and choose Add Variable. Often a control can be tied to a variable, other times, it must be tied to an instance of that control class. For example, with an edit control, the contents of that control could be tied to a **CString** class variable or it could be bound to an instance of the control class **CEdit**. This is the first decision to be made, will the variable be a control class instance or will it be a data member such as an int or string. A list box ought to be tied to an instance of a **CListBox** control, but an edit control can be done either way.

In Figure 7-8, I have right clicked on the edit control and chosen to add a new variable for it. The figure shows the Add Variable dialog.

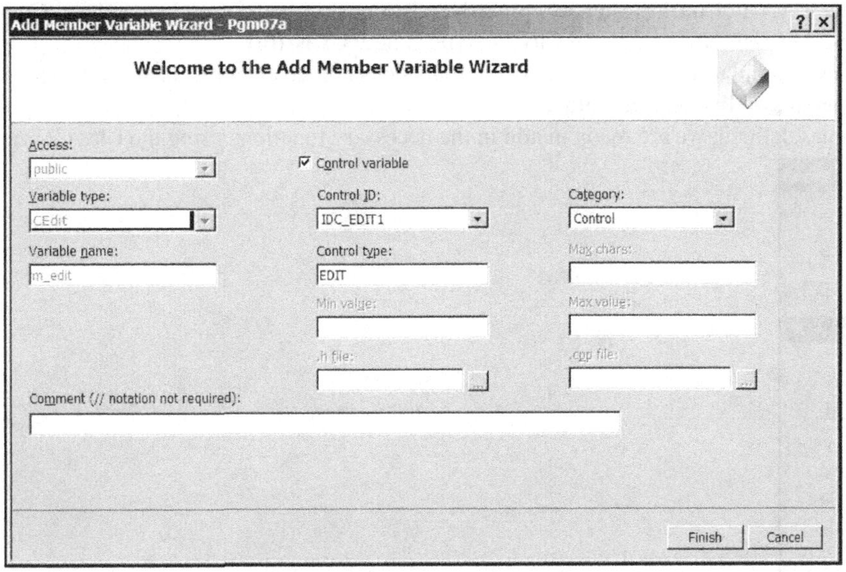

Figure 7-8 Add Variable Dialog for an Edit Control

The default is to add a control class variable, in this case **CEdit**. If a control class is used for an edit control, then you will need to transfer the data into and out of the control. If a **CString** or a number such as an int or double is used, the framework handles the data transfer for you. In the case of an edit control, often it is very convenient to let the framework transfer the data to and from our string or number field. To add a string or number instead of a **CEdit** control, uncheck the Control Variable setting.

Now the Variable type combobox operates. When you click on the arrow and open up the combobox of choices, you have all the supported types, such as a bool, char, int, double. However, the most important one, a string, specifically a **CString** has been omitted! Here is where you can make the transfer buffer a numerical type. However, if you really want a string, then re-check the Control check box and to its right change Category to Value. Now in the Variable type the **CString** appears, along with a number of other possibilities.

Let's examine the variables I added for the Play Dialog. First, in order to keep these critical transfer buffer variables separate from any other class member variables, I usually prefix them with m_ for member. This scheme is used in all the MFC classes for members of a class variable names. If you prefix all of your class member variables with m_, then you cannot tell at a glance which are the key transfer buffers for the controls and which are other ordinary class member variables. Hence, I only use the m_ for controls and their transfer buffers.

In the Play Dialog, I tied the Name edit control, **IDC_EDIT_NAME**, to Enter the name you wish for this variable. I called mine **m_name**. The category defaults to Value which is what we want. Click on the Variable Type combo box. Examine all of the possibilities. Notice that each of these are the exact same data types that were in the text **DDX** macros shown a few pages ago. Since this edit control is to store a person's name, we really do want **CString**.

When you click Ok, notice that now the selected line shows not only the **IDC_EDITNAME**, but also **CString** and

m_name. Further, since this is a string, at the bottom of the window a Maximum Chars edit control has appeared. Here you can limit the total number of characters that this field could contain. It does not count the null terminator.

Next, select the id you entered for the Send Email check box; I used **IDC_CHECK_EMAIL** and click on Add Variable. Notice this time the variable is of type **BOOL**. Enter a name for this variable. I used **m_email**. Click Ok. The transfer buffer for a check box is a **BOOL**. When it is **TRUE**, the check appears. When it is **FALSE**, it is unchecked.

Now select the id for the radio button. Notice that only the id of the first radio button of the group is shown. Then, choose Add Variable. This time, notice that the variable type is **int**. I called this variable **m_color**. The transfer buffer is an **int** which contains the zero-based offset of the radio button that is selected. If the **int** contains 0, then the first radio button of the group is selected. If the **int** contains 2, then it is the third radio button that is on in the group.

Finally, select the id for the list box and choose add variable. The data type is **int** which represents the zero-based index of which string in the list box the user has selected. However, with list boxes, we do not want this as the variable type. Why? There are no strings in the list box as yet. We are going to have to add in those strings. Here comes the catch-22. We must add in the strings into the list box. So the real list box must exist. But the real list box does not exist when the constructor for the dialog class executes. The real list box only comes into existence when the **CDialog::OnInitDialog** function call has finished. So we must add our desired strings into the list box in our derived class's **OnInitDialog** after the base class finishes creation of the real dialog and its controls. This means, that we must dynamically get a pointer to this list box. However, there is an easier way. Click on the Category combo box. Notice that there is another choice—Control. Select Control and enter a name; I used **m_list**. Notice that the variable type is now **CListBox**.

Your view should now be similar to Figure 7.9 below. If yours does not, go ahead and make any needed changes. You should see **m_color**, **m_email**, **m_list**, and **m_name**.

With all of the variables defined, we are ready to add in the necessary functions using the Class Wizard.

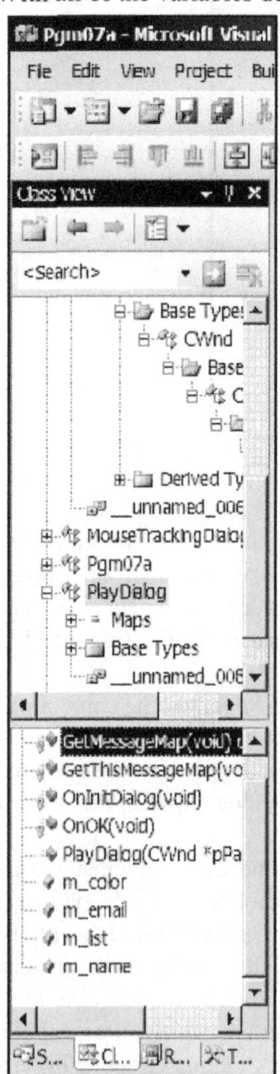

Figure 7-9

In Class View and the PlayDialog class selected, you should also see what member functions have already been added. Specifically, **DoDataExchange** has been automatically added. It handles the automatic coupling of our members with the corresponding control.

However, there are usually a number of other functions that must be overridden. Some of these may be ordinary window messages, such as **WM_SIZE**, for example. Others are virtual functions that do not correspond to the usual message mapping functions. In Class View, right click on the PlayDialog and choose Properties. You should see a very special version of the properties window as shown in Figure 7-10 below. Here, I added a dummy class called Fun. The key thing to notice is the highlighted square box second from the right in the Properties view. This represents functions of **CDialog** that can be overridden. Here I have overridden **OnInitDialog**, a virtual function that is often overridden.

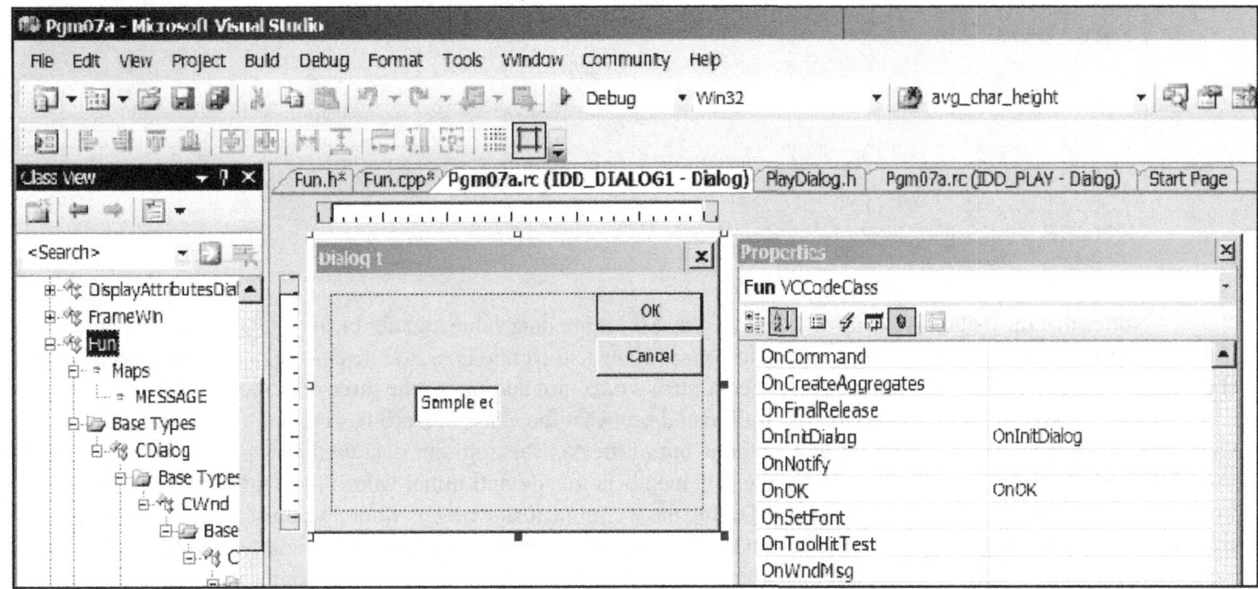

Figure 7-10 The Properties Window in Which Functions Can Be Overridden

The lightening bolt icon represents events, such as a button click, that we can respond to by adding a function to do so, while the icon to its right and just to the left of the override functions represents all of the window messages that we can respond to, again by providing a function. If the function or message that you need to override is in these lists, the Class Wizard can provide it for you. Scroll down the list of possibilities in both categories to get a feeling for what is here. Notice that the Class Wizard only knows about a very tiny fraction of the total number of member functions that are available in a **CWnd** derived class. The Class Wizard can only be used to add or remove functions from within these subsets. If we need a function not in this subset, we must add it manually ourselves. This is the limitation of the Class Wizard.

Scroll down to **WM_INITDIALOG**, select it, and choose Add Function. The Class Wizard immediately adds this function as shown in the bottom left list box labeled Member Functions. With this function, there is no choice in function name because we are overriding an existing member function of **CDialog**.

Finally, find the **IDOK** item in the left side Object Ids list box. Select it. Notice that since it is a button, there are two possibilities that we can respond to: a button click and a button double click. Select the button click and choose Add Function. We need to override this function in order to develop a way to get the data from our dialog class member variable back into the caller's data area(s), **FrameWin** in this case. Notice that this time, you get to provide the name of the function that is called when the Ok button is pressed. The Class Wizard assumes that you will follow the normal naming convention and makes its suggestion for a reasonable name based upon the id of the control. **OnOk** is fine with me, so I clicked Ok. At this point your screen should appear similar to Figure 7.9 above, specifically a function for **OnOk** and for **OnInitDialog**.

If all is okay, now press the Edit Code button. This closes the Class Wizard and Visual Studio now opens the new cpp file we just created with the Class Wizard. Open the **PlayDialog.h** header file. Here is what mine contains.

```
#pragma once
#include "afxwin.h"
#include "resource.h"
// PlayDialog.h : header file
//
/////////////////////////////////////////////////////////////////////////////
// PlayDialog dialog
```

```
class PlayDialog : public CDialog {
// Construction
public:
      PlayDialog(CWnd* pParent = NULL);    // standard constructor
// Dialog Data
      enum { IDD = IDD_PLAY };
      CListBox    m_list;
      CString     m_name;
      BOOL      m_email;
      int         m_color;
// Overrides
      protected:
      virtual void DoDataExchange(CDataExchange* pDX);
// Implementation
protected:
      // Generated message map functions
      virtual BOOL OnInitDialog();
      virtual void OnOK();
      DECLARE_MESSAGE_MAP()
};
```

Notice that the listbox is a control, while the other three are data value transfer buffers. One uses member functions of the **CListBox** class to add the strings that are to appear in the listbox and later, to retrieve the one that has been selected. The dynamic data exchange will transfer the other control's data into and out of the three data members.

Now look at the actual **PlayDialog.cpp** file and see what the Class Wizard has created for us. We actually have a working dialog class that will transfer data into and out of the controls into our data members—well, all except that list box. Notice that the constructor is initializing the data members to a default initial value. The **DoDataExchange** function provides all of the **DDX** macros needed. **OnInitDialog** has a comment showing us where we must add in our coding to add in the strings into the list box. And finally, in **OnOk**, the comments tell us to insert our extra coding before calling the base class **OnOk** function. Here is the location in which we must somehow transfer the data in our data members back to the caller's data areas.

```
// PlayDialog.cpp : implementation file
//
#include "stdafx.h"
#include "pgm07a.h"
#include "PlayDialog.h"
#include "resource.h"
/////////////////////////////////////////////////////////////////////////////
// PlayDialog dialog
PlayDialog::PlayDialog(CWnd* pParent /*=NULL*/)
      : CDialog(PlayDialog::IDD, pParent) {
      m_name = _T("");
      m_email = FALSE;
      m_color = -1;
}

void PlayDialog::DoDataExchange(CDataExchange* pDX) {
      CDialog::DoDataExchange(pDX);
      DDX_Control(pDX, IDC_LIST_CITY, m_list);
      DDX_Text(pDX, IDC_EDITNAME, m_name);
      DDX_Check(pDX, IDC_CHECK_EMAIL, m_email);
}

BEGIN_MESSAGE_MAP(PlayDialog, CDialog)
END_MESSAGE_MAP()
/////////////////////////////////////////////////////////////////////////////
// PlayDialog message handlers
BOOL PlayDialog::OnInitDialog() {
      Cdialog::OnInitDialog();
      // insert our initialization here
      return TRUE;  // return TRUE unless you set the focus to a control
                    // EXCEPTION: OCX Property Pages should return FALSE
```

```
}
void PlayDialog::OnOK() {
      // TODO: Add extra validation here
      CDialog::OnOK();
}
```

Transferring Data from Dialog Data Members to the Caller's Data Members

Okay. We have the first problem solved easily by using the automatic **DDX** transfer mechanism. Data now can flow smoothly between the C++ data members and the real controls of the dialog on the screen. But we still have not addressed the second issue of how does the caller of the dialog get initial values into those C++ members and how do the results get back into the caller's answer areas. Remember that we are going to examine three approaches to dialogs.

The Third Approach in which all of the dialog's data members are public access is the simplest from the view point of the dialog class. Notice in the above **PlayDialog.h** class definition that the Class Wizard built for us, all of the transfer data members have been made public access. Thus, if we were going to implement the **PlayDialog** using the Third Approach, we are done with the dialog coding! All further actions occur in the caller function. When we allocate an instance of the dialog class, the C++ data members are ready for action. The actual real dialog controls, however, are not yet in existence because **DoModal** has not been called which means that **OnInitDialog** has not yet been called.

Further, once **DoModal** has returned with either an **IDOK** or **IDCANCEL**, though the real dialog controls no longer exist, the C++ class still does exist. The following represents how all of the data can be handled—that is, all except the list box strings. Let's look at the **FrameWin** coding for an Update Record type function in which the dialog data members must be given their initial values which are not nulls. In this case, assume **PlayDialog** needs to be passed the initial name and other values. Further, assume that there are many sets of Play data stored in an array of PLAY structures. The PLAY structure is defined this way.

```
enum Color {Red, Green, Blue};
struct PLAY {
 char name[100];
 bool email;
 Color color;
 ...
};
// these two are protected data members of FrameWin
PLAY play[1000]; // the array of Play data
int thisOne;     // index to the current one to be updated
void FrameWin::CmPlayDialog () {
 PlayDialog dlg (this);
 // copy all need data into dialog data members
 dlg.m_name = play[thisOne].name;
 dlg.m_email = play[thisOne].email ? TRUE : FALSE;
 dlg.m_color = (int) play[thisOne].color;
 // ignore list box for now
 if (dlg.DoModal () == IDOK) {
  // copy all data from dialog members into answer area
  play[thisOne].email = dlg.m_email ? true : false;
  play[thisOne].color = (Color) dlg.m_color;
  if (dlg.m_name.GetLength() > 49) {
   // oops
   strncpy (play[thisOne].name, dlg.m_name, 49);
   play[thisOne].name[49] = 0;
  }
  else strcpy (play[thisOne].name, dlg.m_name);
  Invalidate (); // update the screen perhaps
 }
}
```

This method is straightforward, but causes a lot of coding to occur in this function. Imagine what would be in this function's body if there were a dozen data items that needed transferring? This is the drawback of the Third Approach, the caller has to do a lot of coding and the caller must know the exact dialog member variables and their data types and their possible values and ranges and so on. In other words, the dialog is not such a black box any more from an OOP point of view.

The Second Approach migrates this coding into the dialog itself so that the internal workings of the dialog are not being exposed. However, the dialog must have access to a transfer buffer that initially contains the data to be loaded into the controls and which contains the results after Ok is pressed. Note that if Cancel is pressed, this transfer buffer is not updated. In the **OnOk** function, the dialog must have access to the caller's transfer buffer. This generally means that the dialog constructor must be passed a pointer to the caller's transfer buffer or a reference to it. Further, the constructor must then save that pointer in a protected data member so that it is available in **OnInitDialog** (to be able to initialize list boxes) and **OnOk**.

Good design dictates that the **PLAY** structure definition with its **enum** is contained in a separate header file and not in the **FrameWin.h**. Thus, the **PlayDialog** must now include **Play.h** to get access to the structure definition. Here is how the **PlayDialog** class is invoked and how it can be modified for the Second Approach.

```
void FrameWin::CmPlayDialog () {
 PlayDialog dlg (this);
 if (dlg.DoModal () == IDOK) {
  // here play[thisOne] contains the data
  Invalidate ();
 }
}
PlayDialog::PlayDialog (PLAY* ptrp, CWnd* pParent /*=NULL*/)
    : CDialog(PlayDialog::IDD, pParent) {
 m_name = _T("");
 m_email = FALSE;
 m_color = -1;
 ptrplay = ptrp;
 m_name = ptrp->name;
 m_email = ptrp->email ? TRUE : FALSE;
 m_color = (int) ptrp->color;
}
void PlayDialog::OnOK() {
 UpdateData (TRUE); // transfer controls to members
 ptrplay->email = m_email ? true : false;
 ptrplay->color = (Color) m_color;
 if (m_name.GetLength() > 49) {
   strncpy (ptrplay->name, m_name, 49);
   ptrplay->name[49] = 0;
  }
  else strcpy (ptrplay->name, m_name);
 }
 CDialog::OnOK();
}
```

What about situations in which there are only a few simple incoming data fields from **FrameWin**? One could pass the address of each of these to the constructor and have it store a pointer to each item for later use. What about situations in which there are a lot of data members to be transferred to the dialog, perhaps several different structures and even some items that are not part of any structure? In this case, I usually make up a **XFER** structure that contains an instance of everything that needs to be passed, fill it up in the **FrameWin** and pass its address to the dialog. That way, the dialog does not have to store lots of pointers for use in **OnOk**.

In summary, you are going to see both the Second Approach and the Third Approach in widespread use. They are very common. However, you are also likely to see the manual approach also used. So now that we understand the basics of the automatic approaches, let's see how the manual method operates.

The First Approach also must have ways and means of gaining access to the caller's initial data items and a way to store the results back into the caller's answer or transfer buffer. Thus, the data variable must still be defined as they are already in **PlayDialog**. All that changes is there is no **DoDataExchange** function.

```
PlayDialog::PlayDialog (PLAY* ptrp, CWnd* pParent /*=NULL*/)
    : CDialog(PlayDialog::IDD, pParent) {
 ptrplay = ptrp;
 m_name = ptrp->name;
```

```
  m_email = ptrp->email ? TRUE : FALSE;
  m_color = (int) ptrp->color;
 }
 BOOL PlayDialog::OnInitDialog() {
  CDialog::OnInitDialog();
  SetDlgItemText (IDC_EDITNAME, m_name);
or
  SetDlgItemText (IDC_EDITNAME, ptrplay->name);
  ...
  return TRUE;
 }
 void PlayDialog::OnOK() {
  GetDlgItemText (IDC_EDITNAME, ptrplay->name);
  ...
  CDialog::OnOK();
 }
```

When using the manual approach, once the pointer to the caller's transfer buffer is saved, there really is no need, necessarily, to have member data fields because you can transfer directly to and from the caller's buffer. However, you do need to figure out how to manually set each different type of control. Each has a different set of functions to get/set the data in the control.

Okay. So much for "playing" around. We should get some real coding done. So let's examine the dialogs and actions of **Pgm07a** which illustrates these many points and also how to deal with list boxes.

Pgm07a Dialogs to Control Window Actions

In this program, I have implemented an icon to represent the application, one that resembles a tree. I have created a "tree" cursor that looks horrible. Thus, one action the user likely desires at once is the ability to switch back to using the good old arrow cursor. So one dialog box controls switching between the arrow and the tree cursor.

Next, there is a dialog to permit the user to enter their first and last name. The screen display can show which cursor is in use along with the name of the user. However, there is a dialog box that the user can invoke that handles toggling the display of which kind of cursor is in use off and on. The user's name is always visible. But the additional line identifying the cursor is under the user's control.

Next, on which line in the window does the user's name appear? Well actually, I display three lines: a heading line, a blank line, and the user's first and last names. The size of the window at any point in processing dictates the available lines. If the window's height is small, there are only a few lines possible. If the height is large, the name could be on a large number of lines. Thus, a dialog with a list box that shows all available lines permits the user to choose on which line the name is to be displayed.

There is also a simple Help-About dialog which identifies the author of the program. And finally, the user can launch a modeless dialog that tracks mouse cursor locations.

I created these dialogs using many different dialog styles so you can see a variety of appearances. The next series of six figures shows what all of these dialogs look like.

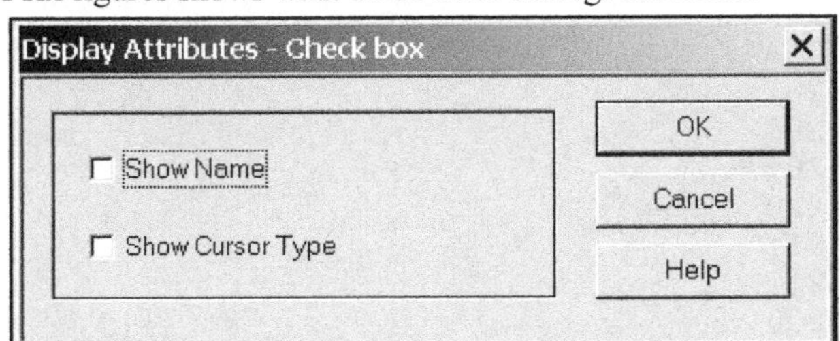

Figure 7.18 The Check Box Show Dialog

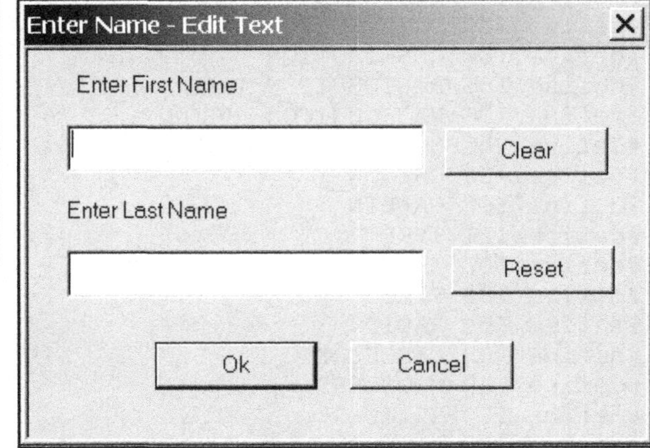

Figure 7.17 The Edit Names Dialog

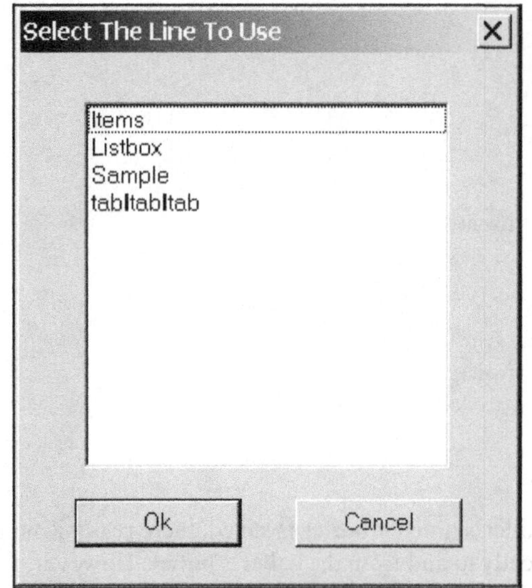

Figure 7.16 The List Box Dialog

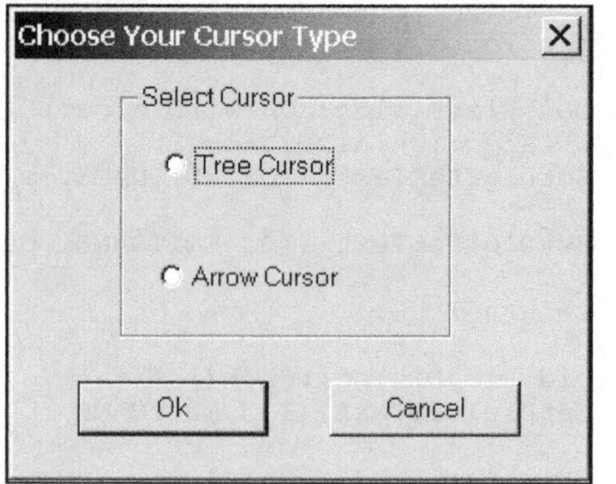

Figure 7.19 The Choose Cursor Dialog

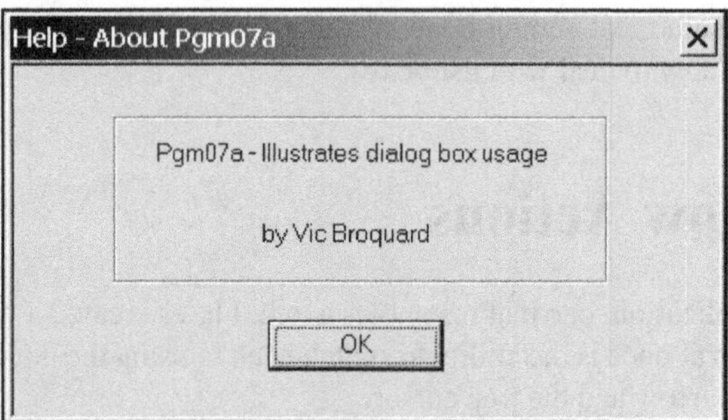

Figure 7.20 The Help About Dialog

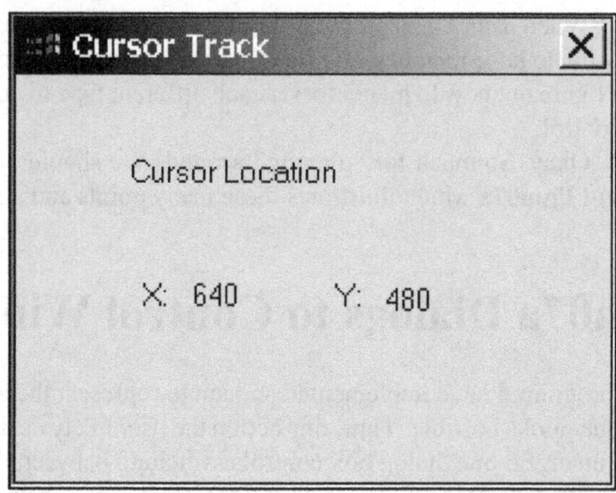

Figure 7.21 The Cursor Location Dialog

Here are the relevant portions of the **resource.h** and RC files.

```
#define CM_CURSOR_DLG                101
#define CM_NAME_DLG                  102
#define CM_ITEM_DLG                  103
#define CM_LINE_DLG                  104
#define CM_LOCATION_DLG              105
#define CM_ABOUT                     106
#define IDC_LISTBOX                  201
#define IDC_CHECK_NAME               202
#define IDC_CHECK_CURSOR             203
#define IDC_FIRSTNAME                204
#define IDC_LASTNAME                 205
#define IDC_CLEARBUTTON              206
#define IDC_RESETBUTTON              207
#define IDC_RADIOBUTTON_TREE         208
#define IDC_RADIOBUTTON_ARROW        209
#define IDC_CURSOR_X                 210
#define IDC_CURSOR_Y                 211
#define IDC_GRPBTN                   212
#define IDI_TREE                     300
#define IDC_TREE                     301
#define IDD_PLAY                     401
#define IDD_RADIO                    501
#define IDD_CHECKBOX                 502
#define IDD_MODELESS                 503
#define IDD_EDITDLG                  504
#define IDD_LISTBOX                  505
#define IDC_EDITNAME                 1000
```

```
#define IDC_RADIO_RED                    1001
#define IDC_RADIO_GREEN                  1002
#define IDC_RADIO_BLUE                   1003
#define IDC_LIST_CITY                    1005
#define IDC_CHECK_EMAIL                  1006
#define IDS_MAINTITLE                    2000
#define IDS_WINNAME                      2001
#define IDS_MSG_QUIT                     2002
#define IDS_MSG_QUERY                    2003
#define IDS_ISTREE                       2004
#define IDS_ISARROW                      2005
#define IDS_NAMEID                       2006
#define IDS_LINEMSG                      2007

/////////////////////////////////////////////////////////////////////////////
//
// Menu
//
MAINMENU MENU DISCARDABLE
BEGIN
    POPUP "&Dialogs"
    BEGIN
        MENUITEM "Choose &Cursor",              CM_CURSOR_DLG
        MENUITEM "Enter &Name",                 CM_NAME_DLG
        MENUITEM "Set &Display Items",          CM_ITEM_DLG
        MENUITEM "Choose Display &Line",        CM_LINE_DLG
        MENUITEM "Show &Location of Cursor",    CM_LOCATION_DLG
    END
    POPUP "&Help"
    BEGIN
        MENUITEM "Help &About",                 CM_ABOUT
    END
END

/////////////////////////////////////////////////////////////////////////////
//
// Dialog
//
IDD_EDITDLG DIALOGEX 23, 81, 189, 114
STYLE DS_MODALFRAME | WS_POPUP | WS_VISIBLE | WS_CAPTION | WS_SYSMENU
EXSTYLE WS_EX_CLIENTEDGE | WS_EX_STATICEDGE
CAPTION "Enter Name - Edit Text"
FONT 8, "MS Sans Serif"
BEGIN
    EDITTEXT        IDC_FIRSTNAME,12,22,110,14
    EDITTEXT        IDC_LASTNAME,12,59,110,14
    PUSHBUTTON      "Ok",IDOK,39,86,50,14
    PUSHBUTTON      "Clear",IDC_CLEARBUTTON,128,23,50,14
    PUSHBUTTON      "Reset",IDC_RESETBUTTON,130,58,50,14
    PUSHBUTTON      "Cancel",IDCANCEL,99,86,50,14
    CTEXT           "Enter First Name",-1,12,6,56,10
    LTEXT           "Enter Last Name",-1,12,43,56,10
END
IDD_ABOUT DIALOGEX 48, 113, 200, 96
STYLE DS_MODALFRAME | DS_3DLOOK | DS_CENTER | WS_POPUP | WS_VISIBLE |
    WS_CAPTION | WS_SYSMENU
EXSTYLE WS_EX_CLIENTEDGE | WS_EX_STATICEDGE
CAPTION "Help - About Pgm07a"
FONT 8, "MS Sans Serif"
BEGIN
    DEFPUSHBUTTON   "OK",IDOK,72,70,50,14
    LTEXT           "by Vic Broquard",IDC_STATIC,70,42,57,8
    LTEXT          "Pgm07a - Illustrates dialog box usage",IDC_STATIC,
                    40,20,128,11
```

```
    GROUPBOX         "",IDC_STATIC,28,10,141,50
END
IDD_RADIO DIALOGEX 34, 29, 150, 106
STYLE DS_MODALFRAME | WS_POPUP | WS_CLIPSIBLINGS | WS_CAPTION | WS_SYSMENU
EXSTYLE WS_EX_STATICEDGE
CAPTION "Choose Your Cursor Type"
FONT 8, "MS Sans Serif"
BEGIN
    CONTROL          "Tree Cursor",IDC_RADIOBUTTON_TREE,"Button",
                BS_AUTORADIOBUTTON | WS_GROUP | WS_TABSTOP,39,22,62,10
    CONTROL          "Arrow Cursor",IDC_RADIOBUTTON_ARROW,"Button",
                     BS_AUTORADIOBUTTON | WS_TABSTOP,38,48,66,15
    PUSHBUTTON       "Ok",IDOK,17,82,50,14
    PUSHBUTTON       "Cancel",IDCANCEL,83,82,50,14
    GROUPBOX         "Select Cursor",IDC_GRPBTN,28,5,87,66,WS_GROUP
END
IDD_CHECKBOX DIALOGEX 32, 94, 207, 66
STYLE DS_MODALFRAME | DS_3DLOOK | DS_CENTER | WS_POPUP | WS_VISIBLE |
    WS_CAPTION | WS_SYSMENU
EXSTYLE WS_EX_CLIENTEDGE
CAPTION "Display Attributes - Check box"
FONT 8, "MS Sans Serif"
BEGIN
    CONTROL          "Show Name",IDC_CHECK_NAME,"Button",
                     BS_AUTOCHECKBOX | WS_TABSTOP,17,16,61,14
    CONTROL          "Show Cursor Type",IDC_CHECK_CURSOR,"Button",
                     BS_AUTOCHECKBOX | WS_TABSTOP,17,35,79,15
    DEFPUSHBUTTON    "OK",IDOK,148,6,50,14
    PUSHBUTTON       "Cancel",IDCANCEL,148,24,50,14
    PUSHBUTTON       "Help",ID_HELP,148,42,50,14
    CONTROL         "",-1,"Static",SS_BLACKFRAME | SS_SUNKEN,7,8,131,48
END
IDD_MODELESS DIALOGEX 34, 51, 134, 89
STYLE DS_3DLOOK | WS_POPUP | WS_VISIBLE | WS_CAPTION | WS_SYSMENU
EXSTYLE WS_EX_STATICEDGE
CAPTION "Cursor Track"
FONT 8, "MS Sans Serif"
BEGIN
    CONTROL          "Cursor Location",-1,"Static",SS_SIMPLE,26,17,56,9
    LTEXT            "X:",-1,29,44,9,9,NOT WS_GROUP
    LTEXT            "640",IDC_CURSOR_X,40,44,25,9,NOT WS_GROUP
    LTEXT            "Y:",-1,72,44,8,8,NOT WS_GROUP
    LTEXT            "480",IDC_CURSOR_Y,83,45,16,8,NOT WS_GROUP
END
IDD_LISTBOX DIALOG DISCARDABLE  20, 38, 148, 153
STYLE DS_MODALFRAME | WS_POPUP | WS_VISIBLE | WS_CAPTION | WS_SYSMENU
CAPTION "Select The Line To Use"
FONT 8, "MS Sans Serif"
BEGIN
    LISTBOX          IDC_LISTBOX,19,14,109,106,LBS_SORT |
                     LBS_NOINTEGRALHEIGHT | WS_VSCROLL | WS_TABSTOP
    PUSHBUTTON       "Ok",IDOK,16,129,50,14
    PUSHBUTTON       "Cancel",IDCANCEL,82,129,50,14
END
/////////////////////////////////////////////////////////////////////////////
//
// Icon
//
// Icon with lowest ID value placed first to ensure application icon
// remains consistent on all systems.
IDI_TREE                ICON    DISCARDABLE     "TREES.ICO"
/////////////////////////////////////////////////////////////////////////////
//
// Cursor
```

```
//
IDC_TREE                    CURSOR   DISCARDABLE     "TREE.CUR"
/////////////////////////////////////////////////////////////////////////////
//
// String Table
//
STRINGTABLE DISCARDABLE
BEGIN
    IDS_MAINTITLE              "Resources and Dialogs - MFC style"
    IDS_WINNAME                "ResourcesPgm"
    IDS_MSG_QUIT               "Do you want to quit the application?"
    IDS_MSG_QUERY              "Query?"
    IDS_ISTREE                 "The cursor is the TREE cursor."
    IDS_ISARROW                "The cursor is the ARROW cursor."
    IDS_NAMEID                 "First Name  and  Last Name"
    IDS_LINEMSG                "Line %02d"
END
```

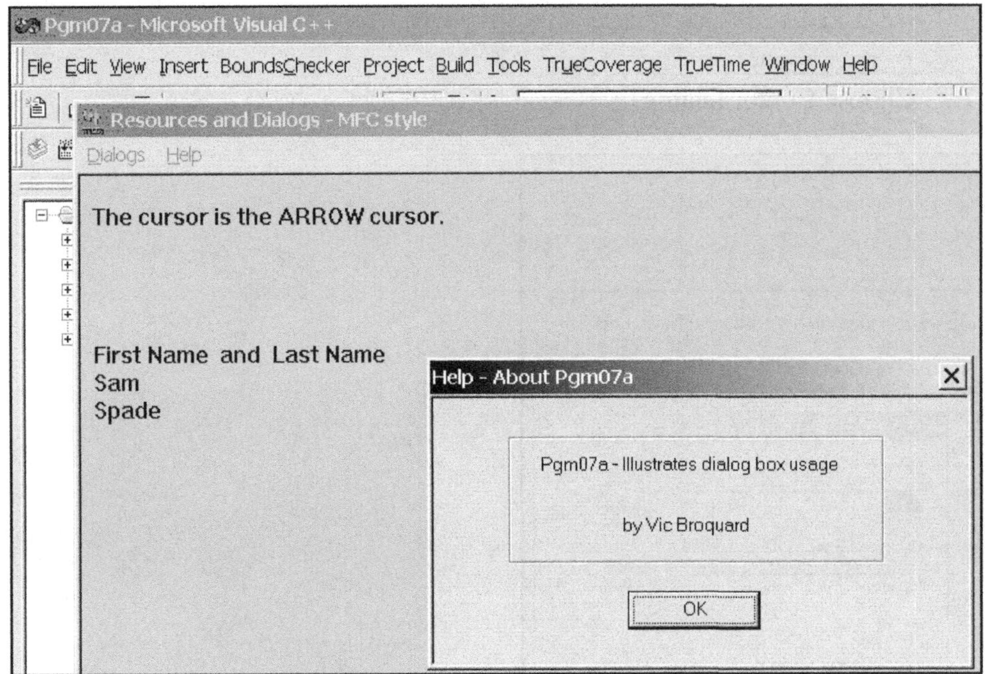

Figure 7.22 Help About Dialog

Next, since I used various dialog styles and options (3D and Centered), let's see how these dialogs actually appear when the program is run. Help About shown in Figure 7.22 is 3D and centered using both the Client and Static edges. Notice that it is centered on the screen, not the application.

The Choose Cursor dialog shown in Figure 7.23 uses a Static Edge and is not centered. The Choose User Name dialog shown in Figure 7.24 uses both a Static and Client Edge.

The Choose Display Attributes Dialog shown in Figure 7.25 has a Client edge, is centered, and is 3D.

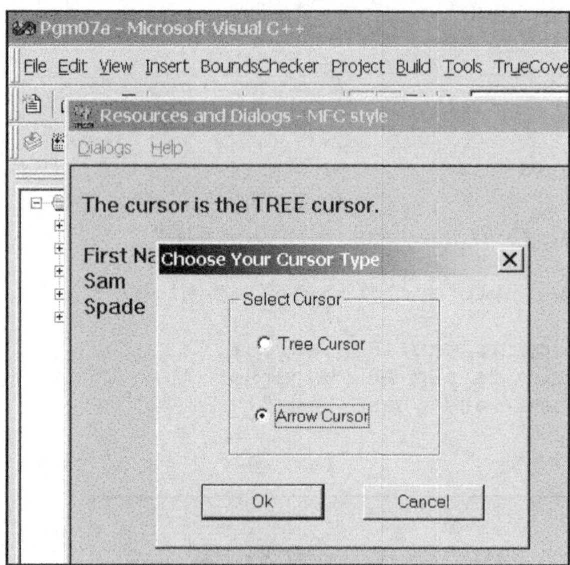

Figure 7.23 Choose Cursor Dialog

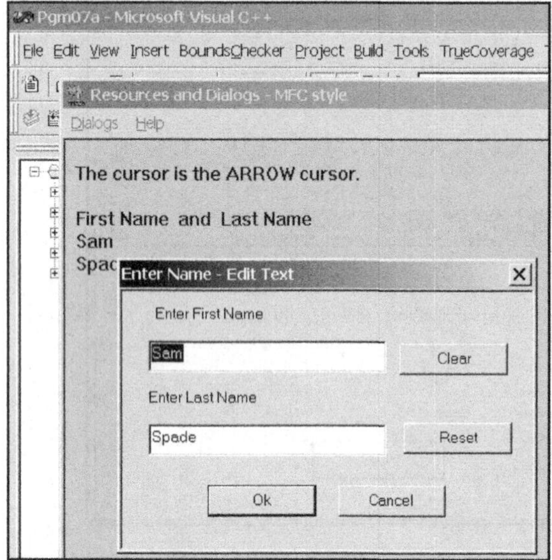

Figure 7.24 Choose User Name Dialog

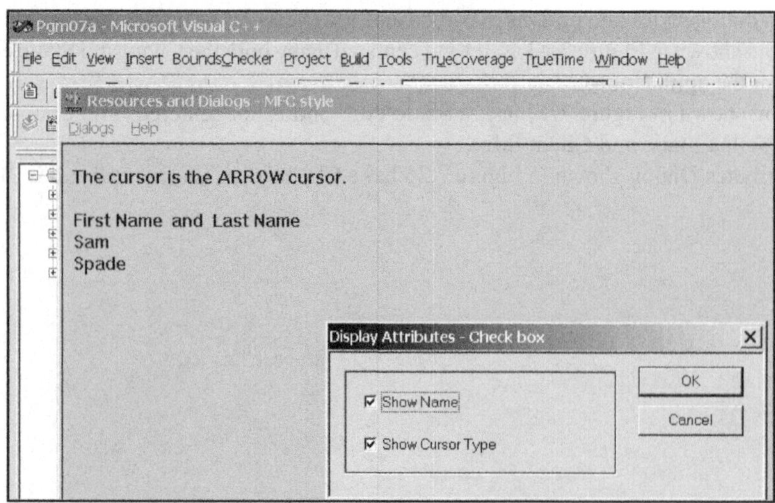

Figure 7.25 Choose Display Attributes Dialog

The Choose Line Dialog shown in Figure 7.26 uses all default style settings.

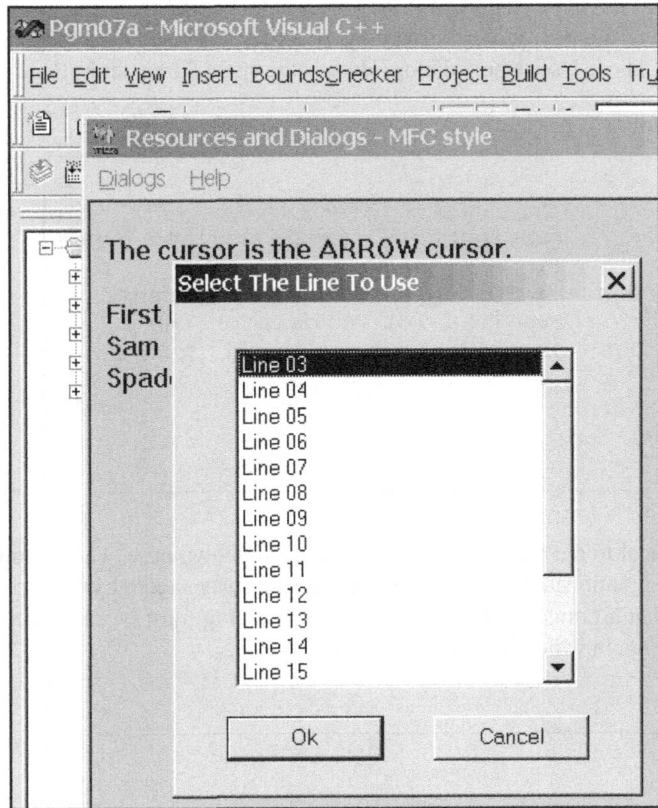

Figure 7.26 Choose Line Dialog

Finally, the Mouse Tracking Dialog in Figure 7.27 uses a 3D look with Static edge.

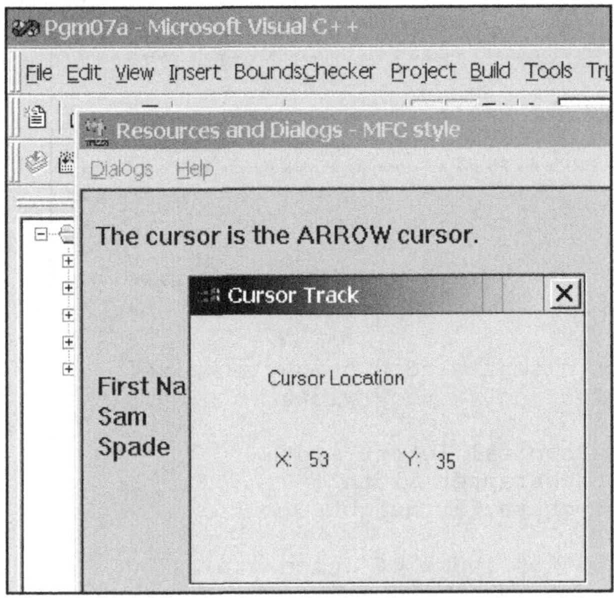

Figure 7.27 Mouse Tracking Modeless Dialog

Sometimes the data to be transferred into and out of a dialog is best handled by passing a pointer to a special transfer buffer structure. If there are numerous values to be passed, of if the values to be passed are within several different structures, of if the data needs to be altered in some manner, such as formatting, before it is given to the dialog, use a transfer structure to simplify it. I did just this with the Choose User Name dialog. Here is the special transfer buffer I made for it.

NamesXfer.h

```
#pragma once

const int MAX_NAME_LEN = 40; // max length - first and last names

// edit dialog transfer buffer - a convenient method to transfer
// data to/from a dialog when there is a lot of data or the
// data is inconvenient to pass or needs to be altered in someway
struct  TRANSFER_NAMES {
 char firstName[MAX_NAME_LEN];
 char lastName[MAX_NAME_LEN];
};
```

The application derived class is identical to the previous chapters and is not shown here. The **FrameWin** class definition defines the basic data. Pay particular attention to those values that are in some way altered by the various dialogs. These are shown in bold face below. Notice that a pointer to the **MouseTrackingDialog** must be saved because it is a modeless dialog and can exist beyond the function in which it is allocated and launched.

FrameWin.h

```
#pragma once
#include "NamesXfer.h"

class MouseTrackingDialog;

/*************************************************************/
/*                                                           */
/* FrameWin Class Definition                                 */
/*                                                           */
/*************************************************************/

class FrameWin : public CFrameWnd {

 /************************************************************/
 /*                                                          */
 /* Class Data Members                                       */
 /*                                                          */
 /************************************************************/

protected:
int  height;         // current client window height in pixels
int  width;          // current client window width in pixels

int  avgCapsWidth;   // average capital letter width
int  avgCharWidth;   // average character width
int  avgCharHeight;  // average character height

int  whichCursor;    // radio button index of which btn is on
int  showName;       // show names when TRUE - for checkboxes
int  showCursor;     // show cursor when TRUE
char firstName[MAX_NAME_LEN]; // user's first name
char lastName[MAX_NAME_LEN];  // user's last name

public: // transfer areas to/from dialogs
// these need to be public so they can be accessed from the dlgs
bool trackOn;        // when true, displays mouse coordinates
```

```
char line[50][10];    // lines for listbox strings
int  lineTot;         // total lines in array that are used
int  lineNumNew;      // set by CmOk of ChooseLineDialog
int  lineNum;         // current line number to show names on

protected:
HCURSOR hcursor;      // current cursor in use
HBRUSH  hbkgrndbrush;// current background brush
MouseTrackingDialog  *ptrMouseTracking; // ptr to modeless dialog

 /************************************************************/
 /*                                                          */
 /* Class Functions:                                         */
 /*                                                          */
 /************************************************************/

public:
              FrameWin ();                  // constructor
              ~FrameWin () {}               // destructor

protected:
afx_msg void  OnPaint ();                   // paint the window
afx_msg int   OnCreate (LPCREATESTRUCT);    // initial class members
afx_msg void  OnDestroy ();                 // delete MouseTracking
afx_msg void  OnClose ();                   // can app quit?
afx_msg void  OnSize (UINT, int, int);      // calc number lines
afx_msg void  OnMouseMove (UINT, CPoint);// track current pos

afx_msg void  CmChooseCursor ();            // choose which cursor
afx_msg void  CmChooseName ();              // enter user name
afx_msg void  CmChooseDisplay ();           // choose what to dsply
afx_msg void  CmChooseLine ();              // pick which line
afx_msg void  CmMouseTracking ();           // start cursor tracking
afx_msg void  CmAbout ();                   // help about dialog

DECLARE_MESSAGE_MAP();
};
```

In the **FrameWin** constructor notice that all of the data members are initialized **before** the call to the **Create** function. Remember that **Create** eventually calls **OnCreate** which sends the first paint message. So some of these must be already set to their initial values. **OnCreate** also illustrates how you can set a different cursor than the one installed during the creation process.

OnDestroy checks to see if there is an instance of the **MouseTrackingDialog** still running when the application is shutting down. If so, it is deleted.

OnSize determines how many lines of text can be shown on the screen with the current window size. It then builds the array **lines** which contain the strings to be shown in the Choose Lines dialog.

OnMouseMove passes the coordinates of the mouse to the Display Tracking dialog, but only if that dialog exists.

Next, come the command handlers that launch the various dialogs. Let's examine these along with the dialogs themselves, from the simplest to the more complex.

```
FrameWin.cpp
```

```
#include "stdafx.h"
#include "framewin.h"
#include "resource.h"
#include "MouseTrackingDialog.h"
#include "ChooseNameDialog.h"
#include "DisplayAttributesDialog.h"
#include "SelectCursorDialog.h"
#include "ChooseLineDialog.h"

/*************************************************************/
```

```
/*                                                              */
/* FrameWin Events Response Table                               */
/*                                                              */
/****************************************************************/

BEGIN_MESSAGE_MAP(FrameWin, CFrameWnd)
 ON_WM_SIZE ()
 ON_WM_PAINT ()
 ON_WM_CREATE ()
 ON_WM_CLOSE ()
 ON_WM_DESTROY ()
 ON_WM_MOUSEMOVE ()
 ON_COMMAND(CM_CURSOR_DLG,   CmChooseCursor)
 ON_COMMAND(CM_NAME_DLG,     CmChooseName)
 ON_COMMAND(CM_ITEM_DLG,     CmChooseDisplay)
 ON_COMMAND(CM_LINE_DLG,     CmChooseLine)
 ON_COMMAND(CM_LOCATION_DLG, CmMouseTracking)
 ON_COMMAND(CM_ABOUT,        CmAbout)
END_MESSAGE_MAP();

/****************************************************************/
/*                                                              */
/* Framewin: Construct the window object                        */
/*                                                              */
/****************************************************************/

FrameWin::FrameWin () : CFrameWnd () {
 ptrMouseTracking = 0; // set no MouseTrackingDialog allocated
 trackOn = false;   // indicate mouse position tracking is not on
 firstName[0] = 0;  // set for no inital user name
 lastName[0]  = 0;
 showName     = FALSE; // init check box xfer buf
 showCursor   = TRUE;  // show cursor type but not names
 lineNum      = 3;     // set default line for showing names

 // set the default cursor to the Tree cursor
 whichCursor = SelectCursorDialog::Tree;


 DWORD style = WS_OVERLAPPEDWINDOW; // set basic window style
 CString title;
 title.LoadString (IDS_MAINTITLE);  // load caption of window

 Create ( AfxRegisterWndClass (
              CS_VREDRAW | CS_HREDRAW,
              AfxGetApp()->LoadStandardCursor (IDC_ARROW),
              ::CreateSolidBrush (GetSysColor(COLOR_WINDOW)),
              AfxGetApp()->LoadIcon (IDI_TREE)),
         title,          // window caption
         style,          // wndclass DWORD style
         rectDefault,    // set initial window position
         0,              // the parent window, here none
         "MAINMENU");    // assign the main menu

 // load the Tree cursor and install it replacing Arrow cursor
 hcursor = ::LoadCursor (AfxGetApp()->m_hInstance,
                         MAKEINTRESOURCE (IDC_TREE));
 ::SetClassLong (m_hWnd, GCL_HCURSOR, (long) hcursor);
}

/****************************************************************/
/*                                                              */
/* OnDestroy: remove dynamically allocated MouseTrackingDialog  */
/*                                                              */
```

```
/********************************************************************/

void FrameWin::OnDestroy () {
 if (ptrMouseTracking) { // only delete it if it still exists
  delete ptrMouseTracking;
 }
 CFrameWnd::OnDestroy ();
}

/********************************************************************/
/*                                                                  */
/* OnCreate: get average character dimensions                       */
/*                                                                  */
/********************************************************************/

int FrameWin::OnCreate (LPCREATESTRUCT lpCS) {
 if (CFrameWnd::OnCreate (lpCS) == -1) return -1;

 TEXTMETRIC  tm;

 // get the system font's characteristics in tm
 CClientDC dc (this);         // acquire a DC
 dc.GetTextMetrics (&tm);     // get the information

 // calculate average character parameters
 avgCharWidth  = tm.tmAveCharWidth;
 avgCharHeight = tm.tmHeight + tm.tmExternalLeading;
 avgCapsWidth  = (tm.tmPitchAndFamily & 1 ? 3 : 2) *
                    avgCharWidth / 2;

 // the following illustrates how to change the background color
 // AFTER it has been set initially in the wndclass structure
 // you need to get the handle of the original brush so that it
 // can be deleted, if not, you will get a memory leak
 hbkgrndbrush = ::CreateSolidBrush (RGB (192, 192, 192));

 // get old brush so we can delete it after installing new brush
 HBRUSH oldbrush = (HBRUSH) ::GetClassLong (m_hWnd,
                                          GCL_HBRBACKGROUND);
 // install new brush
 ::SetClassLong (m_hWnd, GCL_HBRBACKGROUND, (long) hbkgrndbrush);
 ::DeleteObject (oldbrush);

 return 0;
}

/********************************************************************/
/*                                                                  */
/* OnSize: acquire the current dimensions of the client window      */
/*    calc number of available lines for name showing               */
/*                                                                  */
/********************************************************************/

void FrameWin::OnSize (UINT, int cx, int cy) {
 width = cx;  // save current height
 height = cy; // save current width

 char msg[10];
 int  i, j;

 // now dynamically adjust the number of possible lines upon
 // which the names can be displayed:

 // retrieve printf control string "Line %02d"
```

```
 LoadString (AfxGetApp()->m_hInstance, IDS_LINEMSG, msg,
             sizeof(msg));

 // insert line choices into the list box lines strings that
 // will be loaded into the list box
 // -3 for the cursor msgs; -2 since 3 lines of names
 j = height / avgCharHeight - 5;

 if (j<0) j=1; // force at least line 3
 lineTot = j;
 for (i=0; i<j; i++) {
  wsprintf (line[i], msg, i+3);
 }
}

/**************************************************************/
/*                                                            */
/* OnMouseMove: display current mouse position                */
/*                                                            */
/**************************************************************/

void      FrameWin::OnMouseMove (UINT, CPoint pt) {
 // if tracking is on, force the modeless dialog to display pos
 if (trackOn) ptrMouseTracking->ShowPos (pt);
}

/**************************************************************/
/*                                                            */
/* OnPaint: display what the user has selected                */
/*                                                            */
/**************************************************************/

void FrameWin::OnPaint () {
 CPaintDC dc (this);
 CString msg;
 dc.SetBkMode (TRANSPARENT); // let background color show through

 if (showCursor) {
  if (whichCursor == SelectCursorDialog::Tree)
   msg.LoadString (IDS_ISTREE);
  else msg.LoadString (IDS_ISARROW);
  dc.TextOut (avgCharWidth, avgCharHeight, msg);
 }

 if (showName) {
  msg.LoadString (IDS_NAMEID);
  dc.TextOut (avgCharWidth, avgCharHeight*(lineNum), msg);
  dc.TextOut (avgCharWidth, avgCharHeight*(lineNum+1),
              firstName);
  dc.TextOut (avgCharWidth, avgCharHeight*(lineNum+2),
              lastName);
 }
}


/**************************************************************/
/*                                                            */
/* OnClose: determine if the app can be shut down             */
/*                                                            */
/**************************************************************/

void FrameWin::OnClose () {
 CString msgtitle;
 CString msgtext;
```

```
 msgtext.LoadString (IDS_MSG_QUIT);
 msgtitle.LoadString (IDS_MSG_QUERY);
 if (MessageBox (msgtext, msgtitle, MB_YESNO | MB_ICONQUESTION)
     == IDYES) {
  CFrameWnd::OnClose ();
 }
}

/***************************************************************/
/*                                                             */
/* CmAbout: Help About dialog                                  */
/*                                                             */
/***************************************************************/

void      FrameWin::CmAbout () {
 CDialog aboutdlg ("IDD_ABOUT", this);
 aboutdlg.DoModal ();
}

/***************************************************************/
/*                                                             */
/* CmMouseTrack: cursor location modeless dialog activation    */
/*  No data xfer - ShowPos updates dlg controls from mouse move*/
/*                                                             */
/***************************************************************/

void      FrameWin::CmMouseTracking () {
 if (!trackOn) {          // avoid multiple instances of the dlg
  trackOn = true;         // indicate tracking is active
  ptrMouseTracking = new MouseTrackingDialog (this);
  POINT p;
  ::GetCursorPos (&p);     // retrieve current mouse position
  CPoint pt (p);           // convert to CPoint
  ptrMouseTracking->ShowPos (pt);         // display new position
  ptrMouseTracking->ShowWindow (SW_SHOW); // make dialog visible
 }
}

/***************************************************************/
/*                                                             */
/* CmChooseName: enter names dialog                            */
/*   We fill a xfer buffer with the needed data and give to dlg*/
/*   The dlg replaces the xfer buffer with results             */
/*                                                             */
/***************************************************************/

void      FrameWin::CmChooseName () {
 TRANSFER_NAMES  xferEditNames;  // edit names transfer buffer
 // copy into transfer buf the current name in use
 strcpy_s (xferEditNames.firstName, MAX_NAME_LEN, firstName);
 strcpy_s (xferEditNames.lastName, MAX_NAME_LEN, lastName);

 ChooseNameDialog dlg (&xferEditNames, this);
 if (dlg.DoModal () == IDOK) {
  // copy the new data in the xfer buffer to the real db location
  strcpy_s (firstName, MAX_NAME_LEN, xferEditNames.firstName);
  strcpy_s (lastName, MAX_NAME_LEN, xferEditNames.lastName);
  Invalidate(); // force the new name strings to be shown
 }
}

/***************************************************************/
/*                                                             */
/* CmChooseCursor: choose cursor radio button dialog           */
```

```
/*    After creating an instance of the dlg, we must fill the  */
/*    public dlg data member with the initial data; and if ok, */
/*    we must copy the result out of the dlg data member       */
/*                                                             */
/*  Uses a public enum of SelectCursorDialog to id the cursor  */
/*                                                             */
/***************************************************************/

void      FrameWin::CmChooseCursor () {
 SelectCursorDialog dlg (this);
 // store our current settings into dlg's public data member
 dlg.m_which_btn_is_on = whichCursor;

 if (dlg.DoModal () == IDOK) { // create & execute dlg
  // update our members from dlg's public data member
  whichCursor = dlg.m_which_btn_is_on;
  // install the correct cursor
  if (whichCursor == SelectCursorDialog::Tree) {
   hcursor = ::LoadCursor (AfxGetApp()->m_hInstance,
                           MAKEINTRESOURCE (IDC_TREE));
   ::SetClassLong (GetSafeHwnd(), GCL_HCURSOR, (long) hcursor);
  }
  else {
   hcursor = AfxGetApp()->LoadStandardCursor (IDC_ARROW);
   ::SetClassLong (m_hWnd, GCL_HCURSOR, (long) hcursor);
  }
  Invalidate (); // force paint to display msg of new cursor
 }
}

/***************************************************************/
/*                                                             */
/* CmChooseDisplay: choose which items to display in paint     */
/*    After creating an instance of the dlg, we must fill the  */
/*    public dlg data members with the initial data and if ok, */
/*    we must copy the results out of the dlg data members     */
/*                                                             */
/***************************************************************/

void      FrameWin::CmChooseDisplay () {
 DisplayAttributesDialog dlg (this);
 // transfer our current settings into dlg's public members
 dlg.m_showName    = showName;
 dlg.m_showCursor = showCursor;
 if (dlg.DoModal () == IDOK) {    //  create & execute dlg
  // update our members from the dlg's public data members
  showName   = dlg.m_showName ;
  showCursor = dlg.m_showCursor;
  Invalidate (); // repaint window with these options
 }
}

/***************************************************************/
/*                                                             */
/* CmChooseLine: pick which line on which to display name      */
/*    dlg uses GetParent and typecast to FrameWin to access    */
/*    the public data members that contain available lines and */
/*    the line on which to display the name                    */
/*                                                             */
/***************************************************************/

void      FrameWin::CmChooseLine () {
 ChooseLineDialog dlg (this);
 if (dlg.DoModal () == IDOK) {
```

```
  if (lineNumNew >= 0) {          // if OK, set our new line number
   lineNum = lineNumNew + 3;      // save new line number
   Invalidate();                  // force names to show on this line
  }
 }
}
```

The simplest dialog is the Help About dialog. Notice that there is no class for it and that there is no #define for its name, **IDD_ABOUT**, either. This is an example of the simplest possible dialog—one that has no data to be transferred in or out of it. One can just wrap the basic **CDialog** class around it and run it.

```
CDialog aboutdlg ("IDD_ABOUT", this);
aboutdlg.DoModal ();
```

Next, let's look at the Choose Names dialog. This one is an example in which a transfer buffer is used to simplify data transfer. This is a very common approach—copy all the needed fields into a structure instance and pass its address to the constructor who saves it in a protected data member for all the other dialog functions to use as needed. When the dialog completes, the caller must move the results from this structure instance back into their proper variables. **FrameWin** calls it this way.

```
TRANSFER_NAMES  xferEditNames;  // edit names transfer buffer
strcpy_s (xferEditNames.firstName, MAX_NAME_LEN, firstName);
strcpy_s (xferEditNames.lastName, MAX_NAME_LEN, lastName);
ChooseNameDialog dlg (&xferEditNames, this);
if (dlg.DoModal () == IDOK) {
 strcpy_s (firstName, MAX_NAME_LEN, xferEditNames.firstName);
 strcpy_s (lastName, MAX_NAME_LEN, xferEditNames.lastName);
 Invalidate(); // force the new name strings to be shown
}
```

The final **Invalidate** function call is what actually gets the new data painted on the screen.

Here is the Choose Names dialog definition. In bold are the saved transfer buffer pointer and the corresponding C++ dialog data members that are used to transfer the data to the edit controls.

ChooseNameDialog.h

```
#pragma once
#include "resource.h"
#include "NamesXfer.h"

/***************************************************************/
/*                                                             */
/* ChooseNameDialog - enter user first and last name           */
/*  Address of a caller transfer buffer is passed and stored   */
/*  the edit controls are filled from this and results replace */
/*  the original data in the xfer buffer                       */
/*                                                             */
/*  Uses Client Edge and Static Edge styles - no 3d no centered*/
/*                                                             */
/***************************************************************/

class ChooseNameDialog : public CDialog {
// Construction
public:
 ChooseNameDialog(TRANSFER_NAMES* ptrb, CWnd* pParent = NULL);
 TRANSFER_NAMES* ptrnames;

// Dialog Data
 enum { IDD = IDD_EDITDLG };
 Cstring m_firstName;
 Cstring m_lastName;

```

```
// Overrides
protected:
 virtual void DoDataExchange(CDataExchange* pDX);

// Implementation
protected:

 // Generated message map functions
 virtual void OnOK();
 afx_msg void OnReset();
 afx_msg void OnClear();

 DECLARE_MESSAGE_MAP()
};
```

The constructor copies the initial values for the first and last names into the member variables and saves the pointer to the transfer buffer. **DoDataExchange** is called from **OnInitDialog** to load the strings into the edit controls initially. I will discuss the **DDV**, dynamic data validators, later on. Since we need to copy the results back into the passed structure instance, we respond to the Ok button in **OnOk**. The Reset button causes **OnReset** to copy the original data in the transfer buffer back into the edit controls. The Clear button causes the edit controls to be emptied. Notice that I just copy the needed data into the C++ data members and then call **UpdateData** to get the data transferred. This is shown in bold.

ChooseNameDialog.cpp

```
#include "stdafx.h"
#include "pgm07a.h"
#include "ChooseNameDialog.h"

/***************************************************************/
/*                                                             */
/* ChooseNameDialog: enters user's first and last name         */
/*                                                             */
/***************************************************************/

ChooseNameDialog::ChooseNameDialog (TRANSFER_NAMES* ptrb,
                                    CWnd* pParent)
                 : CDialog(ChooseNameDialog::IDD, pParent) {
 m_firstName = ptrb->firstName;
 m_lastName = ptrb->lastName;
 ptrnames = ptrb;
}

void ChooseNameDialog::DoDataExchange(CDataExchange* pDX) {
 CDialog::DoDataExchange(pDX);
 DDX_Text(pDX, IDC_FIRSTNAME, m_firstName);
 DDV_MaxChars(pDX, m_firstName, MAX_NAME_LEN-1);
 DDX_Text(pDX, IDC_LASTNAME, m_lastName);
 DDV_MaxChars(pDX, m_lastName, MAX_NAME_LEN-1);
}

BEGIN_MESSAGE_MAP(ChooseNameDialog, CDialog)
 ON_BN_CLICKED(IDC_RESETBUTTON, OnReset)
 ON_BN_CLICKED(IDC_CLEARBUTTON, OnClear)
END_MESSAGE_MAP()

void ChooseNameDialog::OnOK() {
 UpdateData (TRUE);
 strcpy_s (ptrnames->firstName, MAX_NAME_LEN, m_firstName);
 strcpy_s (ptrnames->lastName, MAX_NAME_LEN, m_lastName);
 CDialog::OnOK();
}

```

```
void ChooseNameDialog::OnReset() {
 m_firstName = ptrnames->firstName;
 m_lastName = ptrnames->lastName;
 UpdateData (FALSE);
}

void ChooseNameDialog::OnClear() {
 m_firstName = "";
 m_lastName = "";
 UpdateData (FALSE);
}
```

The next two dialogs, Choose Display Attributes and Choose Cursor, are handled in much the same way. Both follow the Third Approach in which the caller stored the needed initial values into the public data members before executing the dialog and then the caller retrieves the results from these same data members when the dialog finishes.

For check boxes, the transfer buffer is an **int** containing usually 0 or 1. However, there are really three values possible: **MF_CHECKED, MF_UNCHECKED, MF_GRAYED**. The first yields 0 while the second yields 1.

```
DisplayAttributesDialog.h
```

```
#pragma once
#include "resource.h"

/**************************************************************/
/*                                                            */
/* DisplayAttributesDialog: choose which items to display   */
/*                                                            */
/*  Caller stores initial values and Caller retrieves new ones */
/*                                                            */
/*  Uses Client Edge style and 3d and is centered             */
/*                                                            */
/**************************************************************/

class DisplayAttributesDialog : public CDialog {
// Construction
public:
 DisplayAttributesDialog(CWnd* pParent = NULL);

// Dialog Data
 enum { IDD = IDD_CHECKBOX };
 BOOL m_showCursor;
 BOOL m_showName;

// Overrides
protected:
 virtual void DoDataExchange(CDataExchange* pDX);

// Implementation
protected:

 // Generated message map functions

 DECLARE_MESSAGE_MAP()
};
```

Notice that the dialog is very simple and that we do not even need to respond to the Ok button.

```
DisplayAttributesDialog.cpp
```

```
#include "stdafx.h"
#include "pgm07a.h"
```

```
#include "DisplayAttributesDialog.h"

/***************************************************************/
/*                                                             */
/* DisplayAttributesDialog: choose what is shown on screen     */
/*                                                             */
/***************************************************************/

DisplayAttributesDialog::DisplayAttributesDialog (CWnd* pParent)
                : CDialog (DisplayAttributesDialog::IDD, pParent) {
 m_showCursor = FALSE;
 m_showName = FALSE;
}

void DisplayAttributesDialog::DoDataExchange(CDataExchange* pDX){
 CDialog::DoDataExchange(pDX);
 DDX_Check(pDX, IDC_CHECK_CURSOR, m_showCursor);
 DDX_Check(pDX, IDC_CHECK_NAME, m_showName);
}

BEGIN_MESSAGE_MAP(DisplayAttributesDialog, CDialog)
END_MESSAGE_MAP()
```

The Choose Cursor dialog has one extra twist. Since there are two possible cursors, rather than trying to remember which numerical value means which cursor, I chose to use an enumerated data type. This is a very common action, public class **enums**. It is shown in bold. The transfer buffer for a group of radio buttons is an **int** containing the zero-based offset of which button is on. A value of -1 means no selection has yet been made.

Design Rule 33: It is vitally important that only the first radio button of the group of buttons has the WS_GROUP style attribute in the resource file. It and the remainder of the radio buttons in the group do have the WS_TABSTOP style

SelectCursorDialog.h

```
#pragma once
#include "resource.h"

/***************************************************************/
/*                                                             */
/* SelectCursorDialog: Select which cursor to use              */
/*                                                             */
/* Caller stores initial cursor value before running dialog    */
/* Caller retrieves the new selection                          */
/*                                                             */
/* Uses Static Edge and no 3d no centered                      */
/*                                                             */
/***************************************************************/

class SelectCursorDialog : public CDialog {
// Construction
public:
 SelectCursorDialog(CWnd* pParent = NULL);

 // convenience public enum to determine which button is on
 enum Order {Tree, Arrow};

// Dialog Data
 enum { IDD = IDD_RADIO };
 int  m_which_btn_is_on;

```

```
// Overrides
protected:
 virtual void DoDataExchange(CDataExchange* pDX);

// Implementation
protected:

 // Generated message map functions

 DECLARE_MESSAGE_MAP()
};
```

Again the implementation is very simple because the caller is responsible for setting the initial values and getting the results.

```
SelectCursorDialog.cpp
```

```
#include "stdafx.h"
#include "pgm07a.h"
#include "SelectCursorDialog.h"

/***************************************************************/
/*                                                             */
/* SelectCursorDialog: select which mouse cursor to use        */
/*                                                             */
/***************************************************************/

SelectCursorDialog::SelectCursorDialog (CWnd* pParent)
                    : CDialog(SelectCursorDialog::IDD, pParent) {
 m_which_btn_is_on = -1;
}

void SelectCursorDialog::DoDataExchange(CDataExchange* pDX) {
 CDialog::DoDataExchange(pDX);
 DDX_Radio(pDX, IDC_RADIOBUTTON_TREE, m_which_btn_is_on);
}

BEGIN_MESSAGE_MAP(SelectCursorDialog, CDialog)
END_MESSAGE_MAP()
```

Let's review again how **FrameWin** calls this dialog and how the public **enum** operates. Notice how it sets the dialog's public data before it executes the dialog. Notice also how it obtains the results from the dialog. This is precisely how we must work with the Windows Common dialogs in the next chapter.

```
SelectCursorDialog dlg (this);
dlg.m_which_btn_is_on = whichCursor;
if (dlg.DoModal () == IDOK) { // create & execute dlg
 whichCursor = dlg.m_which_btn_is_on;
 if (whichCursor == SelectCursorDialog::Tree) {
  ...
```

The Choose Line dialog uses a list box which shows text messages indicating on which line the names are to be shown. Sorting is not going to be a problem in this case because of the nature of the strings themselves. They all say Line 03, Line 04, and so on. Since the array of strings was built sequentially, they are in alphabetical order anyway.

A list box must be populated with the strings that it is to show. This must be done when the actual list box exists which is after the **CDialog::OnInitDialog** call is complete. By having the **DDX** mechanism automatically tie the class **CListBox** data member, **m_list**, to the actual list box itself, we can then call member functions to work with the list box. The **AddString** function adds a string (either a **char*** or a **CString**) to the list box. The function **SetCurSel** sets a current selection in the list box. Here I chose to set as the current selection the line that the **FrameWin** is currently using. The function **GetCurSel** returns the current selection. Both of these are zero-based integers. That is, if the user selects the first string in the list box, the index returned is 0. Note that one can also have multi-selection list boxes, but that is beyond this text.

```
ChooseLineDialog.h
```

```
#pragma once
#include "resource.h"

class ChooseLineDialog : public CDialog {
// Construction
public:
 ChooseLineDialog(CWnd* pParent = NULL);

// Dialog Data
 enum { IDD = IDD_LISTBOX };
 ClistBox m_list;

// Overrides
protected:
 virtual void DoDataExchange(CDataExchange* pDX);

// Implementation
protected:

 // Generated message map functions
 virtual void OnOK();
 virtual BOOL OnInitDialog();

 DECLARE_MESSAGE_MAP()
};
```

This implementation shows how a dialog can get a pointer to its parent or caller and then access public data members of the caller. This is a more limited technique because the dialog must include the caller class header and is thus tied directly to a single parent and is not easily reused in other situations. However, this situation does occur, so make sure you follow how this dialog gets access to the **FrameWin** variables.

```
ChooseLineDialog.cpp
```

```
#include "stdafx.h"
#include "pgm07a.h"
#include "ChooseLineDialog.h"

#include "FrameWin.h" // requires intimate knowledge of its data

/***************************************************************/
/*                                                             */
/* ChooseLineDialog - pick which line on which to display names*/
/*                                                             */
/* Uses GetParent to access FrameWin's public data members     */
/* Uses all default styles and no 3d or centered               */
/*                                                             */
/***************************************************************/

ChooseLineDialog::ChooseLineDialog(CWnd* pParent)
                 : CDialog(ChooseLineDialog::IDD, pParent) {
}

void ChooseLineDialog::DoDataExchange(CDataExchange* pDX) {
 CDialog::DoDataExchange(pDX);
 DDX_Control(pDX, IDC_LISTBOX, m_list);
}

```

```
BEGIN_MESSAGE_MAP(ChooseLineDialog, CDialog)
END_MESSAGE_MAP()

void ChooseLineDialog::OnOK() {
 // if no selection is made, abort Ok
 if (m_list.GetCurSel() == LB_ERR) return;

 // get a ptr to the parent
 FrameWin *ptrparent = (FrameWin*) (GetParent ());
 if (!ptrparent) return;

 // save the current user selection index
 ptrparent->lineNumNew = m_list.GetCurSel ();

 CDialog::OnOK();
}

BOOL ChooseLineDialog::OnInitDialog() {
 CDialog::OnInitDialog();

 // get a ptr to the parent
 FrameWin *ptrparent = (FrameWin*) (GetParent ());
 if (!ptrparent) return TRUE;

 // fill up list box from parent's line array
 for (int i=0; i<ptrparent->lineTot; i++) {
  m_list.AddString (ptrparent->line[i]);
  // set the current line in use as the selected one
  if (i+3 == ptrparent->lineNum) m_list.SetCurSel (i);
 }
 return TRUE;
}
```

All of the above were modal dialogs. When they are running, the application is forced to wait until the dialog finishes. Sometimes, the application needs to continue to execute while the dialog is present, as in the Find/Replace dialog. Thus, the Mouse Tracking Dialog is modeless so that it can remain on the screen and actively tracking the mouse while the user does other actions. This means that we must dynamically construct an instance of the dialog and save a class member pointer to it so that access to the dialog is available from other member functions.

Since its purpose is to track the location of the mouse in the **FrameWin**, **OnMouseMove** must somehow get the dialog updated with each new mouse location. This is most easily done my calling a helper function of the dialog, **ShowPos**. Also, note that the user could shut down the application while the dialog is still in operation. Thus, in **OnDestroy**, we must check for this situation and manually delete the dialog.

Another complexity is that when the user closes the dialog, the dialog must somehow communicate that fact to the **FrameWin** so that it ceases to invoke **ShowPos** as the mouse moves. This is accomplished by overriding **OnDestroy** and before actually destroying the dialog, reset the appropriate data items in the **FrameWin** by using **GetParent** to gain access to it.

Similarly, **OnCancel** is overridden to make sure **OnDestroy** is called. Why? Since this is a modeless dialog, the **CDialog::OnCancel** hides the dialog box and does not destroy it. Here, we need it destroyed, not hidden.

The following illustrates the real distinction between modal and modeless dialogs. Modal dialogs have a sequential operation.

constructor + DoModal() + return value => point A

with no other possible functions invoked. At point A, the dialog box is now totally gone. Modeless dialogs are NEVER executed via **DoModal**! They are run as follows.

constructor + Create + ShowWindow => point B
at a later point in time, user closes dialog

At point B the modeless dialog is visible and active and remains fully operational. The box remains visible and potentially active. Only at some later point in time or even application termination, is the box destroyed.

```
MouseTrackingDialog.h
```

```
#pragma once
#include "resource.h"

/***************************************************************/
/*                                                             */
/* MouseTrackingDialog: display mouse position in the FrameWin */
/*                                                             */
/* Modeless dialog - must be created - no data transfer        */
/* separate function to display mouse coordinates              */
/*                                                             */
/* Uses Static Edge and 3d look - no centered                  */
/*                                                             */
/***************************************************************/

class MouseTrackingDialog : public CDialog {
// Construction
public:
 MouseTrackingDialog(CWnd* pParent = NULL);

// Dialog Data
 enum { IDD = IDD_MODELESS };

void      ShowPos (CPoint&);// update coordinates shown on screen
BOOL      DestroyWindow (); // notify parent no longer tracking

protected:

void      OnCancel ();      // must trap and destroy modeless dlg

// Overrides

// Implementation
protected:

 // Generated message map functions

 DECLARE_MESSAGE_MAP()
};
```

In the constructor, we explicitly call the **Create** function. This differs from the modal dialogs in which **DoModal** calls the **Create** function as part of the launching process. Modeless dialogs are created and shown. Modal dialogs are launched with **DoModal**.

Notice in **DestroyWindow** that a pointer to the parent window is obtained again using **GetParent** and cast into a **FrameWin** pointer. The resultant pointer is used to reset **trackOn** back to **false** to cause the **FrameWin** to stop calling the **ShowPos** function as the mouse moves over the client area.

Finally, notice how **ShowPos** is written. This is an example of manual transferring of data into controls. In this case the controls are Static Control. In order for the text in a Static Control to be changed, that control must have an Id number. **SetDlgItemText** then is used to alter the text which is the mouse coordinates.

```
MouseTrackingDialog.cpp
```

```
#include "stdafx.h"
#include "pgm07a.h"
#include "MouseTrackingDialog.h"
#include "FrameWin.h"

/***************************************************************/
/*                                                             */
/* MouseTrackingDialog: display mouse position in the FrameWin */
```

```
/*                                                              */
/* Modeless dialog - must be created - no data transfer         */
/* separate function to display mouse coordinates               */
/*                                                              */
/* Uses Static Edge and 3d look - no centered                   */
/*                                                              */
/****************************************************************/

MouseTrackingDialog::MouseTrackingDialog (CWnd* pParent)
                    : CDialog(MouseTrackingDialog::IDD, pParent) {
 // modeless dialogs must call Create
 Create (IDD_MODELESS, pParent);
}

BEGIN_MESSAGE_MAP(MouseTrackingDialog, CDialog)
END_MESSAGE_MAP()

/****************************************************************/
/*                                                              */
/* DestroyWindow: activated when user closes modeless dialog    */
/*                                                              */
/* reset parent's tracking on indicator to false or off         */
/*                                                              */
/****************************************************************/

BOOL     MouseTrackingDialog::DestroyWindow () {
 // set parent's tracking indicator off to cease sending pos msgs
 // gain access to a pointer to the track_on public member
 FrameWin *ptrparent = (FrameWin*) GetParent ();
 if (ptrparent)
 ptrparent->trackOn = FALSE;
 return CDialog::DestroyWindow ();
}

/****************************************************************/
/*                                                              */
/* OnCancel: handle ESC and closing by calling DestroyWindows   */
/*                                                              */
/* because default handler does not delete the modeless dlg box*/
/* rather it just hides it                                      */
/*                                                              */
/****************************************************************/

void      MouseTrackingDialog::OnCancel () {
 DestroyWindow();  // modeless dlgs must be destroyed
}

/****************************************************************/
/*                                                              */
/* ShowPos: updates the static x,y mouse position fields        */
/*                                                              */
/****************************************************************/

void      MouseTrackingDialog::ShowPos (CPoint &pt) {
 char x[5];
 char y[5];
 _itoa_s (pt.x, x, sizeof(x), 10);
 _itoa_s (pt.y, y, sizeof(y), 10);
 SetDlgItemText (IDC_CURSOR_X, x);
 SetDlgItemText (IDC_CURSOR_Y, y);
}
```

Data Validation

There are some data validator macros, **DDV**, to help ensure that the data being entered into an Edit control is valid. Most simply validate numerical ranges, verifying the number is between **minVal** and **maxVal** inclusive of the endpoints. (If the data type is **UINT**, **DWORD**, or one of the floating point types, typecasts are required on **minVal** and **maxVal**.)

> **Design Rule 34: The DDV function must immediately follow the DDX function for the same control.**

The validator functions are shown below.

```
DDV_MinMaxByte    (CDataExchange* pDX, BYTE value, BYTE minVal,
                   BYTE maxVal);
DDV_MinMaxInt     (CDataExchange* pDX, int value, int minVal,
                   int maxVal);
DDV_MinMaxLong    (CDataExchange* pDX, long value, long minVal,
                   long maxVal);
DDV_MinMaxUInt    (CDataExchange* pDX, UINT value, UINT minVal,
                  UINT maxVal);
DDV_MinMaxDWord   (CDataExchange* pDX, DWORD value, DWORD minVal,
                   DWORD maxVal);
DDV_MinMaxFloat   (CDataExchange* pDX, float const& value,
                   float minVal, float maxVal);
DDV_MinMaxDouble  (CDataExchange* pDX, double const& value,
                   double minVal, double maxVal);
DDV_MaxChars      (CDataExchange* pDX, CString const& value,
                   int nChars);
```

A dialog can also force the **DDX/DDV** operation at other times that on Ok button presses. The **CWnd** member function **UpdateData** causes the data to be transferred as follows.

```
UpdateData (TRUE);
UpdateData (FALSE);
```

where **TRUE** causes the transfer of data from the controls to the dialog transfer buffer and **FALSE** causes the transfer of data to the controls from the dialog transfer buffer.

CDialog::OnOK calls **UpdateData (TRUE);** while **CDialog::OnInitDialog** calls **UpdateData (FALSE);**.

Writing Your Own Data Validator Functions

Frequently, these simple data validators are insufficient for the task at hand. Suppose that an item number was composed of 4 digits, a dash and a letter. When an edit control is used to allow the user to enter the item number, a user-written data validator can ensure that the data is in the proper format.

For example, assume that in the **FrameWin**, we had the following **CString** data items initialized as shown.

```
FrameWin::FrameWin () : CFrameWnd () {
 ...
 strcpy_s (description, sizeof(description), "Pots");
 strcpy_s (itemNum, sizeof(itemNum), "1234-A");
...
```

Next, **OnLaunch** responds to the user clicking on the menu item to update the current data. An instance of the ControlsDialog is launched and is passed the address of the two needed data members.

```
void      FrameWin::OnLaunch() {
 ControlsDialog dlg (&description, &itemNum, this);
 if (dlg.DoModal () == IDOK) {
  Invalidate (); // repaint using new description and itemNum
 }
}
```

The class definition of the **ControlsDialog** is shown below. Notice the new **DDV** function.

```
#pragma once
#include "resource.h"
class ControlsDialog : public CDialog {
public:
 ControlsDialog(CString* ptrd, Cstring* ptri,
                CWnd* pParent = NULL);
 enum { IDD = IDD_DIALOG };
 CString    m_description;
 CString    m_itemNum;
 CString* ptrDescription;
 CString* ptrItemNum;
protected:
 virtual void DoDataExchange(CDataExchange* pDX);
 virtual void OnOK();
 virtual BOOL OnInitDialog();
 void DDV_Fancy(CDataExchange*, CString, int);
 DECLARE_MESSAGE_MAP()
};
```

In the implementation of **ControlsDialog** the pointers are saved. If the corresponding pointer is not null, then its contents are copied into the dialog's members. The in **DoDataExchange**, immediately following the **DDX** for the item number control is the corresponding **DDV** macro for the item number validation.

In the **DDV** function, if the data is invalid, the function sets a flag in the **CDataExchange** instance by calling its **Fail** function and then throws a C++ exception. The MFC C++ exception handling is discussed more fully in a later chapter.

```
#include "stdafx.h"
#include "ControlsDialog.h"
#include "resource.h"
ControlsDialog::ControlsDialog(CString* ptrd, Cstring* ptri,
                               CWnd* pParent)
              : CDialog(ControlsDialog::IDD, pParent) {
 m_description = _T("");
 m_itemNum = _T("");
 ptrDescription = ptrd;
 ptrItemNum = ptri;
 if (ptrDescription) m_description = *ptrDescription;
 if (ptrItemNum) m_itemNum = *ptrItemNum;
}
void ControlsDialog::DoDataExchange(CDataExchange* pDX) {
 CDialog::DoDataExchange(pDX);
 DDX_Text(pDX, IDC_EDIT_FANCY, m_itemNum);
 DDV_Fancy(pDX, m_itemNum, 6);
 DDX_Text(pDX, IDC_EDIT_NAME, m_description);
}
void ControlsDialog::DDV_Fancy(CDataExchange *pDX, CString fancy,
                               int len) {
 if (pDX->m_bSaveAndValidate) {
  int ok = 0;
  if (fancy.GetLength() == len) {
   char *str = fancy.GetBuffer (7);
   if (str[0] >= '0' && str[0] <= '9' &&
       str[1] >= '0' && str[1] <= '9' &&
       str[2] >= '0' && str[2] <= '9' &&
       str[3] >= '0' && str[3] <= '9' &&
       str[4] == '-' &&
       ((str[5] >= 'a' && str[5] <= 'z') ||
        (str[5] >= 'A' && str[5] <= 'Z'))) ;
   else ok = 2;
   fancy.ReleaseBuffer ();
```

```
    }
    else ok = 1;
    if (ok!=0) {
     CString msg;
     if (ok == 1) msg = "Fancy must be 6 characters long";
     else msg = "Fancy must be of the form nnnn-a, where n is"
                "  numeric and a is alpha";
     AfxMessageBox (msg);
     pDX->Fail ();
     AfxThrowUserException ();
    }
  }
}

BEGIN_MESSAGE_MAP(ControlsDialog, CDialog)
END_MESSAGE_MAP()
void ControlsDialog::OnOK() {
 UpdateData (TRUE);
 if (ptrDescription) *ptrDescription = m_description;
 if (ptrItemNum) *ptrItemNum = m_itemNum;
 CDialog::OnOK();
}
```

Sub-classing Controls: Deriving your Own Control Classes

Sometimes even a **DDV** is insufficient to handle the data editing needs of the dialog. Notice that a **DDV** is only called when the user clicks on the Ok button. If the data needs to be edited as the individual keystrokes are being input, then one must derive your own class from **CEdit** and provide that functionality by overriding **OnChar** and other necessary functions. This is known as sub-classing a control.

Sub classing is an advanced topic. But for the curious, one would define an instance of your derived edit class in the dialog definition. Then, use the **DDX** control version, like the list box example above, to have your derived class instance tied into the edit control when it is created.

Programming Problems

Problem Pgm07-1—Acme Inventory Data Entry

We are going to construct an Inventory Data Base system for the ACME Construction Company during the series of programming problems through successive chapters. This initial portion implements the data entry user interface.

The **inventory record** consists of four fields in binary data format; in successive problems, the data is stored in a binary file.

item number: **char [7]**

format: AA-###, where A is any uppercase letter and # is any digit—all three digits must be present as well as both letters and the dash, convert lowercase entries to uppercase

item description: **char [21]**

format: any 20 characters what so ever

quantity on hand: **short int**

item cost: **double**

Make a structure containing these four fields. In the **FrameWin** class, create an instance of an array of 15 of these structures. When the application begins, the array should be empty.

The application should run **maximized** or **minimized only**. Use a light gray background. When the application wants to terminate, if any data has been entered into the array and or if that data has been altered and not yet saved, the query the user and save or terminate based upon the user's response. For now, just pretend that the data has been saved and then terminate. We will add file support in the next version of the problem.

The main menu consists of File, Edit, Font, and Help. The File pop-up menu offers New, Open, Close, Save, SaveAs, Print, Print Setup, and Exit. The Edit pop-up menu offers: Add, Update, and Delete. The Help pop-up menu offers only About. Note that Font is just a menu item, not a pop-up. Use accelerators only if wanted. This problem implements Add, Update, Delete, Exit, and Help menu items only. The others are implemented in the next problem. Create and install a dialog box for Help About as you see fit. When the user selects Edit|Add, execute an Add dialog box with Ok, Cancel, and Clear buttons. The Add dialog box should provide edit controls for entering the four inventory fields in the above order. The Ok button ends the dialog as expected, passing the entered data back. The Cancel button terminates the dialog and sends no data back. The Clear button blanks (zeros) out the edit controls.

Additionally, three data fields must be validated for correct information. Force the item number to conform to the above specifications. The numerical fields, quantity and cost, should be forced to be numerical. Force quantity to be less than or equal to 32,767. You can check for validity of all fields after Ok is pressed. However, data validation is much easier if you use **DDV** data validation macros and corresponding functions. The easiest method of handling the item number is to make your own **DDV** function to handle its validation.

Assume that new records are appended to the end of the array. It the user attempts to add more than the current maximum of 15 records, display an appropriate message box. Make sure that you set the number of records in the array to 0 **before** calling the **Create** function because that function calls **OnCreate** which in turn calls **OnPaint**.

The main window displays of all the records and should contain an appropriate company title, such as, ACME Construction Company, on one line and appropriate column headings above the columns of data.

For extra credit, derive your own class from **CEdit** to perform the data validation as the keystrokes are entered. The easiest way to do this is in your dialog class have an instance of your dreived class, **MyEdit** edit. Then, in **OnInitDialog** after the base class call, tie your instance to the actual physical control by edit. **SubclassDlgItem (IDC_MYEDIT, this);** or use the **DDX** control macro in **DoDataExchange**.

Next, implement the Update and Delete menu choices. Of course, use an update handler to gray out Update and Delete menu items if there are no elements in the array as yet. The first step is to launch a Choose Record to delete or update dialog with a list box showing the item number and description as one long string. If the user makes a selection, then handle it accordingly.

If the user is deleting a record, display a confirmation message box and if Yes, delete that record from the array and repaint the screen. If the user is updating a record, then show the Update dialog. Notice that there is only a slight difference between the Update dialog and the Add dialog. In the update dialog, the dialog caption is different and there is one additional button, the Reset button which resets the four dialog controls back to the original values. Thus, the easiest way to handle the Update and Add dialogs is to make a single AddUpdate dialog and pass it a **bool isUpdate**. If **isUpdate** is on, then set the window text (caption) to reflect that this is an update. Otherwise, leave the original Add title appear as usual. This can be done in **OnInitDialog**. Also in **OnInitDialog**, if this is not an update, then hide the Reset button by getting a pointer to this control by calling **GetDlgItem** passing it the Reset button id. Then, use the returned **CWnd** pointer to call **ShowWindow** passing it **SW_HIDE**.

Chapter 8 Memory, Files, Common Dialog Boxes, Scroll Bars

Introduction

A benefit of Windows is the common look and feel shared by all applications. To achieve this characteristic appearance, Windows provides several **common dialog boxes** that applications should use to handle those basic actions most applications need to do, such as selecting a file to open or choosing a font. The common dialogs include dialogs for file open, file save, search and replace, choose colors, choose fonts, and printing. MFC encapsulates these into classes. But before examining the common dialog specifics, an understanding of how Windows uses memory and the new file system with long filenames must be understood.

Windows and Memory Management

Under the 32-bit versions of Windows, nearly all complexities of memory management have been eliminated! Virtually all of the methods for allocating memory are acceptable, using the **new** function or **malloc** or **falloc**, for example.

In the old days of DOS and Windows 3.1, the system could only access 64K worth of data at one time. That is, the combined data and stack segments of a program could only be 64k in size total. Memory contained within this 64k segment was known as **local**. However, a program could also access memory outside of this 64k segment up to the 640k barrier. Memory outside the original 64k segment was known as **far**. Hence, pointers to data were either **near** pointers or **far** pointers. Windows 3.1 had two different sets of functions to dynamically allocate memory from these two pools: a local allocation and a global allocation. Older C programs used the functions, **malloc** and **falloc,** to allocate local and far memory. Hence, an **LPSTR** is a long or far pointer to a string or a **far char***. The older terminology remains as a reminder of our roots.

On a Win32 platform, a 32-bit platform, a memory address is effectively stored in an **unsigned long** and thus can hold a range of address values up to 4G. However, Windows reserves the upper half of this potential memory for its own usage and allows an application to use the lower half. Thus, our applications can use up to 2G of memory assuming that you have a combination of that much real memory plus swap drive space.

Thus, today all forms of memory allocation are serviced by the same low-level allocation routines. So an application can do an **malloc**, **falloc**, **new**, a Windows **local** alloc or a **global** alloc and all work exactly the same, obtaining a block of memory that is requested, subject to the 2G limit. Thus, my philosophy on which function to use to dynamically allocate needed memory is to use that system that makes the most common sense for the task at hand.

Design Rule 35: Usually all forms of data allocation are equivalent and acceptable, since all memory comes from the one address space.

For example, if I needed to allocate space for an array of **count COSTREC** structures, I would code the allocation this way.

```
COSTREC* arec = new (std::nothrow) COSTREC[count];
```

However, there are some Windows functions that require a Windows globally allocated block of memory, for example the clipboard operations. Thus, we must learn how to use the global allocation functions of Windows.

Windows Global Memory API Functions

Let us examine the API functions to get Windows global memory. Although all memory allocation methods can be used to allocate megabytes under Windows, I am concentrating here on the global method because this procedure is still used when interfacing to some Windows functions such as the clipboard.

When a block of memory is requested, Windows provides a **handle** to the global memory. Only when that memory is locked, does Windows provide a **pointer** to the block. For example, let's say that you needed two large arrays that potentially were to be defined as follows.

```
char   buffer[40000];
CPoint vertices[10000];
```

Under Windows, both could be allocated as shown as automatic storage. Let's allocate them on the global heap. First, in the class definition, include handles to the requests.

```
HANDLE  hbuffer;   // handle to global memory for char array
HANDLE  hvertices;// handle to the memory for CPoint array
```

Next, in the class constructor, request global memory from Windows using the **GlobalAlloc** function.

```
HANDLE   GlobalAlloc (type ID, long amount of memory);
```

The type ID is usually **GMEM_MOVEABLE** for global memory moveable. One could OR in **GMEM_ZEROINIT** if you wish Windows to initialize the memory to zeros. Assuming the following defines, the constructor coding would then be as follows.

```
#define   BUFFER_SIZE   40000
#define   MAX_POINTS    10000
hbuffer = GlobalAlloc (GMEM_MOVEABLE, BUFFER_SIZE);
hvertices = GlobalAlloc (GMEM_MOVEABLE,
                         MAX_POINTS * sizeof (Cpoint));
```

If the handle is 0 or null, then Windows is completely out of memory. Protect your application—**test** the return code.

```
if (!hbuffer || !hvertices) {
 MessageBox ("Try Closing Outstanding Applications",
             "Out of Memory", MB_OK);
}
```

What actions should occur if the allocation fails is application dependent. If the application cannot proceed if the allocation fails, then post a quit message, for example. (This is done in **Pgm08a** in this chapter.)

Design Rule 36: When using the Windows API memory allocation functions, lock the memory one time and unlock it just before freeing it.

Whenever the application needs to use these global memory blocks, they must be locked, or tied to a specific real address. The syntax for the function is shown below.

```
char*  GlobalLock (handle of global memory block);
```

Generally, typecasting is done to the return value to get the pointer into the correct type. So if the handles are not NULL, both handles should be locked to real memory most likely into protected class members.

```
char*   buffer;    // will be used as a string text buffer
CPoint* vertices; // will be used as vertices[j]
buffer = (char*) GlobalLock (hbuffer);
vertices  = (CPoint*) GlobalLock (hvertices);
```

From now on until the destructor is called or the memory is freed, the program can access the memory normally, such as this.

```
buffer[0] = 'A';
vertices[i] = Cpoint(42,42);
```

Before the application terminates, often in the destructor or **OnDestroy**, unlock the memory and free it. The function syntax is shown below.

```
GlobalUnlock (handle of global memory);
GlobalFree (handle of global memory);
```

Here the sequence would be simple this.

```
GlobalUnlock (hbuffer);
GlobalUnlock (hvertices);
GlobalFree   (hbuffer);
GlobalFree   (hvertices);
```

That is all you need do to use megabytes of extended memory under Windows.

However, there is another set of memory allocation functions with which you should be familiar. There were added with Windows 95. They are called the **heap memory** functions.

Suppose that your application needed to dynamically allocate hundreds of thousands of very small quantities of memory when the program runs. Consider what occurs when the program terminates. Suddenly the system must now free all of these small allocations. The result that the user sees is the program takes forever to terminate! An early version of Word Perfect ® ran into this effect. The program took several minutes to terminate as it tried to close a chapter from one of my books. The remedy for such an effect is to use the new heap memory functions.

Design Rule 37: If the application dynamically allocates thousands of memory objects, then consider allocating one sufficiently large chunk from Windows and handling your own suballocations independently of Windows.

Windows New Heap Memory Functions

The new heap memory management functions in Windows allow the creation of a private heap which can be used to eliminate lengthy termination actions of countless delete operations. The new private heap can grow dynamically, allow you to define working sets of data to reduce swapping of virtual memory, and to simplify the deallocation process.

The basic function to allocate a private heap is **HeapCreate**.

```
HANDLE  heap = HeapCreate (DWORD flags, DWORD initsize,
                           DWORD maxsize);
```

where the flags are

```
HEAP_NO_SERIALIZE - for single thread apps to prevent the
                    overhead of exclusion locks from other
                    threads
HEAP_GENERATE_EXCEPTIONS - to have error exceptions thrown
HEAP_ZERO_MEMORY    - to zero the memory
```

The initial size determines the heap's initial size. Use a maximum size of 0 for a heap that can grow or code an upper limit if desired. Save the handle for use in all of the other functions. To destroy the private heap, use this function.

```
HeapDestroy (handle);
```

Now to allocate memory from the private heap, use **HeapAlloc**

```
void* HeapAlloc (HANDLE heaphandle, DWORD flags,
                 DWORD numbytes);
```

The flags often would include **HEAP_ZERO_MEMORY** to have the memory cleared upon allocation. For example, to allocate the **char** buffer from the above example on the private heap, code this.

```
buffer = (char*) HeapAlloc (heap, HEAP_ZERO_MEMORY, 40000);
```

To remove an item from the private heap, use **HeapFree**

```
HeapFree (HANDLE heap, DWORD flags, LPVOID memory_item);
```

And at any time, the validity of the private heap can be checked. Either the entire contents can be validated or a specific allocation on the heap can be validated.

```
BOOL HeapValidate (HANDLE heap, DWORD flags, LPVOID mem);
```

If the **LPVOID** (long pointer to void or just a **void***) memory item is NULL, then the whole private heap is validated. If it points to an item that is allocated in the heap, then that one item is validated. The function returns **TRUE** if all is ok and **FALSE** if the heap contains errors. This could be a useful debugging aid. There are many more uses and functions that can assist debugging.

File Handling Under Windows and Long Filenames

Handling files has become more complex. Under Windows there are several possible file handling systems available, including the older DOS FAT (file allocation table) system used if Windows is booted as DOS in real mode, the protected-mode FAT system (the default often called VFAT for virtual FAT), FAT32, and the NTFS for Windows NT. Obviously, there is a world of difference between the filenames and paths between these systems.

The first time that a file function access a hard disk or volume and whenever a disk is placed in a floppy disk drive, Windows examines the volume to determine which file system is appropriate for that volume. The Windows file system can then access files independently of the underlying file system in use.

Thus, if you need to know the kind of disk, the best approach is to ask Windows which system is in use by calling the **GetVolumeInformation** function.

```
BOOL GetVolumeInformation (
          LPCSTR  rootpath,          LPSTR   volumelabel,
          DWORD   lenvolumelabel,    LPDWORD volsernum,
          LPDWORD maxcomplen,        LPDWORD sysflags,
          LPSTR   filesysname,       DWORD   lenfilesysname);
```

Here, **rootpath** is a string containing the root directory of the volume to be described by this function. If NULL is passed, the root directory of the current volume is used. Upon return, the **volumelabel** string contains the specified volume's label, where **lenvolumelabel** contains the defined length of our **volumelabel** string. The **DWORD** pointed to by **volsernum** contains the DOS volume serial number; if NULL is passed, no volume serial number is returned. Upon return, the **DWORD** pointed to by **maxcomplen** contains the maximum component length. This is defined to be the length of the name between backslashes that form the path. Under Windows and NT, filenames can be up to 256 bytes long (including the null terminator) with a full path including the filename of 260 bytes.

The pointer to the **DWORD sysflags** could likely be a combination of one of the following.

```
FS_CASE_IS_PRESERVED - system will preserve the filename case
FS_CASE_SENSITIVE    - system supports case sensitive filenames
FS_FILE_COMPRESSION  - system supports file-based compression
FS_VOL_IS_COMPRESSED - this volume is a compressed volume
```

Note the last two compression flags are mutually exclusive. On return the string **filesysname** contains the name of the type of file system, FAT, NTFS, and so on. Protected mode FAT and the DOS FAT are not distinguished. If the pointer is NULL, the name is not returned. The **DWORD lenfilesysname** contains the length of our passed **filesysname** string. Note that if one the strings passed is NULL, the function ignores the **DWORD** length field.

Typical coding to obtain which file system is being used on the current disk drive is this.

```
DWORD complen, flags;
char systypename[10];
GetVolumeInformation (NULL, NULL, 0, NULL, &complen, &flags,
                      systypename, sizeof(systypename));
```

If the Protected Mode FAT system is in use, which is the Windows default, the return values are "FAT" and 255 for long names. Actually, one byte must be added to store the null terminator, so the long filename could be 256 bytes. In the Protected Mode FAT system, the full file specification including drive letter, colon, backslash, path, filename.extension, and the null-terminator is 260 bytes. A path specification excluding the filename and extension but including the drive letter, colon and backslash can be 246 characters, leaving room for the standard 8.3 filename and extension.

When an application creates a file or directory that has a long filename, Windows creates an **alias** for the filename that is in the standard DOS 8.3 format. Note that a blank or 0x20 is a possible character in the 8.3 shortened version. (A blank has been a valid DOS 8.3 character, but many programs do not recognize a blank in the filename.) For example, if a WordPad user enters the document long filename of "Memo to Bill Jones on 19 April 1995" Windows attempts to create an alias of "MEMOTO~1.DOC". If this alias is in use, the system tries ~2 and so on. A DIR command at the DOS prompt shows that the filename DOS must use is MEMOTO~1.DOC, while within Windows, the case sensitive long filename is used.

Considering that the application might be connected to a network volume, the **GetVolumeInformation** function should be used to determine which file system is in use on that drive; allocate the length of filenames and paths accordingly. If dynamic allocation of filename strings cannot be done, then use 256 byte strings for the names and 260 bytes for the full path file specification.

Alternatively, use the defined **MAX_PATH** number of characters in the path as is done in all of my sample programs here. I make extensive use of this #define so that I do not have to concern myself with such details.

Design Rule 38: Do not assume that a filename and extension are 8 + 3 bytes long.
Extensions do not have to contain only a maximum of three characters. Use **MAX_PATH**.

Design Rule 39: Do not assume that there are no blanks in the filename nor that there is only one period.

If you need to parse a filename, work from the end of the string backwards looking for the first period. If present, it is the separator for name and extension. (Or use the **_splitpath_s** and **_makepath_s** functions.)

Which File Processing Functions Should Be Used?

Since long filenames are likely to be in use under Windows, the older Windows 3.1 file processing functions should be avoided. (The obsolete Windows 3.1 file I/O functions to avoid include: _lcreat, _lopen, _lclose, _lread, _lwrite, and _llseek.)

Any other file support system is fine to use; use one that makes sense and meets your application's requirements. These include the following file handling systems: C style **fread/fwrite**, **fstream**'s **read/write**, the Win32 **file handle** functions, and the MFC **CFile** functions. But before we examine these latter two new file handling systems, there are several file handling principles that should be understood.

Design Rule 40: Never open a file in one member function and leave it open for later functions.

That is, in response to one Windows message, do not open a file and leave it open once the processing of that message is complete. Doing so makes it much more difficult for applications to share master files. Should the application crash, not only can the file become corrupted, but also memory leaks can result.

Design Rule 41: If the application must work on an individual record basis, the processing cycle should be: open file, seek to the desired record, input/output that record, close the file—all done in one concise series within one member function that responds to one Windows message.

Design Rule 42: If the entire file should be input into a global memory buffer, then input the file in one read operation.

The trick of fast file I/O is to input or output the entire file with one read or write command. This becomes particularly important when inputting large bmp (bit-mapped image) files as we'll do in the next chapter.

Working With the New Windows File Functions

Your practical choices for Windows file operations are to use the new C style Windows file functions, the MFC **CFile** class or even **iostreams**. The Windows' file functions are ideal and fast for handling binary files. However, if you need the facilities of **fgetchar** or **fgets**, you have to write your own functions or use the file **iostreams**. In this book, I use the new Windows file functions.

The basic Windows file functions include: **CreateFile**, **CloseHandle**, **SetFilePointer**, **ReadFile**, and **WriteFile**. Let's examine these one by one. The syntax for **CreateFile** is the most complicated of all of these functions.

```
HANDLE CreateFile (LPCSTR filename, DWORD access, DWORD share,
                   LPSECURITRY_ATTRIBUTES security,
                   DWORD create_flags, DWORD attribs,
                   HANDLE filetemplate);
```

This versatile function opens or creates a file, pipe, communications resource, console, or other disk device. If successful, the file **handle** is returned; if it fails, the value of **INVALID_HANDLE_VALUE** is returned.

The **DWORD access** identifies the access mode which can include ORed values.

```
GENERIC_READ  - allows read access and set file pointer
GENERIC_WRITE - allows write access and set file pointer
```

The **share DWORD** specified file sharing options are these.

```
0                 - prevent file from being shared
FILE_SHARE_READ   - other open operations for read can be done
FILE_SHARE_WRITE  - other open operations for write can be done
```

The **LPSECURITY_ATTRIBUTES** points to the security options. If there are no security options, pass NULL. (This option can be used on NT.)

The **create_flags DWORD** is an important parameter specifying creation details which include these.

```
CREATE_NEW         - create a new file, fails if file exists
CREATE_ALWAYS      - create a new file, overwrites existing file
OPEN_EXISTING      - open existing file, fails if does not exist
OPEN_ALWAYS        - opens a file, if it does not exist, create it
TRUNCATE_EXISTING  - opens existing file, reset to contain 0 bytes
                     must be used with GENERIC_WRITE, fails if the
                     file does not exist
```

The **attribs DWORD** specifies file attributes and includes any combination (all others override the **NORMAL** attribute).

```
FILE_ATTRIBUTE_NORMAL - no attributes, only if no others are used
FILE_ATTRIBUTE_ARCHIVE   - file has the archive bit on
FILE_ATTRIBUTE_HIDDEN    - file has the hidden attribute
FILE_ATTRIBUTE_READONLY  - file has the read only attribute
FILE_ATTRIBUTE_SYSTEM    - file has the system attribute
```

The file template option is an advanced option; use NULL for simple applications.

For example, suppose that **filename** contains the long filename retrieved from the Open common dialog box. The following would open the file for read operations.

```
HANDLE hfile;
hfile = CreateFile (filename, GENERIC_READ, FILE_SHARE_READ,
                    NULL, OPEN_EXISTING, 0, NULL);
if (hfile == INVALID_HANDLE_VALUE) {
  // display error
}
else {
 // read data
}
```

The following would open the existing file, but if the file did not exist, a new one would be created with 0 bytes.

```
HANDLE hfile;
hfile = CreateFile (filename, GENERIC_READ, FILE_SHARE_READ,
                    NULL, OPEN_ALWAYS, 0, NULL);
```

The file close operation is done by **CloseHandle**.

```
CloseHandle (hfile);
```

where **hfile** is a **HANDLE**.

The read operation is done with the **ReadFile** function.

```
BOOL ReadFile (HANDLE hfile, LPVOID buffer, DWORD numbytes,
               LPDWORD ptractualbytes, LPOVERLAPPED ol);
```

The **HANDLE hfile** specifies which file is to be read and it must have been opened with the **GENERIC_READ** option; **buffer** points to the input area; **numbytes** contains the requested number of bytes to input; and **ptractualbytes** points to the **DWORD** that contains the actual number of bytes that were inputted. The **LPOVERLAPPED** is an advanced option and is often NULL. The function returns **TRUE** on success. However, **TRUE** is also returned along with 0 bytes read if the file pointer is beyond the current EOF at the time of the read operation—this **is** the normal EOF condition for which we must test.

If **FALSE** is returned, then the function **GetLastError** returns the cause of the error.

```
DWORD GetLastError();
```

where the return value is one of many possibilities; consult the documentation if you wish to check and display appropriate error messages.

For example, if inventory records were being read in one at a time, then the following C style processing would handle the EOF condition.

```
INV_REC inv_rec[MAX_LIMIT];
int rec_count;
DWORD act_size;
...
rec_count = 0;
while (rec_count < MAX_LIMIT &&
       ReadFile (hfile, &inv_rec[count], sizeof (INV_REC),
      &act_size, NULL) && act_size != 0) rec_count++;
if (rec_count == MAX_LIMIT) {
 // too many records
}
```

Using one read to input the entire file would improve performance. To do so, the **SetFilePointer** function is required, and its syntax is somewhat unusual.

```
DWORD SetFilePointer (HANDLE hfile,
                      LONG low_order_num_bytes_to_move,
                      LONG *high_order_num_bytes_to_move,
                      DWORD method_flags);
```

The potential number of bytes to move could be a 64-bit quantity less 2 bytes. This huge number is broken into two long halves, similar to the way two 16-bit values could be placed into one long. Notice that the high order **DWORD** is passed by address. This high word serves a dual purpose. Upon invocation, the high **DWORD** contains the high order portion of the requested offset. If the function is successful, the high **DWORD** contains the high order portion of the current file offset, also a 64-bit quantity, and the **DWORD** return value contains the low order part. Note that if this high order **DWORD** pointer is NULL, then the function assumes that the file offset cannot exceed a 32-bit (less 2 bytes) length. This would be the most likely case for many applications.

The method flag is one of these possibilities.

```
FILE_BEGIN   - the offset is from the file's beginning
FILE_CURRENT - the offset is from the current file position
FILE_END     - the offset is from the end of the file
```

Should the function fail, the return value is 0xFFFFFFFF which accounts for the "less 2 bytes" in maximum file offsets.

Thus, to input the inventory array as fast as possible, use the following sequence.

```
INV_REC *inv_rec;
HANDLE   hinv_rec;
int      rec_count;
DWORD    actsize;
...
// set to 0 bytes from the eof, returning the file size
DWORD filesize = SetFilePointer (hfile, 0, NULL, FILE_END);
SetFilePointer (hfile, 0, NULL, FILE_BEGIN);
hinv_rec = GlobalAlloc (GMEM_MOVEABLE, filesize);
if (hinv_rec == 0) {
 // display out of memory error
}
inv_rec = (INV_REC*) GlobalLock (hinv_rec);
ReadFile (hfile, inv_rec, filesize, &act_size, NULL);
CloseHandle (hfile);
rec_count = (int) (filesize / sizeof (INV_REC));
```

This approach is often used, particularly in the next chapter when bmp image files are loaded. One could also encapsulate these operations in a C++ class if desired. But the MFC has already done so with the **CFile** class.

The function to write to a file is coded this way.

```
BOOL WriteFile (HANDLE hfile, LPVOID buffer, DWORD num_bytes,
                LPDWORD act_bytes, LPOVERLAPPED lp);
```

The file must have been opened with the **GENERIC_WRITE** option; buffer points to the data to be written; **num_bytes** are to be written; and upon a successful return (**TRUE**), the **DWORD** pointed to by **act_bytes** contains the number of bytes actually written. If the value does not equal the requested number of bytes, then likely the floppy disk contains no more space. (The overlapped option is an advanced feature and should be NULL for our use.)

Some other useful functions include setting the EOF marker and flushing internal buffers. **SetEndOfFile** either truncates or extends a file by marking EOF at the current file pointer position. **FlushFileBuffers** commits any internal buffers by writing them to the file.

```
SetEndOfFile (HANDLE hfile);
FlushFileBuffers (Handle hfile);
```

If there is a chance that the file(s) could be shared, the specific records or bytes that are currently in use can be locked and unlocked when the application is finished with them. A 64-bit offset and 64-bit number of bytes to lock are required.

```
LockFile (HANDLE hfile, DWORD offsetlow, DWORD offhigh,
          DWORD num_bytes_low, DWORD num_bytes_high);
UnlockFile (HANDLE hfile, DWORD offsetlow, DWORD offhigh,
            DWORD num_bytes_low, DWORD num_bytes_high);
```

Functions exist to handle directory/folder operations and to find, delete, and rename files. Consult the documentation for these.

Notice that the file handle I/O operations are all binary in nature and not text oriented, as are the **iostreams**. There are no **getline** function or extraction operators to convert a series of ASCII text characters into an integer, for instance. The file handle method reads and writes blocks of data and is ideally suited to inputting a binary file of **COSTREC** structures or a bmp image file.

The MFC CFile

The MFC encapsulates file handling using a **CFile** class. Its data member is **m_hFile** which is the encapsulated file handle. The class provides a good OOP class for file handling operations.

Instances can be constructed using either of two overloaded constructors. The default ctor does not actually open a file—one would subsequently explicitly call the **Open** function later on. The second ctor not only creates the C++ wrapper but also opens the file much the same way as an **ifstream**.

```
CFile infile;
BOOL infile.Open (const char* filename, UINT openFlags,
                  CFileException* ptrError = 0);
```

or

```
CFile infile (const char* filename, UINT openFlags)
        throw (CFileException);
```

The open flags can be a series of ORed public class **enums** from the following.

CFile::modeCreate–Create a new file. If the file exists, it is truncated to 0 length.

CFile::modeNoTruncate–This is frequently combined with modeCreate. If the file being created already exists, it is not truncated to 0 length.

CFile::modeRead–Opens the file for reading only.

CFile::modeReadWrite–Opens the file for reading and writing.

CFile::modeWrite–Opens the file for writing only.

The above can be combined with the following access qualifiers.

CFile::shareDenyNone–Opens the file without denying other processes read or write access to the file.

CFile::shareDenyRead–Opens the file and denies other processes read access to the file.

CFile::shareDenyWrite–Opens the file and denies other processes write access to the file.

CFile::shareExclusive–Opens the file with exclusive mode, denying other processes both read and write access to the file.

These next two only apply to a derived class. They have no impact at all on a **CFile** because a **CFile** read or write is always a binary block read or write. They are present to provide a framework for a derived class that wishes to implement text file processing, for example.

CFile::typeText—Sets text mode processing
CFile::typeBinary—Sets binary mode

The main difference is that the ctor open can throw a C++ exception if the open fails while the explicit call to open returns a 0 if the file fails to open. Since we have not yet discussed the C++ exception handling within the MFC, we can implement these in a rather simple manner as follows. Here, I am opening the file for input operations.

```
CFile infile;
if (!infile.Open ("MyDataFile.dat",
                  CFile::modeRead | CFile::shareDenyWrite)){
 // message box the failure to open & figure out what to do
 // about it
}
```

Or one can use the following.

```
try {
 CFile infile ("MyDataFile.dat",
               CFile::modeRead | CFile::shareDenyWrite);
}
catch (...) {
 // message box the failure to open & figure out what to do
 // about it
}
```

When you are finished with the file, call the **Close** function.

```
infile.Close ();
```

Seeking operations are very convenient. The two most commonly used functions are **SeekToBegin** which takes no parameters and **SeekToEnd**. **SeekToEnd** also returns the **DWORD** total file size in bytes.

```
infile.SeekToBegin ();
DWORD filesize = infile.SeekToEnd ();
```

The **Read** and **Write** functions take a pointer to the buffer to fill or to output and a **UINT** total number of bytes to I/O. The **Read** function returns the actual number of bytes inputted. If it is less than the requested number, EOF was reached. Both functions can throw an exception if unexpected troubles occur.

```
Write (void* source, UINT numBytes);
UINT Read (void* destination, UINT numBytes);
```

The following illustrates how to input a string of 1000 characters.

```
UINT count;
char buffer[1000];
try {
 count = file.Read (buffer, sizeof(buffer));
}
catch (CArchiveException *ptrex) { // check for EOF
 if (ptrex->m_cause == CArchiveException::endOfFile)
    ptrex->Delete ();
 else { // here some other error occurred
   // you could also display a message box
   throw; // aborts the program
 }
}
if (count != sizeof (buffer)) {
  // unexpected eof occurred, assuming that 1000 bytes were
  // supposed to be in the file
}
```

Much more commonly, the entire file's contents are loaded into dynamically allocated memory, either on a record by record basis or, even faster, the entire file in one read operation. This assumes, of course, that there is sufficient memory to hold the file. Suppose that the file contained an unknown number of **CostRec** records, where **CostRec** is a structure. Assume that **infile** has been opened for read operations. Further, assume that **arec** is defined as a protected data member of

FrameWin in which this coding occurs and is defined as a pointer: **CostRec* arec;**. Also, assume that **numRecs** is a protected **int** of **FrameWin**. The following loads the entire file into memory.

```
numRecs = infile.SeekToEnd () / sizeof (CostRec);
infile.SeekToBegin ();
arec = new CostRec[numRecs];
if (!arec) {
 numRecs = 0;
 // display out of memory
 return;
}
DWORD count;
try {
 count = file.Read (arec, sizeof(CostRec) * numRecs);
}
catch (CArchiveException *ptrex) {
  // display an error message box
  numRecs = 0;
  delete [] arec;
  return;
}
if (count != sizeof(CostRec) * numRecs) {
  // display an error message box
  numRecs = 0;
  delete [] arec;
  return;
}
```

There is, however, an even faster way to handle I/O. It works especially well when one wishes to process the entire file in a read-only fashion. It is called Memory Mapped Files.

Memory Mapped Files

File Mapping treats the file as if it were memory. That is, Windows has opened up their blazingly fast swap file access method to application programs. One opens the input file using the file handle method. Then, one calls the memory mapping functions that converts the file into a "block of memory" whose length is the DOS file size. One has then a simple pointer to the first byte of the file and can access it as if it were memory! Microsoft figures show anywhere from 5 to 10 times faster I/O access to these memory mapped files!

Here is another way to process the **CostRec** instances in a file. I placed everything into a function. But you can rework it any number of more convenient ways. We begin by opening the file the usual way and obtaining the total size for later use. Then, **CreateFileMapping** is called to do the mapping followed by **MapViewOfFile** which provides us with a usable pointer to the beginning of the data.

```
bool  FMapDoSomething (char* filename) {
      HANDLE hfile = CreateFile (filename, GENERIC_READ,
                     FILE_SHARE_READ, 0, OPEN_EXISTING,
                     FILE_ATTRIBUTE_NORMAL, 0);
      if (hfile == INVALID_HANDLE_VALUE)
       return false;
      DWORD filesize = SetFilePointer (hfile, 0, 0, FILE_END);
      SetFilePointer (hfile, 0, 0, FILE_BEGIN);
      // guard against too large a file or a file of 0 bytes
      if (filesize == 0xffffffff || filesize == 0) {
        CloseHandle (hfile);
        return false;
      }
      // attempt to map the file into memory
      HANDLE hhfile = CreateFileMapping (hfile, 0, PAGE_READONLY,
                      0, 0, 0);
      if (hhfile == 0) { // here it failed
        CloseHandle (hfile);
```

```
    return false;
  }
  // now attempt to get a pointer to the first byte
  LPVOID ptrfile = MapViewOfFile (hhfile, FILE_MAP_READ,
                                  0, 0, 0);
  if (!ptrfile) { // here it failed to map
    CloseHandle (hhfile);
    CloseHandle (hfile);
    return false;
  }
  // setup a ptr to mark the end - the first byte not in it
  LPVOID ptrend = (void*) (((BYTE*) ptrfile) + filesize);
  // now do somthing with *ptrfile through *ptrend
  CostRec* arec = (CostRec*) ptrfile; // get an array ptr
  int num = filesize / sizeof (CostRec);
  for (long i=0; i<num; i++) {
    // use arec[i] in some manner
  }
  // clean up actions - undo all the mapping and close file
  UnmapViewOfFile (ptrfile);
  CloseHandle (hhfile);
  CloseHandle (hfile);
  return true;
}
```

If you are interested in pursuing this approach, read up on these Win32 functions. Memory Mapped Files. This is one slick trick used by the "masters" for the fastest possible input operations. In my Hunter Collection Manager Program, I noticed about a 50% decrease in the time that it took to load an image file into memory when using Memory Mapped Files instead of the file handle method!

The MFC Container Classes

We have seen that Windows provides numerous methods for dynamically allocating memory for our needs. Many methods exist for file handling. The rule that I usually follow is to use that method that best suits my needs at that point. However, the MFC also provides several container classes in which to store data. The one that I have used the most in my production coding is the growable array container, **CPtrArray**.

The **CPtrArray** stores an array of void pointers, **void***. That means, you can use it to store an array of absolutely anything. But a typecast is required when accessing a stored pointer. It is an inexpensive array to use because only a pointer is stored. Typically, I dynamically allocate new instances and store their pointers in a **CPtrArray** instance.

While there are many member functions available with this class, only a few are usually needed. After constructing an instance of the **CPtrArray,** new items must be added to the array. This is done with the **Add** function.

```
Add (void* ptritem);
```

Later on, to get access to the ith item, one can use the **GetAt** function or use **[]** subscript notation. Both versions return a NULL pointer if the subscript is out of range or the typecast fails. Let's say that we have stored **CostRec** pointers in the **CPtrArray** called **arec**. The following shows how it can be used.

```
CPtrArray arec;
CostRec* ptrrec = new CostRec;
arec.Add (ptrrec);
ptrrec = (CostRec*) arec.GetAt (0);
ptrrec = (CostRec*) arec[0];
```

When you are done using the array, it must be emptied. This means that you must traverse each element in the array and delete that item. Then, you must remove the internally dynamically allocated array of void pointers using the **RemoveAll** function.

Further, the function **GetSize** returns the number of elements in the array.

Since I frequently need to empty the array for later reuse, I often make a helper function called **EmptyArray**. Here is how the above array of **CostRec** structures can be deleted.

```
void EmptyArray () {
 CostRec* ptrrec;
 for (long j=arec.GetSize()-1; j>=0; j--) {
  ptrrec = (CostRec*) arec.GetAt (j);
  if (!ptrrec) continue;
  delete ptrrec;
 }
 arec.RemoveAll ();
}
```

If you are interested in this class, examine all of the other available member functions. Also look over the other MFC provided container classes. They can be very helpful. **Pgm08a** makes use of a **CPtrArray** to show you a working example.

The MFC Encapsulation of the Windows Common Dialogs

Under the MFC, the class **CFileDialog** encapsulates both the File|Open and File|SaveAs Win32 dialogs. Similarly, the MFC class has the following wrapper classes for the other Win32 common dialogs: **CPrintDialog**, **CFontDialog**, **CColorDialog**, and **CFindReplaceDialog**. To make use of the Windows versions of the common dialogs, add two includes to the precompiled header file **stdafx.h**. For the dialogs add **afxdlgs.h** and also add **afxcmn.h** for the new common controls. Let's begin with the **CFileDialog** class.

The CFileDialog Class

The file open action is frequently done and is found in nearly every application. It involves many interrelated actions involving many dialog controls. Figure 8.1 shows the File Open dialog box.

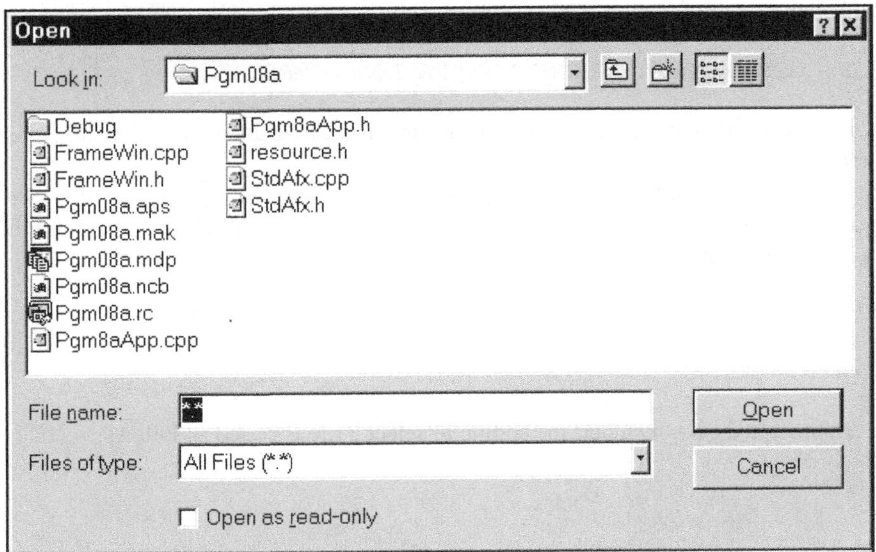

Figure 8.1 The File Open Dialog

Before coding the dialog constructor, several key parameters should be understood since these are used to define the actions we require of the common dialog box. One parameter is the desired **flags**. Among the more frequently used flags are the following.

```
OFN_ALLOWMULTISELECT - allows multiple selections of file namea
OFN_FILEMUSTEXIST    - only allows selection of files that exist
OFN_LONGNAMES        - allow long file names
OFN_PATHMUSTEXIST    - only allows path entries that exist
```

```
OFN_OVERWRITEPROMPT   - save - prompt if overwriting a file
```

The **file filter** is a string that defines one or more pairs of filters. The filters appear in the lower left combo box. Each filter contains a text description followed by the DOS pattern, which, when selected, provides the files in the main list box. The two are separated by a '|' character. For example, the filter string of "All Text Files (*.TXT)|*.*" would request all text files and provide the DOS filter of *.TXT. Multiple pairs can be coded as shown below.

```
"All Files (*.*)|*.*|All Text Files (*.TXT)|*.TXT|"
" All PCX Files (*.PCX)|*.PCX"
```

The **custom filter** is normally null or 0. The **initial directory string** can specify the drive and path to use when the dialog opens, otherwise, the dialog uses the current subdirectory. Remember to include a double \\ in the strings: "\\DOS" for example.

To use the **CFileDialog**, an automatic storage instance of the class is allocated by the constructor.

```
CFileDialog (BOOL open_or_save, // TRUE for Open
                                // FALSE for SaveAs
             LPSTR default_extension,
             LPSTR initial_filename,
             DWORD flags,
             LPSTR filter,
             CWnd *ptrparent);
```

The **BOOL** determines whether the Open (**TRUE**) or SaveAs (**FALSE**) version of the dialog box is used. The **default_extension** string is appended to user entries when the user omits entering one. The **initial_filename** string, if present, appears in the Filename edit box upon dialog launching. Note that if either are NULL, then no extensions are added or no string appears when the dialog begins.

The **flags** ORed identifiers are important and differ between Open and SaveAs. For Open, we commonly use these.

```
OFN_FILEMUSTEXIST | OFN_PATHMUSTEXIST | OFN_LONGNAMES
```

which indicate that the file and path must exist and that the new long filenames are desired if the device supports them. For SaveAs, we commonly use the following.

```
OFN_HIDEREADONLY | OFN_OVERWRITEPROMPT | OFN_LONGNAMES
```

which indicate that no read-only files can be altered, that the Over Write Prompt is desired, and that the new long filenames are desired, if the device supports them.

The filter is often a long string of pairs of file type descriptions for the user and Dir extensions to retrieve them. The two items are separated by a vertical bar (|) and two successive bars (||) indicate the end of the pairs. The following example uses a filter that shows the following in the File Types combo box.

```
All Files (*.*)
CPP Files (*.CPP)
C Files (*.C)
Header Files (*.H*)
```

Assume that **filename** is a protected class member; the coding to select a file is coded as follows.

```
char filename[MAX_PATH];
CFileDialog filedlg (
      TRUE,     // use Open dialog
     "*.CPP", // default extension
     "*.*",    // current file name
     OFN_FILEMUSTEXIST | OFN_PATHMUSTEXIST | OFN_LONGNAMES,
     "All Files (*.*)|*.*|CPP Files (*.CPP)|*.CPP|C Files"
     " (*.C)|*.C|Header Files (*.H*)|*.H*||", this);
if (filedlg.DoModal () == IDOK) { // user has chosen a file
 strcpy (filename, filedlg.GetPathName ());
 // attempt to open the file
 HANDLE hfile = CreateFile (filename, GENERIC_READ,
               FILE_SHARE_READ, NULL,OPEN_EXISTING,
               FILE_ATTRIBUTE_NORMAL, NULL);
 if (hfile==INVALID_HANDLE_VALUE) { // open failed
```

```
 DisplayMsg (IDS_MSG_ERROR, IDS_MSG_FILEOPEN,
             MB_OK | MB_ICONSTOP);
 havefile = FALSE;                    // indicate no file
 return;
}
```

The dialog is executed using **DoModal** and if **IDOK** is returned, a successful choice that exists has been made. Several member functions exist to acquire that portion of the user entry we desire; all return a **CString**. The comments below indicate what portion of the user entry is returned. Assume that the user has entered D:\PGMS\PROBLEM1.CPP.

```
CString GetPathName  (); // returns D:\PGMS\PROBLEM1.CPP
CString GetFileName  (); // returns PROBLEM1
CString GetFileExt   (); // returns CPP
CString GetFileTitle (); // returns PROBELM1.CPP
```

In the above example, the full path with filename is copied into a data member **filename** so that user changes can be later saved.

The CFontDialog

Allowing the user to change fonts introduces another layer of complexity to text displays in the **OnPaint** function. Figure 8.2 shows the Windows common Choose Font dialog box.

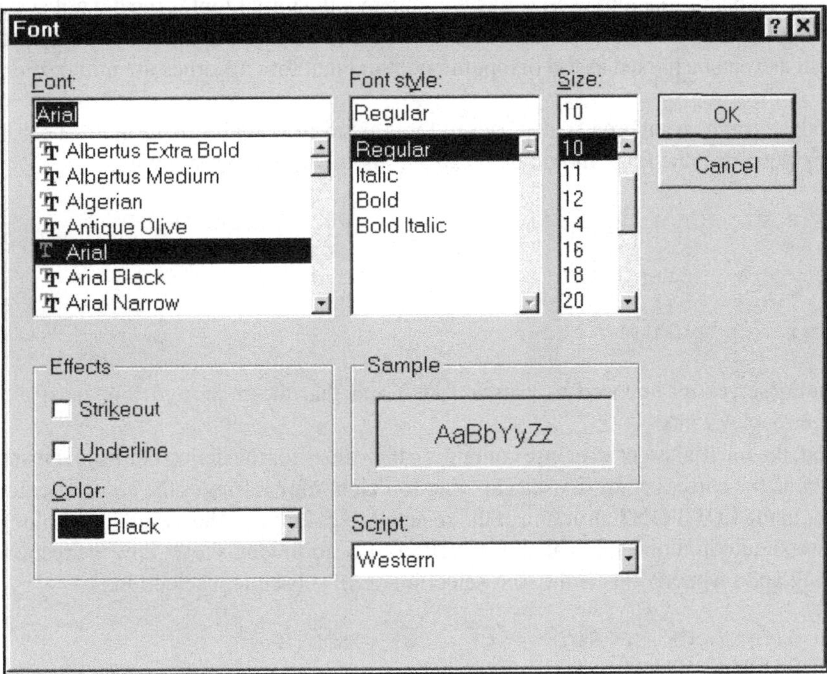

Figure 8.2 The Choose Font Dialog

Until now, when the application begins, the average character dimensions were found and used to control text displays. Since no font changes were allowed, these could be retrieved once and left alone. If you are going to allow font changes, then a more dynamic approach must be taken. We can still set up the application normally as before, assuming the initial font as the standard system font. However, if the user is allowed to change fonts, new members need to be added to the class.

The Win32 **LOGFONT** structure contains all the fields to properly define a specific font. An instance of this structure is used as the transfer buffer to and from the Choose Font common dialog. Specifically, when the Choose Font dialog is created, if we pass it the address of our **LOGFONT** structure instance, then the dialog uses the font defined in it as the initial font to be shown selected in the dialog when it first appears. After the user has made a font selection, a dialog public **LOGFONT** instance contains that font's specifications. We must copy the dialog's **LOGFONT** data into our application's **LOFGONT** instance to make use of the user's choice of font. At this point, we do not need to concern ourselves with exactly what is contained in a **LOGFONT** structure. In a later chapter, we will examine this structure's members.

However, only an actual **CFont** object, which is the actual font, can be selected into our dcs. The **CFont** class has a member function, **CreateFontIndirect** that converts a **LOGFONT** instance into an actual font. Every time that the user selects a new font, we must make a new **CFont** object. Thus, the most convenient way to handle all of these details is to define the following three protected data members in our **FrameWin** class.

```
LOGFONT* ptrlogfont; // user selected font from ChooseFont
CFont*   ptrfont;    // user font to be inserted into a dc
COLORREF fontcolor;  // users chosen font color
```

The pointers are initialized to 0 in the **FrameWin** constructor. The font color from the Choose Font common dialog is a **COLORREF** (a long containing an RGB color value).

As long as the **ptrlogfont** is 0, there is no user-chosen font. We used the default system font that is originally in every dc. If the user chooses a font, then we must dynamically allocate a **LOGFONT** structure and copy the Choose Font data into ours. Next, we allocate a new **CFont** object and call **CreateFontIndirect** to construct the real font based on these specifications in the **LOGFONT** structure.

The **CFontDialog** constructor of the common dialog is defined this way.

```
CFontDialog (LPLOGFONT ptrinitial_logfont, DWORD flags,
             CDC *ptrprinterdc, CWnd *ptrparent);
```

The first time the application responds to a font change menu command, the initial font is the default system font, and the initial pointer is 0. By passing 0 this first time, no default font is selected in the dialog. On subsequent requests, a pointer to the current **LOGFONT** in use can be passed as the first parameter and that font becomes the initial selected font in the dialog.

The flags are important and determine what broad categories of fonts are to be available in the dialog box. For fonts that are going to be used for display purposes, the flags should be set to a combination of the following.

```
CF_FORCEFONTEXIST - gives an error if user selects a non-existent
                    font
CF_SCREENFONTS    - list only screen fonts (not printer)
CF_TTONLY         - TrueType fonts
CF_EFFECTS        _ permit underline, etc
```

These identify the category of fonts (screen as opposed to printer fonts) and that the requested font must exist. The **ptrprinterdc** should be 0 for screen display fonts.

Once the dialog is allocated, the internal **m_cf** structure containing the values for the dialog controls is instantiated. The member field, **rgbColors** contains the current color in use. The function **GetColor** retrieves the color selected by the user, while **m_lf** contains the pointer to the **LOGFONT** structure of the selected font. Initially, the default font color is black; should the user select say yellow, we should initialize the dialog with yellow. The following shows how we respond to the menu item "Choose Font" depending upon whether this is the first selection or all subsequent selections.

```
CFontDialog  dlg (ptrlogfont, CF_EFFECTS | CF_SCREENFONTS |
                  CF_FORCEFONTEXIST, NULL, this);
dlg.m_cf.rgbColors = fontcolor;     // install current color
if (dlg.DoModal () == IDOK) {       // get user font choice
 if (!ptrlogfont) {
  ptrlogfont = new LOGFONT;         // 1st time, create LOGFONT
 }
 else {
  delete ptrfont;
 }
 // copy user choice of font into our LOGFONT instance
 memcpy (ptrlogfont, &(dlg.m_lf), sizeof (LOGFONT));
 fontcolor = dlg.GetColor ();       // save color choice
 // now make our CFont object
 ptrfont = new CFont ();
 ptrfont->CreateFontIndirect (ptrlogfont);
 GetAvgCharDims ();                 // get new average char dims
 SetOurScrollRange ();              // set new scroll range based
```

```
  Invalidate();                       // on new dims, and reshow
 }
}
```

There are some ramifications of the user font change. First, the average character dimensions are now different. Since we must obtain the character dimensions in **OnCreate** as well as here when the font changes, I created a helper function to be called, **GetAvgCharDims**. Further, if the character dimensions have altered, that could impact scrolling. So we must then recall **SetOurScrollRange** to adjust scrolling parameters. Finally, in order for the screen text to be shown in the new font, we must force a repainting of the screen.

The following illustrates how the font is installed and used in **GetAvgCharDims**.

```
  TEXTMETRIC  tm;  // set the system font's characteristics in tm
  CClientDC dc (this);     // acquire a DC
  if (ptrlogfont) { // install any user font
   ptroldfont = dc.SelectObject (ptrfont); // save old one
  }
  dc.GetTextMetrics (&tm); // get the font information
  if (ptrlogfont) {
   dc.SelectObject (ptroldfont); // reinstall old font
  }
  // calculate average character parameters
  avg_char_width = tm.tmAveCharWidth;
  avg_char_height = tm.tmHeight + tm.tmExternalLeading;
  avg_caps_width = (tm.tmPitchAndFamily & 1 ? 3 : 2) *
                    avg_char_width / 2;
```

Similarly in **OnPaint**, the font and its color must be installed.

```
 CPaintDC dc (this);
 // install user font, if any
 if (ptrfont) {
  ptroldfont = dc.SelectObject (ptrfont); // save old font
 }
 dc.SetTextColor (fontcolor);    // install font color
 dc.SetBkMode (TRANSPARENT);     // set so background color shows
...
 // if there is a user font, put the old font back into the dc
 if (ptrfont) {
  dc.SelectObject (ptroldfont);
 }
```

The **CColorDialog** is seldom used and is not discussed here. **The CFindReplaceDialog** is also not discussed in this text, but for a different reason. This dialog only provides the shell coding; if used, the application must supply all of the coding to actually do a "Find" operation, a "Find Next," and the "Replace" action. To fully handle all of these requires a considerable discussion. And in a later chapter, we will see how we can use an Edit control to fully handle all of these actions for us. Finally, the Printer common dialogs are discussed in a later chapter when we deal with printing operations.

Pgm08a: Handling All of the File Menu Choices

We are now in a position to handle all of the File Menu choices (New, Open, Close, Save, SaveAs) that were dummied out in the previous menus of Chapter 6. **Pgm08a** is a Text File Viewer program. That is, it displays the entire contents of any text type of file. In Figure 8.3, **Pgm08a** has used File|Open to open the **FrameWin.h** file for this very program and the user has chosen the Courier New font.

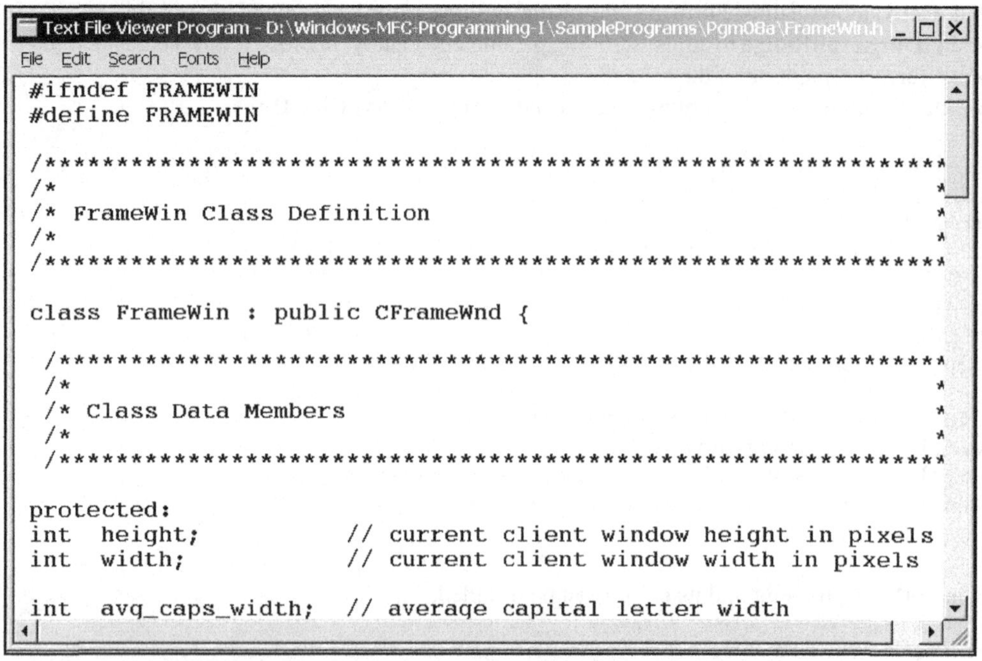

```
Text File Viewer Program - D:\Windows-MFC-Programming-I\SamplePrograms\Pgm08a\FrameWin.h
File  Edit  Search  Fonts  Help
#ifndef FRAMEWIN
#define FRAMEWIN

/**************************************************************
/*                                                            *
/* FrameWin Class Definition                                  *
/*                                                            *
/**************************************************************

class FrameWin : public CFrameWnd {

 /*************************************************************
 /*                                                           *
 /* Class Data Members                                        *
 /*                                                           *
 /*************************************************************

protected:
int  height;          // current client window height in pixels
int  width;           // current client window width in pixels

int  avg_caps_width;  // average capital letter width
```

Figure 8.3 Pgm08a Viewing FrameWin.h with a Courier New Font

In a text file, the line is the basic unit to be shown. Of course, we must be able to handle scrolling in both dimensions. Notice from the figure above that I am using the new style scroll bars created by using **SetScrollInfo**. Obviously, we must store the lines in an array. However, since this is a text file, there is no way to know in advance just how many lines are actually in any given file, some form of a growable array is needed. This is an ideal situation in which to use a **CPtrArray**. Further, since each line is of variable length and since the maximum line length is initially unknown, a **CString** is an ideal candidate to use to store a line because it is effectively a growable array of char.

The resource file looks much as it did in Chapter 6. There is an accelerator table for the Edit menu items. And in the **resource.h** file, I used the (WM_USER + n) method for the menu ID numbers, just for variety. Here are the RC file and the **resource.h** defines from **Pgm08a**.

Listing For File: Pgm08a.rc—Excerpts

```
/////////////////////////////////////////////////////////////////////////////
//
// Menu
//
MAINMENU MENU DISCARDABLE
BEGIN
    POPUP "&File"
    BEGIN
        MENUITEM "&New",                CM_FILENEW
        MENUITEM "&Open...",            CM_FILEOPEN
        MENUITEM "&Close",              CM_FILECLOSE, GRAYED
        MENUITEM SEPARATOR
        MENUITEM "&Save",               CM_FILESAVE, GRAYED
        MENUITEM "Save &As...",         CM_FILESAVEAS, GRAYED
        MENUITEM SEPARATOR
        MENUITEM "&Print...",           CM_FILEPRINT, GRAYED
        MENUITEM "P&rint Setup...",     CM_FILEPRINTERSETUP, GRAYED
        MENUITEM SEPARATOR
        MENUITEM "E&xit\tAlt+F4",       CM_EXIT
```

```
    END
    POPUP "&Edit"
    BEGIN
        MENUITEM "&Undo\tAlt+BkSp",    CM_EDITUNDO, GRAYED
        MENUITEM SEPARATOR
        MENUITEM "Cu&t\tShift+Del",    CM_EDITCUT, GRAYED
        MENUITEM "&Copy\tCtrl+Ins",    CM_EDITCOPY, GRAYED
        MENUITEM "&Paste\tShift+Ins", CM_EDITPASTE, GRAYED
        MENUITEM SEPARATOR
        MENUITEM "Clear &All\tCtrl+Del", CM_EDITCLEAR, GRAYED
        MENUITEM "&Delete\tDel",       CM_EDITDELETE, GRAYED
    END
    POPUP "&Search"
    BEGIN
        MENUITEM "&Find...",           CM_EDITFIND, GRAYED
        MENUITEM "&Replace...",        CM_EDITREPLACE, GRAYED
        MENUITEM "&Next\aF3",          CM_EDITFINDNEXT, GRAYED
    END
    POPUP "&Fonts"
    BEGIN
        MENUITEM "&Font Change",       CM_FONTCHANGE
    END
    POPUP "&Help"
    BEGIN
        MENUITEM "&About...",          CM_HELPABOUT
    END
END
/////////////////////////////////////////////////////////////////////////////
//
// Accelerator
//
MAINMENU ACCELERATORS MOVEABLE PURE
BEGIN
    VK_DELETE,      CM_EDITCUT,             VIRTKEY, SHIFT
    VK_INSERT,      CM_EDITCOPY,            VIRTKEY, CONTROL
    VK_INSERT,      CM_EDITPASTE,           VIRTKEY, SHIFT
    VK_DELETE,      CM_EDITCLEAR,           VIRTKEY, CONTROL
    VK_BACK,        CM_EDITUNDO,            VIRTKEY, ALT
    VK_F3,          CM_EDITFINDNEXT,        VIRTKEY
END

/////////////////////////////////////////////////////////////////////////////
//
// Dialog
//
IDD_ABOUT DIALOG DISCARDABLE  48, 113, 200, 92
STYLE DS_MODALFRAME | WS_POPUP | WS_VISIBLE | WS_CAPTION | WS_SYSMENU
CAPTION "Help - About Pgm08a"
FONT 8, "MS Sans Serif"
BEGIN
    DEFPUSHBUTTON   "OK",IDOK,72,70,50,14
    LTEXT           "by Vic Broquard",IDC_STATIC,70,42,57,8
    LTEXT           "Pgm08a - Common Dialogs, Memory, Files",
                     IDC_STATIC,33,
                    20,130,11
    GROUPBOX        "",IDC_STATIC,28,10,141,50
END
/////////////////////////////////////////////////////////////////////////////
//
// String Table
//
STRINGTABLE DISCARDABLE
BEGIN
    IDS_MAINTITLE    "Text File Viewer Program"
```

```
    IDS_WINNAME       "ViewerPgm"
    IDS_MSG_NOTSAVE   "File has not been saved. Save File now?"
    IDS_MSG_QUIT      "Do you want to quit the application?"
    IDS_MSG_QUERY     "Query?"
    IDS_MSG_ERROR     "Text File Viewer Program - Error Message"
    IDS_MSG_NOMEM    "Out of memory. Close app. Free some memory."
                      " Try again."
    IDS_MSG_FILEERR   "File Save Error. Try File Save As with "
                       "valid filename."
    IDS_MSG_FILEOPEN   "File Open Error. Unable to open the file."
    IDS_MSG_FILEWRT    "File Save Error. Output failed - disk "
                        "full. Try new disk."
END
```

Listing for File: resource.h—Excerpts

```
#define CM_FILENEW              (WM_USER + 102)
#define CM_FILEOPEN             (WM_USER + 103)
#define CM_FILECLOSE            (WM_USER + 104)
#define CM_FILESAVE             (WM_USER + 105)
#define CM_FILESAVEAS           (WM_USER + 106)
#define CM_FILEPRINT            (WM_USER + 107)
#define CM_FILEPRINTERSETUP     (WM_USER + 108)
#define CM_EXIT                 (WM_USER + 109)
#define CM_EDITUNDO             (WM_USER + 110)
#define CM_EDITCUT              (WM_USER + 111)
#define CM_EDITCOPY             (WM_USER + 112)
#define CM_EDITPASTE            (WM_USER + 113)
#define CM_EDITDELETE           (WM_USER + 114)
#define CM_EDITCLEAR            (WM_USER + 115)
#define CM_EDITFIND             (WM_USER + 116)
#define CM_EDITREPLACE          (WM_USER + 117)
#define CM_EDITFINDNEXT         (WM_USER + 118)
#define CM_HELPABOUT            (WM_USER + 119)
#define CM_FONTCHANGE           (WM_USER + 120)
#define IDS_MAINTITLE       2000  // frame window's title
#define IDS_WINNAME         2001  // GetClassName's wndclass name
#define IDS_MSG_NOTSAVE     2002  // file not saved msg
#define IDS_MSG_QUIT        2003  // quit application query msg
#define IDS_MSG_QUERY       2004  // title of quit query messagebox
#define IDS_MSG_ERROR       2005  // error has occurred
#define IDS_MSG_NOMEM       2006  // out of memory
#define IDS_MSG_FILEERR     2007  // file save error
#define IDS_MSG_FILEOPEN    2008  // file open error
#define IDS_MSG_FILEWRT     2009  // file save error - I/O fail
...
```

Pgm08a is rather complex. There are a lot of menu commands that must be implemented. Many effects are interrelated, such as the user selection of a font that impacts scrolling and painting. Painting is impacted by scrolling operations and we must repaint only the minimum number of lines to avoid sluggish, flicker-full displays when scrolling larger files. We must handle the enabling of many menus depending upon whether a file is opened or not.

Just a foot note. Perhaps you had hoped that scrolling would just sort of disappear from view, that it is no longer needed because we can use an Edit control or one of the new MFC supplied scrolling classes. Wrong. If you intend to write applications that run only under Windows NT/2000 or XP, then yes, that is true—you may use these new classes that completely handle scrolling. However, if your application is run under Windows 95/98/ME, all of these are limited to less than 64k worth of data to be scrolled. In other words, you must develop facility in scrolling operations.

Let's begin by looking at all of the member data we need to handle the File Viewer application. The bool variables, **haveFile** and **haveSaved**, track the current overall state of the viewer. The filename string is either a null string when File|New is chosen or contains the name of the file from File|Open.

The pair **lines** and **maxDims**—a **CPtrArray** and a **CSize**—contain the actual file's text lines stored as **CString** instances and the dimensions—the total number of lines and the maximum line width encountered. The total number of lines is found by calling the **GetSize** function of the **CPtrArray**. Finally, six familiar variables track the vertical and horizontal scrolling operations.

Pgm08a's FrameWin Definition

```
#pragma once

/******************************************************************/
/*                                                                */
/* FrameWin Class Definition                                      */
/*                                                                */
/******************************************************************/

class FrameWin : public CFrameWnd {

 /****************************************************************/
 /*                                                              */
 /* Class Data Members                                           */
 /*                                                              */
 /****************************************************************/

protected:
int  height;          // current client window height in pixels
int  width;           // current client window width in pixels

int  avgCapsWidth;    // average capital letter width
int  avgCharWidth;    // average character width
int  avgCharHeight;   // average character height

bool haveFile;        // true when there is a file opened
bool haveSaved;       // true when the file is saved &not changed

char filename[_MAX_PATH]; // the name of the file or null for new

LOGFONT* ptrlogfont;  // the user's chosen font, if any
CFont* ptrfont;       // the CFont to be used in the dc
COLORREF fontcolor;   // the user's chosen font color
CFont* ptroldfont;    // a save area for the dc selection process

CPtrArray lines;      // growable array of CStrings
CSize maxDims;        // maximum scrolling sizes in pixels

// the vertical and horizontal scrolling variables
int numLinesPerPage;
int maxScrollLines;
int currentTopLine;

int numCharsPerLine;
int maxHscrollChars;
int currentStartCol;

 /****************************************************************/
 /*                                                              */
 /* Class Functions:                                             */
 /*                                                              */
 /****************************************************************/

public:
               FrameWin ();
               ~FrameWin () {}

protected:
int  DisplayMsg (UINT, UINT, UINT);  // displays a MessageBox

bool LoadTextFileIntoCStrings (const char* filename);
void ParseFileStringIntoCStrings (char* ptrdata, DWORD size);
```

```
void EmptyArray ();

void SetOurScrollRange (); // set the scrolling ranges
void SaveCheck ();         // query user about saving a file
void SaveFile ();          // save the file
void GetAvgCharDims ();    // gets char dims using user's font
void SetCaption ();        // appends filename to caption

afx_msg void OnPaint ();                    // paint the window
afx_msg int  OnCreate (LPCREATESTRUCT); // initial class members
afx_msg void OnDestroy ();                  // delete fonts & array
afx_msg void OnClose ();                    // can app quit?
afx_msg void OnRButtonDown (UINT, CPoint);  // pop up edit menu
afx_msg void OnSize (UINT flags, int cx, int cy); // reset scroll
afx_msg void OnKeyDown (UINT, UINT, UINT);  // keybd scrolling
afx_msg void OnHScroll (UINT, UINT, CScrollBar*);
afx_msg void OnVScroll (UINT, UINT, CScrollBar*);

// command processors
afx_msg void CmExit ();                // quit the app
afx_msg void CmFontChange ();          // get new user chosen font
afx_msg void CmFileNew ();             // start a new file
afx_msg void CmFileOpen ();            // open an existing file
afx_msg void CmFileClose ();           // close the file
afx_msg void CmFileSave ();            // save the file with samename
afx_msg void CmFileSaveAs ();          // save with new name
afx_msg void CmFilePrint ();           // print the file
afx_msg void CmFilePrinterSetup ();// set up the printer
afx_msg void CmEditUndo ();            // undo last change
afx_msg void CmEditCut ();             // cut to clipboard
afx_msg void CmEditCopy ();            // copy to clipboard
afx_msg void CmEditPaste ();           // paste from the clipboard
afx_msg void CmEditDelete ();          // delete text
afx_msg void CmEditClear ();           // clear text
afx_msg void CmEditFind ();            // find text
afx_msg void CmEditFindNext ();        // find next text
afx_msg void CmEditReplace ();         // find and replace
afx_msg void CmHelpAbout ();           // help about our app

// command enablers
afx_msg void  CmEnableFileOps (CCmdUI*); // enable File menuitems

DECLARE_MESSAGE_MAP();
};
```

Besides the expected menu command handlers, notice that I created a single command enabler that services all of the File menu items, **CmEnableFileOps**. File|Close, for example, is enabled only when a file has been opened or the user has chosen File|New. Note that this is a file viewer not an editor. Thus, File|New is a silly menu item to permit in this program as it only shows an empty screen.

Notice the eight helper functions defined above the command handlers. Since error messages must be displayed from many different locations, I often create a **DisplayMsg** function that is passed the needed id values and it loads the strings, displays the message box and then returns the value that the message box function returns.

When the user chooses to open a second file, the array of lines of the previous file must be removed from the lines array. Hence, I added an **EmptyArray** function.

One caution regarding the naming of the **SetOurScrollRange** function. Its purpose, of course, is to set the ranges of both the horizontal and vertical scroll bars based on the current window dimensions, the amount and size of the text, and the user's chosen font dimensions. But be careful with its name. There is a **CWnd** member function, **SetScrollRange**. One goof we can make is to call **SetOurScrollRange SetScrollRange**. If we do so, then we completely interfere with the window's ability to scroll!

When the user chooses a file to open, we must input that file and store the text lines in our **lines** array. The two functions **LoadTextFileIntoCStrings** and **ParseFileStringIntoCStrings** accomplish that action.

SaveCheck and **SaveFile** handle the frequently needed checking and file save actions. Whenever the file has been altered and the user chooses to open a new file, we must query the user about saving or not saving the changes made to the current file. True, this is File Viewer program and there is no way to alter any of the data. I am just illustrating how this is done. Also note that the file must be saved from two locations: File|Save and File|SaveAs. The only difference between these two is the filename to use. Hence, I wrote one **SaveFile** function that is called from both locations.

A nice touch is appending the name of the file to the window's caption. Since this must be done from several locations, I made a simple helper function to do it, **SetCaption**.

There is a lot of coding here to examine with many interrelated effects. First, let's see the whole implementation. Then after that, let's take a close look at the key operations.

Pgm08a's FrameWin Implementation

```
#include "stdafx.h"
#include "framewin.h"
#include "resource.h"

/***************************************************************/
/*                                                             */
/* FrameWin Events Response Table                              */
/*                                                             */
/***************************************************************/

BEGIN_MESSAGE_MAP(FrameWin, CFrameWnd)
 ON_WM_SIZE ()
 ON_WM_PAINT ()
 ON_WM_CREATE ()
 ON_WM_CLOSE ()
 ON_WM_DESTROY ()
 ON_WM_KEYDOWN()
 ON_WM_VSCROLL ()
 ON_WM_HSCROLL ()
 ON_WM_RBUTTONDOWN ()
 ON_COMMAND(CM_FONTCHANGE,        CmFontChange)
 ON_COMMAND(CM_EXIT,              CmExit)
 ON_COMMAND(CM_FILENEW,           CmFileNew)
 ON_COMMAND(CM_FILEOPEN,          CmFileOpen)
 ON_COMMAND(CM_FILECLOSE,         CmFileClose)
 ON_COMMAND(CM_FILESAVE,          CmFileSave)
 ON_COMMAND(CM_FILESAVEAS,        CmFileSaveAs)
 ON_COMMAND(CM_FILEPRINT,         CmFilePrint)
 ON_COMMAND(CM_FILEPRINTERSETUP,  CmFilePrinterSetup)
 ON_COMMAND(CM_EDITUNDO,          CmEditUndo)
 ON_COMMAND(CM_EDITCUT,           CmEditCut)
 ON_COMMAND(CM_EDITCOPY,          CmEditCopy)
 ON_COMMAND(CM_EDITPASTE,         CmEditPaste)
 ON_COMMAND(CM_EDITCLEAR,         CmEditClear)
 ON_COMMAND(CM_EDITDELETE,        CmEditDelete)
 ON_COMMAND(CM_EDITFIND,          CmEditFind)
 ON_COMMAND(CM_EDITFINDNEXT,      CmEditFindNext)
 ON_COMMAND(CM_EDITREPLACE,       CmEditReplace)
 ON_COMMAND(CM_HELPABOUT,         CmHelpAbout)
 ON_UPDATE_COMMAND_UI(CM_FILECLOSE,      CmEnableFileOps)
 ON_UPDATE_COMMAND_UI(CM_FILESAVE,       CmEnableFileOps)
 ON_UPDATE_COMMAND_UI(CM_FILESAVEAS,     CmEnableFileOps)
 ON_UPDATE_COMMAND_UI(CM_FILEPRINT,      CmEnableFileOps)
 ON_UPDATE_COMMAND_UI(CM_EDITFIND,       CmEnableFileOps)
 ON_UPDATE_COMMAND_UI(CM_EDITREPLACE,    CmEnableFileOps)
 ON_UPDATE_COMMAND_UI(CM_EDITFINDNEXT,   CmEnableFileOps)
END_MESSAGE_MAP();

/***************************************************************/
/*                                                             */
/* Framewin: Construct the window object                       */
```

```
/*                                                                */
/******************************************************************/

FrameWin::FrameWin () : CFrameWnd () {

 LoadAccelTable ("MAINMENU");         // install keybd accelerators

 DWORD style = WS_OVERLAPPEDWINDOW; // set basic window style
 CString title;
 title.LoadString (IDS_MAINTITLE);  // load caption of window
 maxDims = CSize (1,1);             // set a default dimension
 currentTopLine = 0;
 currentStartCol = 0;
 haveFile = haveSaved = false;
 ptrlogfont = 0;
 ptrfont = 0;
 fontcolor = RGB (0, 0, 0);     // set default font color black

 Create ( AfxRegisterWndClass (
              CS_VREDRAW | CS_HREDRAW,
              AfxGetApp()->LoadStandardCursor (IDC_ARROW),
              ::CreateSolidBrush (GetSysColor(COLOR_WINDOW)),
              AfxGetApp()->LoadStandardIcon (IDI_APPLICATION)),
         title,          // window caption
         style,          // wndclass DWORD style
         rectDefault,    // set initial window position
         0,              // the parent window, here none
         "MAINMENU");    // assign the main menu
 SetCaption ();
}

/******************************************************************/
/*                                                                */
/* OnCreate: get average character dimensions                    */
/*                                                                */
/******************************************************************/

int FrameWin::OnCreate (LPCREATESTRUCT lpCS) {
 if (CFrameWnd::OnCreate (lpCS) == -1) return -1;
 GetAvgCharDims ();
 return 0;
}

/******************************************************************/
/*                                                                */
/* DisplayMsg: loads the strings and displays a message box       */
/*                                                                */
/******************************************************************/

int FrameWin::DisplayMsg (UINT id1, UINT id2, UINT flags) {
  CString msg1;
  CString msg2;
  msg1.LoadString (id1);
  msg2.LoadString (id2);
  return MessageBox (msg2, msg1, flags);
}

/******************************************************************/
/*                                                                */
/* OnSize: acquire the current dimensions of the client window */
/*         and reset scrolling ranges                             */
/*                                                                */
/******************************************************************/

```

```
void FrameWin::OnSize (UINT, int cx, int cy) {
 width = cx;  // save current height
 height = cy; // save current width
 SetOurScrollRange ();
}

/*************************************************************/
/*                                                           */
/* SetCaption: appends the filename to the caption           */
/*                                                           */
/*************************************************************/

void FrameWin::SetCaption () {
 CString title;
 title.LoadString (IDS_MAINTITLE); // load caption of window
 if (haveFile) {
  title += " - ";
  if (filename[0] == 0)
   title += "Untitled";
  else
   title += filename;
 }
 else
  title += " - No File Opened";
 SetWindowText (title);           // insert new caption
}

/*************************************************************/
/*                                                           */
/* OnPaint: display what the user has selected               */
/*                                                           */
/*************************************************************/

void FrameWin::OnPaint () {
 CPaintDC dc (this);
 // install user font, if any
 if (ptrfont) {
  ptroldfont = dc.SelectObject (ptrfont); // save old font
 }
 dc.SetTextColor (fontcolor);   // install font color
 dc.SetBkMode (TRANSPARENT);    // set so background color shows

 long i;
 // paint only those lines that are actually needed
 int numlines = lines.GetSize();
 int firstLine = max (0, currentTopLine +
                 dc.m_ps.rcPaint.top / avgCharHeight - 1);
 int lastLine = min (numlines, 1 + currentTopLine +
                 dc.m_ps.rcPaint.bottom / avgCharHeight);

 for (i=firstLine; i<lastLine; i++) {
  CString* ptrs = (CString*) lines.GetAt(i);
  if (!ptrs) continue;
  dc.TextOut (avgCharWidth * (1 - currentStartCol),
             avgCharHeight * (-currentTopLine + i), *ptrs);
 }

 // if there is a user font, put the old font back into the dc
 if (ptrfont) {
  dc.SelectObject (ptroldfont);
 }
}

/*************************************************************/
```

```
/*                                                                */
/* GetAvgCharDims: retrieve current font's average dimensions    */
/*                                                                */
/*****************************************************************/

void      FrameWin::GetAvgCharDims () {

  TEXTMETRIC  tm;  // set the system font's characteristics in tm

  CClientDC dc (this);    // acquire a DC

  if (ptrlogfont) { // install any user font
   ptroldfont = dc.SelectObject (ptrfont); // save old one
  }

  dc.GetTextMetrics (&tm); // get the font information

  if (ptrlogfont) {
   dc.SelectObject (ptroldfont); // reinstall old font
  }

  // calculate average character parameters
  avgCharWidth = tm.tmAveCharWidth;
  avgCharHeight = tm.tmHeight + tm.tmExternalLeading;
  avgCapsWidth = (tm.tmPitchAndFamily & 1 ? 3 : 2) *
                  avgCharWidth / 2;
}

/*****************************************************************/
/*                                                                */
/* CmFontChange: get users font request and implement it         */
/*                                                                */
/*****************************************************************/

void      FrameWin::CmFontChange () {

 CFontDialog  dlg (ptrlogfont, CF_EFFECTS | CF_SCREENFONTS |
                  CF_FORCEFONTEXIST, NULL, this);
 dlg.m_cf.rgbColors = fontcolor;   // install current color

 if (dlg.DoModal () == IDOK) {     // get user font choice
  if (!ptrlogfont) {
   ptrlogfont = new LOGFONT;       // 1st time, create LOGFONT
  }
  else {
   delete ptrfont;
  }
  // copy user choice of font into our LOGFONT instance
  memcpy (ptrlogfont, &(dlg.m_lf), sizeof (LOGFONT));
  fontcolor = dlg.GetColor ();     // save color choice
  // now make our CFont object
  ptrfont = new CFont ();
  ptrfont->CreateFontIndirect (ptrlogfont);

  GetAvgCharDims ();               // get new average char dims
  SetOurScrollRange ();            // set new scroll range based
  Invalidate();                    // on new dims, and reshow
 }
}

/*****************************************************************/
/*                                                                */
/* SetOurScrollRange: sets the horiz and vert scrolling ranges   */
/*       using the new SCROLLINFO structure                       */
```

```
/*                                                                 */
/*******************************************************************/

void FrameWin::SetOurScrollRange () {
 // calculate new max vertical range bassed on current size
 numLinesPerPage = height / avgCharHeight;
 maxScrollLines = max (0, maxDims.cy - numLinesPerPage + 1);

 // adjust thumb line position - could now exceed bottom pos
 currentTopLine = min (currentTopLine, maxScrollLines);

 // set up scroll range and position of the thumb bar
 SCROLLINFO si;
 si.cbSize = sizeof (si);
 si.fMask = SIF_ALL;
 si.nMin = 0;
 si.nMax = maxDims.cy;
 si.nPage = numLinesPerPage;
 si.nPos = currentTopLine; // initial position at the start
 SetScrollInfo (SB_VERT, &si, TRUE);

 numCharsPerLine = width / avgCharWidth;
 maxHscrollChars = max (0, maxDims.cx - numCharsPerLine);
 currentStartCol = min (currentStartCol, maxHscrollChars);
 si.nMax = maxDims.cx;
 si.nPage = numCharsPerLine;
 si.nPos = currentStartCol; // initial position at the start
 SetScrollInfo (SB_HORZ, &si, TRUE);
}

/*******************************************************************/
/*                                                                 */
/* LoadTextFileIntoCStrings: load a text file into an array of */
/*     CStrings - it sets the maDims to the max number of chars*/
/*     of the longest line and the number of lines in the file */
/*                                                                 */
/*******************************************************************/

bool FrameWin::LoadTextFileIntoCStrings (const char* filename) {
 // open the file
 HANDLE hfile = CreateFile (filename, GENERIC_READ,
                            FILE_SHARE_READ, 0, OPEN_EXISTING,
                            FILE_ATTRIBUTE_NORMAL, 0);
 if (hfile == INVALID_HANDLE_VALUE)
  return false;

 // obtain the file size in bytes
 DWORD filesize = SetFilePointer (hfile, 0, 0, FILE_END);
 SetFilePointer (hfile, 0, 0, FILE_BEGIN);

 // guard against too large a file or a file of 0 bytes
 if (filesize == 0xffffffff || filesize == 0) {
  CloseHandle (hfile);
  return false;
 }

 // allocate an array of char to hold the file +1 for null byte
 char* ptrdata = new char[filesize + 1];
 if (!ptrdata) {
  DisplayMsg (IDS_MSG_NOMEM, IDS_MSG_ERROR, MB_ICONSTOP | MB_OK);
  CloseHandle (hfile);
  return false;
 }

```

```
 // input the file into array of char
 DWORD act_size;
 ReadFile (hfile, ptrdata, filesize, &act_size, NULL);
 ptrdata[filesize] = 0;
 CloseHandle (hfile);

 // convert the array of char into individual CStrings
 // setting the maxDims member as a byproduct
 ParseFileStringIntoCStrings (ptrdata, filesize + 1);

 delete [] ptrdata; // remove obsolete array
 return true;
}

/***************************************************************/
/*                                                             */
/* ParseFileStringIntoCStrings: find each string in the file   */
/*    and store in a new CString and add it to the array       */
/*    when done, maxDims is set to the number of lines and the */
/*    maximum width of any line encountered                    */
/*                                                             */
/***************************************************************/

void FrameWin::ParseFileStringIntoCStrings (char* ptrdata,
                                            DWORD filesize) {
 long maxWidth = 1;
 char* ptrstart = ptrdata;
 char* ptrend = ptrdata + filesize;
 char* ptrthis;

 // for each line in the text block
 while (ptrstart < ptrend) {
  ptrthis = ptrstart;
  // search for ending <CR> <LF> codes
  while (ptrthis < ptrend) {
   if (*ptrthis == '\r') {
    *ptrthis++ = 0;          // replace <CR> with null
    if (*ptrthis == '\n')
     ptrthis++;              // skip over the next <LF>
    break;                   // stop and store this string
   }
   ptrthis++;
  }
  // create a new CString and copy the found string into it
  CString* ptrs = new CString;
  *ptrs = ptrstart;
  lines.Add (ptrs);   // add this new CString to the array
  // replace maximum line length in chars if needed
  if (ptrs->GetLength() > maxWidth)
   maxWidth = ptrs->GetLength();
  // reset ptrstart to the start of the next line in the block
  ptrstart = ptrthis;
 }
 // save the dimensions found for this file's data
 maxDims.cy = lines.GetSize ();
 maxDims.cx = maxWidth;
}

/***************************************************************/
/*                                                             */
/* OnDestroy: remove the array of CString lines                */
/*                                                             */
/***************************************************************/

```

```
void FrameWin::OnDestroy () {
 EmptyArray ();
 if (ptrlogfont) delete ptrlogfont;
 if (ptrfont) delete ptrfont;
 CFrameWnd::OnDestroy ();
}

/***************************************************************/
/*                                                             */
/* EmptyArray: remove all CStrings from the array              */
/*                                                             */
/***************************************************************/

void FrameWin::EmptyArray () {
 for (int i=lines.GetSize()-1; i>=0; i--) {
  CString* ptrs = (CString*) lines.GetAt (i);
  if (ptrs) delete ptrs;
 }
 lines.RemoveAll ();
}

/***************************************************************/
/*                                                             */
/* OnClose: determine if the app can be shut down              */
/*                                                             */
/***************************************************************/

void FrameWin::OnClose () {
 if (haveFile && !haveSaved)
  SaveCheck (); // save file if needed
 if (DisplayMsg (IDS_MSG_QUERY, IDS_MSG_QUIT, MB_YESNO |
                 MB_ICONQUESTION) == IDYES)
  CFrameWnd::OnClose ();
}

/***************************************************************/
/*                                                             */
/* SaveCheck: query user about needed file save                */
/*                                                             */
/***************************************************************/

void      FrameWin::SaveCheck () {
 // based on user request and whether or not file has a name,
 // send save msgs
 if (DisplayMsg (IDS_MSG_QUERY, IDS_MSG_NOTSAVE, MB_YESNO |
                 MB_ICONQUESTION) == IDYES) {
  if (strcmp (filename, "")==0)
      SendMessage (WM_COMMAND, CM_FILESAVEAS, 0L);
  else
      SendMessage (WM_COMMAND, CM_FILESAVE, 0L);
 }
}

/***************************************************************/
/*                                                             */
/* OnKeyDown: provide a keyboard scroller interface            */
/*                                                             */
/***************************************************************/

void FrameWin::OnKeyDown (UINT key, UINT, UINT) {

 // check for and handle any possible keyboard scroll request

 switch (key) {
```

```
  case VK_UP:    // requests scroll up 1 line
   SendMessage (WM_VSCROLL, SB_LINEUP, 0L); break;

  case VK_DOWN:  // requests scroll down 1 line
   SendMessage (WM_VSCROLL, SB_LINEDOWN, 0L); break;

  case VK_LEFT:  // requests scroll left 1 col
   SendMessage (WM_HSCROLL, SB_LINEUP, 0L); break;

  case VK_RIGHT: // requests scroll right 1 col
   SendMessage (WM_HSCROLL, SB_LINEDOWN, 0L); break;

  case VK_PRIOR: // request scroll 1 page up
   SendMessage (WM_VSCROLL, SB_PAGEUP, 0L); break;

  case VK_NEXT:  // request scroll 1 page down
   SendMessage (WM_VSCROLL, SB_PAGEDOWN, 0L); break;

  case VK_END:   // request goto the bottom
   SendMessage (WM_HSCROLL, SB_PAGEDOWN, 0L); break;

  case VK_HOME:  // request goto the top
   SendMessage (WM_HSCROLL, SB_PAGEUP, 0L);  break;
 }
}

/****************************************************************/
/*                                                              */
/* OnVScroll: scroll window vertically                          */
/*                                                              */
/****************************************************************/

void FrameWin::OnVScroll (UINT type, UINT pos, CScrollBar*) {
 int numLinesToScroll;

 switch (type) {

  case SB_LINEUP:     // scroll up 1 line
   numLinesToScroll = -1; break;

  case SB_LINEDOWN:   // scroll 1 line down
   numLinesToScroll = 1; break;

  case SB_PAGEUP:     // scroll 1 page up
   numLinesToScroll = min (-1, -numLinesPerPage); break;

  case SB_PAGEDOWN:   // scroll 1 page down
   numLinesToScroll = max (1, numLinesPerPage); break;

  case SB_THUMBTRACK: // follow thumb bar
   numLinesToScroll = pos - currentTopLine; break;

  default:
   numLinesToScroll = 0;
 }

 numLinesToScroll = max (-currentTopLine,
                      min (numLinesToScroll,
                          maxScrollLines - currentTopLine));

 if (numLinesToScroll !=0) {
  currentTopLine +=numLinesToScroll;
  ScrollWindow (0, -avgCharHeight * numLinesToScroll, 0, 0);
```

```
  SCROLLINFO si;
  si.cbSize = sizeof (si);
  si.fMask = SIF_POS;
  si.nPos = currentTopLine; // initial position at the start
  SetScrollInfo (SB_VERT, &si, TRUE);
 }
}

/********************************************************************/
/*                                                                  */
/* OnHScroll: scroll window horizontally                            */
/*                                                                  */
/********************************************************************/

void FrameWin::OnHScroll (UINT type, UINT pos, CScrollBar*) {
 int numCharsToScroll;
 switch (type) {

  case SB_LINEUP:    // scroll 1 col left
   numCharsToScroll = -1; break;

  case SB_LINEDOWN:  // scroll 1 col right
   numCharsToScroll = 1; break;

  case SB_PAGEUP:    // scroll 1 page left
   numCharsToScroll = -8; break;

  case SB_PAGEDOWN:   // scroll 1 page right
   numCharsToScroll = 8; break;

  case SB_THUMBTRACK: // follow thumb bar
   numCharsToScroll = pos - currentStartCol; break;

  default:
   numCharsToScroll = 0;
 }

 numCharsToScroll = max (-currentStartCol,
                      min (numCharsToScroll,
                        maxHscrollChars - currentStartCol));
 if (numCharsToScroll !=0) {
  currentStartCol +=numCharsToScroll;
  ScrollWindow (-avgCharWidth * numCharsToScroll, 0, 0, 0);
  SCROLLINFO si;
  si.cbSize = sizeof (si);
  si.fMask = SIF_POS;
  si.nPos = currentStartCol; // initial position at the start
  SetScrollInfo (SB_HORZ, &si, TRUE);
 }
}

/********************************************************************/
/*                                                                  */
/* OnRButtonDown: popup edit menu as a floating menu                */
/*                                                                  */
/********************************************************************/

void FrameWin::OnRButtonDown (UINT, CPoint point) {
 CMenu *ptrmenu  = GetMenu ();              // point to main menu
 CMenu *ptrpopup = ptrmenu->GetSubMenu (1);// point to edit popup
 ClientToScreen (&point);                   // convert coordinates
 ptrpopup->TrackPopupMenu (0, point.x, point.y, this, 0);
}
```

```
/*******************************************************************/
/*                                                                 */
/* SaveFile: write the file                                        */
/*                                                                 */
/*******************************************************************/

void FrameWin::SaveFile () {
 HANDLE hfile = CreateFile (filename, GENERIC_WRITE, 0, NULL,
             CREATE_ALWAYS, FILE_ATTRIBUTE_NORMAL, NULL);
 if (hfile==INVALID_HANDLE_VALUE) {
  DisplayMsg (IDS_MSG_ERROR, IDS_MSG_FILEERR, MB_OK|MB_ICONSTOP);
  return;
 }

 CString buf; // this string will hold the entire file
 // build up buf by adding <CR><LF> codes at the end of each line
 CString* ptrs;
 for (int i=0; i<lines.GetSize(); i++) {
  ptrs = (CString*) lines.GetAt (i);
  if (!ptrs) continue;
  buf += *ptrs;
  buf += "\r\n";
 }

 // obtain a pointer to the buf so we can write it out
 DWORD sz = buf.GetLength();
 char* buffer = buf.GetBuffer (sz);
 DWORD asize;
 // write the whole file - note in this case, one could write
 // from buf directly without converting it into an char*
 if (!WriteFile (hfile, buffer, sz, &asize, NULL)
     || asize != sz) {
  DisplayMsg (IDS_MSG_FILEWRT, IDS_MSG_ERROR, MB_ICONSTOP|MB_OK);
 }

 buf.ReleaseBuffer ();
 CloseHandle (hfile);
 haveSaved = true;
}

/*******************************************************************/
/*                                                                 */
/* CmFileNew: open a new file                                      */
/*                                                                 */
/*******************************************************************/

void FrameWin::CmFileNew () {
 // if the file has not been saved, ask the user and handle
 if (haveFile && !haveSaved)
  SaveCheck();
 EmptyArray ();              // remove all lines from the array
 filename[0] = 0;            // set no filename
 haveFile  = true;           // set have a new file
 haveSaved = false;          // that has not been saved
 currentTopLine = 0;
 currentStartCol = 0;
 maxDims = CSize (1,1);
 SetCaption ();
 SetOurScrollRange ();       // reset scroll bar range for newfile
 Invalidate();               // and clear screen
}

/*******************************************************************/
/*                                                                 */
```

```
/* CmFileOpen: open an existant file                              */
/*                                                                */
/******************************************************************/

void FrameWin::CmFileOpen () {
 // if the file has not been saved, ask the user and handle
 if (haveFile && !haveSaved)
  SaveCheck();

 // create new transfer buffer
 CFileDialog filedlg (TRUE,     // use Open dialog
                      "*.CPP", // default extension
                      "*.*",    // current file name
           OFN_FILEMUSTEXIST | OFN_PATHMUSTEXIST | OFN_LONGNAMES,
           "All Files (*.*)|*.*|CPP Files (*.CPP)|*.CPP|C Files"
           " (*.C)|*.C|Header Files (*.H*)|*.H*||", this);

 // get user's file choice
 if (filedlg.DoModal () == IDOK) { // user has chosen a file
  strcpy_s (filename, sizeof(filename), filedlg.GetPathName ());
  EmptyArray ();  // remove all prior lines
  // load the new file into the array
  if (!LoadTextFileIntoCStrings (filename)) {
   DisplayMsg (IDS_MSG_FILEOPEN,IDS_MSG_ERROR,MB_ICONSTOP|MB_OK);
   haveFile = false;    // indicate no file
   return;
  }

  haveFile = true;         // set have a file
  haveSaved = true;        // set file is saved because not changed
  currentTopLine = 0;
  currentStartCol = 0;
  SetCaption ();
  SetOurScrollRange ();    // set new scrollbar range
  Invalidate ();           // and display new file
 }
}

/******************************************************************/
/*                                                                */
/* CmFileClose: close an opened file                              */
/*                                                                */
/******************************************************************/

void FrameWin::CmFileClose () {
 // if the file is not yet saved, ask user and handle
 if (haveFile && !haveSaved)
  SaveCheck();
 haveFile  = false;       // set no file
 haveSaved = false;       // set not saved
 EmptyArray ();
 filename[0] = 0;
 currentTopLine = 0;
 currentStartCol = 0;
 SetCaption ();
 SetOurScrollRange ();    // set new scrollbar range
 Invalidate ();           // clear screen
}

/******************************************************************/
/*                                                                */
/* CmFileSave: save an existant file                              */
/*                                                                */
/******************************************************************/
```

```

void FrameWin::CmFileSave () {
 // if there is a file, either save it or
 // if no filename, use saveas
 if (haveFile) {
  if (strcmp (filename, "") == 0)
   SendMessage (WM_COMMAND, CM_FILESAVEAS, 0L);
  else SaveFile();
 }
}

/*****************************************************************/
/*                                                               */
/* CmFileSaveAs: Save an existant file with a new name           */
/*                                                               */
/*****************************************************************/

void FrameWin::CmFileSaveAs () {
 if (haveFile) {
  // set up transfer buffer
  CFileDialog filedlg (FALSE,    // use SaveAs dialog
                      "*.CPP", // default extension
                      "*.*",   // current file name
          OFN_HIDEREADONLY | OFN_OVERWRITEPROMPT | OFN_LONGNAMES,
          "All Files (*.*)|*.*|CPP Files (*.CPP)|*.CPP|C Files"
          " (*.C)|*.C|Header Files (*.H*)|*.H*||", this);
  // install current name
  strcpy_s (filedlg.m_ofn.lpstrFile, MAX_PATH, filename);

  if (filedlg.DoModal () == IDOK) { // user has chosen a file
   strcpy_s (filename, sizeof(filename), filedlg.GetPathName ());
   SaveFile ();                     // save the file
   SetCaption ();
  }
 }
}

/*****************************************************************/
/*                                                               */
/* CmEnableFileOps: enables/disables File operations menu items*/
/*                                                               */
/*****************************************************************/

void      FrameWin::CmEnableFileOps (CCmdUI *ptrenabler) {
 ptrenabler->Enable (haveFile);
}

/*****************************************************************/
/*                                                               */
/* CmHelpAbout: shows who wrote this app                         */
/*                                                               */
/*****************************************************************/

void      FrameWin::CmHelpAbout () {
 CDialog aboutdlg ("IDD_ABOUT", this);
 aboutdlg.DoModal ();
}

/*****************************************************************/
/*                                                               */
/* CmExit: user is trying to quit the app                        */
/*                                                               */
/*****************************************************************/

```

```
void       FrameWin::CmExit () {
 PostMessage (WM_CLOSE);
}

/*************************************************************/
/*                                                           */
/* The following are just shells to be later implemented     */
/*                                                           */
/*************************************************************/

void       FrameWin::CmEditFind () {
 MessageBox ("Find not implemented", "Search - Find",
             MB_ICONINFORMATION | MB_OK);
}

void       FrameWin::CmEditReplace () {
 MessageBox ("Replace not implemented", "Search - Replace",
             MB_ICONINFORMATION | MB_OK);
}

void       FrameWin::CmEditFindNext () {
 MessageBox ("Find Next not implemented", "Search Find Next",
             MB_ICONINFORMATION | MB_OK);
}

void       FrameWin::CmFilePrint () {
 if (haveFile)
  MessageBox ("Print not implemented",
             "File Print", MB_ICONINFORMATION | MB_OK);
}

void       FrameWin::CmFilePrinterSetup () {
 MessageBox ("Printer Setup not implemented",
            "File PrinterSetup", MB_ICONINFORMATION | MB_OK);
}

void       FrameWin::CmEditUndo () {
 MessageBox ("Edit Undo not implemented", "Edit Undo",
             MB_ICONINFORMATION | MB_OK);
}

void       FrameWin::CmEditCut () {
 MessageBox ("Edit Cut not implemented", "Edit Cut",
             MB_ICONINFORMATION | MB_OK);
}

void       FrameWin::CmEditCopy () {
 MessageBox ("Edit Copy not implemented", "Edit Copy",
             MB_ICONINFORMATION | MB_OK);
}

void       FrameWin::CmEditPaste () {
 MessageBox ("Edit Paste not implemented", "Edit Paste",
             MB_ICONINFORMATION | MB_OK);
}

void       FrameWin::CmEditDelete () {
 MessageBox ("Edit Delete not implemented", "Edit Delete",
             MB_ICONINFORMATION | MB_OK);
}

void       FrameWin::CmEditClear () {
 MessageBox ("Edit Clear not implemented", "Edit Clear",
             MB_ICONINFORMATION | MB_OK);
```

```
}
```

The constructor initializes the application to no file in use and no user font chosen. Thus, when the window appears, we see just an empty white window, or whatever window color the user has chosen in his Windows Color Scheme. **OnCreate** calls **GetAvgCharDims** to obtain the character dimensions of the default system font. If you wanted the program to open a specific file when it begins, then **OnCreate** could post a File|Open message or explicitly call the **LoadTextFileIntoCStrings** function passing it the filename to use. Of course, do not forget to call **SetOurScrollRange** after the file is loaded.

One annoying action is coding the numerous Message Boxes that display the various messages. For convenience, I have defined a helper function called **DisplayMsg** that is passed the two message IDs and the ORed flags; it loads the strings and returns the return value from the **MessageBox** function. This is a clever convenience trick many of us use to eliminate repetitive coding sequences.

```
int FrameWin::DisplayMsg (UINT id1, UINT id2, UINT flags) {
  CString msg1;
  CString msg2;
  msg1.LoadString (id1);
  msg2.LoadString (id2);
  return MessageBox (msg2, msg1, flags);
}
```

The sequence of steps to perform in response to the File|New menu selection is this. Remember, there could be a file already opened and altered. So first, see if any existing file must be saved and save it if the user desires. The array must be emptied. The scrolling variables must be reset to the top left of the area and the new scrolling ranges reset. For a File|New operation, the scroll bars would then disappear. Since the screen may have the previous file's text displayed on it, we must force a repaint to show the empty screen.

```
if (haveFile && !haveSaved) SaveCheck();
EmptyArray ();              // remove all lines from the array
strcpy (filename, "");      // set no filename
haveFile  = true;           // set have a new file
haveSaved = false;          // that has not been saved
current_top_line = 0;
current_start_col = 0;
maxDims = CSize(1,1);
SetCaption ();
SetOurScrollRange ();       // reset scroll bar range for newfile
Invalidate();               // and clear screen
```

Notice that no provision whatsoever is made to actually enter any data or modify any data.

The member function that responds to the File|Open menu selection is more complex. The common Open File dialog box is executed to obtain the new filename. If the user clicks OK, then we can retrieve the file name and go on to open the file and input the lines. In this example, several filters are provided for *.C, *.CPP, and all types of header files *.H*.

```
if (haveFile && !haveSaved) SaveCheck();
CFileDialog filedlg (TRUE,     // use Open dialog
                    "*.CPP", // default extension
                    "*.*",   // current file name
          OFN_FILEMUSTEXIST | OFN_PATHMUSTEXIST | OFN_LONGNAMES,
          "All Files (*.*)|*.*|CPP Files (*.CPP)|*.CPP|C Files"
          " (*.C)|*.C|Header Files (*.H*)|*.H*||", this);
if (filedlg.DoModal () == IDOK) { // user has chosen a file, so
 strcpy (filename, filedlg.GetPathName ());
 EmptyArray ();
 if (!LoadTextFileIntoCStrings (filename)) {
  DisplayMsg (IDS_MSG_FILEOPEN,IDS_MSG_ERROR,MB_ICONSTOP|MB_OK);
  haveFile = false;      // indicate no file
  return;
 }
 haveFile = true;
```

```
 haveSaved = true;
 current_top_line = 0;
 current_start_col = 0;
 SetCaption ();
 SetOurScrollRange ();
 Invalidate ();
}
```

Next, let's examine how the text file is actually input and then broken down into individual lines. The function **LoadTextFileIntoCStrings** is passed the filename string to open. I use the new Win32 file handle system. The DOS file offset pointer is positioned to the end of the file which returns the file size in bytes. Don't forget to reposition it back to the start of the file before attempting to input the data. Then I allocate a character string that is file size plus one byte in length so there is room for the null terminator. The file is then input in one read operation, a null terminator inserted and the file is closed. **ParseFileStringIntoCStrings** is called to do the work of separating the lines and adding them into the array. Once that is done, the character buffer is no longer needed and is deleted.

```
HANDLE hfile = CreateFile (filename, GENERIC_READ,
                           FILE_SHARE_READ, 0, OPEN_EXISTING,
                           FILE_ATTRIBUTE_NORMAL, 0);
if (hfile == INVALID_HANDLE_VALUE)
 return false;
DWORD filesize = SetFilePointer (hfile, 0, 0, FILE_END);
SetFilePointer (hfile, 0, 0, FILE_BEGIN);
...
char* ptrdata = new char[filesize + 1];
...
DWORD act_size;
ReadFile (hfile, ptrdata, filesize, &act_size, NULL);
ptrdata[filesize] = 0;
CloseHandle (hfile);
ParseFileStringIntoCStrings (ptrdata, filesize+1);
delete [] ptrdata; // remove obsolete array
```

ParseFileStringIntoCStrings, which is passed the pointer to the file character array and its length, must find each line in the array, store that in a new **CString,** and add it to the **CPtrArray lines**. The **GetSize** function can be used to tell how many lines are in the array for vertical scrolling. As each line is found, I track the maximum number of characters on any line, which is needed for horizontal scrolling.

At the start, **ptrstart** points to the beginning of a line, the very first byte. The end of that line is marked by a <CR> and <LF> pair of bytes. So I use a working pointer to move sequentially along the buffer looking for the byte with the <CR> in it. When I find it, I replace it with a null terminator. Now **ptrstart** really does point to a null terminated string.

```
long maxWidth = 1;
char* ptrstart = ptrdata;
char* ptrend = ptrdata + filesize;
char* ptrthis;
while (ptrstart < ptrend) {
 ptrthis = ptrstart;
 while (ptrthis < ptrend) {
  if (*ptrthis == '\r') {
   *ptrthis++ = 0;          // replace <CR> with null
   if (*ptrthis == '\n')
    ptrthis++;              // skip over the next <LF>
   break;                   // stop and store this string
  }
  ptrthis++;
 }
```

At this point, I allocate a new **CString** to hold this string, copy the found string into it, and add it to the array. I also check to see if this string is longer than the current maximum length of any string encountered thus far. To go on to the next line, I reset **ptrstart** to the value in the working pointer which is pointing to the first byte after the <LF> code.

```
  CString* ptrs = new CString;
  *ptrs = ptrstart;
  lines.Add (ptrs);
  if (ptrs->GetLength() > maxWidth)
   maxWidth = ptrs->GetLength();
  ptrstart = ptrthis;
 }
```

When the loop finished at the end of the entire buffer holding the whole file, I save the maximum dimensions for use in the scrolling operations.

```
 maxDims.cy = lines.GetSize ();
 maxDims.cx = maxWidth;
```

In contrast, the **SaveFile** function is vastly simpler. I open the output file using the new Win32 file handle system. Next, each line in the array must have the <CR><LF> codes appended to it. So that I can perform just one file write operation to gain speed, I must concatenate all of the strings into one large string. The **CString** is ideal for this. Notice how I iterate through each element in the array. Remember, it is an array of void pointers. So when you get access to the ith element, it must be typecast to the correct data type. If that dynamic cast cannot be done, then the pointer is 0.

```
 HANDLE hfile = CreateFile (filename, GENERIC_WRITE, 0, NULL,
            CREATE_ALWAYS, FILE_ATTRIBUTE_NORMAL, NULL);
...
 CString buf; // this string will hold the entire file
 CString* ptrs;
 for (int i=0; i<lines.GetSize(); i++) {
  ptrs = (CString*) lines.GetAt (i);
  if (!ptrs) continue;
  buf += *ptrs;
  buf += "\r\n";
 }
```

Now, I can write the entire file in one output operation. To illustrate how to gain access to the **char*** array that the **CString** is encapsulating, I coded the following.

```
 DWORD sz = buf.GetLength();
 char* buffer = buf.GetBuffer (sz);
 DWORD asize;
 if (!WriteFile (hfile, buffer, sz, &asize, NULL)
     || asize != sz) {
... display an error message
 buf.ReleaseBuffer ();
 CloseHandle (hfile);
 haveSaved = true;
```

But I could have saved several lines of coding my just writing from the **CString** directly. The **CString** class has an **LPCSTR** typecast function that does the necessary conversion.

```
WriteFile (hfile, buf, sz, &asize, NULL)
```

Using MFC's CScrollBar to Scroll a Text Window

Now let's examine the interrelated scrolling actions including **OnPaint**. Scrolling can be done by using the normal size scroll bars or by using the new **SCROLLINFO** method in which the size of the thumb bar is representative of the amount to be scrolled. I used the new **SCROLLINFO** method in **Pgm08a**.

Our use of scroll bars is complicated by factors that affect the current range. Perhaps the largest factor is the total number of lines in the file. Assume that 20 lines can be shown on the screen. If a file contains 100 lines, the vertical scroll bar should have a range of 0 to 80. If you let range from 0 to 100, you would get that peculiar effect of scrolling to the bottom only to find the last line is now just off the top of the screen. By limiting the range to total lines minus the number on the screen at one time, when you scroll to the bottom, the last line of the file is at the bottom of the screen.

Notice also that the number of possible lines per current screen size also depends on the font that is in use as well as the current client window size. Different fonts have differing average character dimensions, particularly the font point size. The other factor that affects the range of scroll bars is the current size or dimension of the window.

The scroll range, both horizontal and vertical, must be set from a number of locations within the program. Thus, I created a **SetOurScrollRange** function to do the work. This function is called from a number of places.

A. **OnSize** calls it to reset the scroll bars' current range in response to changing window dimensions.

B. **CmFontChange** calls it whenever the user changes the fonts; of course, **GetAvgCharDims** must be called before setting the scroll ranges.

C. **CmFileOpen** and **CmFileNew** and **CmFileClose** must call it to adjust the scroll bars' range based upon the number of lines in the file.

Under the MFC, a **CWnd** automatically installs scroll bars if the window is created with a **WNDCLASS** style that includes the **WS_VSCROLL** and/or **WS_HSCROLL**. The **CWnd** class contains the key scrolling functions, particularly the **GetScrollPos**, **SetScrollPos**, **SetScrollRange**, and **ScrollWindow**. The scroll bar range must be recalculated whenever there is a font change, a window size change, or a file new or open request. Therefore, **SetOurScrollRange** is invoked from **OnSize**, **CmFontChange**, **CmFileOpen**, **CmFileNew**, and **CmFileClose**. If the range of a scroll bar becomes 0, the scroll bar is automatically hidden. Whenever the range of a scroll bar is above 0, the scroll bar becomes visible.

The calculations to determine the amount of scroll range needed are the same ones with which you are already familiar. They are shown below. The **height** and **width** are set in **OnSize**. The **CSize maxDims** is set when the file is loaded and contains the number of lines and the maximum number of characters on the longest line.

For Vertical Scrolling:
```
numLinesPerPage = height / avgCharHeight;
maxScrollLines = max (0, maxDims.cy - numLinesPerPage + 1);
currentTopLine = min (currentTopLine, maxScrollLines);
```

For Horizontal Scrolling:
```
numCharsPerLine = width / avgCharWidth;
maxHscrollChars = max (0, maxDims.cx - numCharsPerLine);
currentStartCol = min(currentStartCol, maxHscrollChars);
```

The **SetOurScrollRange** function begins by making the above calculations. The next step depends on which type of scroll bar your desire. If you wish the older style in which the thumb bar always remains the same small size, then code the following next.
```
SetScrollRange (SB_VERT, 0, maxScrollLines, FALSE);
SetScrollPos (SB_VERT, currentTopLine, TRUE);
SetScrollRange (SB_HORZ, 0, maxHscrollChars, FALSE);
SetScrollPos (SB_HORZ, currentStartCol, TRUE);
```

To avoid unnecessary scroll bar flickering, if the range and position of the thumb bar are going to both be adjusted in quick succession, as done here, set the **BOOL** for repainting to **FALSE** on the first function and then **TRUE** on the last. In this manner, the scroll bar is only redrawn one time.

In **Pgm08a**, I wish to illustrate the newer style scroll bars with the proportioned thumb bar sizes. So in this case a call to **SetScrollInfo** must be made for each scroll bar, passing a filled in **SCROLLINFO** structure. The **CWnd SetScrollInfo** function is coded this way.

```
SetScrollInfo (SB_VERT or SB_HORZ, &si, TRUE);
```
where **si** is an instance of the **SCROLLINFO** structure. Its members include
```
WORD fMask - an ORed series specifying which of the following members are valid
int  nMin  - the minimum scroll amount - usually 0
int  nMax  - the maximum scroll amount in pixels
int  nPage - the number of pixels in a page or screen height
int  nPos  - the current thumb bar position
```

The flags for the **WORD** that specify which are to be used include these.
```
SIF_PAGE            - use the page amount to set page size
```

```
SIF_POS              - set the position, use nPos
SIF_RANGE            - set the range, use nMin and nMax
SIF_DISABLENOSCROLL - disable the scroll bar
SIF_ALL              - all of these are valid
```

So for vertical scroll range setting, we use the following.

```
SCROLLINFO si;
si.cbSize = sizeof (si);
si.fMask = SIF_ALL;
si.nMin = 0;
si.nMax = maxDims.cy;
si.nPage = numLinesPerPage;
si.nPos = currentTopline; // initial position at the start
SetScrollInfo (SB_VERT, &si, TRUE);
```

Followed by this for horizontal scrolling

```
si.nMax = maxDims.cx;
si.nPage = numCharsPerLine;
si.nPos = currentStartCol; // initial position at the start
SetScrollInfo (SB_HORZ, &si, TRUE);
```

Under the MFC, our applications must process and handle scroll bar messages just as was done in the C API style back in Chapters 2 and 3. The message map entries are **OnVScroll** and **OnHScroll**.

```
BEGIN_MESSAGE_MAP(FrameWin, CFrameWnd)
 ON_WM_VSCROLL ()
 ON_WM_HSCROLL ()
END_MESSAGE_MAP()
```

The prototypes for these two messages in the class header are these.

```
afx_msg void  OnHScroll (UINT type, UINT pos, CScrollBar*);
afx_msg void  OnVScroll (UINT type, UINT pos, CscrollBar*);
```

Here the scroll **type** is one of the standard **SB_** scroll message ids while the **pos** or position is the current position of the thumb bar.

The vertical scrolling function **OnVScroll** first sets the number of lines to scroll based upon the **SB_** scroll message ids. The number of lines to scroll is either one line for up/down one line or the number of lines per page for page up/down or the relative number of lines from the current top to the thumb bar position when tracking the thumb bar. This potential amount, as usual, is then forced into range based upon the current top line position in the file and the maximum amount of scrolling possible.

```
int numLinesToScroll;
switch (type) {
 case SB_LINEUP:      // scroll up 1 line
  numLinesToScroll = -1; break;
 case SB_LINEDOWN:    // scroll 1 line down
  numLinesToScroll = 1; break;
 case SB_PAGEUP:      // scroll 1 page up
  numLinesToScroll = min (-1, -num_lines_per_page); break;
 case SB_PAGEDOWN:    // scroll 1 page down
  numLinesToScroll = max (1, num_lines_per_page); break;
 case SB_THUMBTRACK: // follow thumb bar
  numLinesToScroll = pos - current_top_line; break;
 default:
  numLinesToScroll = 0;
}
numLinesToScroll = max (-current_top_line,
                      min (numLinesToScroll,
                          max_scroll_lines - current_top_line));
```

In **OnHScroll**, the number of characters to horizontally scroll is give by these choices.

```
int num_chars_to_scroll;
```

```
switch (type) {
 case SB_LINEUP:     // scroll 1 col left
  num_chars_to_scroll = -1; break;
 case SB_LINEDOWN:   // scroll 1 col right
  num_chars_to_scroll = 1; break;
 case SB_PAGEUP:     // scroll 1 page left
  num_chars_to_scroll = -8; break;
 case SB_PAGEDOWN:    // scroll 1 page right
  num_chars_to_scroll = 8; break;
 case SB_THUMBTRACK: // follow thumb bar
  num_chars_to_scroll = pos - current_start_col; break;
 default:
  num_chars_to_scroll = 0;
}
num_chars_to_scroll = max (-current_start_col,
                      min (num_chars_to_scroll,
                        max_hscroll_chars - current_start_col));
```

Finally, if there really are lines to scroll or any horizontal characters to scroll, the new top line is calculated or the new current start column is calculated and the **CWnd** function **ScrollWindow** is invoked. This function requires the amount to reposition the window in both x and y dimensions. For vertical scrolling, the zero is passed for the x dimension. And the y dimension is passed the **negative** of the number of lines to scroll multiplied by the average character height. The last two **NULL** or **0** parameters are the address of a **(RECT** or **CRect)** rectangular area of the client area to be scrolled and the address of any clipping rectangle **(RECT** or **Crect)**.

So for vertical scrolling we have these lines.

```
if (numLinesToScroll !=0) {
 current_top_line +=numLinesToScroll;
 ScrollWindow (0, -avg_char_height*numLinesToScroll, 0, 0);
```

And for horizontal scrolling, we code the following.

```
if (num_chars_to_scroll !=0) {
 current_start_col +=num_chars_to_scroll;
 ScrollWindow (-avg_char_width*num_chars_to_scroll, 0, 0, 0);
```

The final steps in either **OnVSchroll** or **OnHScroll** depend upon the style of the scroll bars. If you are using the older style bars, then we do the following.

```
SetScrollPos (SB_VERT, current_top_line, TRUE);
```

and

```
SetScrollPos (SB_HORZ, current_start_col, TRUE);
```

However, if the new style scroll bars are in use, we must again call **SetScrollInfo** to set the new thumb bar position. Since that is the only value that is changing, the setup is shorter. For the vertical scrolling case, we code this.

```
SCROLLINFO si;
si.cbSize = sizeof (si);
si.fMask = SIF_POS;
si.nPos = current_top_line; // initial position at the start
SetScrollInfo (SB_VERT, &si, TRUE);
```

And for horizontal scrolling, we code this.

```
SCROLLINFO si;
si.cbSize = sizeof (si);
si.fMask = SIF_POS;
si.nPos = current_start_col; // initial position at the start
SetScrollInfo (SB_HORZ, &si, TRUE);
```

Now exactly what happens when the **ScrollWindow** is executed? Suppose that twenty-five lines were painted on the screen. Assume that the user scrolls down one line. It does not make sense for Windows to invalidate the whole screen. Actually, twenty-four lines are already visible and only one line must be new. Hence, Windows, based upon the area of the screen to be scrolled, does a **BitBlt** (Bit Block Transfer—see Chapter 9) or a graphics copy of that portion of the screen that contains the still needed twenty-four lines, copying that block up one line or one average character height, overlaying the existing image. Thus, the first twenty-four lines are now just where they should be for the scrolled effect. Windows now issues a paint message for the only remaining invalid rectangle that occupied by the bottom line. Smart paint routines **must** take advantage of this and only display that **one** needed line, creating a very smooth text scroll.

The problem with this approach is that it places a great deal of extra coding into the paint routine just to determine which line or series of lines in the entire file need to be displayed at what portion on the screen. But it is not hard to do.

In the **OnPaint** function, when we acquire our paint dc, Windows inserts into that instance the information we need in some public data members. Within a **CPaintDC**, the paint information is stored in the member **m_ps** which is the **PAINTSTRUCT** instance. One of its members is the invalid rectangle known as **rcPaint**. As **OnPaint** begins, remember that any user font must be selected into the dc along with any user chosen font color.

```
CPaintDC dc (this);
if (ptrfont) {
 ptroldfont = dc.SelectObject (ptrfont);
}
dc.SetTextColor (fontcolor);
dc.SetBkMode (TRANSPARENT);
```

Rather than try to figure out at which character within a line to begin painting, I just repaint the entire line. Trying to determine which character has pitfalls because of variable pitched fonts. Okay. So how do we determine what to paint?

Well, ignoring for a moment the invalid rectangle given in **m_ps.rcPaint**, we would begin with the current top line and end after one screen's worth of lines, current top line + the number of lines per screen + 1. Why +1? Well, window heights are often not a precise multiple of the average character height. In essence, then, one may well be showing the top portion of another line at the very bottom of the window. So the +1 allows for that effect. However, we must guard against trying to paint more lines than are actually in the array. Conceivably, the current top line + number of lines per screen could exceed the total number of lines in the data. So we must use the minimum of those two values so our line subscript does not go out of range.

To only paint those lines that are actually needed as indicated by **m_ps.rcPaint**, we must add to the actual starting line index the number of lines that the **m_ps.rcPaint.top** value represents—that is, divide **m_ps.rcPaint.top** by the average character height. Similarly, we must end at the current top line plus **m_ps.rcPaint.bottom** divided by the average character height. It is most convenient to make two variables for these two values.

```
long i;
int numlines = lines.GetSize();
int firstLine = max (0, current_top_line +
                 dc.m_ps.rcPaint.top / avg_char_height - 1);
int lastLine = min (numlines, 1 + current_top_line +
                 dc.m_ps.rcPaint.bottom / avg_char_height);
```

That was the hard part. The actual painting code is now a simple loop. But, when done, do not forget to select back into the dc the original default font.

```
for (i=firstLine; i<lastLine; i++) {
 CString* ptrs = (CString*) lines.GetAt(i);
 if (!ptrs) continue;
 dc.TextOut (avg_char_width * (1 - current_start_col),
          avg_char_height * (-current_top_line + i), *ptrs);
}
if (ptrfont) {
 dc.SelectObject (ptroldfont);
}
```

Some Additional Considerations About Pgm08a

When you run the application, pay attention to the limitations that are present. How could we insert coding so that one could enter text, change text, or even find and locate text? The clipboard functions are implemented in Chapter 13. There should be a mouse selection or placement of an editing insertion point.

What about memory requirements? This solution is actually is good shape. The **CPtrArray** can grow as large as needed. Each item in the array is a **CString**, which is also growable. The only memory limitations are the total amount of available memory and swap drive space.

In **Pgm08a**, many command handlers such as that for Edit|Cut were shelled out and not implemented. One constructs larger applications **one** function at a time. When setting up menus and their corresponding handlers and enabler functions, it is common practice to code shell dummies as done here in **Pgm08a**. Later on when the basic application is working, a programmer then begins to add the actual code to these shelled functions.

Scrolling Only a Portion of a Window and the RecalcLayout Function: Pgm08b

Sometimes only a portion of a window area ought to be scrolled. Perhaps there is a company logo or heading displayed at the top portion of the window that should remain fixed while the rest of the screen scrolls. When the **ScrollWindow** function is called, the last two parameters are the address of a scrolling area rectangle and a clipping rectangle. Until now, we passed 0 for them, indicating neither were present. Thus, the entire window client area was scrolled.

In order to scroll a portion of a window while the remainder is untouched, a rectangle must define that portion that is to be scrolled. And the address of that rectangle is passed as the last two parameters to **ScrollWindow**. In **Pgm08b**, the name of the file being viewed is displayed in the "header" zone at the top of the client window, outlined in red. The remainder of the window becomes the scrolling area.

It is vitally important to restructure **OnPaint** to use x and y coordinated that are based on the scrolling area rectangle. In other words, we use the scrolling area's top and left coordinates as the base numbers to which we then add in the current line's coordinates. Failure to compute the (x, y) coordinates for **TextOut** calls often results in strange portions of the window being scrolled.

However, there is another factor that ought to be considered at this point so that proper scrolling techniques can be learned initially without having to be drastically altered when more features are added to the application. I am specifically referring to the addition of tool bars. In chapter 11, we will add various tool bars and a status bar to our applications. Unfortunately, the **FrameWin** considers these decorations as just another child window. So **OnSize** reports the total client window dimensions. The decorations lie inside that area! **GetClientArea** also reports the total window size. So if one uses those dimensions, one ends up scrolling the tool bars and status bar! While it is an interesting trick, it is not acceptable in application scrolling. Immediately, one must drastically alter scrolling methodology. I find that this is an unacceptable learning twist!

Thus, since we are learning the proper method of scrolling here, let's modify our approach to include this bizarre behavior that we will encounter very shortly. That way, we will not have to alter our scrolling logic at all when we add in the fancy decorations—the tool bars and status bar. The key to scrolling logic that works in all situations is the **CFrameWnd** function called **RecalcLayout**.

RecalcLayout is defined to be a virtual void member function of the **CFrameWnd** class. It is called by the framework at various times whenever the window needs adjusting because a new child has been added or the window resized or the tool bars have been repositioned. In other words, it is called by the framework when any event that potentially could result in a change of dimensions occurs. It takes one **BOOL** parameter that defaults to **TRUE** which notifies the active in-place item that the frame has changed size.

If we override this function, the MFC provides another function that we can call that returns the real client area. It is called **RepositionBars**. Normally, **RepositionBars** does just that, it repositions and redraws all of the tool bars and status bar. However, if it is passed the **enum CWnd::reposQuery**, then it does not reposition anything but instead calculates what remains of the client area which is the "real" client area, as far as we are concerned.

To do scrolling properly such that you will never have to redesign the entire process when tool bars are added, we must take this effect into account now. In our **FrameWin** class, define two **CRect** objects. I called them the **RealClientArea** and **ScrollArea**.

They obtain their values from within our **RecalcLayout** function. After calling the base class which actually does the repositioning operation, **RepositionBars** passing it the query identifier so that it fills the **RealClientArea CRect** with the "real" client area. In that function call, the identifiers **AFX_IDW_CONTROLBAR_FIRST** and **AFX_IDW_CONTROLBAR_LAST** specify the range of identifiers used by our tool bars.

```
void FrameWin::RecalcLayout (BOOL bNotify) {
 CFrameWnd::RecalcLayout (bNotify );
 // calculate real client area
 RepositionBars (AFX_IDW_CONTROLBAR_FIRST,
                 AFX_IDW_CONTROLBAR_LAST, 0, CWnd::reposQuery,
                 &RealClientArea );
```

Now we must set the **ScrollArea CRect** to the dimensions of the scrolling portion. But the corners of the rectangle must be based upon those of the **RealClientArea** corners. In this example, the heading area displays one line which is the filename. I added four extra pixels for spacing above and below the text. The **CRect SetRect** function provides a convenient way to set the four values. Notice that each of the four values are based on the **RealClientArea** corners.

```
 // for example allow for headings avg char height + 4
 ScrollArea.SetRect (RealClientArea.left,
                     RealClientArea.top + avg_char_height + 5,
                     RealClientArea.right, RealClientArea.bottom);
```

With these two rectangles initialize or reset to the new dimensions, we can now set the scrolling ranges. Remember that any change in the actual dimensions may force a change in the scrolling range. After calling **SetOurScrollRange**, invalidate the **RealClientRect** to force the client window to be repainted using these new or modified dimensions.

```
 SetOurScrollRange();
 InvalidateRect (RealClientArea, TRUE); // force a repaint
}
```

In **SetOurScrollRange**, there are only two small changes to be made. We can no longer use the total client window size as reported in **OnSize** to determine the maximum lines per page and the number of characters per line. Instead we must use the dimensions of the **ScrollArea**.

```
      numLinesPerPage = ScrollArea.Height()  / avgCharHight;
      numCharsPerLine = ScrollArea.Width()  / avgCharWidth;
```

In **OnSize**, we should call **RecalcLayout**. Later on, when the tool bars are installed, we can dispense with calling it from **OnSize**. The call is just this.

```
      RecalcLayout (TRUE);
```

In **OnVScroll**, the **ScrollWindow** function call now passes the address of the **ScrollArea** as the rectangle to scroll and clip.

```
      ScrollWindow (0, -avgCharHeight * numLinesToScroll,
                    &ScrollArea, &ScrollArea);
```

And similarly in **OnHScroll**, we have this call.

```
      ScrollWindow (-avgCharWidth * numCharsToScroll, 0,
                    &ScrollArea, &ScrollArea);
```

The real work comes in the restructuring of **OnPaint** to only use (x, y) coordinates that are based upon either the **RealClientArea** for the headings or **ScrollArea** for the actual text lines of the file we are viewing.

To draw the red rectangle outline for the headings, I created a red pen and selected it into the dc, saving the old pen. Then I made a **CRect** object of the proper dimensions. Note that the dimensions are all expressed in terms of **RealClientArea** and **ScrollArea** values highlighted in bold. The **TexOut** coordinates are in terms of **RealClientArea**. It would be a major mistake to use absolute coordinates, such as 0 or **avg_char_height** because the tool bar may very well be occupying that space of the client window!

```
 CPen red;
 CPen* ptroldpen;
 red.CreatePen (PS_SOLID, 1, RGB (255, 0, 0));
      ptroldpen = dc.SelectObject (&red);
 CRect head = CRect (RealClientArea.left, RealClientArea.top, RealClientArea.right,
ScrollArea.top-1);
 dc.Rectangle (&head);
 if (haveFile) {
  CString name;
  if (filename[0] == 0)
   name = "Untitled";
  else
   name = filename;
  dc.TextOut (RealClientArea.left+2, RealClientArea.top+1, name);
 }
```

```
else
 dc.TextOut (RealClientArea.left+2, RealClientArea.top+1,
             "No File Opened Yet");
dc.SelectObject (ptroldpen);
```

After printing the heading, the next step is to install a clipping region so that no errant drawing can be done over the top of this heading area. After allocating an instance of **CRgn**, I called **CreateRectRgnIndirect** passing it the **ScrollArea** rectangle on which to model the region. Then, use the **SelectClipRgn** function to install the clipping region. From this point onwards, nothing can be drawn outside the region which is the **ScrollArea** rectangle.

```
CRgn rclip;
rclip.CreateRectRgnIndirect (&ScrollArea);
dc.SelectClipRgn (&rclip);
```

Now go ahead and determine the first and last lines that need to be repainted as before. The changes lie in the (x, y) coordinates passed to the **TexOut** call. These must use **ScrollArea** as a base.

```
int numlines = lines.GetSize();
int firstLine = max (0, currentTopLine +
                dc.m_ps.rcPaint.top / avgCharHeight - 1);
int lastLine = min (numlines, 1 + currentTopLine +
                dc.m_ps.rcPaint.bottom / avgCharHeight);
for (i=firstLine; i<lastLine; i++) {
 CString* ptrs = (CString*) lines.GetAt(i);
 if (!ptrs) continue;
 dc.TextOut (ScrollArea.left +
                avgCharWidth * (1 - currentStartCol),
             ScrollArea.top +
              avgCharHeight * (-currentTopLine + i), *ptrs);
}
```

In summary, if you always set up your scrolling coding in a similar manner, overriding **RecalcLayout** to establish the real dimensions of the client area and then force all painting and scrolling to be in terms of these rectangles, scrolling will be a breeze.

An alternative approach is to derive another class, say **ChildWin** from **CWnd**. Then, install an instance of the **ChildWin** as the client window of the **FrameWnd**. All of the text, the array, the scrolling and the painting are moved from the **FrameWin** into the **ChildWin** class. The **CFrameWnd** class does properly handle the resizing of the **ChildWin** when it is a child of the frame. One then only need worry about the heading rectangle and the setting up a scrolling rectangle to avoid scrolling the headings in the **ChildWin**. The **FrameWin** can still respond to the File menu items but likely passes the requests on down to the child.

Console Debugging Window: Another Trick of the Masters

By now you have discovered that it is very difficult to debug **OnPaint** coding and scrolling actions because every time the debugger window pops up, it forces a total repaint of the application window. You cannot step through the instructions of **OnPaint** and see what it is doing on the screen. The only effective way to debug an **OnPaint** routine is through the use of a second monitor, which Visual Studio does support. However, there is an alternative approach that provides some help.

When your application starts, it can open a DOS Console Window. This window looks just like the DOS console windows that most all of your previous programs have been using. An application can use C style **cprintf** statements to display informative information to the console window during the debug run. In order to use the console output functions, we must include <**conio.h**>.

Obviously, we do not want this console window appearing in the Release version, only during debug runs. When you select the Debug build, the compiler defines a symbol **_DEBUG** which we can test. Thus, we surround all of these console output instructions with such a check.

```
#ifdef _DEBUG
_cprintf ("FrameWin ctor - now calling Create\r\n");
#endif
```

When using the **cprintf** function, you must supply the end of line DOS codes which are a carriage return followed by a line feed code. These are **\r** and **\n** respectively. The **cprintf** function takes the usual C output control specifications to display an **int**, a **long**, a **double**, a **char** and a **string**: %d %ld %f %c %s.

Figure 8.4 shows **Pgm08b** scrolling a file along with the console window behind it.

When the program terminates, the console window also closes. So in order to examine its contents in detail, set a break point in **OnDestroy** on the base class call. Then, when the application terminates, this is about the last function to be called. You can then study in detail or copy portions of the console window for later examination.

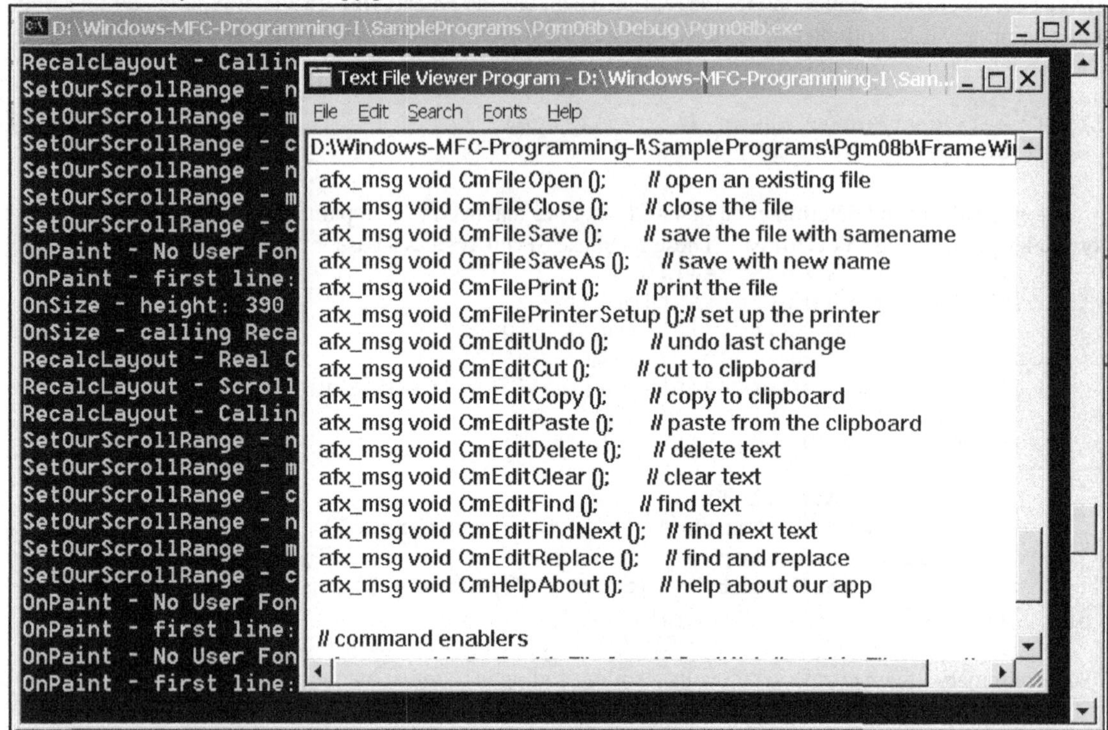

Figure 8.4 Pgm08b with the Black Console Window

Here is the output from a sample run of **Pgm08b**. Notice the detailed information given when a scroll action is requested along with the **OnPaint** data. Interestingly, you can also follow along the other function call sequences as the application first starts up.

The Console Window's Output

```
FrameWin ctor - now calling Create
RecalcLayout - Real Client Area 0 0 756 466
RecalcLayout - Scroll Area 0 -842150446 756 466
RecalcLayout - Calling SetOurScrollRange
OnSize - height: 446 width: 756
OnSize - calling RecalcLayout
RecalcLayout - Real Client Area 0 0 756 446
RecalcLayout - Scroll Area 0 -842150446 756 446
RecalcLayout - Calling SetOurScrollRange
SetOurScrollRange - num lines per page: -1
SetOurScrollRange - max scroll lines: 3
SetOurScrollRange - current top line: 0
SetOurScrollRange - num chars per line: 0
SetOurScrollRange - max hscroll: 1
SetOurScrollRange - current start column: 0
SetOurScrollRange - num lines per page: -1
SetOurScrollRange - max scroll lines: 3
SetOurScrollRange - current top line: 0
SetOurScrollRange - num chars per line: 0
SetOurScrollRange - max hscroll: 1
SetOurScrollRange - current start column: 0
```

```
OnCreate - calls GetAvgCharDims
GetAvgCharDims: height: 20 width: 9
SetCaption called with this title:
Text File Viewer Program - No File Opened
OnSize - height: 446 width: 756
OnSize - calling RecalcLayout
RecalcLayout - Real Client Area 0 0 756 446
RecalcLayout - Scroll Area 0 25 756 446
RecalcLayout - Calling SetOurScrollRange
OnSize - height: 466 width: 756
OnSize - calling RecalcLayout
RecalcLayout - Real Client Area 0 0 756 466
RecalcLayout - Scroll Area 0 25 756 466
RecalcLayout - Calling SetOurScrollRange
SetOurScrollRange - num lines per page: 22
SetOurScrollRange - max scroll lines: 0
SetOurScrollRange - current top line: 0
SetOurScrollRange - num chars per line: 84
SetOurScrollRange - max hscroll: 0
SetOurScrollRange - current start column: 0
SetOurScrollRange - num lines per page: 22
SetOurScrollRange - max scroll lines: 0
SetOurScrollRange - current top line: 0
SetOurScrollRange - num chars per line: 84
SetOurScrollRange - max hscroll: 0
SetOurScrollRange - current start column: 0
OnPaint - No User Font Chosen Yet
OnPaint - first line: 0 last line: 0
CmEnableFileOps - entered - have file: 0
CmEnableFileOps - entered - have file: 0
CmEnableFileOps - entered - have file: 0
CmEnableFileOps - entered - have file: 0
ParseFileStringIntoCStrings - number lines: 112
ParseFileStringIntoCStrings - max width in chars: 65
CmFileOpen - file loaded is called: D:\Windows-MFC-Programming-I\
          SamplePrograms\Pgm08b\FrameWin.h
CmFileOpen - calling SetCaption and SetOurScrollRange
SetCaption called with this title:
Text File Viewer Program - D:\Windows-MFC-Programming-I\SamplePro
          \Pgm08b\FrameWin.h
OnSize - height: 466 width: 736
OnSize - calling RecalcLayout
RecalcLayout - Real Client Area 0 0 736 466
RecalcLayout - Scroll Area 0 25 736 466
RecalcLayout - Calling SetOurScrollRange
SetOurScrollRange - num lines per page: 22
SetOurScrollRange - max scroll lines: 91
SetOurScrollRange - current top line: 0
SetOurScrollRange - num chars per line: 81
SetOurScrollRange - max hscroll: 0
SetOurScrollRange - current start column: 0
SetOurScrollRange - num lines per page: 22
SetOurScrollRange - max scroll lines: 91
SetOurScrollRange - current top line: 0
SetOurScrollRange - num chars per line: 81
SetOurScrollRange - max hscroll: 0
SetOurScrollRange - current start column: 0
OnPaint - No User Font Chosen Yet
OnPaint - first line: 0 last line: 24
OnVScroll: num lines to scroll: 22
OnPaint - No User Font Chosen Yet
OnPaint - first line: 22 last line: 46
OnVScroll: num lines to scroll: 0
OnVScroll: num lines to scroll: 1
```

```
OnPaint - No User Font Chosen Yet
OnPaint - first line: 44 last line: 47
OnVScroll: num lines to scroll: 0
OnSize - height: 465 width: 736
OnSize - calling RecalcLayout
RecalcLayout - Real Client Area 0 0 736 465
RecalcLayout - Scroll Area 0 25 736 465
RecalcLayout - Calling SetOurScrollRange
SetOurScrollRange - num lines per page: 22
SetOurScrollRange - max scroll lines: 91
SetOurScrollRange - current top line: 23
SetOurScrollRange - num chars per line: 81
SetOurScrollRange - max hscroll: 0
SetOurScrollRange - current start column: 0
OnPaint - No User Font Chosen Yet
OnPaint - first line: 22 last line: 47
OnSize - height: 460 width: 678
OnSize - calling RecalcLayout
RecalcLayout - Real Client Area 0 0 678 460
RecalcLayout - Scroll Area 0 25 678 460
RecalcLayout - Calling SetOurScrollRange
SetOurScrollRange - num lines per page: 21
SetOurScrollRange - max scroll lines: 92
SetOurScrollRange - current top line: 23
SetOurScrollRange - num chars per line: 75
SetOurScrollRange - max hscroll: 0
SetOurScrollRange - current start column: 0
OnPaint - No User Font Chosen Yet
OnPaint - first line: 22 last line: 47
OnSize - height: 453 width: 530
OnSize - calling RecalcLayout
RecalcLayout - Real Client Area 0 0 530 453
RecalcLayout - Scroll Area 0 25 530 453
RecalcLayout - Calling SetOurScrollRange
OnSize - height: 433 width: 530
OnSize - calling RecalcLayout
RecalcLayout - Real Client Area 0 0 530 433
RecalcLayout - Scroll Area 0 25 530 433
RecalcLayout - Calling SetOurScrollRange
SetOurScrollRange - num lines per page: 20
SetOurScrollRange - max scroll lines: 93
SetOurScrollRange - current top line: 23
SetOurScrollRange - num chars per line: 58
SetOurScrollRange - max hscroll: 7
SetOurScrollRange - current start column: 0
SetOurScrollRange - num lines per page: 20
SetOurScrollRange - max scroll lines: 93
SetOurScrollRange - current top line: 23
SetOurScrollRange - num chars per line: 58
SetOurScrollRange - max hscroll: 7
SetOurScrollRange - current start column: 0
OnPaint - No User Font Chosen Yet
OnPaint - first line: 22 last line: 45
OnSize - height: 418 width: 412
OnSize - calling RecalcLayout
RecalcLayout - Real Client Area 0 0 412 418
RecalcLayout - Scroll Area 0 25 412 418
RecalcLayout - Calling SetOurScrollRange
SetOurScrollRange - num lines per page: 19
SetOurScrollRange - max scroll lines: 94
SetOurScrollRange - current top line: 23
SetOurScrollRange - num chars per line: 45
SetOurScrollRange - max hscroll: 20
SetOurScrollRange - current start column: 0
```

```
OnPaint - No User Font Chosen Yet
OnPaint - first line: 22 last line: 44
OnHScroll: num chars to scroll: 1
OnPaint - No User Font Chosen Yet
OnPaint - first line: 23 last line: 44
OnHScroll: num chars to scroll: 0
OnHScroll: num chars to scroll: 8
OnPaint - No User Font Chosen Yet
OnPaint - first line: 23 last line: 44
OnHScroll: num chars to scroll: 0
CmFontChange - user has selected a new font
CmFontChange - calling GetAvgCharDims, SetOurScrollRange
GetAvgCharDims: height: 24 width: 9
SetOurScrollRange - num lines per page: 16
SetOurScrollRange - max scroll lines: 97
SetOurScrollRange - current top line: 23
SetOurScrollRange - num chars per line: 45
SetOurScrollRange - max hscroll: 20
SetOurScrollRange - current start column: 9
OnPaint - Using User Font
OnPaint - first line: 22 last line: 41
CmEnableFileOps - entered - have file: 1
CmEnableFileOps - entered - have file: 1
CmEnableFileOps - entered - have file: 1
CmEnableFileOps - entered - have file: 1
CmEnableFileOps - entered - have file: 1
CmFileClose - file closed
CmFileOpen - calling SetCaption and SetOurScrollRange
SetCaption called with this title:
Text File Viewer Program - No File Opened
SetOurScrollRange - num lines per page: 16
SetOurScrollRange - max scroll lines: 97
SetOurScrollRange - current top line: 0
SetOurScrollRange - num chars per line: 45
SetOurScrollRange - max hscroll: 20
SetOurScrollRange - current start column: 0
OnPaint - Using User Font
OnPaint - first line: 0 last line: 0
OnPaint - Using User Font
OnPaint - first line: 0 last line: 0
OnDestroy - calling base class
```

To open the console window, add one function call to **AllocConsole** in the **CWinApp** derived class before you begin to create the actual **FrameWin**.

```
BOOL  Pgm08b::InitInstance () {
#ifdef _DEBUG
 if (!AllocConsole())
  AfxMessageBox ("Opps. Failed to make console window",
                 MB_ICONSTOP | MB_OK);
#endif
 m_pMainWnd = new FrameWin;
```

The function returns **FALSE** if it fails to create the console window. If this occurs, I display a simple message and continue.

Here is the complete coding for the **FrameWin** class of **Pgm08b**. Notice the two new **CRect** objects in the class defintion: **RealClientArea** and **ScrollArea**.

```
Pgm08b's FrameWin Implementation
```

```
#include "stdafx.h"
#include <conio.h>
#include "framewin.h"
#include "resource.h"
```

. . .

```
/*************************************************************/
/*                                                           */
/* Framewin: Construct the window object                     */
/*                                                           */
/*************************************************************/

FrameWin::FrameWin () : CFrameWnd () {

 LoadAccelTable ("MAINMENU");        // install keybd accelerators

 DWORD style = WS_OVERLAPPEDWINDOW; // set basic window style
 CString title;
 title.LoadString (IDS_MAINTITLE);  // load caption of window
 maxDims = CSize (1,1);             // set a default dimension
 currentTopLine = 0;
 currentStartCol = 0;
 haveFile = haveSaved = false;
 ptrlogfont = 0;
 ptrfont = 0;
 fontcolor = RGB (0, 0, 0);     // set default font color black

#ifdef _DEBUG
_cprintf ("FrameWin ctor - now calling Create\r\n");
#endif

 Create ( AfxRegisterWndClass (
              CS_VREDRAW | CS_HREDRAW,
              AfxGetApp()->LoadStandardCursor (IDC_ARROW),
              ::CreateSolidBrush (GetSysColor(COLOR_WINDOW)),
              AfxGetApp()->LoadStandardIcon (IDI_APPLICATION)),
         title,         // window caption
         style,         // wndclass DWORD style
         rectDefault,   // set initial window position
         0,             // the parent window, here none
         "MAINMENU");   // assign the main menu
 SetCaption ();
}

/*************************************************************/
/*                                                           */
/* OnCreate: get average character dimensions                */
/*                                                           */
/*************************************************************/

int FrameWin::OnCreate (LPCREATESTRUCT lpCS) {
 if (CFrameWnd::OnCreate (lpCS) == -1) return -1;
#ifdef _DEBUG
_cprintf ("OnCreate - calls GetAvgCharDims\r\n");
#endif
 GetAvgCharDims ();
 return 0;
}
```

. . .

```
/*************************************************************/
/*                                                           */
/* OnSize: acquire the current dimensions of the client window */
/*         and reset scrolling ranges                        */
/*                                                           */
/*************************************************************/

void FrameWin::OnSize (UINT, int cx, int cy) {
 width = cx;  // save current height
 height = cy; // save current width
```

```
#ifdef _DEBUG
_cprintf ("OnSize - height: %d width: %d\r\n", height, width);
_cprintf ("OnSize - calling RecalcLayout\r\n");
#endif
 RecalcLayout (TRUE);
}

/***************************************************************/
/*                                                             */
/* SetCaption: appends the filename to the caption             */
/*                                                             */
/***************************************************************/

void FrameWin::SetCaption () {
 CString title;
 title.LoadString (IDS_MAINTITLE);  // load caption of window
 if (haveFile) {
  title += " - ";
  if (filename[0] == 0)
   title += "Untitled";
  else
   title += filename;
 }
 else
  title += " - No File Opened";
 SetWindowText (title);
#ifdef _DEBUG
_cprintf ("SetCaption called with this title:\r\n");
_cprintf ("%s\r\n", title);
#endif
}

/***************************************************************/
/*                                                             */
/* OnPaint: display what the user has selected                 */
/*                                                             */
/***************************************************************/

void FrameWin::OnPaint () {
 CPaintDC dc (this);
 // install user font, if any
 if (ptrfont) {
  ptroldfont = dc.SelectObject (ptrfont); // save old font
 }
 dc.SetTextColor (fontcolor);   // install font color
 dc.SetBkMode (TRANSPARENT);    // set so background color shows

#ifdef _DEBUG
_cprintf ("OnPaint - %s\r\n", ptrfont ? "Using User Font" :
           "No User Font Chosen Yet");
#endif

 CPen red;
 CPen* ptroldpen;
 red.CreatePen (PS_SOLID, 1, RGB (255, 0, 0));
 ptroldpen = dc.SelectObject (&red);
 CRect head = CRect (RealClientArea.left, RealClientArea.top,
                     RealClientArea.right, ScrollArea.top-1);
 dc.Rectangle (&head);
 if (haveFile) {
  CString name;
  if (filename[0] == 0)
   name = "Untitled";
```

```
  else
   name = filename;
  dc.TextOut (RealClientArea.left+2, RealClientArea.top+1, name);
 }
 else
  dc.TextOut (RealClientArea.left+2, RealClientArea.top+1,
              "No File Opened Yet");
 dc.SelectObject (ptroldpen);
 CRgn rclip;
 rclip.CreateRectRgnIndirect (&ScrollArea);
 dc.SelectClipRgn (&rclip);
 long i;
 // paint only those lines that are actually needed
 int numlines = lines.GetSize();
 int firstLine = max (0, currentTopLine +
                 dc.m_ps.rcPaint.top / avgCharHeight - 1);
 int lastLine = min (numlines, 1 + currentTopLine +
                 dc.m_ps.rcPaint.bottom / avgCharHeight);
#ifdef _DEBUG
_cprintf ("OnPaint - first line: %d last line: %d\r\n",
          firstLine, lastLine);
#endif
 for (i=firstLine; i<lastLine; i++) {
  CString* ptrs = (CString*) lines.GetAt(i);
  if (!ptrs) continue;
  dc.TextOut (ScrollArea.left
              + avgCharWidth * (1 - currentStartCol),
              ScrollArea.top +
              avgCharHeight * (-currentTopLine + i), *ptrs);
 }
 // if there is a user font, put the old font back into the dc
 if (ptrfont) {
  dc.SelectObject (ptroldfont);
 }
}
/*************************************************************/
/*                                                           */
/* RecalcLayout: overridden function to obtain the real client */
/*               area - less any tool bars and status bar areas*/
/*                                                           */
/*************************************************************/
void FrameWin::RecalcLayout (BOOL bNotify) {
 CFrameWnd::RecalcLayout (bNotify );
 // calculate real client area
 RepositionBars (AFX_IDW_CONTROLBAR_FIRST,
                 AFX_IDW_CONTROLBAR_LAST, 0, CWnd::reposQuery,
                 &RealClientArea );
 // for example allow for headings avg char height + 4
 ScrollArea.SetRect (RealClientArea.left,
                     RealClientArea.top + avgCharHeight + 5,
                     RealClientArea.right, RealClientArea.bottom);
#ifdef _DEBUG
_cprintf ("RecalcLayout - Real Client Area %d %d %d %d\r\n",
          RealClientArea.left, RealClientArea.top,
          RealClientArea.right, RealClientArea.bottom);
```

```
_cprintf ("RecalcLayout - Scroll Area %d %d %d %d\r\n",
          ScrollArea.left, ScrollArea.top,
          ScrollArea.right, ScrollArea.bottom);
_cprintf ("RecalcLayout - Calling SetOurScrollRange\r\n");
#endif
 SetOurScrollRange();
 InvalidateRect (RealClientArea, TRUE); // force a repaint
}

/***************************************************************/
/*                                                             */
/* GetAvgCharDims: retrieve current font's average dimensions  */
/*                                                             */
/***************************************************************/

void FrameWin::GetAvgCharDims () {

  TEXTMETRIC  tm;  // set the system font's characteristics in tm

  CClientDC dc (this);    // acquire a DC

  if (ptrlogfont) { // install any user font
   ptroldfont = dc.SelectObject (ptrfont); // save old one
  }

  dc.GetTextMetrics (&tm); // get the font information

  if (ptrlogfont) {
   dc.SelectObject (ptroldfont); // reinstall old font
  }

  // calculate average character parameters
  avgCharWidth = tm.tmAveCharWidth;
  avgCharHeight = tm.tmHeight + tm.tmExternalLeading;
  avgCapsWidth = (tm.tmPitchAndFamily & 1 ? 3 : 2) *
                 avgCharWidth / 2;
#ifdef _DEBUG
_cprintf ("GetAvgCharDims: height: %d width: %d\r\n",
          avgCharHeight, avgCharWidth);
#endif
}

/***************************************************************/
/*                                                             */
/* CmFontChange: get users font request and implement it       */
/*                                                             */
/***************************************************************/

void      FrameWin::CmFontChange () {
 CFontDialog  dlg (ptrlogfont, CF_EFFECTS | CF_SCREENFONTS |
                   CF_FORCEFONTEXIST, NULL, this);
 dlg.m_cf.rgbColors = fontcolor;    // install current color

 if (dlg.DoModal () == IDOK) {      // get user font choice
  if (!ptrlogfont) {
   ptrlogfont = new LOGFONT;        // 1st time, create LOGFONT
  }
  else {
   delete ptrfont;
  }
  // copy user choice of font into our LOGFONT instance
  memcpy (ptrlogfont, &(dlg.m_lf), sizeof (LOGFONT));
  fontcolor = dlg.GetColor ();      // save color choice
  // now make our CFont object
```

```
  ptrfont = new CFont ();
  ptrfont->CreateFontIndirect (ptrlogfont);
#ifdef _DEBUG
_cprintf ("CmFontChange - user has selected a new font\r\n");
_cprintf ("CmFontChange - calling GetAvgCharDims, SetOurScrollRan
#endif
  GetAvgCharDims ();                // get new average char dims
  SetOurScrollRange ();             // set new scroll range based
  Invalidate();                     // on new dims, and reshow
 }
}

/*************************************************************/
/*                                                           */
/* SetOurScrollRange: sets the horiz and vert scrolling ranges */
/*      using the new SCROLLINFO structure                   */
/*                                                           */
/*************************************************************/

void FrameWin::SetOurScrollRange () {
 if (!avgCharHeight) return; // avoid division by 0 at start up
 // calculate new max vertical range bassed on current size
 numLinesPerPage = ScrollArea.Height() / avgCharHeight;
 maxScrollLines = max (0, maxDims.cy -numLinesPerPage+1);

 // adjust thumb line position - could now exceed bottom pos
 currentTopLine = min (currentTopLine, maxScrollLines);

 // set up scroll range and position of the thumb bar
 SCROLLINFO si;
 si.cbSize = sizeof (si);
 si.fMask = SIF_ALL;
 si.nMin = 0;
 si.nMax = maxDims.cy;
 si.nPage = numLinesPerPage;
 si.nPos = currentTopLine; // initial position at the start
 SetScrollInfo (SB_VERT, &si, TRUE);

 numCharsPerLine = ScrollArea.Width() / avgCharWidth;
 maxHscrollChars = max (0, maxDims.cx - numCharsPerLine);
 currentStartCol = min (currentStartCol, maxHscrollChars);
 si.nMax = maxDims.cx;
 si.nPage = numCharsPerLine;
 si.nPos = currentStartCol; // initial position at the start
 SetScrollInfo (SB_HORZ, &si, TRUE);
#ifdef _DEBUG
_cprintf ("SetOurScrollRange - num lines per page: %d\r\n",
          numLinesPerPage);
_cprintf ("SetOurScrollRange - max scroll lines: %d\r\n",
          maxScrollLines);
_cprintf ("SetOurScrollRange - current top line: %d\r\n",
          currentTopLine);
_cprintf ("SetOurScrollRange - num chars per line: %d\r\n",
          numCharsPerLine);
_cprintf ("SetOurScrollRange - max hscroll: %d\r\n",
          maxHscrollChars);
_cprintf ("SetOurScrollRange - current start column: %d\r\n",
          currentStartCol);
#endif
}
...
/*************************************************************/
/*                                                           */
```

```
/* ParseFileStringIntoCStrings: find each string in the file   */
/*     and store in a new CString and add it to the array      */
/*     when done, maxDims is set to the number of lines and the */
/*     maximum width of any line encountered                   */
/*                                                              */
/***************************************************************/

void FrameWin::ParseFileStringIntoCStrings (char* ptrdata,
                                            DWORD filesize) {
 long maxWidth = 1;
 char* ptrstart = ptrdata;
 char* ptrend = ptrdata + filesize;
 char* ptrthis;

 // for each line in the text block
 while (ptrstart < ptrend) {
  ptrthis = ptrstart;
  // search for ending <CR> <LF> codes
  while (ptrthis < ptrend) {
   if (*ptrthis == '\r') {
    *ptrthis++ = 0;          // replace <CR> with null
    if (*ptrthis == '\n')
     ptrthis++;              // skip over the next <LF>
    break;                   // stop and store this string
   }
   ptrthis++;
  }
  // create a new CString and copy the found string into it
  CString* ptrs = new CString;
  *ptrs = ptrstart;
  lines.Add (ptrs);    // add this new CString to the array
  // replace maximum line length in chars if needed
  if (ptrs->GetLength() > maxWidth)
   maxWidth = ptrs->GetLength();
  // reset ptrstart to the start of the next line in the block
  ptrstart = ptrthis;
 }
 // save the dimensions found for this file's data
 maxDims.cy = lines.GetSize ();
 maxDims.cx = maxWidth;
#ifdef _DEBUG
_cprintf ("ParseFileStringIntoCStrings - number lines: %d\r\n",
          maxDims.cy);
_cprintf ("ParseFileStringIntoCStrings - max width in chars: %d\r
          maxDims.cx);
#endif
}

/***************************************************************/
/*                                                              */
/* OnDestroy: remove the array of CString lines                 */
/*                                                              */
/***************************************************************/

void FrameWin::OnDestroy () {
 EmptyArray ();
 if (ptrlogfont) delete ptrlogfont;
 if (ptrfont) delete ptrfont;
#ifdef _DEBUG
_cprintf ("OnDestroy - calling base class\r\n");
#endif
 CFrameWnd::OnDestroy ();
}
/***************************************************************/
```

```
/*                                                              */
/* OnVScroll: scroll window vertically                          */
/*                                                              */
/****************************************************************/

void FrameWin::OnVScroll (UINT type, UINT pos, CScrollBar*) {
 int numLinesToScroll;

 switch (type) {

  case SB_LINEUP:      // scroll up 1 line
   numLinesToScroll = -1; break;

  case SB_LINEDOWN:    // scroll 1 line down
   numLinesToScroll = 1; break;

  case SB_PAGEUP:      // scroll 1 page up
   numLinesToScroll = min (-1, -numLinesPerPage); break;

  case SB_PAGEDOWN:    // scroll 1 page down
   numLinesToScroll = max (1, numLinesPerPage); break;

  case SB_THUMBTRACK: // follow thumb bar
   numLinesToScroll = pos - currentTopLine; break;

  default:
   numLinesToScroll = 0;
 }

 numLinesToScroll = max (-currentTopLine,
                         min (numLinesToScroll,
                              maxScrollLines - currentTopLine));
#ifdef _DEBUG
_cprintf ("OnVScroll: num lines to scroll: %d\r\n",
          numLinesToScroll);
#endif
 if (numLinesToScroll !=0) {
  currentTopLine +=numLinesToScroll;
  ScrollWindow (0, -avgCharHeight*numLinesToScroll,
                &ScrollArea, &ScrollArea);
  SCROLLINFO si;
  si.cbSize = sizeof (si);
  si.fMask = SIF_POS;
  si.nPos = currentTopLine; // initial position at the start
  SetScrollInfo (SB_VERT, &si, TRUE);
 }
}

/****************************************************************/
/*                                                              */
/* OnHScroll: scroll window horizontally                        */
/*                                                              */
/****************************************************************/

void FrameWin::OnHScroll (UINT type, UINT pos, CScrollBar*) {
 int numCharsToScroll;
 switch (type) {

  case SB_LINEUP:     // scroll 1 col left
   numCharsToScroll = -1; break;

  case SB_LINEDOWN:  // scroll 1 col right
   numCharsToScroll = 1; break;

```

```
  case SB_PAGEUP:     // scroll 1 page left
   numCharsToScroll = -8; break;

  case SB_PAGEDOWN:    // scroll 1 page right
   numCharsToScroll = 8; break;

  case SB_THUMBTRACK: // follow thumb bar
   numCharsToScroll = pos - currentStartCol; break;

  default:
   numCharsToScroll = 0;
 }

 numCharsToScroll = max (-currentStartCol,
                         min (numCharsToScroll,
                           maxHscrollChars - currentStartCol));
#ifdef _DEBUG
_cprintf ("OnHScroll: num chars to scroll: %d\r\n",
          numCharsToScroll);
#endif
 if (numCharsToScroll !=0) {
  currentStartCol +=numCharsToScroll;
  ScrollWindow (-avgCharWidth*numCharsToScroll, 0,
                &ScrollArea, &ScrollArea);
  SCROLLINFO si;
  si.cbSize = sizeof (si);
  si.fMask = SIF_POS;
  si.nPos = currentStartCol; // initial position at the start
  SetScrollInfo (SB_HORZ, &si, TRUE);
 }
}
```

...

```
/*****************************************************************/
/*                                                               */
/* SaveFile: write the file                                      */
/*                                                               */
/*****************************************************************/

void FrameWin::SaveFile () {
 HANDLE hfile = CreateFile (filename, GENERIC_WRITE, 0, NULL,
             CREATE_ALWAYS, FILE_ATTRIBUTE_NORMAL, NULL);
 if (hfile==INVALID_HANDLE_VALUE) {
  DisplayMsg (IDS_MSG_ERROR, IDS_MSG_FILEERR, MB_OK|MB_ICONSTOP);
  return;
 }

 CString buf; // this string will hold the entire file
 // build up buf by adding <CR><LF> codes at the end of each line
 CString* ptrs;
 for (int i=0; i<lines.GetSize(); i++) {
  ptrs = (CString*) lines.GetAt (i);
  if (!ptrs) continue;
  buf += *ptrs;
  buf += "\r\n";
 }

 // obtain a pointer to the buf so we can write it out
 DWORD sz = buf.GetLength();
 char* buffer = buf.GetBuffer (sz);
 DWORD asize;
 // write the whole file - note in this case, one could write
 // from buf directly without converting it into an char*
 if (!WriteFile (hfile, buffer, sz, &asize, NULL)
     || asize != sz) {
```

```
  DisplayMsg (IDS_MSG_FILEWRT, IDS_MSG_ERROR, MB_ICONSTOP|MB_OK);
 }

 buf.ReleaseBuffer ();
 CloseHandle (hfile);
 haveSaved = true;
#ifdef _DEBUG
_cprintf ("SaveFile - file has been saved\r\n");
#endif
}

/***************************************************************/
/*                                                             */
/* CmFileNew: open a new file                                  */
/*                                                             */
/***************************************************************/

void FrameWin::CmFileNew () {
 // if the file has not been saved, ask the user and handle
 if (haveFile && !haveSaved)
  SaveCheck();
 EmptyArray ();            // remove all lines from the array
 filename[0] = 0;          // set no filename
 haveFile  = true;         // set have a new file
 haveSaved = false;        // that has not been saved
 currentTopLine = 0;
 currentStartCol = 0;
 maxDims = CSize(1,1);
#ifdef _DEBUG
_cprintf ("CmFileNew - a new file is setup\r\n");
_cprintf ("CmFileNew - calling SetCaption and SetOurScrollRange\r
#endif
 SetCaption ();
 SetOurScrollRange ();     // reset scroll bar range for newfile
 Invalidate();             // and clear screen
}

/***************************************************************/
/*                                                             */
/* CmFileOpen: open an existant file                           */
/*                                                             */
/***************************************************************/

void FrameWin::CmFileOpen () {
 // if the file has not been saved, ask the user and handle
 if (haveFile && !haveSaved)
  SaveCheck();

 // create new transfer buffer
 CFileDialog filedlg (TRUE,    // use Open dialog
                     "*.CPP", // default extension
                     "*.*",   // current file name
          OFN_FILEMUSTEXIST | OFN_PATHMUSTEXIST | OFN_LONGNAMES,
          "All Files (*.*)|*.*|CPP Files (*.CPP)|*.CPP|C Files"
          " (*.C)|*.C|Header Files (*.H*)|*.H*||", this);

 // get user's file choice
 if (filedlg.DoModal () == IDOK) { // user has chosen a file, so
  strcpy_s (filename, sizeof(filename), filedlg.GetPathName ());
  EmptyArray ();  // remove all prior lines
  // load the new file into the array
  if (!LoadTextFileIntoCStrings (filename)) {
   DisplayMsg (IDS_MSG_FILEOPEN,IDS_MSG_ERROR,MB_ICONSTOP|MB_OK);
   haveFile = false;     // indicate no file
```

```
   return;
  }

  haveFile = true;        // set have a file
  haveSaved = true;       // set file is saved because not changed
  currentTopLine = 0;
  currentStartCol = 0;
#ifdef _DEBUG
_cprintf ("CmFileOpen - file loaded is called: %s\r\n", filename)
_cprintf ("CmFileOpen - calling SetCaption and SetOurScrollRange\
#endif
  SetCaption ();
  SetOurScrollRange (); // set new scrollbar range
  Invalidate ();        // and display new file
 }
}

/*****************************************************************/
/*                                                               */
/* CmFileClose: close an opened file                             */
/*                                                               */
/*****************************************************************/

void FrameWin::CmFileClose () {
 // if the file is not yet saved, ask user and handle
 if (haveFile && !haveSaved)
  SaveCheck();
 haveFile  = false;     // set no file
 haveSaved = false;     // set not saved
 filename[0] = 0;
 EmptyArray ();
 currentTopLine = 0;
 currentStartCol = 0;
#ifdef _DEBUG
_cprintf ("CmFileClose - file closed\r\n");
_cprintf ("CmFileOpen - calling SetCaption and SetOurScrollRange\
#endif
 SetCaption ();
 SetOurScrollRange (); // set new scrollbar range
 Invalidate ();        // clear screen
}
```

...

```
/*****************************************************************/
/*                                                               */
/* CmEnableFileOps: enables/disables File operations menu items*/
/*                                                               */
/*****************************************************************/

void      FrameWin::CmEnableFileOps (CCmdUI *ptrenabler) {
#ifdef _DEBUG
_cprintf ("CmEnableFileOps - entered - have file: %d\r\n",
          haveFile ? 1 : 0);
#endif
 ptrenabler->Enable (haveFile);
}
```

Note in **SetOurScrollRange**, we must first check for division by 0. This effect occurs only in Release builds because the timing of the initial messages being sent to our application is different than that in a Debug build. Comment out this line and make a release build and try to run the application.

Programming Problems

Problem Pgm08-1: Revised Acme Inventory Data Entry

In this version of the problem, we add file support and scrolling. The data base file is commonly called **invmast.dat**. I have provided two test data files called Invmast.dat and Invmast-small.dat. The larger file is about 64k in size while the smaller is only 1k. These are **binary** files, so make sure that you set the structure alignment project option to **byte** alignment.

Modify the program to work with as many records as will fit in a 64K global memory array of inventory structures. (The structure should be 7 + 21 + 2 + 8 = 38 bytes long, so you could probably enter up to 1,724 records.) Note that this limit is an artificial, arbitrary barrier. If you prefer to use a growable container to avoid this arbitrary limitation, do so. You could use a **CPtrArray**.

Of course, this now means that vertical scroll bars must be added so that the user can scroll the screen display. Watch out for scrolling of the heading and column heading lines! Realistically, they should not scroll. This means that when you call **ScrollWindow**, the last two parameters, which have been 0 to date, now must be the address of the scrolling rectangle. More on this shortly.

Implement the File menu choices. The File pop-up menu offers New, Open, Close, Save, SaveAs, Print, Print Setup, and Exit. Print and Print Setup remain unimplemented as yet. But provide implementations for the others as follows.

When the application starts, begin by having a New file. Into the caption, append " - Untitled Data Base File". If the user saves the new file, replace the caption with " - filename". If the user selects Open, present the common File Open dialog using *.dat as the only filter—the only file type available to open. If the user selects a file to open, append that filename to the caption. If a SaveAs operation is required, present the common File SaveAs dialog. If the user chooses Close, then append to the caption " - No File Opened Yet". This means that you must have a mechanism to track whether or not there is a file opened or newed. This then, impacts the Add, Update, and Delete menu items in that they should be grayed out if there is no file newed or opened.

You should track whether or not any changes have been made to an existing file so that you can prompt the user about saving unsaved data at the appropriate times.

Finally, install an application icon of your own design to represent the application when minimized.

It is vitally important that you use **Pgm08b** as your scrolling model. In the next version of this problem, tool bars and a status bar will be added. Unless you wish to totally rewrite all of your display and scrolling code, design your **OnPaint** and scrolling code similar to **Pgm08b**. Specifically, override **RecalcLayout** as I have done and have it find the real client rectangle. Define your actual scrolling area based solely on the real client rectangle coordinates. When you issue the **ScrollWindow** call, pass the address of your actual scrolling area to that function. In **OnPaint**, in all drawing functions use the real client rectangle's coordinates as a base for all heading items and use the scrolling rectangle's coordinates as a base for all detail text lines. If you do so, then adding the tool bars and the status bar will be relatively painless. If you do not follow this, adding them is very likely to be a nightmare.

For extra credit, **highlight** the current record on the screen. When a record is selected for updating and the update has completed, position the screen display so that record is shown on the screen and highlighted. After a record is added, position and highlight the new record similarly. Do what you like after a deletion, likely make the next sequential record after the one deleted highlighted.

For extra credit, add mouse support. When the user clicks on a line, select that line and highlight it. If the user double clicks on a line, launch the Update dialog using that line's data in the dialog. Additionally, if the user right clicks on a selected line, pop-up a menu asking whether the user wishes to Update or Delete that line. Should the user press the del key when a line is highlighted, display the "are you sure you want to delete this entry" message box.

Chapter 9 Graphics, The GDI Package

Introduction

The Graphical Device Interface (GDI) is one of the more powerful features of Windows. The number and complexity of graphics operations that can be done are exceedingly large. Therefore, I have chosen to limit the function coverage to the basic drawing set while still discussing the power features.

Graphics construction at the hardware level is not only a complex undertaking but highly device dependent. The many SuperVGA cards all have significant differences and capabilities. Recall the Tic Tac Toe game. From a programming point of view, we merely wanted an O drawn and invoked the **Ellipse** function. Windows isolates our program from the specific hardware, handling the ellipse construction. If the graphics coprocessor can draw an ellipse, Windows instructs it to do so. On the other hand, if the hardware cannot, Windows proceeds to calculate the individual points of the ellipse and has the hardware plot the resultant points. The visual effect is the same; the ellipse is drawn.

Windows manages this separation by "device independent graphics," insulating programmer from the board dependent specifics. The fundamental building block that enables Windows to perform this separation is the device driver, the .DRV files. Driver files access the hardware of the video display. We know that SuperVGA monitors are capable of several very different graphics modes with differing number of colors present (2-color, 4-color, 16-color, and 256-color, true color) and differing screen resolutions (640x480, 800x600, and 1024x768). Normally, the color mode and resolution are the user's choice. This is done via Windows Control Panel application. Beginning with Windows 95, the display resolution and colors can be dynamically altered without closing down all applications and restarting Windows! Now a new complexity has entered, namely all Windows applications should be able to handle display changes in a dynamic fashion. Not only can the resolution and number of colors be affected but also the average character dimensions, because the fonts can be altered based on the display driver. **Pgm09a** responds to this new Windows message, **WM_DISPLAYCHANGE** adjusting for all three factors.

> **Design Rule 43: All Windows applications that are in anyway affected by dynamic alterations to the screen resolution or number of colors or fonts must respond to the WM_DISPLAYCHANGE message and be able to dynamically adjust for such changes, including the potential impact upon fonts.**

Since I have been using a **GetAvgCharDims** function to acquire font dimensions in the sample programs, it is very easy to respond. In response to the **WM_DISPLAYCHANGE** message, I can call **GetAvgCharDims** and then **Invalidate** to update the screen.

Graphics are composed of two differing points of view: **raster** and **vector** graphics. Raster graphics is concerned with drawing individual pixel points; most PC displays are raster devices. Vector graphics is concerned with drawing lines; most plotters are vector devices. Windows, by virtue of being device independent, allows an application to access the hardware from both points of view. In other words, although the video display only plots points, your application can direct that a line be drawn from point A to point B; Windows handles the details. If the device can handle vector graphics, Windows has little to do except pass along to the device the line request. If the device can only handle raster graphics, Windows proceeds to calculate the individual pixels that need to be shown and requests the series of pixels that represent the line be shown.

The Device Context

The programming key to this independence is the device context (DC). Whenever you want to display anything, you must obtain a handle to a DC first. In doing so, Windows inserts into that DC many current "attributes" that determine how the GDI functions are to be handled on the specific display device. In addition to the items we have seen so far, such as the pen and brush, these attributes also include such items as the display resolution and the color mode. These attributes allow an application to call a GDI function and pass it the least number of parameters to define that action. (You do not have to pass the drawing color and the background color, for example.)

There are several methods of getting the handle to a DC. The most common method is in response to **WM_PAINT** messages as we have been doing extensively thus far and create a **CpaintDC**.

```
void OnPaint () {
 CPaintDC dc(this);
 ...
}
```

Here you can only draw in the invalid client rectangle area.

At other times, you can get a handle to the whole client area by using a **CclientDC**.

```
CClientDC dc (this);
```

The client DC allows drawing anywhere within the client area of the application.

You can gain access to the entire area owned by the window (in other words the frame window and its client window), including the border, title bar, menu bar, and so on by using a **CwindowDC**.

```
CWindowDC dc (m_hWnd);
```

With a window DC, you can access or draw anywhere within the entire window of the application. Of course, if you draw over the menu bar, Windows immediately sends your frame window a paint message to redraw the menu bar.

Access to the entire screen in provided by the following C API call.

```
hdc = CreateDC ("DISPLAY", NULL, NULL, NULL);
```

or

```
hdc = CreateDC (0);
...
ReleaseDC (hwnd, hdc);
```

You can now paint anywhere on the screen. It is impolite to do so, for then all other windows are sent subsequent "repaint themselves" messages.

Finally, there is a very powerful DC type known as a **memory DC**. Memory DCs contain all of the information that would normally be displayed on the screen, rather like a memory image of the screen image. A memory DC is the key to fancy graphics operations. For example, suppose that it takes several seconds for your application to draw the current complex image in the client area. Do you really want the user to "watch the build up" as the bits and pieces are slowly drawn on the screen DC? And what about scrolling? Suppose that your final image is larger than the client area and you have installed scroll bars. Do you want the user to wait several seconds whenever he or she scrolls? Memory DCs solve all of these problems.

You draw to the memory DC just as if it were a normal DC, but nothing appears on the screen. When you have finished drawing the image, you then copy that **portion** of the memory DC onto the screen DC that you desire. Instantly, the correct portion of the final image appears. Now when a scroll is requested, you merely copy the new correct portion of the memory image onto the screen DC. The copy operation is called a **BitBlt** or bit block transfer, and is one of the power features of the GDI.

Using memory DCs add a professional touch to your graphics application. The only drawback is that the memory DC can take up a significant amount memory, depending upon the color mode and resolution. For example, a memory DC for an image that is to be in 256-colors at 1024x768 resolution occupies more than 780K! Later in this chapter I demonstrate how to use a memory DC.

One important note. For every DC that you request, be sure that you **ReleaseDC**, or **delete** the pointer to the **new**ed DC or have the destructor called. Under Windows 3.1, there were only five real device contexts total with which to serve all running applications as well as itself. Thus, if you fail to give back a DC repeatedly, Windows 3.1 quickly crashed. While Windows 95 has improved the DC count, avoid failures to give back real DCs or you can easily run the system out of DCs. On the other hand, the number of memory DCs is limited only by available memory.

Obtaining the Device Capabilities

The function **GetDeviceCaps** provides access to all of the device capabilities.

```
int value = dc.GetDeviceCaps (index);
```

There are 28 index identifiers with many sub identifiers. Consult your documentation for a full discussion of all of the capabilities and their identifiers. In normal use, only a few are really needed by those applications that require specific knowledge of the color mode or resolution currently in use.

```
HORZRES   - width of the display in pixels
VERTRES   - height of the display in pixels
BITSPIXEL - number of color bits per pixel
PLANES    - number of color planes
```

Detecting the color mode requires specific knowledge of the different architectures. For now, some generalities are these. If the color bits per pixel is 8 and the number of color planes is 1, you are in 256-color mode. If the number of planes is 4 and the color bits per pixel is 4, you are in the 16 color mode.

Saving DCs

Before using a DC, say in **OnPaint**, normally one installs several items. So far, we have installed our own brushes and pens and fonts, and set the various aspects for drawing text. Every time **OnPaint** is invoked, we must reelect all these back into the paint DC. These actions take a bit of time. If you were to save that DC all set up properly once, then whenever **OnPaint** was invoked, all you would need to do is restore that DC and paint.

By setting in **wndclass.Style** the **CS_OWNDC** attribute, each window class you create from this registered class has its own private DC that exists until the window is destroyed. Initialization of the owned DC is normally done during **WM_CREATE** message processing, that is, during **OnCreate**. Whenever you request a paint DC or a **GetDC** operation, it is the owned DC that is returned. (It is not the DC that is returned for the screen DCs, of course.) The cost of having your own permanent DC is about 800 bytes of memory permanently assigned to the DC.

You must still **ReleaseDC** whenever exiting a C API style function. This is automatically done when the destructor is called in the MFC. Another even broader approach is to use the **wndclass.Style CS_CLASSDC**. Here any window, even in another instance of the application that is running, share the same DC. The first instance begun sets up the DC that it and all other launched instances share this one DC. Of course, when you change say the text color in one window, suddenly the text color changes in all other instances. Sometimes this is desirable; others, a disaster.

Mapping Modes and Viewport Versus Window Coordinates

The DC mapping mode represents the fundamental method of drawing graphics. The basic parameters consist of a mapping unit (often the pixel), the (x, y) values given in these mapping units, and the origin of the coordinate system. Windows supports eight different mapping modes; the default and the most frequently encountered mode is **MM_TEXT**.

In the **MM_TEXT** mapping mode, the logical unit is the pixel. Thus, all (x, y) coordinate values are interpreted to be in pixels. The coordinate system's origin is the upper left corner of the screen. Increasing positive x values go to the right; negative, to the left. Increasing positive y values go down; negative y values go up. Notice that this is the reverse of most math graphs that have the positive y axis going up. It takes a bit of getting used to. In the other mapping modes, the unit of measurement varies among: .1 mm, .01 mm, .01 inch, .001 inch, 1/1440 inch. In many of these, the positive y axis goes upwards as expected.

There are three coordinate systems in use. **Whole window coordinates**, such as used when using a **GetWindowDC** function, are based on (0, 0) being the upper left corner of the sizing or frame window. **Client area coordinates**, which we have used predominately to this point, have (0, 0) at the upper left corner of the client window. **Full screen coordinates** use (0, 0) as the upper left corner of the screen.

The mapping mode determines how Windows converts or "maps" logical coordinates specified in the GDI functions into specific device coordinates on the screen. In other words, the mapping mode determines how the **window or logical coordinates** are converted into **viewport or device coordinates**.

And here we have a clash of nomenclature. In most graphics packages, the term viewport refers to the clipping region. However, in Windows, the **viewport coordinates** are in pixels and are usually given in terms of the client area or window, unless using a window or screen DC. The **window or logical coordinates** are specified in the logical unit of the mapping mode with the appropriate origin and direction of the axis appropriate to the mode. There are many Window functions to convert from one scheme into another. Often, scaling can be done to make images "fit." Table 9.1 shows the available mapping modes.

Table 1 The Mapping Modes

Mapping Mode Identifiers	Logical Unit	Increasing Coordinate Values X-axis	Y-axis
MM_TEXT	Pixel	Right	Down
MM_ANISOTROPIC	Arbitrary x!=y	Selectable	Selectable
MM_ISOTROPIC	Arbitrary x==y	Selectable	Selectable
MM_TWIPS	1/1440 inch	Right	Up
MM_LOMETRIC	.1 mm	Right	Up
MM_HIMETRIC	.01mm	Right	Up
MM_LOENGLISH	.01 inch	Right	Up
MM_HIENGLISH	.001 inch	Right	Up

Note that a **twip** means a twentieth of a point and a point is a printer's unit of measurement equal to 1/72 of an inch. Since these more exotic mapping modes are so seldom used, I examine only the common **MM_TEXT** mode in this chapter. In a later chapter on printing, I examine the two isotropic and twip modes.

In **MM_TEXT** mode, the origin point (0, 0) can be changed, but the scaling factor or "extent" is fixed at 1 to 1. That is, 1 pixel in window or logical coordinates (either x or y) is 1 pixel in the viewport or device coordinates. Thus, to convert from window or logical coordinates to the viewport or device coordinates, use the following formulae.

```
x viewport = x window - x window origin + x viewport origin;
y viewport = y window - y window origin + y viewport origin;
```

Under Windows, the origin points can be adjusted via the following functions.

```
CPoint SetViewportOrg (int x, int y);
CPoint SetViewportOrg (CPoint pt);
CPoint GetViewportOrg ();
CPoint SetWindowOrg   (int x, int y);
CPoint SetWindowOrg   (CPoint pt);
CPoint GetWindowOrg   ();
```

These functions have the effect of altering where the origin (0, 0) is found. Use one of the two but **not** both on the same window. Either set the viewport origin or set the window origin.

Suppose that you wished to display a graph whose plot included equal ranges along the plus and minus sides of both the x-axis and y-axis, such as a graph of a trigonometric function. If you just used the default setup, only the positive values would be displayed and then upside down, because only the positive quadrant of the full graphical image is on the screen. The remedy is to move the viewport origin to the center of the client window area with positive y going up. By invoking **SetViewportOrg**, the window's logical point (0, 0) is displayed in the center of the client area. Now all four quadrants of the trig plot are visible.

```
CPoint pt, oldpt;
pt.x = width/2;
pt.y = height/2;
oldpt = dc.SetViewportOrg (pt);
```

or

```
oldpt = dc.SetViewportOrg (width/2, height/2);
```

That is, the logical coordinates range from -**width/2** to +**width**/2 and from -**height/2** to +**height/2**. If you wanted to display a title at the top of the client window, use the following coordinates.

```
dc.TextOut (-width/2, -height/2, "Graph Title");
```

To use the **SetWindowOrg**, use negative values to achieve the same effect.

```
dc.SetWindowOrg (-width/2, -height/2);
```

Shifting viewport origins is one method of responding to a "scroll" request with graphical images. The drawback to this approach is that the entire image must be redrawn or all text displayed, letting Windows handle all of the clipping. Using a memory DC provides a better scheme. Only in the two "scalable" isotropic modes can the viewport or window **extent** be changed; in all other modes, the scale factor is always 1:1. The two isotropic modes are very useful when scaling the screen onto a printed page. The extent can be altered via the functions shown below.

```
CSize SetViewportExt (CSize new);
CSize SetViewportExt (int cx, int cy);
CSize GetViewportExt ();
CSize SetWindowExt   (CSize new);
CSize SetWindowExt   (int cx, int cy);
CSize GetWindowExt   ();
```

GDI Objects Rules of Use

Recall the earlier Design Rules concerning GDI objects.

1. Delete all GDI objects that you create

2. Do not delete GDI objects while they are selected in a valid DC

3. Do not delete stock objects; if you do, Windows ignores it.

Often, one must save the old object when a new object is created and selected into a DC. Later just before the DC is to be destroyed, the old object or the original object is selected back into the DC, the new object deleted, and the DC destroyed.

If many objects are selected into a DC, it can be annoying to have to save all of the corresponding original objects and then later reelect the old one back into the DC. The **CDC** based classes provide a pair of functions for quick restoration.

```
int  SaveDC ();
BOOL RestoreDC (int saveid);
```

When the DC is saved onto the stack, a save ID number is returned for later use in the restore function. The DC can be saved as frequently as desired. However, since they are saved on the stack, there should be a matching number of restores. All GDI objects and the mapping mode are saved and restored.

Pens

When you invoke many drawing functions, those functions utilize the currently selected pen and brush. Let's examine their creation more fully. Windows provides the stock pens **WHITE_PEN** and **BLACK_PEN**. (There is an **NULL_PEN** that does not draw.) Again, stock objects do not need to be deleted.

When you create your own pens, three parameters are required: the color, the width, and the style. The width is in pixels. The style is one of the following identifiers.

```
PS_SOLID              - solid pen
PS_DASH               - only with width 1
PS_DOT                - only with width 1
PS_DASHDOT            - only with width 1
PS_DASHDOTDOT         - only with width 1
PS_NULL - null pen    - only with width 1
PS_INSIDEFRAME        - a solid pen used in drawing a bounding
                        rectangle whose dimension are shrunk to
                        fit within the bounding rectangle
```

Under the MFC, you can explicitly call the **CreatePen** function or call the overloaded constructor. Generally, if you define an instance of a **CPen** as a class member, you need to call **CreatePen** in the class constructor. However, if you dynamically allocate the pen, use the overloaded constructor version.

```
CPen redPen (PS_SOLID, 1, RGB (255, 0, 0)); // solid red pen
CPen p;
p.CreatePen (PS_SOLID, 1, RGB (255, 0, 0)); // solid red pen
```

The sequence of use is as follows.
create the logical pen
SelectObject the pen into the DC

draw with the DC
select in another or restore the original pen
when **ReleaseDC** or when a new pen is selected, **delete** the pen

What appears between the dots and dashes on the fancier pens? The color depends upon the background mode. If it is **OPAQUE**, Windows fills the spaces with the background color. If it is **TRANSPARENT**, Windows does not fill at all, so whatever color is there is still there. The default background color is white, so very often we use the **SetBkColor** function with **SetBkMode** as we have done in previous **OnPaint** functions.

Brushes

A brush is an 8x8 pixel bitmap used repeatedly to cover an area. For a pure black brush, the bit patterns are all 0's; for a white brush, the patterns are all 1's. Windows also creates dithered colored or gray patterns. In black and white mode, alternating 0's and 1's in the pattern would yield a visual effect of medium gray. More 1's than 0's, a lighter gray; more 0's than 1's, a darker gray. This dithering effect is a result of the eye's inability to differentiate the colors of individual pixels when they are so tiny.

When using colors, the effects are much more difficult to predict, unless you have a background in art, specifically in additive color mixing. Although Windows normally uses only 16 solid colors (in the 16-color mode), many more than 16 colors may be produced, well simulated actually, by dithering. Suppose that you alternated red and green in the 8x8 pixel brush pattern. The visual effect would be an entirely different color, yellow, unless you took a magnifying glass to the screen. Thus, although you may have created a solid brush, if Windows cannot display that color, because it is not one of the basic 16 colors, Windows attempts to create a dithered pattern that closely approximates your request. When running in True Color mode, Windows can create a brush of your specific color.

There is also a series of hatch patterns that can be used in brush creation. The hatch brush identifiers include the following.

```
HS_HORIZONTAL - horizontal lines
HS_VERTICAL   - vertical lines
HS_FDIAGONAL  - forward slanting diagonal lines ///
HS_BDIAGONAL  - back slanting diagonal lines \\\
HS_CROSS      - cross hatch pattern rather like +++
HS_DIAGCROSS  - diagonal cross pattern rather like xxxx
```

To create a brush, use any of the following. Again, you can create a brush in the constructor or wait and invoke the appropriate create function later on.

```
CBrush brush1 (RGB (255, 255, 0));
CBrush brush2 (HS_HORIZONTAL, RGB (255, 255, 0));
CBrush brush;
brush.CreateSolidBrush (RGB (255, 255, 0));
brush.CreateHatchBrush (HS_HORIZONTAL, RGB (255, 255, 0));
brush.CreatePatternBrush (CBitmap *object);
```

Drawing Graphical Images

The number of possible functions to draw objects is quite extensive. Let's cursorily examine several these.

To draw a line from (x1, yl) to (x2, y2) specify the coordinates separately or construct a **CPoint** object. Specifically, **MoveTo** is used to position the pen to a point without drawing; **LineTo** draws a line from where the pen currently is located to the passed point. Under the MFC, both **MoveTo** and **LineTo** can take either a pair of (x, y) integer values or a **CPoint** object.

```
dc.MoveTo (x, y);
dc.MoveTo (point);
dc.LineTo (x, y);
dc.LineTo (point);
```

Therefore, when storing lines, often arrays of **CPoint** or **POINT** structures are used. However, there is a much better method for drawing lines—the **Polyline** function. This function draws a series of connected lines from an array of points.

```
CPoint       linearray[MAX_POINTS];
dc.Polyline (linearray, number_of_points);
```

Another workhorse is the **Polygon** function. This function is passed an array of points that, when connected, form a multi-sided object. Additionally, a line is drawn from the last point back to the first point if they are not the same point. The interior is filled with the current background color.

```
dc.Polygon (arraypoints, number_of_points);
```

where the array is an array of **CPoint** objects. Windows clips as usual.

Windows has other functions to draw: **Arc, AngleArc, Chord, Ellipse, FillRect, FrameRect, InvertRect, Pie, Rectangle, RoundRect, SetPixel**, and others—all are encapsulated in the **CDC** classes.

Under Windows 3.1, all coordinates and numbers of points were 16-bit quantities. Under the later versions of Windows, all coordinates and numbers of points are 32-bit integers. That is, the world (x, y) coordinates can range from -2,147,483,648 to 2,147,483,647. Unfortunately, the Windows 95/98/ME GDI is still 16-bit at heart; it truncates the 32-bit values to 16-bit! So if you wish to use the larger ranges, run under Windows NT/2000. This helps my cartography applications.

The Drawing Modes or ROPS and Clipping Regions

Windows provides a set of **drawing modes** that specify how the drawing pen is to interact with the canvas or background underneath the pen. The default is **R2_COPYPEN** in which the pen's color is directly copied onto the screen overlaying all colors beneath it. Actually, what Windows does to plot a pixel from the pen at a specific (x, y) point is to perform a bitwise Boolean operation on the pen's color and the screen's pixel color. This process is known as a **binary raster operation** or **ROP**. There are sixteen **ROPS** possible shown in Table 2, and the **ROP** to use is set using the **SetROP2** function.

```
int dc.SetROP2 (id_value); // returns old ROP2 mode
```

Table 2 The Sixteen R2 Ops (Binary Raster Operations)

```
ID                Action

R2_COPYPEN       - Pixel is the pen's color
R2_NOTCOPYPEN    - Pixel is the inverse of the pen's color
R2_BLACK         - Pixel is always binary 0, usually black
R2_WHITE         - Pixel is always binary 1, usually white
R2_XORPEN        - Pixel = pen XOR screen pixel - colors that are
                   in the pen and screen pixel but not in both
R2_NOTXORPEN     - Pixel = NOT (pen XOR screen pixel) - the inverse
                   of the colors of an XOR
R2_MASKNOTPEN    - Pixel = (NOT pen) AND screen pixel - combination
                   of colors common to both the screen and the
                   inverse of the pen
R2_MASKPEN       - Pixel = pen AND screen pixel - combination of
                   the colors common to both pen and screen pixels
R2_MASKPENNOT    - Pixel = pen AND (NOT screen pixel) - combination
                  of colors common to the pen and inverse of screen
R2_NOTMASKPEN    - Pixel = NOT (pen AND screen) - inverse of the
                   R2_MASKPEN color
R2_MERGEPEN      - Pixel = pen OR screen pixel - combination of
                   both the pen and screen color
R2_MERGENOTPEN   - Pixel = (NOT pen) OR screen - combination of
                   screen and the inverse of the pen
R2_MERGEPENNOT   - Pixel = NOT (screen) AND pen - combination of
                   colors common to both the pen and the inverse of
                   the screen
R2_NOTMERGEPEN   - Pixel = NOT (pen OR screen) - the inverse of
                   R2_MERGEPEN
R2_NOP           - Pixel is unchanged
R2_NOT           - Pixel is the inverse of the screen color
```

Normally, the default of just copying the pen's color onto the screen is what is wanted. Perhaps the next frequently used **ROP** is **R2_XORPEN**, where the pen's color is exclusively ORed with the background pixel's color. This is frequently used in animation because the **XOR** logic has a peculiar property: if the same pixel is plotted the same way a second time, the drawn object disappears and the original background reappears. This technique is often used to display a moving cursor. **XOR** plot the cursor at position 1. When it is to move, re-plot the same cursor at point 1 and the background that was overlaid by the cursor reappears. (See the palette discussion below for the meaning of color inversion.)

What is meant by the "inverse color?" In black and white mode, black inverts to white and vice-versa. However, when color enters, it becomes more complex. If the video mode is in 4-color (unlikely) or 16-color, the **ROPS** apply to each of the color planes (4 in the case of 16-color mode). The results can be specifically calculated. However, when in the 256-color mode, the bits that define the colors can be user-defined. Windows defines a set of 21 system colors (Chapter 5). These colors are in the 256-color color palette as well, unless the application has replaced them. Generally, the colors are grouped into a dark set of ten and the light set of ten. To invert, switch from one set to the other; a dark blue might invert to a lighter blue, for example. Here the best guidance is to experiment.

Other features of the GDI include establishing clipping regions. The default is the client area, and during an **OnPaint** request, the invalid portion of the client region. However, you can establish other particular regions for clipping within the client area. Once set up and selected into the DC, Windows automatically clips any drawing activities within that region as well.

The Mighty BitBlt

BitBlt stands for a bit block transfer, which is an exceedingly fast method of copying all or part of a bitmap onto a canvas, retaining the original dimensions or stretching them in some manner. **BitBlts** simply copy bitmap bits extraordinarily quickly. Another form of the **ROP** is used with **BitBlts** because there are now three items that could combine to form the final colors: the source image, the selected brush, and the background screen or canvas being painted. This **tertiary ROP** has 256 possibilities—most do not even have a name or ID. Only a few are really used. The commonly used ones are **PATCOPY**, **SRCCOPY**, **BLACKNESS**, and **WHITENESS**. There are several versions of the **BitBlt**.

The first is **PatBlt**—a pattern block transfer. It is used to set a rectangular area to a constant value or color. The background brush is used along with another **ROP** method of combining the colors. Since **PatBlt** uses only a destination DC and a brush, only a subset of 16 of the 256 **ROPS** is valid. Most often, **PATCOPY** is used when only the brush color is wanted. Other useful ones include **BLACKNESS** and **WHITENESS**.

```
dc.PatBlt (x, y, width, height, PATCOPY);
```

The **BitBlt** function operates like the **PatBlt** but introduces a second DC and its coordinates.

```
dc.BitBlt (x, y, width, height, sourcedc, srcex, srcey, ROP);
```

Although all 256 **ROP** possibilities exist, the most frequently used **ROP** is **SRCCOPY**—copy the source unaltered to the destination. **BitBlt** has many uses. You can copy objects from one place in the client area to another area. You can copy objects from another DC to the client area DC. You can copy to/from a memory DC. The only limiting factor is that the dimensions must be the same. In other words no stretching—expansion or contraction—can be done.

StretchBlt is used when you need to alter the resultant dimensions. You can also flip the image vertically or horizontally. Also, when there is a **color mode** difference between the image bitmap and the actual display DC (say going from a 256-color bitmap onto a 16-color display), **StretchBlt** can be used, although the performance is very poor.

```
dc.StretchBlt (x, y, width, height, sourcedc, srcex, srcey,
                          srcewidth, srceheight, ROP);
```

When shrinking a bitmap, **StretchBlt** must combine two or more rows or columns of pixels into one. Three possible methods exist and are set by using **SetStretchBlt**.

```
dc.SetStretchBltMode (mode);
```

where the mode is one of these.

BLACKONWHITE - the default, if two or more pixels have to be combined, a logical AND is performed on the pixels - black pixels tend to dominate

WHITEONBLACK - uses a logical OR on the pixels - white pixels tend to dominate

COLORONCOLOR - eliminates pixels, so whatever one is used has its original color - best for color bitmaps as it avoids color distortion

Creating Memory DCs

To create a memory DC, two items are needed: a model DC to emulate and a bitmap work area with the desired dimensions. Most often, the memory DC or portions of it will, at some point, be copied to the real client window DC. Therefore, it is **vital** that the memory DC parallel exactly the DC upon which it will ultimately be displayed. Windows API provides functions for just this purpose.

C API Style:

```
HDC      dc     = CreateDC ("DISPLAY", NULL, NULL, NULL);
HDC      memdc  = CreateCompatibleDC (dc);
HBITMAP membmp = CreateCompatibleBitmap (dc, int width,
                   int height);
DeleteDC (dc);
HBITMAP oldbmp = SelectObject (memdc, membmp);
```

First, **CreateDC** is used to construct a DC for a specific device, most often for a printer. However, when the keyword string "**DISPLAY**" is used as the device, a DC is constructed based upon the current display driver and display settings, such as resolution and color type. This DC is then used as the model DC to be emulated by the memory DC. Next, **CreateCompatibleDC** constructs a memory DC based upon the real display DC. The canvas of the memory DC now has a bitmap consisting of just **one** pixel. So, next, a bitmap canvas on which to paint must be constructed with the dimensions that we want. The bitmap also must match the display color type and resolution. **CreateCompatibleBitmap** does just that, modeling itself upon the model DC and using our provided dimensions. The new bitmap must be selected into the memory DC, while saving the old bitmap. Later on, when the memory DC and bitmap are to be destroyed, the old bitmap must be selected back into the memory DC; then both the memory DC and bitmap can be deleted. When DCs are created, they must be deleted. Note this subtly: with **GetDC,** use **ReleaseDC** to remove it, but with **CreateDC** use **DeleteDC** to remove it.

With the memory DC constructed, **any** function that uses a **hdc** can draw on it. Pens and brushes can be selected into the memory DC. Rectangles drawn, polygons painted, and so on. Of course, nothing appears on the screen; it is all in the memory DC and its bitmap. In the paint processing, the memory DC or portions of it is **BitBlt**ed onto the screen in whatever location you want.

Windows through the Control Panel|Display permits the user to change the display resolution and colors and font sizes **without** closing all applications and restarting Windows. Now suddenly **all** running applications must adapt to the new display. Windows sends all applications two **WM_DISPLAYCHANGE** messages. The **wparam** is 0 on the first message indicating that the display characteristics are going to be changed. The second message contains 1 indicating the display has now been changed. Windows applications should respond to this second message, if for no other reason than to reacquire the average character dimensions or screen paints can be garbled. However, if the application is using a memory DC modeled on the screen, that entire model in now **invalid**. The memory DC and its bitmap must be destroyed and a new pair constructed modeled on the new display characteristics.

Under the MFC, the **CDC** encapsulates the memory DC. Where can this creation be done? At any point where a DC can be constructed that is similar to what is needed. Since the process must only be done one time, unless the display changes, it is often done in **OnCreate**.

```
CClientDC dc (this);   // get a dc to model
ptrmemdc = new CDC;
ptrmemdc->CreateCompatibleDC (&dc);
ptrmembitmap = new CBitmap;
ptrmembitmap->CreateCompatibleBitmap (&dc, width, height);
ptrmemdc->SelectObject(ptrmembitmap);
```

or

```
CDC *ptrmemDC = new CDC;
ptrmemdc->CreateDC ("DISPLAY", NULL, NULL, NULL);
...
ptrmemdc->DeleteDC ();
```

Normally, the **ptrmemdc** and the **ptrmembitmap** variables are class members. In the class destructor or in the **DestroyWindow** function, the objects are deleted.

```
if (ptrmemdc)
 delete ptrmemdc;
if (ptrmembitmap)
 delete ptrmembitmap;
```

As with the C API Style, after the DC is created, it has an installed bitmap of 1 pixel. We must allocate a bitmap of the proper size and that is compatible with the current display. There is no sense in having a 256-color bitmap when you are running in 16-color mode. Later in this chapter when we discuss the display of BMP files, I show how one could display with mixed color modes.

Lastly, it is a good idea to install a clipping region so that Windows can automatically clip while drawing on this memory DC.

```
// install a clipping region if desired
CRgn* ptrregn = new CRgn();
CRect rec (0, 0, width, height);
ptrregn->CreateRectRgnIndirect (&rec);
ptrmemdc->SelectClipRgn (ptrregn);
```

Notice that the **CRgn** class encapsulates a region object which can be constructed from a **CRect** object by using the **CreateRectRgnIndirect**. **SelectClipRgn** is then used to select it into the memory DC. And now when any drawing is done on the memory DC, Windows provides proper clipping.

Since the memory DC and its associated bitmap may occupy considerable memory, especially with large bitmaps on a 256-color display, some thought should be made concerning the lifetime of the DC. If the application only needs to display the image, one might take the approach of construct the memory DC, perform the drawing operations on it, **BitBlt** it to the screen, and then delete the memory DC. On the other hand, if the application needs to scroll the image or otherwise needs to keep the memory DC available because of frequent usage, then use protected members to store the pointers to the DC and its bitmap; allocate it once and delete it in the destructor.

Alternatively, one could define all of these objects in the class definition file, removing the pointer versions. However, it is easier to respond to display changes and other events if you have control over when the objects are deleted and created.

Pgm09a: Graphics Scrolling, Memory DCs and Handling Display Changes

Pgm09a illustrates how to perform **smooth** scrolling on a graphics window by the use of a memory DC. All drawing is done on the memory DC. Then, the portion that can fit in the client area is **BitBlted** onto the client area. Whenever the user scrolls, the current thumb bar position is used to **BitBlt** the corresponding rectangle from the memory DC. When the scrolling unit is a single pixel, a very smooth scroll results. The **BitBlt** blazes so that the user can drag the thumb bar and we can keep up! Figure 9.1 shows what the program looks like on the screen.

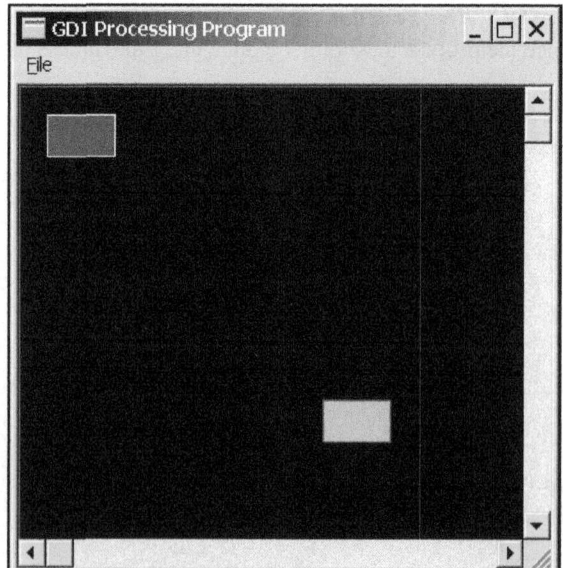

Figure 9.1 Pgm09a Using a Memory DC for Smooth Graphics Scrolling

This program also responds to display mode changes made dynamically by the user through the Control Panel|Display dialog. The new average character dimensions are acquired and the memory DC is deleted and then reallocated, modeled on the new display mode.

Setting Up an Application-wide Information Class

In larger applications, some data may be needed throughout many different window classes. Such items as the full screen dimensions, the display color mode, and the presence or absence of a mouse are commonly needed data. Rather than maintaining duplicate copies of these items as members of the different window classes or continually using the API functions to retrieve them, it makes sense to make these items broadly available. Often, such fields are made global/external in nature. However, with C++ there is a better alternative for indiscriminate use of global data: **static public** members that are initialized by **static** functions.

Try to organize such broadly needed information into meaningful groups. The above type of screen fields might be classed as "system information," while the fields required to maintain a 256-color palette might be in another group. Here, I created a **SysInfo** class to encapsulate the system information. **SysInfo** contains six **static public** data members, including **screenWidth** and **screenHeight** that hold the full screen dimensions, **mouse** which is **true** when a mouse is present, and three fields to contain the color mode information. These system values are gathered by a **static** member function **InitSysInfo** which is invoked from the **CWinApp** derived class and also from the function responding to **WM_DISPLAYCHANGE** messages.

Now suppose that in a non-Windows class function, say **DateTime**, a message must be displayed. That class, **DateTime**, does not have access to **CWnd** or **CWinApp** member functions or data. Hence, no message box actions. Well, it could call the API version, passing 0 for the parent **hwnd**. The MFC provides for just such eventualities with these global macros.

```
CWinApp* AfxGetApp ();    // returns a pointer to the app object
HANDLE   AfxGetInstanceHandle (); // gets handle to this instance
HANDLE   AfxGetResourceHandle (); // gets handle to app resources
```

Even though no actual instances of this class will be allocated, a dummy constructor must be provided. The class has one **static** function, **InitSysInfo**, whose purpose is to initialize the **static** system data. Although I used C API style to create the DC, it could have been done using a **CDC** class this way.

```
CDC dc ();
dc.CreateDC ("DISPLAY", NULL, NULL, NULL);
screen_width = dc.GetDeviceCaps (HORZRES);
...
```

SysInfo Class Definition

```
#pragma once

/***************************************************************/
/*                                                             */
/* SysInfo Class Definition: system wide objects              */
/*                                                             */
/***************************************************************/

class SysInfo {

 /**************************************************************/
 /*                                                            */
 /* Static and Public Access Data Members:                     */
 /*                                                            */
 /**************************************************************/

public:

 static bool mouse;                  // true = mouse present
```

```
 static int  screenWidth;        // screen x dimension in pels
 static int  screenHeight;       // screen y dimension in pels
 static int  screenBitsPixel;    // screen bits per pixel
 static int  screenNumPlanes;    // screen number of bit planes
 static int  screenPalette;      // screen number of colors
 /*************************************************************/
 /*                                                           */
 /* Functions:                                                */
 /*                                                           */
 /*************************************************************/
public:
            SysInfo () {}           // dummy constructor
 static bool InitSysInfo ();        // initialize the static data
};
```

SysInfo Class Implementation

```
#include "stdafx.h"
#include "sysinfo.h"   // class header
/**************************************************************/
/*                                                            */
/* SysInfo: system wide objects - static public members       */
/*                                                            */
/**************************************************************/
// static members
bool SysInfo::mouse;              // TRUE = mouse present
int  SysInfo::screenWidth;        // screen x dimension in pels
int  SysInfo::screenHeight;       // screen y dimension in pels
int  SysInfo::screenBitsPixel;    // screen bits per pixel
int  SysInfo::screenNumPlanes;    // screen number of bit planes
int  SysInfo::screenPalette;      // screen number of colors
/**************************************************************/
/*                                                            */
/* InitSysInfo: initializes static values                     */
/*              returns true if it is successful              */
/*                                                            */
/**************************************************************/
bool SysInfo::InitSysInfo () {
 // get system-wide mouse and screen settings
 mouse = GetSystemMetrics(SM_MOUSEPRESENT) ? true : false;
 HDC hdc = CreateDC  ("DISPLAY", NULL, NULL, NULL);
 screenWidth     = GetDeviceCaps (hdc, HORZRES);
 screenHeight    = GetDeviceCaps (hdc, VERTRES);
 screenBitsPixel = GetDeviceCaps (hdc, BITSPIXEL);
 screenNumPlanes = GetDeviceCaps (hdc, PLANES);
 screenPalette   = GetDeviceCaps (hdc, SIZEPALETTE);
 DeleteDC (hdc);
 return true; // successful
}
```

Pgm09a Implementation

The variable **mapsize** represents the maximum size of the graphics display area. For scrolling and displaying, the canvas extends from 0 to 400 pixels, square. Since this value could be set in various ways, I also inserted some code to force the map size to not exceed the current screen capabilities. If you do a maximize operation, then the entire map is shown with no scroll bars. This map size is passed to the **FrameWin** constructor from the **CWinApp** derived class, **Pgm09a**.

```
// get system-wide mouse and screen settings
SysInfo::InitSysInfo ();

int mapsize = 400;  // set default map size
// guarantee dimension does not exceed screen capacity in
// the current mode
mapsize = SysInfo::screenHeight < mapsize?
                  SysInfo::screenHeight : mapsize;
// construct new frame window
m_pMainWnd = new FrameWin (mapsize);
```

Now examine the **FrameWin** class definition. I defined several pens and brushes. This is also a common technique used in larger applications. If the application needs to frequently and repeatedly create pens and brushes, doing so once saves time and coding. Also if one is going to do much real drawing, an array of points is needed. Although I really do not need to do so here, I have allocated space for a large array of points from global memory to illustrate using global memory allocations with the GDI functions. The member **hlparray** is the handle to the global memory array and the member **lp** is the locked pointer. Note that I did not name it **ptrlp** because its main use is in the array style: **lp[i].x**. Next, the pointers to the memory DC and memory bitmap are defined.

The number of member functions is few and one half of them center around the memory DC and display change actions. **ConstructMemDC** creates the compatible memory DC. **RemoveMemDC** deletes the memory DC. **DrawMemDC** performs the actual GDI drawing operations on the memory DC. **OnCreate** invokes **GetAvgCharDims**, **ConstructMemDC** and **DrawMemDC**. Should the display mode be dynamically altered, **RemoveDC** is called followed by these two again. **OnSize** resets any scroll bar range based on the current child window dimensions.

Pgm09a's FrameWin Definition

```
#pragma once

/***************************************************************/
/*                                                             */
/* FrameWin Class Definition                                   */
/*                                                             */
/***************************************************************/

class FrameWin : public CFrameWnd {

 /***************************************************************/
 /*                                                             */
 /* Class Data Members                                          */
 /*                                                             */
 /***************************************************************/

protected:

CPen        whitePen;   // a set of pens
CPen        redPen;
CPen        bluePen;
CPen        greenPen;

CBrush      blackBrush; // a set of brushes
CBrush      blueBrush;
CBrush      grayBrush;

int          arraySize;   // set to 500 CPoint objects
```

```
HANDLE       hlparray;     // handle of global lp array for points
CPoint*      lp;           // locked ptr of lp array of x,y points
CDC*         ptrmemdc;         // memory device context for drawing
CBitmap*     ptrmembitmap;     // memory bitmap of drawing
CRgn*        ptrregn;          // clipping region
CRect        fullWindow;       // max sized window
CRect        displayWindow;    // current display window size
CPoint       scrollPosition;   // offset from full window to 0,0 of
                               // paint's display window
int          currentVpel;      // current vertical scroll offset
int          currentHpel;      // current horizontal scroll offset
int          numVpelsToScroll;
int          numHpelsToScroll;
int          maxVscrollPels;   // max num vertical pels to scroll
int          maxHscrollPels;   // max num horiz pels to scroll
int          avgCharWidth;     // average character width
int          avgCharHeight;    // average character height
int          avgCapsWidth;     // average capital's width
 /*************************************************************/
 /*                                                           */
 /* Class Functions:                                          */
 /*                                                           */
 /*************************************************************/
public:
              FrameWin (int mapsz);
             ~FrameWin () {}
protected:
 void  GetAvgCharDims ();   // get the average character dims
 void  RemoveMemDC ();      // delete memory DC objects
 void  ConstructMemDC ();   // construct new memory DC
 void  DrawMemDC ();        // draw objects on memory DC
afx_msg void OnPaint ();                     // paint the window
afx_msg int  OnCreate (LPCREATESTRUCT); // initial class members
afx_msg void OnDestroy ();                   // delete fonts & array
afx_msg void OnSize (UINT flags, int cx, int cy); // reset scroll
afx_msg void OnKeyDown (UINT, UINT, UINT);  // keybd scrolling
afx_msg void OnHScroll (UINT, UINT, CScrollBar*);
afx_msg void OnVScroll (UINT, UINT, CScrollBar*);
//user has changed display settings, so need to rebuild
afx_msg LRESULT OnDisplayChange (WPARAM, LPARAM);
// command processors
afx_msg void CmExit ();              // quit the app
DECLARE_MESSAGE_MAP();
};
```

Notice in particular how the function that responds to the **WM_DISPLAYCHANGE** message is defined. It returns 0 if it handles the message; **wparam** contains 0 or 1 indicating the display mode is going to be changed and then that it has now changed. Normally, I pass along the “is going to change” message and actually respond when the display has actually changed.

Now examine the **FrameWin** class implementation. In the constructor, all of the various pens and brushes are created. The **full_window** represents the maximum size rectangle of the graphics area, while **display_window** represents the current client area rectangle whose dimensions are altered in **OnSize** processing. Scroll bars are added just as they were when processing text. The actual range is set in **OnSize**, based upon the current client area dimensions.

The global points array is allocated with room for 500 points; I need five points! In **OnSize**, the current client area dimensions are retrieved and stored in **display_window**. Should the user resize the window so that the display area exceeds the graphic image **mapsize**, the **display_window** rectangle is forced to not exceed the **mapsize**. Then, the scroll bar ranges are set based on the number of pixel difference between the actual **mapsize** (**full_window**) and the current size (**display_window**).

ConstructMemDC allocates the memory DC, exactly as discussed above. A compatible DC is created based upon the client DC. A compatible bitmap is created based upon the full screen dimensions. After the bitmap is selected into the memory DC, a clipping region is defined and installed. Now the memory DC is ready for use.

DrawMemDC does the actual drawing. The global memory line points array, **lp**, is locked and filled with a series of points that trace the map size dimensions. **FillRect** clears out the previous drawing and set our background color of black. To show how to use Windows globally allocated memory with GDI functions, **Polyline** uses the **lp** array to draw a red line around the border of the graphics area. I used the **lp** array so that you could see how one might handle drawing actions with large amounts of data. Next, a series of colored rectangles is drawn.

OnPaint now becomes simple. If **ptrmemdc** exists, then a **BitBlt** copies the image portion onto the screen. When you experiment with this application, notice how fast and smooth the graphics scroll actually is. With a small amount of effort, your graphics handling can be quite professional.

I did not check and display error messages should some of the allocations fail just to keep the example shorter.

Pgm09a's FrameWin Implementation

```
#include "stdafx.h"
#include "framewin.h"
#include "resource.h"
#include "SysInfo.h"

/***************************************************************/
/*                                                             */
/* FrameWin Events Response Table                              */
/*                                                             */
/***************************************************************/

BEGIN_MESSAGE_MAP(FrameWin, CFrameWnd)
 ON_WM_SIZE ()
 ON_WM_PAINT ()
 ON_WM_CREATE ()
 ON_WM_DESTROY ()
 ON_WM_KEYDOWN()
 ON_WM_VSCROLL ()
 ON_WM_HSCROLL ()
 ON_COMMAND(CM_EXIT, CmExit)
 ON_MESSAGE(WM_DISPLAYCHANGE, OnDisplayChange)
END_MESSAGE_MAP();

/***************************************************************/
/*                                                             */
/* Framewin: Construct the window object                       */
/*                                                             */
/***************************************************************/

FrameWin::FrameWin (int mapsize) : CFrameWnd () {
 // construct the objects needed for drawing
 whitePen.CreatePen (PS_SOLID, 1, RGB (255, 255, 255));
 redPen.CreatePen (PS_SOLID, 1, RGB (255, 0, 0));
 bluePen.CreatePen (PS_SOLID, 1, RGB (0, 0, 255));
 greenPen.CreatePen (PS_SOLID, 1, RGB (0, 255, 0));

 blackBrush.CreateSolidBrush(RGB (0, 0, 0));
 blueBrush.CreateSolidBrush(RGB (0, 0, 255));
```

```
 grayBrush.CreateSolidBrush(RGB (192, 192, 192));

 fullWindow.top     = fullWindow.left      = 0;
 fullWindow.right   = fullWindow.bottom    = mapsize;

 displayWindow.top  = displayWindow.bottom = 0;
 displayWindow.left = displayWindow.right  = 0;

 // allocate from global memory an array of 500 CPoint objects
 arraySize = 500;
 hlparray = GlobalAlloc (GMEM_MOVEABLE,
                         arraySize * sizeof (CPoint));
 ptrmemdc     = 0;
 ptrmembitmap = 0;
 ptrregn      = 0;
 currentVpel = 0;
 currentHpel = 0;

 // set up the items needed to create the window
 DWORD style = WS_OVERLAPPEDWINDOW | WS_VSCROLL | WS_HSCROLL;
 CRect rect (0, 0, mapsize, mapsize);
 CString title;
 title.LoadString (IDS_MAINTITLE);
 Create (AfxRegisterWndClass (
              CS_VREDRAW | CS_HREDRAW,
              AfxGetApp()->LoadStandardCursor (IDC_ARROW),
              (HBRUSH) GetStockObject (BLACK_BRUSH),
              AfxGetApp()->LoadStandardIcon (IDI_APPLICATION)),
          title,              // window caption
          style,              // wndclass DWORD style
          rect,               // set initial window position
          0,                 // the parent window, here none
         "MAINMENU");        // assign the main menu
}

/*************************************************************/
/*                                                           */
/* OnCreate: build the memory dc and bitmap and drawing once  */
/*                                                           */
/*************************************************************/

int FrameWin::OnCreate (LPCREATESTRUCT lpCS) {
 if (CFrameWnd::OnCreate (lpCS) == -1) return -1;
 GetAvgCharDims ();
 ConstructMemDC ();
 DrawMemDC ();
 return 0;
}

/*************************************************************/
/*                                                           */
/* OnSize: acquire the current dimensions of the client window */
/*         and reset scrolling ranges                        */
/*                                                           */
/*************************************************************/

void FrameWin::OnSize (UINT, int, int) {
 GetClientRect (&displayWindow); // get new window size
 // force new display size not to exceed full map window size
 if (displayWindow.bottom>fullWindow.bottom)
     displayWindow.bottom=fullWindow.bottom;

 if (displayWindow.right>fullWindow.right)
     displayWindow.right=fullWindow.right;
```

```

 // based on size of current display and max full window map size
 // set the scrolling range
 maxVscrollPels = fullWindow.bottom - displayWindow.bottom;
 maxHscrollPels = fullWindow.right  - displayWindow.right;
 currentVpel = min (currentVpel, maxVscrollPels);
 currentHpel = min (currentHpel, maxHscrollPels);

 SetScrollRange (SB_VERT, 0, maxVscrollPels, FALSE);
 SetScrollPos (SB_VERT, currentVpel, TRUE);
 SetScrollRange (SB_HORZ, 0, maxHscrollPels, FALSE);
 SetScrollPos (SB_HORZ, currentHpel, TRUE);
}

/******************************************************************/
/*                                                                */
/* OnPaint: display what's appropriate from the memory dc         */
/*                                                                */
/******************************************************************/

void FrameWin::OnPaint () {
 CPaintDC dc (this);
 if (ptrmemdc)
  // display the memDC onto that portion of the display window
  // using bitblt tocopy from memory to the client area dc
  dc.BitBlt (displayWindow.left, displayWindow.top,
             displayWindow.right - displayWindow.left,
             displayWindow.bottom - displayWindow.top,
             ptrmemdc, currentHpel, currentVpel, SRCCOPY);
}

/******************************************************************/
/*                                                                */
/* GetAvgCharDims: retrieve current font's average dimensions     */
/*                                                                */
/******************************************************************/

void FrameWin::GetAvgCharDims () {
 TEXTMETRIC  tm;  // set the system font's characteristics in tm
 CClientDC dc (this);    // acquire a DC
 dc.GetTextMetrics (&tm); // get the font information
 // calculate average character parameters
 avgCharWidth = tm.tmAveCharWidth;
 avgCharHeight = tm.tmHeight + tm.tmExternalLeading;
 avgCapsWidth = (tm.tmPitchAndFamily & 1 ? 3 : 2) *
                  avgCharWidth / 2;
}

/******************************************************************/
/*                                                                */
/* OnDestroy: remove the array and memory dc and bitmap           */
/*                                                                */
/******************************************************************/

void FrameWin::OnDestroy () {
 if (hlparray)
  GlobalFree(hlparray);
 RemoveMemDC ();
 CFrameWnd::OnDestroy ();
}

/******************************************************************/
/*                                                                */
/* OnDisplayChange: user has changed the display settings, so     */
```

```
/*                   we must update totally rebuild the memory dc  */
/*                                                                 */
/*****************************************************************/

LRESULT FrameWin::OnDisplayChange (WPARAM which, LPARAM lp) {
 LRESULT retcd = CFrameWnd::OnDisplayChange (which, lp);
 if (which == 1) {
  SysInfo::InitSysInfo (); // reinitialize system information
  GetAvgCharDims ();       // reacquire the character dimensions
  RemoveMemDC ();          // delete old memory DC
  ConstructMemDC ();       // build new memory DC
 }
 return retcd;
}

/*****************************************************************/
/*                                                               */
/* RemoveMemDC: delete all memory DC items and reset ptrs to 0 */
/*                                                               */
/*****************************************************************/

void      FrameWin::RemoveMemDC () {
 if (ptrmemdc)
  delete ptrmemdc;
 if (ptrmembitmap)
  delete ptrmembitmap;
 if (ptrregn)
  delete ptrregn;
 ptrmemdc = 0;
 ptrmembitmap = 0;
 ptrregn = 0;
}

/*****************************************************************/
/*                                                               */
/* ConstructMemDC: builds a memory DC and bitmap for drawing   */
/*                                                               */
/*****************************************************************/

void      FrameWin::ConstructMemDC () {
 CClientDC dc (this);
 ptrmemdc = new CDC ();
 ptrmemdc->CreateCompatibleDC (&dc); // create the memory dc
 ptrmembitmap = new CBitmap ();      // create a bitmap for memdc
 ptrmembitmap->CreateCompatibleBitmap (&dc,
   SysInfo::screenWidth, SysInfo::screenHeight); // a large one
 ptrmemdc->SelectObject(ptrmembitmap); // put  bitmap into memDC

 //install clipping region if desired, not needed in this example
 ptrregn = new CRgn();
 CRect rec (0, 0, SysInfo::screenWidth, SysInfo::screenHeight);
 ptrregn->CreateRectRgnIndirect (&rec); // define the region
 ptrmemdc->SelectClipRgn (ptrregn);     // set up clipping region
}

/*****************************************************************/
/*                                                               */
/* DrawMemDC: draws graphical images into the memory DC        */
/*                                                               */
/*****************************************************************/

void FrameWin::DrawMemDC () {
 lp = (CPoint*) GlobalLock(hlparray);  // lock down array
 // clear out whole previous image
```

```
 CRect rec (0, 0, SysInfo::screenWidth, SysInfo::screenHeight);
 ptrmemdc->FillRect (&rec, &blackBrush);

 // draw a red line around full window area
 // here I am illustrating the use of the array and global memory
 // it would be vastly easier just to call Rectangle()
 lp[0].x=0;                   lp[0].y=0;
 lp[1].x=0;                   lp[1].y=fullWindow.right-1;
 lp[2].x=fullWindow.right-1; lp[2].y=fullWindow.right-1;
 lp[3].x=fullWindow.right-1; lp[3].y=0;
 lp[4].x=0;                   lp[4].y=0;
 ptrmemdc->SelectObject (&redPen); // install red pen to draw box
 ptrmemdc->Polyline (lp, 5);        // draw red line around edge

 // draw a series of rectangles the easy way
 ptrmemdc->SelectObject (&whitePen);
 ptrmemdc->SelectObject(&blueBrush);
 // white around blue center
 ptrmemdc->Rectangle (20, 20, 70, 50);

 ptrmemdc->SelectObject (&redPen);
 // red around blue center
 ptrmemdc->Rectangle (320, 320, 370, 350);

 ptrmemdc->SelectObject (&grayBrush);
 // red around gray center
 ptrmemdc->Rectangle (220, 220, 270, 250);

 GlobalUnlock(hlparray);  // unlock global memory lp array
}

/***************************************************************/
/*                                                             */
/* OnKeyDown: provide a keyboard scroller interface            */
/*                                                             */
/***************************************************************/

void FrameWin::OnKeyDown (UINT key, UINT, UINT) {
 switch (key) {

  case VK_UP:     // requests scroll up 1 line
   SendMessage (WM_VSCROLL, SB_LINEUP, 0L); break;

  case VK_DOWN:   // requests scroll down 1 line
   SendMessage (WM_VSCROLL, SB_LINEDOWN, 0L); break;

  case VK_LEFT:   // requests scroll left 1 col
   SendMessage (WM_HSCROLL, SB_LINEUP, 0L); break;

  case VK_RIGHT: // requests scroll right 1 col
   SendMessage (WM_HSCROLL, SB_LINEDOWN, 0L); break;

  case VK_PRIOR: // request scroll 1 page up
   SendMessage (WM_VSCROLL, SB_PAGEUP, 0L); break;

  case VK_NEXT:  // request scroll 1 page down
   SendMessage (WM_VSCROLL, SB_PAGEDOWN, 0L); break;

  case VK_END:    // request goto the bottom
   SendMessage (WM_HSCROLL, SB_PAGEDOWN, 0L); break;

  case VK_HOME:  // request goto the top
   SendMessage (WM_HSCROLL, SB_PAGEUP, 0L);  break;
 }
```

```
}

/********************************************************************/
/*                                                                  */
/* OnVScroll: scroll window vertically                              */
/*                                                                  */
/********************************************************************/

void FrameWin::OnVScroll (UINT type, UINT pos, CScrollBar*) {
 switch (type) {
  case SB_LINEUP:     // scroll up 1 line
   numVpelsToScroll = -1; break;

  case SB_LINEDOWN:   // scroll 1 line down
   numVpelsToScroll = 1; break;

  case SB_PAGEUP:     // scroll 1 page up
   numVpelsToScroll = -8; break;

  case SB_PAGEDOWN:   // scroll 1 page down
   numVpelsToScroll = 8; break;

  case SB_THUMBTRACK: // follow thumb bar
   numVpelsToScroll = pos - currentVpel; break;

  default:
   numVpelsToScroll = 0;
 }
 numVpelsToScroll = max (-currentVpel,
                      min (numVpelsToScroll,
                           maxVscrollPels - currentVpel));
 if (numVpelsToScroll !=0) {
  currentVpel +=numVpelsToScroll;
  ScrollWindow (0, -numVpelsToScroll, NULL, NULL);
  SetScrollPos (SB_VERT, currentVpel, TRUE);
 }
}

/********************************************************************/
/*                                                                  */
/* OnHScroll: scroll window horizontally                            */
/*                                                                  */
/********************************************************************/

void FrameWin::OnHScroll (UINT type, UINT pos, CScrollBar*) {
 switch (type) {
  case SB_LINEUP:    // scroll 1 col left
   numHpelsToScroll = -1; break;

  case SB_LINEDOWN:  // scroll 1 col right
   numHpelsToScroll = 1; break;

  case SB_PAGEUP:    // scroll 1 page left
   numHpelsToScroll = -8; break;

  case SB_PAGEDOWN:   // scroll 1 page right
   numHpelsToScroll = 8; break;

  case SB_THUMBTRACK: // follow thumb bar
   numHpelsToScroll = pos - currentHpel; break;

  default:
   numHpelsToScroll = 0;
 }
```

```
 numHpelsToScroll = max (-currentHpel,
                         min (numHpelsToScroll,
                              maxHscrollPels - currentHpel));
 if (numHpelsToScroll !=0) {
  currentHpel +=numHpelsToScroll;
  ScrollWindow (-numHpelsToScroll, 0, NULL, NULL);
  SetScrollPos (SB_HORZ, currentHpel, TRUE);
 }
}

/*************************************************************/
/*                                                           */
/* CmExit: user is trying to quit the app                    */
/*                                                           */
/*************************************************************/

void      FrameWin::CmExit () {
 PostMessage (WM_CLOSE);
}
```

Next, let's get even fancier and add the ability to load and display bitmap images. However, let us extend the simple "show it on the screen" to include some "hot" display methods designed to generate user interest.

DIBs and Color Palettes

The bitmaps that we have used so far and those from **CreateBitmap** and **LoadBitmap** are stored in a Windows **device dependent bitmap** or **DDB** under the control of the GDI and must be compatible with the video display (or printer).

Bitmaps can also be stored in files with the usual extension of bmp. They are saved in a **device independent bitmap** format or **DIB**. The DIB stores all of the pixels in a manner that is not dependent upon the actual device and specifically not on the color-mode of the device. Special consideration must be given to the DIB's possible color palette. This is because the actual method of storing the color palette and the method of storing the pixel's color varies completely between the different color modes in which the image could be stored. Common DIB color modes include 2-color (monochrome), 16-color, 256-color, 32K, 64K, and 16M (true-color). The DIB stores this information in a common, uniform format that is totally independent of the display's current color mode selected by the computer user.

When saved on disk, a DIB has the extension bmp although some applications save them with a dib extension; both are equivalent. DIBs are not GDI objects under Windows; therefore, normal GDI drawing functions cannot be performed on them. Under the MFC prior to Visual C++ Version 7, there is no DIB class. In Version 7, there is a **CImage** class to handle many common types of image files, not just bmps. So for now, we must create one ourselves.

Windows provides a method to convert DIBs into DDBs. When converted, the color palette is adjusted to fit the real color mode in use, such as 16-color or 256-color or true color. The layout of the DIB file is a bit awkward. A **BITMAPFILEHEADER** structure is the first item in the BMP file and contains the characters "BM" in the first two bytes in the field called **byType**; the member **bfSize** member contains the file size; the member **bfOffBits** contains the offset to the actual bitmap bits from the beginning of the file. Next comes the **BITMAPINFOHEADER** structure that provides the details of this bitmap's organization, including the width and height and color mode and so on; it is variable in size. If the color palette is present, it comes next. Finally, come the actual bits that make up the image.

Remember that these bmp files are often quite large, hundreds of K. A high resolution, 256-color, full screen image has 786,432 bytes of pixels! In the 26M color mode, that number quadruples. When read into memory, these DIBs are often referred to as **packed DIB memory format**. As such, they consist of **BITMAPINFOHEADER**, a color table if present, and the bits themselves; the file header is discarded.
A bmp file begins with the **BITMAPFILEHEADER** structure which is used to control the input of the rest of the file. It is never actually saved in memory beyond the initial loading of the file. It is shown in Table 3.

Table 3—The Bmp File Header Structure (BITMAPFILEHEADER)

```
WORD     bfType;        // must be BM
DWORD    bfSize;        // size of file in bytes
WORD     bfReserved1;   // must be 0
WORD     bfReserved2;   // must be 0
DWORD    bfOffBits;     // byte offset from file start to the
                        // bits array
```

Following the file header structure comes a **BITMAPINFO** structure that contains information about the dimensions and color format of a device-independent bitmap (DIB). Its layout is shown in Table 4. It contains two structure members: the **BITMAPINFOHEADER** structure followed by the color table array of **RGBQUAD** structures, **if** there is a color table present in this bmp file.

Table 4—The BITMAPINFO Structure

```
The BITMAPINFO Structure:
BITMAPINFOHEADER bmiHeader;
RGBQUAD          bmiColors[1];
The BITMAPINFOHEADER Structure:
DWORD   biSize;          // size of this structure in bytes
LONG    biWidth;         // bitmap width in pixels
LONG    biHeight;        // bitmap height in pixels
WORD    biPlanes;        // target device # of planes - must
                         // be set to 1
WORD    biBitCount;      // number of bits per pixel 1, 4, 8,
                         // 16, 24, or 32
// the fields below here may not be present or they may be
// all be 0 - they are seldom used
DWORD   biCompression;   // indicates a compressed bitmap
DWORD   biSizeImage;     // size in bytes of the image
LONG    biXPelsPerMeter; // horz resolution in pels per meter
                         // of target display for best views
LONG    biYPelsPerMeter; // vert resolution in pels per meter
                         // of target display for best view
DWORD   biClrUsed;       // number of color indexes actually
                         // used in this image
DWORD   biClrImportant;  // number of colors that are
                         // important to render this bitmap
RGBQUAD bmiColors[1];    // the first RGBQUAD color structure
```

Note that the fields below the **biBitCount** may all be zero or even omitted; use the **biSize** member to determine the structure's exact length. When creating a bmp file, if you wish to ignore these fields below **biBitCount**, then set them all to zeros. While run-length encoding for data compression is possible, I have never seen one that is compressed. After the **BITMAPINFOHEADER** structure comes the color table which defines the precise colors to be used in this DIB. Generally a color value is specified by a **RGBQUAD** structure as shown in Table 5.

Table 5—The RGBQUAD Structure

```
The RGBQUAD Structure:
    BYTE    rgbBlue;
    BYTE    rgbGreen;
    BYTE    rgbRed;
    BYTE    rgbReserved; // always 0
```

The color table, if present, is set up a bit unusually because it can hold a variable number of **RGBQUAD** color structures, depending upon the number of unique colors in the bitmap image. The official color table structure begins at the end of the **BITMAPINFO** and is defined as containing only the first element in the color table. Immediately after this first **RGBQUAD** structure in the **BITMAPINFO** structure come the remainder of the variable number of color **RGBQUAD** structures.

If this is one of the three true color image files, 32K, 64K or 16M, there is no color table present. The first color pixel bits begin at this location where the color table would otherwise begin.

The color table is followed immediately by the actual bitmap bits, as an array of **BYTE** data (**unsigned char**) which can be one, two, three or four bytes for each pixel, depending on the color mode of the image. The best method to unravel the color table is to add **biSize** to the location of the **BITMAPINFOHEADER**, yielding the possible start of the color table. Then, compare that location to the **bfOffBits** member. If they are equal, there is **no** color table present. The difference between the two locations divided by the size of an **RGBQUAD** structure (four bytes) yields the number of color table entries actually stored. Alternatively, if the **biClrUsed** is actually present and non-zero, its value can be used. In **Pgm09b**, I check for this field's presence and use its value if non-zero.

Using DIBs requires solving several problems, including how to input the file in a usable form, how the color palette operates, how to construct and install a proper color palette for the DIB, and how to get the image onto the screen. Let's examine these issues one by one. Under the MFC, the first challenge is to actually input the DIB into a dynamically allocated memory area.

There are other input considerations. I am ignoring OS2 Presentation Manager style bitmaps which have a slightly different set of headers. The bitmap bits that contain the individual pixel colors can be a very large array. Often some form of data compression can be used to reduce that volume of data. **Run Length Encoding**, **RLE**, is one of the most common techniques used to compress images. Operating upon one scan line (one row of pixels) at a time, the basic idea is to replace a series of identical color values with a count of the number of duplicate color values and that color value. So that 10 consecutive blue bits would be replaced by 10 x blue. RLE is the basis of the PCX file format; however, RLE is only infrequently used in bmp files. Hence, I am ignoring image compression here.

First, let's examine how the DIBs are input; then how the color palettes are handled; lastly how to work with DIBs in memory DCs. Under the MFC, we must write our own **CDib** class. I have purposely kept the class extremely simply so that the basic principles can easily be seen. Examine the class header file.

CDib Class Definition

```
#pragma once

/***************************************************************/
/*                                                             */
/* CDib Class Definition                                       */
/*                                                             */
/***************************************************************/

class CDib {

 /*************************************************************/
 /*                                                           */
 /* Class Data Members                                        */
 /*                                                           */
 /*************************************************************/

public:
 enum NumColors {Colors2, Colors16, Colors256, Colors16T,
                 Colors24T, Colors32T, Unknown};
protected:

 BYTE* ptrDib;                  // ptr to the DIB
 NumColors numColors;           // the number of colors in this DIB
 int numColorTableEntries;      // number of color table entries
 int numColorsUsed;             // number of colors actually used
 int actualNumColorsInTable;    // real number of colors in table
 int colorTableSize;            // number of bytes in color table
 int bmWidth;                   // bmp width
 int bmHeight;                  // bmp height
 BYTE* ptrBits;   // the addr of the bits for manual manipulation
 LPBITMAPINFO ptrBmInfo;        // addr of BITMAPINFO structure
 CPalette* ptrPalette;          // the palette, if any

 /*************************************************************/
 /*                                                           */
 /* Class Functions:                                          */
 /*                                                           */
 /*************************************************************/
```

```

public:

       CDib (const char*); // makes a memory DIB from a .BMP file
      ~CDib ();            // removed the DIB and palette

bool         IsValid () const;    // true if DIB is loaded &ready
CPalette*    GetPalette () const; // returns any palette in use
BYTE*        GetDibBitsAddr () const;// returns ptr to data bits
int          GetDibWidth () const;   // returns width of DIB
int          GetDibHeight () const;  // returns height of DIB
LPBITMAPINFO GetBitmapInfo () const; // returns ptr to BITMAPINFO
int          GetBitSize () const; // gets the size of image bit
NumColors    GetNumColors () const;

protected:
void  ReadDibFile (const char*); // input the DIB file & make DIB
void  MakePalette ();            // makes color palette from DIB
};
```

Many of the data members and member functions return needed information about the image, such as the image's dimensions and its color mode. I began the class with a public class enumerated data type that defines the actual color mode of the image. The constructor controls all of the loading operations. It calls **ReadDibFile** to load the image. The image itself is stored in the member **ptrdib**. This pointer actually points to the **BITMAPINFO** portion of the file. The member **ptrBits** is adjusted to point further down into the data to the actual start of the pixel data bits. If there is a color palette for this image, it is built as part of the initial loading process and a pointer to the **CPalette** instance is stored and passed to client programs as requested via **GetPalette**. The **IsValid** function allows client programs to check on the success of the initial loading process since a constructor cannot return any value and since I did not want to introduce C++ exception processing at this point in the text.

The destructor is responsible for deleting the image portion, **ptrdib**, and any palette, **ptrPalette**. If a console window is present, key information about this bmp file is displayed during the loading operation.

CDib Class Implementation

```
#include "stdafx.h"
#include <conio.h>

#include "cdib.h"

/***************************************************************/
/*                                                             */
/* CDib: Load the DIB into a memory CDib object                */
/*                                                             */
/***************************************************************/

CDib::CDib (const char *filename) {
 ptrPalette = 0;
#ifdef _DEBUG
 _cprintf ("CDib: Opening File: %s\r\n", filename);
#endif
 ReadDibFile (filename); // attempt the loading of the DIB file
}

/***************************************************************/
/*                                                             */
/* ~CDib: Delete the CDib object                               */
/*                                                             */
/***************************************************************/

CDib::~CDib () {
 if (ptrDib) delete [] ptrDib;
 if (ptrPalette) delete ptrPalette;
```

```
}

/**************************************************************/
/*                                                            */
/* ReadDibFile: loads a .BMP file into a dib                  */
/*                                                            */
/**************************************************************/

void CDib::ReadDibFile (const char *filename) {
 BITMAPFILEHEADER bmfh;
 DWORD            dwDibSize;
 DWORD            actsz;

 // open the file .BMP
 HANDLE hfile = CreateFile (filename, GENERIC_READ,
                  FILE_SHARE_READ, NULL, OPEN_EXISTING, 0, NULL);
 if (hfile == INVALID_HANDLE_VALUE) {
  ptrDib = 0;
  return;
 }

 // input the BITMAPFILEHEADER structure
 ReadFile (hfile, (LPSTR) &bmfh, sizeof (BITMAPFILEHEADER),
           &actsz, NULL);
 if (actsz != sizeof (BITMAPFILEHEADER)) {
  CloseHandle (hfile);
  ptrDib = 0;
  return;
 }

 // verify it is a .BMP file
 if (bmfh.bfType != * (WORD *) "BM") {
  CloseHandle (hfile);
  ptrDib = 0;
  return;
 }

 // calculate the size of the file less the file header
 // and allocate memory for the dib
 dwDibSize = bmfh.bfSize - sizeof (BITMAPFILEHEADER);
 ptrDib = new BYTE [dwDibSize];
 if (!ptrDib) {
  CloseHandle (hfile);
  return;
 }

 // read in the rest of the DIB - could be huge amount of bytes
 // for a large .BMP file
 ReadFile (hfile, (LPSTR) ptrDib, dwDibSize, &actsz, NULL);
 CloseHandle (hfile);
 if (actsz != dwDibSize) {
  delete [] ptrDib;
  ptrDib = 0;
  return;
 }

 // check the validity of the size of the info header
 // - fail OS2 bitmaps
 if (((BITMAPINFOHEADER*) ptrDib)->biSize <=
     sizeof(BITMAPCOREHEADER)) {
  delete [] ptrDib;
  ptrDib = 0;
  return;
 }
```

```

 // calc the theoretical number of colors in the color palette
 WORD bitcount = ((BITMAPINFOHEADER*) ptrDib)->biBitCount;
#ifdef _DEBUG
 _cprintf ("CDib: biBitCount: %ld\r\n", bitcount);
#endif
 // some chance that the biClrUsed field is really there
 numColorsUsed = ((BITMAPINFOHEADER*) ptrDib)->biClrUsed;
 // set class color table values
 switch (bitcount) {
  case 1:
   numColorTableEntries = 2;
   numColors = Colors2;
   break;
  case 4:
   numColorTableEntries = 16;
   numColors = Colors16;
   break;
  case 8:
   numColorTableEntries = 256;
   numColors = Colors256;
   break;
  case 16:
   numColorTableEntries = 0;
   numColors = Colors16T;
   break;
  case 24:
   numColorTableEntries = 0;
   numColors = Colors24T;
   break;
  case 32:
   numColorTableEntries = 0;
   numColors = Colors32T;
   break;
  default:
   numColorTableEntries = 0;
   numColors = Unknown;
 }
#ifdef _DEBUG
 _cprintf ("CDib: color results\r\n");
 _cprintf (" numColors enum: %d\r\n", numColors);
 _cprintf (" numColorTableEntries: %d\r\n", numColorTableEntries)
 _cprintf (" numColorsUsed: %d\r\n", numColorsUsed);
#endif
 // set basic image statistics
 actualNumColorsInTable = numColorsUsed ? numColorsUsed :
                          numColorTableEntries;
 colorTableSize = actualNumColorsInTable * sizeof (RGBQUAD);

 ptrBmInfo = (LPBITMAPINFO) ptrDib;
 ptrBits = ptrDib + ((BITMAPINFOHEADER*) ptrDib)->biSize +
           colorTableSize;
 bmHeight = ((BITMAPINFOHEADER*) ptrDib)->biHeight;
 bmWidth = ((BITMAPINFOHEADER*) ptrDib)->biWidth;

 MakePalette (); // make any needed color palette
}

/***************************************************************/
/*                                                             */
/* MakePalette: constructs logical color palette               */
/*                                                             */
/***************************************************************/

```

```
void CDib::MakePalette () {
 // no palettes for the higher color images
 if (numColors > Colors256) return;
 if (!IsValid ()) return;

 LPLOGPALETTE ptrpal;
 HANDLE       hpal; // handle for the palette in memory

 // allocate a LOGPALETTE for the # of colors in use such as
 // 16-color,256-color
 hpal = GlobalAlloc (GHND, sizeof (LOGPALETTE) +
               actualNumColorsInTable * sizeof (PALETTEENTRY));
 ptrpal = (LPLOGPALETTE) GlobalLock (hpal);
 if (!ptrpal) return;

 // fill up the LOGPALETTE structure by copying from the
 // dib color array
 ptrpal->palNumEntries = (unsigned short) actualNumColorsInTable;
 ptrpal->palVersion = 0x300;

 LPBITMAPINFO ptrinfo = GetBitmapInfo();
 for (int i=0; i<actualNumColorsInTable; i++) {
  ptrpal->palPalEntry[i].peRed = ptrinfo->bmiColors[i].rgbRed;
  ptrpal->palPalEntry[i].peGreen =ptrinfo->bmiColors[i].rgbGreen;
  ptrpal->palPalEntry[i].peBlue = ptrinfo->bmiColors[i].rgbBlue;
  ptrpal->palPalEntry[i].peFlags = 0;
 }

 // fill in the palette by creating the palette from LOGPALETTE
 ptrPalette = new CPalette;
 ptrPalette->CreatePalette (ptrpal);

 // now delete the LOGPALETTE which is no longer needed
 GlobalUnlock (hpal);
 GlobalFree (hpal);
}

/***************************************************************/
/*                                                             */
/* GetDibWidth: returns pixel width of image                   */
/*                                                             */
/***************************************************************/

int CDib::GetDibWidth () const {
 return (!IsValid ()) ? 0 : bmWidth;
}

/***************************************************************/
/*                                                             */
/* GetDibHeight: returns pixel height of image                 */
/*                                                             */
/***************************************************************/

int CDib::GetDibHeight () const {
 return (!IsValid ()) ? 0 : bmHeight;
}

/***************************************************************/
/*                                                             */
/* GetDibBitsAddr: rets the addr of the color bits of the image*/
/*                                                             */
/***************************************************************/

BYTE*  CDib::GetDibBitsAddr () const {
```

```
 return (!IsValid ()) ? 0 : ptrBits;
}

/***************************************************************/
/*                                                             */
/* GetBitmapInfo:  returns the addr of the BITMAPINFO data     */
/*                                                             */
/***************************************************************/

LPBITMAPINFO CDib::GetBitmapInfo () const {
 return (!IsValid ()) ? 0 : ptrBmInfo;
}

/***************************************************************/
/*                                                             */
/* GetNumColors: returns the image color type                  */
/*                                                             */
/***************************************************************/

CDib::NumColors CDib::GetNumColors () const {
 return numColors;
}

/***************************************************************/
/*                                                             */
/* GetPalette: returns the color palette, if any               */
/*                                                             */
/***************************************************************/

CPalette* CDib::GetPalette () const {
 return ptrPalette;
}

/***************************************************************/
/*                                                             */
/* GetBitSize: returns the number of bytes for one pixel       */
/*                                                             */
/***************************************************************/

int CDib::GetBitSize () const {
 switch (numColors) {
  case Colors2:
  case Colors16:
  case Colors256:
   return 1;
  case Colors16T:
   return 2;
  case Colors24T:
   return 3;
  case Colors32T:
   return 4;
  default:
   return 1;
 }
}

/***************************************************************/
/*                                                             */
/* IsValid: returns TRUE is DIB is loaded properly             */
/*                                                             */
/***************************************************************/

bool CDib::IsValid () const {
 return (ptrDib) ? true : false;
```

```
285 }
```

The constructor invokes **ReadDibFile** to actually input the DIB. There, **CreateFile** attempts to open the file for **GENERIC_READ** operations. If successful, the **BITMAPFILEHEADER** structure in read into an automatic storage instance of the structure. Verification of the first two bytes is done to ensure that they contain a DIB signature—"BM". Next, the actual size of the DIB is found by subtracting the size of the file header structure from the **bfSize**, the total file size. Based upon the DIB size, memory is allocated to hold the DIB and stored in **ptrdib**. One **ReadFile** operation is requested to input the rest of the entire BMP file! Remember that this could be requesting several hundred thousand bytes. The file is therefore loaded into memory as fast as possible. One other validity check is then performed on the **BITMAPINFOHEADER** portion to verify that **biSize** is at least 16 bytes or more, that is, it is not an OS2 bitmap.

Next, the number of colors present in the color table is calculated. The theoretical number of colors in the color table, **numColorTableEntries**, and the color are determined from the **biBitCount** member. If **biBitCount** contains a 1, then this is a 2-color image and **numColorTableEntries** is set to 2. If it contains a 4, then this is a 16-color image and the table contains 16 entries. If it contains an 8, then this is a 256-color image and the color table could contain 256 entries. If it contains a 16, then this is a 32K color mode image and there is no color table present. In these higher color modes, the actual pixel data contains the RGB color values. If it contains a 24, then this is a 64K color image with no color table. And if it contains a 32, then this is a true color, 16M color image with no color table. If there is the possibility of a color table present, then we must determine its size.

If the **biClrUsed** field is present and is non-zero, I store it in **numColorsUsed** and I use its value as the actual number of colors in the table. The member **actualNumColorsInTable** is then set depending upon these various values. For convenience only, I calculate the total size of the color table and save it in **colorTableSize**. Using these values, I set the pointer to the actual color pixel data and the image dimensions. Finally, we must deal with making a color palette for client program use, if there is one.

MakePalette initializes the **CPalette** pointer to 0. If **numColors**, the image color depth field, is greater than 256-colors or if the load failed, then there is no palette. Before we examine how to construct the palette, let's examine some palette details.

Handling Color: The Palettes

The original color system was the **RGB** triplet stored in an **unsigned long** called a **COLORREF** type. Red intensity is stored in the right most byte. Moving leftward, next is the green intensity byte, then the blue. The leftmost byte contains the type that could be one of three possibilities.

```
type = 0 => an explicit RGB color value in the other three bytes
       1 => a logical color palette index number
       2 => an RGB value from a color palette stored elsewhere
```

How does an **RGB** triplet actually define the color that appears on the screen? To understand exactly how Windows handles color palettes, we must examine briefly how the hardware handles color in the 256-color mode. Examine Figure 9.2 for an overview of this complex process.

A pixel's color on an analog monitor is created by the combined intensities from the red, green, and blue guns. The intensity for each color gun comes from an 18-bit value (RGB) stored in the VGA DAC or digital to analog converter. The DAC holds an array of 256 RGB table entries referenced by a byte color number ranging from 0 to 255. This byte can be the color byte coming from the bitmap data bits or DIB. If so, the method is said to be using DAC **index** numbers. When specifying an index, we get whatever color is currently loaded into that DAC color table entry. More frequently, we wish to specify a specific RGB color. (With DIBs we can choose to use RGB or color index methods.)

DOS programs are used to direct DAC manipulation, for it is extremely easy to insert whatever color values are desired. In fact, DOS programs often **animate** the palette by inserting a specific set of colors, say for a daytime color scene and then periodically reduced the DAC color values by say 10 units every few seconds. When the DAC values change, on the next CRT refresh cycle, the entire image is now redisplayed using the slightly darker colors. This gives the appearance of sunset. This is called **Palette Animation** and can be done under Windows as well. The only problem is that under Windows, an application **never** has direct access to the DAC.

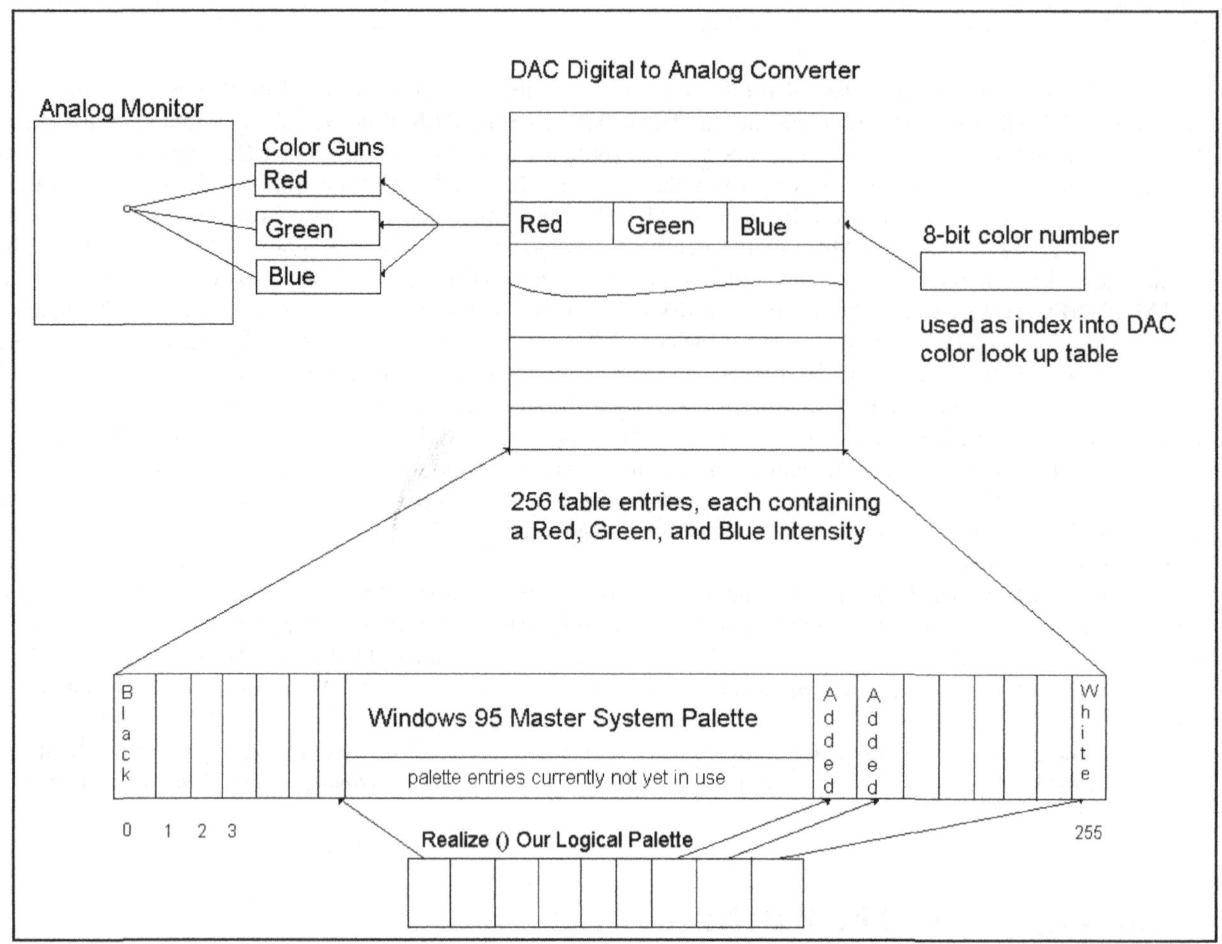

Figure 9.2 How Colors Are Displayed — Using the System Palette and Logical Color Palette

Instead, Windows, to enable device independent programming, maintains **one** master color palette with the DAC colors in it. Windows handles the transfer of the master palette colors into the DAC. The master palette has 256 entries in it corresponding to those of the DAC itself. Master palette index 0 is **always** black and index 255 is **always** white. These two colors can never be changed.

Windows also has its twenty-one system colors loaded into the first ten and last 10 palette entries with the middle 235 available for application use. (Specifically indices 0-9 and 246-255 are used.) By using the API functions **GetSysColor** and **SetSysColor**, an application can get the current system colors in use and set them to other colors. Note that these twenty-one colors are user-adjustable from the Control Panel applet by choosing ready-made schemes such as Arizona or by custom design.

Note that now we can understand the raster operations that "invert" colors. If a pixel currently is using DAC index 0x00, then its inverse in DAC index 0xFF; if it was using index 0x0F, the inverse is DAC index 0xF0. While the inverse is defined for black and white, with colors, they are not. This is why Windows uses the first ten and last ten. They are inverses of each other. If inverse raster operations are important to your 256-color application, then lay out your color scheme accordingly.

When you request a pen or brush using RGB values, Windows tries to match your request with an entry currently in the master palette, adding new entries if needed. However, if your application needs the use of a color palette, as we now do to display a DIB in its proper colors, an application private **logical color palette** must be used. (There is no method to access Windows's master palette directly with the exception of the Direct-X development platform.)

After an application has constructed its desired logical palette, it must instruct Windows to insert or **map** the logical palette onto its master palette. This mapping is a quite complex operation, but the basic idea is to determine a sort of cross index so that, when the application requests color 5 from its logical palette, Windows substitutes the correct entry from the master table. This mapping process is done in response to the **RealizePalette** API function.

Now consider what could happen if several application windows are on the screen concurrently, each requesting its own logical palette to be mapped onto the master palette. We launch our application requesting that its palette be mapped and suddenly there is no more room in the master palette! Windows handles this by performing the best match possible, which, if many different colors are currently available, can result in a satisfactory dithered color.

On the other hand, suppose that the first launched application has replaced all the system colors (except black and white, of course) and filled all 236 other slots with 254 different shades of red. When we launch our application and request our logical palette be mapped with **RealizePalette**, only reds, black and white are available—our application is likely to look quite bizarre! In fact, the entire desktop appears bizarre as well. It is not polite to replace the twenty-one system colors unless the application is running and **only** running in full screen mode (so no one can see the bizarre effect).

In this case, a full master palette, since our application has the input focus, Windows provides another option—to replace the colors in its master table. This is done by first invoking **UnrealizePalette** before attempting to realize our logical palette. Once done, the application with the 254 shades of red now looks bizarre, but it does not have the input focus. Should you task switch to the red application, it now regains the input focus and Windows permits it to reset the master palette once more to 254 shades of red and our application now looks strange. The messages to which a palette using application should consider responding are **WM_QUERYNEWPALETTE** sent when our application regains the input focus and **WM_PALETTECHANGED** sent after another application has changed the palette which allows us to re-realize our palette to for the best appearance under the circumstances. For the MFC palettes, use the **UnrealizeObject** function if **CGdiObject** which is a base class of **CPalette**.

Windows maps each color to this extended system palette as follows.

1. If a color in the user's logical palette matches a color already in the master system palette, that color is mapped to the existing system palette index or offset from the start of the 256 colors. Index 0 points to the first color in the 256 color palette.
2. If a color in the user's logical palette does not match, then that color is added to the extended system palette, if there is still room for it (236 possibilities).
3. When the extended system logical palette is full, the user's color is matched to the nearest or closest matching color that is already in the 256 extended system palette.
4. When there are several applications with logical palettes, Windows maps the logical palette of the topmost window into the extended system palette.

A logical palette is similar to a hardware palette. It is a table of RGB colors, the number of entries corresponding to the color mode. If you are using the 256-color mode, the logical palette contains 256 **RGB** values. The **COLORREF** item as stored in a logical palette is called the **PALETTEENTRY** structure and the logical palette is the **LOGPALETTE** structure that also contains 1 **PALETTEENTRY** (a bit unusual coding). The **CPalette** class maintains the logical palette, encapsulating the **LOGPALETTE** structure. The **LOGPALETTE** structure contains the following members.

```
WORD palVersion;             // usually 0x0300
WORD palNumEntries;          // number of colors in the palette
PALETTEENTRY palPalEntry[1]; // an array of color entries
```

Provision is made for an array of palette entries; only the first is actually defined in the structure. Thus, when allocating a **LOGPALETTE** structure, allocate memory for two **WORD**s plus the number of colors to be in the palette times the size of a **PALETTEENTRY** structure. The **PALETTEENTRY** structure is defined as shown below.

```
BYTE peRed;
BYTE peGreen;
BYTE peBlue;
BYTE peFlags;
```

The flags can be one of the following.

```
0              - for a normal color palette entry of RGB values
PC_EXPLICIT    - treat low word as an index into hardware palette
PC_NOCOLLAPSE  - do not map this entry to any existing color
PC_RESERVED    - reserved for animation effect and is to be
                 altered often
```

These flags are very important. Normally we use a flag of 0 for RGB palette values. However, if the color bits are to be used as a direct index reference into the DAC (assuming the correct colors are already there via the master palette), use **PC_EXPLICIT**. If dithered and nearest matching colors are not desired, use **PC_NOCOLLAPSE**. And for palette animation special effects, use **PC_RESERVED**. When Windows encounters either of these latter types, it **must** make a palette entry slot available for that color. The following standard coding determines if the current display driver supports logical palettes.

```
if ( (dc.GetDeviceCaps (RASTERCAPS) & RC_PALETTE) &&
     (dc.GetDeviceCaps (DRIVERVERSION) >= 0x0300) )
{ does support log palettes}
else { does not}
```

To create a logical 256-color palette, for example, one would define it as follows.

```
#define NUMCOLOR 256
LOGPALETTE  *ptrlogpal;
ptrlogpal = (LOGPALETET *) new char[sizeof (LOGPALETTE) +
            (NUMCOLOR - 1) * sizeof (PALETTEENTRY) ];
// -1 because logpalette has 1 paletteentry within it
ptrlogpal->palVersion = 0x0300;
ptrlogpal->palNumEntries = NUMCOLOR;
```

Next, you would need to install the color RGB values. There are many ways to give these palette entries their color RGB values. You could load in a palette saved on disk. You could initialize them as follows.

```
for (int i = 0; i<NUMCOLOR; i++) {
 ptrlogpal->palPalEntry[i].peRed = i;
 ptrlogpal->palPalEntry[i].peGreen = 0;
 ptrlogpal->palPalEntry[i].peBlue = 0;
 ptrlogpal->palPalEntry[i].peFlags = 0;
}
```

Next, the palette is ready for implementation. Construct the logical palette object and then realize it.

```
CPalette *ptrpalette = new CPalette ();
dc.CreatePalette (ptrlogpal);
dc.SelectPalette (ptrpalette, 0);
// where 0 = foreground palette, 1 = background palette
dc.RealizePalette();
```

At this point, the logical palette is merged into the system extended logical palette. The palette messages sent by Windows that an application using logical palettes should respond to are these.

```
BEGIN_MESSAGE_MAP(...
 ON_WM_QUERYNEWPALETTE ()
 ON_WM_PALETTECHANGED ()
 ON_MESSAGE(WM_DISPLAYCHANGE, OnDisplayChange)
END_MESSAGE_MAP()

// not us, so realize onto their pallette
afx_msg void OnPaletteChanged (Cwnd *ptr to win that changed
                               the palette);
// install our own colors, we are active
afx_msg void OnQueryNewPalette ();
LRESULT OnDisplayChange (WPARAM, LPARAM);
```

Whenever your application gains the input focus, becomes the active task, Windows first gives your application an opportunity to install its own colors in the system logical palette, before the window is displayed and activated. Thus, in **OnQueryNewPalette** you should at least do the following.

```
BOOL      MainWin::OnQueryNewPalette () {
 CDC *ptrdc = GetDC ();
 CPalette *ptroldpal = ptrdc->SelectPalette (ptrpalette, FALSE);
 UINT i = ptrdc->RealizePalette ();
 ReleaseDC (ptrdc);
 if (i) InvalidateRect(NULL, TRUE);
 return TRUE;
}
```

When another window changes the palette, all other windows are sent the palette changed message. If you want your application, when it is not active, to have the best possible colors in the new color scheme, you would respond to these messages with similar coding as given in the query processing.

```
void      MainWin::OnPaletteChanged (CWnd *ptrwin) {
 if (ptrwin != this) OnQueryNewPalette ();
```

```
}
```

There are many other Windows API and MFC functions for manipulating palettes. Consult the documentation as the need arises.

Now, return to the **MakePalette** function of the **CDib** class above. Windows provides **LPLOGPALETTE** which is a pointer to a **LOGPALETTE** structure. Our first step is to allocate a **LOGPALETTE** structure sufficiently large enough to hold all of the color entries contained in the bmp file's color table. I used a global memory allocation to illustrate how global memory is used; any other method of dynamically allocating the table is equally as valid.

```
hpal = GlobalAlloc (GHND, sizeof (LOGPALETTE) +
                actualNumColorsInTable * sizeof (PALETTEENTRY));
ptrpal = (LPLOGPALETTE) GlobalLock (hpal);
```

Next, the structure instance is filled in using the values from the bmp file's color table.

```
ptrpal->palNumEntries = (unsigned short) actualNumColorsInTable;
ptrpal->palVersion = 0x300;
LPBITMAPINFO ptrinfo = GetBitmapInfo();
for (int i=0; i<actualNumColorsInTable; i++) {
 ptrpal->palPalEntry[i].peRed = ptrinfo->bmiColors[i].rgbRed;
 ptrpal->palPalEntry[i].peGreen =ptrinfo->bmiColors[i].rgbGreen;
 ptrpal->palPalEntry[i].peBlue = ptrinfo->bmiColors[i].rgbBlue;
 ptrpal->palPalEntry[i].peFlags = 0;
}
```

With the **LOGPALETTE** instance created, the actual MFC **CPalette** instance is allocated and created using the **LOGPALETTE** instance.

```
ptrPalette = new CPalette;
ptrPalette->CreatePalette (ptrpal);
GlobalUnlock (hpal);
GlobalFree (hpal);
```

Methods to Display the DIB Image

There are a number of approaches to actually getting the DIB image on the screen. They vary according to the applications needs. The number of times the image is to be displayed, the speed required, and game animation are the major factors.

The SetDIBitsToDevice Method

If the image is to be painted one time only, the image could be displayed directly from the **CDib** class using the C API function **SetDIBitsToDevice**.

```
SetDIBitsToDevice (dc.m_hDC, 0, 0, dibrect.right, dibrect.bottom,
               current_hpel, -current_vpel, 0, dibrect.bottom,
               ptrdib-> GetDibBitsAddr (), ptrdib->GetBitmapInfo (),
               DIB_RGB_COLORS);
```

Design Rule 44: The DIB origin (0, 0) is at the lower left corner of the DIB bits array, not the upper left!

Yes, DIBs are indeed upside down. Thus, if you are using scroll bars similar to the earlier presentations, then the y scroll distance must be negated when using **SetDIBitsToDevice.**

The **SetDIBitsToDevice** approach has two drawbacks: speed versus the color palette hindrance and the inability to draw upon the DIB using GDI functions. If the color-mode of the image in the DIB and the color-mode of the video driver are the same, no problem. However, if these two are different, then every time the bits are set, the color palette must be adjusted, realizing colors. Specifically, Windows takes each color in the DIB and attempts to find the nearest matching color that the current video display is capable of producing. Sometimes, this is exceedingly slow when converting 24-bit color DIBs to say 16-color.

When using **SetDIBitsToDevice** there is one very important consideration to make—whether to use the DIB's color palette or not. If the DIB's color palette is not installed prior to setting the bitmap bits **and** if that DIB uses some colors that are not matchable on the current palette in use, the resultant display has very weird colors, rather like a "solarized" photograph. On the other hand, if the colors are matchable, the image appears with its expected colors. In Pgm09b, you can experiment with this effect. In the paint routine, I attempt to construct the DIB's color palette, install it, and realize it before the **SetDIBitsToDevice** invocation. If the palette cannot be constructed, I display a message box. Simply comment out the palette construction and subsequent destruction lines and rebuilt and open one of the photographic BMP files. You can see how displaying DIBs without their correct color palette appears.

Two Methods of Constructing a Memory DC

The next approach of getting the image on the screen uses a memory DC. The idea is to convert the DIB into a DDB once. Then, all display can be done from the memory dc. This results in a significant speed boost plus the ability to use GDI functions directly on the memory DC and its bitmap. **BitBlts** are used to display all or parts of the image. If you are going to allow scrolling or other actions that may require a total redisplay of the DIB, it is faster to go ahead and perform these color conversion activities one time. That is, go ahead and convert the DIB image into a normal **memory DC and bitmap**. This could be done by constructing a memory DC as we have done previously. Run **Pgm09b** and load in a larger image using both menu load options. Try dragging the thumb bar and performing a fast scroll. You will notice the memory DC implementation is significantly better.

However, if one simply constructs a compatible bitmap and copies the DIB bits into the DDB bitmap, the color palette information is lost! Thus, there are two methods for constructing the memory copy—one that loses color palette information and one that preserves the DIB color palette. Which method is used depends upon the actual colors used in the DIB and the colors in the normal application palette.

Memory DC Method 1 For Converting DIBs into DDBs With Possible Color Loss Using SetDIBits

```
CClientDC dc (this);                  // dc to copy
ptrmemdc = new CDC();                 // the memory dc
ptrmemdc->CreateCompatibleDC (&dc);// copy client dc
ptrbitmap = new CBitmap ();      // create the bitmap for memdc
ptrbitmap->CreateCompatibleBitmap (&dc, dibrect.Width(),
                                        dibrect.Height());
ptrmemdc->SelectObject (ptrbitmap); // insert bitmap into memdc
// one time conversion of DIB color bits to the compatible DC
SetDIBits (ptrmemdc->m_hDC, HBITMAP (ptrbitmap->m_hObject), 0,
           dibrect.Height(), ptrdib->GetDibBitsAddr (),
           ptrdib->GetBitmapInfo (),
           DIB_RGB_COLORS);            // copy dib bits into bitmap
dc.BitBlt (actrect.left, actrect.top, actrect.Width(),
           actrect.Height(), ptrmemdc, current_hpel,
           current_vpel, SRCCOPY);
```

These actions would be done once; then in the **Paint** routine, the new palette is installed and a **BitBlt** makes the transfer, assuming scroll bars are present. Notice that the y scroll position is now **not** negated, since we are now using a real DDB in memory. The new palette must be selected into the Paint DC. The realization of the palette installs the colors. The **BitBlt** uses the client area rectangle as before.

Memory DC Method 2 For Converting DIBs into DDBs With No Color Loss Using CreateDIBitmap

If there is to be no color loss, then obviously a color palette must be constructed. Another API function is needed, one that will take each DIB color bit and convert it into matching color in the selected palette as well as construct the DDB bitmap. This is the **CreateDIBitmap** function which, if successful, returns an **HBITMAP** that can then be selected into the memory DC. This function is not encapsulated in the MFC; we must use the C API style function whose syntax is as follows.

```
HBITMAP CreateDIBitmap (HDC dc, BITMAPINFOHEADER* ptrheader,
            CBM_INIT, BYTE* ptrbmbits, BITMAPINFO* ptrinfo,
            DIB_RGB_COLORS);
```

The flag **CBM_INIT** causes the actual conversion and copying of the bitmap bits. Normally, the **DIB_RGB_COLORS** flag is used, indicating that the color palette contains RGB values. The alternative is **DIB_PAL_COLORS** which indicates the color palette contains actual DAC palette index numbers.

Under the MFC, the sequence for memory DC construction prior to **BitBlt**ing in the **Paint** function is as follows.

```
CClientDC dc (this);
ptrpalette = new CPalette ();
ptrdib->MakePalette (ptrpalette);
if (ptrpalette) {
 ptrmemdc = new CDC();
 ptrmemdc->CreateCompatibleDC (&dc);
 ptrmemdc->SelectPalette (ptrpalette, FALSE);
 dc.SelectPalette (ptrpalette, FALSE);
 dc.RealizePalette ();
 hbmp = CreateDIBitmap   (dc.m_hDC,
             (BITMAPINFOHEADER*)(ptrdib->GetBitmapInfo()),
              CBM_INIT, ptrdib->GetDibBitsAddr(),
              ptrdib->GetBitmapInfo (), DIB_RGB_COLORS);
 if (hbmp != 0) SelectObject (ptrmemdc->m_hDC,hbmp);
}
```

This is the approach taken in **Pgm09b** to load the bmp file into a memory dc. With this approach, you can use the normal GDI functions to draw on the memory dc. However, you cannot access directly any of the bitmap bits. When writing games, this is a serious drawback because games typically perform manipulations directly on the image bits themselves.

Method for Constructing Memory DCs for Game Animation: DIBSection

This last approach yields the maximum performance needed for fast action games. What is needed is a memory DC that can be directly drawn upon using the GDI functions, one that can be **BitBlt**ed directly to the screen as fast as DOS games and one in which the application has nearly complete control over the color palette. Enter the **CreateDIBSection** function which gives us the best implementation short of using the Direct-X Games Development API.

Under Windows and Windows NT, the **CreateDIBSection** function creates a very special **HBITMAP** that is tied nearly directly to the hardware. When a **BitBlt** is done, there is **no** palette translation. The bits within the bitmap are assumed to be palette indices mapped directly to Windows' Master Palette. The **BitBlt** simply copies the bits directly onto the screen, resulting in the absolute fastest **BitBlt**ing in Windows! Additionally, the application has **direct access** to the bitmap bits for any desired manipulation as well as the ability to use normal GDI drawing functions on the bitmap. Indeed, this is a very special bitmap.

Using a DC model (usually a screen or window DC) that has installed any needed palette and using a **BITMAPINFO** structure that defines the dimensions and color table, if any, to be used, the function constructs the bitmap. (There are other advanced options that are ignored here.)

```
// returned address of the bitmap's bits for direct access
BYTE *ptrbits;
HBITMAP = CreateDIBSection (HDC dc, BITMAPINFO* ptrbm,
          DIB_RGB_COLORS, (void**) &ptrbits, NULL, 0);
```

If direct manipulation if the bits is desired, save the returned address of the bits, **ptrbits**.

A bmp file can be loaded into a **DIBSection** in **Pgm09b** if desired. You can experiment with the differences between using a memory dc and a **DIBSection**. A simple memory dc is usually sufficiently fast enough for most operations. However, if you need the fastest possible action and/or direct access to the actual bits within the image, use a **DIBSection**.

Bitmap Special Effects Displays

While most applications just display the images and go on, for a more professional and "catchy look," bitmap images can be displayed using several special effects. Generally, these effects are used once as the original graphic image is first displayed. If you wish to use special effects, then the second approach, converting all the way into a DDB in a memory DC is needed. Among the easier effects to implement are the following.

The **Vertical Crush** effect begins by showing only the left and right edges and then successively displays the remaining lines until the center is reached.

The **Horizontal Crush** effect displays the top and bottom lines and then the other lines moving toward the center are displayed last.

The **Diagonal** effect begins the display in the upper left corner and slowly displays the image along a diagonal line until the bottom right corner is reached.

The **Spiral In** effect begins at the outer edges and displays successive areas in a spiral inward motion until the center is reached.

The **Spiral Out** effect begins at the center of the image and displays successive areas in a circular, spiral manner outward to all edges. (My second favorite.)

The **Skip Horizontal** effect alternates drawing vertical columns moving from the left to right and right to left. Each set skips over the next adjacent column, leaving a hole. When one pass is done, it repeats in a similar manner displaying those that were skipped on the first pass.

The **Skip Vertical** effect operates similarly drawing pairs of rows from the top down and bottom up, each time skipping the next adjacent row, leaving a hole every other row. The next pass displays these missing rows.

The **Skip DiagonalSquares** displays the image diagonally in small squares, omitting every other square, creating a checkerboard appearance. The second pass then fills in these missing squares.

The **Skip Rectangles** effect draws a thin rectangle at the maximum dimensions of the image, then moves inward skipping over the would-be next rectangle, creating a rectangle hole. On the last pass the missing rectangles are displayed. (This is my favorite effect.)

There are many more possibilities than these few I have shown. An excellent reference to how to create these and other special effects in C style, including how to input the BMP file, is a series of articles by Charles Mirho, Window/DOS Developer's Journal, Feb, Mar, May 1994, Vol 5 nos: 2, 3, 5. I have used three of his C style routines adapting them for MFC use. Additionally, I have adapted four routines from a set of C style effects in an article by Saurabh Dixit, Creating Special-Effect Bitmaps, in Dr. Dobb's Sourcebook, March/April 1995; the article has some additional effects.

Pgm09b: DIB (BMP) File Display with Fancy Effects

Sample program **Pgm09b** displays DIBs (bmp files) with scroll bars as needed in either of the two display formats just discussed. Then, the image can be displayed using any of the special effects. Once that image has been displayed using the effect, should you scroll the image or resize the window, the bitmap is redrawn normally.

Pgm09b permits the bmp file to be loaded and shown in three ways including the fast DIB Section. The loading method is controlled via the menu. You can test loading the bitmap as a DIB and by converting it into a memory DC. All special effects require the memory DC, so if it has not been converted from a DIB, the choice of any special effect forces the conversion process.

Each special effect can be chosen from the menu. However, since there are so many, I added an Animation Sequence menu item, which is enabled after any bitmap has been loaded. If animation is selected, I display in sequence all of the animation effects, one by one, rapid fire.

However, as processors and video display hardware get faster and faster, we must have a means of slowing sown these effects or else they display so fast you cannot observe the effect. Another menu item brings up a time delay dialog that allows you to slow the effect down. All times are in milliseconds. If you have a fast video card and a 1.6G processor, try entering a 50 millisecond delay.

In the **Bmps** subdirectory along with the sample programs are several bmp files for display. (Yes, I took these photographs.) The File Open dialog uses this as the initial directory to display. If the user selects a different subdirectory, then the next time the File Open dialog is launched, that different subdirectory is used as the initial directory. There is a Devil's Tower photograph that I have stored in four formats: 2-color, 16-color, 256-color and 16M (true color).

Open one of the Devil's Tower images and run the animation sequence to see all of the display effects. The resource file is very simple and is not reproduced here in the text. Neither is the actual coding of the **SetTimeDelay** dialog class; it is exceedingly simple. The application class opens the DOS console window and is also not shown. However, to understand how the automation operates, we need to see the resource.h #define numbers.

```
#define CM_NORMAL                     1127
#define CM_CRUSH_VERT                 1128
#define CM_CRUSH_HORZ                 1129
#define CM_DIAGONAL                   1130
#define CM_SPIRAL_IN                  1131
#define CM_SPIRAL_OUT                 1132
#define CM_SKIPHORIZ                  1133
#define CM_SKIPVERT                   1134
#define CM_SKIPDIAGSQR                1135
#define CM_SKIPRECTANGLES             1136
```

Notice that all of the identifiers are in sequence beginning with **CM_NORMAL**. Thus, if we have an integer effect number, we can cycle through all of the effects merely by incrementing the effect number. When that number goes beyond the last command id value, we are done.

Figure 9.3 Pgm09b Displaying Devils-16M Bmp File

Figure 9.3 shows the normal display of an image. Here is the **FrameWin** header file.

FrameWin Definition for Pgm09b

```
#pragma once

class CDib;

/***************************************************************/
/*                                                             */
/* FrameWin Class Definition                                   */
/*                                                             */
/***************************************************************/

class FrameWin : public CFrameWnd {

 /**************************************************************/
 /*                                                            */
 /* Class Data Members                                         */
 /*                                                            */
 /**************************************************************/

```

```
protected:

char     filename[MAX_PATH]; // filename of .BMP file
char     initDir[MAX_PATH];  // open dlg initial dir to show

CDib*    ptrDib;             // pointer a DIB in memory
CDC*     ptrMemDC;           // a memory DC for the .BMP file
HBITMAP  hbmp;               // a bitmap for the memory DC
CPalette* ptrPalette;        // the palette for the memory dc

int      effectType;         // type of effect, 0 = normal

CRect    dibRect;            // dimensions of dib
CRect    actRect;            // dimensions of client area

CRect    fullWindow;         // max sized window
CRect    displayWindow;      // current dsply window onto full win

int      currentVpel;        // current vertical scroll offset
int      currentHpel;        // current horizontal scroll offset
int      numVpelsToScroll;
int      numHpelsToScroll;
int      maxVscrollPels;     // max num pels vertical to scroll
int      maxHscrollPels;     // max num pels horizontal to scroll

bool     animate;    // true when going thru effects automatically
DWORD    delayTime;  // milliseconds delay to slow effects down

 /****************************************************************/
 /*                                                              */
 /* Class Functions:                                             */
 /*                                                              */
 /****************************************************************/

public:
              FrameWin ();
             ~FrameWin ();

protected:
afx_msg void  CmLoadFromDib ();  // display BMP directly from dib
afx_msg void  CmLoadFromMemoryDC (); // display from a memory DC
afx_msg void  CmLoadFromDIBSection ();// display from DIB Section
afx_msg void  CmCrushVert ();         // crush effect vertical
afx_msg void  CmCrushHorz ();         // crush effect horizontal
afx_msg void  CmDiagonal ();          // diagonal effect
afx_msg void  CmNormal ();            // display normally
afx_msg void  CmSpiralIn ();          // spiral in effect
afx_msg void  CmSpiralOut ();         // spiral out effect
afx_msg void  CmSkipHoriz ();         // skip horizontal effect
afx_msg void  CmSkipVert ();          // skip vertical effect
afx_msg void  CmSkipDiagSquares ();   // skip diagonal squares
afx_msg void  CmSkipRectangles ();    // skip rectangles effect
afx_msg void  CmAnimate ();           // start animation sequence
afx_msg void  CmEnableAnimate (CCmdUI*);// enable animate effects
afx_msg void  CmExit ();              // quit
afx_msg void  CmTimeDelay ();         // set effects delay time

afx_msg void  OnPaint ();             // display the image
afx_msg void  OnSize (UINT, int, int);
afx_msg void  OnKeyDown (UINT, UINT, UINT);
afx_msg void  OnHScroll (UINT, UINT, CScrollBar*);
afx_msg void  OnVScroll (UINT, UINT, CScrollBar*);

afx_msg LRESULT OnDisplayChange (WPARAM, LPARAM);
```

```

void Pause ();
void EffectDiagonal(CDC &);      // perform diagonal effect
void EffectCrush (CDC &);        // perform crush effect
void EffectSpiral (CDC &);       // perform spiral effect
void EffectSkipHoriz (CDC &);    // perform skip horizontal
void EffectSkipVert (CDC &);     // perform skip vertical
void EffectSkipDiagSquares (CDC &);// perform skip diagonal sqs
void EffectSkipRectangles (CDC &); // perform skip rectangles

void UpdateCaption ();           // include BMP filename in title
void SetOurScrollRange ();       // adjust scroll range
void RemoveObject ();            // deletes all dib objects
void ConvertToMemoryDC ();       // convert dib to memory DC
void ConvertToGameDC ();         // convert dib to DIB Section DC
void LoadBMPFile ();             // loads a .BMP file into a dib

DECLARE_MESSAGE_MAP();
};
```

All of the work is done in the **FrameWin** class with support from the **CDib** class. The member **filename** stores the full path and name of the loaded file; further, the filename is appended to the main window's caption on the title bar, just as you would see in Paintbrush. The **effecttype** member contains the effect identifiers, which are the same identifiers as used in the menu item ids. The implementation is rather lengthy because of all the special effects, 1167 lines long. My handy formatter program that makes these listings can only handle up to 999 lines. Thus, we either live with truncated line numbers beyond that point, or I must reduce the coding line length. I chose to live with the truncated line lengths.

FrameWin Implementation for Pgm09b

```
#include "stdafx.h"
#include <conio.h>
#include "framewin.h"
#include "resource.h"
#include "CDib.h"
#include "SetDelayTimeDlg.h"

/*****************************************************************/
/*                                                               */
/* FrameWin Events Response Table                                */
/*                                                               */
/*****************************************************************/

BEGIN_MESSAGE_MAP(FrameWin, CFrameWnd)
 ON_WM_SIZE ()
 ON_WM_PAINT ()
 ON_WM_VSCROLL ()
 ON_WM_KEYDOWN()
 ON_WM_HSCROLL ()
 ON_COMMAND(CM_EXIT,                 CmExit)
 ON_COMMAND(CM_LOAD_FROM_DIB,        CmLoadFromDib)
 ON_COMMAND(CM_LOAD_FROM_MEMORYDC,CmLoadFromMemoryDC)
 ON_COMMAND(CM_LOAD_GAME_MEMORYDC,CmLoadFromDIBSection)
 ON_COMMAND(CM_CRUSH_VERT,           CmCrushVert)
 ON_COMMAND(CM_CRUSH_HORZ,           CmCrushHorz)
 ON_COMMAND(CM_DIAGONAL,             CmDiagonal)
 ON_COMMAND(CM_NORMAL,               CmNormal)
 ON_COMMAND(CM_SPIRAL_IN,            CmSpiralIn)
 ON_COMMAND(CM_SPIRAL_OUT,           CmSpiralOut)
 ON_COMMAND(CM_SKIPHORIZ,            CmSkipHoriz)
 ON_COMMAND(CM_SKIPVERT,             CmSkipVert)
 ON_COMMAND(CM_SKIPDIAGSQR,          CmSkipDiagSquares)
 ON_COMMAND(CM_SKIPRECTANGLES,       CmSkipRectangles)
```

```
 ON_COMMAND(CM_ANIMATE,            CmAnimate)
 ON_COMMAND(CM_TIMEDELAY,          CmTimeDelay)
 ON_UPDATE_COMMAND_UI(CM_ANIMATE, CmEnableAnimate)
 ON_MESSAGE(WM_DISPLAYCHANGE, OnDisplayChange)
END_MESSAGE_MAP();

/*****************************************************************/
/*                                                               */
/* Framewin: Construct the window object                         */
/*                                                               */
/*****************************************************************/

FrameWin::FrameWin () : CFrameWnd () {
 strcpy_s (initDir, sizeof(initDir), "..\\bmps");
 filename[0]  = 0;
 effectType   = CM_NORMAL;
 ptrDib       = 0;
 ptrMemDC     = 0;
 ptrPalette   = 0;
 hbmp         = 0;
 currentVpel  = 0;
 currentHpel  = 0;
 animate      = false;
 delayTime    = 1;

 DWORD style = WS_OVERLAPPEDWINDOW | WS_VSCROLL | WS_HSCROLL;
 CRect rect (10, 10, 600, 450);
 CString title;
 title.LoadString (IDS_FRAMETITLE);

 Create (AfxRegisterWndClass (
              CS_VREDRAW | CS_HREDRAW,
              AfxGetApp()->LoadStandardCursor (IDC_ARROW),
              (HBRUSH) GetStockObject (LTGRAY_BRUSH),
              AfxGetApp()->LoadStandardIcon (IDI_APPLICATION)),
        title, style, rect, 0, "MAINMENU");
}

/*****************************************************************/
/*                                                               */
/* ~FrameWin: destructor - remove allocated items                */
/*                                                               */
/*****************************************************************/

FrameWin::~FrameWin () {
 RemoveObject ();
}

/*****************************************************************/
/*                                                               */
/* RemoveObject: delete all items associated with a dib          */
/*                                                               */
/*****************************************************************/

void      FrameWin::RemoveObject () {
 if (ptrDib)      delete ptrDib;
 if (ptrMemDC)    delete ptrMemDC;
 if (hbmp)        DeleteObject (hbmp);
 ptrDib     = 0;  // and reset to none loaded
 ptrMemDC   = 0;
 ptrPalette = 0;
 hbmp       = 0;
}

```

```
/**************************************************************/
/*                                                            */
/* CmExit:  shut down                                         */
/*                                                            */
/**************************************************************/

void      FrameWin::CmExit () {
 PostMessage (WM_CLOSE);
}

/**************************************************************/
/*                                                            */
/* OnSize: get current dimensions & adjust scrolling          */
/*                                                            */
/**************************************************************/

void      FrameWin::OnSize (UINT a, int b, int c) {

 CFrameWnd::OnSize    (a, b, c);
 GetClientRect (&actRect); // get new window size
 SetOurScrollRange ();     // set scroll ranges based on new size
}

/**************************************************************/
/*                                                            */
/* OnDisplayChange: user has changed the display settings     */
/*                                                            */
/**************************************************************/

LRESULT   FrameWin::OnDisplayChange (WPARAM which, LPARAM lp) {
 LRESULT retcd = CFrameWnd::OnDisplayChange (which, lp);
 if (which == 1) {
  RemoveObject ();                  // remove any previous objects
  if (filename[0] !=0) {            // if there was a .BMP file
   ptrDib = new CDib (filename);    // attempt to load the file
   if (!ptrDib || !ptrDib->IsValid ())
    MessageBox("Invalid Bitmap File - Try Again",
               "Bitmap File Error", MB_OK);
   else {
    // set up the dib size in a rectangle
    dibRect.left = dibRect.top = 0;
    dibRect.right = ptrDib->GetDibWidth();
    dibRect.bottom = ptrDib->GetDibHeight();
   }
  }
  effectType = CM_NORMAL;           // reset to normal effects
  Invalidate ();                    // repaint window
 }
 return retcd;
}

/**************************************************************/
/*                                                            */
/* LoadBMPFile: loads in a BMP file into a dib                */
/*                                                            */
/**************************************************************/

void      FrameWin::LoadBMPFile () {
 RemoveObject ();
 CFileDialog filedlg (TRUE, // use Open dialog
                 "*.BMP",   // default extension
                 "*.BMP",   // current file name
    OFN_HIDEREADONLY | OFN_FILEMUSTEXIST | OFN_NOREADONLYRETURN |
    OFN_LONGNAMES,
```

```
    "Bitmap Files (*.BMP)|*.bmp|Bitmap Files (*.DIB)|*.DIB||",
    this);
 // install last initial dir to use
 filedlg.m_ofn.lpstrInitialDir = initDir;

 // get user's file choice
 if (filedlg.DoModal () == IDOK) {  // user has chosen a file, so
  strcpy_s (filename, sizeof(filename), filedlg.GetPathName ());
  ptrDib = new CDib (filename);     // attempt to load the file
  if (!ptrDib || !ptrDib->IsValid ())
   MessageBox("Invalid Bitmap File - Try Again",
              "Bitmap File Error", MB_OK);
  else {
   // set up the dib size in a rectangle
   dibRect.left = dibRect.top = 0;
   dibRect.right = ptrDib->GetDibWidth();
   dibRect.bottom = ptrDib->GetDibHeight();
  }
 }
}

/**************************************************************/
/*                                                            */
/* ConvertToMemoryDC: convert a dib to memory DC              */
/*                                                            */
/**************************************************************/

void       FrameWin::ConvertToMemoryDC () {
 // skip this action, should the dib not be there
 if (!ptrDib || !ptrDib->IsValid ()) return;
 CClientDC dc (this);                 // dc to copy
 ptrPalette =ptrDib->GetPalette();
 ptrMemDC = new CDC();                // the memory dc
 ptrMemDC->CreateCompatibleDC (&dc);  // copy client dc
 if (ptrPalette) {          // install the palette if there is one
  ptrMemDC->SelectPalette (ptrPalette, FALSE);
  dc.SelectPalette (ptrPalette, FALSE);
  dc.RealizePalette ();
 }

 // construct a DDB from the DIB using the realized palette
 hbmp = CreateDIBitmap (dc.m_hDC,
        (BITMAPINFOHEADER*)(ptrDib->GetBitmapInfo()),
        CBM_INIT, ptrDib->GetDibBitsAddr(),
        ptrDib->GetBitmapInfo (), DIB_RGB_COLORS);
 // it successful, install DDB bitmap into the memory DC
 if (hbmp != 0) SelectObject (ptrMemDC->m_hDC,hbmp);
 if (!ptrMemDC || !hbmp) {
  MessageBox("Cannot create MemoryDC",
             "Error In Conversion of Dib", MB_OK);
  RemoveObject (); // if not all created, delete all objects
  return;
 }
}

/**************************************************************/
/*                                                            */
/* ConvertToGameDC: convert a dib to DIB Section Game memory DC*/
/*                  removes the dib if it fails to convert    */
/*                                                            */
/**************************************************************/

void       FrameWin::ConvertToGameDC () {
 // skip this action, should the dib not be there
```

```
 if (!ptrDib || !ptrDib->IsValid ()) return;
 if (ptrDib->GetNumColors() <= CDib::Colors16) {
  MessageBox ("Currently converting a 2-color or 16-color image"
              " to a DIBSection is not supported",
              "Error: Performing a Memory DC Conversion Instead",
              MB_ICONINFORMATION | MB_OK);
  ConvertToMemoryDC ();
  return;
 }
 CClientDC dc (this);                   // dc to copy
 ptrPalette = ptrDib->GetPalette();
 ptrMemDC = new CDC();                  // the memory dc
 ptrMemDC->CreateCompatibleDC (&dc);    // copy client dc
 if (ptrPalette) {  // if there is a palette, then use it
  dc.SelectPalette (ptrPalette, FALSE);// into the real DC
  dc.RealizePalette ();                 // realize the palette
 }

 // construct a DIB Section from the DIB
 // save ptrbits pointer if you want direct access to bits
 BYTE *ptrbits;
 hbmp = CreateDIBSection (dc.GetSafeHdc(),
        ptrDib->GetBitmapInfo (),
        DIB_RGB_COLORS, (LPVOID*) &ptrbits, NULL, 0);
 // if successful, install DIB Section bitmap into the memory DC
 if (hbmp) { // now copy in the actual bit map bits
  long h = ptrDib->GetDibHeight();
  long w = ptrDib->GetDibWidth ();
  SelectObject (ptrMemDC->m_hDC,hbmp);
  long s = ptrDib->GetBitSize ();
  long sz = h * w * s;
  BYTE* ptrDibBits = ptrDib->GetDibBitsAddr();
  memcpy (ptrbits, ptrDibBits, sz);
 }
 if (!ptrMemDC || !hbmp) {
  MessageBox("Cannot create DIB Section Memory DC",
             "Error In Conversion of Dib", MB_OK);
  RemoveObject ();
  return;
 }
}

/***************************************************************/
/*                                                             */
/* UpdateCaption: include .BMP filename in title               */
/*                                                             */
/***************************************************************/

void      FrameWin::UpdateCaption () {
 CString newtitle;
 newtitle.LoadString (IDS_FRAMETITLE);
 newtitle += " - ";
 newtitle += filename;
 SetWindowText (newtitle);  // install new concatenated title
}

/***************************************************************/
/*                                                             */
/* CmEnableAnimate: if BMP loaded, enables animate sequence    */
/*                                                             */
/***************************************************************/

void      FrameWin::CmEnableAnimate (CCmdUI *ptrenabler) {
 ptrenabler->Enable (ptrDib && ptrDib->IsValid() ? 1 : 0);
```

```
}

/*****************************************************************/
/*                                                               */
/* CmAnimate: cycle through all effects                          */
/*                                                               */
/*****************************************************************/

void      FrameWin::CmAnimate () {
 if (ptrDib && ptrDib->IsValid() && !ptrMemDC)
  ConvertToMemoryDC ();
 animate = true;
 effectType = CM_CRUSH_VERT;
#ifdef _DEBUG
_cprintf ("Animate starts with: %d\r\n", effectType);
#endif
 Invalidate ();
}

/*****************************************************************/
/*                                                               */
/* CmTimeDelay: get user's time delay in milliseconds            */
/*                                                               */
/*****************************************************************/

void FrameWin::CmTimeDelay () {
 SetDelayTimeDlg dlg (this);
 dlg.m_delay = delayTime;
 if (dlg.DoModal () == IDOK) {
  delayTime = dlg.m_delay;
 }
}

/*****************************************************************/
/*                                                               */
/* Pause: pause the requested number of milliseconds             */
/*                                                               */
/*****************************************************************/

void FrameWin::Pause () {
 DWORD endTicks = GetTickCount() + delayTime;
 DWORD ticks = GetTickCount();
 // delay the requested number of seconds
 while (ticks < endTicks)
  ticks = GetTickCount ();
}

/*****************************************************************/
/*                                                               */
/* CmLoadFromDib: Load a BMP file and display from a DIB         */
/*                                                               */
/*****************************************************************/

void      FrameWin::CmLoadFromDib () {
 LoadBMPFile ();                     // load the dib file
 if (ptrDib && ptrDib->IsValid ()) { // successful load?
  if (effectType!=CM_NORMAL)          // if not normal load, then
   ConvertToMemoryDC ();              // finish conversion
  if (ptrDib->IsValid ()) {           // still a success, finish up
   currentVpel = 0;                  // clear scroll position
   currentHpel = 0;
   SetOurScrollRange ();              // adjust the scroll bar range
   UpdateCaption ();                  // insert filename into title
   Invalidate();                      // force the image to be shown
```

```
  }
 }
}

/************************************************************/
/*                                                          */
/* CmLoadFromMemoryDC: Load in a BMP file into a memory DC  */
/*                                                          */
/************************************************************/

void      FrameWin::CmLoadFromMemoryDC () {
 LoadBMPFile ();            // load the .BMP file
 if (!ptrDib || !ptrDib->IsValid ()) return;
 ConvertToMemoryDC ();      // convert to memory dc
 if (ptrDib->IsValid()) {   // still a success?
  currentVpel = 0;         // clear scroll position
  currentHpel = 0;
  SetOurScrollRange ();     // yes, so adjust the scroll range
  UpdateCaption ();         // insert the filename into the title
  effectType = CM_NORMAL;   // set for normal type display
  Invalidate();             // force image to be displayed
 }
}

/************************************************************/
/*                                                          */
/* CmLoadFromDIBSection: Load in a BMP file into a Game     */
/*                       DIB Section mem DC                 */
/*                                                          */
/************************************************************/

void      FrameWin::CmLoadFromDIBSection () {
 LoadBMPFile ();            // load the .BMP file
 if (!ptrDib || !ptrDib->IsValid ()) return;
 ConvertToGameDC ();        // convert to DIB Section game mem dc
 if (ptrDib->IsValid()) {   // still a success?
  currentVpel = 0;         // clear scroll position
  currentHpel = 0;
  SetOurScrollRange ();     // yes, so adjust the scroll range
  UpdateCaption ();         // insert the filename into the title
  effectType = CM_NORMAL;   // set for normal type display
  Invalidate();             // force image to be displayed
 }
}

/************************************************************/
/*                                                          */
/* CmNormal: set up for normal display of bitmap            */
/*                                                          */
/************************************************************/

void      FrameWin::CmNormal () {
 effectType = CM_NORMAL; // signal normal display chosen
 Invalidate ();          // force redisplay
}

/************************************************************/
/*                                                          */
/* CmCrushVert: set up for vertical crush effect            */
/*                                                          */
/************************************************************/

void      FrameWin::CmCrushVert () {
 effectType = CM_CRUSH_VERT;  // signal vertical crush requested
```

```
 if (ptrDib && ptrDib->IsValid() && !ptrMemDC)
  ConvertToMemoryDC ();
 Invalidate(); // force vertical crush effect
}
/***************************************************************/
/*                                                             */
/* CmCrushHorz: set up for horizontal crush effect             */
/*                                                             */
/***************************************************************/
void      FrameWin::CmCrushHorz () {
 effectType = CM_CRUSH_HORZ;  // horizontal crush effect request
 if (ptrDib && ptrDib->IsValid() && !ptrMemDC)
  ConvertToMemoryDC ();
 Invalidate(); // force horizontal crush effect
}
/***************************************************************/
/*                                                             */
/* CmDiagonal: set up for a diagonal effect                    */
/*                                                             */
/***************************************************************/
void      FrameWin::CmDiagonal () {
 effectType = CM_DIAGONAL; // signal diagonal effect requested
 if (ptrDib && ptrDib->IsValid() && !ptrMemDC)
  ConvertToMemoryDC ();
 Invalidate(); // force the diagonal effect to occur
}
/***************************************************************/
/*                                                             */
/* CmSprialIn: set up for a spiral in effect                   */
/*                                                             */
/***************************************************************/
void      FrameWin::CmSpiralIn () {
 effectType = CM_SPIRAL_IN; // signal spiral in requested
 if (ptrDib && ptrDib->IsValid() && !ptrMemDC)
  ConvertToMemoryDC ();
 Invalidate(); // force the sprial in effect to occur
}
/***************************************************************/
/*                                                             */
/* CmSprialOut: set up for a spiral out effect                 */
/*                                                             */
/***************************************************************/
void      FrameWin::CmSpiralOut () {
 effectType = CM_SPIRAL_OUT; // signal sprial out requested
 if (ptrDib && ptrDib->IsValid() && !ptrMemDC)
  ConvertToMemoryDC ();
 Invalidate(); // force the spiral out effect to occur
}
/***************************************************************/
/*                                                             */
/* CmSkipHoriz: setup for a skip horizontal effect             */
/*                                                             */
/***************************************************************/
void      FrameWin::CmSkipHoriz () {
```

```
 effectType = CM_SKIPHORIZ; // skip horizontal effect requested
 if (ptrDib && ptrDib->IsValid() && !ptrMemDC)
  ConvertToMemoryDC ();
 Invalidate(); // force the diagonal effect to occur
}

/*************************************************************/
/*                                                           */
/* CmSkipVert: setup for a skip vertical effect              */
/*                                                           */
/*************************************************************/

void      FrameWin::CmSkipVert () {
 effectType = CM_SKIPVERT; // skip vertical effect requested
 if (ptrDib && ptrDib->IsValid() && !ptrMemDC)
  ConvertToMemoryDC ();
 Invalidate(); // force the diagonal effect to occur
}

/*************************************************************/
/*                                                           */
/* CmSkipDiagSquares: setup for a skip diagonal squares effect */
/*                                                           */
/*************************************************************/

void      FrameWin::CmSkipDiagSquares () {
 effectType = CM_SKIPDIAGSQR; //  skip diagonal squares effect
 if (ptrDib && ptrDib->IsValid() && !ptrMemDC)
  ConvertToMemoryDC ();
 Invalidate(); // force the diagonal effect to occur
}

/*************************************************************/
/*                                                           */
/* CmSkipRectangles: set up for a skip rectangles effect     */
/*                                                           */
/*************************************************************/

void      FrameWin::CmSkipRectangles () {
 effectType = CM_SKIPRECTANGLES; // skip rectangles effect
 if (ptrDib && ptrDib->IsValid() && !ptrMemDC)
  ConvertToMemoryDC ();
 Invalidate(); // force the diagonal effect to occur
}

/*************************************************************/
/*                                                           */
/* OnPaint: draw once - then scroll the memDC                */
/*                                                           */
/*************************************************************/

void      FrameWin::OnPaint () {
 CPaintDC  dc(this);
 if (!ptrDib || !ptrDib->IsValid()) return;

 if (ptrPalette) { // if there is a user palette, use it
  dc.SelectPalette (ptrPalette, 0); // insert the dib's palette
  dc.RealizePalette();                // cause palette to be set up
 }

 if (effectType == CM_NORMAL) {
  if (ptrMemDC)                       // paint from memory DC
   // copy the memory image to the screen adjusted by scroll bar
   dc.BitBlt (actRect.left, actRect.top, actRect.Width(),
```

```
                actRect.Height(), ptrMemDC, currentHpel,
                currentVpel, SRCCOPY);
  else                              // paint from the dib directly
   // dib origin is backwards in height - copy dib bits to screen
   ::SetDIBitsToDevice (dc.GetSafeHdc(), 0, 0, dibRect.right,
                dibRect.bottom, currentHpel, -currentVpel, 0,
                dibRect.bottom, ptrDib-> GetDibBitsAddr (),
                ptrDib->GetBitmapInfo (), DIB_RGB_COLORS);
  return;
 }

 if (currentVpel + currentHpel > 0) { // if image is scrolled
  // reset to upper left corner
  ScrollWindow (-currentHpel, -currentVpel, NULL, NULL);
  SetScrollPos (SB_VERT, 0, TRUE);  // reset scroll pos to 0,0
  SetScrollPos (SB_HORZ, 0, TRUE);
  currentVpel = currentHpel = 0;
 }

 switch (effectType) {  // handle the specific effect signaled
   case CM_DIAGONAL:                    // diagonal effect
    EffectDiagonal (dc); break;         // perform the effect
   case CM_CRUSH_VERT:                  // vertical crush effect
   case CM_CRUSH_HORZ:                  // horizontal crush effect
    EffectCrush (dc); break;            // perform the effect
   case CM_SPIRAL_IN:                   // sprial in effect
   case CM_SPIRAL_OUT:                  // sprial out effect
    EffectSpiral (dc); break;           // perform the effect
   case CM_SKIPHORIZ:
    EffectSkipHoriz (dc); break;        // perform the effect
   case CM_SKIPVERT:
    EffectSkipVert (dc); break;         // perform the effect
   case CM_SKIPDIAGSQR:
    EffectSkipDiagSquares (dc); break; // perform the effect
   case CM_SKIPRECTANGLES:
    EffectSkipRectangles (dc); break;  // perform the effect
 }

 if (animate) {                       // if animation is on, then
  effectType++;                       // set for next effect

#ifdef _DEBUG
_cprintf ("effect type: %d Last one is: %d\r\n", effectType,
          CM_SKIPRECTANGLES+1);
#endif

  if (effectType == CM_SKIPRECTANGLES+1) { // all done?

#ifdef _DEBUG
_cprintf ("animate stopping: %d Last one is: %d\r\n", effectType,
          CM_SKIPRECTANGLES+1);
#endif

   effectType = CM_NORMAL;            // yes, so set for normal
   animate = false;                   // turn off animation
  }
  Invalidate ();                      // display next effect
 }
}

/*************************************************************/
/*                                                           */
/* The following 3 routines have been adapted from a series of */
/*      articles:                                            */
```

```
/*                                                               */
/* Charles Mirho, Windows/Dos Developers Journal Feb, Mar,      */
/*        and May 1994  Vol 5, Nos: 2, 3, 5                      */
/*                                                               */
/* In all, the speed and effectiveness can be controlled by     */
/* adjusting the numpels field. Trouble arises from those       */
/* images that are not even multiples of the numpels;           */
/* unBitBlted streaks result.                                   */
/*                                                               */
/*****************************************************************/

/*****************************************************************/
/*                                                               */
/* EffectDiagonal: perform diagonal bitmap display              */
/*                                                               */
/*****************************************************************/

void      FrameWin::EffectDiagonal (CDC & dc) {

 int numpels = 2;        // user adjustable width of diagonal line
 // set right and bottom limits to image size minus one diagonal
 // width numpels
 int rightstop  = dibRect.right  - numpels;
 int bottomstop = dibRect.bottom - numpels;
 int startrow, startcol, col, row;
 startcol = 0;                  // begin at top left corner, go
 while (startcol <= rightstop) {// until diagonal is at right top
  col = startcol;        // edge; set at this begin column and
  row = 0;               // then for all rows until the bottom
  while (col >= 0 && row <=bottomstop) {
   // copy diagonal squares in that line
   dc.BitBlt (col, row, numpels, numpels, ptrMemDC, col, row,
              SRCCOPY);
   col -= numpels;       // from current starting column back to 0
   row += numpels;       // and all rows to bottom - diag width
  }
  startcol += numpels;  // going from column 0 to right edge
  Pause ();
 }
 startrow = numpels;    // repeat for bottom right diagonals
 while (startrow <= bottomstop) { // going from top right corner
  col = rightstop;       // showing all column squares on one row
  row = startrow;        // then moving down one more row
  while (col >= 0 && row <= bottomstop) {
   // show all col and rows on this diag
   dc.BitBlt (col, row, numpels, numpels, ptrMemDC, col, row,
              SRCCOPY);
   col -= numpels;       // move back towards center diagonal col
   row += numpels;       // move down to next row to make diagonal
  }
  startrow += numpels;  // repeat for next diagonal line
  Pause ();
 }
}

/*****************************************************************/
/*                                                               */
/* EffectCrush: perform vertical or horizontal crush effect     */
/*                                                               */
/*****************************************************************/

void      FrameWin::EffectCrush (CDC &dc) {
 int x, y, left, top, right, bot, numpels;
 numpels = 2;            // user adjustable line width
```

```
 left = top = 0;        // set left and top to beginning of image
 // set right and bottom points to image size less the chosen
 // line width
 right = dibRect.right  - numpels;
 bot   = dibRect.bottom - numpels;

 if (effectType == CM_CRUSH_VERT) { // do vertical crush here
  while (top < bot) {      // for all rows until top meets bottom
   for (x=left; x<=right; x+=numpels) // copy all cols in top row
    dc.BitBlt (x, top, numpels, numpels, ptrMemDC, x, top,
               SRCCOPY);
   top += numpels;         // set top row down one for next pass
   for (x=left; x<=right; x+=numpels) // copy all cols in bot row
    dc.BitBlt (x, bot, numpels, numpels, ptrMemDC, x, bot,
               SRCCOPY);
   bot -= numpels;         // set for next bottom row up one
   Pause ();
  }
 }
 else {                    // do horizontal crush here
  while (left < right) {   // for all cols until left meets right
   for (y=top; y<=bot; y+=numpels) // copy all rows in right col
    dc.BitBlt (right, y, numpels, numpels, ptrMemDC, right, y,
               SRCCOPY);
   right -= numpels;       // set inward for right next column
   for (y=top; y<=bot; y+=numpels) // copy all rows in left col
    dc.BitBlt (left, y, numpels, numpels, ptrMemDC, left, y,
               SRCCOPY);
   left += numpels;        // set inward for next left column
   Pause ();
  }
 }
}

/****************************************************************/
/*                                                              */
/* EffectSpiral: perform inward or outward spiral effect        */
/*                                                              */
/****************************************************************/

void      FrameWin::EffectSpiral (CDC &dc) {
 int left = 0, top = 0, right, bot, numpels, x, y, width, height;
 numpels = 2; // user adjustable line width
 // set width, right, height, bot to img size - chosen line width
 right = width  = dibRect.right - numpels;
 bot   = height = dibRect.bottom - numpels;

 // both effects done by drawing successive rectangles going
 // inward or outward
 if (effectType == CM_SPIRAL_IN) {   // do sprial in here
  // draw all sides - repeat until both meet in the center
  while (left < right && top < bot) {
   for (x=left; x<=right; x+=numpels)
    // show all squares on top row
    dc.BitBlt (x, top, numpels, numpels, ptrMemDC, x, top,
               SRCCOPY);
   top += numpels;            // move down for next top row
   for (y=top; y<=bot; y+=numpels)
    // show all squares on right side
    dc.BitBlt (right, y, numpels, numpels, ptrMemDC, right, y,
               SRCCOPY);
   right -= numpels;          // move to left for next right side
   for (x=right; x>=left; x-=numpels)
    // show all squares on bottom side
```

```
   dc.BitBlt (x, bot, numpels, numpels, ptrMemDC, x, bot,
              SRCCOPY);
  bot -= numpels;          // move upward for next bottom row
  for (y=bot; y>=top; y-=numpels)
   // show all squares on left side
   dc.BitBlt (left, y, numpels, numpels, ptrMemDC, left, y,
              SRCCOPY);
  left += numpels;  // move to right for next left side
  Pause ();
 }
}
else { // do sprial out here - draw all sides by displaying the
 // very center portion that is not an even multiple of rects
 left = (width/2) - (width/2) % numpels;
 right = left;
 top = (height/2) - (height/2) % numpels;
 bot = top;
 dc.BitBlt (left, top, numpels, numpels, ptrMemDC, left, top,
            SRCCOPY);

 // now display all rectangles from center outward
 while (bot < height || right < width) {
  // go until both dimensions complete
  if (top > 0) {      // are there any more top rows to do?
   top -= numpels;    // yes, move up one row
   for (x=left; x<=right; x+=numpels)
    // show all columns on this row
    dc.BitBlt (x, top, numpels, numpels, ptrMemDC, x, top,
               SRCCOPY);
  }
  if (right < width) {
   // are there any more right cols to do
   right += numpels; // yes, move to right one column
   for (y=top; y<=bot; y+=numpels)
    // show all rows on right side
    dc.BitBlt (right, y, numpels, numpels, ptrMemDC, right, y,
               SRCCOPY);
  }
  if (bot < height) {
   // are there any more bottom rows
   bot += numpels;    // yes, move down one row
   for (x=right; x>=left; x-=numpels)
    // show all columns on this row
    dc.BitBlt (x, bot, numpels, numpels, ptrMemDC, x, bot,
               SRCCOPY);
  }
  if (left >0) {
   // are there any more left cols to do
   left -= numpels;  // yes, move left one column
   for (y=bot; y>=top; y-=numpels)
    // show all rows on left side
    dc.BitBlt (left, y, numpels, numpels, ptrMemDC, left, y,
               SRCCOPY);
  }
  Pause ();
 }
}
}

/***************************************************************/
/*                                                             */
/* The following 4 routines have been adapted from an article: */
/*                                                             */
/* Saurabh Dixit, Creating Special-Effect Bitmaps,             */
```

```
/*   Dr. Dobb's Sourcebook   March/April, 1995                      */
/*                                                                  */
/* Original article is done is C style and has more effects         */
/*                                                                  */
/********************************************************************/

/********************************************************************/
/*                                                                  */
/* EffectSkipHoriz: perform a skip horizontal effect                */
/*                                                                  */
/********************************************************************/

void      FrameWin::EffectSkipHoriz (CDC &dc) {
 int curleft, curright, numpieces, width, height;
 int colwidth = 4;          // user adjustable width of the strips
 int twocolwidths = 2 * colwidth; // left-right col inc amount
 width  = dibRect.right;   // bitmap's total width
 height = dibRect.bottom;  // bitmap's total height
 numpieces = width / colwidth; // get num pieces of colwidth size

 // set the curright column starting point
 if (width % colwidth) {
  // set the middle point when width is not exact multiple of
  // chosen column width
  if (numpieces % 2)
   curright = numpieces * colwidth;     // odd number of pieces
  else
   curright = (numpieces-1) * colwidth; // even number of pieces
 }
 else {
  // set the middle point when width is an exact multiple of
  // column width
  if (numpieces % 2)
   curright = width - twocolwidths;     // odd number of pieces
  else
   curright = width - colwidth;         // even number of pieces
 }
 // set current right starting column to the first column
 curleft  = 0;
 while (curright > 0 || curleft < width) { // for all pieces,
  // copy the current left vertical strip to screen
  dc.BitBlt (curleft, 0, colwidth, height, ptrMemDC, curleft, 0,
             SRCCOPY);
  // copy the current right vertical strip to screen
  dc.BitBlt(curright, 0, colwidth, height, ptrMemDC, curright, 0,
            SRCCOPY);
  // get next pair of strips skipping over one column
  curleft  += twocolwidths; // skip over one column to the right
  curright -= twocolwidths; // skip over one column to the left
  Pause ();
 }
}

/********************************************************************/
/*                                                                  */
/* EffectSkipVert: perform a skip vertical effect                   */
/*                                                                  */
/********************************************************************/

void      FrameWin::EffectSkipVert (CDC &dc) {
 int curtop, curbot, numpieces, width, height;
 int rowheight = 2;         // user adjustable num pels in one row
 // amt to add to get to next row to show
 int tworowheight = 2 * rowheight;
```

```
 width  = dibRect.right;             // bitmap actual width
 height = dibRect.bottom;            // bitmap actual height
 numpieces = height / rowheight;     // number of rows possible

 // set starting bottom row
 if (height % rowheight) {
  // calc starting bottom when bitmap height is not an exact
  // multiple of row height
  if (numpieces % 2)
   curbot = numpieces * rowheight; // odd number of row pairs
  else                             // even number of row pairs
   curbot = (numpieces - 1) * rowheight;
 }
 else {
  // calc starting bottom when bitmap height is an exact
  // multiple of row height
  if (numpieces % 2)
   curbot = height - tworowheight; // odd number of row pairs
  else
   curbot = height - rowheight;    // even number of row pairs
 }
 curtop = 0;                      // set current starting top row
 while (curbot > 0 || curtop < height) { // for all rows,
  // copy the current top row to the screen
  dc.BitBlt (0, curtop, width, rowheight, ptrMemDC, 0, curtop,
             SRCCOPY);
  // copy the current bottom row to the screen
  dc.BitBlt (0, curbot, width, rowheight, ptrMemDC, 0, curbot,
             SRCCOPY);
  curtop += tworowheight;          // skip over one row down
  curbot -= tworowheight;          // skip over one row up
  Pause ();
 }
}

/*************************************************************/
/*                                                           */
/* EffectSkipDiagSquares: perform skip diagonal squares effect */
/*                                                           */
/*************************************************************/

void      FrameWin::EffectSkipDiagSquares (CDC &dc) {

 int   i, left, top, numlines, width, height;
 width  = dibRect.right;      // actual bitmap width
 height = dibRect.bottom;     // actual bitmap height

 // set up the size parameter - can be user adjustable, but both
 // the width and height must be even multiples of this value
 // because it is a square element
 int size;
 // I have set up four chances to automatically figure the size
 // - you can hard hard code for a single known bitmap
 if (width%4 == 0 && height%4 == 0) size = 4;
 else if (width%3 == 0 && height%3 == 0) size = 3;
 else if (width%2 == 0 && height%2 == 0) size = 2;
 else size = 1;

 // set the number of lines to do
 numlines = (width + height) / size - 1;
 for (i=1; i<=numlines; i++) { // divide into even/odd
  if (i % 2) {                 // this is an odd line number
   left = i * size;            // set left position of first square
   if (left > width)
```

```
     left = width;            // constrain to max width of bitmap
    top = (i - left / size + 1) * size; // starting top square pos
    // copy all squares in this line skipping over adjacent square
    while (top <= height) {
     // copy each square to the screen
     dc.BitBlt (left-size, top-size, size, size, ptrMemDC,
                left-size, top-size, SRCCOPY);
     left -= size; // skip over adjacent squares
     top  += size;
    }
   }
   else {                     // this is an even line number
    // set starting left pos, depending upon odd or even number
    // of squares
    if ((width + height) / size % 2) left = width + (2-i) * size;
    else left = width + (1 - i) * size;
    top = height;            // fix starting top to real bottom row
    while (left <= width) {
     // copy each square to the screen
     dc.BitBlt (left-size, top-size, size, size, ptrMemDC,
                left-size, top-size, SRCCOPY);
     left += size; // skip over adjacent squares
     top  -= size;
    }
   }
   Pause ();
  }
}

/**************************************************************/
/*                                                            */
/* EffectSkipRectangles: perform a skip rectangles effect     */
/*                                                            */
/**************************************************************/

void      FrameWin::EffectSkipRectangles (CDC &dc) {
 int xl, yl, halfsize, minsize, xr, yr;
 int inwidth, inheight, outwidth, outheight, width, height;
 width  = dibRect.right; // actual bitmap width
 height = dibRect.bottom;// actual bitmap height
 bool stilldrawing;      // true while there is still a set to do
 xl = 0;
 yl = 0;
 // get the smaller dimension
 minsize = (width>height ? height : width);
 //set x right to 1/2 min size based on min dimension even or odd
 // which is the center of the image
 xr = minsize % 2 ? (minsize / 2) : (minsize / 2) + 1;
 if (xr % 2 == 0)
  xr ++;                 // if x right is even multiple of 2, add 1
 yr = xr;
 // save approximate center for terminating inward pass
 halfsize = xr;
 while (xl <= halfsize || yl <= halfsize) {
  stilldrawing = false;
  // since can be uneven number and center is approx
  // if any inner or outer rectangle is drawn, set to true
  // and make another pass - draw the rectangle going inward
  // 4 separate BitBlts - one for each side
  if (xl <= halfsize && yl <= halfsize) {
   inwidth  = width  - (xl * 2);
   inheight = height - (yl * 2);
   // top edge
   dc.BitBlt (xl, yl, inwidth, 1, ptrMemDC, xl, yl,SRCCOPY);
```

```
   // left edge
   dc.BitBlt (xl, yl, 1, inheight, ptrMemDC, xl, yl,SRCCOPY);
   // bottom edge
   dc.BitBlt (xl, yl+inheight, inwidth+1, 1, ptrMemDC,xl,
              yl+inheight,SRCCOPY);
   // right edge
   dc.BitBlt (xl+inwidth, yl, 1, inheight+1, ptrMemDC,
              xl+inwidth, yl,SRCCOPY);
   stilldrawing = true;
  }
  // draw the rectangle going outward - 4 separate BitBlts
  // - one for each side
  if (xr >= 0 && yr >= 0) {
   // shifting is a faster way to multiply by 2
   outwidth  = width  - (xr << 1);
   outheight = height - (yr << 1);
   // top edge
   dc.BitBlt (xr, yr, outwidth, 1, ptrMemDC, xr, yr, SRCCOPY);
   // left edge
   dc.BitBlt (xr, yr, 1, outheight, ptrMemDC, xr, yr, SRCCOPY);
   // bottom edge
   dc.BitBlt (xr, yr+outheight, outwidth+1, 1, ptrMemDC, xr,
              yr+outheight, SRCCOPY);
   // right edge
   dc.BitBlt (xr+outwidth, yr, 1, outheight+1, ptrMemDC,
              xr+outwidth, yr, SRCCOPY);
   stilldrawing = true;
  }
  // if either were drawn, try next set until none left
  if (stilldrawing) {
   xl += 2;        // skip a rectangle moving inward
   yl += 2;
   xr -= 2;        // skip a rectangle moving outward
   yr -= 2;
  }
  else break;      // finally drawn all on this set, stop
  Pause ();
 }
}

/************************************************************/
/*                                                          */
/* SetOurScrollRange: if image is present, reset scroll range */
/*                                                          */
/************************************************************/

void      FrameWin::SetOurScrollRange () {
 if (!ptrDib || !ptrDib->IsValid())
  return;                          // only adjust if file is opened

 int x = dibRect.right - actRect.right;      // set diff in widths
 if (x<0) x = 0;                             // min is 0
 int y = dibRect.bottom - actRect.bottom;    // set diff in height
 if (y<0) y = 0;                             // min is 0
 maxVscrollPels = y;
 maxHscrollPels = x;
 currentVpel = min (currentVpel, maxVscrollPels);
 currentHpel = min (currentHpel, maxHscrollPels);
 SetScrollRange (SB_VERT, 0, maxVscrollPels, FALSE);
 SetScrollPos (SB_VERT, currentVpel, TRUE);
 SetScrollRange (SB_HORZ, 0, maxHscrollPels, FALSE);
 SetScrollPos (SB_HORZ, currentHpel, TRUE);
}
```

```
/***************************************************************/
/*                                                             */
/* OnKeyDown: provide a keyboard scroller interface            */
/*                                                             */
/***************************************************************/

void      FrameWin::OnKeyDown (UINT key, UINT, UINT) {
 // check for and handle any possible keyboard scroll request
 switch (key) {

  case VK_UP:    // requests scroll up 1 line
   SendMessage (WM_VSCROLL, SB_LINEUP, 0L); break;

  case VK_DOWN:  // requests scroll down 1 line
   SendMessage (WM_VSCROLL, SB_LINEDOWN, 0L); break;

  case VK_LEFT:  // requests scroll left 1 col
   SendMessage (WM_HSCROLL, SB_LINEUP, 0L); break;

  case VK_RIGHT: // requests scroll right 1 col
   SendMessage (WM_HSCROLL, SB_LINEDOWN, 0L); break;

  case VK_PRIOR: // request scroll 1 page up
   SendMessage (WM_VSCROLL, SB_PAGEUP, 0L); break;

  case VK_NEXT:  // request scroll 1 page down
   SendMessage (WM_VSCROLL, SB_PAGEDOWN, 0L); break;

  case VK_END:   // request goto the bottom
   SendMessage (WM_HSCROLL, SB_PAGEDOWN, 0L); break;

  case VK_HOME:  // request goto the top
   SendMessage (WM_HSCROLL, SB_PAGEUP, 0L);  break;
 }
}

/***************************************************************/
/*                                                             */
/* OnVScroll: scroll window vertically                         */
/*                                                             */
/***************************************************************/

void FrameWin::OnVScroll (UINT type, UINT pos, CScrollBar*) {
 switch (type) {

  case SB_LINEUP:      // scroll up 1 line
   numVpelsToScroll = -1; break;

  case SB_LINEDOWN:    // scroll 1 line down
   numVpelsToScroll = 1; break;

  case SB_PAGEUP:      // scroll 1 page up
   numVpelsToScroll = -8; break;

  case SB_PAGEDOWN:    // scroll 1 page down
   numVpelsToScroll = 8; break;

  case SB_THUMBTRACK: // follow thumb bar
   numVpelsToScroll = pos - currentVpel; break;

  default:
   numVpelsToScroll = 0;
 }
 numVpelsToScroll = max (-currentVpel,
```

```
                       min (numVpelsToScroll,
                            maxVscrollPels - currentVpel));
  if (numVpelsToScroll !=0) {
   currentVpel +=numVpelsToScroll;
   ScrollWindow (0, -numVpelsToScroll, NULL, NULL);
   SetScrollPos (SB_VERT, currentVpel, TRUE);
  }
 }

/*****************************************************************/
/*                                                               */
/* OnHScroll: scroll window horizontally                         */
/*                                                               */
/*****************************************************************/

void FrameWin::OnHScroll (UINT type, UINT pos, CScrollBar*) {
  switch (type) {

   case SB_LINEUP:     // scroll 1 col left
    numHpelsToScroll = -1; break;

   case SB_LINEDOWN:   // scroll 1 col right
    numHpelsToScroll = 1; break;

   case SB_PAGEUP:     // scroll 1 page left
    numHpelsToScroll = -8; break;

   case SB_PAGEDOWN:    // scroll 1 page right
    numHpelsToScroll = 8; break;

   case SB_THUMBTRACK: // follow thumb bar
    numHpelsToScroll = pos - currentHpel; break;

   default:
    numHpelsToScroll = 0;
  }
  numHpelsToScroll = max (-currentHpel,
                       min (numHpelsToScroll,
                            maxHscrollPels - currentHpel));
  if (numHpelsToScroll !=0) {
   currentHpel +=numHpelsToScroll;
   ScrollWindow (-numHpelsToScroll, 0, NULL, NULL);
   SetScrollPos (SB_HORZ, currentHpel, TRUE);
  }
 }
```

The constructor initializes all members to 0, particularly the pointers to the bmp objects: **ptrdib, ptrmemdc, hbmp**, and **ptrpalette**. The default **effecttype** is **CM_NORMAL**. The function **RemoveObject** deletes any of these objects that may exist. The **OnSize** member acquires the current client area rectangle, **actrect**, and then invokes the **SetOurScrollRange** function to reset the scroll bar ranges. In **SetOurScrollRange**, the unit is again 1 pixel and the x, y ranges are the differences in the DIB's actual dimensions and that of the current client area rectangle.

The **LoadBMPFile** function follows the general form discussed above. The **ConvertToMemoryDC** function handles the remaining conversions, as needed.

The **UpdateCaption** function illustrates how to append to the main window's title bar. Often, when a window is maximized, the caption is modified. "DIB Processing" is the normal caption. Whenever a file is loaded, the full path/filename is appended. I retrieve the caption string from the resource file, append a " - " and the filename to it. Then the caption is changed.

```
SetWindowText (newtitle); // install new concatenated title
```

Bmp files are loaded in response to one of two load menu items. The normal DIB request invokes **LoadBMPFile**. Then, if special effects are turned on, it invokes **ConvertToMemoryDC** just as if the user had chosen the second menu choice, "Load into memory." Both functions after a successful file load, then call **SetOurScrollRange** and **UpdateCaption** before **Invalidate** forces the image to be painted. The various menu item responses for the special effects simply set the **effecttype** to the correct effect ID, complete the conversion to a memory DC if required, and **Invalidate** to cause the image to be displayed with that effect.

The **OnPaint** function does nothing if there is no file loaded. The **effecttype** is cased. For all of the special effects cases, the palette is first realized, if present, and then the appropriate effects function invoked. For the normal display, the coding is as discussed above. Remember that when using **SetDIBitsToDevice**, any scroll y offsets must be negated due to the reversal of the y axis. Notice again that after the display is complete, the last thing **OnPaint** does is set the **effecttype** back to **CM_NORMAL**, so that the user can scroll and use the image normally.

A study of how the special effects are coded is left to the reader to explore—study the code and my comments. The basic idea is to construct small square blocks of dimensions **numpels** and **BitBlt** them to the paint dc. Following Mirho's examples, I have not included special handling for the bitmaps whose dimensions are not an even multiple of the **numpels** block size. The results are less than satisfactory for those cases. To see the effect, try using "arches.bmp" which has an odd width. The odd dimension effect can be greatly minimized by setting **numpels** smaller. Try using 1 pel. Speed of display is also a consideration. The larger the **numpels**, the faster the effect. The diagonal effect goes very slowly with **numpels** = 1.

With the faster processors and speedy video cards, I had to insert a **Pause** function after each iteration of the effects drawing. The function **GetTickCount** returns the number of milliseconds that have elapsed since Windows was started. To pause for a specific number of milliseconds, get the initial tick count and add in the number of milliseconds desired, storing the result in **endTicks**. Then, write a simple loop that keeps calling **GetTickCount** until the tick count is equal to or greater than the **endTicks** value.

The New CImage Class

The MFC has added a new class for viewing bmp images as well as jpg, gif, and png, CImage. To load in a supported image file, call the Load function, which inputs the image file and attempts to store it in a DIBSection for total access. If successful, the bits are directly accessible as well as normal image properties, such as width and height. The class also attempts to construct its own device context, much like a memory DC. Hence, it has its own special BitBlt function that is used to copy the image onto the screen.

In Pgm09c, I have removed the CDib class and inserted an instance of the CImage class as our data member. When the user chooses the Load File menu choice, after retrieving his or her selection from the File Open dialog, I pass it on to the CImage Load function. Once it has loaded the image, I then fill up our dibRect structure with its dimensions and Invalidate the window so that the image is displayed in OnPaint.

This then removes quite a lot of other coding and functions. The only tricky item is that the many BitBlt function calls have to be reversed. That is, it was paint's dc.BitBlt passing it the memory dc address. Now it is image.BitBlt passing it paint's dc.

Since most of the coding is the same, only selected portions are shown here. Please examine the source code more fully. The stdafx.h file contains the new include file, <atlimage.h>.

FrameWin Definition for Pgm09c

```
#pragma once

/*****************************************************************/
/*                                                               */
/* FrameWin Class Definition                                     */
/*                                                               */
/*****************************************************************/

class FrameWin : public CFrameWnd {

 /***************************************************************/
 /*                                                             */
```

```
/* Class Data Members                                          */
/*                                                             */
/***************************************************************/

protected:

char     filename[MAX_PATH]; // filename of .BMP file
char     initDir[MAX_PATH];  // open dlg initial dir to show

CImage   image;              // the class to hold the image

int      effectType;         // type of effect, 0 = normal

CRect    dibRect;            // dimensions of dib
CRect    actRect;            // dimensions of client area

CRect    fullWindow;         // max sized window
CRect    displayWindow;      // current dsply window onto full win

int      currentVpel;        // current vertical scroll offset
int      currentHpel;        // current horizontal scroll offset
int      numVpelsToScroll;
int      numHpelsToScroll;
int      maxVscrollPels;     // max num pels vertical to scroll
int      maxHscrollPels;     // max num pels horizontal to scroll

bool     animate;    // true when going thru effects automatically
DWORD    delayTime;  // milliseconds delay to slow effects down
...
```

FrameWin Implementation for Pgm09c

```
...
/***************************************************************/
/*                                                             */
/* OnDisplayChange: user has changed the display settings      */
/*                                                             */
/***************************************************************/

LRESULT   FrameWin::OnDisplayChange (WPARAM which, LPARAM lp) {
 LRESULT retcd = CFrameWnd::OnDisplayChange (which, lp);
 if (which == 1) {
  if (filename[0] !=0) {
   image.Load (filename);
   if (image.IsNull()) {
    AfxMessageBox ("Error file is not loaded. Try another image",
    return retcd;
   }
   // set up the dib size in a rectangle
   dibRect.left = dibRect.top = 0;
   dibRect.right = image.GetWidth();
   dibRect.bottom = image.GetHeight();
   effectType = CM_NORMAL;          // reset to normal effects
   Invalidate ();                   // repaint window
  }
 }
 return retcd;
}

/***************************************************************/
/*                                                             */
/* LoadFile: loads in a BMP file and displays it               */
/*                                                             */
```

```
/*************************************************************/

void      FrameWin::CmLoadFile () {
 CFileDialog filedlg (TRUE, // use Open dialog
                 "*.BMP",   // default extension
                 "*.BMP",   // current file name
    OFN_HIDEREADONLY | OFN_FILEMUSTEXIST | OFN_NOREADONLYRETURN |
    OFN_LONGNAMES,
    "Bitmap Files (*.BMP)|*.bmp|Bitmap Files (*.DIB)|*.DIB||",
    this);
 // install last initial dir to use
 filedlg.m_ofn.lpstrInitialDir = initDir;

 // get user's file choice
 if (filedlg.DoModal () == IDOK) {  // user has chosen a file, so
  strcpy_s (filename, sizeof(filename), filedlg.GetPathName ());
  image.Load (filedlg.GetPathName ());
  if (image.IsNull()) {
   AfxMessageBox ("Error file is not loaded. Try another image",
   return;
  }
  // set up the dib size in a rectangle
  dibRect.left = dibRect.top = 0;
  dibRect.right = image.GetWidth();
  dibRect.bottom = image.GetHeight();
  Invalidate(TRUE);
 }
}
...
/*************************************************************/
/*                                                           */
/* CmCrushVert: set up for vertical crush effect             */
/*                                                           */
/*************************************************************/

void      FrameWin::CmCrushVert () {
 effectType = CM_CRUSH_VERT;  // signal vertical crush requested
 Invalidate(); // force vertical crush effect
}
...
/*************************************************************/
/*                                                           */
/* OnPaint: draw once - then scroll the memDC                */
/*                                                           */
/*************************************************************/

void      FrameWin::OnPaint () {
 CPaintDC  dc(this);
 if (image.IsNull()) return;


 if (effectType == CM_NORMAL) {
  //copy the memory image to the screen adjusted by scroll bar
  image.BitBlt (dc, actRect.left, actRect.top, actRect.Width(),
             actRect.Height(),currentHpel, currentVpel, SRCCOPY);
  return;
 }

 if (currentVpel + currentHpel > 0) { // if image is scrolled
  // reset to upper left corner
  ScrollWindow (-currentHpel, -currentVpel, NULL, NULL);
  SetScrollPos (SB_VERT, 0, TRUE);  // reset scroll pos to 0,0
  SetScrollPos (SB_HORZ, 0, TRUE);
  currentVpel = currentHpel = 0;
```

```
 }

 switch (effectType) {  // handle the specific effect signaled
   case CM_DIAGONAL:                      // diagonal effect
    EffectDiagonal (dc); break;           // perform the effect
   case CM_CRUSH_VERT:                    // vertical crush effect
   case CM_CRUSH_HORZ:                    // horizontal crush effect
    EffectCrush (dc); break;              // perform the effect
   case CM_SPIRAL_IN:                     // sprial in effect
   case CM_SPIRAL_OUT:                    // sprial out effect
    EffectSpiral (dc); break;             // perform the effect
   case CM_SKIPHORIZ:
    EffectSkipHoriz (dc); break;          // perform the effect
   case CM_SKIPVERT:
    EffectSkipVert (dc); break;           // perform the effect
   case CM_SKIPDIAGSQR:
    EffectSkipDiagSquares (dc); break; // perform the effect
   case CM_SKIPRECTANGLES:
    EffectSkipRectangles (dc); break;  // perform the effect
 }

 if (animate) {                        // if animation is on, then
  effectType++;                        // set for next effect

#ifdef _DEBUG
_cprintf ("effect type: %d Last one is: %d\r\n", effectType,
          CM_SKIPRECTANGLES+1);
#endif

  if (effectType == CM_SKIPRECTANGLES+1) { // all done?

#ifdef _DEBUG
_cprintf ("animate stopping: %d Last one is: %d\r\n", effectType,
          CM_SKIPRECTANGLES+1);
#endif

   effectType = CM_NORMAL;             // yes, so set for normal
   animate = false;                    // turn off animation
  }
  Invalidate ();                       // display next effect
 }

}

/***************************************************************/
/*                                                             */
/* The following 3 routines have been adapted from a series of */
/*       articles:                                             */
/*                                                             */
/* Charles Mirho, Windows/Dos Developers Journal Feb, Mar,     */
/*         and May 1994  Vol 5, Nos: 2, 3, 5                   */
/*                                                             */
/* In all, the speed and effectiveness can be controlled by    */
/* adjusting the numpels field. Trouble arises from those      */
/* images that are not even multiples of the numpels;          */
/* unBitBlted streaks result.                                  */
/*                                                             */
/***************************************************************/

/***************************************************************/
/*                                                             */
/* EffectDiagonal: perform diagonal bitmap display             */
/*                                                             */
/***************************************************************/
```

```

void       FrameWin::EffectDiagonal (CDC & dc) {

 int numpels = 2;          // user adjustable width of diagonal line
 // set right and bottom limits to image size minus one diagonal
 // width numpels
 int rightstop  = dibRect.right  - numpels;
 int bottomstop = dibRect.bottom - numpels;
 int startrow, startcol, col, row;
 startcol = 0;                     // begin at top left corner, go
 while (startcol <= rightstop) {// until diagonal is at right top
  col = startcol;          // edge; set at this begin column and
  row = 0;                 // then for all rows until the bottom
  while (col >= 0 && row <=bottomstop) {
   // copy diagonal squares in that line
   image.BitBlt (dc, col, row, numpels, numpels,  col, row,
              SRCCOPY);
   col -= numpels;         // from current starting column back to 0
   row += numpels;         // and all rows to bottom - diag width
  }
  startcol += numpels;  // going from column 0 to right edge
  Pause ();
 }
 startrow = numpels;     // repeat for bottom right diagonals
 while (startrow <= bottomstop) { // going from top right corner
  col = rightstop;         // showing all column squares on one row
  row = startrow;          // then moving down one more row
  while (col >= 0 && row <= bottomstop) {
   // show all col and rows on this diag
   image.BitBlt (dc, col, row, numpels, numpels,  col, row,
              SRCCOPY);
   col -= numpels;         // move back towards center diagonal col
   row += numpels;         // move down to next row to make diagonal
  }
  startrow += numpels;  // repeat for next diagonal line
  Pause ();
 }
}
...
```

Programming Problems

Problem Pgm09-1—Revised Tic Tac Toe Program

Revise the Tic Tac Toe program as follows. Using Paintbrush or any other image editor, make two bmp images. One represents the X and one represents the O. Make them both the same size and be as fancy with them as desired.

Revise the **ChildWin** class, which is responsible for displaying the X or O value, to **BitBlt** either the X or O image when a player makes their box selection. Since the frame window can be resized by the user which in turn resizes all of the child windows, use **StretchBlt** to do the actual painting of the image onto the child window client area.

Problem Pgm09-2—The Random Square Special Effect

Revise **Pgm09b** to handle another special effect, the Random Square. Divide up the image into small squares whose dimensions are of your choice. Construct a 2-d array of type **bool** to represent the 2-d arrangement of the squares of the image. When the row and column **bool** value is **false**, the corresponding square of the image has not been shown on the screen. When the **bool** is **true**, it has already been shown.

When the user chooses this Random Effect, seed the random number generator with the current time and obtain a random row and column number within the range allowed by the total number of rows and columns in which you have divided the image. If the corresponding **bool** is **false**, **BitBlt** that square to the screen and set the bool to true. If the corresponding **bool** is **true**, then adopt some method of finding the next not yet shown square and show it. When all squares have been shown, the process is finished. Experiment with the visual effect created using different sized squares.

Chapter 10 Control Bars, Status Bars, Tool Boxes, and Child Client Windows

Introduction

With the basics down, now it's time for the fancier effects that can turn a plain application into a dynamic display. The MFC class library provides support for easily adding many convenience features to your Windows application. They include **status bars**, **control bars** or **tool bars**, and **tool boxes** which may be fixed or floating on the screen.

A status bar normally appears at the bottom of the window and displays program-defined messages as well as hint messages for menus and tool bar buttons. Status bars also may contain smaller display windows for the status of special keys such as the Scroll Lock, Cap Lock, and Num Lock keys. Status bars are useful for displaying key information, such as the page number, line number, and column number of the caret in a text processing application. Because of the smaller, variable width font used to display messages, more than 80 character messages can be displayed.

Control bars, also known as tool bars, often contain small bitmap buttons that represent menu items providing a shortcut or a fast method of making selections. Usually there are buttons for File|New, File|Open, and so on. Because the function or purpose of a button may not be obvious to a user, **flyover hints** and **tool tips** can be provided. Many tool bar images do not readily express what they are to do to beginners (or old timers for that matter) When the mouse cursor is over a button (or when a menu item is highlighted), the corresponding hint string appears in either on the status bar at the bottom of the screen; these are called **flyover hints**. Additionally, a one or two word **tool tip** can pop-up just beside a button if the user keeps the mouse cursor over a button for about a second.

Finally, tool boxes provide a convenient wrapper for any number of additional buttons (but not exclusively buttons) such as providing a selection of pen widths and brush colors. Paintbrush, for example, has a tool box of color selections, drawing pen widths, and bitmapped buttons representing the current mode of operation such as cut, text, line drawing, and rectangle drawing. The simplest tool boxes are fixed in location. However, for any professional application, the user ought be able to move the tool box to any wanted screen location and hide and reshow the tool box as needed.

When the tool bar or box is fixed to one of the four sides of the frame window, they are said to be **docked**. When these tool bars are not docked but are being positioned somewhere within the client area, they are said to be **floating**.

Under the MFC, docking and floating tool bars are easy to create because the framework handles most all of the details. The tool bar can be docked at one of the four sides or can be "torn off" or floating and moved anywhere desired by the user.

In Figure 10.1 you can see what the drawing application program for this chapter, **Pgm10a**, looks like with the fancy controls. Notice that, initially, the main tool bar is docked at the top and that I have added a text message beneath each button. The tool box of line widths and colors is docked on the right side. The status bar is on the bottom.

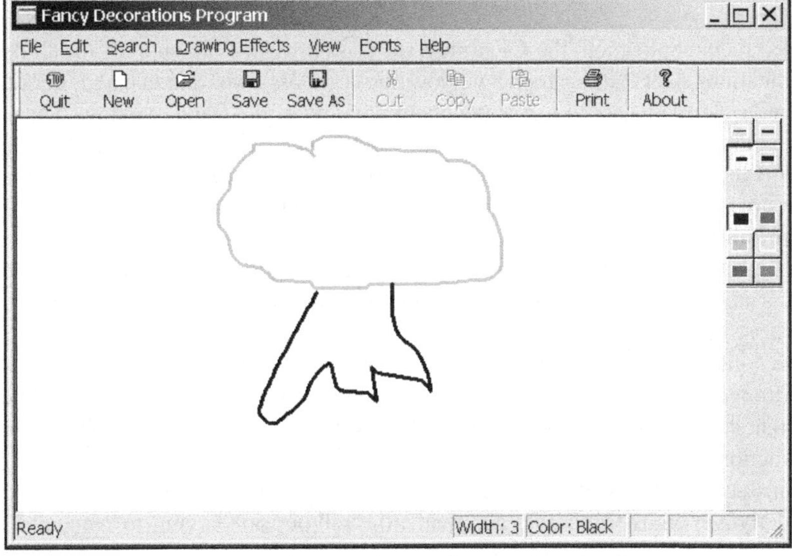

Figure 10.1 Pgm10a with Both Tool Bars Docked

When the mouse is not over any of the buttons, a "Ready" message appears on the status bar. Notice also that the initial color and line width selections are shown in two separate panes in the status bar. To their right are "status" boxes for Scroll Lock, Num Lock, and Caps Lock.

In Figure 10.2, I have undocked both tool bars and have the mouse hovering over the Open button. Notice the tool tip that appears just below the button and the flyover hint on the status bar.

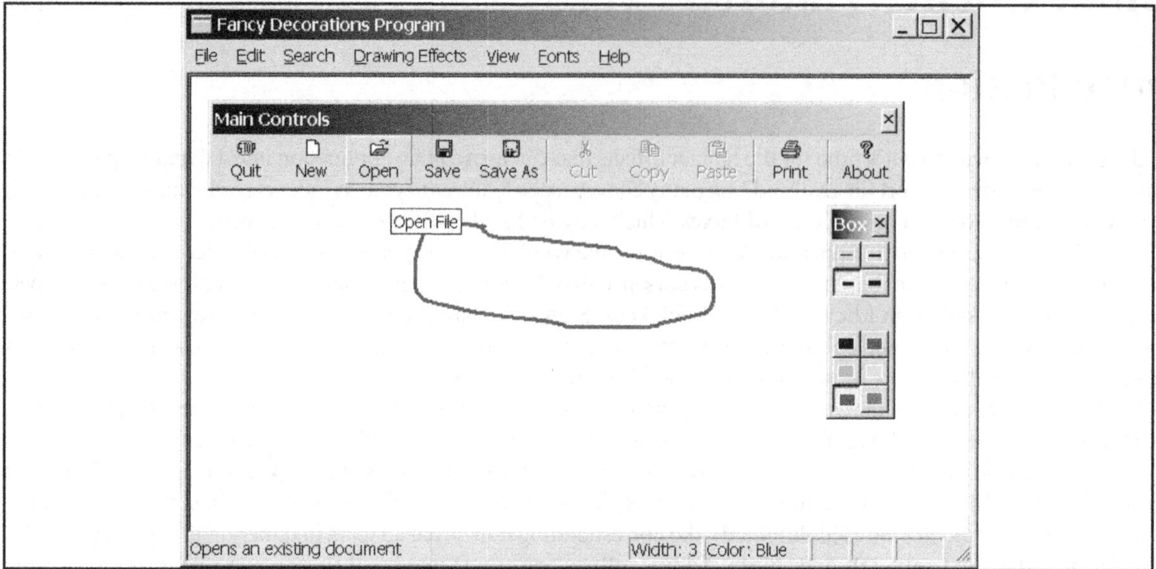

Figure 10.2 Pgm10a with Both Tool Bars Undocked and Mouse Over Open Button

When undocked, both tool bars appear similar to a modeless dialog box. Further, both floating windows have a title or caption. Notice that the current selections in the tool box appear depressed while all others appear normal. In contrast, with the new Rebar style main tool bar, a selected button appears raised above the bar—the Open button in this case. The mouse cursor is not visible in the screen capture, Figure 10.2.

All of these items are often referred to as decorations. In this chapter, all of the basic decorations are covered. Again, there are many variations possible, including placing text edit controls, list boxes, and combo boxes into control bars. Once you are comfortable with the basics, you can experiment with even fancier decorations.

Division of Labors: Adding a Client Window Class

Our simpler applications to date consisted of a single frame window which handled all of the processing details. Perhaps you have noticed that they have become huge in size? It is time that we begin a division of labor—that is, break the application down into smaller components.

When decorations are added to an application, the **CFrameWnd** class provides full support for all decorations. Thus, we typically structure our applications such that our frame window derived class owns and manages our decorations. Then, we add another **CWnd** or similar derived class to act as the client window of the frame window. Thus, the frame window class handles the menu, tool bars and status bar while the client window handles the real work of the application.

In this chapter, the client portion illustrates the basic principles of drawing or scribbling in my case. However, no attempt is made to save or somehow store any drawing actually done. In fact, if a repaint is done, the entire canvas is wiped clean by the background erase of **OnPaint**.

The basic **CFrameWnd** class handles all of the decorations via our class member instances of the decoration classes. The basic classes for tool bars and status bars are **CToolBar** and **CStatusBar**. We can, of course, create a tool box that is derived from the **CToolBar** class. The **CToolBar** class provides support for flyover hints as well as tool tips. Instead of menu commands to reposition the control bar or tool boxes, **CToolBar** utilizes user dragging. If a control bar initially located at the top of the window is dragged, the control bar becomes a floating window. If it is dragged sufficiently close to any side, it is then "docked" on that side. Hence, we have the term **dockable** tool bars. The MFC framework, via the **CFrameWnd**, handles all of this functionality.

The only restriction is that instances of **CToolBar** must be child windows of a **CFrameWnd** derived class and not a **CWnd** in order for tool tips and flyover hints to operate automatically without our having to manually code such functionality.

This does impact the design somewhat. A large percentage of the buttons on the main (top) tool bar control file operations. Others control the Edit operations, which directly concern the child drawing window. However, the tool box of line widths and pen colors directly impacts only the child window operations. Yet, because of the framework, these tool bars must be under the control of the frame window. However, by responding to **OnCmdMsg** and routing all messages first to the **DrawWin** child window, we could let that window take care of all of these details, such as enabling items and so on. If we did that, then, in terms of breaking the work load down between classes, we are in effect moving everything that was in the frame window down into the client window and we have accomplished no simplification or work load sharing!

Instead, we will let the frame window class be fully in charge of the decorations including such mundane things as enabling menu items and buttons and responding to button pressed. Those that the frame window derived class cannot fully handle can be given to the **DrawWin** child window to handle by the **SendMessage** mechanism. In fact, we can invent our own, application-specific messages to send!

Using the App Wizard to Create Shell Programs

When we begin to add in toolbars, it is wise to allow the App Wizard to create a working framework, one that is guaranteed to at least compile and run with a visible toolbar and status bar.

Let's see what that first shell is by making a play project. Choose File-New Project and select MFC Application. Enter a name, here I chose Pgm10a. Next a lengthy series of property pages appears allowing us to tailor what our shell program contains. We have many selections to make and to uncheck. Click Application Type first. Choose Single Document and uncheck Document View Architecture and Use UNICODE libraries. Click the Next button to go to the database support page. None is the database default, which is what we desire. Click Next once more. Here on the User Interface page, you can tailor various items. Notice that a toolbar and status bar are the defaults. I suggest you make two projects varying the type of toolbar selected: Standard Docking and Standard Docking Browser Style. In this example, I did not check Browser Style. Click Next. On the Advanced Features page, uncheck all items and click Next.

On the Generated Classes page, we cannot change the names of the generated classes, but we can change their filenames. If you have noticed, all of the MFC classes begin with a 'C' for Class. Unfortunately, the App Wizard also uses this naming convention for our own application classes. I think that it is very wise to never begin our own classes with a C prefix. That way, anyone can tell at a glance which are the MFC classes and which are those that we have written. We can always edit the generated coding and change class names later on, so click Finish and the wizard builds our shell application.

Now click Build and then execute the shell application. Figure 10-3 shows mine.

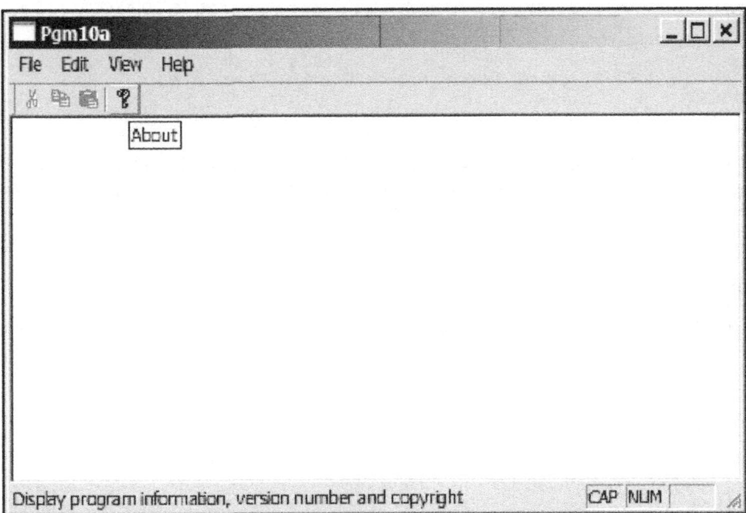

Figure 10-3 The Shell Application for Pgm10a

Notice that we have a toolbar with greyed buttons for Cut, Copy, and Paste. However, I floated the mouse over the Help About button. Notice that a small pop-up tooltip window appears saying "About." On the status bar is the Flyover Hint message which is rather lengthy. It is displayed with a variable pitch font so one can show rather lengthy hint messages in the available space. On the status bar's right side are the indicators. I turned on Cap Lock as well as Num Lock. Essentially, these are toggle switch messages that relay the status of Caps, Num, and Scroll lock keys. There is also a gripper bar on the very right side of the status bar for easy re-sizing of the window. A beginning menu is also available. The Help-About item displays an About dialog box.

One slick feature is on the View menu. Toolbar and Statusbar are checked menu items. That is, if you select one, it hides that item and shows no check. Selecting that one again, makes the toolbar or statusbar re-appear and re-checks the menu item. Finally, grab the toolbar and drag it out into the open client window area. It undocks from the top and becomes floating. However, it does not have a caption when undocked; it should have a caption such as Main Toolbar. Try docking the toolbar on the other sides of the frame window. Notice that the frame window only allows docking on the top or on the right side. Where a floating toolbar is allowed to dock is totally under the programmer's control.

Now let's look at the code that was generated by the App Wizard, beginning with **stdafx.h**. Obviously, it is overly complicated.

```
//stdafx.h : include file for standard system include files,
// or project specific include files that are used frequently,
// but are changed infrequently
#pragma once
#ifndef _SECURE_ATL
#define _SECURE_ATL 1
#endif
#ifndef VC_EXTRALEAN
#define VC_EXTRALEAN            // Exclude rarely-used stuff from Windows headers
#endif
// Modify the following defines if you have to target a platform prior to the ones specified below.
// Refer to MSDN for the latest info on corresponding values for different platforms.
#ifndef WINVER                          // Allow use of features specific to Windows XP or later.
#define WINVER 0x0501           // Change this to the appropriate value to target other versions of
Windows.
#endif
#ifndef _WIN32_WINNT            // Allow use of features specific to Windows XP or later.

#define _WIN32_WINNT 0x0501     // Change this to the appropriate value to target other versions of
Windows.
#endif
#ifndef _WIN32_WINDOWS                  // Allow use of features specific to Windows 98 or later.
#define _WIN32_WINDOWS 0x0410 // Change this to the appropriate value to target Windows Me or later.
#endif
#ifndef _WIN32_IE                       // Allow use of features specific to IE 6.0 or later.
#define _WIN32_IE 0x0600        // Change this to the appropriate value to target other versions of IE.
#endif
#define _ATL_CSTRING_EXPLICIT_CONSTRUCTORS    // some CString constructors will be explicit
// turns off MFC's hiding of some common and often safely ignored warning messages
#define _AFX_ALL_WARNINGS
#include <afxwin.h>           // MFC core and standard components
#include <afxext.h>           // MFC extensions
#ifndef _AFX_NO_OLE_SUPPORT
#include <afxdtctl.h>           // MFC support for Internet Explorer 4 Common Controls
#endif
#ifndef _AFX_NO_AFXCMN_SUPPORT
#include <afxcmn.h>                     // MFC support for Windows Common Controls
#endif // _AFX_NO_AFXCMN_SUPPORT
```

Looking this over and re-examining the **stdafx.h** file that we have been using, there really is no real difference, save limiting our programs to XP only, instead of Win2000 or better. I chose to replace this file with our simpler one from our earlier programs.

Now examine the **CWinApp** header file.

```
// Pgm10a.h : main header file for the Pgm10a application
//
#pragma once
#ifndef __AFXWIN_H__
	#error "include 'stdafx.h' before including this file for PCH"
#endif
#include "resource.h"       // main symbols
// CPgm10aApp:
// See Pgm10a.cpp for the implementation of this class
//
class CPgm10aApp : public CWinApp
{
public:
	CPgm10aApp();
// Overrides
public:
	virtual BOOL InitInstance();
// Implementation
public:
	afx_msg void OnAppAbout();
```

```
        DECLARE_MESSAGE_MAP()
};
extern CPgm10aApp theApp;
```

Notice that the wizard generated coding has the application class responding to the Help-About request, showing that dialog. Hence, there is a command message in the message map to invoke **OnAppAbout**.

One trick that is commonly done is to include the line

`extern CPgm10aApp theApp;`

Any file that includes this entry has total access to the public interface of the application class by using the name **theApp**.

Here is the implementation file.

```
// Pgm10a.cpp : Defines the class behaviors for the application.
//
#include "stdafx.h"
#include "Pgm10a.h"
#include "MainFrm.h"
#ifdef _DEBUG
#define new DEBUG_NEW
#endif
// CPgm10aApp
BEGIN_MESSAGE_MAP(CPgm10aApp, CWinApp)
        ON_COMMAND(ID_APP_ABOUT, &CPgm10aApp::OnAppAbout)
END_MESSAGE_MAP()
// CPgm10aApp construction
CPgm10aApp::CPgm10aApp()
{
        // TODO: add construction code here,
        // Place all significant initialization in InitInstance
}
// The one and only CPgm10aApp object
CPgm10aApp theApp;
// CPgm10aApp initialization
BOOL CPgm10aApp::InitInstance()
{
        CWinApp::InitInstance();
        // Standard initialization
        // If you are not using these features and wish to reduce the size
        // of your final executable, you should remove from the following
        // the specific initialization routines you do not need
        // Change the registry key under which our settings are stored
        // TODO: You should modify this string to be something appropriate
        // such as the name of your company or organization
        SetRegistryKey(_T("Local AppWizard-Generated Applications"));
        // To create the main window, this code creates a new frame window
        // object and then sets it as the application's main window object
        CMainFrame* pFrame = new CMainFrame;
        if (!pFrame)
              return FALSE;
        m_pMainWnd = pFrame;
        // create and load the frame with its resources
        pFrame->LoadFrame(IDR_MAINFRAME,
              WS_OVERLAPPEDWINDOW | FWS_ADDTOTITLE, NULL,
              NULL);
        // The one and only window has been initialized, so show and update it
        pFrame->ShowWindow(SW_SHOW);
        pFrame->UpdateWindow();
        // call DragAcceptFiles only if there's a suffix
        //  In an SDI app, this should occur after ProcessShellCommand
        return TRUE;
}

// CPgm10aApp message handlers
// CAboutDlg dialog used for App About
```

```
class CAboutDlg : public CDialog
{
public:
	CAboutDlg();
// Dialog Data
	enum { IDD = IDD_ABOUTBOX };
protected:
	virtual void DoDataExchange(CDataExchange* pDX);	// DDX/DDV support
// Implementation
protected:
	DECLARE_MESSAGE_MAP()
};
CAboutDlg::CAboutDlg() : CDialog(CAboutDlg::IDD)
{
}
void CAboutDlg::DoDataExchange(CDataExchange* pDX)
{
	CDialog::DoDataExchange(pDX);
}
BEGIN_MESSAGE_MAP(CAboutDlg, CDialog)
END_MESSAGE_MAP()
// App command to run the dialog
void CPgm10aApp::OnAppAbout()
{
	CAboutDlg aboutDlg;
	aboutDlg.DoModal();
}
```

First, let's remove the registry key coding, that is totally unneeded for any of our applications. Dealing with the registry is an advanced topic. Cleaning up **InitInstance**, we are left with this coding:

```
BOOL CPgm10aApp::InitInstance() {
	CWinApp::InitInstance();
	CMainFrame* pFrame = new CMainFrame;
	if (!pFrame) return FALSE;
	m_pMainWnd = pFrame;
	pFrame->LoadFrame(IDR_MAINFRAME,
		WS_OVERLAPPEDWINDOW | FWS_ADDTOTITLE, NULL,
		NULL);
	pFrame->ShowWindow(SW_SHOW);
	pFrame->UpdateWindow();
	return TRUE;
}
```

This coding is dynamically allocating the new frame window, but is using a different approach to creating it. The **LoadFrame** function loads in the window and ties a number of features together via the boldfaced id, **IDR_MAINFRAME**. It is usually intended for the Document View architecture, where the frame window, toolbar, main menu and child views are all launched together as a package and bound together. We will deal with the style option, **FWS_ADDTOTITLE** when we cover the doc-view architecture. All that I chose to eliminate from this coding is the registry setting line.

Finally, I chose to rename the class from **CPgm10aApp** to **Pgm10a** to maintain a uniform naming convention across all of these examples.

Instead of diving into the coding of the other classes, let's examine the graphical portions and then the coding required to implement the toolbar, statusbar, and a floating toolbox of colors. However, I did go ahead and globally change the class name to FrameWin to be consistent with all of our sample programs thus far.

The MFC Implementation of Decorations

A tool bar generally contains many bitmap buttons that represent menu items. Further, the MFC provides many standard bitmaps to be used with the common File, Edit, and Search menu items, such as open, new, print, cut, paste, and find. When a button represents one of these common actions, such as File|New or Edit|Cut, it is very wise to copy and reuse the Microsoft provided standard images. To this end, Microsoft provides two easy ways to get them.

One way to get to these standard tool bar images is to use the Application Wizard and let it generate a dummy application. Then, open up the generated tool bar and copy the needed button images into your own application's tool bar.

Another way to get them is to track down the many resources Microsoft has provided with the on line documentation. Their location varies from release to release. Sometimes these files have not been loaded onto disk from the original install CDs.

On my machine, they are located in "Microsoft Visual Studio .NET\ Common7\ Graphics." Other sub-folders contain icons and cursors that you can insert into your application as well. There are two sizes of buttons. The usual ones are 16x15 pixels in size.

Figure 10.4 The Tool Bar Bmp File for Pgm10a

The tool bar itself consists of a consecutive series of these small bmp images. Figure 10.4 shows the actual tool bar bmp image for **Pgm10a**.

Figure 10.5 The Tool Box Bmp File

Figure 10.5 shows the tool box bmp file. Notice that neither of these bmp image strips look remotely like the actual tool bars shown in Figure 10.1 and 10.2!

The **CToolBar** class loads in the bmp image strip and then generates the visible tool bar based on our construction details. There are two ways that we can code the construction details: the old style and the new style. The main tool bar in **Pgm10a** uses the new style while the tool box uses the old style. This way you can see how both are accomplished.

With either method, a **separator** adds a gap between the buttons, simulating a group effect. The framework provides the separator via a special identifier. In the tool box, I used two separators in a row to produce the appearance of two columns per row.

The place to begin is how to get the tool bar image strip built in the first place. One very easy and convenient method is to copy another sample application's tool bar and modify it. Feel free to copy those that I have provided with this text. Another way is to choose the Insert|New Resource|Toolbar menu item.

Using the Resource Editor to Add a New Tool Bar

When you right click on the rc file and choose Add New Resource and then toolbar, the Resource Editor begins a new tool bar. Figure 10.6 shows the editing screen immediately after choosing this menu command. This is the new style of toolbar creation; there is also an older method as well.

You are presented with three views. The one at the top is how the tool bar appears. The button that you are currently editing has a dotted focus rectangle around it. The small image on the left is what this image really looks like. The large image on the right side is the actual image zoomed or greatly magnified so that you can effectively draw your button. Each button on the strip is 16x15 pixels in size. Now draw in your fancy button.

If you also open up another sample tool bar or bmp in the Resource Editor, you can copy and paste onto this new image.

When you have the new button image looking the way you want it, then double click on the image of that button in the top view—it is the one with the dotted focus rectangle around it. Double clicking opens the property's box for this button. Here in the button property's box is where you assign then command ID number that the button is to represent or send when pressed. Also, here is where you can enter the flyover hint string and tool tip.

The first portion of the string is what becomes the flyover hint. The flyover hint is separated from the corresponding tool tip by a new line code, a \n. The tool tip text comes after the new line code. Keep tool tips fairly short, just a few words.

The flyover hint can be rather lengthy. Figure 10.7 shows the property control after I have double clicked on the button in the top view. I also entered the command id and the corresponding text strings to use.

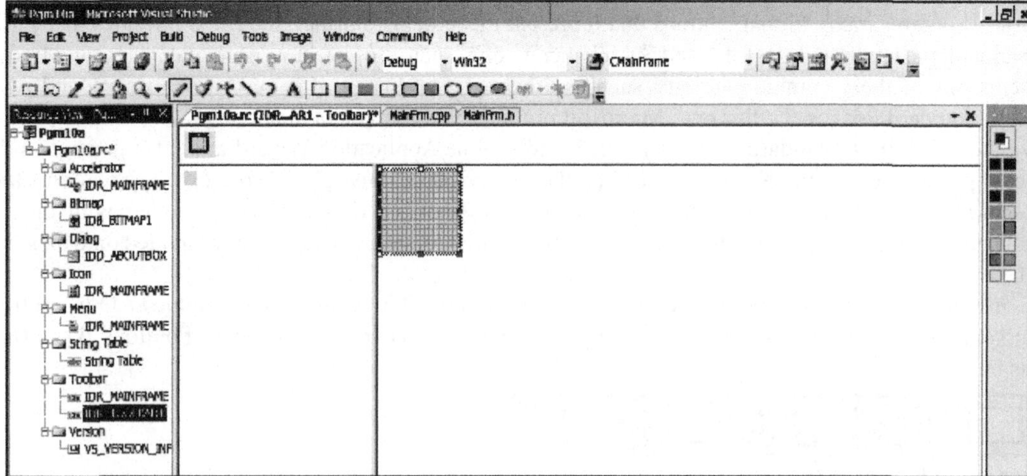

Figure 10-6 Creating a New Toolbar

To get to the next button to edit, simply click on the new empty button to the right of the one just finished. You can also drag one button to another location on the strip, that is, you can move them around by dragging. Alternatively, you can do edit-cut and paste.

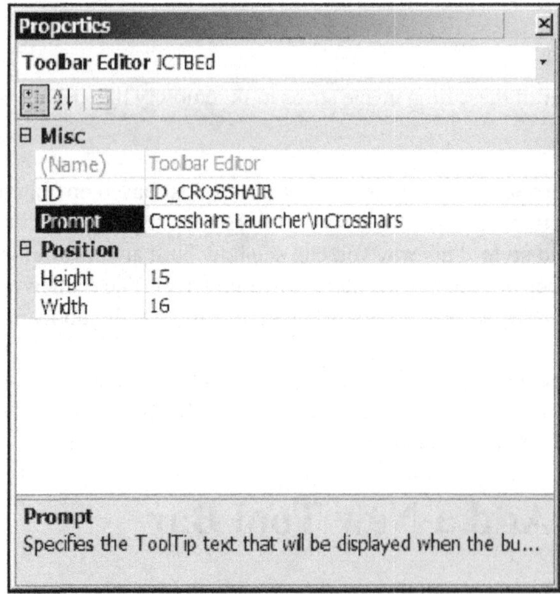

Figure 10-7 Setting Properties of a Button

Before we go much farther in this process, let's examine the actual RC file and **resource.h** file for **Pgm10a** that I added to so we can see what is being created. Remember that there are two styles for the tool bar correlations of buttons to their corresponding commands. Both are illustrated with this sample program.

Here is the relevant portion of the **resource.h** file. It contains the command id values.

```
#define IDD_ABOUTBOX              100
#define IDR_MAINFRAME             128
#define IDR_Pgm10aTYPE            129
#define IDB_TOOLBOX                 3      // the tool box bitmap
#define CM_FONTCHANGE    (WM_USER + 101)
#define CM_FILENEW       (WM_USER + 103)
#define CM_FILEOPEN      (WM_USER + 104)
```

```
#define CM_FILESAVE      (WM_USER + 105)
#define CM_FILESAVEAS    (WM_USER + 106)
#define CM_FILEPRINT            (WM_USER + 107)
#define CM_FILEPRINTERSETUP     (WM_USER + 108)
#define CM_EXIT                 (WM_USER + 109)
#define CM_EDITUNDO             (WM_USER + 110)
#define CM_EDITCUT              (WM_USER + 111)
#define CM_EDITCOPY             (WM_USER + 112)
#define CM_EDITPASTE            (WM_USER + 113)
#define CM_EDITCLEAR            (WM_USER + 114)
#define CM_EDITFIND             (WM_USER + 115)
#define CM_EDITREPLACE          (WM_USER + 116)
#define CM_EDITFINDNEXT         (WM_USER + 117)
#define CM_LINECHANGE           (WM_USER + 118)
#define CM_COLORCHANGE          (WM_USER + 119)
#define CM_LINE1                (WM_USER + 121)
#define CM_LINE2                (WM_USER + 122)
#define CM_LINE3                (WM_USER + 123)
#define CM_LINE4                (WM_USER + 124)
#define CM_COLORA               (WM_USER + 125)
#define CM_COLORB               (WM_USER + 126)
#define CM_COLORC               (WM_USER + 127)
#define CM_COLORD               (WM_USER + 128)
#define CM_COLORE               (WM_USER + 129)
#define CM_COLORF               (WM_USER + 130)
#define ID_LINEWIDTH        1000
#define ID_LINECOLOR        1001
#define IDS_MSG_QUIT         2001
#define IDS_MSG_QUERY        2002
```

Notice the **IDR_MAINFRAME** generated by the App Wizard. This id is used to identify several different items so that the **LoadFrame** function can install the frame window and all its resources. This id is the id of the toolbar bmp image, the toolbar button ids, the main menu, the accelerator table, and the application caption title string. Thus, **LoadFrame** with this one id can load in all the needed resources of the frame window. I added **IDB_TOOLBOX** to define the floating toolbox of pen widths and colors.

Notice the numerical values for the four line width identifiers. If we take the command id that is sent when any given line width button is pressed and subtract **CM_LINE1** and add 1 to it, we have the actual line width in pixels.

```
linewidth = CM_LINE4 - CM_LINE1 + 1;
```

yields 4 pixels.

Similarly, the command id values for the six colors are all in a row. If we have an array of color values, then subtracting the base value, **CM_COLORA** from the command id sent by a color button press yields a zero-based offset that can be used as an index into the color array.

The **ID_LINEWIDTH** and **ID_LINECOLOR** identifiers are used to reserve two panes on the far right of the statusbar for our use. Here I will show the current width and color in use.

The corresponding RC file is interesting. It begins with the inclusion of the two tool bar image files and the program icon.

```
/////////////////////////////////////////////////////////////////////////////
//
// Icon
//
// Icon with lowest ID value placed first to ensure app icon
// remains consistent on all systems.
IDR_MAINFRAME           ICON       "res\\Pgm10a.ico"
/////////////////////////////////////////////////////////////////////////////
//
// Bitmap
//
IDR_MAINFRAME           BITMAP     "res\\Toolbar.bmp"
IDB_TOOLBOX             BITMAP     "res\\TOOLBOX.BMP"
/////////////////////////////////////////////////////////////////////////////
```

```
//
// Toolbar
//
IDR_MAINFRAME TOOLBAR  16, 15
BEGIN
    BUTTON      ID_APP_EXIT
    BUTTON      CM_FILENEW
    BUTTON      CM_FILEOPEN
    BUTTON      CM_FILESAVE
    BUTTON      CM_FILESAVEAS
    SEPARATOR
    BUTTON      CM_EDITCUT
    BUTTON      CM_EDITCOPY
    BUTTON      CM_EDITPASTE
    SEPARATOR
    BUTTON      CM_FILEPRINT
    SEPARATOR
    BUTTON      ID_APP_ABOUT
END
```

The above Toolbar section is the new style way of tying each button to the corresponding command id value that is sent when the button is pushed. These values are in the **same order** as the button images on the bmp tool bar strip. **ID_APP_EXIT** is the framework's command id to be sent when the very first button on the far left of the tool bar is pressed or when the app termination has been requested. The key word, **SEPARATOR**, instructs the **CToolBar** to leave a standard spacer gap at this point in the resultant tool bar. Separators are used to group similar buttons together, such as the File group from the Edit group.

Next, comes the main menu. Notice that these same command id values are used in the menu, such as **CM_FILENEW**.

Design Rule 45: A tool bar button should always have a corresponding menu item. The reason for this is for user Accessibility. It should also have a corresponding String table entry for flyover hints and tool tips, if desired.

For some people, a Windows application is best controlled via hot keys and menu selection. For others that can use a mouse, the tool bar is faster. Here is the menu. Notice that the menu id is IDR_MAINFRAME. I also used the framework's ids for exit and help about, shown in bold face.

```
IDR_MAINFRAME MENU
BEGIN
    POPUP "&File"
    BEGIN
        MENUITEM "&New",                  CM_FILENEW
        MENUITEM "&Open...",              CM_FILEOPEN
        MENUITEM "&Save",                 CM_FILESAVE, GRAYED
        MENUITEM "Save &As...",           CM_FILESAVEAS, GRAYED
        MENUITEM SEPARATOR
        MENUITEM "&Print...",             CM_FILEPRINT, GRAYED
        MENUITEM "P&rint Setup...",   CM_FILEPRINTERSETUP, GRAYED
        MENUITEM SEPARATOR
        MENUITEM "E&xit\tAlt+F4",         ID_APP_EXIT
    END
    POPUP "&Edit"
    BEGIN
        MENUITEM "&Undo\tAlt+BkSp",       CM_EDITUNDO, GRAYED
        MENUITEM SEPARATOR
        MENUITEM "Cu&t\tShift+Del",       CM_EDITCUT, GRAYED
        MENUITEM "&Copy\tCtrl+Ins",       CM_EDITCOPY, GRAYED
        MENUITEM "&Paste\tShift+Ins",     CM_EDITPASTE, GRAYED
        MENUITEM SEPARATOR
        MENUITEM "Clear &All\tCtrl+Del",  CM_EDITCLEAR, GRAYED
    END
    POPUP "&Search"
```

```
    BEGIN
        MENUITEM "&Find...",                 CM_EDITFIND, GRAYED
        MENUITEM "&Replace...",              CM_EDITREPLACE, GRAYED
        MENUITEM "&Next\aF3",                CM_EDITFINDNEXT, GRAYED
    END
    POPUP "&Drawing Effects"
    BEGIN
        POPUP "Line &Width"
        BEGIN
            MENUITEM "1 Pixel",              CM_LINE1
            MENUITEM "2 Pixels",             CM_LINE2
            MENUITEM "3 Pixels",             CM_LINE3
            MENUITEM "4 Pixels",             CM_LINE4
        END
        POPUP "Line &Color"
        BEGIN
            MENUITEM "&Black",               CM_COLORA
            MENUITEM "&Red",                 CM_COLORB
            MENUITEM "&Green",               CM_COLORC
            MENUITEM "&Yellow",              CM_COLORD
            MENUITEM "B&lue",                CM_COLORE
            MENUITEM "&Purple",              CM_COLORF
        END
    END
    POPUP "&View"
    BEGIN
        MENUITEM "&Toolbar",                 ID_VIEW_TOOLBAR
        MENUITEM "&Status Bar",              ID_VIEW_STATUS_BAR
        MENUITEM "Tool &Box",                IDB_TOOLBOX
    END
    POPUP "&Fonts"
    BEGIN
        MENUITEM "&Font Change",             CM_FONTCHANGE
    END
    POPUP "&Help"
    BEGIN
        MENUITEM "&About...",                ID_APP_ABOUT
    END
END
// Accelerator
//
IDR_MAINFRAME ACCELERATORS
BEGIN
    VK_DELETE,      CM_EDITCUT,              VIRTKEY, SHIFT
    VK_INSERT,      CM_EDITCOPY,             VIRTKEY, CONTROL
    VK_INSERT,      CM_EDITPASTE,            VIRTKEY, SHIFT
    VK_DELETE,      CM_EDITCLEAR,            VIRTKEY, CONTROL
    VK_BACK,        CM_EDITUNDO,             VIRTKEY, ALT
    VK_F3,          CM_EDITFINDNEXT,         VIRTKEY
END
```

Notice that a new pop-up has been added, View. The View menu provides check marked items to hide and show the tool bar, tool box and the status bar. This way, when space becomes a premium, the user can hide the bars to gain a larger screen area. When they are needed, they can be reshown.

Design Rule 46: Always provide a Hide and Show View menu item for every tool bar and status bar in the application.

The framework provides the complete mechanism to hide and show both the main tool bar and the status bar. To invoke that functionality, we provide the special MFC identifiers, **ID_VIEW_TOOLBAR** and **ID_VIEW_STATUS_BAR**. These are reserved MFC identifiers. When the user selects either of these menu items, the framework automatically hides or shows the corresponding item and handles placing a check mark on the corresponding View menu item.

In this program, we have an additional tool box, whose id is **IDB_TOOLBOX**. Notice that we can use this framework functionality for our other tool bars by placing the id of the image bitmap strips here on the View menu. The framework will then handle hiding and showing the tool box for us. However, we must also implement another short command enabler function to take care of the check mark on the menu item.

```
// String Table
//
STRINGTABLE DISCARDABLE
BEGIN
    ID_INDICATOR_EXT            "EXT"
    ID_INDICATOR_CAPS           "CAP"
    ID_INDICATOR_NUM            "NUM"
    ID_INDICATOR_SCRL           "SCRL"
    ID_INDICATOR_OVR            "OVR"
    ID_INDICATOR_REC            "REC"
END
```

In order to display the "on" status of the Caps Lock key or Scroll Lock, we must provide the string text we wish displayed in the corresponding pane in the status bar, such as CAP or SCRL. However, we must use the MFC provided identifiers for these strings. If we use the above identifiers, then the framework automatically handles displaying the requested indicator's status. We do not have to code anything else to have these fully operational. True, here in a graphical drawing program, none of these indicators have any real use. However, in a text editing situation, they are very meaningful.

```
STRINGTABLE DISCARDABLE
BEGIN
    IDR_MAINFRAME               "Pgm10a Fancy Decorations Program"
    AFX_IDS_APP_TITLE           "Pgm10a Fancy Decorations Program"
    AFX_IDS_IDLEMESSAGE         "Ready"
END
```

Next, in the String table are strings with the same identifiers as the menu items and tool bar buttons. These strings become the flyover hints and tool tips that the framework automatically displays when the mouse is over one of these buttons or menu commands. Notice that a specific command id is used in potentially four places: on a menu item, on a menu accelerator, on a tool bar button, and on a string table entry. It is this command id that binds all of these together.

```
STRINGTABLE DISCARDABLE
BEGIN
    CM_FONTCHANGE  "Select new font\nFont Change"
    CM_FILENEW     "Creates a new document\nNew File"
    CM_FILEOPEN    "Opens an existing document\nOpen File"
    CM_FILESAVE    "Saves this document\nSave"
    CM_FILESAVEAS  "Saves this document with a new name\nSave As"
    CM_FILEPRINT   "Print this document\nPrint"
    CM_FILEPRINTERSETUP      "Setup the printer\nPrint Setup"
    CM_EDITUNDO    "Reverses the last operation\nUndo Last Change"
...
    CM_LINE1  "Select 1 pixel line width\nLine width 1"
    CM_LINE2  "Select 2 pixels line width\nLine width 2"
    CM_LINE3  "Select 3 pixels line width\nLine width 3"
    CM_LINE4  "Select 4 pixels line width\nLine width 4"
    CM_COLORA "Select Black as the drawing color\nColor: Black"
    CM_COLORB "Select Red as the drawing color\nColor: Red"
    CM_COLORC "Select Green as the drawing color\nColor: Green"
    CM_COLORD "Select Yellow as the drawing color\nColor: Yellow"
    CM_COLORE "Select Blue as the drawing color\nColor: Blue"
    CM_COLORF "Select Purple as the drawing color\nColor: Purple"
    IDB_TOOLBOX        "Hide or Show Tool Box\\bHide/Show Tool Box"
    ID_VIEW_TOOLBAR      "Show or hide the toolbar\nToggle ToolBar"
    ID_VIEW_STATUS_BAR "Show or hide the status bar\nToggle "
                         "StatusBar"
```

Another important set of strings must also be in the String table. Now that we are beginning to make use of some framework supplied features, we must include some MFC built-in id values in the String table. The first string with the id of **AFX_IDS_IDLEMESSAGE** is displayed whenever the mouse is not on some other menu or tool bar button. Typically, we display a flyover hint of "Ready." These others are some other strings that the framework may require, depending upon user interactions.

```
    AFX_IDS_IDLEMESSAGE "Ready"
    ID_NEXT_PANE       "Switch to the next window pane\nNext Pane"
    ID_PREV_PANE       "Switch back to the previous window "
                       "pane\nPrevious Pane"
    ID_WINDOW_SPLIT    "Split the active window into panes\nSplit"
    AFX_IDS_SCSIZE         "Change the window size"
    AFX_IDS_SCMOVE         "Change the window position"
    AFX_IDS_SCMINIMIZE     "Reduce the window to an icon"
    AFX_IDS_SCMAXIMIZE     "Enlarge the window to full size"
    AFX_IDS_SCNEXTWINDOW "Switch to the next document window"
    AFX_IDS_SCPREVWINDOW "Switch to the previous document window"
    AFX_IDS_SCCLOSE        "Close the active window and prompts to"
                           " save the documents"
    AFX_IDS_SCRESTORE      "Restore the window to normal size"
    AFX_IDS_SCTASKLIST     "Activate Task List"
    ID_LINEWIDTH               "Width: 1"
    ID_LINECOLOR               "Color: black"
END
```

These last two strings contain some initial default text that is to be displayed in the two user informational panes on the status bar. They are needed because they provide the initial width of each of these panes. The framework makes sure that each user pane is sufficiently wide enough to hold the above text.

Implementing Decorations in the FrameWin Class

Let's begin by examining the construction and use of the normal main tool bar and status bar which are created using the new style approach. Then, with the basics down, we'll look at the tool box construction which is created using the older style method. Examine the **FrameWin** class definition. I have highlighted the key items.

FrameWin Definition

```
// MainFrm.h : interface of the FrameWin class
//
#pragma once
#include "DrawWin.h"
#include "CToolBox.h"

/***************************************************************/
/*                                                             */
/* FrameWin Class Definition                                   */
/*                                                             */
/***************************************************************/

class FrameWin : public CFrameWnd {

 /*************************************************************/
 /*                                                           */
 /* Class Data Members                                        */
 /*                                                           */
 /*************************************************************/

protected:

CStatusBar m_wndStatusBar; // our status bar
```

```
CToolBar    m_wndToolBar;    // our normal tool bar
CToolBox    m_wndToolBox;    // tool box of line widths and colors
DrawWin     m_wndView;       // the client window for drawing

int         linesel;    // current line width selection
int         colorsel;   // current color selection

 /*********************************************************/
 /*                                                       */
 /* Class Functions                                       */
 /*                                                       */
 /*********************************************************/

public:
 FrameWin();
protected:
 DECLARE_DYNAMIC(FrameWin)

// Attributes
public:

// Operations
public:

// Overrides
public:
 virtual BOOL PreCreateWindow (CREATESTRUCT& cs);
 virtual BOOL OnCmdMsg (UINT nID, int nCode, void* pExtra,
                       AFX_CMDHANDLERINFO* pHandlerInfo);

// Implementation
public:
 virtual ~FrameWin();
#ifdef _DEBUG
 virtual void AssertValid() const;
 virtual void Dump(CDumpContext& dc) const;
#endif

// Generated message map functions
protected:
 afx_msg int  OnCreate(LPCREATESTRUCT lpCreateStruct);
 afx_msg void OnSetFocus(CWnd *pOldWnd);
 afx_msg void OnClose ();
         int  DisplayMsg (int, int, UINT);

//             command processors
afx_msg void  CmLines (UINT);   // process line width btn presses
afx_msg void  CmColors (UINT);  // process color btns presses
// enabler sets the selected width button down - all others up
afx_msg void  OnUpdateToolBoxLines (CCmdUI*);
// enabler sets the selected color button down - all others up
afx_msg void  OnUpdateToolBoxColors (CCmdUI*);

// handles hiding and showing and the checkmark on View Tool Box
afx_msg void  OnUpdateViewToolBox (CCmdUI*);

//             dummy command processors - enables some buttons
afx_msg void  CmFontChange ();
afx_msg void  CmFileNew ();
afx_msg void  CmFileOpen ();
afx_msg void  CmFileSave ();
afx_msg void  CmFileSaveAs ();
afx_msg void  CmFilePrint ();
afx_msg void  CmFilePrinterSetup ();
```

```

 DECLARE_MESSAGE_MAP()
};
```

Notice that **FrameWin** defines four key member instances: **CStatusBar m_wndStatusBar, CToolBar m_wndToolBar, CToolBox m_wndToolBox, and DrawWin m_wndView**. In all four cases, when an instance of **FrameWin** is allocated, the compiler calls the default constructors to allocate the C++ wrapper portion, the Interface Object. In **OnCreate**, after the frame window has been constructed, we must explicitly call each of these four objects' create functions.

The other two data members are tracking the current line width selection and the current color chosen by the user: **linesel** and **colorsel**. When a tool box button is pressed, the frame window obtains the new setting, sends a notification message of that change on down to the **DrawWin**, and displays the new setting on the status bar.

Control Bar and Status Bar Construction

The **FrameWin** constructor sets the current line width to 1 and the current color to the index for black. Notice that the familiar coding to call create is no longer present here. LoadFrame now handles that operation. The next function is **OnCreate**. It is here that all of the decorations are created. Let's examine the sequences and function calls needed for the new style tool bars and the status bar. Then, we will see how it is done by using the old style approach for our tool box.

As always, the first action in **OnCreate** is to call the proper base class to actually build the frame window. Next, we call the **Create** function for the **DrawWin** child window. If it should fail to construct, I displayed a short message on the Debugger's Output window using the **TRACE0** macro. The **TRACE0** macro displays a string only when compiled in the DEBUG mode. It has no effect in a RELEASE build. (There are several other forms of the TRACE macro if you are interested in using it.)

```
if (CFrameWnd::OnCreate(lpCreateStruct) == -1)
 return -1;
// create a view to occupy the client area of the frame
if (!m_wndView.Create(NULL, NULL, AFX_WS_DEFAULT_VIEW,
 CRect(0, 0, 0, 0), this, AFX_IDW_PANE_FIRST, NULL))
{
 TRACE0("Failed to create view window\n");
 return -1;
}
```

This looks like a typical call to a **Create** function. The initial size of the window specified by the **CRect** object is utterly irrelevant; it is just a place holder here. The frame window will shortly be resizing all of its child windows to fit within the actual dimensions of the frame window.

There are two special MFC identifiers here: **AFX_WS_DEFAULT_VIEW** and **AFX_IDW_PANE_FIRST**. Normally the first parameter to **Create** is the return value from **AfxRegisterWndClass**. Here, it is 0 along with the window name second parameter. The MFC has several built-in, predefined, preregistered classes for our use. **AFX_WS_DEFAULT_VIEW** is one of them. It provides a default child window style. The second special identifier is being used as the unique child window identifier. By using this special identifier, **AFX_IDW_PANE_FIRST**, the framework will completely maintain that window for us, resizing it as the frame resizes, even destroying and deleting it for us when the frame window is destroyed. If you have a second or third or fourth child window, simple give them successive identifiers based on this initial one. That is, a second child window would be given the id of **AFX_IDW_PANE_FIRST + 1**, and so on.

Next, the main tool bar is created using the new style method which means that the corresponding command identifiers that the buttons represent are defined in the resource file as a **TOOLBAR** with the same identifier as the tool bar image.

```
// new style tool bar creation with button defs in the rc file
if (!m_wndToolBar.CreateEx (this, TBSTYLE_FLAT, WS_CHILD |
          WS_VISIBLE | CBRS_TOP | CBRS_GRIPPER | CBRS_TOOLTIPS |
          CBRS_FLYBY | CBRS_SIZE_DYNAMIC) ||
    !m_wndToolBar.LoadToolBar(IDR_MAINFRAME)) {
 TRACE0 ("Failed to create the main toolbar\n");
```

```
  return -1;
 }
```

This creates the toolbar. However, by also setting the button text, we can create fancier buttons. These are adding a text message that appears below the buttons.

```
 // for normal tool bar buttons, omit these lines
 // these lines set the text below each button
 m_wndToolBar.SetButtonText (0, "Quit");
 m_wndToolBar.SetButtonText (1, "New");
 m_wndToolBar.SetButtonText (2, "Open");
 m_wndToolBar.SetButtonText (3, "Save");
 m_wndToolBar.SetButtonText (4, "Save As");
 m_wndToolBar.SetButtonText (6, "Cut");
 m_wndToolBar.SetButtonText (7, "Copy");
 m_wndToolBar.SetButtonText (8, "Paste");
 m_wndToolBar.SetButtonText (10, "Print");
 m_wndToolBar.SetButtonText (12, "About");
 m_wndToolBar.SetSizes (CSize(55,40), CSize(16,15));
 // this sets the total size of the combined image and text
```

This rather lengthy statement calls the extended create function so that some additional style values can be set, and, if the creation is successful, the actual image file is loaded using the **LoadToolBar** function. The buttons then correspond to the RC file's corresponding **TOOLBAR** grouping. Some of the extended style values are as follows.

TBSTYLE_FLAT—Creates a flat toolbar in which both the toolbar and the buttons are transparent and hot-tracking is enabled. Button text appears under button bitmaps. When the mouse is over a button, the button appears raised.

TBSTYLE_LIST—Creates a flat toolbar with button text to the right of the bitmap and is otherwise identical to TBSTYLE_FLAT.

TBSTYLE_TRANSPARENT—Creates a transparent toolbar in which the toolbar is transparent but the buttons are not.

TBSTYLE_WRAPABLE—Creates a toolbar that can have multiple lines of buttons. Toolbar buttons can "wrap" to the next line when the toolbar becomes too narrow to include all buttons on the same line. We will use this one with the tool box.

There are a number of control bars identifiers as well. Some of these include the following.

```
CBRS_TOOLTIPS—displays tool tips
CBRS_FLYBY—display flyby hints
CBRS_GRIPPER—shows a gripper bar for dragging
CBRS_SIZE_DYNAMIC—the bar is variable in size and can be resided by the user
CBRS_SIZE_FIXED—the bar is fixed in size and cannot be resized by the user
CBRS_TOP—the bar is at the top of the frame
CBRS_BOTTOM—the bar is at the bottom of the frame
CBRS_LEFT—the bar is at the left side of the frame
CBRS_RIGHT—the bar is at the right side of the frame
CBRS_ALIGN_ANY—allows control to be docked on any side
CBRS_ALIGN_TOP—allows control to be docked at top of frame
CBRS_ALIGN_BOTTOM— allows control to be docked on bottom of frame
CBRS_ALIGN_LEFT—allows control to be docked on left of frame
CBRS_ALIGN_RIGHT—allows control to be docked on right of frame
CBRS_BORDER_TOP—draws a top border around control
CBRS_BORDER_BOTTOM—draws a bottom border around control
CBRS_BORDER_LEFT—draws a left border around control
CBRS_BORDER_RIGHT—draws a right border around control
```

If you pass 0 to **CreateEx** instead of **TBSTYLE_FLAT**, then you get the normal old style buttons that appear raised when not in use and appear depressed when pressed. Go ahead and try it out; see the difference.

The **SetButtonText** is passed the zero-based offset of the button along with the test to show. Do not forget to include each separator in the numerical count. The last function call, **SetSizes**, tells the bar what the correct total size of each button should be. I determined this value by trial and error. It is based primarily on the length of the largest text message. If you leave these lines out, then the tool bar consists only of the tiny 16x15 button images.

There are some additional function calls that must be made for the tool bar to operate, but these are done after constructing the tool box and status bar. The status bar construction is done this way.

```
if (!m_wndStatusBar.Create(this) ||
  !m_wndStatusBar.SetIndicators(indicators,
    sizeof(indicators)/sizeof(UINT)))
{
  TRACE0("Failed to create status bar\n");
  return -1;       // fail to create
}
```

In contrast to a tool bar create, the status bar is simple. However, the additional panes must be installed by calling **SetIndicators**. In the global area of the **FrameWin.cpp** file, a global array of unsigned integers called **indicators** must be defined.

```
static UINT indicators[] = {
  ID_SEPARATOR,
  ID_LINEWIDTH,   // pane for line width message
  ID_LINECOLOR,   // pane for line color message
  ID_INDICATOR_CAPS,
  ID_INDICATOR_NUM,
  ID_INDICATOR_SCRL,
};
```

The **static** keyword makes this global array called indicators known only in this cpp file. Without that qualifier, this array could be accessed from any other cpp file by use of the **extern** keyword.

The **ID_SEPARATOR** is used to allow a bit of a separation from the far left large pane where the flyover hints are displayed. Notice that I included the identifiers for the two new panes that are to show the current line width and color in use. These are followed by the status indicator ids. Notice that all of these ids must have a corresponding String table entry. The construction uses the width of each corresponding string to automatically size each pane.

The old style method is used to create the tool box.

```
if (!m_wndToolBox.Create (this, WS_CHILD | WS_VISIBLE |
                    CBRS_SIZE_FIXED | CBRS_TOP | CBRS_TOOLTIPS |
   // substitute CBRS_SIZE_DYNAMIC for CBRS_SIZE_FIXED to see
   // user adjustable number of columns when box is floating
                    CBRS_FLYBY, IDB_TOOLBOX)
        || !m_wndToolBox.LoadBitmap (IDB_TOOLBOX)
        || !m_wndToolBox.SetButtons (buttons_box,
                           sizeof(buttons_box)/sizeof(UINT))) {
  TRACE0 ("Failed to create the tool box\n");
  return -1;
}
m_wndToolBox.SetButtons .SetColumns (2); // set tool box numcols
```

Here the **Create** function is used because I do not want the new raised button when pressed effect. Notice that this tool box is using the **CBRS_SIZE_FIXED** flag. That is because I always want to have the tool box shown with two columns per each row. With four line width buttons and six color choice buttons, no other number of columns per row looks good, in my opinion. If you want to experiment, change this flag to **CBRS_SIZE_DYNAMIC** and undock the tool box and resize it.

Instead of calling the **LoadToolBar** function, the old style method calls **LoadBitmap** to load in the image file. The corresponding command identifiers and separators are established via the **SetButtons** function that uses another global unsigned integer array of command identifiers, called **buttons_box**.

```
static UINT BASED_CODE buttons_box[] = {
  CM_LINE1,
  CM_LINE2,
  CM_LINE3,
  CM_LINE4,
  ID_SEPARATOR,
  ID_SEPARATOR,
```

```
   CM_COLORA,
   CM_COLORB,
   CM_COLORC,
   CM_COLORD,
   CM_COLORE,
   CM_COLORF,
};
```

The **SetColumns** function can be called to adjust the number of columns desired, here 2. However, that is also the default that I coded in the derived class constructor, so that this call is really not needed here. The **CToolBox** derived class is very simple and is used to align the buttons into columns. So let's defer examining that class until the remainder of tool bar construction is finished.

Next, we **must** handle the docking situation. This is a two-step process. Each tool bar **must** be notified where it is allowed to dock, top, bottom, left, and right. Then, the frame window itself **must** be notified where we are going to allow tool bars to be docked. Notice that both calls are needed. Both the tool bar class and the frame window class have an **EnableDocking** function.

```
m_wndToolBar.EnableDocking (CBRS_ALIGN_ANY);
m_wndToolBox.EnableDocking (CBRS_ALIGN_ANY);
EnableDocking (CBRS_ALIGN_ANY);
```

Next, we should specify where the tool bars are to be initially docked when the application launches using the **DockControlBar** function.

```
DockControlBar (&m_wndToolBar, AFX_IDW_DOCKBAR_TOP);
DockControlBar (&m_wndToolBox, AFX_IDW_DOCKBAR_RIGHT);
```

The first parameter is the address of the tool bar to be docked and the second is a **UINT** specifying where to dock it. It can be one of the following

```
AFX_IDW_DOCBAR_TOP
AFX_IDW_DOCBAR_BOTTOM
AFX_IDW_DOCBAR_LEFT
AFX_IDW_DOCBAR_RIGHT
```

The next step programmers often overlook. A window caption should be installed. Otherwise, should a user undocks the tool bar, the tool bar floating window has no caption!

```
m_wndToolBar.SetWindowText (_T("Main Controls"));
m_wndToolBox.SetWindowText (_T("Box"));
```

Sometimes, the initial size of a status bar pane is not sufficiently large enough to hold the largest status message. A pane can be enlarged by calling the **SetPaneInfo** function and specifying a new total width.

```
statusbar.SetPaneInfo (2,ID_LINECOLOR, 0, 80);
```

The last step in **OnCreate** is to send a notification message of the current line width and color choice in use. We can **invent** our own messages to send. Make up a command id value that is unique as usual. The meaning of the **wparam** and **lparam** can be anything that we desire. In this case, I chose to have **wparam** contain the new line width or color selection index. **lparam** is not used.

```
m_wndView.SendMessage (CM_LINECHANGE, linesel, 0L);
m_wndView.SendMessage (CM_COLORCHANGE, colorsel, 0L);
```

In the receiving window class, the message map entry for an invented new message is **ON_MESSAGE**.

```
ON_MESSAGE(CM_LINECHANGE, CmLineChange)
ON_MESSAGE(CM_COLORCHANGE, CmColorChange)
```

And the prototypes for these new message handlers are as follows.

```
afx_msg LRESULT CmLineChange (WPARAM, LPARAM);
afx_msg LRESULT CmColorChange (WPARAM, LPARAM);
```

They are passed the **wparam** and **lparam** values. The **LRESULT** or **long** return value indicates whether or not the function handled the message. A return value of 0 means that the message was handled.

The _T is one of several data-type mappings, defined in **TCHAR.H**, which provide for proper encoding of data independent of the encoding platform. While we normally use the default generic encoding scheme, some applications may wish to use the UNICODE form. By defining your constant data using the data-type mappings, defining or undefining the constant _UNICODE and recompiling, you can switch between encoding schemes. The data-type mappings for the default generic text types consist of the following.

Generic-Text Data Type Mappings

_TCHAR	char
_TINT	int
_TSCHAR	signed char
_TUCHAR	unsigned char
_TXCHAR	char
_T or _TEXT	No effect (removed by preprocessor)

If you examine the MFC code, you will see these various data-type mappings in action.

From now on, the framework handles all of the docking and hint actions. When the cursor is over a button for about a second, tool tips are displayed. The instant the cursor is over the button, flyover hints appear. How are the hints found? From a string resource that has the same string ID as the button ID. A tool tip comes after the flyover hint separated by a newline code, \n. For example, the hint string for File|Open might be this.

```
CM_FILEOPEN, "Opens an existing file\nOpen"
```

Remember that tool tips should only be one or two words while flyover hints can be quite lengthy.

The Tool Box Derived Class

The derived **CToolBox** class must handle the placement of the buttons into rows of 2 columns each. While each of the ten objects on the tool bar image look like buttons, they should operate as if they were two sets of radio buttons with the current selections remaining in the depressed state. Each of the buttons must have the **TBBS_CHECKBOX** style added to it when the button is created. Thus, to easily constrain the box to two columns and initialize the buttons' style, I have derived a **CToolBox** class from **CToolBar**. Additionally, a static array of color strings is defined for use in displaying the current color selection on the status bar.

CToolBox Class Definition

```
#pragma once

/*******************************************************************/
/*                                                                 */
/* CToolBox Class Definition                                       */
/*                                                                 */
/*******************************************************************/

class CToolBox : public CToolBar {

 /*****************************************************************/
 /*                                                               */
 /* Class Data Members                                            */
 /*                                                               */
 /*****************************************************************/

public:

static const char colors[6][7]; // the colors represented

protected:

UINT     m_nColumns;             // number of columns of buttons

 /*****************************************************************/
```

```
 /*                                                             */
 /* Class Functions:                                            */
 /*                                                             */
 /**************************************************************/

public:

         CToolBox ();                  // constructor
virtual ~CToolBox () {}

void     SetColumns (UINT nColumns); // set the number of columns
UINT     GetColumns ();              // get the number of columns

DECLARE_MESSAGE_MAP()
};
```

The other data member is the number of columns the tool box currently has. The constructor specifies that there are to be two columns per row initially. Also, the constructor initializes the four margin widths of the base **CToolBar** class. I find using only 1 pixel yields a pleasing border, while 4 pixels seems too great a space for my tastes. **GetColumns** returns the current number of columns. All the real work is done in **SetColumns** which must actually layout the buttons into the indicated number of columns.

```
CToolBox Class Implementation
```

```
#include "stdafx.h"
#include "CToolBox.h"

const char CToolBox::colors[6][7] = {
                 "Black","Red","Green","Yellow","Blue","Purple"};

/**************************************************************/
/*                                                            */
/* CToolBox Events Response Table                             */
/*                                                            */
/**************************************************************/

BEGIN_MESSAGE_MAP(CToolBox, CToolBar)
END_MESSAGE_MAP()

/**************************************************************/
/*                                                            */
/* CToolBox Constructor                                       */
/*                                                            */
/**************************************************************/

CToolBox::CToolBox () {
 m_nColumns        = 2; // set for two columns
 m_cxLeftBorder    = 1; // set a margin
 m_cxRightBorder   = 1; // these fields belong to the base
 m_cyTopBorder     = 1; // CToolBar class
 m_cyBottomBorder  = 1;
}

/**************************************************************/
/*                                                            */
/* GetColumns: return the number of columns in use            */
/*                                                            */
/**************************************************************/

UINT CToolBox::GetColumns () {
 return m_nColumns;
}
```

```

/*************************************************************/
/*                                                           */
/* SetColumns: layout the box using the passed num of columns */
/*             and set each button with the radio btn style  */
/*             and layout the column breaks where needed     */
/*                                                           */
/*************************************************************/

void      CToolBox::SetColumns (UINT numcols) {
 m_nColumns = numcols;
 // get total number buttons to do
 int numbtns = GetToolBarCtrl ().GetButtonCount ();
 // for each button, install checkbox style
 // for each button that begins a new row, install wrapped style
 for (int i=0; i<numbtns; i++) {
  UINT style = GetButtonStyle (i);  // get current button style
  BOOL wrap = (((i + 1) % numcols) == 0);// find column wrap spot
  if (wrap) style |= TBBS_WRAPPED;  // enable wrapped on this one
  else style &= ~TBBS_WRAPPED;      // or disable wrapped
  style |= TBBS_CHECKBOX;           // add in the check box style
  SetButtonStyle (i, style);        // and save as it's new style
 }
 Invalidate ();
 // force toolbar to use new layout
 GetParentFrame ()->RecalcLayout ();
}
```

The function **GetToolBarCtrl** retrieves a pointer to the base class of the **CToolBar**, the Windows **CToolBarCtrl**. **GetButtonCount** retrieves the number of buttons currently installed so we can iterate through all buttons, at least adding in the **TBBS_CHECKBOX** style. Each button's style is retrieved by the **GetButtonStyle** function and is reset by **SetButtonStyle**. Since the buttons are in order, a simple % (remainder or mod) operation can tell us when to add the **TBBS_WRAPPED** style. Since potentially you might want to have more or fewer columns, the code dynamically removes and adds the wrapped style.

Just for your information, the button styles include the following.

button types:

```
TBBS_BUTTON    - defines a push button
TBBS_SEPARATOR - defines a separator button
TBBS_CHECKBOX  - defines a pushbutton that acts like a
                 checkmark
```

button states:

```
TBBS_PRESSED   - show in the pressed state
TBBS_CHECKED   - show in the checked state
TBBS_ENABLED   - enable the button
```

Also for your information, the Windows control bar, **CToolBarCtrl**, from which **CToolBar** is derived, uses the very same actual toolbox bitmap strip of button images. However, much more information is required than just the command ID that corresponds to a button. A new structure, **TBBUTTON**, has the following members that more completely define a button.

```
int iBitmap;     // zero-based index of button image
int idCommand;   // command ID sent when button is pressed
BYTE fsState;    // button state
BYTE fsStyle;    // button style
DWORD dwData;    // application defined value
int iString;     // zero-based index of label string, if any
```

The button state flags is an ORed combination of one or more of the following.

```
TBSTYLE_ENABLED - button is enabled - normal active state
TBSTYLE_CHECKED - button is displayed as pressed or checked
TBSTYLE_PRESSED - button is being pressed right now
TBSTYLE_WRAP    - a line break follows this button
```

```
TBSTYLE_HIDDEN  - button is not visible (for separators)
TBSTYLE_INDETERMINATE - button is grayed
```

The button style is an ORed combination of one or more of the following.

```
TBSTYLE_BUTTON - a standard pushbutton
TBSTYLE_CHECK  - toggles between checked and unchecked serves
                 both radio buttons and check box styles
TBSTYLE_CHECKGROUP - creates a check button in a group that
                     stays pressed until another button in
                     that group is pressed
TBSTYLE_GROUP  - similar to check group
TBSTYLE_SEP    - creates a separator control - not visible
```

Other style options include these.

```
TBSTYLE_TOOLTIPS   - causes tool tips to be used
TBSTYLE_WRAPABLE   - control can have multiple lines of buttons
```

If the button displays text, an index into an array of strings must be provided so the control can find the text to display. There is no **CWnd** style set text type of function. The ten buttons and two separators could then be defined as follows.

```
    TBBUTTON buttons_box[] = {
 {0, CM_LINE1,  TBSTATE_ENABLED, TBSTYLE_CHECKGROUP, 0, NULL },
 {1, CM_LINE2,  TBSTATE_ENABLED, TBSTYLE_CHECKGROUP, 0, NULL },
 {2, CM_LINE3,  TBSTATE_ENABLED, TBSTYLE_CHECKGROUP, 0, NULL },
 {3, CM_LINE4,  TBSTATE_ENABLED, TBSTYLE_CHECKGROUP, 0, NULL },
 {0, 0,         TBSTATE_ENABLED, TBSTYLE_SEP,        0, NULL},
 {0, 0,         TBSTATE_ENABLED, TBSTYLE_SEP,        0, NULL},
 {4, CM_COLORA, TBSTATE_ENABLED, TBSTYLE_CHECKGROUP, 0, NULL },
 {5, CM_COLORB, TBSTATE_ENABLED, TBSTYLE_CHECKGROUP, 0, NULL },
 {6, CM_COLORC, TBSTATE_ENABLED, TBSTYLE_CHECKGROUP, 0, NULL },
 {7, CM_COLORD, TBSTATE_ENABLED, TBSTYLE_CHECKGROUP, 0, NULL },
 {8, CM_COLORE, TBSTATE_ENABLED, TBSTYLE_CHECKGROUP, 0, NULL },
 {9, CM_COLORF, TBSTATE_ENABLED, TBSTYLE_CHECKGROUP, 0, NULL }
};
```

The MFC Message Map Entries for a Consecutive Range of Command IDs

The MFC message map macros offer two "range of ID commands"—one for a consecutive series of commands and one for the corresponding command enabler functions. The macros are called **ON_COMMAND_RANGE** and **ON_UPDATE_COMMAND_UI_RANGE**.

These message macros take three operands instead of the normal two. The first operand is the beginning command ID of the range of messages; the second operand is the last ID in the consecutive range; and the third operand is the member function to be invoked. That is why I have used successive command ID numbers in the resource header file for **CM_LINE1** through **CM_LINE4** and for **CM_COLORA** through **CM_COLORF**. The **FrameWin** message map to respond to the ten buttons becomes simply this.

```
BEGIN_MESSAGE_MAP(FrameWin, CFrameWnd)
 ON_COMMAND_RANGE(CM_LINE1, CM_LINE4, CmLines)
 ON_COMMAND_RANGE(CM_COLORA, CM_COLORF, CmColors)
END_MESSAGE_MAP()
```

When the two member functions are invoked, the actual command ID number that corresponds to the button that was pressed is passed as a **UINT**, unlike a normal command handler which has no parameters. Thus, the function prototypes appear in the class header file as follows.

```
afx_msg void CmLines (UINT);
afx_msg void CmColors (UINT);
```

It becomes a simple matter to calculate the line width and color index numbers from command IDs. Once the new line width or color index is known, then a **WM_MESSAGE** or a user message is sent to the **DrawWin** window. With user messages, **WPARAM** and **LPARAM** are used to pass additional user-defined information. Here, **wparam** contains either the line width or the color index. For **CmLines**, we have the following.

```
void      FrameWin::CmLines (UINT cmd) {
 linesel = cmd - CM_LINE1 + 1;
 m_wndView.SendMessage (CM_LINECHANGE, linesel, 0L);
 char msg[20];
 wsprintf (msg, "Width: %d", linesel);
 statusbar.SetPaneText (1, msg);
}
```

Back in the to the **DrawWin**, the new message is accessed this way.

```
ON_MESSAGE(CM_COLORCHANGE, CmColorChange);
afx_msg LRESULT  CmColorChange (WPARAM, LPARAM);
```

Displaying Information on the Status Bar

The above also shows how to display information in one of our panes on the status bar. The **SetPaneText** function is passed the zero-based pane number and the new text to display.

```
m_wndStatusBar.SetPaneText (1, msg);
```

The third parameter to **SetPaneText** is a **BOOL** that defaults to **TRUE**. When **TRUE**, the pane is invalidated so the new text can be painted. This is usually what we want.

Sometimes, an application has many such items to display on the status bar. In such cases, you might create a **DisplayOnStatusBar** function that is passed all the items to display.

Sometimes, a child window or some other class wishes to display some text on the status bar. If the status bar instance is public access, then it can readily be done. The global function **AfxGetApp** returns a pointer to the **CWinApp** whose data member **m_pMainWnd** points to the main frame window. A pointer to any child window, which includes the draw window, tool box, control bar, and the status bar, in this case, can be obtained by passing that window's ID to the **GetDescendantWindow** function. What is not so obvious is that the internal ID for the status bar is **AFX_IDW_STATUS_BAR**.

```
CStatusBar *ptrbar = (CStatusBar*) AfxGetApp()->m_pMainWnd->
                    GetDescendantWindow (AFX_IDW_STATUS_BAR);
char msg[80];
wsprintf (msg, "Draw: line width: %d - Color: %s",
         linewidth, col[colnum]);
ptrbar->SetPaneText (0, msg);
```

The above displays the message in the flyover hint area. Of course, this is a transitory message since as soon as you move the mouse over another control, it is replaced with the current flyover hint.

The drawback of doing the status bar updating in these other locations than the **FrameWin** owning class is having to remember the status bar display techniques. What I often do in such cases is create a **FrameWin** helper function, such as **DisplaySBMsg** that is passed the string text and does the displaying. This has the benefit of encapsulating all of the status bar actions to the **FrameWin** owner class.

Hiding and Showing Tool Boxes

If the ID of the menu item to hide/show the toolbox is the bmp resource ID number, the framework can handle hiding and showing our tool box with only a small effort on our part. To the message map, add two entries.

```
ON_UPDATE_COMMAND_UI(IDB_TOOLBOX, OnUpdateViewToolBox)
ON_COMMAND_EX(IDB_TOOLBOX, OnBarCheck)
```

The command enabler actually handles the check mark. If the box is currently visible, the enabler passes **TRUE** to the **SetCheck** enabler function. If not, **FALSE** is passed and no check mark is displayed.

```
void FrameWin::OnUpdateViewToolBox (CCmdUI *ptrui) {
 ptrui->SetCheck ((toolbox.GetStyle() & WS_VISIBLE) != 0);
}
```

The second entry in the message map is lifted from the MFC framework coding and handles the work of actually hiding or reshowing the tool box as if it were any other normal tool bar. The undocumented **ON_COMMAND_EX** macro works similarly to the usual **ON_COMMAND** except that it passes control to internal framework command targets. Specifically in this case, the framework function **OnBarCheck** handles the desired hide/show operations for us. If we use this magic, then we do not have to do any coding to hide or reshow our tool box.

Here is the complete **FrameWin** coding.

FrameWin Implementation

```
// FrameWin.cpp : implementation of the FrameWin class
//

#include "stdafx.h"
#include "Pgm10a.h"
#include "FrameWin.h"

#ifdef _DEBUG
#define new DEBUG_NEW
#endif

IMPLEMENT_DYNAMIC(FrameWin, CFrameWnd)

BEGIN_MESSAGE_MAP(FrameWin, CFrameWnd)
 ON_WM_CREATE()
 ON_WM_SETFOCUS()
 ON_WM_CLOSE ()
 ON_COMMAND(CM_FONTCHANGE, CmFontChange)
 ON_COMMAND(CM_FILENEW, CmFileNew)
 ON_COMMAND(CM_FILEOPEN, CmFileOpen)
 ON_COMMAND(CM_FILESAVE, CmFileSave)
 ON_COMMAND(CM_FILESAVEAS, CmFileSaveAs)
 ON_COMMAND(CM_FILEPRINT, CmFilePrint)
 ON_COMMAND(CM_FILEPRINTERSETUP, CmFilePrinterSetup)
 ON_UPDATE_COMMAND_UI(IDB_TOOLBOX, OnUpdateViewToolBox)
 ON_COMMAND_EX(IDB_TOOLBOX, OnBarCheck)
 ON_COMMAND_RANGE(CM_LINE1, CM_LINE4, CmLines)
 ON_COMMAND_RANGE(CM_COLORA, CM_COLORF, CmColors)
 ON_UPDATE_COMMAND_UI_RANGE(CM_LINE1, CM_LINE4,
                            OnUpdateToolBoxLines)
 ON_UPDATE_COMMAND_UI_RANGE(CM_COLORA, CM_COLORF,
                            OnUpdateToolBoxColors)
END_MESSAGE_MAP()

static UINT indicators[] =
{
 ID_SEPARATOR,           // status line indicator
 ID_LINEWIDTH,
 ID_LINECOLOR,
};
```

```

/***************************************************************/
/*                                                             */
/* Old Style Method of Tool Bar Construction                   */
/*                                                             */
/***************************************************************/

static UINT BASED_CODE buttons_box[] = {
  CM_LINE1,
  CM_LINE2,
  CM_LINE3,
  CM_LINE4,
  ID_SEPARATOR,
  ID_SEPARATOR,
  CM_COLORA,
  CM_COLORB,
  CM_COLORC,
  CM_COLORD,
  CM_COLORE,
  CM_COLORF,
};

/***************************************************************/
/*                                                             */
/* FrameWin Class construction                                 */
/*                                                             */
/***************************************************************/

FrameWin::FrameWin() {
 linesel = 1;          // set initial pen width
 colorsel = 0;         // set initial black color
}

FrameWin::~FrameWin() {
}

/***************************************************************/
/*                                                             */
/* OnCreate: build and install all tool bars and status bar    */
/*                                                             */
/***************************************************************/

int FrameWin::OnCreate(LPCREATESTRUCT lpCreateStruct)
{
 if (CFrameWnd::OnCreate(lpCreateStruct) == -1)
  return -1;
 // create a view to occupy the client area of the frame
 if (!m_wndView.Create(NULL, NULL, AFX_WS_DEFAULT_VIEW,
  CRect(0, 0, 0, 0), this, AFX_IDW_PANE_FIRST, NULL))
 {
  TRACE0("Failed to create view window\n");
  return -1;
 }

 // new style tool bar creation with button defs in the rc file
 if (!m_wndToolBar.CreateEx (this, TBSTYLE_FLAT, WS_CHILD |
           WS_VISIBLE | CBRS_TOP | CBRS_GRIPPER | CBRS_TOOLTIPS |
           CBRS_FLYBY | CBRS_SIZE_DYNAMIC) ||
     !m_wndToolBar.LoadToolBar(IDR_MAINFRAME)) {
  TRACE0 ("Failed to create the main toolbar\n");
  return -1;
 }

 // for normal tool bar buttons, omit these lines
```

```
 // these lines set the text below each button
 m_wndToolBar.SetButtonText (0, "Quit");
 m_wndToolBar.SetButtonText (1, "New");
 m_wndToolBar.SetButtonText (2, "Open");
 m_wndToolBar.SetButtonText (3, "Save");
 m_wndToolBar.SetButtonText (4, "Save As");
 m_wndToolBar.SetButtonText (6, "Cut");
 m_wndToolBar.SetButtonText (7, "Copy");
 m_wndToolBar.SetButtonText (8, "Paste");
 m_wndToolBar.SetButtonText (10, "Print");
 m_wndToolBar.SetButtonText (12, "About");
 m_wndToolBar.SetSizes (CSize(55,40), CSize(16,15));
 // this sets the total size of the combined image and text

 if (!m_wndStatusBar.Create(this) ||
  !m_wndStatusBar.SetIndicators(indicators,
    sizeof(indicators)/sizeof(UINT)))
 {
  TRACE0("Failed to create status bar\n");
  return -1;      // fail to create
 }

 //now create the tool box using the old style method
 if (!m_wndToolBox.Create (this, WS_CHILD | WS_VISIBLE |
                     CBRS_SIZE_FIXED | CBRS_TOP | CBRS_TOOLTIPS |
   // substitute CBRS_SIZE_DYNAMIC for CBRS_SIZE_FIXED to see
   // user adjustable number of columns when box is floating
                     CBRS_FLYBY, IDB_TOOLBOX)
        || !m_wndToolBox.LoadBitmap (IDB_TOOLBOX)
        || !m_wndToolBox.SetButtons (buttons_box,
                             sizeof(buttons_box)/sizeof(UINT))) {
  TRACE0 ("Failed to create the tool box\n");
  return -1;
 }

 // the following is not really needed in this case
 // the ctor has set it to 2 already
 m_wndToolBox.SetColumns (2); // set the tool box to 2 columns

 // now notify tool bars to accept any form of docking
 m_wndToolBar.EnableDocking (CBRS_ALIGN_ANY);
 m_wndToolBox.EnableDocking (CBRS_ALIGN_ANY);

 // notify the framewindow of docking requirements
 EnableDocking (CBRS_ALIGN_ANY);

 // dock main tool bar at the top and the tool box on the right
 DockControlBar (&m_wndToolBar, AFX_IDW_DOCKBAR_TOP);
 DockControlBar (&m_wndToolBox, AFX_IDW_DOCKBAR_RIGHT);

 // insert captions to be shown when the tool bars are floating
 m_wndToolBar.SetWindowText (_T("Main Controls"));
 m_wndToolBox.SetWindowText (_T("Box"));

 // set the max width of the color status bar pane
 m_wndStatusBar.SetPaneInfo (2,ID_LINECOLOR, 0, 80);

 // notify DrawWin of the initial line width and color selections
 m_wndView.SendMessage (CM_LINECHANGE, linesel, 0L);
 m_wndView.SendMessage (CM_COLORCHANGE, colorsel, 0L);

 return 0;
}

```

```
/********************************************************************/
/*                                                                  */
/* PreCreateWindow: adjust window style                             */
/*                                                                  */
/********************************************************************/

BOOL FrameWin::PreCreateWindow(CREATESTRUCT& cs)
{
 if( !CFrameWnd::PreCreateWindow(cs) )
  return FALSE;
 // TODO: Modify the Window class or styles here by modifying
 //  the CREATESTRUCT cs

 cs.dwExStyle &= ~WS_EX_CLIENTEDGE;
 cs.lpszClass = AfxRegisterWndClass(0);
 return TRUE;
}

// FrameWin diagnostics
#ifdef _DEBUG
void FrameWin::AssertValid() const { CFrameWnd::AssertValid(); }
void FrameWin::Dump(CDumpContext& dc) const{CFrameWnd::Dump(dc);}
#endif //_DEBUG

/********************************************************************/
/*                                                                  */
/* OnSetFocus: pass focus down to the DrawWin                       */
/*                                                                  */
/********************************************************************/

void FrameWin::OnSetFocus (CWnd* /*pOldWnd*/) {
 // forward focus to the view window
 m_wndView.SetFocus();
}

/********************************************************************/
/*                                                                  */
/* OnCmdMsg: pass messages on down to the DrawWin as well           */
/*                                                                  */
/********************************************************************/

BOOL FrameWin::OnCmdMsg (UINT nID, int nCode, void* pExtra,
                         AFX_CMDHANDLERINFO* pHandlerInfo) {
 // let the view have first crack at the command
 if (m_wndView.OnCmdMsg(nID, nCode, pExtra, pHandlerInfo))
  return TRUE;
 // otherwise, do default handling
 return CFrameWnd::OnCmdMsg(nID, nCode, pExtra, pHandlerInfo);
}

/********************************************************************/
/*                                                                  */
/* OnUpdateViewToolBox: command enabler for check mark on           */
/*        Menu View Tool Box - handles hiding and showing           */
/*                                                                  */
/********************************************************************/

void      FrameWin::OnUpdateViewToolBox (CCmdUI *ptrui) {
 // place check mark on menu item if tool box is now visible
 ptrui->SetCheck ((m_wndToolBox.GetStyle() & WS_VISIBLE) != 0);
}

/********************************************************************/
/*                                                                  */
```

```
/* CmLines: handle any of the line button presses               */
/*          get new line width, display on status bar           */
/*          and send a message to DrawWin                        */
/*                                                               */
/*****************************************************************/

void      FrameWin::CmLines (UINT cmd) {
 // line width is the command ID less the command ID of line 1 +1
 linesel = cmd - CM_LINE1 + 1;
 // send the new line width to DrawWin using a private message
 m_wndView.SendMessage (CM_LINECHANGE, linesel, 0L);
 // display new width on the status bar
 char msg[20];
 wsprintf (msg, "Width: %d", linesel);
 m_wndStatusBar.SetPaneText (1, msg);
}

/*****************************************************************/
/*                                                               */
/* CmColors: handle any of the color button presses              */
/*          get new line color, display on status bar           */
/*          and send a message to DrawWin                        */
/*                                                               */
/*****************************************************************/

void      FrameWin::CmColors (UINT cmd) {
 //color idx is the command ID less the command ID of first color
 colorsel = cmd - CM_COLORA;
 // send the color number to DrawWin using a private message
 m_wndView.SendMessage (CM_COLORCHANGE, colorsel, 0L);
 // Display color choice on the status bar
 char msg[20];
 wsprintf (msg, "Color: %s", CtoolBox::colors[colorsel]);
 m_wndStatusBar.SetPaneText (2, msg);
}

/*****************************************************************/
/*                                                               */
/* OnUpdateToolBoxLines: set pressed state for current line     */
/*            width button and sets all others to not pressed   */
/*                                                               */
/*****************************************************************/

void      FrameWin::OnUpdateToolBoxLines (CCmdUI *ptrui) {
 ptrui->SetRadio ((UINT)(linesel + CM_LINE1 -1) == ptrui->m_nID);
}

/*****************************************************************/
/*                                                               */
/* OnUpdateToolBoxColors: set pressed state for current brush   */
/*                    color button and all others to unpressed */
/*                                                               */
/*****************************************************************/

void      FrameWin::OnUpdateToolBoxColors (CCmdUI *ptrui) {
 ptrui->SetRadio ((UINT)(colorsel + CM_COLORA) == ptrui->m_nID);
}

/*****************************************************************/
/*                                                               */
/* OnClose:  determine if the app can be shut down              */
/*                                                               */
/*****************************************************************/

```

```
void      FrameWin::OnClose () {
 if (DisplayMsg (IDS_MSG_QUERY, IDS_MSG_QUIT,
                 MB_YESNO | MB_ICONQUESTION) == IDYES)
  CFrameWnd::OnClose ();
}

/***************************************************************/
/*                                                             */
/* DisplayMsg: displays error message and return user response */
/*                                                             */
/***************************************************************/

int       FrameWin::DisplayMsg (int id1, int id2, UINT flags) {

 char msg1[80];
 char msg2[80];
 LoadString (AfxGetApp()->m_hInstance, id1, msg1, sizeof(msg1));
 LoadString (AfxGetApp()->m_hInstance, id2, msg2, sizeof(msg2));
 return MessageBox (msg2, msg1, flags);
}

/***************************************************************/
/*                                                             */
/* A Series of dummy command handlers so that all buttons are  */
/*             not grayed out                                  */
/*                                                             */
/***************************************************************/

void      FrameWin::CmFileNew () {
 MessageBox ("File New is not yet implemented", "File New",
             MB_ICONINFORMATION | MB_OK);
}
void      FrameWin::CmFileOpen () {
 MessageBox ("Open not implemented", "File Open",
             MB_ICONINFORMATION | MB_OK);
}
void      FrameWin::CmFileSave () {
 MessageBox ("Save not implemented","File Save",
             MB_ICONINFORMATION | MB_OK);
}
void      FrameWin::CmFileSaveAs () {
 MessageBox ("SaveAs not implemented", "File SaveAs",
             MB_ICONINFORMATION|MB_OK);
}
void      FrameWin::CmFilePrint () {
 MessageBox ("Print not implemented","File Print",
             MB_ICONINFORMATION | MB_OK);
}
void      FrameWin::CmFilePrinterSetup () {
 MessageBox ("Printer Setup not implemented",
            "File PrinterSetup",
             MB_ICONINFORMATION | MB_OK);
}
void      FrameWin::CmFontChange () {
 MessageBox ("Font change not implemented", "Font Change",
             MB_ICONINFORMATION | MB_OK);
}
```

The DrawWin Client Window and Capturing the Mouse

When drawing, capturing the mouse is often required. When the user presses the left button, we draw a line from where the cursor is currently located to all of the subsequent positions to which the mouse is moved while the left button remains held down. While that button is pressed, we **cannot** allow any other mouse events to be passed to **any** other window or control. Therefore, we **capture** all mouse events for the duration of the drawing cycle. The complicating factor is that drawing involves three separate mouse events and, therefore, three separate event functions. These are **OnLButtonDown**, **OnMouseMove**, and **OnLButtonUp**. The **bool** member **buttondown** is used to communicate between these three functions.

When the left button is pressed, **OnLButtonDown** does nothing if **buttondown** is **true** avoiding double click problems. If not, then a new pen is created using the current selections of line width and color and a **CClientDC** is gotten upon which to draw. The mouse actions are captured. The pen is positioned to the position where the left button was pressed and **buttondown** set to **true**. This then gives us a good idea of what data members and functions the **DrawWin** must have. Here is the class definition.

DrawWin Class Definition

```
#pragma once

/***************************************************************/
/*                                                             */
/* DrawWin Class Definition                                    */
/*                                                             */
/***************************************************************/

class DrawWin : public CWnd {

 /**************************************************************/
 /*                                                            */
 /* Class Data Members                                         */
 /*                                                            */
 /**************************************************************/

protected:
 COLORREF   colors[6];  // the possible colors array
 COLORREF   linecolor;  // current drawing pen color
 int        colnum;     // current pen color array index
 int        linewidth;  // current pen width
 bool       buttondown; // true if leftbutton is down for drawing
 CPen*      ptrpen;     // the current drawing pen
 CClientDC* ptrdc;      // the current drawing DC

 /**************************************************************/
 /*                                                            */
 /* Class Functions                                            */
 /*                                                            */
 /**************************************************************/

public:
              DrawWin ();
afx_msg void  OnPaint (); // paint backgrd white
virtual BOOL  PreCreateWindow(CREATESTRUCT& cs); // make window

protected:

afx_msg void  OnLButtonDown (UINT, CPoint); // begin drawing
afx_msg void  OnLButtonUp (UINT, CPoint);   // end drawing
afx_msg void  OnMouseMove (UINT, CPoint);   // continue drawing

afx_msg LRESULT CmLineChange (WPARAM, LPARAM);
afx_msg LRESULT CmColorChange (WPARAM, LPARAM);

DECLARE_MESSAGE_MAP()
```

```
};
```

What is perhaps not immediately obvious is just how we actually create the window in the first place. In this case, the window creation is done in **PreCreateWindow**. Let's examine the complete coding and then discuss the actual key drawing portions in detail.

DrawWin Class Implementation

```
#include "stdafx.h"
#include "Pgm10a.h"
#include "DrawWin.h"
#include "resource.h"

/*******************************************************************/
/*                                                                 */
/* Message Map                                                     */
/*                                                                 */
/*******************************************************************/

BEGIN_MESSAGE_MAP(DrawWin,CWnd )
 ON_WM_PAINT ()
 ON_WM_LBUTTONDOWN ()
 ON_WM_LBUTTONUP()
 ON_WM_MOUSEMOVE()
 ON_MESSAGE(CM_LINECHANGE, CmLineChange)
 ON_MESSAGE(CM_COLORCHANGE, CmColorChange)
END_MESSAGE_MAP()

/*******************************************************************/
/*                                                                 */
/* DrawWin: setup all initial values                               */
/*                                                                 */
/*******************************************************************/

DrawWin::DrawWin() {
 buttondown = false;            // signal not drawing now
 ptrpen     = 0;                // set no current pen
 ptrdc      = 0;                // or DC for drawing

 // initialize possible colors
 colors[0]  = RGB (0,0,0);       // Black
 colors[1]  = RGB (255, 0,0);    // LtRed
 colors[2]  = RGB (0, 255, 0);   // LtGreen
 colors[3]  = RGB (255, 255,0);  // LtYellow
 colors[4]  = RGB (0, 0, 255);   // LtBlue
 colors[5]  = RGB (255, 0,255);  // LtMagenta
 linecolor  = colors[2];         // set beginning pen color
 colnum     = 2;                 // set initial pen color index
 linewidth  = 2;                 // set initial pen width
}

/*******************************************************************/
/*                                                                 */
/* PreCreateWindow: register class for automatic OnCreate          */
/*                                                                 */
/*******************************************************************/

BOOL DrawWin::PreCreateWindow(CREATESTRUCT& cs) {
 if (!Cwnd::PreCreateWindow(cs)) return FALSE;
 cs.dwExStyle |= WS_EX_CLIENTEDGE;
 cs.style &= ~WS_BORDER;
 cs.lpszClass = AfxRegisterWndClass (
    CS_HREDRAW | CS_VREDRAW | CS_DBLCLKS,
```

```
     ::LoadCursor(NULL, IDC_ARROW),
     reinterpret_cast<HBRUSH>(COLOR_WINDOW+1), NULL);
 return TRUE;
}

/********************************************************************/
/*                                                                  */
/* OnLButtonDown: begin drawing                                     */
/*                                                                  */
/********************************************************************/

void DrawWin::OnLButtonDown (UINT, CPoint point) {
 if (!buttondown) {      // avoid multiple invocations by dblclick
  buttondown = true;              // signal drawing
  ptrdc  = new CClientDC (this);// get new draw DC
  linecolor = colors[colnum];    // set line RGB color to use
  ptrpen = new CPen (PS_SOLID, linewidth, linecolor);
  ptrdc->SelectObject (ptrpen); // install pen in DC
  SetCapture ();            // capture all mouse movements for draw
  ptrdc->MoveTo (point);  // set pen to starting point for draw
 }
}

/********************************************************************/
/*                                                                  */
/* OnLButtonUp: stop drawing the line                               */
/*                                                                  */
/********************************************************************/

void DrawWin::OnLButtonUp (UINT, CPoint) {
 if (buttondown) {
  if (ptrdc) delete ptrdc;    // stop drawing - remove GDI objects
  if (ptrpen) delete ptrpen; // if flurry of clicks, avoids crash
  buttondown = false;         // signal not drawing
  ReleaseCapture ();          // and release mouse
 }
}

/********************************************************************/
/*                                                                  */
/* OnMouseMove: draw a line to mouse position                       */
/*                                                                  */
/********************************************************************/

void DrawWin::OnMouseMove (UINT, CPoint point) {
 if (buttondown)
  ptrdc->LineTo (point); // draw line to here given by point
}

/********************************************************************/
/*                                                                  */
/* CmLineChange: receives a new line width from tool box            */
/*                                                                  */
/********************************************************************/

LRESULT DrawWin::CmLineChange (WPARAM line, LPARAM) {
 linewidth = line;
 return 0;
}

/********************************************************************/
/*                                                                  */
/* CmColorChange: receives a new color from tool box                */
/*                                                                  */
```

```
/********************************************************************/

LRESULT DrawWin::CmColorChange (WPARAM color, LPARAM) {
 colnum = color;
 return 0;
}

/********************************************************************/
/*                                                                  */
/* OnPaint: just repaint the background white                       */
/*                                                                  */
/********************************************************************/

void DrawWin::OnPaint() {
 CPaintDC dc(this); // minimalist paint
}

```

First, how is the child window created? The ctor only sets the pointers to 0 and **buttondown** to **false**, meaning no drawing is in progress. It also sets up the RGB color values for the six color choices. It is in **PreCreateWindow** that the actual **Create** call is made. I tweak the default window style a bit, removing borders and adding a client edge. Experiment and see what the difference is if the client edge is not added.

```
cs.dwExStyle |= WS_EX_CLIENTEDGE;
cs.style &= ~WS_BORDER;
cs.lpszClass = AfxRegisterWndClass (
   CS_HREDRAW | CS_VREDRAW | CS_DBLCLKS,
   ::LoadCursor(NULL, IDC_ARROW), HBRUSH(COLOR_WINDOW+1), NULL);
```

The create structure's **lpszClass** is assigned the registered class. The remainder of the construction is then automatic. It becomes very streamlined indeed.

The only significant coding is how to actually implement the drawing process. It begins with a left button press. It is vital that we only perform the starting sequence one time when no drawing is in progress because we must allocate a **CClientDC** on which to perform all subsequent drawing. We must keep this dc in existence until the left button is released. That is, the dc, for the first time, is going to exist across message handler functions.

```
if (!buttondown) {
 buttondown = true; // signal drawing
```

It is vital that the very first action is to turn on the **buttondown bool** at once. This **bool** prevents further invocations of the following coding that allocates the dc and so on. Why? Users can click the left button rapidly many times in succession. A volley of **WM_LBUTTONDOWN** messages hit our application and this function in particular. If we do not lock out all subsequent requests at once, we can easily end up executing the following coding multiple times and thus leak dcs! There are only a finite number of dcs available!

Next, allocate the dc and get it ready for operations. This also means we must allocate a new pen of the proper width and color. The alternative would be to hold in our class a set of "premade" pens, which is prohibitively large—4 widths of 6 colors, or 24 pens!

```
  ptrdc   = new CClientDC (this);// get new draw DC
  linecolor = colors[colnum];    // set line RGB color to use
  ptrpen = new CPen (PS_SOLID, linewidth, linecolor);
  ptrdc->SelectObject (ptrpen); // install pen in DC
```

With the dc ready for drawing, we capture the mouse and move the pen to the point at which the left button was pressed down.

```
  SetCapture ();           // capture all mouse movements for draw
  ptrdc->MoveTo (point);   // set pen to starting point for draw
 }
```

The **SetCapture** is crucial. We intend to draw a line from this point to wherever the mouse is moved by responding to **OnMouseMove** messages. What happens if the user moves the mouse over the frame window? Obviously, our client dc cannot continue to paint over the frame components—it is a client dc not a window dc. However, consider what happens if the user releases the left button while over the frame window? The **WM_LBUTTONUP** message is sent to the frame window and not the **DrawWin** and so we never do get a chance to delete this dc or to ever end the initial drawing operation. The user could never draw again until they managed to send a **WM_LBUTTONUP** message to the **DrawWin**. It is worse than all this. Suppose that our application was not maximized and that the user dragged the mouse over another application and released the left button there? Now our application does not even get the mouse message! Thus, it is imperative that **DrawWin** be sent every mouse message from now on until the left button is released.

Whenever the mouse moves a line is drawn from the current pen position to the new mouse position in **OnMouseMove**.

```
if (buttondown) ptrdc->LineTo (point);
```

Finally, when the button is released, drawing halts; it is vital that the mouse be released for obvious reasons.

```
if (buttondown) {
 if (ptrdc) delete ptrdc;     // stop drawing - remove GDI objects
 if (ptrpen) delete ptrpen;  // if flurry of clicks, avoids crash
 buttondown = false;          // signal not drawing
 ReleaseCapture ();           // and release mouse
}
```

Actually, some way to store the lines that are being created is needed so that **OnPaint** could reproduce the lines when required and so that the drawing could be saved either as a series of lines or as a DIB in a bmp file. See the **Scribble** MFC sample program for details on how this could be done.

RecalcLayout: Painting the Client Area of FrameWin Itself

Pgm10a completely avoided the frame window client dimensions problem by having a **CWnd** derived child window that acted as a client for the frame window. What is the problem that was avoided?

When a frame window has decorations, the space occupied by those bars is not removed from the available client area as reported by **GetClientArea** or the **OnSize** reported window dimensions. Thus, if the main tool bar is docked at the top of the frame window, its height is **not** removed from the client rectangle. Thus, in the frame window's **OnPaint**, a y coordinate of 0 is located underneath the tool bar! If the tool bar was 40 pixels in height, then the top 40 pixels of whatever was displayed using a y value of 0 to 40 would be hidden behind the tool bar. Worse still, if scrolling was not aware of this, then the tool bar and status bar would scroll upwards as well!

The **CFrameWnd** class has an internal function, **RecalcLayout,** that the framework calls whenever any of the child windows are resized or when the frame window is resized. The function handles the layout of the decorations within the new size constraints. However, the function **RepositionBars** can be called with a special identifier to obtain the real client area. That is, the client area of the frame window minus the space occupied by all of the decorations.

In **Pgm08b** of chapter 8,we saw how the **RecalcLayout** function can be overridden to fill up a **CRect** with the real client area. There we coded the following.

```
void FrameWin::RecalcLayout (BOOL bNotify) {
 CFrameWnd::RecalcLayout (bNotify );
 RepositionBars (AFX_IDW_CONTROLBAR_FIRST,
                 AFX_IDW_CONTROLBAR_LAST, 0, CWnd::reposQuery,
                 &RealClientArea );
```

The key parameter is **Cwnd::reposQuery** which bypasses re-laying out of the decorations and instead fills the passed **RealClientArea CRect** with the actual real client area available.

Then, in **OnPaint** or any where else that painting was done, one must base all coordinates upon **RealClientArea.left** and **RealClientArea.top**. The following displays the kth **msg** string on the kth line from the top of the real client area.

```
dc.TextOut (RealClientArea.left + avg_char_width,
            RealClientArea.top + avg_char_height * k, msg[k]);
```

If you intend to do any actual painting in your frame window's **OnPaint**, then please review how this function was utilized in **Pgm08b**.

Programming Problems

Pgm10-1—Revised Acme Inventory Data Entry with Decorations

This problem extends the ongoing development of the Inventory Data Base system for the ACME Construction Company using Problem **Pgm08-1** as a base. Modify the application as follows.

1. Construct a dockable toolbar, statusbar and tool tips in the frame window.
You may use the common Microsoft supplied buttons for the standard menu buttons, if desired. Create your own buttons for Add, Update, and Delete. (Be sure that you have a menu item selection for each button.) The main tool bar should at least have buttons for File|New, File|Open, File|Save, Font Change, Add, Update, Delete, and Help|About. You may add additional buttons as desired.

2. Instead of having a main window heading with the appropriate company title, place the company heading on the status bar in a separate pane.
Append to the company title on the status bar or create an additional pane for the following.
Record nnnn
where nnnn is the record number that is the current record. The current record is defined as the first record, when the file is first opened; the record just scrolled to; the record just added; the record just updated. For a delete, you can define the current record any way you like.

3. Add support for a Mark Up Percentage
Next, consider that the **cost** field is really the wholesale cost. Occasionally, the user may wish to view the display in terms of maximum profit. Maximum profit on a single item is defined as the total cost times the markup. For example, if the markup is 20%, .2 is used. For one record, the maximum profit is defined to be the **qty** * **cost** * **markup**. This maximum profit is to be displayed in a fifth, rightmost column for each record. Note that maximum profit is calculated and never stored in the file. When the user wishes to see the maximum profit, display that additional field on each line on the screen. (The easiest method is to calculate each during the screen paint, line by line.)

4. Construct a **floating** tool box and allow the user to hide and to reshow the tool box. It can begin docked if desired. The tool box includes a group of six buttons (two columns with three rows) representing the following maximum profit markup percentages.
normal - no max profits are shown on the screen
max profit of .1
max profit of .125
max profit of .15
max profit of .175
max profit of .2
When the app begins, the normal button is in effect and no maximum profits are displayed on the screen. Whenever any max profit button is pressed, update the display on the screen appropriately.

5. Additionally, on the right side of the status bar include the total expected profits, found by summing all of the maximum profits from all records in the file.

6. Implement the Choose Fonts menu item.
Allow the user to choose any font desired and with any point size. This directly impacts scrolling as well as painting.

Chapter 11 The Multiple Document Interface

Introduction

Windows provides two generalized interfaces designed to simplify the handling of one or more documents, where a document normally is thought of as a text file, but can be literally any kind of data. The two interfaces are called the **SDI** and **MDI**—single document interface and the multiple document interface. The major difference between the two is that the MDI provides the programmer and user with the tools with which to work and manage many documents concurrently.

Figure 11.1 shows our first MDI sample program, **Pgm11a**, in operation. The fancy decorations have been brought forward. Two previous applications have been converted into MDI child windows: the graphics GDI scroll program from Chapter 9 and the draw program from Chapter 10 complete with tool box. Two separate instances of each type have been opened.

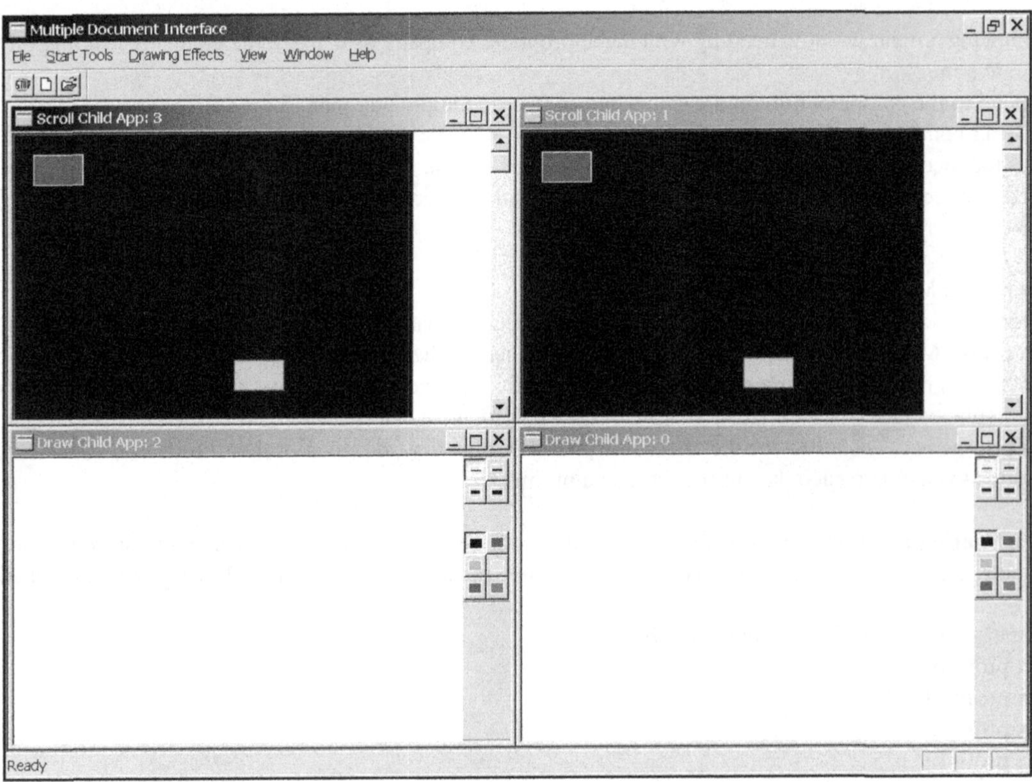

Figure 11.1 Pgm11a — MDI Application with Four Child Windows Open

The MDI framework introduces three new window types. The normal frame window is now derived from **CMDIFrameWnd** which owns the main tool bar and status bar. The client area of the MDI frame window is occupied by an instance of the **MDIClient** window. The MFC does not have a class to encapsulate this window because the basic functionality of the **MDIClient** almost never needs to be extended. Each of the child windows are derived from **CMDIChildWnd** which in turn is derived from **CFrameWnd**.

The MDI framework supports a new pop-up menu called "Windows", which has been pulled down in Figure 11.2. The MDI framework fully handles all of the "Windows" menu items without any coding from us. The MDI child windows can be Cascaded or Tiled (tiled is shown in these figures). When several documents are iconized, the MDI framework arranges them for you. In Figure 11.3, I launched another three documents and then minimized three documents of the seven. One can switch to a different document by clicking anywhere in that document.

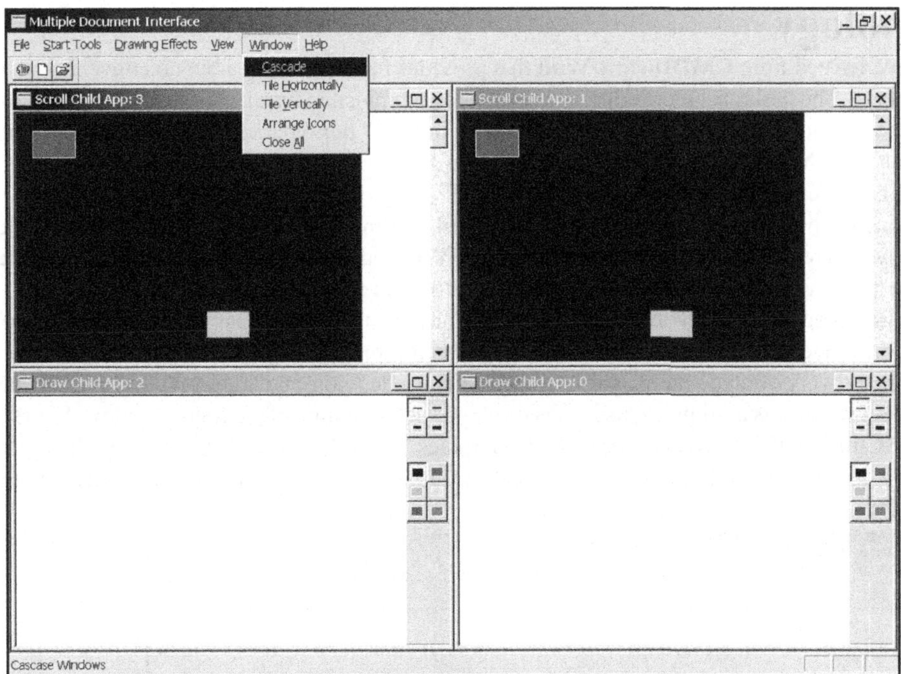

Figure 11.2 Pgm11a With the Window Menu Pulled Down

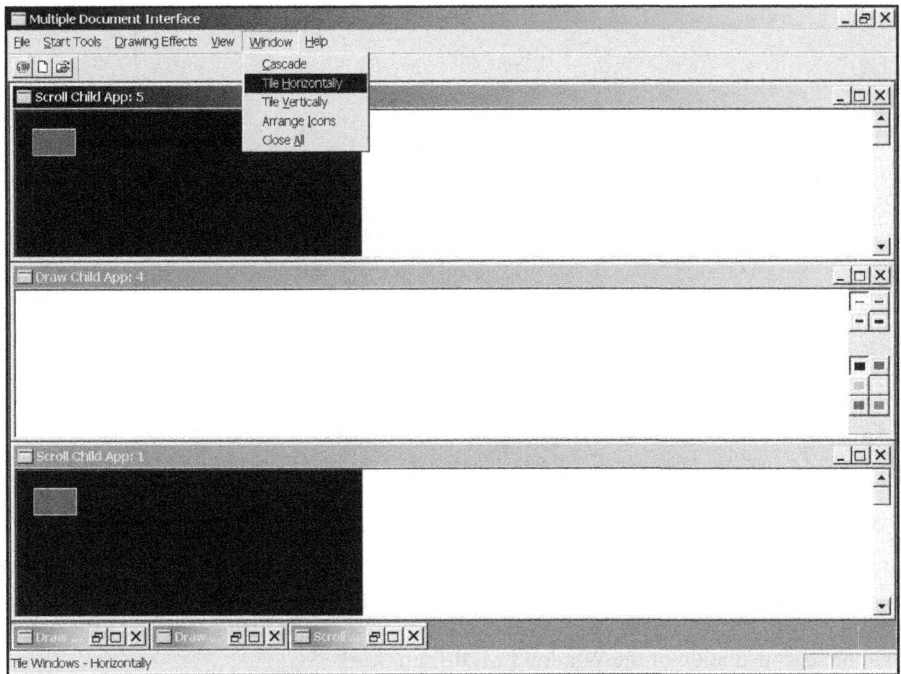

Figure 11.3 Pgm11a With Window Menu With Seven Child Windows

Each document window normally has its own system caption or title bar with a control bar and min/max buttons. Thus, each child window has the full use of a normal system menu with Close and Move along with the ability to minimize itself and most importantly to maximize itself just as if that one document were the only one running.

The **MDIClient** window, the invisible client area of the **MDIFrameWnd**, is not just limited to the size of the screen or even the size of the **MDIFrameWnd**. Rather the client window is a virtual canvas with world coordinates of +- 32,767 pixels wide. The MDI framework creates a mini-desktop on which to organize windows objects or documents.

MDI Terminology

The main window is now derived from **CMDIFrameWnd** that provides the desktop area but no conventional window on which to display documents. The desktop-like window is managed by an invisible instance of the **MDIClient** window that provides the processing of all document windows, handling the "Windows" pop-up menu, and allocates new instances of documents. There is only one **MDIClient** window that manages all of the other document windows. It normally is not encapsulated in a C++ class; we just use the API default.

Each separate document is an instance of a **CMDIChildWnd** window. There can be nearly unlimited child windows opened, subject only to system resources. Note that the **CMDIChildWnd** class is derived from a **CFrameWnd not Cwnd**. Thus, the child windows have resizeable frame borders, a title bar, tool bars, and a status bar.

The **CMDIFrameWnd** window **always** has a menu bar which should have at least the "Windows" pop-up menu. **CMDIChildWnd** windows have no menu bars. Rather they receive menu commands passed on down to them from the MDI frame window. They can and very often do merge some of their own needed pop-up menus onto the main menu bar.

When a document window is minimized, its icon is displayed at the bottom of the frame window. If no special icon is provided in the **CMDIChildWnd** derived class, as with the Graphics Scroll, MDI substitutes a standard minimized icon.

When a document is maximized, it takes over the entire frame window area; its controls merge with the frame window as shown in Figure 12.4.

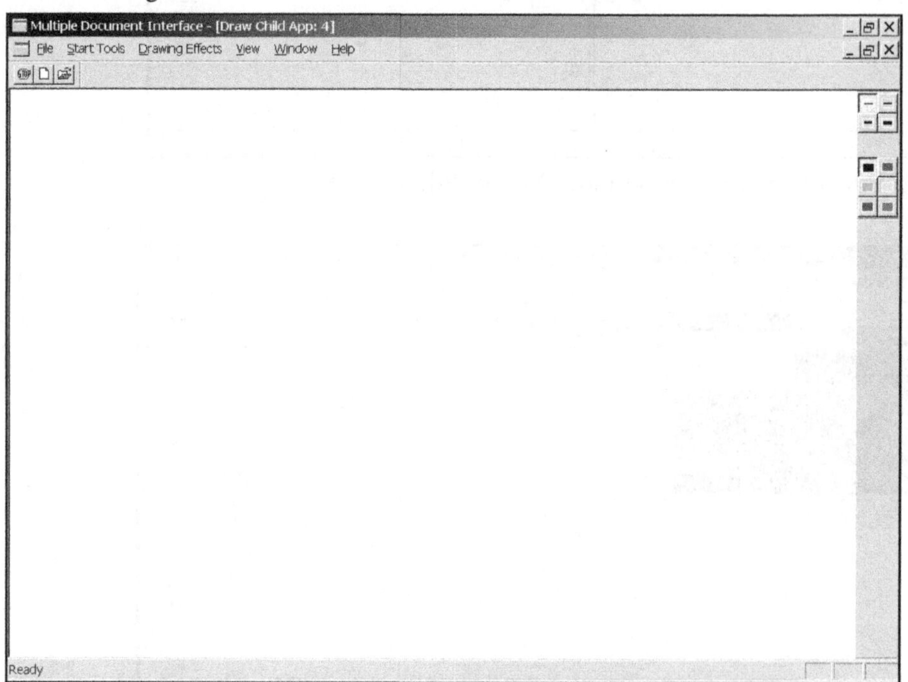

Figure 11.4 Pgm11a with Draw Child Maximized

The **MDIClient** window serves as the **parent window** for all of the MDI children, **not** the frame window, as one might expect. Since the client window can be huge in size, children can be placed far off screen and gotten to by scrolling. Or the client can be reduced in size, restricting the area in which the children can be displayed. The MFC implementation, as expected, is a fairly simple encapsulation of the Windows MDI framework.

Pgm11a: Overview

Unlimited numbers (except by resources) of two different types of MDI child windows can be launched: **DrawWin** and **ScrollWin**. In general, any application that we have coded up to this point could become a MDI child window. Notice that the MDI child window is derived from a frame window class.

So the starting point for conversion to MDI is to change the base class from **CFrameWnd** to **CMDIChildWnd**. For the Scroll Window application, this conversion process is very simple. For the Draw Window, the process is immensely more complex because of the tool box.

In the program in Chapter 10, there is only one instance of **DrawWin** and only one tool box. Now there can be numerous instances of **DrawWin** and the tool box as well. The main menu should have the familiar "hide/show tool box" menu item located under the View pop-up menu. If there are no **DrawWin** client windows, this hid/show menu item should not be on the main menu. It should only be present when one or more **DrawWin** have been launched.

To handle this effect, we take advantage of the ability of a child MDI window to install its own menu additions **while** it is the **active** child. So when a Scroll Window is reactivated, the hide/show tool boxes menu item is grayed. The ability of the MDI to manage child menus becomes vital. In this version, the tool box's status is determined dynamically using **CWnd** member functions to inquire whether the tool box is currently visible or not.

Contrast the appearance/disappearance and the enabling of the hide/show tool box menu item with the pop-up menu for Drawing Effects that permit choosing the line width and color. This large pop-up menu is defined in the main application menu and is always present, even if there are no child windows opened. However, when no DrawWin windows are opened, all these menus are greyed out.

Minimization of the **DrawWin** creates another problem. Since the icon is within the client window, if a tool box is present, then the tool box would be appended to the icon representing the window. It certainly looks funny to see an icon with a tool box appended to it! Thus, we must be able to detect when our Draw window is about to become minimized so that we can hide the tool box. Conversely, we must be able to detect when that window is about to be restored so that we can make the tool box visible once more.

Further, each of the **DrawWin** child window's can have its tool box undocked. Consider what happens when the tool box is floating and its parent **DrawWin** is moved or resized? If we do nothing about this, then a given **DrawWin** can have its associated tool box located far outside the child window itself, adding to the confusion. In this case, I have chosen to force the tool box to be repositioned near the top left corner of the moving **DrawWin**.

As we examine how to code for the MDI, you will now see why we have been coding in so general a manner, dividing the workload among the application, frame, and window classes. It was done for easy insertion into the MDI framework.

The MFC Implementation of MDI, Pgm11a

From a design viewpoint, separating each MDI child class from the overall MDI frame window offers great benefits. No longer does the frame window class have to directly manage objects for its child windows, such as the tool box palette in Pgm10a.

Each separate MDI child class has its own source and header files. Since they are derived from a frame window, they can have and maintain their own tool boxes, control bars, and so on. But what about their own resources? It would be very practical for each MDI child class to have their own resource files as well. In a large company project, it is impractical for many programers working on separate portions of the application to all share the very same RC file. Coordinating programmer modifications to the RC file would be a nightmare task!

However, by now you should have realized that the Developer Studio expects one resource file (RC) and it saves the identifiers in one file, **resource.h**. How can we have multiple resource files and corresponding resource header files?

How to Have Multiple Resource Files

We keep the main resource file known as **Pgm11a.rc** with **resource.h** as its header. To construct another resource file for say **DrawWin**, in the Solution Explorer right click on the project and choose Add New and choose resource file. Enter a new name, such as DrawWin.rc or ScrollWin.rc. Unfortunately, the corresponding resource header files are named resource1.h and resource2.h.

It becomes important to keep the numerical values of items in each of the three resource files different. I chose to use 2000 for string items in the FrameWin resource file and 2100 and 2200 for the other two string resource files.

A large project with many programmers often makes use of this technique, with each portion of the project utilizing its own resource file. When setting up a larger project, one can make subfolders for different portions of the project. For example, one might have an \Image subfolder that contains all of the cpp, header, and resource files for the series of Image classes of the application. In such a manner, one can organize a project that consists of hundreds of classes and many resource files.

Pgm11a.rc, excerpts

```
IDR_MAINFRAME              ICON                    "res\\Pgm11a.ico"
IDR_MAINFRAME              BITMAP                  "res\\Toolbar.bmp"
IDR_MAINFRAME MENU
BEGIN
```

```
    POPUP "&File"
    BEGIN
        MENUITEM "E&xit\tAlt+F4",                   ID_APP_EXIT
    END
    POPUP "&Start Tools"
    BEGIN
        MENUITEM "&Draw",                           CM_DRAW
        MENUITEM "&Scroll",                         CM_SCROLL
    END
    POPUP "&Drawing Effects"
    BEGIN
        POPUP "Line &Width"
        BEGIN
            MENUITEM "1 Pixel",                         CM_LINE1
            MENUITEM "2 Pixels",                        CM_LINE2
            MENUITEM "3 Pixels",                        CM_LINE3
            MENUITEM "4 Pixels",                        CM_LINE4
        END
        POPUP "Line &Color"
        BEGIN
            MENUITEM "&Black",                          CM_COLORA
            MENUITEM "&Red",                            CM_COLORB
            MENUITEM "&Green",                          CM_COLORC
            MENUITEM "&Yellow",                         CM_COLORD
            MENUITEM "B&lue",                           CM_COLORE
            MENUITEM "&Purple",                         CM_COLORF
        END
    END
    POPUP "&View"
    BEGIN
        MENUITEM "&Toolbar",                        ID_VIEW_TOOLBAR
        MENUITEM "&Status Bar",                     ID_VIEW_STATUS_BAR
        MENUITEM SEPARATOR
    END
    POPUP "&Window"
    BEGIN
        MENUITEM "&Cascade",                        CM_CASCADECHILDREN, GRAYED
        MENUITEM "Tile &Horizontally",              CM_TILECHILDRENH, GRAYED
        MENUITEM "Tile &Vertically",                CM_TILECHILDRENV, GRAYED
        MENUITEM "Arrange &Icons",                  CM_ARRANGEICONS, GRAYED
        MENUITEM "Close &All",                      CM_CLOSECHILDREN, GRAYED
    END
    POPUP "&Help"
    BEGIN
        MENUITEM "&About...",                       ID_APP_ABOUT
    END
END
IDD_ABOUTBOX DIALOGEX 0, 0, 235, 55
STYLE DS_SETFONT | DS_MODALFRAME | DS_FIXEDSYS | WS_POPUP | WS_CAPTION | WS_SYSMENU
CAPTION "About Pgm11a"
FONT 8, "MS Shell Dlg", 0, 0, 0x1
BEGIN
    ICON            IDR_MAINFRAME,IDC_STATIC,11,17,20,20
    LTEXT           "Pgm11a Version 1.0",IDC_STATIC,40,10,119,8,SS_NOPREFIX
    LTEXT           "Illustrates Multiple Doc Interface",IDC_STATIC,40,25,119,8
    DEFPUSHBUTTON   "OK",IDOK,178,7,50,16,WS_GROUP
END
STRINGTABLE
BEGIN
    IDR_MAINFRAME           "Pgm11a"
    CM_DRAW                 "Launch Draw Window\nStart Draw"
    CM_SCROLL               "Launch Scroll Window\nStart Scroll"
    CM_CASCADECHILDREN      "Cascase Windows"
    CM_TILECHILDRENH        "Tile Windows - Horizontally"
```

```
    CM_TILECHILDRENV        "Tile Windows - Vertically"
    CM_ARRANGEICONS         "Arrange Icons"
    CM_CLOSECHILDREN        "Close All Windows"
    CM_LINE1                "Select 1 pixel line width\nLinewidth 1"
    CM_LINE2                "Select 2 pixels line width\nLinewidth 2"
    CM_LINE3                "Select 3 pixels line width\nLinewidth 3"
    CM_LINE4                "Select 4 pixels line width\nLinewidth 4"
    CM_COLORA               "Select Black as the drawing color\nBlack"
    CM_COLORB               "Select Red as the drawing color\nRed"
    CM_COLORC               "Select Green as the drawing color\nGreen"
    CM_COLORD              "Select Yellow as the drawing color\nYellow"
    CM_COLORE               "Select Blue as the drawing color\nBlue"
    CM_COLORF             "Select Purple as the drawing color\nPurple"
    IDS_MSG_QUIT            "Do you want to quit the application?"
    IDS_MSG_QUERY           "Query?"
    IDS_DRAW                "Draw Child App: "
    IDS_SCROLL              "Scroll Child App: "
END
```

resource.h, excerpts

```
#define IDD_ABOUTBOX                    100
#define IDR_MAINFRAME                   128
#define CM_DRAW                         1124
#define CM_SCROLL                       1125
#define CM_CASCADECHILDREN              1128
#define CM_TILECHILDRENH                1129
#define CM_TILECHILDRENV                1130
#define CM_ARRANGEICONS                 1131
#define CM_CLOSECHILDREN                1132
#define IDS_MSG_QUIT                    2001
#define IDS_MSG_QUERY                   2002
#define IDS_DRAW                        2003
#define IDS_SCROLL                      2004
#define CM_LINE1                        1145
#define CM_LINE2                        1146
#define CM_LINE3                        1147
#define CM_LINE4                        1148
#define CM_COLORA                       1149
#define CM_COLORB                       1150
#define CM_COLORC                       1151
#define CM_COLORD                       1152
#define CM_COLORE                       1153
#define CM_COLORF                       1154
```

DrawWin.rc, excerpts

```
IDB_TOOLBOX          BITMAP             "..\\res\\TOOLBOX.BMP"
STRINGTABLE
BEGIN
    IDB_TOOLBOX             "Hide/Show Tool &Box"
    IDS_DRAWQUIT            "Ok to close this drawing?"
    IDS_DRAWTITLE           "Make a Drawing"
    IDS_DRAW_MSG_QUERY     "Do you want to close this drawing window?"
END
```

DrawWinRC.h, excerpts

```
#define IDB_TOOLBOX                     3
#define IDS_DRAWQUIT                    2200
#define IDS_DRAWTITLE                   2201
#define IDS_DRAW_MSG_QUERY              2202
```

ScrollWin.rc, excerpts

```
STRINGTABLE DISCARDABLE
BEGIN
```

```
    IDS_SCROLL_QUIT          "Query"
    IDS_SCROLL_QUIT_MSG      "Ok to close this scroll window?"
    IDS_SCROLLTITLE          "Graphics Scroll Window"
END
```

ScrollWinRC.h, excerpts

```
#define IDS_SCROLL_QUIT                   2101
#define IDS_SCROLL_QUIT_MSG               2102
#define IDS_SCROLLTITLE                   2103
```

Handling the "Windows" Pop-up Menu Items

The MFC implementation is merely a cover wrapper over the Windows C API MDI framework. The framework has some built-in command IDs for processing the "Windows" menu items such as Cascade, Tile, and so on. These are shown below.

```
Built-in IDs           Description      CMDIFrameWin function invoked

ID_WINDOW_TILE_VERT - vertically    - MDITile (MDITILE_VERTICAL);
ID_WINDOW_TILE_HORZ - horizontally - MDITile (MDITILE_HORIZONTAL);
ID_WINDOW_CASCADE   - cascade       - MDICascade ();
ID_WINDOW_ARRANGE   - icon arrange - MDIIconArrange ();
```

If you do **not** use these predefined IDs, then in the command response function, invoke the **CMDIFrameWnd** functions indicated above. In **Pgm11a**, I used the usual **CM_** style identifiers. Thus, in the **FrameWin** cpp file, in response to these menu commands, I had to explicitly invoke the above API functions as well as add String table values for these **CM_** items.

On the other hand, had I used the above built-in IDs and included the **afxres.rc** file which has the corresponding String table entries for these, then I would need no coding at all for these Windows pop-up menu items. The default framework would handle them automatically.

The Implementation of the MDI Frame Window Class

I began this example by using the App Wizard to create a new project. This time, I checked using Multiple documents. Otherwise, make all the same settings as in Chapter 10. The App Wizard then created an overly complex project, in that it created a CWnd derived class to be the client window of the CMDIChildWnd class. It also assumed all classes would be dynamically created based on a single ID value and that the app class would be handling File-New operations. Hence, once the skeleton framework was built, I began deleting the excess baggage. In essence, the application class remains nearly the same as the last chapter, handling the Help-About dialog and launching the frame window instance.

Look first to the main frame window class, **FrameWin**, which is derived from **CMDIFrameWnd**. The derived **CMDIFrameWnd** class **must** create an instance of the Windows API default MDI client window. Further, the launching and maintenance of the child windows is done by the derived **CMDIFrameWnd** class. Remember too, that the **CMDIFrameWnd** is also responsible for the tool bar and status bar.

To facilitate closing all of the MDI children at one time without forcing the user to respond to numerous "Can Close" queries, the **public bool fastClose** is defined. It is **public** so that the MDI child windows can access it. The member **numChildren** not only is used to count the current number of MDI children but also it is used as the number to be appended to the children window titles.

The Windows API encapsulates two additional functions in **CMDIFrameWnd** that assist in moving between MDI child windows. They are called **MDIGetActive** and **MDINext**.

```
CMDIChildWnd *  MDIGetActive (BOOL ptrismaximized);
void            MDINext ();
```

MDIGetActive returns a pointer to the currently active MDI child window with the **BOOL** pointed to by **ptrismaximized** set to **TRUE** is that MDI child is currently maximized. The function **MDINext** deactivates the current MDI child and makes the MDI child window that is immediately behind it the now active MDI child. Thus, one could envision a loop such as this.

```
CMDIChild *ptrchild = MDIGetActive (NULL);
while (ptrchild != NULL) {
 ...
 MDINext ();
 ptrchild = MDIGetActive (NULL);
}
```

The Windows implementation of **MDINext** always returns a pointer to the next window. So if there are two children, the function returns a pointer to the other one endlessly and the above code can present an infinite loop. Further, if MDI children are iconized, they are **not** in the loop and seem to be bypassed. But there is a failsafe way to determine if there are no more MDI children of a specific type—have the MDI frame window who launched them keep a tally.

Examine the **FrameWin** definition file noting the new MDI functions. I also added another inline function to return the number of children, the field that is used to append to child window titles. It is not an accurate count of the true number of MDI children, however. Suppose six MDI children are launched and then children numbered 1 and 2 are deleted. The number of children cannot be set to four because if another MDI child were launched, it would then be given the number 4 to append to its title. Now there would be two child windows numbered 4!

```
FrameWin Class Definition
```

```
/***************************************************************/
/*                                                             */
/* FrameWin Definition of CMDI Frame Window                    */
/*                                                             */
/***************************************************************/

class FrameWin : public CMDIFrameWnd {

 /**************************************************************/
 /*                                                            */
 /* Data Members                                               */
 /*                                                            */
 /**************************************************************/

public:
bool       fastClose;    // avoid lots of query prompts when true

protected:
int        numChildren; // count of MDI children
CStatusBar statusbar;
CToolBar   toolbar;

 /**************************************************************/
 /*                                                            */
 /* Functions                                                  */
 /*                                                            */
 /**************************************************************/

public:
                FrameWin ();        // init child win counts
               ~FrameWin () {}      // destructor - do nothing

protected:

afx_msg int     OnCreate(LPCREATESTRUCT); // make tool & status bar
afx_msg void    OnClose ();             // determines if app can quit
int             DisplayMsg (int, int, UINT); // shows a message box

//              command processors
afx_msg void    CmExit ();     // shut app down - close all children
afx_msg void    CmDraw ();     // launch the draw client window
afx_msg void    CmScroll ();   // launch the scroll client
afx_msg void    CmHelpAbout (); // help about our app

```

```
//              MDI Children Functions
afx_msg void CmCascadeChildren (); // cascade all windows
afx_msg void CmTileChildrenH ();   // tile windows horizontally
afx_msg void CmTileChildrenV ();   // tile windows vertically
afx_msg void CmArrangeIcons ();    // arrange minimized icons
afx_msg void CmCloseChildren ();   // close all child windows

int GetChildCount (); // get total number of MDI child windows

DECLARE_MESSAGE_MAP()
};
```

The **FrameWin** MDI implementation begins in the constructor by creating the MDI frame window and initializing the child count to zero. **OnCreate** now must create the MDI client window. To do so, a pointer to the Windows pop-up menu is required. Notice how I obtain that pointer.

```
CMenu* ptrmenu = new CMenu ();
ptrmenu->LoadMenu ("MAINMENU");
// construct the MDI hidden client window using the main menu
// pointing it to the Window pop-up
CreateClient (lpCS, ptrmenu->GetSubMenu(4));
delete ptrmenu;
```

Once the MDI client window is created, the **OnCreate** sequence continues with old style tool bar and status bar construction similar to the coding seen in the last chapter.

```
if (toolbar.Create (this) &&
    toolbar.LoadBitmap (IDB_MAINFRAME) &&
    toolbar.SetButtons (buttons, sizeof(buttons)/sizeof(UINT)))
  if (statusbar.Create (this) &&
      statusbar.SetIndicators (indicators, sizeof(indicators) /
                               sizeof(UINT))) ;
  else return -1;
else return -1;
toolbar.SetBarStyle (
            toolbar.GetBarStyle() | CBRS_TOOLTIPS | CBRS_FLYBY);

toolbar.SetWindowText (_T("Main Controls"));
toolbar.EnableDocking (CBRS_ALIGN_ANY);
EnableDocking (CBRS_ALIGN_ANY);
DockControlBar (&toolbar);
```

Let's first see the entire coding and then analyze the specific sequences required to launch the child windows and how the fast close mechanism operates.

FrameWin Class Implementation

```
#include "stdafx.h"
#include "FrameWin.h"
#include "ScrollWin.h"
#include "DrawWin.h"
#include "resource.h"    // pick up resource IDs

/***************************************************************/
/*                                                             */
/* tool bar buttons and status bar buttons                     */
/*                                                             */
/* control bar buttons - IDs are command buttons               */
/* same order as in the bitmap 'toolbar.bmp'                   */
/*                                                             */
/***************************************************************/

```

```
static UINT BASED_CODE buttons[] = {

  ID_APP_EXIT,
  CM_DRAW,
  CM_SCROLL,
};

static UINT BASED_CODE indicators[] = {
  ID_SEPARATOR,            // status line indicator
  ID_INDICATOR_CAPS,
  ID_INDICATOR_NUM,
  ID_INDICATOR_SCRL,
};

/*****************************************************************/
/*                                                               */
/* FrameWin Message Map                                          */
/*                                                               */
/*****************************************************************/

BEGIN_MESSAGE_MAP(FrameWin, CMDIFrameWnd)
 ON_WM_CREATE ()
 ON_WM_CLOSE ()
 ON_COMMAND(CM_DRAW,              CmDraw)
 ON_COMMAND(CM_SCROLL,            CmScroll)
 ON_COMMAND(CM_CASCADECHILDREN,   CmCascadeChildren)
 ON_COMMAND(CM_TILECHILDRENH,     CmTileChildrenH)
 ON_COMMAND(CM_TILECHILDRENV,     CmTileChildrenV)
 ON_COMMAND(CM_ARRANGEICONS,      CmArrangeIcons)
 ON_COMMAND(CM_CLOSECHILDREN,     CmCloseChildren)
END_MESSAGE_MAP()

/*****************************************************************/
/*                                                               */
/* Framewin: Construct the window object                         */
/*                                                               */
/*****************************************************************/

FrameWin::FrameWin () {
 CString title;
 title.LoadString (IDR_MAINFRAME);
 // create the MDI frame window
 Create (NULL, title, WS_OVERLAPPEDWINDOW, rectDefault, NULL,
         MAKEINTRESOURCE(IDR_MAINFRAME));
 fastClose   = false;// set no express close in operation
 numChildren = 0;    // set num children to 0 for title additions
}

/*****************************************************************/
/*                                                               */
/* OnCreate: construct the status and tool box - insert menu     */
/*                                                               */
/*****************************************************************/

int FrameWin::OnCreate (LPCREATESTRUCT lpCS) {
 // construct from resource file the main menu to be used
 CMenu *ptrmenu;
 ptrmenu = new CMenu ();
 ptrmenu->LoadMenu (IDR_MAINFRAME);

 // construct the MDI hidden client window using the main menu
 // pointing it to the Window pop-up
 CreateClient (lpCS, ptrmenu->GetSubMenu(4));
 delete ptrmenu;
```

```

 // attempt to build control bar and status bar using old style
 if (toolbar.Create (this) &&
     toolbar.LoadBitmap (IDR_MAINFRAME) &&
     toolbar.SetButtons (buttons, sizeof(buttons)/sizeof(UINT)))
  if (statusbar.Create (this) &&
      statusbar.SetIndicators (indicators, sizeof(indicators) /
                               sizeof(UINT))) ;
  else return -1;
 else return -1;

 // all ok, so set for hints and tool tips wanted
 toolbar.SetBarStyle (
            toolbar.GetBarStyle() | CBRS_TOOLTIPS | CBRS_FLYBY);

 // insert captions to be shown when the tool bars are floating
 toolbar.SetWindowText (_T("Main Controls"));

 // now notify control to accept any form of docking
 toolbar.EnableDocking (CBRS_ALIGN_ANY);

 // notify the framewindow of docking requirements
 EnableDocking (CBRS_ALIGN_ANY);

 // and dock control bar at top
 DockControlBar (&toolbar);

 return 0;
}

/*************************************************************/
/*                                                           */
/* CmDraw: Launch a new DrawWin with its tool box            */
/*                                                           */
/*************************************************************/

void FrameWin::CmDraw () {
 CString title;
 char msg[10];
 // construct modified window title appending id number to title
 title.LoadString (IDS_DRAW);
 _itoa_s (numChildren, msg, sizeof(msg), 10);
 title += msg;
 // allocate a draw MDI child window
 DrawWin *ptrwin = new DrawWin ();
 // now create the draw MDI child window using many default args
 if (!ptrwin->Create (NULL, title)) {
  delete ptrwin;
  return;
 }
 numChildren++;
 ptrwin->ShowWindow (SW_SHOW); // and make child visible
 // no attempt to make this one maxed if previous one was maxed
}

/*************************************************************/
/*                                                           */
/* CmScroll: Launch a new client window for scrolling        */
/*                                                           */
/*************************************************************/

void FrameWin::CmScroll () {
 CString title;
 char msg[10];
```

```
 // construct modified window title appending id number to title
 title.LoadString (IDS_SCROLL);
 _itoa_s (numChildren, msg, sizeof(msg), 10);
 title += msg;
 CMDIChildWnd *ptrcurwin = MDIGetActive ();
 // allocate new scroll window with a map size of 400 pixels
 ScrollWin *ptrwin = new ScrollWin (400);
 // now call the Create function using many default arguments
 if (!ptrwin->Create (0, title)) {
  delete ptrwin;
  return;
 }
 numChildren++;
 ptrwin->ShowWindow (SW_SHOW);              // make child visible

 // if the previous child was maximized, then make new one maxed
 if (ptrcurwin)
  if (ptrcurwin->GetStyle() & WS_MAXIMIZE)
   ptrwin->MDIMaximize();
}

/***************************************************************/
/*                                                             */
/* CmCloseChildren: close children with no child close prompts */
/*                                                             */
/***************************************************************/

void FrameWin::CmCloseChildren () {
 fastClose = true;              // turn on express close option
 // find the current active child
 CMDIChildWnd *ptrwin = MDIGetActive ();
 while (ptrwin) {               // for all MDI children:
  ptrwin->MDIDestroy ();        // destroy the child window
  MDINext();                    // make the next child active
  ptrwin = MDIGetActive ();     // and get a ptr to next active one
 }
 fastClose = false;             // turn off express close option
 numChildren = 0;               // set all child win counts to 0
}

/***************************************************************/
/*                                                             */
/* The 5 MDI Child Window arrangement functions                */
/*                                                             */
/***************************************************************/

void FrameWin::CmCascadeChildren () {
 MDICascade ();
}
void FrameWin::CmTileChildrenH () {
 MDITile (MDITILE_HORIZONTAL);
}
void FrameWin::CmTileChildrenV () {
 MDITile (MDITILE_VERTICAL);
}
void FrameWin::CmArrangeIcons () {
 MDIIconArrange ();
}
int FrameWin::GetChildCount () {
 return numChildren;
}


/***************************************************************/
```

```
/*                                                                */
/* OnClose: query user if we can terminate the application        */
/*                                                                */
/******************************************************************/

void FrameWin::OnClose () {
 if (DisplayMsg (IDS_MSG_QUERY, IDS_MSG_QUIT, MB_YESNO |
        MB_ICONQUESTION) == IDYES)
  DestroyWindow ();
}

/******************************************************************/
/*                                                                */
/* DisplayMsg: shows a MessageBox and returns its retcode         */
/*                                                                */
/******************************************************************/

int FrameWin::DisplayMsg (int id1, int id2, UINT flags) {
 CString msg1, msg2;
 msg1.LoadString (id1);
 msg2.LoadString (id2);
 return MessageBox (msg2, msg1, flags);
}

```

Launching an MDI Child Window

There are several ways to launch child windows. If the child is a text editor, for example, you could use the File|New and File|Open menu items to launch the editor with that file. I show how this can be done in the next chapter. Here, I provide a button and menu item for each type of child. When either the menu selection or the button to launch the child window, Draw or Scroll, is pressed the command **CM_DRAW** or **CM_SCROLL** is sent to the MDI client for handling in either the **CmDraw** or **CmScroll** functions. The two functions only differ in the actual allocation of the new child window itself. The **ScrollWin** constructor accepts the desired **mapsize**.

Notice that each instance of either the Draw document or the Scroll object has a **unique** title that helps identify which is which. Since it is the frame window's responsibility to launch another child document, it also should provide a method to help that child in uniquely identifying itself in that child's title bar. Very often a number is appended to the name of the document title. If you are using an actual file new or open, the filename can serve as the unique identifier.

The general procedure for launching child MDI windows begins with creating a string from the current **numberChildren** count that is subsequently passed to the child constructor. In **CmDraw** the child's title is loaded from the resource file and the current number of children is appended to the end of the title. A new instance of the **DrawWin** class is allocated and its **Create** function invoked. Notice that the MDI child window **Create** function provides NULL default arguments for most of the parameters, making it very easy to invoke **Create**. If the creation was successful, the number of children is incremented and the new child window made visible. Do not forget to actually call its **ShowWindow** function, for that is what actually makes the child window visible.

```
CString title;
char msg[10];
title.LoadString (IDS_DRAW);
_itoa_s (numchildren, msg, sizeof(msg), 10);
title += msg;
DrawWin *ptrwin = new DrawWin ();
if (!ptrwin->Create (NULL, title)) {
 delete ptrwin;
 return;
}
numChildren++;
ptrwin->ShowWindow (SW_SHOW);
```

CmScroll coding is exactly parallel. However, at the very end of the sequence, an additional loop is coded. When the current child window is maximized and when the user chooses to launch another child window, ideally, the new child window should also be maximized when it first appears. By getting the active MDI child window and checking whether or not its current style has the **WS_MAXIMIZE** flag turned on, we can maximize the new child window. The function to maximize an MDI child window is **MDIMaximize**.

```
 CMDIChildWnd *ptrcurwin = MDIGetActive ();
 if (ptrcurwin)
  if (ptrcurwin->GetStyle() & WS_MAXIMIZE)
   ptrwin->MDIMaximize();
}
```

Experiment with the effect. Launch any child window of **Pgm11a** and then maximize it. Now launch a new Scroll child and then a new Draw child. The effect is very visible.

The Fast Close Operation

When the user requests that a specific window or document be closed, that class provides its own **OnClose** function to decide if work needs to be saved and so on. However in MDI, the user can have a dozen documents active and then select close the application or from the Windows pop-up—Close All Windows. Here, the frame window's **OnClose** is called and it invokes what it sees as the only client window, the MDI Client window. So it calls the MDI Client window's **OnClose**, which in turn, one by one, invokes each of the dozen document's **OnClose** functions. Pity the "poor user," who, at this point, must respond to a dozen "Do you want to close this window" queries.

The solution is to implement a "fast close" operation that attempts to bypass all of these child window queries. To do this, the **FrameWin** defines a **bool fastClose** that is initially set to **false**. Each child window's **OnClose** function can check this **bool**. When the child window is closing, if that **bool** is **true**, then the child window would only prompt the user if it was necessary to save work.

In the **FrameWin** class, the **CmCloseChildren** function is called whenever all windows are going to be shut down, either from the frame window (Alt-F4 for example) or from the Window|Close All. In **CmCloseChildren fastclose** is set to **true** so that all of the closing MDI child windows can check it to avoid displaying unneeded "Can Close" messages. Remember that the children can still display a message if file contents need to be saved. At this point, the function should loop through all MDI children attempting to destroy them.

```
 fastClose = true;            // turn on express close option
 CMDIChildWnd *ptrwin = MDIGetActive ();
 while (ptrwin) {             // for all MDI children:
  ptrwin->MDIDestroy ();      // destroy the child window
  MDINext();                  // make the next child active
  ptrwin = MDIGetActive ();   // and get a ptr to next active one
 }
 fastClose = false;           // turn off express close option
 numChildren = 0;             // set all child win counts to 0
```

A few pages ago, we looked at this kind of loop which could be an infinite loop. This time, however, when a pointer to the next MDI child is obtained, the **MDIDestroy** function is called, removing that window. Thus, this loop will end when all of the MDI child windows are destroyed. **MDIGetActive** will eventually return 0 when there are no more MDI child windows left. At this point, we can safely reset the number of children to 0 along with the **fastClose bool**.

Converting ScrollWin from Pgm09a into a CMDIChildWnd

Now we must convert the scrolling window from **Pgm09a** into a **CMDIChildWnd, ScrollWin**. First, construct the resource files as given above. Next, I have removed the **SysInfo** class from the implementation, substituting **screenXpels** and **screenYpels** for the screen dimensions. **ScrollWin** is now derived from **CMDIChildWnd**. To accommodate MDI, the **CmExit** functionality is moved to **OnClose**; and functions **Create** and **OnDestroy** are added to install the modified title and notify the MDI frame of **ScrollWin** termination.

```
 ScrollWin Class Definition
```

```
#pragma once

/********************************************************************/
/*                                                                  */
/* ScrollWin: Display a Graphic Scroll Window                       *
/*                                                                  */
/********************************************************************/

class ScrollWin : public CMDIChildWnd {

 /******************************************************************/
 /*                                                                */
 /* Class Data Members                                             */
 /*                                                                */
 /******************************************************************/

protected:

CPen        whitePen;    // a set of pens
CPen        redPen;
CPen        bluePen;
CPen        greenPen;

CBrush      blackBrush; // a set of brushes
CBrush      blueBrush;
CBrush      grayBrush;

int          arraySize;    // set to 500 CPoint objects
HANDLE       hlparray;     // handle of global lp array for points
CPoint*      lp;           // locked ptr of lp array of x,y points

CDC*         ptrmemdc;         // memory device context for drawing
CBitmap*     ptrmembitmap;     // memory bitmap of drawing
CRgn*        ptrregn;          // clipping region

CRect        fullWindow;       // max sized window
CRect        displayWindow;    // current display window size
CPoint       scrollPosition;   // offset from full window to 0,0 of
                               // paint's display window

int          screenXpels;      // screen's X dimension
int          screenYpels;      // screen's Y dimension

int          currentVpel;      // current vertical scroll offset
int          currentHpel;      // current horizontal scroll offset
int          numVpelsToScroll;
int          numHpelsToScroll;
int          maxVscrollPels;  // max num vertical pels to scroll
int          maxHscrollPels;  // max num horiz pels to scroll

int          avgCharWidth;     // average character width
int          avgCharHeight;    // average character height
int          avgCapsWidth;     // average capital's width

 /******************************************************************/
 /*                                                                */
 /* Class Functions:                                               */
 /*                                                                */
 /******************************************************************/

public:
               ScrollWin (int mapsize = 400);  // constructor

```

```
protected:

 void  GetAvgCharDims ();     // get the average character dims
 void  RemoveMemDC ();        // delete memory DC objects
 void  ConstructMemDC ();     // construct new memory DC
 void  DrawMemDC ();          // draw objects on memory DC

afx_msg void  OnClose ();     // can close this draw window
afx_msg void  OnDestroy (); // destroy all objects
afx_msg void  OnPaint ();
afx_msg int   OnCreate (LPCREATESTRUCT); // construct memory dc
afx_msg void  OnSize (UINT, int, int);   // reset scrolling size
afx_msg void  OnKeyDown (UINT, UINT, UINT); // keybd interface
afx_msg void  OnHScroll (UINT, UINT, CScrollBar*);
afx_msg void  OnVScroll (UINT, UINT, CScrollBar*);

//user has changed display settings, so need to rebuild
afx_msg LRESULT OnDisplayChange (WPARAM, LPARAM);

DECLARE_MESSAGE_MAP()
};
```

In the **ScrollWin** implementation, the constructor now only performs initialization duties, allocating pens and brushes, defining the window and scrolling rectangles, and similar actions. Recall that the **FrameWin** now actually calls the **ScrollWin Create**. In **OnCreate**, once the window element is constructed, the full screen dimensions are acquired; this replaces the **SysInfo** class which before had maintained the screen dimensions.

In **OnClose**, which is invoked when the user attempts to close this window, the MDI frame's **fastClose** member must be checked to determine if a Close All is currently in effect. The **CWnd** function **GetParentFrame** is used to obtain a pointer to the **CMDIFrameWnd**; it must be cast back into a **FrameWin** pointer so that **fastclose** can be accessed. Notice that **MDIDestroy** is called if the window is to close.

```
void  ScrollWin::OnClose () {
 FrameWin *ptrparent = (FrameWin*) (GetParentFrame());
 if (ptrparent->fastClose == FALSE) {
  CString title, msg;
  title.LoadString (IDS_SCROLL_QUIT);
  msg.LoadString (IDS_SCROLL_QUIT_MSG);
  if (MessageBox (msg, title, MB_YESNO | MB_ICONQUESTION)
      == IDYES) {
   MDIDestroy ();
  }
 }
}
```

Here is the complete **ScrollWin** implementation. Notice how easily it converts into an MDI child window.

ScrollWin Class Implementation

```
#include "StdAfx.h"
#include "ScrollWin.h"   // class definition
#include "resource2.h" // pick up resource id numbers
#include "FrameWin.h"

/***************************************************************/
/*                                                             */
/* Message Map                                                 */
/*                                                             */
/***************************************************************/

BEGIN_MESSAGE_MAP(ScrollWin, CMDIChildWnd)
 ON_WM_CREATE()
 ON_WM_DESTROY()
```

```
 ON_WM_CLOSE()
 ON_WM_KEYDOWN()
 ON_WM_VSCROLL ()
 ON_WM_HSCROLL ()
 ON_WM_SIZE ()
 ON_WM_PAINT ()
 ON_MESSAGE(WM_DISPLAYCHANGE, OnDisplayChange)
END_MESSAGE_MAP()

/**************************************************************/
/*                                                            */
/* ScrollWin: make pens, brushes, and setup scrolling sizes   */
/*                                                            */
/**************************************************************/

ScrollWin::ScrollWin (int mapsize) : CMDIChildWnd () {
 // construct the objects needed for drawing
 whitePen.CreatePen (PS_SOLID, 1, RGB (255, 255, 255));
 redPen.CreatePen (PS_SOLID, 1, RGB (255, 0, 0));
 bluePen.CreatePen (PS_SOLID, 1, RGB (0, 0, 255));
 greenPen.CreatePen (PS_SOLID, 1, RGB (0, 255, 0));

 blackBrush.CreateSolidBrush(RGB (0, 0, 0));
 blueBrush.CreateSolidBrush(RGB (0, 0, 255));
 grayBrush.CreateSolidBrush(RGB (192, 192, 192));

 fullWindow.top     = fullWindow.left      = 0;
 fullWindow.right   = fullWindow.bottom    = mapsize;

 displayWindow.top  = displayWindow.bottom = 0;
 displayWindow.left = displayWindow.right  = 0;

 // allocate from global memory an array of 500 CPoint objects
 arraySize = 500;
 hlparray = GlobalAlloc (GMEM_MOVEABLE,
                         arraySize * sizeof (CPoint));
 ptrmemdc     = 0;
 ptrmembitmap = 0;
 ptrregn      = 0;
 currentVpel = 0;
 currentHpel = 0;
}

/**************************************************************/
/*                                                            */
/* OnCreate: build the memory dc and bitmap and drawing once  */
/*                                                            */
/**************************************************************/

int ScrollWin::OnCreate (LPCREATESTRUCT lpCS) {
 if (CMDIChildWnd::OnCreate (lpCS) == -1) return -1;
 GetAvgCharDims ();
 CClientDC dc (this);
 screenXpels = dc.GetDeviceCaps (HORZRES);
 screenYpels = dc.GetDeviceCaps (VERTRES);
 ConstructMemDC ();
 DrawMemDC ();
 return 0;
}

/**************************************************************/
/*                                                            */
/* OnSize: acquire the current dimensions of the client window */
/*         and reset scrolling ranges                         */
```

```
/*                                                              */
/****************************************************************/

void ScrollWin::OnSize (UINT, int, int) {
GetClientRect (&displayWindow); // get new window size
 // force new display size not to exceed full map window size
 if (displayWindow.bottom>fullWindow.bottom)
     displayWindow.bottom=fullWindow.bottom;

 if (displayWindow.right>fullWindow.right)
     displayWindow.right=fullWindow.right;

 // based on size of current display and max full window map size
 // set the scrolling range
 maxVscrollPels = fullWindow.bottom - displayWindow.bottom;
 maxHscrollPels = fullWindow.right  - displayWindow.right;
 currentVpel = min (currentVpel, maxVscrollPels);
 currentHpel = min (currentHpel, maxHscrollPels);

 SetScrollRange (SB_VERT, 0, maxVscrollPels, FALSE);
 SetScrollPos (SB_VERT, currentVpel, TRUE);
 SetScrollRange (SB_HORZ, 0, maxHscrollPels, FALSE);
 SetScrollPos (SB_HORZ, currentHpel, TRUE);
}

/****************************************************************/
/*                                                              */
/* OnPaint: display what's appropriate from the memory dc      */
/*                                                              */
/****************************************************************/

void ScrollWin::OnPaint () {
 CPaintDC dc (this);
 if (ptrmemdc)
  // display the memDC onto that portion of the display window
  // using bitblt tocopy from memory to the client area dc
  dc.BitBlt (displayWindow.left, displayWindow.top,
             displayWindow.right - displayWindow.left,
             displayWindow.bottom - displayWindow.top,
             ptrmemdc, currentHpel, currentVpel, SRCCOPY);
}

/****************************************************************/
/*                                                              */
/* GetAvgCharDims: retrieve current font's average dimensions  */
/*                                                              */
/****************************************************************/

void ScrollWin::GetAvgCharDims () {
 TEXTMETRIC  tm;  // set the system font's characteristics in tm
 CClientDC dc (this);    // acquire a DC
 dc.GetTextMetrics (&tm); // get the font information
 // calculate average character parameters
 avgCharWidth = tm.tmAveCharWidth;
 avgCharHeight = tm.tmHeight + tm.tmExternalLeading;
 avgCapsWidth = (tm.tmPitchAndFamily & 1 ? 3 : 2) *
                  avgCharWidth / 2;
}

/****************************************************************/
/*                                                              */
/* OnDestroy: remove the array and memory dc and bitmap        */
/*                                                              */
/****************************************************************/
```

```

void ScrollWin::OnDestroy () {
 if (hlparray)
  GlobalFree(hlparray);
 RemoveMemDC ();
 CMDIChildWnd::OnDestroy ();
}

/***************************************************************/
/*                                                             */
/* OnClose: check if can close andd handle fast closing        */
/*                                                             */
/***************************************************************/

void  ScrollWin::OnClose () {
 FrameWin *ptrparent = (FrameWin*) (GetParentFrame());
 if (ptrparent->fastClose == FALSE) {
  CString title, msg;
  title.LoadString (IDS_SCROLL_QUIT);
  msg.LoadString (IDS_SCROLL_QUIT_MSG);
  if (MessageBox (msg, title, MB_YESNO | MB_ICONQUESTION)
      == IDYES) {
   MDIDestroy ();
  }
 }
}

/***************************************************************/
/*                                                             */
/* OnDisplayChange: user has changed the display settings, so  */
/*                  we must update totally rebuild the memory dc */
/*                                                             */
/***************************************************************/

LRESULT ScrollWin::OnDisplayChange (WPARAM which, LPARAM lp) {
 LRESULT retcd = CMDIChildWnd::OnDisplayChange (which, lp);
 if (which == 1) {
  CClientDC dc (this);
  screenXpels = dc.GetDeviceCaps (HORZRES);
  screenYpels = dc.GetDeviceCaps (VERTRES);
  GetAvgCharDims ();       // reacquire the character dimensions
  RemoveMemDC ();          // delete old memory DC
  ConstructMemDC ();       // build new memory DC
 }
 return retcd;
}

/***************************************************************/
/*                                                             */
/* RemoveMemDC: delete all memory DC items and reset ptrs to 0 */
/*                                                             */
/***************************************************************/

void ScrollWin::RemoveMemDC () {
 if (ptrmemdc)
  delete ptrmemdc;
 if (ptrmembitmap)
  delete ptrmembitmap;
 if (ptrregn)
  delete ptrregn;
 ptrmemdc = 0;
 ptrmembitmap = 0;
 ptrregn = 0;
}
```

```

/**************************************************************/
/*                                                            */
/* ConstructMemDC: builds a memory DC and bitmap for drawing  */
/*                                                            */
/**************************************************************/

void ScrollWin::ConstructMemDC () {
 CClientDC dc (this);
 ptrmemdc = new CDC ();
 ptrmemdc->CreateCompatibleDC (&dc); // create the memory dc
 ptrmembitmap = new CBitmap ();      // create a bitmap for memdc
 ptrmembitmap->CreateCompatibleBitmap (&dc,
               screenXpels, screenYpels); // a large one
 ptrmemdc->SelectObject(ptrmembitmap); // put  bitmap into memDC

 //install clipping region if desired, not needed in this example
 ptrregn = new CRgn();
 CRect rec (0, 0, screenXpels, screenYpels);
 ptrregn->CreateRectRgnIndirect (&rec); // define the region
 ptrmemdc->SelectClipRgn (ptrregn);     // set up clipping region
}

/**************************************************************/
/*                                                            */
/* DrawMemDC: draws graphical images into the memory DC       */
/*                                                            */
/**************************************************************/

void ScrollWin::DrawMemDC () {
 lp = (CPoint*) GlobalLock(hlparray);  // lock down array
 // clear out whole previous image
 CRect rec (0, 0, screenXpels, screenYpels);
 ptrmemdc->FillRect (&rec, &blackBrush);

 // draw a red line around full window area
 // here I am illustrating the use of the array and global memory
 // it would be vastly easier just to call Rectangle()
 lp[0].x=0;                     lp[0].y=0;
 lp[1].x=0;                     lp[1].y=fullWindow.right-1;
 lp[2].x=fullWindow.right-1; lp[2].y=fullWindow.right-1;
 lp[3].x=fullWindow.right-1; lp[3].y=0;
 lp[4].x=0;                     lp[4].y=0;
 ptrmemdc->SelectObject (&redPen); // install red pen to draw box
 ptrmemdc->Polyline (lp, 5);       // draw red line around edge

 // draw a series of rectangles the easy way
 ptrmemdc->SelectObject (&whitePen);
 ptrmemdc->SelectObject(&blueBrush);
 // white around blue center
 ptrmemdc->Rectangle (20, 20, 70, 50);

 ptrmemdc->SelectObject (&redPen);
 // red around blue center
 ptrmemdc->Rectangle (320, 320, 370, 350);

 ptrmemdc->SelectObject (&grayBrush);
 // red around gray center
 ptrmemdc->Rectangle (220, 220, 270, 250);

 GlobalUnlock(hlparray);  // unlock global memory lp array
}

/**************************************************************/
```

```
/*                                                              */
/* OnKeyDown: provide a keyboard scroller interface             */
/*                                                              */
/****************************************************************/

void ScrollWin::OnKeyDown (UINT key, UINT, UINT) {
 switch (key) {

  case VK_UP:     // requests scroll up 1 line
   SendMessage (WM_VSCROLL, SB_LINEUP, 0L); break;

  case VK_DOWN:   // requests scroll down 1 line
   SendMessage (WM_VSCROLL, SB_LINEDOWN, 0L); break;

  case VK_LEFT:   // requests scroll left 1 col
   SendMessage (WM_HSCROLL, SB_LINEUP, 0L); break;

  case VK_RIGHT: // requests scroll right 1 col
   SendMessage (WM_HSCROLL, SB_LINEDOWN, 0L); break;

  case VK_PRIOR: // request scroll 1 page up
   SendMessage (WM_VSCROLL, SB_PAGEUP, 0L); break;

  case VK_NEXT:  // request scroll 1 page down
   SendMessage (WM_VSCROLL, SB_PAGEDOWN, 0L); break;

  case VK_END:    // request goto the bottom
   SendMessage (WM_HSCROLL, SB_PAGEDOWN, 0L); break;

  case VK_HOME:  // request goto the top
   SendMessage (WM_HSCROLL, SB_PAGEUP, 0L);  break;
 }
}

/****************************************************************/
/*                                                              */
/* OnVScroll: scroll window vertically                          */
/*                                                              */
/****************************************************************/

void ScrollWin::OnVScroll (UINT type, UINT pos, CScrollBar*) {
 switch (type) {
  case SB_LINEUP:      // scroll up 1 line
   numVpelsToScroll = -1; break;

  case SB_LINEDOWN:    // scroll 1 line down
   numVpelsToScroll = 1; break;

  case SB_PAGEUP:      // scroll 1 page up
   numVpelsToScroll = -8; break;

  case SB_PAGEDOWN:    // scroll 1 page down
   numVpelsToScroll = 8; break;

  case SB_THUMBTRACK: // follow thumb bar
   numVpelsToScroll = pos - currentVpel; break;

  default:
   numVpelsToScroll = 0;
 }
 numVpelsToScroll = max (-currentVpel,
                      min (numVpelsToScroll,
                           maxVscrollPels - currentVpel));
 if (numVpelsToScroll !=0) {
```

```
  currentVpel +=numVpelsToScroll;
  ScrollWindow (0, -numVpelsToScroll, NULL, NULL);
  SetScrollPos (SB_VERT, currentVpel, TRUE);
 }
}

/***************************************************************/
/*                                                             */
/* OnHScroll: scroll window horizontally                       */
/*                                                             */
/***************************************************************/

void ScrollWin::OnHScroll (UINT type, UINT pos, CScrollBar*) {
 switch (type) {
  case SB_LINEUP:     // scroll 1 col left
   numHpelsToScroll = -1; break;

  case SB_LINEDOWN:   // scroll 1 col right
   numHpelsToScroll = 1; break;

  case SB_PAGEUP:     // scroll 1 page left
   numHpelsToScroll = -8; break;

  case SB_PAGEDOWN:    // scroll 1 page right
   numHpelsToScroll = 8; break;

  case SB_THUMBTRACK: // follow thumb bar
   numHpelsToScroll = pos - currentHpel; break;

  default:
   numHpelsToScroll = 0;
 }
 numHpelsToScroll = max (-currentHpel,
                      min (numHpelsToScroll,
                           maxHscrollPels - currentHpel));
 if (numHpelsToScroll !=0) {
  currentHpel +=numHpelsToScroll;
  ScrollWindow (-numHpelsToScroll, 0, NULL, NULL);
  SetScrollPos (SB_HORZ, currentHpel, TRUE);
 }
}
```

Converting Pgm10a's DrawWin to a CMDIChildWnd

Converting Chapter 10's **DrawWin** into a MDI child is more difficult for three reasons. We must supply the hide/show menu. The ownership of the tool box must be moved into the MDI child window from the **FrameWin** class. Much of the original frame window and main window classes must be merged back into one MDI child window.

DrawWin illustrates two approaches to menu handling. With the simple hide/show tool box menu item, I chose to have the **DrawWin** class install that menu item when the very first **DrawWin** child is launched. Similarly, when the last **DrawWin** child is removed, the menu item is removed. In order to track the number of instances of **DrawWin** that are in existence, I added a static data member, **numdraw**. This integer is incremented in the **DrawWin** constructor and decremented in **OnDestroy**. **numdraw** is this a reference counter.

The second menu approach handles the entire pop-up menu for Drawing Effects. Here manually creating this entire pop-up menu would have been tedious. I chose to place it in the main frame window menu instead. In a later chapter, we will see a third approach in which the framework automatically merges a child window's menu with the main frame window's menu.

To dynamically add this new hide/show tool box menu item, we maintain a static count of the number of launched instances. When the first instance of the Draw MDI child is launched, it can gain access to the main frame window's menu and then the View pop-up group. If the new menu item is not yet on the menu (which would be the case when the first Draw child is launched), the Draw child can append the hide/show menu item. Subsequent Draw children can check the instance count and if non-zero, the hide/show menu item is already installed, avoiding numerous hide/show menu items in the View pop up menu. Alternatively, each child could check the static count of windows. To remove that menu item, when the Draw child is destroyed, it can check the instance count and if now zero, remove the menu item.

Look over the **DrawWin** class header file and notice that there are very few changes needed beyond moving coding from the old frame window class into the **DrawWin** class. Let's examine the implementation step by step. Note that the **CToolBox** class is exactly the same as in Chapter 10 and is not shown below.

DrawWin Class Definition

```
#pragma  once

#include "CToolBox.h"

/***************************************************************/
/*                                                             */
/* DrawWin Class Definition                                    */
/*                                                             */
/***************************************************************/

class DrawWin : public CMDIChildWnd {

 /**************************************************************/
 /*                                                            */
 /* Class Data Members                                         */
 /*                                                            */
 /**************************************************************/

protected:

 static int numdraw;     // total number of draw children active

 COLORREF   colors[6];   // the possible colors array
 COLORREF   linecolor;   // current drawing pen color
 int        colnum;      // current pen color array index
 int        linewidth;   // current pen width
 bool       buttondown;  // true if leftbutton is down for drawing
 CPen*      ptrpen;      // the current drawing pen
 CClientDC* ptrdc;       // the current drawing DC
 CToolBox   toolbox;     // client window's tool box

 /**************************************************************/
 /*                                                            */
 /* Class Functions                                            */
 /*                                                            */
 /**************************************************************/

public:
                 DrawWin (); // set initial line width & color
afx_msg void     OnPaint (); // paint background white

protected:
afx_msg void     OnClose ();                     // check if can close
afx_msg int      OnCreate(LPCREATESTRUCT); // construct tool box
afx_msg void     OnDestroy ();         // remove allocated menus & child

// remove tool box when minimized
afx_msg void     OnSize (UINT, int, int);

// reshow tool box when restoring
afx_msg BOOL     OnQueryOpen ();

// reposition tool box as win moves
```

```
afx_msg void  OnMove (int, int);

afx_msg void  OnLButtonDown (UINT, CPoint); // begin drawing
afx_msg void  OnLButtonUp (UINT, CPoint);   // end drawing
afx_msg void  OnMouseMove (UINT, CPoint);   // continue drawing

int    DisplayMsg (int, int, UINT);    // display a message
void   UpdateStatusBar ();             // display msg on status bar

// check mark hide/show tool box
afx_msg void  OnUpdateViewToolBox (CCmdUI*);
afx_msg void  CmLines (UINT);    // process all line width btns
afx_msg void  CmColors (UINT);   // process all color btns presses
afx_msg void  OnUpdateToolBoxLines (CCmdUI*); //enable line width
afx_msg void  OnUpdateToolBoxColors (CCmdUI*);//enable color btns

DECLARE_MESSAGE_MAP()
};
```

The first time only positioning of the tool box does not need to be done because the MDI child is now a frame window; it is initially placed on the right side of the draw window. Next, the handling of whether or not to install our hide/show menu item is controlled by the static **numdraw** initially zero.

The pop-up menu layout or **menu description** is vital not only for proper handling of MDI menus but also for OLE operations (Object Linking and Embedding). The genesis of the menu description is OLE. Historically, there had to be a common way for child windows to modify the main menu even when that child had absolutely no idea of what was in the main menu. OLE's big problem is how to link or embed a paintbrush image in a text document, for example, because the menu structures are totally different.

The solution is to generalize the **significance** of the various pop-up menus that appear on the menu bar. OLE defines six logical groups in the order they appear on the menu bar.

1 File Group
2 Edit Group
3 Container Group
4 Object Group
5 Window Group
6 Help Group

Each group may contain 0, 1, or more pop up menus. Normally, the file group contains only the File menu that we have been using throughout all of our examples. The Edit group often contains two pop-ups—one for Edit (cut and paste) and one for Search (find and replace). Windows and Help each usually contain one pop-up menu. The Window pop-up is nearly always the MDI group, perhaps with additions. The container group often contains the pop-up menu that enables the user to control the various decorations, such as the View menu we have been using. And the object group provides one document specific set of pop-up menus. For example, in the Write application, the Character, Paragraph, and Document pop-up menus are object group specific menus.

This is a **logical** grouping of pop-up menus. On the menu bar, they all appear one after the other. For example in Write the main menu appears this way.

```
File Edit Find Character Paragraph Document Help
```

The number of pop-up menus within the six group scheme is this: 1 2 0 3 0 1, or 1 in File, 2 in Edit, none in Container, 3 in Object, none in Window, and 1 in Help.

When dealing with OLE, it is precisely this line of integers that is being provided to the **OleSetMenuDescr** function, which notifies the menu manager how to group the pop-up menus. Examine again the **Pgm11a.rc** file and find the menu layout. We asked for the following pop-up menus.

```
File  Start Tools  Drawing Tools  View  Window  Help
```

Following the OLE scheme, the file group has one pop-up; Edit group has none; the container group has one, the Start Tools; the object group has one, the Drawing Tools; the Windows group has two, View and Window; and the Help group has one. Once we have set up this logical scheme, it becomes very easy for all child windows to modify the main menu at will. Child windows can then add and delete both groups and menu items. Looking over the categories, most frequently a child window would like to add an Object group for those pop up menus that are unique to it. Ok, so this isn't a text on OLE, but you should still consider in which groups you place your menu items.

The installation of the menu item is done in **OnCreate** after the call to the base class is complete. If there are no instances yet, access is made to the main menu by dynamically obtaining a pointer to the main **CMDIFrameWnd** and, using the member function **GetMenu** which returns a pointer to the main menu, an instance of **CMenu** is obtained. This pointer is then used to get a further pointer to the "View" pop-up menu at offset 3, using **GetSubMenu** which also returns a **CMenu** pointer.

```
if (numdraw==0) {
 CMenu *ptrmenu = AfxGetApp()->m_pMainWnd->GetMenu ();
 CMenu *ptrsmenu = ptrmenu->GetSubMenu (3);
 char menuitem[40];
 LoadString (AfxGetApp()->m_hInstance, IDB_TOOLBOX, menuitem,
                                       sizeof(menuitem));
 ptrsmenu->AppendMenu (MF_ENABLED | MF_STRING, IDB_TOOLBOX,
                       menuitem);
}
```

Then, load in the hide/show tool box message string from the resource file. Finally, use the **CMenu** function **AppendMenu** to install it.

Conversely, in **OnDestroy** if this is the last **DrawWin** child, the menu item must be removed. If **numdraw** is now zero, obtain a pointer first to the main menu as was done in **OnCreate** and, from that, get a pointer to the View pop-up menu. Then, use the **DeleteMenu** function to remove the hide/show tool box menu item by passing it the command ID and the **MF_BYCOMMAND** identifier.

```
if (numdraw==0) {
 CMenu *ptrmenu = AfxGetApp()->m_pMainWnd->GetMenu ();
 CMenu *ptrsmenu = ptrmenu->GetSubMenu (3);
 ptrsmenu->DeleteMenu (IDB_TOOLBOX, MF_BYCOMMAND);
}
```

The tool box requires more action on our part only when it has become floating; while docked, the **CMDIFrameWnd** handles it. Therefore, we must be able to detect when **DrawWin** is about to be minimized and hide the tool bar before iconization occurs. Otherwise, the tool box ends up appended to a corner of the iconized window. Later, when the icon is about to be restored, we must re-show the tool box. (Note that one could create another **bool** member to keep track of whether the window was hidden by the user before the minimization request and upon restoration, preserve that setting. Here upon restoration, the tool box always reappears.)

When a window is about to become minimized, the **WM_SYSCOMMAND** is sent with the **SC_MINIMIZE** flag enabled. As a result, the **OnSysCommand** function was often used to check for minimization. Be careful using this message handler because minimization can also occur using a mouse double click on the title bar. When the user presses the left mouse button on the title bar, a **WM_SYSCOMMAND** message is sent but the flags have nearly all possibilities set! This occurs because the user could next begin dragging the window (a Move) or could double click (Maximize/Restore), for example. So here again is the single click, drag, or double click on an object problem we examined earlier. Since Windows does not know before hand for certain the exact meaning of the first left button down on the title bar just yet, many of the flags are set. Windows then begins a potential Move window operation but quickly alters it to a Maximize or Restore operation. The end result is that if you only check the flags for **SC_MINIMIZED**, you may respond to a non-existent request as the user is actually moving the window.

In this application, only the fact that the application is now minimized is needed so that we can hide the tool box. A far safer place to check for this occurrence is in **OnSize**. A **WM_SIZE** message is also sent to the window after it has been minimized notifying the window that it is now iconized. The flags are set to the identifier **SIZE_MINIMIZED**. Thus, in **OnSize** check for iconization and if so, hide the tool box. Next, whenever an iconized window is about to be restored, Windows sends that window a **WM_QUERYOPEN** message to see if it wishes to restore; if it does, it returns **TRUE**. Therefore, respond to **OnQueryOpen** messages to restore the tool box.

In **OnSize** if the MDI child has become iconized, and if the tool box is visible, I send the hide message.

```
if (flags & SIZE_MINIMIZED)
 if (toolbox.GetStyle() & WS_VISIBLE)
  SendMessage (WM_COMMAND, IDB_TOOLBOX, 0L);
```

In **OnMove**, which is invoked whenever the MDI child window is moved, if the tool box is visible, where should the tool box be repositioned if at all? If you ignore the tool box during the movement of the corresponding child window, one can end up with the tool box being located far outside the child frame! This effect is shown in Figure 11.7.

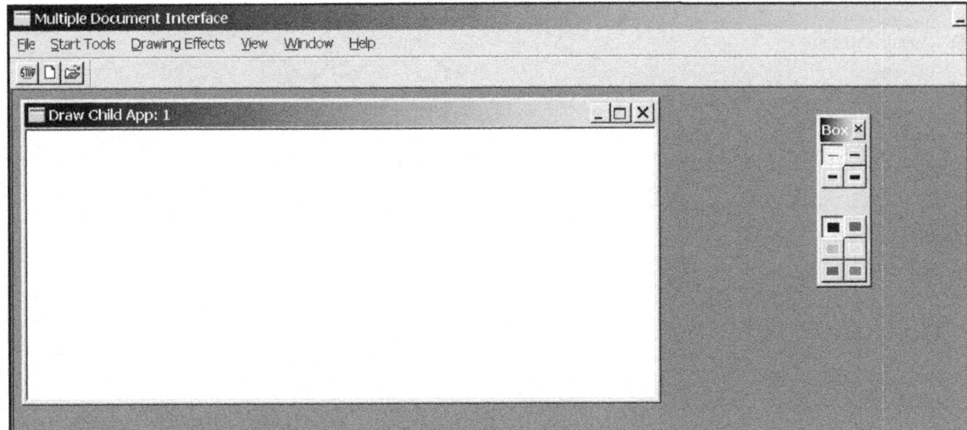

Figure 11.7 Floating Tool Box Far Outside Its Child Window Owner

One way to handle this behavior is to reposition the tool box say at the upper left corner of the child window when it is moved. To illustrate this, uncomment out the following coding in **OnMove**. If the tool box exists and is floating, obtain the needed system metrics and call the **FloatControlBar** function to move it.

```
if (toolbox.GetSafeHwnd () && toolbox.IsFloating ()) {
 CRect r;
 GetWindowRect (&r);
 r.left += GetSystemMetrics (SM_CXFRAME) * 2;
 r.top += GetSystemMetrics (SM_CYFRAME)*2 +
          GetSystemMetrics (SM_CYCAPTION);
 FloatControlBar (&toolbox, CPoint (r.left, r.top));
}
```

Figure 11.8 shows this effect after moving the window.

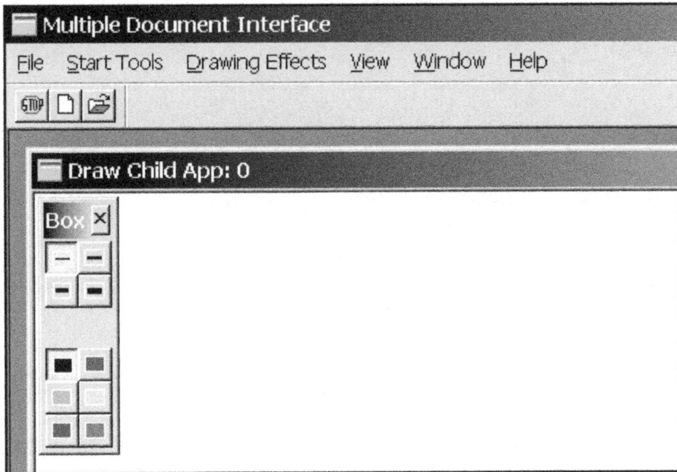

Figure 11.8 Repositioning the Floating Tool Box

Finally, in **OnQueryOpen**, when the MDI window is about to be restored, I send the re-show tool box message.

```
SendMessage (WM_COMMAND, IDB_TOOLBOX, 0L);
return CMDIChildWnd::OnQueryOpen ();
```

Here is the complete coding for the **DrawWin**.

```
DrawWin Class Implementation
```

```
#include "StdAfx.h"
#include "DrawWin.h"
#include "FrameWin.h"
#include "resource1.h"
#include "resource.h"

/*************************************************************/
/*                                                           */
/* Old Style Method of Tool Bar Construction                 */
/*                                                           */
/*************************************************************/

static UINT BASED_CODE buttons_box[] = {
  CM_LINE1,
  CM_LINE2,
  CM_LINE3,
  CM_LINE4,
  ID_SEPARATOR,
  ID_SEPARATOR,
  CM_COLORA,
  CM_COLORB,
  CM_COLORC,
  CM_COLORD,
  CM_COLORE,
  CM_COLORF,
};

/*************************************************************/
/*                                                           */
/* Message map                                               */
/*                                                           */
/*************************************************************/

BEGIN_MESSAGE_MAP(DrawWin, CMDIChildWnd)
 ON_WM_CREATE ()
 ON_WM_PAINT ()
 ON_WM_DESTROY ()
 ON_WM_LBUTTONDOWN ()
 ON_WM_LBUTTONUP()
 ON_WM_MOUSEMOVE()
 ON_WM_CLOSE()
 ON_WM_SIZE()
 ON_WM_MOVE()
 ON_WM_QUERYOPEN()
 ON_UPDATE_COMMAND_UI(IDB_TOOLBOX, OnUpdateViewToolBox)
 ON_COMMAND_EX(IDB_TOOLBOX, OnBarCheck)
 ON_COMMAND_RANGE(CM_LINE1, CM_LINE4, CmLines)
 ON_COMMAND_RANGE(CM_COLORA, CM_COLORF, CmColors)
 ON_UPDATE_COMMAND_UI_RANGE(CM_LINE1, CM_LINE4,
                            OnUpdateToolBoxLines)
 ON_UPDATE_COMMAND_UI_RANGE(CM_COLORA, CM_COLORF,
                            OnUpdateToolBoxColors)
END_MESSAGE_MAP()

// number of DrawWin - controls hide/show menu item
int   DrawWin::numdraw = 0;

/*************************************************************/
/*                                                           */
/* Drawwin: Construct the window object                      */
/*                                                           */
/*************************************************************/

DrawWin::DrawWin () {
```

```
 colnum      = 0;                 // set initial black color
 linewidth   = 1;                 // set initial line width of 1

 buttondown  = false;             // signal not drawing now
 ptrpen      = 0;                 // set no current pen
 ptrdc       = 0;                 // or DC for drawing

 // initialize possible colors
 colors[0]   = RGB (0,0,0);       // Black
 colors[1]   = RGB (255, 0,0);    // LtRed
 colors[2]   = RGB (0, 255, 0);   // LtGreen
 colors[3]   = RGB (255, 255,0);  // LtYellow
 colors[4]   = RGB (0, 0, 255);   // LtBlue
 colors[5]   = RGB (255, 0,255);  // LtMagenta
 linecolor   = colors[colnum];    // set beginning pen color
}

/***************************************************************/
/*                                                             */
/* OnDestroy: possibly remove the hide show menu               */
/*                                                             */
/***************************************************************/

void DrawWin::OnDestroy () {

 numdraw--;          // dec number of draw children
 if (numdraw==0) {
  // must remove our menu item for hide/show tool box
  // get access to menu and remove hide/show menu item
  CMenu *ptrmenu = AfxGetApp()->m_pMainWnd->GetMenu ();
  CMenu *ptrsmenu = ptrmenu->GetSubMenu (3);
  ptrsmenu->DeleteMenu (IDB_TOOLBOX, MF_BYCOMMAND);
 }
 // now continue destroying this MDI child
 CMDIChildWnd::OnDestroy ();
}

/***************************************************************/
/*                                                             */
/* OnCreate: construct our tool box                            */
/*                                                             */
/***************************************************************/

int DrawWin::OnCreate (LPCREATESTRUCT lpCS) {

 int retcd;
 if ((retcd = CMDIChildWnd::OnCreate (lpCS)) !=0) return -1;

 if (numdraw==0) {
  // this is the first, so install hide/show tool box menu item
  // acquire the main menu & then the offset 3 (4th) pop up menu
  // so that we can append the hide/show tool box item if needed
  CMenu *ptrmenu = AfxGetApp()->m_pMainWnd->GetMenu ();
  CMenu *ptrsmenu = ptrmenu->GetSubMenu (3);
  // so load in a new menu item and install in View menu
  char menuitem[40];
  LoadString (AfxGetApp()->m_hInstance, IDB_TOOLBOX, menuitem,
                                        sizeof(menuitem));
  ptrsmenu->AppendMenu (MF_ENABLED | MF_STRING, IDB_TOOLBOX,
                        menuitem);
 }
 numdraw++;

 // construct tool box: create, load its bitmap,
```

```
 // and assign its command IDs
 if (toolbox.Create (this, WS_CHILD | WS_VISIBLE |
                     CBRS_SIZE_FIXED | CBRS_TOP | CBRS_TOOLTIPS |
                     CBRS_FLYBY, IDB_TOOLBOX)
     && toolbox.LoadBitmap (IDB_TOOLBOX)
     && toolbox.SetButtons (buttons_box, sizeof(buttons_box)
                            / sizeof(UINT)));
 else return -1;

 toolbox.SetColumns (2); // set 2 columns

 // now notify control to accept any form of docking
 toolbox.EnableDocking (CBRS_ALIGN_ANY);

 // notify the framewindow of docking requirements
 EnableDocking (CBRS_ALIGN_ANY);

 // and dock both control bar and tool box at top
 DockControlBar (&toolbox, AFX_IDW_DOCKBAR_RIGHT);

 // insert captions to be shown when the tool bars are floating
 toolbox.SetWindowText(_T("Box"));

 // display initial pen color and width on the status bar
 UpdateStatusBar ();
 return retcd;
}

/*************************************************************/
/*                                                           */
/* UpdateStatusBar: show width and color on the status bar   */
/*                                                           */
/*************************************************************/

void DrawWin::UpdateStatusBar () {
 // this display will be temporary only
 // it will be overlaid by next hints
 // first get a pointer to status bar
 CStatusBar *ptrbar = (CStatusBar*) AfxGetApp()->m_pMainWnd->
                       GetDescendantWindow (AFX_IDW_STATUS_BAR);
 char msg[80]; // construct a message for the status bar
 wsprintf (msg, "Draw: line width: %d - Color: %s",
           linewidth, CToolBox::colors[colnum]);
 ptrbar->SetPaneText (0, msg); // and display the message
}

/*************************************************************/
/*                                                           */
/* OnSize: on going minimized, hide any visible tool box     */
/*                                                           */
/*************************************************************/

void DrawWin::OnSize (UINT flags, int width, int height) {
 CMDIChildWnd::OnSize (flags, width, height);
 if (flags & SIZE_MINIMIZED)      // check if we are now minimized
  if (toolbox.GetStyle() & WS_VISIBLE)  // is tool box visible
   SendMessage (WM_COMMAND, IDB_TOOLBOX, 0L); // yes, so hide it
}

/*************************************************************/
/*                                                           */
/* OnMove: force tool box to reposition when parent moves    */
/*                                                           */
/*************************************************************/
```

```

void DrawWin::OnMove (int x, int y) {
 CMDIChildWnd::OnMove (x, y);
// if (toolbox.GetSafeHwnd () && toolbox.IsFloating ()) {
//  CRect r;
//  GetWindowRect (&r);
//  r.left += GetSystemMetrics (SM_CXFRAME) * 2;
//  r.top += GetSystemMetrics (SM_CYFRAME)*2 +
//           GetSystemMetrics (SM_CYCAPTION);
//  FloatControlBar (&toolbox, CPoint (r.left, r.top));
// }
}

/****************************************************************/
/*                                                              */
/* EvQueryOpen: when restoring from icon, reshow tool box       */
/*                                                              */
/****************************************************************/

BOOL DrawWin::OnQueryOpen () {
 SendMessage (WM_COMMAND, IDB_TOOLBOX, 0L);// force show tool box
 return CMDIChildWnd::OnQueryOpen (); // and continue the Restore
}

/****************************************************************/
/*                                                              */
/* CmLines: handle any of the line button presses               */
/*                                                              */
/****************************************************************/

void DrawWin::CmLines (UINT cmd) {
 // line width is the command ID less the command ID of line 1 +1
 linewidth = cmd - CM_LINE1 + 1;
 UpdateStatusBar (); // display new choice on status bar
}

/****************************************************************/
/*                                                              */
/* CmColors: handle any of the color button presses             */
/*                                                              */
/****************************************************************/

void DrawWin::CmColors (UINT cmd) {
 // color idx = command number less the command ID of first color
 colnum = cmd - CM_COLORA;
 UpdateStatusBar (); // display new color choice on status bar
}

/****************************************************************/
/*                                                              */
/* OnUpdateViewToolBox: handles the check mark on menu item     */
/*                                                              */
/****************************************************************/

void DrawWin::OnUpdateViewToolBox (CCmdUI *ptrui) {
 // place check mark on menu item is tool box is now visible
 ptrui->SetCheck ((toolbox.GetStyle() & WS_VISIBLE) != 0);
}

/****************************************************************/
/*                                                              */
/* OnUpdateToolBoxLines: set line button as pressed             */
/*                                                              */
/****************************************************************/
```

```

void DrawWin::OnUpdateToolBoxLines (CCmdUI *ptrui) {
 ptrui->SetRadio (
       (UINT) (linewidth + CM_LINE1 -1) == ptrui->m_nID ? 1 : 0);
}

/*************************************************************/
/*                                                           */
/* OnUpdateToolBoxColors: set color button as pressed        */
/*                                                           */
/*************************************************************/

void DrawWin::OnUpdateToolBoxColors (CCmdUI *ptrui) {
 ptrui->SetRadio (
             (UINT)(colnum + CM_COLORA) == ptrui->m_nID ? 1 : 0);
}

/*************************************************************/
/*                                                           */
/* OnLButtonDown: begin drawing                              */
/*                                                           */
/*************************************************************/

void DrawWin::OnLButtonDown (UINT, CPoint point) {
 if (!buttondown) {     // avoid multiple invocations by dblclick
  buttondown = true;            // signal drawing
  ptrdc  = new CClientDC (this);// get new draw DC
  linecolor = colors[colnum];   // set line RGB color to use
  ptrpen = new CPen (PS_SOLID, linewidth, linecolor);
  ptrdc->SelectObject (ptrpen); // install pen in DC
  SetCapture ();          // capture all mouse movements for draw
  ptrdc->MoveTo (point);  // set pen to starting point for draw
 }
}

/*************************************************************/
/*                                                           */
/* OnLButtonUp: stop drawing the line                        */
/*                                                           */
/*************************************************************/

void DrawWin::OnLButtonUp (UINT, CPoint) {
 if (buttondown) {
  if (ptrdc) delete ptrdc;   // stop drawing - remove GDI objects
  if (ptrpen) delete ptrpen; // if flurry of clicks, avoids crash
  buttondown = false;        // signal not drawing
  ReleaseCapture ();         // and release mouse
 }
}

/*************************************************************/
/*                                                           */
/* OnMouseMove: draw a line to mouse position                */
/*                                                           */
/*************************************************************/

void DrawWin::OnMouseMove (UINT, CPoint point) {
 if (buttondown)
  ptrdc->LineTo (point); // draw line to here given by point
}

/*************************************************************/
/*                                                           */
/* OnPaint: just repaint the background white                */
```

```
/*                                                                  */
/********************************************************************/

void DrawWin::OnPaint() {
 CPaintDC dc(this); // minimalist paint
}

/********************************************************************/
/*                                                                  */
/* OnClose: query user if we can terminate this drawing             */
/*                                                                  */
/********************************************************************/

void DrawWin::OnClose () {
 if (((FrameWin*) GetParentFrame())->fastClose == FALSE)
  if (DisplayMsg (IDS_DRAW_MSG_QUERY, IDS_DRAWQUIT, MB_YESNO |
              MB_ICONQUESTION) == IDYES)
   MDIDestroy ();
}

/********************************************************************/
/*                                                                  */
/* DisplayMsg: shows a MessageBox and returns its retcode           */
/*                                                                  */
/********************************************************************/

int DrawWin::DisplayMsg (int id1, int id2, UINT flags) {
 CString msg1, msg2;
 msg1.LoadString (id1);
 msg2.LoadString (id2);
 return MessageBox (msg2, msg1, flags);
}
```

So with a minimal effort, both **ScrollWin** and **DrawWin** have been converted into MDI children. MDI supports a very complex application environment. If you always develop your projects with the division of labors as we have been doing in the preceding chapters, only minor changes are required to install that application into a larger MDI application. The next step is to examine how to install text editors as MDI children and then how to conduct cut and paste operations, in other words using the clipboard.

Programming Problems

None

Chapter 12 A Text Editor, Fonts, and Clipboard Operations

Introduction

In this chapter, we explore how an actual text editor can be written. It is one thing to be able to view a text file in a window; it is quite another to provide full text editing capabilities. Such editing would include maintaining a caret and current insertion point within the text, processing **OnChar** messages to obtain the next character, storing and displaying that character and handling the usual arrow keys, insert key, delete key, backspace rubout key, and the tab key. A complete implementation of all of these features would be quite a project, especially when the user is in total control of what font (fixed, variable, and point size) is used.

However, if the file to be edited is sufficiently small, a **CEdit** control can provide all of this functionality with virtually no coding on our part! A **CEdit** control can have the multi-line flag set which causes the control to properly handle <CR><LF> codes by moving to column 1 of the next line when these codes are encountered. Of course, to be workable, the **CEdit** control must be resized to occupy the entire client area of the window. If the proposed **EditWin** class is derived from **CMDIChildWnd**, then the client area is easily obtained from **OnSize** because there are no tool bars to confuse the issue of the real client area.

Since the user very likely wishes to control the font in use, we ought to gain a better understanding of fonts and their metrics and usage.

Finally, we should also implement clipboard operations as well so that the user can use Cut/Copy/Paste operations. When a **CEdit** control is used, that class provides several functions that completely handle these operations; they are called **Cut**, **Copy**, and **Paste**. However, handling graphical clipboard operations is more involved. So we will add clipboard operations to the **DrawWin** class from the last chapter to see how it is done.

The Use of The CEdit Control as a Main Window

In a dialog box, the **CEdit** control provides all the needed text editing services. In fact, the **CEdit** control can be designated a multi-line control so that many separate lines could be shown. When a full-fledged text editing operation is required, one often used trick is to make the **CEdit** control become the client window! Once we install a **CEdit** control as the client window, all of the powerful features are readily available.

One **major** consideration is that the **CEdit** control cannot handle more than 64K worth of text; often, considerably less. The MFC has a **static UINT nMaxSize** set to 64K-2 bytes, unrealistically high. In practice, do not expect to get more than about 32K into a **CEdit** control. If we can live with this shortcoming, we gain enormous functionality from **CEdit** and other derived classes.

This size restriction applies only to Windows 95/98/ME. Under Windows NT/2000, the **CEdit** control may contain up to 2G of text, depending upon the amount of memory and the size of the swap drive.

When we get into the View classes two chapters from now, we will discover that the MFC also provides a number of other classes that aid our application creation. The **CScrollView** class automatically handles scrolling with no coding on our part. Again, unfortunately, it is also subject to this same maximum amount of data or 32,767 lines. If the amount of data to be edited or displayed is not too large, then these controls and classes can be used with a minimal amount of effort on our part.

Just like any other child window such as the tool bar, we maintain an instance of the **CEdit** control as one of our data members, along with the tool box and status bar instances.

```
CEdit   editwin; // our CEdit main window
```

The **CEdit** control is usually created in the **OnCreate** function of the MDI child frame window.

```
CRect rect;
GetClientRect (&rect);
if (!editwin.Create (WS_CHILD | WS_VISIBLE | ES_AUTOHSCROLL |
                     ES_AUTOVSCROLL | ES_MULTILINE |
                     ES_WANTRETURN | WS_VSCROLL | WS_HSCROLL,
                     rect, this, EDITWINDOW)) {
 DisplayMsg (IDS_MSG_ERROR, IDS_MSG_NOMEM, MB_OK);
 return -1;
}
```

The style identifiers are crucial. For a multi-line control, use **ES_MULTILINE**. If **ES_AUTOVSCROLL** and **ES_AUTOHSCROLL** are added, the control automatically handles all scrolling operations. Further, if **WS_VSCROLL** and **WS_HSCROLL** are added, then scroll bars are shown and used automatically. We need to do nothing for proper scrolling. If the scroll bars are not added, then the auto scrolling flags permit the user to scroll by using the arrow keys, scrolling one line or character at a time. The **ES_WANTRETURN** is also crucial. This flag notifies the control to properly interpret the <CR><LF> codes, or end line codes, as line breaks. Without this flag turned on, these control codes display as little black squares.

The **EDITWINDOW** is a made up id used to identify the Edit control (in case of multiple **CEdit** controls). The rectangle provides the location and most importantly, the dimensions of the control, often set to the actual client window size. We must override **OnSize** to readjust the dimensions of the control when the user resizes the window.

```
void EditWin::OnSize (UINT, int width, int height) {
 if (editwin.GetSafeHwnd())
  editwin.MoveWindow (0, 0, width, height, TRUE);
}
```

However, since **OnSize** is called several times during the construction of a window, it is likely that at the very beginning our **CEdit** control has not yet been created. That is, the real interface element has not been created; there is no **hwnd**. Thus, we must guard against an attempt to move a window which does not yet exist. By calling the **GetSafeHwnd** function, we can tell if this control has had its interface element created or not. Only if the real Win32 Edit control exists does the **MoveWindow** function get called.

When the MDI child window first appears, the **CEdit** control should be given the focus. If this is not done, then the user must click somewhere within the visible control in order to begin editing.

```
void EditWin::OnSetFocus(CWnd*) {
      editwin.SetFocus();
}
```

Text must be transferred into and out of the Edit control during File New, Open, Save, and SaveAs operations. When an Edit control is used in a dialog, we normally use the automatic data transfer method to put text into the control and retrieve its contents. However, now we must manually perform these actions. The member functions for the text transfer are provided from base classes. Under MFC, the **CEdit** class is derived from **CScrollbar** and from **CWnd** and it uses the **CWnd** member functions **GetWindowText** and **SetWindowText**.

```
      editwin.GetWindowText (charbuffer, numberbytes);
      editwin.SetWindowText (charbuffer);
```

where **charbuffer** is an array of char sufficiently large enough to hold the data. The **CWnd** member function **GetWindowTextLength** returns the number of bytes in the control. Often the two are combined to retrieve the text.

```
      editwin.GetWindowText (buf, editwin.GetWindowTextLength ());
```

The **GetWindowTextLength** function can also be used to assist in enabling/graying the File Save, SaveAs, and other Edit menu items. If the length is zero, there is nothing to save, for example.

When the window is closing, we need to know if the data in the control has been modified since it was placed into the control so that we can prompt the user before closing. The MFC function **GetModify** returns **TRUE** if the data has been altered. We can check for this situation this way.

```
      if (editwin.GetSafeHwnd() &&editwin.GetModify())
        SaveCheck();
```

After a save and when the text is first transferred into the Edit control, any previous setting of the control's modify flag must be cleared. The **CEdit** control maintains a modified flag to track whether or not any changes have been made. We can alter that flag using the **SetModify** function.

```
editwin.SetModify (FALSE); // set CEdit not modified yet
```

The Edit control maintains an undo buffer to facilitate removal of the last change. Again, when text is first loaded into the Edit control, any previous contents of the Edit control must be removed.

```
editwin.EmptyUndoBuffer (); // clear CEdit's undo buffer
```

The Edit control can also report on the current number of lines in the text of the control.

```
int totlines = editwin.GetLineCount ();
```

Finally, when the user changes fonts, the Edit control must be notified of the font change and requested to use the new font. Communication is handled through the **SendMessage** function passing the **WM_SETFONT** message to the Edit control. The message passes a handle to the font as the **wparam** parameter and zero for the **lparam**. We must also call its Invalidate function to make the control repaint its contents in the new font.

```
hfont = CreateFontIndirect (ptrlogfont);
editwin.SendMessage (WM_SETFONT, (WPARAM) hfont, 0L);
editwin.Invalidate ();
```

Given these member functions, a **CEdit** control can easily be installed as a main window providing quite acceptable text editing capabilities. **CEdit** also provides easy-to-use clipboard operations which we will examine shortly. Again, the main restriction is the Windows 95/98/ME limit of 30K to 64K.

All About Fonts

Windows supports many kinds of fonts. Some fonts have been hand-tuned to give optimum viewing on a display. Others are designed for best use on plotter devices. A few fonts give their best results on the printed page. Usually, these special type fonts do not view well when used on devices for which they were not hand-tuned. Also, because of the hand-tuning process, they are available only in a few specific point sizes.

On the other hand since Windows 3.1, the use of TrueType fonts in documents has become widespread. These fonts are completely scalable offering the user virtually any point sizes. However, when printing scalable fonts, especially on a laser printer, they must be properly scaled to fit the printer resolution. If they are not, you may see your page rendered in microscopic letters! Note that TrueType fonts sent to a dot matrix printer are considered bit mapped graphical images and printed as slowly as a paintbrush image.

Note that one might think that the solution would be to decide what **printer** font is going to be used and then install that font as the **screen** display font. However, this approach also does not work because many printer fonts are small. If displayed directly on the screen, they would be illegible. Why? The CRT is often viewed from a distance of about 24 inches from the eye while the printed page is often viewed from an eye distance of 10-12 inches. Thus, magnification becomes a problem. When Windows renders a font, it considers the display surface. For example, if the user specifies an 8 point font, when Windows constructs the font for a screen display, it scales the font to become legible. Yet, when that same font is constructed for a printer display, Windows uses the correct point size. If Windows did not do this scaling, many printer fonts would be illegible on the screen.

Font Details

Windows provides six stock fonts shown in Table 12.1, which define a particular typeface and size. Use the following to select them.

```
dc.SelectStockObject (font ID);
```

Table 12.1 The Windows Stock Fonts

```
SYSTEM_FONT          - a proportional ANSI character set used in menus,
                       dialog boxes, message boxes, and title bars
SYSTEM_FIXED_FONT    - fixed-pitch ANSI font compatible with early
                       versions of Windows - all chars have the same
                       width
```

```
OEM_FIXED_FONT       - often called the terminal font, used for
                       windowed DOS apps using text character based
                       modes
ANSI_FIXED_FONT      - a Courier font smaller than the system of
                       terminal fonts
ANSI_VAR_FONT        - either a Helvetica or Times Roman variable width
                       font usually smaller than the system font
DEVICE_DEFAULT_FONT  - a built-in or most suitable font for a specific
                       device - for a CRT there is none usually, so it
                       uses the system font - for printers, such as a
                       dot-matrix, it is often the default text mode
                       font
```

Fonts fall into two broad categories called **GDI fonts** and **device fonts**. Often, they have the file extension FON while the newer TrueType fonts are stored in two files with extensions of TTF and FOT. The GDI fonts are those that are to be displayed on the screen and come in three broad kinds: **raster fonts**, **stoke fonts**, and **TrueType fonts**.

Raster fonts are stored as a bitmap pixel pattern representing the character. Each raster font is designed for a specific size. Some slight scaling can be done in integer multiples of the original size by duplicating the pixels, but generally the results look poor. Thus, raster fonts are normally used in specifically available sizes and are often referred to as non-scalable fonts. They have two slight advantages: they display faster since they are just a bitmap to **BitBlt** and they have been hand-tuned to present the best legibility.

Stroke fonts are created by drawing lines and are only found in use with plotter devices.

TrueType fonts are completely scalable; they are stored as a set of curves and lines, with hints for scaling effects. Once a specific height and width are set, Windows "rasterizes" the font into the proper bitmap for display; then it is ready for use. This rasterizing process takes a bit of time, but only needs to be done once. The font is stored in memory. TrueType fonts are almost as legible or "good" as the raster fonts, but offer complete scalability.

If you are trying to match the printer's fonts so that you are displaying in the WYSIWYG manner, TrueType is required.

A font is a collection of characters in a particular typeface and size. The term **typeface** denotes only the style. (Note that in the printing world, typeface includes the style, bold, underlining, and the size—a complete package.) There are many styles, but the most common include: Courier, Helvetica, Times Roman. (Note that the typeface names are copyrighted; therefore, Windows modifies the font ever so slightly and assigns another similar name to that font.) The Windows family of typefaces are called: Modern, Roman, Swiss, Script, and Decorative.

The differences lie in several areas: **stroke width**, **type of pitch**, and **the use of serifs**. **Stroke** widths that make up the characters can be fixed or variable. **Pitch** can be fixed (all characters have the same width) or variable (different widths for the characters). Therefore, if a font has a fixed stroke width, it usually also has a fixed pitch. A **serif** is a small extra line that finishes off character strokes yielding a different look to the character. The term **sans serif** means without any serifs. The Table 12.2 illustrates the Windows font identifiers and a representative sample is used in the Typefaces column.

Table 12.2 Windows Fonts and Samples

ID names	Pitch	Serifs	Typefaces
FF_MODERN	fixed	-	Courier, Elite, Pica
FF_SWISS	variable	no	Helvetica
FF_ROMAN	variable	Yes	Times Roman
FF_SCRIPT	-	-	[illegible]
FF_DECORATIVE	-	-	Wingdings
FF_DONTCARE	-	-	any

What exact font is available depends upon the video display driver, what fonts you have loaded, what printer driver is installed, what font add-on packages are installed, and changes you have made to the default settings in the WIN.INI file.

The size of a character font is given in units of **points** that are about 1/72 inch and measures the height of a character. A size of 10 points means that the character's height is 10/72 of an inch. Windows defines another term, a **twip**, which is a twentieth of a point, 1/1440 inch. In the raster fonts, each pixel is an integral number of logical twips in size.

One cannot use the point size to accurately determine the size on the display screen because of the internal aspect ratio of that specific monitor. If you choose a font size of 24 points, then those characters are formed 24 pixels high. However, **only** on a monitor that displays 72 pixels per physical inch will those characters really appear as 24 real points high. Often the scale factor for the monitors is about 40% larger than 1 inch to account for the magnification needed so that the monitor can be viewed from about 2 feet away. However, when the characters are displayed on the printer, they are exactly 24 points or 24/72 inches high. The printer canvas contains real inches.

There is a mapping mode **MM_TWIPS** in which you would get an accurate rendering; the characters would be really 24/72 inch high. But it is seldom used, because most common printer fonts would be rendered too small to be easily read. Instead, the **MM_ANISOTROPIC** or **MM_ISTROPIC** modes are used. The anisotropic mode can have different scales in the x and y directions, while the isotropic mode has the same scale in both directions. If you wish to approach WYSIWYG, the screen display should be **MM_ANISOTROPIC**.

The LOGFONT and TEXTMETRIC Structures

Fonts are described by a **LOGFONT** structure. To create a font, you create an instance of the **LOGFONT** structure and initialize the fields to your desired requirements. When you execute the create font functions, Windows attempts to match your requested font with the best available matching font: the one that comes the closest to your criteria in the **LOGFONT** object. Once the real font is created, Windows inserts the real characteristics of that font back into the **LOGFONT** structure for your use. When we use the common font dialog, the results are returned in a **LOGFONT** structure.

Design Rule 47: Note that the closest matching process only occurs at the point the font is actually inserted into the DC (dc.SelectObject), not on font creation!

Normally for choosing font type of actions, you would use the common font dialog. It is much easier than doing those actions "by hand." However, you may need to create the printer fonts and even a matching display font, if you are attempting WYSIWYG. Table 12.3 shows the Windows definition of the **LOGFONT** structure.

Table 12.3 The LOGFONT Structure

```
#define LF_FACESIZE          32
struct LOGFONT {
 int      lfHeight;          // height in logical units, a negative value
                             // means the units are in points
 int      lfWidth;           // the avg width in logical units
 int      lfEscapement;      // 0 normally
 int      lfOrientation;     // 0 normally
 int      lfWeight;          // FW_NORMAL (400) or FW_BOLD (700)
 BYTE     lfItalic;          // italics font if non-zero
 BYTE     lfUnderline;       // underline font if non-zero
 BYTE     lfStrikeOut;       // strikeout font if non-zero
 BYTE     lfCharSet;         // ANSI_CHARSET (0), DEFAULT_CHARSET (1),
                             // SYMBOL_CHARSET (2), OEM_CHARSET (255)
 BYTE     lfOutPrecision;    // OUT_DEFAULT_PRECIS output match precision
 BYTE     lfClipPrecision;   // CLIP_DEFAULT_PRECIS clip match precision
 BYTE     lfQuality;         // DRAFT_QUALITY or PROOF_QUALITY
 BYTE     lfPitchAndFamily;// combined values for pitch and family:
                             // FF_DONTCARE, FF_MODERN, FF_ROMAN
                             // FF_SWISS, FF_SCRIPT, FF_DECORATIVE
                             // ORed with one of these:
                            // DEFAULT_PITCH, FIXED_PITCH, VARIABLE_PITCH
 char lfFaceName[LF_FACESIZE]; // typeface name of the font
};
```

When you insert your choices, Windows attempts the best matching font. Table 12.5 gives you some guidelines to aid you in making intelligent choices.

Table 12.5 Guidelines When Constructing Fonts

```
 lfCharSet - ANSI_CHARSET gives raster or TrueType fonts
             OEM-CHARSET gives only the terminal font
             SYMBOL_CHARSET gives Wingdings font
 FIXED_PITCH - gives only fixed width fonts, no variable width fonts
 if lfFaceName is 0, then the family becomes an important factor
 if a raster font is requested, the lfHeight is matched, even if a
             smaller height has to be increased
 if a raster font is requested with PROOF_QUALITY, then height is less
             important than quality
```

Very often, the width is 0, letting the height alone determine the font. This is done to prevent awkward letter shapes during the scaling process. If you specify a height of say 12 and a width of 42, then each letter is going to be stretched in width and be very weird looking as well as hard to read. When the width is 0, Windows scales the width to be proportional to the height. And this is normally what we desire.

After the font is created and selected into a DC, the text metrics structure contains the current information on the font. Table 12.6 shows the **TEXTMETRIC** structure.

Table 12.6 The TEXTMETRIC Structure

```
struct TEXTMETRIC {
int  tmHeight;            // height of the character cell and is equal
                          // to the sum of the tmAscent and tmDescent
int  tmAscent;            // height of the character cell measured from
                          // the baseline
int  tmDescent;           // height of the cell measured from the
                          // baseline to the bottom of the cell
int  tmInternalLeading;   // the amount of internal leading - equal to
                          // the cell height (tmHeight) minus the
                          // maximum height of any character in the
                          // font but not including the height of
                          // accent marks
int  tmExternalLeading;   // recommended amount of leading for this
                          // font and is the whitespace above all
                          // characters and accent marks
int  tmAveCharWidth;      // average width of characters in the font
                          // roughly the width of the letter "X"
int  tmMaxCharWidth;      // the max width of any character in the font
int  tmWeight;            // the weight of the font
BYTE tmItalic;            // nonzero indicates an italic font
BYTE tmUnderlined;        // nonzero indicates an underlined font
BYTE tmStruckOut;         // nonzero indicates struck through font
BYTE tmFirstChar;         // value of the first character in the set
BYTE tmLastChar;          // value of the last character in the set
BYTE tmDefaultChar;       // character to be substituted for characters
                          // that are not in the font
BYTE tmBreakChar;         // character that is used to separate words
BYTE tmPitchAndFamily;    // identifies the font pitch and its family
BYTE tmCharSet;           // identifies the character set:
                          //  ANSI_CHARSET, SYMBOL_CHARSET, OEM_CHARSET
int  tmOverhang;          // nonzero if the driver simulates bold or
                          // italics represents any additional width of
                          // the character
int  tmDigitizedAspectX;  // horizontal aspect ratio for which this
                          // font was designed
int  tmDigitizedAspectY;  // vertical aspect ration for which this font
                          // was designed
};
```

The pitch portion of the byte field **tmPitchAndFamily** is different from the corresponding **LOGFONT** member. The low nibble contains one or more pitch identifiers stored differently than in the **LOGFONT** member. Mask the pitch nibble (AND) with the identifier **TMPF_FIXED_PITCH**; if the bit is ON, it is a variable font, otherwise it's a fixed font.

Similarly mask and test for **TMPF_VECTOR** (on means a vector font), **TMPF_DEVICE** (on means a device font), and **TMPF_TRUETYPE** (on means TrueType).

The point size is reflected in the **tmHeight** member. In other words, the point size does not include the spacing between lines, which is known as **line spacing**. While a typographer determines the shape and size of a character for a given point size, the typesetter actually determines the line spacing which can be based upon the point size, font color, line length, maximum character size and so on. Windows provides a suggested or reasonable value for the line spacing in the member **tmExternalLeading**. Thus, the vertical spacing between lines from a programming point of view would be the sum of **tmHeight** and **tmExternalLeading**. Most fields parallel those of the **LOGFONT**.

Additionally, the **GetDeviceCaps** function returns similar information. Figure 12.1 shows the basic values for a Hewlett Packard LaserJet 4 Plus.

```
HORZSIZE      Width in millimeters:              203
VERTSIZE      Height in millimeters:             271
HORZRES       Width in pixels:                  4800
VERTRES       Height in raster lines:           6396
BITSPIXEL     Color bits per pixel:                1
PLANES        Number of color planes:              1
NUMBRUSHES    Number of device brushes:           -1
NUMPENS       Number of device pens:              80
NUMMARKERS    Number of device markers:            0
NUMFONTS      Number of device fonts:              4
NUMCOLORS     Number of device colors:             2
PDEVICESIZE   Size of device structure:         5104
ASPECTX       Relative width of pixel:           600
ASPECTY       Relative height of pixel:          600
ASPECTXY      Relative diagonal of pixel:        849
LOGPIXELSX    Horizontal dots per inch:          600
LOGPIXELSY    Vertical dots per inch:            600
SIZEPALETTE   Number of palette entries:           0
NUMRESERVED   Reserved palette entries:            0
COLORRES      Actual color resolution:             0
```

Figure 12.1 **GetDeviceCaps** Results for a HP LaserJet 4 Plus

Notice that the printer has an equal number of dots per inch vertically and horizontally as shown in the **LOGPIXELSX** and **LOGPIXELSY** entries. **HORZRES** and **VERTRES** provide the page size in pixels.

If you are attempting WYSIWYG, then, when handling the Choose Font dialog, you can restrict the user's selections by using key flags. Under the MFC you can set the flags to an ORed combination of the following.

```
CF_ANSIONLY          - allows ANSI sets only
CF_FIXEDPITCHONLY - allows only fixed pitch sets
CF_SCALABLEONLY     - allows scalable fonts only
CF_TTONLY           - allows TrueType fonts only
CF_PRINTERFONTS     - allows printer fonts only
CF_SCREENFONTS      - allows screen fonts only
CF_BOTH             - allows both printer fonts and display fonts
CF_WYSIWYG          - allows only fonts that are available on
                      both printer and screen
CF_EFFECTS          - allows color, underline, and strike through
CF_FORCEFONTEXIST - errors if user selects a nonexistent font
CF_INITLOGFONTSTRUCT - sets dialog controls from a LOGFONT
```

These IDs can be ORed and passed to the **CFontDialog** constructor. This is what we have been doing all along.

```
ptrdlg = new CFontDialog (NULL,
          CF_EFFECTS | CF_PRINTERFONTS | CF_FORCEFONTEXIST,
          ptrprinterDC, this);
```

Under the MFC, we have been copying the user's selection that is stored in the **CFontDialog** into our local **LOGFONT** copy and building a font from it.

```
LOGFONT logfont;
CFont font;
font.CreateFontIndirect (&logfont);
```

Pgm12a: A Text Editor and Graphics Clipboard Operations Program

Before we tackle the clipboard operations, let's implement these features thus far discussed. **Pgm12a** is another MDI example. The main MDI frame allows for editing a new text file, opening an existing text file, or launching a new Draw client. The two MDI child frames are **EditWin** and **DrawWin** respectively. Figure 12.2 shows **Pgm12a** in action with one of each opened.

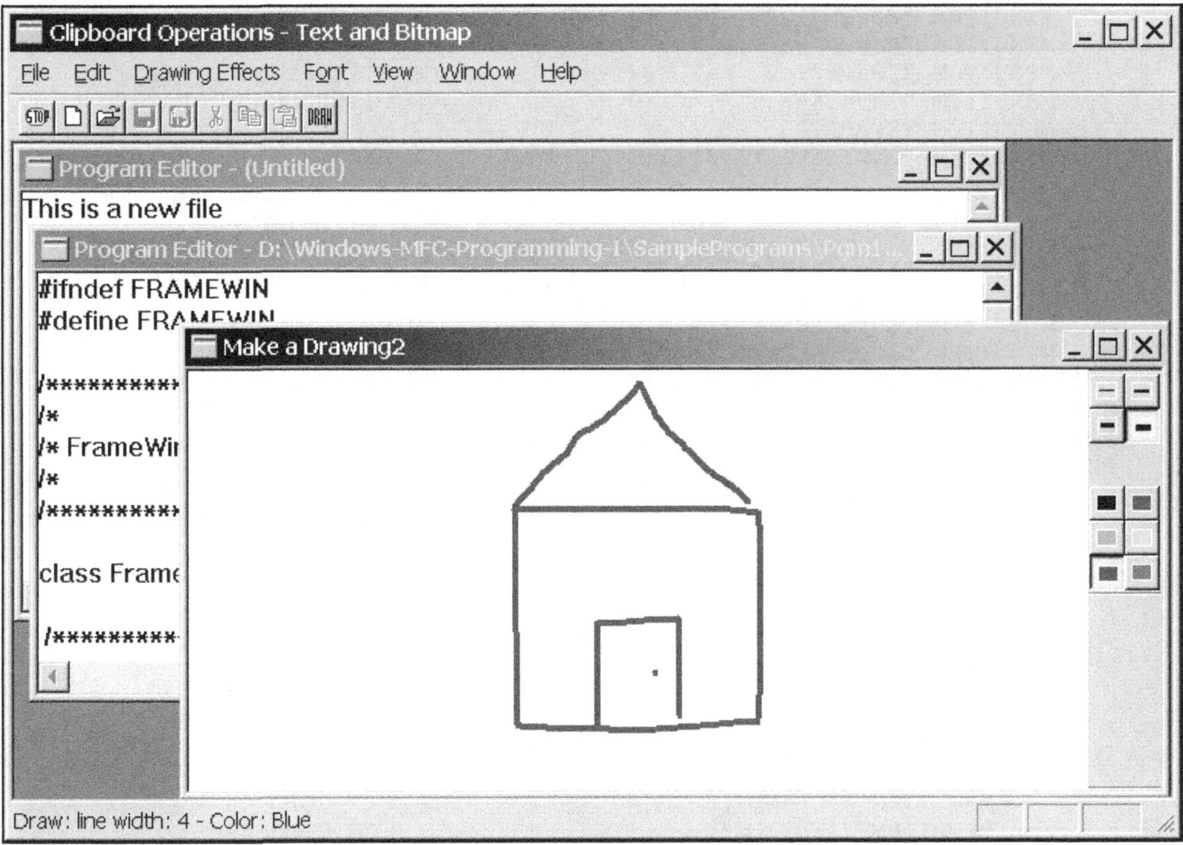

Figure 12.2 Pgm12a with Three Child Windows in Operation

The **DrawWin** class has been brought forward from the previous example in the last chapter. Code has been added to support clipboard operations which we will examine in the next section.

The **EditWin** class is derived from **CMDIChildWnd** and has a **CEdit** control as its client window. Its constructor is given a string containing the filename. For a File|New operation, the string is a null string. For File|Open the string is the filename chosen by the user from the common File Open Save dialog.

The tool bar contains icons for launching these three types of child windows along with the usual Edit Cut/Copy/Paste operations. Similarly, the main menu consists of the File and Edit group first. These are followed by the operations group containing the Drawing Effects and Fonts pop-up menus. Fonts are enabled by the **EditWin** instances while the Drawing Effects are activated by **DrawWin** instances. On the left side of the menu bar come the expected View, Window and Help groups.

Again, I utilized separate RC files for the main application, **Pgm12a.rc**, and for each of the client classes, **EditWin.rc** and **DrawWin.rc**. Here are the relevant portions of these resource files.

From **Pgm12a.rc**

```
/////////////////////////////////////////////////////////////////////////////
//
// Bitmap
//
IDB_MAINFRAME           BITMAP  MOVEABLE PURE    "TOOLBAR.BMP"
/////////////////////////////////////////////////////////////////////////////
//
// Menu
//
MAINMENU MENU DISCARDABLE
BEGIN
    POPUP "&File"
    BEGIN
        MENUITEM "&New",                        CM_FILENEW
        MENUITEM "&Open...",                    CM_FILEOPEN
        MENUITEM "New &Draw",                   CM_DRAW
        MENUITEM "&Save",                       CM_FILESAVE, GRAYED
        MENUITEM "Save &As...",                 CM_FILESAVEAS, GRAYED
        MENUITEM SEPARATOR
        MENUITEM "E&xit\tAlt+F4",               CM_EXIT
    END
    POPUP "&Edit"
    BEGIN
        MENUITEM "&Undo\tAlt+BkSp",             CM_EDITUNDO, GRAYED
        MENUITEM SEPARATOR
        MENUITEM "Cu&t\tShift+Del",             CM_EDITCUT, GRAYED
        MENUITEM "&Copy\tCtrl+Ins",             CM_EDITCOPY, GRAYED
        MENUITEM "&Paste\tShift+Ins",           CM_EDITPASTE, GRAYED
    END
    POPUP "&Drawing Effects"
    BEGIN
        POPUP "Line &Width"
        BEGIN
            MENUITEM "1 Pixel",                     CM_LINE1
            MENUITEM "2 Pixels",                    CM_LINE2
            MENUITEM "3 Pixels",                    CM_LINE3
            MENUITEM "4 Pixels",                    CM_LINE4
        END
        POPUP "Line &Color"
        BEGIN
            MENUITEM "&Black",                      CM_COLORA
            MENUITEM "&Red",                        CM_COLORB
            MENUITEM "&Green",                      CM_COLORC
            MENUITEM "&Yellow",                     CM_COLORD
            MENUITEM "B&lue",                       CM_COLORE
            MENUITEM "&Purple",                     CM_COLORF
        END
    END
    POPUP "F&ont"
    BEGIN
        MENUITEM "&Choose Font",                CM_FONTCHANGE
    END
    POPUP "&View"
    BEGIN
        MENUITEM "&Toolbar",                    ID_VIEW_TOOLBAR
        MENUITEM "&Status Bar",                 ID_VIEW_STATUS_BAR
        MENUITEM SEPARATOR
    END
    POPUP "&Window"
    BEGIN
```

```
        MENUITEM "&Cascade",                CM_CASCADECHILDREN, GRAYED
        MENUITEM "Tile &Horizontally",      CM_TILECHILDRENH, GRAYED
        MENUITEM "Tile &Vertically",        CM_TILECHILDRENV, GRAYED
        MENUITEM "Arrange &Icons",          CM_ARRANGEICONS, GRAYED
        MENUITEM "C&lose All",              CM_CLOSECHILDREN, GRAYED
    END
    POPUP "&Help"
    BEGIN
        MENUITEM "&About...",                    CM_HELPABOUT
    END
END
/////////////////////////////////////////////////////////////////////////////
//
// String Table
//
STRINGTABLE DISCARDABLE
BEGIN
    ID_INDICATOR_EXT        "EXT"
    ID_INDICATOR_CAPS       "CAP"
    ID_INDICATOR_NUM        "NUM"
    ID_INDICATOR_SCRL       "SCRL"
    ID_INDICATOR_OVR        "OVR"
    ID_INDICATOR_REC        "REC"
    CM_DRAW                 "Launch Draw Window\nLaunch Draw"
    CM_HELPABOUT            "About the Fancy Dialog application"
    CM_EXIT                 "Quit, prompt to save the documents\nExit App"
    CM_CASCADECHILDREN      "Cascase Windows"
    CM_TILECHILDRENH        "Tile Windows - Horizontally"
    CM_TILECHILDRENV        "Tile Windows - Vertically"
    CM_ARRANGEICONS         "Arrange Icons"
    CM_CLOSECHILDREN        "Close All Windows"
    CM_FILENEW              "Creates a new document\nNew Document"
    CM_FILEOPEN             "Opens an existing document\nOpen Document"
    CM_FILESAVE             "Saves this document\nSave"
    CM_FILESAVEAS           "Saves this document with a new name\nSave As"
    CM_EDITUNDO             "Reverses the last operation\nUndo Last Change"
    CM_EDITCUT     "Cuts the selection and puts it on the Clipboard\nCut Selection"
    CM_EDITCOPY    "Copies the selection and puts it on the Clipboard\nCopy Selection"
    CM_EDITPASTE   "Inserts the clipboard contents at the insertion point\nPaste"
    ID_VIEW_TOOLBAR         "Hide/Show Tool Bar"
    ID_VIEW_STATUS_BAR      "Hide/Show Status Bar"
    AFX_IDS_IDLEMESSAGE     "Ready"
    IDS_MAINTITLE           "Clipboard Operations - Text and Bitmap"
    IDS_MSG_QUIT            "Do you want to quit the application?"
    IDS_MSG_QUERY           "Query?"
    CM_FONTCHANGE           "Choose Font\nChoose Font"
END
```

From **DrawWin.rc**

```
/////////////////////////////////////////////////////////////////////////////
//
// Bitmap
//
IDB_TOOLBOX             BITMAP  MOVEABLE PURE   "TOOLBOX.BMP"
/////////////////////////////////////////////////////////////////////////////
//
// String Table
//
STRINGTABLE DISCARDABLE
BEGIN
    CM_LINE1                "Select 1 pixel line width\nLinewidth 1"
    CM_LINE2                "Select 2 pixels line width\nLinewidth 2"
    CM_LINE3                "Select 3 pixels line width\nLinewidth 3"
    CM_LINE4                "Select 4 pixels line width\nLinewidth 4"
    CM_COLORA               "Select Black as the drawing color\nBlack"
    CM_COLORB               "Select Red as the drawing color\nRed"
```

```
    CM_COLORC                   "Select Green as the drawing color\nGreen"
    CM_COLORD                   "Select Yellow as the drawing color\nYellow"
    CM_COLORE                   "Select Blue as the drawing color\nBlue"
    CM_COLORF                   "Select Purple as the drawing color\nPurple"
    IDB_TOOLBOX                 "Hide/Show Tool &Box"
    IDS_DRAWQUIT                "Ok to close this drawing?"
    IDS_DRAWTITLE               "Make a Drawing"
END
```

From **EditWin.rc**

```
STRINGTABLE
BEGIN
 IDS_EDIT,          "Program Editor - "
 IDS_MSG_NOTSAVE,   "File has not been saved. Save File now?"
 IDS_MSG_ERROR,     "Edit Program - Error Message"
 IDS_MSG_NOMEM,     "Out of memory. Close app. Free some memory. Try again."
 IDS_MSG_FILEERR,   "File Save Error. Try File Save As with valid filename."
 IDS_MSG_FILEOPEN,  "File Open Error. Try again with valid filename."
 IDS_MSG_FILEREAD,  "File Open Error. Unable to input the file."
 IDS_MSG_FILEWRT,   "File Save Error. Output failed - disk full. Try new disk."
 IDS_MSG_FILEBIG,   "We can only handle files up to 65,535 bytes long."
 IDS_MSG_EDIT,      "Program Editor - Quit Query"
 IDS_MSG_EDITQUIT,  "Do you want to quit editing this file?"
END
```

The **CMDIFrameWnd** class, **FrameWin**, is almost identical to the frame window class from **Pgm11a**. Support has been added for the new **EditWin** class. It responds to File|New and File|Open menu commands.

```
FrameWin.h Definition of the CMDIFrameWnd Class

#pragma once

/***************************************************************/
/*                                                             */
/* FrameWin Definition of MDI Frame Window                     */
/*                                                             */
/***************************************************************/

class FrameWin : public CMDIFrameWnd {

 /**************************************************************/
 /*                                                            */
 /* Data Members                                               */
 /*                                                            */
 /**************************************************************/

public:
bool        fastclose;   // avoid lots of query prompts when true

protected:
int         numchildren; // count of MDI children
CStatusBar  statusbar;   // our status bar
CToolBar    toolbar;     // our tool bar

 /**************************************************************/
 /*                                                            */
 /* Functions                                                  */
 /*                                                            */
 /**************************************************************/

public:
               FrameWin ();       // init child win counts
              ~FrameWin () {}     // destructor - do nothing
```

```

protected:
afx_msg int    OnCreate(LPCREATESTRUCT); // make tool & status bar
afx_msg void   OnClose ();            // determines if app can quit
int            DisplayMsg (int, int, UINT); // shows a message box

//             command processors
afx_msg void   CmExit ();             // terminate app
afx_msg void   CmDraw ();             // launch draw client window
afx_msg void   CmHelpAbout ();        // help about our app
afx_msg void   CmFileNew ();          // start new text file
afx_msg void   CmFileOpen ();         // open existing text file

//             MDI Children Functions
afx_msg void   CmCascadeChildren (); // cascade all windows
afx_msg void   CmTileChildrenH ();    // tile windows horizontally
afx_msg void   CmTileChildrenV ();    // tile windows vertically
afx_msg void   CmArrangeIcons ();     // arrange minimized icons
afx_msg void   CmCloseChildren ();    // close all child windows

int GetChildCount (); // get total number of MDI child windows

DECLARE_MESSAGE_MAP()
};
```

The implementation of **Pgm12a**'s **FrameWin** is nearly the same as in **Pgm11a**. The only significant changes are the command handlers for the File|New and File|Open menu items.

FrameWin.cpp Implementation of the CMDIFrameWnd Class

```
#include "stdafx.h"
#include "FrameWin.h"
#include "EditWin.h"
#include "DrawWin.h"
#include "resource.h"
#include "DrawWinRC.h"
#include "EditWinRC.h"

/***************************************************************/
/*                                                             */
/* tool bar buttons and status bar buttons                     */
/*                                                             */
/* control bar buttons - IDs are command buttons               */
/* same order as in the bitmap 'toolbar.bmp'                   */
/*                                                             */
/***************************************************************/

static UINT BASED_CODE buttons[] = {
  CM_EXIT,
  CM_FILENEW,
  CM_FILEOPEN,
  CM_FILESAVE,
  CM_FILESAVEAS,
  CM_EDITCUT,
  CM_EDITCOPY,
  CM_EDITPASTE,
  CM_DRAW,
};

static UINT BASED_CODE indicators[] = {
  ID_SEPARATOR,            // status line indicator
  ID_INDICATOR_CAPS,
  ID_INDICATOR_NUM,
```

```
  ID_INDICATOR_SCRL,
};

/**************************************************************/
/*                                                            */
/* FrameWin Message Map                                       */
/*                                                            */
/**************************************************************/

BEGIN_MESSAGE_MAP(FrameWin, CMDIFrameWnd)
 ON_WM_CREATE ()
 ON_WM_CLOSE ()
 ON_COMMAND(CM_EXIT,             CmExit)
 ON_COMMAND(CM_FILENEW,          CmFileNew)
 ON_COMMAND(CM_FILEOPEN,         CmFileOpen)
 ON_COMMAND(CM_DRAW,             CmDraw)
 ON_COMMAND(CM_HELPABOUT,        CmHelpAbout)
 ON_COMMAND(CM_CASCADECHILDREN, CmCascadeChildren)
 ON_COMMAND(CM_TILECHILDRENH,    CmTileChildrenH)
 ON_COMMAND(CM_TILECHILDRENV,    CmTileChildrenV)
 ON_COMMAND(CM_ARRANGEICONS,     CmArrangeIcons)
 ON_COMMAND(CM_CLOSECHILDREN,    CmCloseChildren)
END_MESSAGE_MAP()

/**************************************************************/
/*                                                            */
/* Framewin: Construct the window object                      */
/*                                                            */
/**************************************************************/

FrameWin::FrameWin () {
 CString title;
 title.LoadString (IDS_MAINTITLE);
 // create the MDI frame window
 Create (NULL, title, WS_OVERLAPPEDWINDOW, rectDefault, NULL,
         "MAINMENU");
 fastclose   = false;// set no express close in operation
 numchildren = 0;     // set num children to 0 for title additions
}

/**************************************************************/
/*                                                            */
/* OnCreate: construct status and tool bars                   */
/*                                                            */
/**************************************************************/

int FrameWin::OnCreate (LPCREATESTRUCT lpCS) {
 // construct from resource file the main menu to be used
 CMenu *ptrmenu;
 ptrmenu = new CMenu ();
 ptrmenu->LoadMenu ("MAINMENU");

 // construct the MDI hidden client window using the main menu
 // pointing it to the Window pop-up
 CreateClient (lpCS, ptrmenu->GetSubMenu(5));
 delete ptrmenu;

 // attempt to build control bar and status bar using old style
 if (toolbar.Create (this) &&
     toolbar.LoadBitmap (IDB_MAINFRAME) &&
     toolbar.SetButtons (buttons, sizeof(buttons)/sizeof(UINT)))
  if (statusbar.Create (this) &&
      statusbar.SetIndicators (indicators, sizeof(indicators) /
                               sizeof(UINT))) ;
```

```
  else return -1;
 else return -1;

 // all ok, so set for hints and tool tips wanted
 toolbar.SetBarStyle (
             toolbar.GetBarStyle() | CBRS_TOOLTIPS | CBRS_FLYBY);

 // insert captions to be shown when the tool bars are floating
 toolbar.SetWindowText (_T("Main Controls"));

 // now notify control to accept any form of docking
 toolbar.EnableDocking (CBRS_ALIGN_ANY);

 // notify the framewindow of docking requirements
 EnableDocking (CBRS_ALIGN_ANY);

 // and dock control bar at top
 DockControlBar (&toolbar);

 return 0;
}

/*************************************************************/
/*                                                           */
/* CmDraw: Launch new child window for drawing, with a tool box*/
/*                                                           */
/*************************************************************/

void      FrameWin::CmDraw () {
 CString title;
 char msg[10];
 // construct modified window title appending id number to title
 title.LoadString (IDS_DRAWTITLE);
 itoa (numchildren, msg, 10);
 title += msg;
 // allocate a draw MDI child window
 DrawWin *ptrwin = new DrawWin ();
 // now create the draw MDI child window using many default args
 if (!ptrwin->Create (NULL, title)) {
  delete ptrwin;
  return;
 }
 numchildren++;
 ptrwin->ShowWindow (SW_SHOW); // and make child visible
 // no attempt to make this one maxed if previous one was maxed
}

/*************************************************************/
/*                                                           */
/* CmFileOpen: open an existent file                         */
/*                                                           */
/*************************************************************/

void FrameWin::CmFileOpen () {
 CFileDialog filedlg (TRUE,     // use Open dialog
                      "*.CPP", // default extension
                      "*.*",   // current file name
           OFN_FILEMUSTEXIST | OFN_PATHMUSTEXIST | OFN_LONGNAMES,
           "All Files (*.*)|*.*|CPP Files (*.CPP)|*.CPP|C Files "
       "(*.C)|*.C|Header Files (*.H*)|*.H*||", this);

 // get user's filename choice
 if (filedlg.DoModal () == IDOK) { // user has chosen a file, so
  CString filename;
```

```
  filename = filedlg.GetPathName (); // extract its filename
  // construct a caption that includes this filename
  CString title;
  title.LoadString (IDS_EDIT);
  title += filename;
  // allocate a child edit window that opens this file
  EditWin *ptrwin = new EditWin (filename);
  if (!ptrwin->Create (NULL, title)) {
   delete ptrwin;
   return;
  }
  ptrwin->ShowWindow (SW_SHOW); // cause window to be visible
  numchildren++;
 }
}

/***************************************************************/
/*                                                             */
/* CmFileNew: new file to edit                                 */
/*                                                             */
/***************************************************************/

void FrameWin::CmFileNew () {
 // create "untitled" window caption
 CString title;
 title.LoadString (IDS_EDIT);
 title += "(Untitled)";
 CString filename;
 // allocate a child edit window
 EditWin *ptrwin = new EditWin (filename);
 if (!ptrwin->Create (NULL, title)) { // create the MDI child
  delete ptrwin;
  return;
 }
 ptrwin->ShowWindow (SW_SHOW); // cause window to be visible
 numchildren++;
}

/***************************************************************/
/*                                                             */
/* CmCloseChildren: close children with no child close prompts */
/*                                                             */
/***************************************************************/

void FrameWin::CmCloseChildren () {
 fastclose = true;             // turn on express close option
 // find the current active child
 CMDIChildWnd *ptrwin = MDIGetActive ();
 while (ptrwin) {              // for all MDI children:
  ptrwin->MDIDestroy ();       // destroy the child window
  MDINext();                   // make the next child active
  ptrwin = MDIGetActive ();    // and get a ptr to next active one
 }
 fastclose = false;            // turn off express close option
 numchildren = 0;              // set all child win counts to 0
}

/***************************************************************/
/*                                                             */
/* The 5 MDI Child Window arrangement functions                */
/*                                                             */
/***************************************************************/

void FrameWin::CmCascadeChildren () {
```

```
 MDICascade ();
}
void FrameWin::CmTileChildrenH () {
 MDITile (MDITILE_HORIZONTAL);
}
void FrameWin::CmTileChildrenV () {
 MDITile (MDITILE_VERTICAL);
}
void FrameWin::CmArrangeIcons () {
 MDIIconArrange ();
}
int FrameWin::GetChildCount () {
 return numchildren;
}

/*************************************************************/
/*                                                           */
/* OnClose: query user if we can terminate the application   */
/*                                                           */
/*************************************************************/

void FrameWin::OnClose () {
 if (DisplayMsg (IDS_MSG_QUERY, IDS_MSG_QUIT, MB_YESNO |
        MB_ICONQUESTION) == IDYES)
  DestroyWindow ();
}

/*************************************************************/
/*                                                           */
/* DisplayMsg: shows a MessageBox and returns its retcode    */
/*                                                           */
/*************************************************************/

int FrameWin::DisplayMsg (int id1, int id2, UINT flags) {
 CString msg1, msg2;
 msg1.LoadString (id1);
 msg2.LoadString (id2);
 return MessageBox (msg2, msg1, flags);
}

/*************************************************************/
/*                                                           */
/* CmHelpAbout: shows who wrote this app                     */
/*                                                           */
/*************************************************************/

void FrameWin::CmHelpAbout () {
 // informational dialog - show About dialog
 CDialog aboutdlg ("IDD_ABOUT", this);
 aboutdlg.DoModal ();
}

/*************************************************************/
/*                                                           */
/* CmExit:  determine if the app can be shut down            */
/*                                                           */
/*************************************************************/

void FrameWin::CmExit () {
 PostMessage (WM_CLOSE);
}
```

Let's examine how instances of the **EditWin** are launched. An instance of **CFileDialog** is created in response to File|Open. If the user makes a file selection, then the window caption string is constructed by concatenating "Program Editor" with the actual filename.

```
void FrameWin::CmFileOpen () {
 CFileDialog filedlg (TRUE,     // use Open dialog
                      "*.CPP", // default extension
                      "*.*",   // current file name
           OFN_FILEMUSTEXIST | OFN_PATHMUSTEXIST | OFN_LONGNAMES,
           "All Files (*.*)|*.*|CPP Files (*.CPP)|*.CPP|C Files "
       "(*.C)|*.C|Header Files (*.H*)|*.H*||", this);
 if (filedlg.DoModal () == IDOK) {
  CString filename;
  filename = filedlg.GetPathName (); // extract its filename
  CString title;
  title.LoadString (IDS_EDIT);
  title += filename;
```

Now an instance of the **EditWin** is allocated and passed this new title. If the C++ wrapper is successfully created, then the **Create** function is called, once again, adopting many of the default arguments. Finally, **ShowWindow** is called to make this child visible.

```
  EditWin *ptrwin = new EditWin (filename);
  if (!ptrwin->Create (NULL, title)) {
   delete ptrwin;
   return;
  }
  ptrwin->ShowWindow (SW_SHOW);
  numchildren++;
 }
}
```

When responding to the File|New command, the process is simpler but parallel. Here the title string contains the text "Untitled."

```
void FrameWin::CmFileNew () {
 CString title;
 title.LoadString (IDS_EDIT);
 title += "(Untitled)";
 CString filename;
 EditWin *ptrwin = new EditWin (filename);
 if (!ptrwin->Create (NULL, title)) {
  delete ptrwin;
  return;
 }
 ptrwin->ShowWindow (SW_SHOW);
 numchildren++;
}
```

The **EditWin** is derived from **CMDIChildWnd**. The few data members contain the **CEdit** control which fills the client area of this window and the user-chosen font, if any.

EditWin.h Definition

```
#pragma once

/***************************************************************/
/*                                                             */
/* EditWin Class Definition                                    */
/*                                                             */
/***************************************************************/

class EditWin : public CMDIChildWnd {
```

```

 /************************************************************/
 /*                                                          */
 /* Class Data Members                                       */
 /*                                                          */
 /************************************************************/

protected:
CEdit    editwin;     // the CEdit main window
CString  filename;    // full path file spec
LOGFONT* ptrlogfont; // the user's chosen font, if any

 /************************************************************/
 /*                                                          */
 /* Class Functions:                                         */
 /*                                                          */
 /************************************************************/

public:
             EditWin (CString& filename);  // constructor
            ~EditWin () {}                 // destructor

protected:

afx_msg int  OnCreate (LPCREATESTRUCT); // create CEdit & load
afx_msg void OnDestroy ();              // save file, delete font
afx_msg void OnClose ();                // save query
afx_msg void OnSetFocus(CWnd* pOldWnd); // give CEdit the focus
afx_msg void OnSize (UINT, int, int);   // reposition CEdit

             // utility functions
        void SaveCheck ();             // query user - save file
        void SaveFile ();              // save the file
        int  DisplayMsg (int, int, UINT); // display message box
        void SetNoFileErr (int, UINT); // dsply error and no file

             // command processors
afx_msg void CmFontChange ();      // get new user chosen font
afx_msg void CmFileSave ();        // save the file with same name
afx_msg void CmFileSaveAs ();      // save with new name
afx_msg void CmEditUndo ();        // undo last change
afx_msg void CmEditCut ();         // cut to clipboard
afx_msg void CmEditCopy ();        // copy to clipboard
afx_msg void CmEditPaste ();       // paste from the clipboard

             // command enablers
afx_msg void CmEnableEditUndo (CCmdUI*); // enable/disable Undo
afx_msg void CmEnableEditCut  (CCmdUI*); // enable/disable Cut
afx_msg void CmEnableEditCopy (CCmdUI*); // enable/disable Copy
afx_msg void CmEnableEditPaste (CCmdUI*);// enable/disable Paste

DECLARE_MESSAGE_MAP()
};
```

The implementation follows the discussion above. In **OnCreate**, the **CEdit** control is created and in **OnSize**, it is resized to fill the current client area. Also, in **OnCreate**, if the user has chosen a file to edit, the file is opened and inputted into a global memory area and then given to the **CEdit** control to show. The **CEdit** control copies the text so we can delete this memory once **SetWindowText** has completed. If the user chooses File|Save, we can retrieve the revised text from the **CEdit** control and write it to the file. Study these member functions; make sure that you understand and follow the interrelationships. In the next section, we examine the clipboard operations.

```
EditWin.cpp Implementation
```

```
#include "stdafx.h"
#include "FrameWin.h"
#include "EditWin.h"
#include "resource.h"
#include "EditWinRC.h"

/***************************************************************/
/*                                                             */
/* EditWin Messsage Map                                        */
/*                                                             */
/***************************************************************/

BEGIN_MESSAGE_MAP(EditWin, CMDIChildWnd)
 ON_WM_CREATE ()
 ON_WM_DESTROY ()
 ON_WM_CLOSE()
 ON_WM_SETFOCUS()
 ON_WM_SIZE()
 ON_COMMAND(CM_FONTCHANGE,         CmFontChange)
 ON_COMMAND(CM_FILESAVE,           CmFileSave)
 ON_COMMAND(CM_FILESAVEAS,         CmFileSaveAs)
 ON_COMMAND(CM_EDITUNDO,           CmEditUndo)
 ON_COMMAND(CM_EDITCUT,            CmEditCut)
 ON_COMMAND(CM_EDITCOPY,           CmEditCopy)
 ON_COMMAND(CM_EDITPASTE,          CmEditPaste)
 ON_UPDATE_COMMAND_UI(CM_EDITUNDO, CmEnableEditUndo)
 ON_UPDATE_COMMAND_UI(CM_EDITCUT,  CmEnableEditCut)
 ON_UPDATE_COMMAND_UI(CM_EDITCOPY, CmEnableEditCopy)
 ON_UPDATE_COMMAND_UI(CM_EDITPASTE,CmEnableEditPaste)
END_MESSAGE_MAP()

/***************************************************************/
/*                                                             */
/* EditWin: Construct the window object - save file name       */
/*                                                             */
/***************************************************************/

EditWin::EditWin (CString& filenm) : CMDIChildWnd () {
 ptrlogfont = 0;     // no user font chosen as yet
 filename = filenm; // save the filename
}

/***************************************************************/
/*                                                             */
/* OnDestroy: save file if modified & wanted, delete user font */
/*                                                             */
/***************************************************************/

void EditWin::OnDestroy () {
 if (editwin.GetSafeHwnd() && editwin.GetModify ())
  SaveCheck (); // save file if needed
 if (ptrlogfont) delete ptrlogfont;
 CMDIChildWnd::OnDestroy ();
}

/***************************************************************/
/*                                                             */
/* CmFontChange: choose font dialog                            */
/*                                                             */
/***************************************************************/

void EditWin::CmFontChange () {
 CFontDialog  dlg (ptrlogfont, CF_EFFECTS | CF_SCREENFONTS |
```

```
                    CF_FORCEFONTEXIST, NULL, this);
 if (dlg.DoModal () == IDOK) {      // get user font choice
  if (!ptrlogfont) {
   ptrlogfont = new LOGFONT;        // 1st time, create LOGFONT
  }
  // copy user choice of font into our LOGFONT instance
  memcpy (ptrlogfont, &(dlg.m_lf), sizeof (LOGFONT));
  // build the font and give it to the CEdit control
  HFONT hfont = ::CreateFontIndirect (ptrlogfont);
  editwin.SendMessage (WM_SETFONT, (WPARAM) hfont, 0);
  editwin.Invalidate ();
 }
}

/*************************************************************/
/*                                                           */
/* OnCreate: create the CEdit control - load in the file or  */
/*           set up an empty new file                        */
/*                                                           */
/*************************************************************/

int EditWin::OnCreate (LPCREATESTRUCT lpCS) {
 int retcd = CMDIChildWnd::OnCreate (lpCS); // create our window
 CRect rect;
 GetClientRect (&rect);
 // allocate a CEdit control as a client window
 if (!editwin.Create (WS_CHILD | WS_VISIBLE | ES_AUTOHSCROLL |
             ES_AUTOVSCROLL | ES_MULTILINE | ES_WANTRETURN |
             WS_VSCROLL | WS_HSCROLL, rect, this, EDITWINDOW)) {
  // if not able to build CEdit, display error
  DisplayMsg (IDS_MSG_ERROR, IDS_MSG_NOMEM, MB_OK);
  return -1;
 }

 // load a null file or load the real file into the CEdit control
 if (filename.GetLength() == 0) {
  editwin.SetWindowText (0);     // send new text to CEdit window
  editwin.SetModify (FALSE);     // set CEdit not modified yet
  editwin.EmptyUndoBuffer ();    // clear CEdit's undo buffer
  return retcd;
 }

 // attempt to open the file
 HANDLE hfile = CreateFile (filename, GENERIC_READ, 0, NULL,
                    OPEN_EXISTING, FILE_ATTRIBUTE_NORMAL, NULL);
 if (hfile == INVALID_HANDLE_VALUE) {
  // file create failed, so show error msg and install null file
  SetNoFileErr (IDS_MSG_FILEOPEN , MB_OK | MB_ICONSTOP);
  return -1;
 }

 // get file size and reset DOS offset back to the beginning
 DWORD filesize = SetFilePointer (hfile, 0L, NULL, FILE_END);
 SetFilePointer (hfile, 0L, NULL, FILE_BEGIN);

 // CEdit can handle upto 64K absolute maximum
 if (filesize > 65535L) {
  // show err and install null file
  SetNoFileErr (IDS_MSG_FILEBIG, MB_OK);
  CloseHandle (hfile);
  return -1;
 }

 // allocate a file input buffer - add one for NULL terminator
```

```
 // Note that any dynamic memory allocation method is ok to use
 HANDLE  hbuffer = GlobalAlloc (GMEM_MOVEABLE, filesize + 1);
 if (!hbuffer) {  // error, not enough memory for buffer
  // show err and install null file
  SetNoFileErr (IDS_MSG_NOMEM, MB_OK | MB_ICONSTOP);
  CloseHandle (hfile);
  return -1;
 }
 // get locked ptr to global buffer
 char *ptrbuf = (char*) GlobalLock (hbuffer);

 // input the whole file
 DWORD actsz;
 ReadFile (hfile, ptrbuf, filesize, &actsz, NULL);
 CloseHandle (hfile);

 if (actsz != filesize) { // check for input read error
  // show err and install null file
  SetNoFileErr (IDS_MSG_FILEREAD, MB_OK | MB_ICONSTOP);
  GlobalUnlock (hbuffer); // remove the global memory
  GlobalFree   (hbuffer);
  return -1;
 }

 // install the text file into the CEdit control
 ptrbuf [filesize] = 0;       // insert null terminator for CEdit
 editwin.SetWindowText (ptrbuf); // set CEdit to new text
 editwin.SetModify (FALSE);      // set CEdit to unmodified
 editwin.EmptyUndoBuffer ();     // clear CEdit's undo buffer
 GlobalUnlock (hbuffer);         // unlock file buffer
 GlobalFree   (hbuffer);         // and free global memory
 return retcd;
}

/*************************************************************/
/*                                                           */
/* SetNoFileErr: display file open error                     */
/*               and install null file in CEdit              */
/*                                                           */
/*************************************************************/

void EditWin::SetNoFileErr (int id2, UINT flags) {
 DisplayMsg (IDS_MSG_ERROR, id2, flags); // display the error msg
 filename = "";                 // install untitled new file
 editwin.SetWindowText (0);     // send null text to CEdit window
 editwin.SetModify (FALSE);     // set CEdit not modified yet
 editwin.EmptyUndoBuffer ();    // clear CEdit's undo buffer
}

/*************************************************************/
/*                                                           */
/* OnSize: resize the CEdit client                           */
/*                                                           */
/*************************************************************/

void EditWin::OnSize (UINT, int width, int height) {
 if (editwin.GetSafeHwnd())
  editwin.MoveWindow (0, 0, width, height, TRUE);
}

/*************************************************************/
/*                                                           */
/* OnSetFocus: pass the focus on down to the child window    */
/*                                                           */
```

```
/*************************************************************/

void EditWin::OnSetFocus(CWnd*) {
 editwin.SetFocus();
}

/*************************************************************/
/*                                                           */
/* SaveCheck: query user about needed file save              */
/*                                                           */
/*************************************************************/

void EditWin::SaveCheck () {
 // based on user request and whether or not file has a name,
 // send ourselves the save messages
 if (DisplayMsg (IDS_MSG_QUERY, IDS_MSG_NOTSAVE,
                 MB_YESNO | MB_ICONQUESTION) == IDYES) {
  if (filename.GetLength() == 0)
      SendMessage (WM_COMMAND, CM_FILESAVEAS, 0L);
  else
      SendMessage (WM_COMMAND, CM_FILESAVE, 0L);
 }
}

/*************************************************************/
/*                                                           */
/* CmFileSave: save an existent file                         */
/*                                                           */
/*************************************************************/

void EditWin::CmFileSave () {
 // if no name, use SaveAs otherwise use SaveFile
 if (filename.GetLength()==0)
  SendMessage (WM_COMMAND, CM_FILESAVEAS, 0L);
 else SaveFile();
}

/*************************************************************/
/*                                                           */
/* SaveFile: write the file                                  */
/*                                                           */
/*************************************************************/

void EditWin::SaveFile () {
 // allocate a buffer based upon current size of text in CEdit
 long filesize = editwin.GetWindowTextLength ();
 HANDLE hbuffer = GlobalAlloc (GMEM_MOVEABLE, filesize);
 if (hbuffer==NULL) {   // error, not enough memory for buffer
  DisplayMsg (IDS_MSG_ERROR, IDS_MSG_NOMEM, MB_OK | MB_ICONSTOP);
  return;
 }
 char* buf = (char*) GlobalLock (hbuffer);

 // transfer the updated text from CEdit control into global buf
 editwin.GetWindowText (buf, filesize);

 // open the file, replacing any existing file
 HANDLE hfile = CreateFile (filename, GENERIC_WRITE, 0, NULL,
                     CREATE_ALWAYS, FILE_ATTRIBUTE_NORMAL, NULL);
 if (hfile == INVALID_HANDLE_VALUE) {
  DisplayMsg (IDS_MSG_ERROR,IDS_MSG_FILEERR, MB_OK| MB_ICONSTOP);
  GlobalUnlock (hbuffer);
  GlobalFree (hbuffer);
  return;
```

```
 }

 // write the whole file
 DWORD actsz;
 WriteFile (hfile, buf, filesize, &actsz, NULL);
 CloseHandle (hfile);      // close file and delete global memory
 GlobalUnlock (hbuffer);
 GlobalFree   (hbuffer);

 if (actsz != (DWORD) filesize) // if write fails, show error
  DisplayMsg (IDS_MSG_ERROR, IDS_MSG_FILEWRT, MB_OK|MB_ICONSTOP);
 else
  editwin.SetModify (FALSE);    // set CEdit to unmodified
}

/*************************************************************/
/*                                                           */
/* CmFileSaveAs: Save an existent file with a new name       */
/*                                                           */
/*************************************************************/

void EditWin::CmFileSaveAs () {
 CFileDialog filedlg (FALSE,   // use SaveAs dialog
                      "*.CPP", // default extension
                      "*.*",   // current file name
          OFN_HIDEREADONLY | OFN_OVERWRITEPROMPT | OFN_LONGNAMES,
          "All Files (*.*)|*.*|CPP Files (*.CPP)|*.CPP|C Files"
          " (*.C)|*.C|Header Files (*.H*)|*.H*||", this);
 // install current file name
 strcpy (filedlg.m_ofn.lpstrFile, filename);
 if (filedlg.DoModal () == IDOK) {  // user has chosen a file, so
  filename = filedlg.GetPathName ();// extract its filename
  SaveFile ();                      // save the file
  CString title;                    // construct window title
  title.LoadString (IDS_EDIT);
  title += filename;
  SetWindowText (title);            // install new title
 }
}

/*************************************************************/
/*                                                           */
/* OnClose:  query user if we can terminate                  */
/*                                                           */
/*************************************************************/

void EditWin::OnClose () {
 if (editwin.GetSafeHwnd() && editwin.GetModify ())
  SaveCheck (); //save file if needed
 if (((FrameWin*) GetParentFrame())->fastclose == FALSE) {
  if (DisplayMsg (IDS_MSG_QUERY, IDS_MSG_EDITQUIT,
                  MB_YESNO | MB_ICONQUESTION) == IDYES) {
   MDIDestroy ();
  }
 }
}

/*************************************************************/
/*                                                           */
/* DisplayMsg: displays error message and return user response */
/*                                                           */
/*************************************************************/

int EditWin::DisplayMsg (int id1, int id2, UINT flags) {
```

```
 CString msg1, msg2;
 msg1.LoadString (id1);
 msg2.LoadString (id2);
 return MessageBox (msg2, msg1, flags);
}

/***************************************************************/
/*                                                             */
/* CmEnableEditUndo: enables/disables edit undo menu item      */
/*                                                             */
/***************************************************************/

void EditWin::CmEnableEditUndo (CCmdUI *ptrenabler) {
 ptrenabler->Enable (editwin.CanUndo());
}

/***************************************************************/
/*                                                             */
/* CmEnableEditCut: enables/disables edit cut menu item        */
/*                                                             */
/***************************************************************/

void EditWin::CmEnableEditCut (CCmdUI *ptrenabler) {
 ptrenabler->Enable (editwin.GetSel()>0? 1: 0);
}

/***************************************************************/
/*                                                             */
/* CmEnableEditCopy: enables/disables edit copy menu item      */
/*                                                             */
/***************************************************************/

void EditWin::CmEnableEditCopy (CCmdUI *ptrenabler) {
 ptrenabler->Enable (editwin.GetSel()>0? 1: 0);
}

/***************************************************************/
/*                                                             */
/* CmEnableEditPaste: enables/disables edit paste menu item    */
/*                                                             */
/***************************************************************/

void EditWin::CmEnableEditPaste (CCmdUI *ptrenabler) {
 ptrenabler->Enable (IsClipboardFormatAvailable (CF_TEXT));
}

/***************************************************************/
/*                                                             */
/* CmEditCut: Remove text data and place on clipboard          */
/*                                                             */
/***************************************************************/

void EditWin::CmEditCut () {
 editwin.Cut (); // cut it to clipboard
}

/***************************************************************/
/*                                                             */
/* CmEditCopy: copy text to clipboard                          */
/*                                                             */
/***************************************************************/

void EditWin::CmEditCopy () {
 editwin.Copy (); // copy it to clipboard
```

```
}

/*******************************************************************/
/*                                                                 */
/* CmEditPaste: Paste text from the clipboard                      */
/*                                                                 */
/*******************************************************************/

void EditWin::CmEditPaste () {
 if (IsClipboardFormatAvailable (CF_TEXT))
  editwin.Paste (); // paste from clipboard
}

/*******************************************************************/
/*                                                                 */
/* CmEditUndo: Undo last change                                    */
/*                                                                 */
/*******************************************************************/

void EditWin::CmEditUndo () {
 editwin.Undo ();
}
```

While **DrawWin** has changed little from the last chapter, for completeness and to aid understanding of the clipboard operations, here is the complete coding. The new data members all handle the clipboard operations.

DrawWin.h Definition

```
#pragma once

#include "CToolBox.h"

/*******************************************************************/
/*                                                                 */
/* DrawWin Class Definition                                        */
/*                                                                 */
/*******************************************************************/

class DrawWin : public CMDIChildWnd {

 /******************************************************************/
 /*                                                                */
 /* Class Data Members                                             */
 /*                                                                */
 /******************************************************************/

protected:

 static int numdraw;     // total number of draw children active

 COLORREF   colors[6];   // the possible colors array
 COLORREF   linecolor;   // current drawing pen color
 int        colnum;      // current pen color array index
 int        linewidth;   // current pen width
 bool       lbuttondown;// true if leftbutton is down for drawing
 CPen*      ptrpen;      // the current drawing pen
 CClientDC* ptrdc;       // the current drawing DC
 CToolBox   toolbox;     // client window's tool box

 CClientDC *ptrselectdc;// the current selection DC
 CRect      select_rect;// the selection rectangle for cut/paste

 bool       hideshow;    // true when tool box is visible
```

```
 bool        rbuttondown;// true when in select mode
 bool        selected;   // true when image is selected
 bool        paste;      // true when pasting from the clipboard

 /*************************************************************/
 /*                                                           */
 /* Class Functions                                           */
 /*                                                           */
 /*************************************************************/

public:
                 DrawWin (); // set initial line width & color
afx_msg void  OnPaint (); // paint background white

protected:
afx_msg void  OnClose ();                   // check if can close
afx_msg int   OnCreate(LPCREATESTRUCT); // construct tool box
afx_msg void  OnDestroy ();      // remove allocated menus & child

// remove tool box when minimized
afx_msg void  OnSize (UINT, int, int);

// reshow tool box when restoring
afx_msg BOOL  OnQueryOpen ();

// reposition tool box as win moves
afx_msg void  OnMove (int, int);

afx_msg void  OnLButtonDown (UINT, CPoint); // begin drawing
afx_msg void  OnLButtonUp (UINT, CPoint);   // end drawing
afx_msg void  OnMouseMove (UINT, CPoint);   // continue drawing

int   DisplayMsg (int, int, UINT);   // display a message
void  UpdateStatusBar ();            // display msg on status bar

// check mark hide/show tool box
afx_msg void  OnUpdateViewToolBox (CCmdUI*);

afx_msg void  CmLines (UINT);   // process all line width btns
afx_msg void  CmColors (UINT);  // process all color btns presses
afx_msg void  OnUpdateToolBoxLines (CCmdUI*); //enable line width
afx_msg void  OnUpdateToolBoxColors (CCmdUI*);//enable color btns


afx_msg void  OnRButtonDown (UINT, CPoint); // begin selection
afx_msg void  OnRButtonUp (UINT, CPoint);   // end selection
        void  ShowFocusRect (bool);// fix up focus rect & show it
        void  ToClipboard (); // copy to clipboard

afx_msg void  CmEditCut ();    // cut selected image to clpbd
afx_msg void  CmEditCopy ();   // copy selected image to clpbd
afx_msg void  CmEditPaste (); // paste from clipboard
afx_msg void  CmEnableEditCut   (CCmdUI*); // enable/disable Cut
afx_msg void  CmEnableEditCopy  (CCmdUI*); // enable/disable Copy
afx_msg void  CmEnableEditPaste (CCmdUI*);// enable/disable Paste

DECLARE_MESSAGE_MAP()
};
```

Here is the complete implementation of **DrawWin**. Again, we will look at the clipboard operations next.

```
DrawWin.cpp Implementation
```

```
#include "stdafx.h"

#include "FrameWin.h"
#include "DrawWin.h"
#include "DrawWinRC.h"
#include "resource.h"

/*************************************************************/
/*                                                           */
/* Old Style Method of Tool Bar Construction                 */
/*                                                           */
/*************************************************************/

static UINT BASED_CODE buttons_box[] = {
  CM_LINE1,
  CM_LINE2,
  CM_LINE3,
  CM_LINE4,
  ID_SEPARATOR,
  ID_SEPARATOR,
  CM_COLORA,
  CM_COLORB,
  CM_COLORC,
  CM_COLORD,
  CM_COLORE,
  CM_COLORF,
};

/*************************************************************/
/*                                                           */
/* Message map                                               */
/*                                                           */
/*************************************************************/

BEGIN_MESSAGE_MAP(DrawWin, CMDIChildWnd)
 ON_WM_CREATE ()
 ON_WM_PAINT ()
 ON_WM_DESTROY ()
 ON_WM_LBUTTONDOWN ()
 ON_WM_LBUTTONUP()
 ON_WM_MOUSEMOVE()
 ON_WM_CLOSE()
 ON_WM_SIZE()
 ON_WM_MOVE()
 ON_WM_QUERYOPEN()
 ON_UPDATE_COMMAND_UI(IDB_TOOLBOX, OnUpdateViewToolBox)
 ON_COMMAND_EX(IDB_TOOLBOX, OnBarCheck)
 ON_COMMAND_RANGE(CM_LINE1, CM_LINE4, CmLines)
 ON_COMMAND_RANGE(CM_COLORA, CM_COLORF, CmColors)
 ON_UPDATE_COMMAND_UI_RANGE(CM_LINE1, CM_LINE4,
                            OnUpdateToolBoxLines)
 ON_UPDATE_COMMAND_UI_RANGE(CM_COLORA, CM_COLORF,
                            OnUpdateToolBoxColors)
 ON_WM_RBUTTONDOWN ()
 ON_WM_RBUTTONUP()
 ON_COMMAND(CM_EDITCUT,             CmEditCut)
 ON_COMMAND(CM_EDITCOPY,            CmEditCopy)
 ON_COMMAND(CM_EDITPASTE,           CmEditPaste)
 ON_UPDATE_COMMAND_UI(CM_EDITCUT,   CmEnableEditCut)
 ON_UPDATE_COMMAND_UI(CM_EDITCOPY,  CmEnableEditCopy)
 ON_UPDATE_COMMAND_UI(CM_EDITPASTE, CmEnableEditPaste)
END_MESSAGE_MAP()

// number of DrawWin - controls hide/show menu item
```

```
int    DrawWin::numdraw = 0;

/*****************************************************************/
/*                                                               */
/* Drawwin: Construct the window object                          */
/*                                                               */
/*****************************************************************/

DrawWin::DrawWin () {
 colnum      = 0;                  // set initial black color
 linewidth   = 1;                  // set initial line width of 1

 ptrpen      = 0;                  // set no current pen
 ptrdc       = 0;                  // or DC for drawing

 // initialize possible colors
 colors[0]   = RGB (0,0,0);        // Black
 colors[1]   = RGB (255, 0,0);     // LtRed
 colors[2]   = RGB (0, 255, 0);    // LtGreen
 colors[3]   = RGB (255, 255,0);   // LtYellow
 colors[4]   = RGB (0, 0, 255);    // LtBlue
 colors[5]   = RGB (255, 0,255);   // LtMagenta
 linecolor   = colors[colnum];     // set beginning pen color

 lbuttondown = false;              // indicate not drawing
 rbuttondown = false;              // indicate not selecting
 paste       = false;              // indicate not pasting
 selected    = false;              // indicate not selected
}

/*****************************************************************/
/*                                                               */
/* OnDestroy: possibly remove the hide show menu                 */
/*                                                               */
/*****************************************************************/

void DrawWin::OnDestroy () {

 numdraw--;           // dec number of draw children
 if (numdraw==0) {
  // must remove our menu item for hide/show tool box
  // get access to menu and remove hide/show menu item
  CMenu *ptrmenu = AfxGetApp()->m_pMainWnd->GetMenu ();
  CMenu *ptrsmenu = ptrmenu->GetSubMenu (4);
  ptrsmenu->DeleteMenu (IDB_TOOLBOX, MF_BYCOMMAND);
 }
 // now continue destroying this MDI child
 CMDIChildWnd::OnDestroy ();
}

/*****************************************************************/
/*                                                               */
/* OnCreate: construct our tool box                              */
/*                                                               */
/*****************************************************************/

int DrawWin::OnCreate (LPCREATESTRUCT lpCS) {

 int retcd;
 if ((retcd = CMDIChildWnd::OnCreate (lpCS)) !=0) return -1;

 if (numdraw==0) {
  // this is the first, so install hide/show tool box menu item
  // acquire the main menu & then the offset 4 (5th) pop up menu
```

```
   // so that we can append the hide/show tool box item if needed
   CMenu *ptrmenu = AfxGetApp()->m_pMainWnd->GetMenu ();
   CMenu *ptrsmenu = ptrmenu->GetSubMenu (4);
   // so load in a new menu item and install in View menu
   char menuitem[40];
   LoadString (AfxGetApp()->m_hInstance, IDB_TOOLBOX, menuitem,
                                       sizeof(menuitem));
   ptrsmenu->AppendMenu (MF_ENABLED | MF_STRING, IDB_TOOLBOX,
                         menuitem);
  }
  numdraw++;

  // construct tool box: create, load its bitmap,
  // and assign its command IDs
  if (toolbox.Create (this, WS_CHILD | WS_VISIBLE |
                      CBRS_SIZE_FIXED | CBRS_TOP | CBRS_TOOLTIPS |
                      CBRS_FLYBY, IDB_TOOLBOX)
      && toolbox.LoadBitmap (IDB_TOOLBOX)
      && toolbox.SetButtons (buttons_box, sizeof(buttons_box)
                             / sizeof(UINT)));
  else return -1;

  toolbox.SetColumns (2); // set 2 columns

  // now notify control to accept any form of docking
  toolbox.EnableDocking (CBRS_ALIGN_ANY);

  // notify the framewindow of docking requirements
  EnableDocking (CBRS_ALIGN_ANY);

  // and dock both control bar and tool box at top
  DockControlBar (&toolbox, AFX_IDW_DOCKBAR_RIGHT);

  // insert captions to be shown when the tool bars are floating
  toolbox.SetWindowText(_T("Box"));

  // display initial pen color and width on the status bar
  UpdateStatusBar ();
  return retcd;
 }

/***************************************************************/
/*                                                             */
/* UpdateStatusBar: show width and color on the status bar     */
/*                                                             */
/***************************************************************/

void DrawWin::UpdateStatusBar () {
 // this display will be temporary only
 // it will be overlaid by next hints
 // first get a pointer to status bar
 CStatusBar *ptrbar = (CStatusBar*) AfxGetApp()->m_pMainWnd->
                        GetDescendantWindow (AFX_IDW_STATUS_BAR);
 char msg[80]; // construct a message for the status bar
 wsprintf(msg,"Draw: line width: %d - Color: %s", linewidth,
          CToolBox::colors[colnum]);
 ptrbar->SetPaneText (0, msg); // and display the message
}

/***************************************************************/
/*                                                             */
/* OnSize: on going minimized, hide any visible tool box       */
/*                                                             */
/***************************************************************/
```

```

void DrawWin::OnSize (UINT flags, int width, int height) {
 CMDIChildWnd::OnSize (flags, width, height);
 if (flags & SIZE_MINIMIZED)     // check if we are now minimized
  if (toolbox.GetStyle() & WS_VISIBLE)  // is tool box visible
   SendMessage (WM_COMMAND, IDB_TOOLBOX, 0L); // yes, so hide it
}

/*****************************************************************/
/*                                                               */
/* OnMove: force tool box to reposition when parent moves       */
/*                                                               */
/*****************************************************************/

void DrawWin::OnMove (int x, int y) {
 CMDIChildWnd::OnMove (x, y);
// if (toolbox.GetSafeHwnd () && toolbox.IsFloating ()) {
//  CRect r;
//  GetWindowRect (&r);
//  r.left += GetSystemMetrics (SM_CXFRAME) * 2;
//  r.top += GetSystemMetrics (SM_CYFRAME)*2 +
//           GetSystemMetrics (SM_CYCAPTION);
//  FloatControlBar (&toolbox, CPoint (r.left, r.top));
// }
}

/*****************************************************************/
/*                                                               */
/* EvQueryOpen: when restoring from icon, reshow tool box       */
/*                                                               */
/*****************************************************************/

BOOL DrawWin::OnQueryOpen () {
 SendMessage (WM_COMMAND, IDB_TOOLBOX, 0L);// force show tool box
 return CMDIChildWnd::OnQueryOpen (); // and continue the Restore
}

/*****************************************************************/
/*                                                               */
/* CmLines: handle any of the line button presses               */
/*                                                               */
/*****************************************************************/

void DrawWin::CmLines (UINT cmd) {
 // line width is the command ID less the command ID of line 1 +1
 linewidth = cmd - CM_LINE1 + 1;
 UpdateStatusBar (); // display new choice on status bar
}

/*****************************************************************/
/*                                                               */
/* CmColors: handle any of the color button presses             */
/*                                                               */
/*****************************************************************/

void DrawWin::CmColors (UINT cmd) {
 // color idx = command number less the command ID of first color
 colnum = cmd - CM_COLORA;
 UpdateStatusBar (); // display new color choice on status bar
}

/*****************************************************************/
/*                                                               */
/* OnUpdateViewToolBox: handles the check mark on menu item     */
```

```
/*                                                                  */
/********************************************************************/

void DrawWin::OnUpdateViewToolBox (CCmdUI *ptrui) {
 // place check mark on menu item is tool box is now visible
 ptrui->SetCheck ((toolbox.GetStyle() & WS_VISIBLE) != 0);
}

/********************************************************************/
/*                                                                  */
/* OnUpdateToolBoxLines: set line button as pressed                 */
/*                                                                  */
/********************************************************************/

void DrawWin::OnUpdateToolBoxLines (CCmdUI *ptrui) {
 ptrui->SetRadio (
       (UINT) (linewidth + CM_LINE1 -1) == ptrui->m_nID ? 1 : 0);
}

/********************************************************************/
/*                                                                  */
/* OnUpdateToolBoxColors: set color button as pressed               */
/*                                                                  */
/********************************************************************/

void DrawWin::OnUpdateToolBoxColors (CCmdUI *ptrui) {
 ptrui->SetRadio (
             (UINT)(colnum + CM_COLORA) == ptrui->m_nID ? 1 : 0);
}

/********************************************************************/
/*                                                                  */
/* OnPaint: just repaint the background white                       */
/*                                                                  */
/********************************************************************/

void DrawWin::OnPaint() {
 CPaintDC dc(this); // minimalist paint
}

/********************************************************************/
/*                                                                  */
/* OnClose: query user if we can terminate this drawing             */
/*                                                                  */
/********************************************************************/

void DrawWin::OnClose () {
 if (((FrameWin*) GetParentFrame())->fastclose == FALSE)
  if (DisplayMsg (IDS_MSG_QUERY, IDS_DRAWQUIT, MB_YESNO |
             MB_ICONQUESTION) == IDYES)
   MDIDestroy ();
}

/********************************************************************/
/*                                                                  */
/* DisplayMsg: shows a MessageBox and returns its retcode           */
/*                                                                  */
/********************************************************************/

int DrawWin::DisplayMsg (int id1, int id2, UINT flags) {
 CString msg1, msg2;
 msg1.LoadString (id1);
 msg2.LoadString (id2);
 return MessageBox (msg2, msg1, flags);
```

```
}
/***************************************************************/
/*                                                             */
/* CmEditCut: cut the selected graphic image area to clipboard */
/*                                                             */
/***************************************************************/
void DrawWin::CmEditCut () {
 if (selected) {// when image is selected, select_rect holds dims
  ToClipboard (); // send image to clipboard, say is a cut
  // perform cut => set image rectangle to background color
  HDC hourdc = ::GetDC(m_hWnd);      // get a hdc to model
  ::PatBlt (hourdc, select_rect.left, select_rect.top,
          select_rect.Width(), select_rect.Height() , WHITENESS);
  ::ReleaseDC (m_hWnd, hourdc);      // release the dc
  selected = false; // indicate image is no longer selected
 }
}
/***************************************************************/
/*                                                             */
/* CmEditCopy: copy selection to the clipboard                 */
/*                                                             */
/***************************************************************/
void DrawWin::CmEditCopy () {
 if (selected) {// when image is selected, select_rect holds dims
  ToClipboard ();// send image to clipboard & say not a cut
  selected = false;   // indicate image is no longer selected
 }
}
/***************************************************************/
/*                                                             */
/* ToClipboard: send image to clipboard                        */
/*                                                             */
/***************************************************************/
void DrawWin::ToClipboard () {
 // set selected image dims
 int height = select_rect.bottom - select_rect.top;
 int width  = select_rect.right - select_rect.left;
 // remove selection dotted frame
 HDC hourdc = ::GetDC(m_hWnd);            // get a hdc to model
 ::DrawFocusRect (hourdc, &select_rect); // remove dotted frame
 // make a copy of the selected area
 HDC hmemdc = ::CreateCompatibleDC (hourdc);
 HBITMAP bm = ::CreateCompatibleBitmap (hourdc, width, height);
 HBITMAP obm;
 obm = (HBITMAP)::SelectObject (hmemdc, bm);// install new bitmap
 // copy our image to memory copy
 ::BitBlt (hmemdc,0, 0, width, height, hourdc, select_rect.left,
           select_rect.top, SRCCOPY);
 ::SelectObject (hmemdc, obm);         // remove our copy bitmap
 ::DeleteDC (hmemdc);                  // delete the compatible dc
 ::ReleaseDC (m_hWnd, hourdc);         // remove the model dc
 // now copy it to the clipboard
 VERIFY(OpenClipboard ());
 VERIFY(::EmptyClipboard ());
 VERIFY(::SetClipboardData (CF_BITMAP, bm));
```

```
 VERIFY(::CloseClipboard ());
}

/*************************************************************/
/*                                                           */
/* CmEditPaste: paste from the clipboard                     */
/*                                                           */
/*************************************************************/

void DrawWin::CmEditPaste () {
 // if it is graphical bitmap
 if (::IsClipboardFormatAvailable (CF_BITMAP)) {
  paste = true;    // signal paste operation in progress
  // acquire the cross cursor
  HCURSOR hcross = LoadCursor (NULL, IDC_CROSS);
  // install the cross cursor
  SetClassLong (m_hWnd, GCL_HCURSOR, (long) hcross);
 }
}

/*************************************************************/
/*                                                           */
/* CmEnableEditCut: enable cut when there is a selection     */
/*                                                           */
/*************************************************************/

void DrawWin::CmEnableEditCut (CCmdUI* ptrcmd) {
 ptrcmd->Enable (selected);
}

/*************************************************************/
/*                                                           */
/* CmEnableEditCopy: enable copy when there is a selection   */
/*                                                           */
/*************************************************************/

void DrawWin::CmEnableEditCopy (CCmdUI* ptrcmd) {
 ptrcmd->Enable (selected);
}

/*************************************************************/
/*                                                           */
/* CmEnableEditPaste: enable paste when there is a bitmap on */
/*                      the clipboard                        */
/*                                                           */
/*************************************************************/

void DrawWin::CmEnableEditPaste (CCmdUI* ptrcmd) {
 // is there a graphics bitmap on the clipboard?
 ptrcmd->Enable (::IsClipboardFormatAvailable (CF_BITMAP));
}

/*************************************************************/
/*                                                           */
/* OnLButtonDown: begin drawing or paste or deselect rectangle */
/*                                                           */
/*************************************************************/

void DrawWin::OnLButtonDown (UINT, CPoint point) {
 // handle paste process requested first, if requested
 if (paste) {
  if (OpenClipboard ()==0)  // someone else using clipboard
   return;
  // get the bitmap
```

```
  HBITMAP hbm = (HBITMAP) GetClipboardData (CF_BITMAP);
  ASSERT (hbm); // verify exists - debugging only
  // make compatible memory dc to copy this onto the screen
  HDC hourdc = ::GetDC(m_hWnd);
  HDC hmemdc = ::CreateCompatibleDC (hourdc);
  HBITMAP obm = (HBITMAP)::SelectObject (hmemdc, hbm);
  BITMAP bm;
  // retrieve bm section sp we can get the size of the image
  ::GetObject(hbm, sizeof(bm), &bm);
  int width = bm.bmWidth;
  int height = bm.bmHeight;
  // copy our image to memory copy
  ::BitBlt (hourdc, point.x, point.y, width, height, hmemdc,
            0, 0, SRCCOPY);
  ::SelectObject (hmemdc, obm); // remove clipboard's bitmap
  ::DeleteDC (hmemdc);          // delete the compatible dc
  ::ReleaseDC (m_hWnd, hourdc); // release the model dc
  CloseClipboard ();            // close down the clipboard
  paste = false;                // indicate no longer pasting
  // reinstall main arrow cursor
  HCURSOR harrow = LoadCursor (NULL, IDC_ARROW);
  SetClassLong (m_hWnd, GCL_HCURSOR, (long) harrow);
 }

 // next check for a deselect process being requested
 else if (selected) {
  // if an image is selected, deselect it
  CClientDC dc (this);
  // remove the dotted select rectangle
  dc.DrawFocusRect (&select_rect);
  selected = false; // indicate image is no longer selected
 }

 // finally handle any requested draw operation
 else if (!lbuttondown) {
  lbuttondown = true;           // lock out subsequent clicks
  ptrdc = new CClientDC (this); // get new draw DC
  linecolor = colors[colnum];   // install current color
  ptrpen = new CPen (PS_SOLID, linewidth, linecolor);
  ptrdc->SelectObject (ptrpen); // install pen in DC
  SetCapture ();            // capture all mouse movements for draw
  ptrdc->MoveTo (point);    // set pen to starting point for draw
 }
}

/*****************************************************************/
/*                                                               */
/* OnLButtonUp: stop drawing the line                            */
/*                                                               */
/*****************************************************************/

void DrawWin::OnLButtonUp (UINT, CPoint) {
 if (lbuttondown) {
  if (ptrdc) delete ptrdc;   // stop drawing - remove GDI objects
  if (ptrpen) delete ptrpen; // if flurry of clicks, avoids crash
  lbuttondown = false;       // signal not drawing
  ReleaseCapture ();         // and release mouse
 }
}

/*****************************************************************/
/*                                                               */
/* OnRButtonDown: begin selection mode                           */
/*                                                               */
```

```
/********************************************************************/

void DrawWin::OnRButtonDown (UINT, CPoint point) {
 // avoid multiple invocations
 if (!rbuttondown && !paste) {
  rbuttondown = true;          // signal selection mode activated
  ptrselectdc = new CClientDC (this);    // get our DC
  // remove old selected dotted rectangle
  if (selected) ptrselectdc->DrawFocusRect (&select_rect);
  // calc start point
  select_rect.SetRect (point.x, point.y, point.x, point.y);
  SetCapture(); // capture all mouse movements
 }
}

/********************************************************************/
/*                                                                  */
/* OnRButtonUp: stop selection of image                             */
/*                                                                  */
/********************************************************************/

void DrawWin::OnRButtonUp (UINT, CPoint) {
 if (rbuttondown) {      // end select mode
  rbuttondown = false;  // signal no longer selecting
  delete ptrselectdc;   // remove our select dc
  ReleaseCapture ();    // free up the mouse

  ShowFocusRect (true); // fix up possible upside down coords

  // calculate current dimensions of image
  int height = select_rect.bottom - select_rect.top;
  int width  = select_rect.right - select_rect.left;

  if (width == 0 && height == 0) // avoid a NULL selection
   return;

  selected = true; // signal there has been a selection made
 }
}

/********************************************************************/
/*                                                                  */
/* OnMouseMove: draw a line to mouse position or                    */
/*              extend selection rect position                      */
/*                                                                  */
/********************************************************************/

void DrawWin::OnMouseMove (UINT, CPoint point) {
 // draw line requested
 if (lbuttondown)
  ptrdc->LineTo (point); // draw a line from here to point

 // extend image selection dimensions requested
 else if (rbuttondown) {
  ShowFocusRect (false);  // remove previous selection frame
  // calculate new image dimensions
  select_rect.SetRect (select_rect.left, select_rect.top,
                       point.x, point.y);
  // show the focus rect even if upside down
  ShowFocusRect (false);
 }
}

/********************************************************************/
```

```
/*                                                              */
/* ShowFocusRect: handle displaying Focus Rect, even when it    */
/*                can be upside down                            */
/*                                                              */
/****************************************************************/

void DrawWin::ShowFocusRect (bool fixit) {
 bool fixleft = false, fixtop = false;
 int temp;

 // since the selection image could be reversed,
 //normalize reversed dims
 if (select_rect.right - select_rect.left < 0) {
  temp = select_rect.right;
  select_rect.right = select_rect.left;
  select_rect.left = temp;
  fixleft = true;
 }
 if (select_rect.bottom - select_rect.top < 0) {
  temp = select_rect.bottom;
  select_rect.bottom = select_rect.top;
  select_rect.top = temp;
  fixtop = true;
 }

 if (fixit) return; // final fix up done, do not show rectangle

 // draw new selection frame
 ptrselectdc->DrawFocusRect (&select_rect);

 // now unfix it so user can continue upside down
 if (fixleft) {
  temp = select_rect.right;
  select_rect.right = select_rect.left;
  select_rect.left = temp;
 }
 if (fixtop) {
  temp = select_rect.bottom;
  select_rect.bottom = select_rect.top;
  select_rect.top = temp;
 }
}
```

Clipboard Operations

Accessing the clipboard to exchange data between applications and to provide cut and paste operations are extremely easy to do. Built-in support for the clipboard is provided by the MFC. And in fact, **CEdit** controls provide this clipboard support automatically with virtually no user coding required.

Data can be stored on the clipboard in several formats. Table 12.7 shows the more common clipboard formats.

Table 12.7 Common Clipboard Formats

Format	Description
CF_TEXT	- null-terminated ASCI text with <CRLF>
CF_BITMAP	- device dependent bitmaps
CF_DIB	- device independent bitmaps
CF_PALETTE	- color palette, usually with dibs
CF_WAVE	- .WAV sound data
CF_PRIVATEFIRST	- the first type of totally program defined data
CF_PRIVATELAST	- the highest user defined clipboard format type

Notice that an application can cut and paste nearly anything desired, such as data base records, spreadsheet information, and so on merely by using a clipboard type within the range of the last two identifiers. In this chapter I examine the two most commonly encountered formats—**CF_TEXT** and **CF_BITMAP**. The general cycle of action to be followed when using the clipboard is a simple one.

For Pastes:

```
if the clipboard contains data of the type desired,
    open the clipboard
    copy the clipboard data into your own data member
    close the clipboard
```

For Cut and Copy:

```
if there is a selection made,
    open the clipboard
    create a copy of your data
    give that copy permanently to the clipboard
    close the clipboard
```

The close operation is vital. During the entire time that your application has the clipboard opened, **no** other applications can access the clipboard.

Design Rule 48: Always close the clipboard when finished copying, cutting, or pasting.

Design Rule 49: When giving an object to the Clipboard, Windows takes complete ownership of that object. Do not attempt to use or reference that object after giving it to the Clipboard. If you need to reference that object, make a global memory copy and give Windows that copy.

The only complicating factor to clipboard access is the requisite **selection** of the data to be cut/copied. If the data is text, for simplicity, we can let the **CEdit** control handle the selection process internally. But for graphics, we must implement the selection process ourselves. The method I use here emulates the method of graphics selection in the Paintbrush application. Let's begin with the simpler of the two types, text.

Handling Text with the Clipboard

The **CEdit** class provides automatic support for Clipboard operations including Cut, Copy, and Paste along with Undo. These operations are automatically handled by **CEdit** members **if** the menu command handlers invoke the **CEdit** functions for copy/cut/paste and so on.

The **CEdit** control provides the following member functions that handle the Edit pop-up menu operations; we need only to invoke them. Assume that **editwin** is the **CEdit** control.

Edit Undo:	`if (editwin.CanUndo ()) editwin.Undo ();`
Edit Cut:	`editwin.Cut ();`
Edit Copy:	`editwin.Copy ();`
Edit Paste:	`editwin.Paste ();`
Edit Clear:	`editwin.Clear ();`

For Cut/Copy actions in functions **CmEditCut** and **CmEditCopy**, by using some functionality of the **CEdit** control, we do not have to perform the text selection actions. Instead, we call the member function **GetSel** which fills up two integers with the corresponding positions of the beginning and ending selected data. These are similar to subscripts in a character string array.

```
int startpos, endpos;
editwin.GetSel (startpos, endpos);
```

The two positions are passed by reference and contain the offsets of the selected text within the edit buffer of the control. If **endpos** is 0, none is selected.

With the MFC, the cut/copy process is simplified by using the **CEdit** provided functions **Cut** and **Copy**.

```
editwin.Copy ();
editwin.Cut ();
```

These two **CEdit** functions perform the sequence of opening, clearing, copying the data, and closing the clipboard for us.

The paste operation of **CmEditPaste** is equally simple to perform. The first step is to verify that text is available which is done by using the **IsClipboardFormatAvailable** function, which does not require the clipboard to be opened.

```
BOOL IsClipboardFormatAvailable (CF_TEXT);
```

Here, the function is passed an ORed series of acceptable clipboard formats the application can handle. The **CEdit** function **Paste** handles all of the work for us and typical coding becomes simply this.

```
if (IsClipboardFormatAvailable (CF_TEXT))
  editwin.Paste (); // paste from clipboard
```

Handling Bitmaps on the Clipboard

Transferring bitmaps to and from the clipboard requires much more effort on our part because there is no automatic selection process for us to use. Therefore, I begin by discussing exactly how the process should occur from the user's perspective. My model is the Paintbrush program.

Paintbrush has a bitmap button on its tool box to select cut/copy operations. Rather than add in that complexity, I use a common alternative method, right mouse button presses. The standard Windows method for selection of a graphical area for cut/paste operations involved pressing the right button at the upper left corner and dragging to the lower right corner. As the mouse is being dragged, a dotted frame or rectangle appears around the selected portion of the image. When the button is released, one sees the dotted frame outlining the selected area.

If the button is re-pressed, then that original selection is replaced by this beginning of a new one, repeated until the user is satisfied. At which point, the menu item cut or copy is selected; note that these menu items are enabled whenever a selection has been made and is outlined by the dotted frame rectangle. After the cut/copy is selected, that portion of the image is copied onto the clipboard. The dotted frame then disappears. If a cut was requested, the dotted rectangle is filled with the background color, white here.

When a bitmap image is on the clipboard, the Edit| Paste menu item becomes enabled with Cut and Copy disabled. After the Paste menu item is selected, some means must be used to remind the user that he or she must go on to select the point at which to paste the image. Here I use a simple change of the mouse cursor from the arrow to the cross. The user is expected to position the mouse cursor to the desired insertion point and press the left button. The bitmap is copied onto the current window, using that point as the origin point for the upper left corner of the clipboard bitmap. Once the paste is done, the cursor is changed back to the normal arrow. Note that as long as the bitmap remains on the clipboard, the Paste menu item remains enabled.

Drawing the dotted frame or rectangle is quite easy using the **DrawFocusRect** function.

```
dc.DrawFocusRect (&select_rect); // draw dotted frame
```

Here **select_rect** is a **CRect** containing the current dimensions of the frame. The actual drawing is done by the Windows API function of the same name called from the MFC member function, **DrawFocusRect**, using XOR logic to plot the dotted lines.

XOR logic is a commonly used graphical trick. If an image is plotted by XORing the pixel colors, then if the same image is plotted at the same location a second time using XOR, the original colors reappear and the image disappears. For example, using the simpler 4-color mode, we have the following.

```
           pixel color bits
screen:          01  blue
object:    XOR 10   green
           ------
new obj:         11  red  <--- the new object appears red
object:    XOR 10   green
           ------
                 01  blue <--- the original blue is back
```

Some texts actually set the ROP2 value to XOR before the invocation of the **DrawFrameRect** function similar to this.

```
dc.SetROP2 (R2_XORPEN);
```

However, this is not needed because the Windows API **DrawFocusRect** function that the MFC invokes inline always sets this just before drawing the focus rectangle.

Thus, the selection sequence consists of initially drawing the dotted frame. If the user moves the mouse, first redraw the original frame and then the new frame modified by the mouse cursor's position. Tight control over operations is needed, since the left button press can mean three different things: paste here, de-select current selected area, or draw. Therefore, four control **bool** members are used.

```
bool lbuttondown, rbuttondown, paste, selected;
```

paste is **true** only when the user has selected Edit|Paste.
selected is **true** only while an image area is currently selected which is that time between releasing the right button and either the next left button press to de-select, another right button press to de-select and re-select a new area, or the cut/copy menu items are selected.
rbuttondown is **true** only while the right button is down and we're not in paste mode.
lbuttondown is **true** only during a draw operation.

The coding sequence in the **OnLButtonDown** function must check for paste operations first and handle if found. If paste is not in effect, then it checks if any area is selected to so that it can determine if a de-selection action is required. Finally, if the left button is not down, the draw operation can commence.

Beyond providing the **CmEditCut**, **CmEditCopy**, and **CmEditPaste** functions, three command enablers must be used to properly enable these menu items. For the cut/copy operations, the selected **bool** member is all that is required. The paste enabler must check the current contents of the clipboard to see if a bitmap is present.

By checking the clipboard every time, the enabler solves another communication problem for us. If the user task switches to another application, such as PaintBrush and copies say **leaves.bmp** to the clipboard, when the user task switches back to our draw window, our application needs to know that there is now a bitmap currently on the clipboard. Therefore, by continual checking, the enabler correctly notifies our application of the bitmap's presence.

Let's begin our examination of the revised **DrawWin** class with the three enablers. For the cut/copy enablers (**CmEnableEditCut** and **CmEnableEditCopy**), they simply return the status of the **selected bool**. Remember, **selected** is **true** only when the user has made a graphical selection.

```
ptrcmd->Enable (selected);
```

The **CmEnableEditPaste** checks the current contents of the clipboard looking for the presence of a bitmap.

```
ptrcmd->Enable (::IsClipboardFormatAvailable (CF_BITMAP));
```

Next, let's look at the selection process, involving the right button. **OnRButtonDown** only activates when there is not a right button press in progress and when paste is chosen. Obtain a DC to our client window. If there is a currently selected area on the screen indicated by **selected** being **true**, it must be removed by using **DrawFocusRect** with the current **select_rect** values that makes the frame disappear. Then, the new beginning upper left position is calculated and installed into the **select_rect** and the mouse events captured. The new **CRect** function **SetRect** conveniently resets a new value into the rectangle object.

```
if (!rbuttondown && !paste) {
 rbuttondown = true;
 ptrselectdc = new CClientDC (this);
 if (selected)
  ptrselectdc->DrawFocusRect (&select_rect);
 select_rect.SetRect (point.x, point.y, point.x, point.y);
 SetCapture();
}
```

Next, the user drags the mouse to the desired ending lower right position. **OnMouseMove** handles the successive removal of the previous dotted frame and display of the new frame. Again, I use the **SetRect** function to reset new values into the rectangle object.

```
if (lbuttondown)
 ptrdc->LineTo (point);
else if (rbuttondown) {
```

```
 ShowFocusRect (false);
 select_rect.SetRect (select_rect.left, select_rect.top,
                      point.x, point.y);
 ShowFocusRect (false);
}
```

Finally, the right button is released and **OnRButtonUp** is invoked to finish off the selection process by setting **rbuttondown** back to **false**, removing the DC, releasing the mouse, calling **ShowFocusRect** (request permanent fix of coordinates), calculating the image width and height, and if the dimensions are not zero, setting **selected** to true.

```
if (rbuttondown) {
 rbuttondown = false;
 delete ptrselectdc;
 ReleaseCapture ();
 ShowFocusRect (true);
 int height = select_rect.bottom - select_rect.top;
 int width  = select_rect.right - select_rect.left;
 if (width == 0 && height == 0) return;
 selected = true;
}
```

Did you notice the new function in both **OnMouseMove** and **OnRButtonUp** called **ShowFocusRect**? This function provides a final nice touch on the selection process. Often the user drags backwards or from the right to the left or even upside down. Our calculated dimensions based upon right—left coordinates are negative. **DrawFocusRect** fails when the coordinates are backwards! Rather than just rejecting the negative widths and heights, the **select_rect** coordinates should just be reversed and the Focus Rectangle drawn. If the reversed coordinates are not re-reversed, the user is not able to select more than one pixel dimensions. Thus, while the user is still dragging the focus rectangle, **ShowFocusRect** must reverse, show, and re-reverse the coordinates. However, when the right button up message comes, the coordinates must be permanently reversed. The **ShowFocusRect** function is as follows.

```
void      DrawWin::ShowFocusRect (bool fixit) {
 bool fixleft = false, fixtop = false;
 int temp;
 if (select_rect.right - select_rect.left < 0) {
  temp = select_rect.right;
  select_rect.right = select_rect.left;
  select_rect.left = temp;
  fixleft = true;
 }
 if (select_rect.bottom - select_rect.top < 0) {
  temp = select_rect.bottom;
  select_rect.bottom = select_rect.top;
  select_rect.top = temp;
  fixtop = true;
 }
 if (fixit) return;
 ptrselectdc->DrawFocusRect (&select_rect);
 if (fixleft) {
  temp = select_rect.right;
  select_rect.right = select_rect.left;
  select_rect.left = temp;
 }
 if (fixtop) {
  temp = select_rect.bottom;
  select_rect.bottom = select_rect.top;
  select_rect.top = temp;
 }
}
```

Now let us examine the cut and copy operation via the menu items. **CmEditCut** and **CmEditCopy** are nearly identical save for the removal of the image when cut is chosen. Therefore, I replaced the common coding with a helper function, **ToClipboard**.

In **CmEditCopy** if **selected** is **true**, then I must make a bitmap copy of the selected area of our window. To do so,

I need to use a **BitBlt** onto a memory DC to give to Windows to be placed onto the clipboard. Therefore, I get a client DC and a memory DC based upon our client dc. Once the current selected rectangle dimensions are converted into a width and height, the dotted frame that shows the selected area must be removed.

```
void      DrawWin::CmEditCopy () {
 if (selected) {
  ToClipboard (false);
  selected = false;
 }
}
void      DrawWin::ToClipboard () {
 int height = select_rect.bottom - select_rect.top;
 int width  = select_rect.right - select_rect.left;
 HDC hourdc = ::GetDC(m_hWnd);
 ::DrawFocusRect (hourdc, &select_rect);
```

Then, the bitmap is allocated based upon the current dimensions and inserted into the memory dc.

```
 HDC hmemdc = ::CreateCompatibleDC (hourdc);
 HBITMAP bm = ::CreateCompatibleBitmap (hourdc, width,
               height);
 HBITMAP obm;
 obm = (HBITMAP)::SelectObject (hmemdc, bm);
```

And the copy is made using **BitBlt**. With the bitmap copy completed, these objects are removed.

```
 ::BitBlt (hmemdc,0, 0, width, height, hourdc,
          select_rect.left, select_rect.top, SRCCOPY);
 ::SelectObject (hmemdc, obm);
 ::DeleteDC (hmemdc);
 ::ReleaseDC (m_hWnd, hourdc);
```

The actual transfer to the clipboard is done using the C API clipboard functions.

```
 VERIFY(OpenClipboard ());
 VERIFY(::EmptyClipboard ());
 VERIFY(::SetClipboardData (CF_BITMAP, bm));
 VERIFY(::CloseClipboard ());
}
```

The VERIFY and ASSERT Macros

The **ASSERT** macro is strictly a debugging macro; it has no effect in a Release build. The macro is passed a test condition. If that test condition fails or is false, an assertion message box appears at run time. Personally, I seldom use an **ASSERT** because of the fact that it has no effect in the Release production version of the program. If I feel that something could cause an error, I prefer to check for that situation and handle accordingly. I hate "mostly working" programs. Hence, you have seen my style, check for situations and display an error message in a message box.

In contrast, the **VERIFY** macro operates in both the Debug and Release builds. If the test condition fails or is zero, then a message box to that effect appears at run time. Thus, I chose to wrap each of the C API clipboard function calls with a **VERIFY**. If any of the four steps fails, the user is alerted to the failure.

Handling a Cut Operation

If the Cut menu item was selected, after the same above sequence of calling **ToClipboard** is done, the actual Cut is done by using **PatBlt** to replace the **select_rect** area with the background color.

```
HDC hourdc = ::GetDC(m_hWnd);
::PatBlt (hourdc, select_rect.left, select_rect.top,
        select_rect.Width(), select_rect.Height() , WHITENESS);
::ReleaseDC (m_hWnd, hourdc);
```

Notice that I have used the C API versions of these graphics functions. They are just simple and convenient. However, I could also have used the MFC encapsulation of these various functions as well.

Handling the Paste Operation

When the **CmEditPaste** function is invoked by selecting the Edit|Paste menu item, if the clipboard contains bitmap data, **paste** is set to **true**. Some means must be provided to ensure the user realizes that he or she is to select the desired point upon which to paste the image. Changing the cursor should alert the user to a paste operation.

When Edit|Paste is chosen, I change the arrow cursor into the cross cursor. However, since the cursor must remain as the cross across messages and potential task switches, the safest approach is to install the cross cursor in the window's **WNDCLASS**, using **SetClassLong**. Thus, the coding of the **CmEditPaste** is only the short sequence.

```
if (::IsClipboardFormatAvailable (CF_BITMAP)) {
 paste = true;
 HCURSOR hcross = LoadCursor (NULL, IDC_CROSS);
 SetClassLong (m_hWnd, GCL_HCURSOR, (long) hcross);
}
```

The actual copy from the clipboard and insertion onto the window is done when the left button is pressed. **OnLButtonDown** now has the added responsibility of signaling where to paste and must be handled before checking for de-selection and normal drawing. In **OnLButtonDown**, first check for paste operation in effect, then check for a deselection request, and if neither, it must be a draw request.

To handle the paste action, a **BitBlt** is used to copy from the clipboard copy onto our DC. This means that I need to place the bitmap into a memory dc and **BitBlt** from the memory DC onto our client window DC. Do not forget to close the clipboard. And the paste operation is complete. Clean up involves setting **paste** back to **false** and restoring the normal cursor. So **OnLButtonDown** is done this way.

```
if (paste) {
 if (OpenClipboard ()==0) return;
 HBITMAP hbm = (HBITMAP) GetClipboardData (CF_BITMAP);
 ASSERT (hbm);
 HDC hourdc = ::GetDC(m_hWnd);
 HDC hmemdc = ::CreateCompatibleDC (hourdc);
 HBITMAP obm = (HBITMAP)::SelectObject (hmemdc, hbm);
 BITMAP bm;
 ::GetObject(hbm, sizeof(bm), &bm);
 int width = bm.bmWidth;
 int height = bm.bmHeight;
 ::BitBlt (hourdc, point.x, point.y, width, height, hmemdc,
        0, 0, SRCCOPY);
 ::SelectObject (hmemdc, obm);
 ::DeleteDC (hmemdc);
 ::ReleaseDC (m_hWnd, hourdc);
 CloseClipboard ();
 paste = false;
 HCURSOR harrow = LoadCursor (NULL, IDC_ARROW);
 SetClassLong (m_hWnd, GCL_HCURSOR, (long) harrow);
}
```

OnLButtonDown then handles any de-select request that is occurring if **selected** is currently **true**. To de-select, the **DrawFocusRect** function must XOR the current **select_rect** to remove the dotted frame

```
else if (selected) {
 CClientDC ourdc (this);
 ourdc.DrawFocusRect (&select_rect);
 selected = false;
}
```

Finally, **OnLButtonDown** can then go on with the normal draw process.

```
else if (!lbuttondown) {
 lbuttondown = true;
 ptrdc  = new CClientDC (this);
 linecolor = colors[colnum];
 ptrpen = new CPen (PS_SOLID, linenum, linecolor);
 ptrdc->SelectObject (ptrpen);
```

```
   SetCapture ();
   ptrdc->MoveTo (point);
}
```

Programming Problems

Pgm12-1—Revised Acme Inventory Data Entry with Clipboard Support

Once again, we are going to revise the Acme Inventory Data Entry program. Using **Pgm10-1** as the base of operations, add clipboard support. When a record is selected, that is, when it is highlighted, permit the user to cut or copy it to the clipboard. When a record is deleted, place that record on the clipboard.

The easiest way to implement this is by storing an instance of the Inventory structure on the clipboard. This means that you should use the data type clipboard identifier of **CF_PRIVATEFIRST**.

When there is any data of type **CF_PRIVATEFIRST** on the clipboard, enable Edit|Paste. If the user wishes to paste, do so by appending the clipboard record onto the end of the array.

Thoroughly test these changes.

Pgm12-2—Revised Acme Inventory Data Entry with Undo-Redo Support

Once again, we are going to revise the Acme Inventory Data Entry program. Using **Pgm10-1** as the base of operations, add support for two new Edit menu items: Undo and Redo. To implement these, you will need two instances of a stack class, one for each of these operations.

Every time a record is Added, Updated or Deleted, place sufficient information onto the Undo stack so that the user could undo that addition, modification or deletion. The easiest way to implement this is to create a helper structure that contains an instance of the Inventory record structure and other members that enable you to undo that operation, such as a code that indicates add, update or delete and perhaps a record number.

When an Undo is selected, place sufficient information onto the Redo stack to enable the user to change his or her mind and redo what was just undone.

Thoroughly test these changes to the application.

Chapter 13 Basic Printing Operations

Introduction

Ever had a programming nightmare? Well, printing documents under Windows is bad, really bad; but it could be a lot worse. The MFC does help speed the process. Perhaps the most significant problem facing the programmer is the vast number of different printers, each with their own printing protocol. Consider the task of writing a DOS application that prints a document that includes both text and graphics. How do you handle the printing process? Windows attempts to solve this nasty situation by providing device independent printing. Still, it remains a tricky, confusing arena.

The Design of Printing Operations

The File pop-up menu often offers four menu items for the user: File|Print, File|Page Setup, File|Preview and File|Print Setup. The File|Preview operation is discussed in depth in Chapter 15. The printer setup operation displays the Windows common printer setup dialog box in which the user can select the current printer to be used, set the current default printer, and set some printer options such as landscape mode. When File|Print is chosen, the Windows common print dialog box is displayed. From this dialog, the user selects the specific details for this print run, including Portrait/Landscape, image dithering, which pages and how many copies, for example. Once the user selects Ok, the printing process begins. An "Abort Printing Process" dialog box appears for the duration of the printing process. Should the user select the abort button, the print is canceled. Under the MFC, the programmer must supply the Abort dialog when printing outside of the document-view architecture.

The MFC is designed around a high-level document-view architecture, which is covered in detail in Chapter 15. In the document-view scheme, the document class encapsulates the actual application data while the one or more view classes encapsulates the onscreen images of that data. For example, a document class could hold the data of a spreadsheet, while one view class could display the table form and another view class could display the data in a graphical format. This scheme is complex, adds considerable overhead to the application, and, based upon my experience teaching programmers new to Windows programming, is extremely difficult to understand until the basics of Windows programming are known. While the document-view approach can simplify somewhat the basic printing process for the programmer, let's ignore this approach initially and examine several direct printing methods because not every application is a document-view application.

Printing Method 1: Printing a Mixed Page of Text and Graphics from the Screen Paint Function

Suppose that one has a screen containing a mixture of text and graphical images to be printed. The paint function is already rendering the page on the screen by drawing upon the passed screen DC. A common approach to printing such a page is to present the paint function with a printer DC and have that same code render the page on the printer. The paint function does not even know that it is actually printing! It just draws on the presented DC. The big benefit is avoidance of duplicated coding. The disadvantage is the method works well only when what is onscreen is what is to be printed. It becomes quite awkward when such things as headings, column headings, foot notes and page numbers are required.

Printing Method 2: Printing Multiple Page Documents or Printing Reports

Normally, the phrase "multiple page document" suggests a letter, memo, or a chapter in a book. However, it can equally represent a spreadsheet, a database, mailing labels, or custom designed invoices! In other words, a "multiple page document" is the **norm**. The printed pages representing mailing labels or custom designed forms may never even have an equivalent "onscreen" display. Database systems and spreadsheets, to a lesser extent, often generate various types of printed reports. Under the MFC, report-specific functions can be used to actually render reports on the printer.

Scaling the Page

There is a major difference in scale between the screen image and the printed page; screen images have a different scale than the printer. If a square occupying 1/4 of the client area is drawn on the screen, when drawn directly on a printer, the printed square it is not proportionately the same. Screen resolution is often 640x480 or 1024x768 pixels, covering from about 10 inches (a 14" monitor) to 12.5 inches (a 17" monitor). Each printer has a specific resolution given in dots per inch (dpi) with a constant page size of 8½ by 11 inches. Dot-matrix printers typically have a resolution of about 120 dpi, while laser printers may have 300 dpi to 600 dpi or more. Consider a line 120 pixels long drawn on a 14" monitor in VGA resolution (640x480) that appears about 1.5 inches long; that same line is rendered about 1 inch long on a dot-matrix printer at 120 dpi and about 1/3 or 1/6 inch long on a laser printer (120/300 or 120/600). Thus, when drawing graphical images, the two relative scales must be considered.

Normally, the print functions use the **MM_TEXT** mapping mode where one logical unit, the pixel, is one physical unit, the pixel. This one-to-one correspondence is what is causing the scaling difficulties. The mapping mode best suited for printers is **MM_ANISOTROPIC** (or possibly **MM_ISOTROPIC**) because in this mode, the program can specify its own units, that is, scale one or both of the axises.

Using Fonts

The font used to render the page plays a very critical role in the printing process. The chosen font affects the actual speed that the printer can print the page (particularly true for dot-matrix printers) and it affects the scaling process. Consider the dismal speed of a dot matrix printer displaying a graphical image; it may take minutes to display even one page. Yet, if only printer built-in fonts are used, a dot matrix printer can print text as fast as it does under DOS. On the other hand since Windows 3.1, the use of TrueType fonts in documents has become widespread. These fonts are completely scalable offering the user many point sizes. However, when printing scalable fonts, especially on a laser printer, they must be properly scaled to fit the printer resolution. If they are not, you may see your page rendered in microscopic letters! Note that TrueType fonts sent to a dot matrix printer are considered bit mapped graphical images and printed as slowly as a paintbrush image. On dot matrix printers, only those built-in fonts print at text speeds.

Note that one might think that the solution would be to decide what **printer** font is going to be used and then install that font as the **screen** font. However, this approach also does not work because many printer fonts are small; if displayed directly on the screen, they would be illegible. Why? The CRT is often viewed from a distance of about 24 inches from the eye while the printed page is often viewed from an eye distance of 10-12 inches. Thus, magnification becomes a problem. When Windows renders a font, it considers the display surface. For example, if the user specifies an 8-point font, when Windows constructs the font for a screen display, it scales the font to become legible. Yet, when that same font is constructed for a printer display, Windows uses the correct point size. If Windows did not do this scaling, many printer fonts would be illegible on the screen. Hence, some form of scaling must be done when printing.

The Print Spooling Process

Windows implements a GDI interface, **Escape**, to handle printing. (Most printers use an escape sequence to enable/disable various special effects and options.) Several crucial sub-functions include **StartDoc**, **EndDoc**, and **NewFrame** that begin a document, stop printing a document, and begin a new page by ending the last page with the issuance of the formfeed code to the printer. C API style coding directly accesses these **Escape** functions. The MFC in the document-view approach completely encapsulates these low level operations, but does not do so outside of the document-view. For printing in such circumstances, I utilize these **Escape** functions.

The printing process is a complex interaction between the GDI, the printer device driver (.DRV file) for the specific printer, and the Print Manager program. The complex chain of events begins with the print request. The GDI first builds a temporary disk file containing all of the GDI commands required to construct the printout. These commands are constructed from our functions that display the text and graphical images on the printer DC. Then, this metafile of GDI commands for the entire document is read back and, together with the printer driver, Windows creates another temporary disk file of the specific printer commands needed to render the pages. When this is complete (**EndDoc**), the Print Manager can then begin to the process all over with another job that is ready to be printed. Meanwhile, the Print Manager then inputs the temporary rendered file and spools it to the actual printer. These two temporary files can become quite large, many megabytes. If at any point the disk becomes full, an error is raised.

A process called **banding** can reduce the overhead of these temporary files and speed up the process. The idea is to divide a page into a series of printing bands or rectangles and process each directly, creating only the actual file to be passed to the Print Manager to be spooled directly to the printer. Often the application just redisplays the whole page, letting the clipping process dictated by the banding rectangle handle what is really to be printed within that band. (The alternative is to have a "band smart" printing function, vastly more complex.) Although the page is completely displayed for each band, there is still an increase in speed from not having to create and read back the GDI metafile for the page. Also the required disk space may be as much as halved.

Pgm13a : Printing Method 1, Using a Dual Purpose Render Function

Figure 13.1 shows **Pgm13a** in operation. The screen display is what is going to be printed, properly scaled to be proportionately the same. There are a sample text message and a rectangle graphic. When you run the program, notice carefully the proportions of the rectangle versus the screen size. The printout should be similar, scaling the rectangle accordingly. Resize the window and reprint.

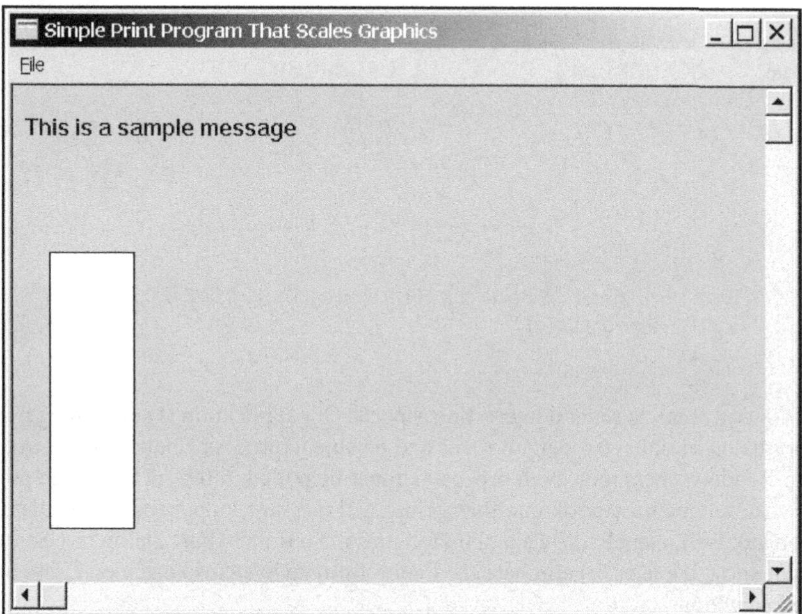

Figure 13.1 **Pgm13a** in Operation Using Render Function

One method to create printed output for a page in a device independent manner is rather clever, if not confusing. The window that owns the page to be printed has an **OnPaint** function which normally creates that page on the client area via constructing a **CPaintDC** device context and rendering the text and graphics data. When printing, the application constructs a printing DC and renders the same data to it. Both **OnPaint** and the printing function must display the same information in the same manner. Therefore, we write **one** generalized **Render** function that is passed a pointer to the **CDC** to use and it displays the data onto that DC. When we get to the document-view, we will see that this is precisely what the MFC actually does, only **Render** becomes **OnDraw**.

When not running under the MFC's document-view, printing operations more closely parallel the C API. Examine the **Pgm13a.rc** file. Notice that an "Abort Printing" dialog box must be created. The "Abort Printing" dialog appears at the start of the printing process and is removed when the document is finished printing. While the dialog is active, the user can press the Cancel button, terminating the printing process.

Pgm13a.rc

```
/////////////////////////////////////////////////////////////////////////////
```

```
//
// Menu
//
MAINMENU MENU DISCARDABLE
BEGIN
    POPUP "&File"
    BEGIN
        MENUITEM "&Choose Font",              CM_FONTCHANGE
        MENUITEM SEPARATOR
        MENUITEM "&Print...",                 CM_FILEPRINT, GRAYED
        MENUITEM "P&rint Setup...",           CM_FILEPRINTERSETUP, GRAYED
        MENUITEM SEPARATOR
        MENUITEM "E&xit\tAlt+F4",             CM_EXIT
    END
END
/////////////////////////////////////////////////////////////////////////////
//
// Dialog
//
PRINTINGDLG DIALOG DISCARDABLE  40, 40, 120, 40
STYLE WS_POPUP | WS_VISIBLE | WS_CAPTION | WS_SYSMENU
CAPTION "Printer Routine"
BEGIN
    CTEXT           "Printing Document",-1,4,6,120,12
    DEFPUSHBUTTON   "Cancel",IDCANCEL,44,22,32,14,WS_GROUP
END
/////////////////////////////////////////////////////////////////////////////
//
// String Table
//
STRINGTABLE DISCARDABLE
BEGIN
    IDS_MAINTITLE           "Simple Print Program That Scales Graphics"
    IDS_WINNAME             "Print Program 1"
END
```

Implementation of the Abort dialog presents several interesting aspects. Our application is performing its printing operations. Simultaneously, the Abort dialog must have the input focus and be able to process a button press. In order for two independent processes to receive Windows messages, both processes **must** be polled in the API message processing loop. Thus, the Abort dialog must provide a temporary hook into the normal API message loop, peeking into the message queue looking for messages that belong to itself, namely the Cancel button press. So if the Abort dialog has established a hook into the message queue, it cannot allow the user to terminate the dialog from its System|Close menu item or Alt-F4 because it is not in the message processing loop.

How can the System menu be changed to gray out "Close?" Access to the System menu is provided by a **CWnd** member function, **GetSystemMenu** which is passed a **BOOL**. When the **BOOL** is **FALSE**, a copy of the current System menu is provided upon which modifications can be made. When **TRUE**, the default System menu is reinstalled. Here, we wish to gray or disable the Close menu item whose ID is **SC_CLOSE**.

```
GetSystemMenu(FALSE)->EnableMenuItem (SC_CLOSE, MF_GRAYED);
```

Next, consider what must occur if the user does press the Cancel button. A **bool** flag, here called **userabort**, must be set. Additionally, the actual C API style message peek function must have access to this **bool** to avoid sending the Abort dialog messages after the Cancel button is pressed. Therefore, this **bool** must be external in scope. Finally, since the Abort dialog has the input focus, when the Cancel button is pressed, the focus must be returned to the application itself. This is done by the **EnableWindow** member function of **Cwnd**.

```
GetParent ()->EnableWindow (TRUE);
```

Here **TRUE** enables the window and **FALSE** disables it.

Examine the **PrintingDlg** class definition and implementation for the Abort Dialog.

PrintDlg.h Definition

```
#pragma once

/*************************************************************/
/*                                                           */
/* PrintingDlg: Display Modeless "Cancel Printing" dlg box   */
/*                                                           */
/*************************************************************/

class PrintingDlg : public CDialog {

public:
          PrintingDlg ();    // constructor of modeless dlg
BOOL      OnInitDialog ();   // disable "system "Close" menu item
void      OnCancel ();       // re-enable main window

DECLARE_MESSAGE_MAP()
};
```

PrintDlg.cpp Implementation

```
#include "stdafx.h"
#include "printdlg.h"

extern bool userabort; // access to "C" style abort indicator

/***************************************************************/
/*                                                             */
/* PrintingDlg Message Map - handle responses                  */
/*                                                             */
/***************************************************************/

BEGIN_MESSAGE_MAP(PrintingDlg, CDialog)
  ON_COMMAND (IDCANCEL, OnCancel)
END_MESSAGE_MAP()

/***************************************************************/
/*                                                             */
/* PrintingDlg: construct the dialog                           */
/*                                                             */
/***************************************************************/

PrintingDlg::PrintingDlg () :CDialog () {
 Create ("PRINTINGDLG");
}

/***************************************************************/
/*                                                             */
/* OnInitDialog: disable system menu item: Close               */
/*                                                             */
/***************************************************************/

BOOL PrintingDlg::OnInitDialog () {
 GetSystemMenu(FALSE)->EnableMenuItem (SC_CLOSE, MF_GRAYED);
 return TRUE;
}

/***************************************************************/
/*                                                             */
/* OnCancel: re-enable main window to cancel printing operation*/
/*                                                             */
/***************************************************************/
```

```

void PrintingDlg::OnCancel () {
 // signal abort to the replaced message processor
 userabort = true;
 GetParent ()->EnableWindow (TRUE); // re-activate parent window
 CDialog::OnCancel ();              // cancel the dialog box
}
```

When the dialog is being constructed, in **OnInitDialog** normally transfer buffers and perhaps controls are initialized. Here, the System menu's Close menu item is grayed. The dialog has one message in its message map: **OnCancel**. When the Cancel button is pressed, the notification flag, **userabort**, is set and the parent widow is once again given the input focus. The dialog is then terminated by invoking the **CDialog** base class member function **OnCancel**. In normal circumstances, the abort printing dialog box is destroyed by using **DestroyWindow** as the successful printing process terminates. Another useful function is **EndDialog** which posts a message to close the dialog and can be used anywhere in the entire dialog processing system to terminate a dialog.

```
EndDialog (int returncode);
```

Next, examine the **FrameWin** class definition and implementation to see the Abort dialog's message peek function.

FrameWin Class Definition

```
#pragma once

/********************************************************************/
/*                                                                  */
/* FrameWin: displays text and graphics to be printed               */
/*                                                                  */
/********************************************************************/

class FrameWin : public CFrameWnd {

 /******************************************************************/
 /*                                                                */
 /* Class Data Members                                             */
 /*                                                                */
 /******************************************************************/

protected:

int       avgCapsWidth;  // average capital letter width
int       avgCharWidth;  // average character width
int       avgCharHeight; // average character height

LOGFONT*  ptrLogFont;      // user selected font from dialog
CFont*    ptrFont;         // the user font
COLORREF  fontColor;       // the font's color

 /******************************************************************/
 /*                                                                */
 /* Class Functions:                                               */
 /*                                                                */
 /******************************************************************/

public:
                FrameWin (); // constructor
               ~FrameWin (); // destructor

protected:

afx_msg int    OnCreate (LPCREATESTRUCT); // gets avg char dims
afx_msg void   OnPaint ();
afx_msg void   CmFontChange ();      // get new font
```

```
afx_msg void  CmFilePrint ();         // print the page
afx_msg void  CmFilePrinterSetup ();// set up the printer
afx_msg void  CmExit ();              // shut down

void GetAvgCharDims ();               // get avg char dims
bool HandlePrinting (CPrintDialog*);// do the actual printing
void Render (CDC*);                 // either paint or print screen

DECLARE_MESSAGE_MAP()
};
```

FrameWin Class Implementation

```
#include "stdafx.h"
#include "framewin.h"
#include "resource.h"
#include "printdlg.h"

/***************************************************************/
/*                                                             */
/* Externals: the printing dialog and abort flag               */
/*                                                             */
/***************************************************************/

static HWND  hprintdlg;  // for the msg handler
bool         userabort;  // abort when true

/***************************************************************/
/*                                                             */
/* AbortProc: replacement msg handler for printing abort dialog*/
/*                                                             */
/***************************************************************/

// While printing, the Printing dialog box is displayed with a
// Cancel button. This routine replaces the normal message
// handling mechanism, until printing is done or the Cancel
// button is pressed.

int APIENTRY AbortProc (HDC, int) {
 MSG msg;
 while (!userabort && PeekMessage (&msg, NULL, 0, 0, PM_REMOVE)){
  if (!hprintdlg || !IsDialogMessage(hprintdlg, &msg)) {
   TranslateMessage(&msg);
   DispatchMessage(&msg);
  }
 }
 return !userabort;
}

/***************************************************************/
/*                                                             */
/* FrameWin Events Response Table                              */
/*                                                             */
/***************************************************************/

BEGIN_MESSAGE_MAP(FrameWin, CFrameWnd)
 ON_WM_CREATE ()
 ON_WM_PAINT ()
 ON_COMMAND(CM_FONTCHANGE,         CmFontChange)
 ON_COMMAND(CM_EXIT,               CmExit)
 ON_COMMAND(CM_FILEPRINT,          CmFilePrint)
 ON_COMMAND(CM_FILEPRINTERSETUP, CmFilePrinterSetup)
END_MESSAGE_MAP()
```

```

/**************************************************************/
/*                                                            */
/* Framewin: Construct the window object                      */
/*                                                            */
/**************************************************************/

FrameWin::FrameWin () : CFrameWnd () {
 CString title;
 title.LoadString (IDS_MAINTITLE);
 DWORD style = WS_OVERLAPPEDWINDOW | WS_VSCROLL | WS_HSCROLL;
 CRect rect (10, 10, 600, 450);

 LoadAccelTable ("MAINMENU");
 ptrLogFont = 0;               // no user font yet
 ptrFont = 0;
 fontColor = RGB (0, 0, 0);    // set default font color black

 Create ( AfxRegisterWndClass (
              CS_VREDRAW | CS_HREDRAW,
              AfxGetApp()->LoadStandardCursor (IDC_ARROW),
              (HBRUSH) GetStockObject (LTGRAY_BRUSH),
              AfxGetApp()->LoadStandardIcon (IDI_APPLICATION)),
         title, style, rect, 0, "MAINMENU");
}

/**************************************************************/
/*                                                            */
/* OnCreate: get average character height and width           */
/*                                                            */
/**************************************************************/

int FrameWin::OnCreate (LPCREATESTRUCT lpCS) {
 int retcd = CFrameWnd::OnCreate (lpCS);
 GetAvgCharDims ();
 return retcd;
}

/**************************************************************/
/*                                                            */
/* ~FrameWin: remove any user font                            */
/*                                                            */
/**************************************************************/

FrameWin::~FrameWin () {
 if (ptrLogFont) delete ptrLogFont;
 if (ptrFont) delete ptrFont;
}

/**************************************************************/
/*                                                            */
/* GetAvgCharDims: get average character height and width     */
/*                                                            */
/**************************************************************/

void FrameWin::GetAvgCharDims () {
  TEXTMETRIC  tm;
  CClientDC dc (this);
  CFont* ptroldfont = 0;
  if (ptrFont)                  // install any user font
   ptroldfont = dc.SelectObject (ptrFont);
  dc.GetTextMetrics (&tm);      // get the font information
  if (ptrFont)                  // remove user font
   dc.SelectObject (ptroldfont);
```

```

  // calculate average character parameters
  avgCharWidth  = tm.tmAveCharWidth;
  avgCharHeight = tm.tmHeight + tm.tmExternalLeading;
  avgCapsWidth  = (tm.tmPitchAndFamily & 1 ? 3 : 2) *
                    avgCharWidth / 2;
}

/***************************************************************/
/*                                                             */
/* OnPaint: displays text and a graphic for printing           */
/*                                                             */
/***************************************************************/

void FrameWin::OnPaint () {
 CPaintDC  dc(this);
 Render (&dc);
}

/***************************************************************/
/*                                                             */
/* Render: display screen on device or on the printer          */
/*                                                             */
/***************************************************************/

void FrameWin::Render (CDC *ptrdc) {
 CFont* ptroldfont = 0;
 if (ptrFont)           // install any user font
  ptroldfont = ptrdc->SelectObject (ptrFont);

 ptrdc->SetTextColor (fontColor);// install font color
 ptrdc->SetBkMode (TRANSPARENT); // set so background color shows

 ptrdc->TextOut (avgCharWidth, avgCharHeight,
                 "This is a sample message");
 ptrdc->Rectangle (avgCharWidth*3, avgCharHeight*6,
                   avgCharWidth*10, avgCharHeight*16);

 if (ptrFont)           // remove user font
  ptrdc->SelectObject (ptroldfont);
}

/***************************************************************/
/*                                                             */
/* CmFontChange: get users font request and implement it       */
/*                                                             */
/***************************************************************/

void FrameWin::CmFontChange () {
 CFontDialog  *ptrdlg;
 ptrdlg = new CFontDialog (ptrLogFont, CF_EFFECTS |
                  CF_SCREENFONTS | CF_FORCEFONTEXIST, NULL, this);
 ptrdlg->m_cf.rgbColors = fontColor;  // install current color
 if (ptrdlg->DoModal () == IDOK) {     // get user font choice
  if (!ptrLogFont)
   ptrLogFont = new LOGFONT;           // 1st time, create LOGFONT
  // copy user font choice
  memcpy (ptrLogFont, &(ptrdlg->m_lf), sizeof (LOGFONT));
  fontColor = ptrdlg->GetColor ();     // save color choice
  if (ptrFont) delete ptrFont;         // remove old font, if any
  ptrFont = new CFont ();              // make a new font
  ptrFont->CreateFontIndirect (ptrLogFont);
  GetAvgCharDims ();                   // get new avg char dims
  Invalidate();                        // force repaint
```

```
 }
 delete ptrdlg;
}

/***********************************************************/
/*                                                         */
/* CmFilePrint: print an existing file                     */
/*                                                         */
/***********************************************************/

void FrameWin::CmFilePrint () {
 CPrintDialog printdlg (FALSE, PD_USEDEVMODECOPIES, this);
 // initialize dialog controls
 printdlg.m_pd.nMinPage = 1;
 printdlg.m_pd.nMaxPage = 1;
 printdlg.m_pd.nFromPage = 1;
 printdlg.m_pd.nToPage = 1;
 printdlg.m_pd.nCopies = 1;

 if (printdlg.DoModal () == IDCANCEL) return; // if cancel, quit

 if (!HandlePrinting (&printdlg))
  MessageBox ("Unable to print the document", "Printer Section",
             MB_OK | MB_ICONEXCLAMATION);
}

/***********************************************************/
/*                                                         */
/* HandlePrinting: print the document                      */
/*                                                         */
/***********************************************************/

bool FrameWin::HandlePrinting (CPrintDialog *ptrprintdlg) {
 bool printerror = false;
 userabort = false;

 // setup a printer DC by attaching the printer from the common
 // dialog which has already created one for us
 CDC  *ptrprinterDC = new CDC;
 ptrprinterDC->Attach (ptrprintdlg->GetPrinterDC ());

 // setup a printing cancel dialog box
 PrintingDlg  *ptrprintingdlg = new PrintingDlg ();
 // set the external hwnd for abort proc
 hprintdlg = ptrprintingdlg->m_hWnd;

 // attempt to install the abort procedure
 if (ptrprinterDC->SetAbortProc (AbortProc) < 0) {
  ptrprintingdlg->DestroyWindow (); // failed, remove abort dlg
  delete ptrprintingdlg;            // remove dialog object
  delete ptrprinterDC;              // remove printer DC
  return false;
 }

 // print the document
 DOCINFO doc;        // used by Windows for printing document msg
 doc.cbSize = sizeof(DOCINFO);
 doc.lpszDocName = "Printing the screen";
 doc.lpszOutput = NULL;
 doc.lpszDatatype = NULL;
 doc.fwType = 0;

 // setup scaling factors
 CSize oldwinext, oldprintext;
```

```
 int   oldmode;
 CRect clrect;
 GetClientRect(clrect);        // get size of the display window
 CSize clsize = clrect.Size(); // the size of the screen
 // get the size of the printed page
 CSize pagesize (ptrprinterDC->GetDeviceCaps (HORZRES),
                 ptrprinterDC->GetDeviceCaps (VERTRES));

 // the main print processing loop - start the document
 if (::StartDoc (ptrprinterDC->m_hDC, &doc) >0) {
  // set for begin page
  if (::StartPage (ptrprinterDC->m_hDC) >0) {
   // install current scaling - Windows resets it in StartPage
   // each time, so we must re-install our scaling for each page
   oldmode  = ptrprinterDC->SetMapMode (MM_ISOTROPIC);
   oldwinext = ptrprinterDC->SetWindowExt (clsize);
   oldprintext = ptrprinterDC->SetViewportExt (pagesize);

   // actually go print the page
   Render (ptrprinterDC);

   // replace the original DC values
   ptrprinterDC->SetWindowExt (oldwinext);
   ptrprinterDC->SetViewportExt (oldprintext);
   ptrprinterDC->SetMapMode (oldmode);

   // signal end of page and check for errors
   if (::EndPage (ptrprinterDC->m_hDC) >=0)
    ::EndDoc (ptrprinterDC->m_hDC); // signal end of document
   else printerror = true;
  }
  else printerror = true;
 }
 else printerror = true;

 // if abort pressed, set focus back to our window
 if (!userabort) EnableWindow (TRUE); // restore main wnd action

 delete ptrprinterDC;
 ptrprintingdlg->DestroyWindow ();
 delete ptrprintingdlg;
 return !printerror && !userabort; // return success code
}

/***************************************************************/
/*                                                             */
/* CmFilePrinterSetup: set up the printer parameters           */
/*                                                             */
/***************************************************************/

void FrameWin::CmFilePrinterSetup () {
 CPrintDialog printdlg (TRUE, PD_USEDEVMODECOPIES, this);
 printdlg.DoModal ();
}

/***************************************************************/
/*                                                             */
/* CmExit: determine if the app can be shut down               */
/*                                                             */
/***************************************************************/

void FrameWin::CmExit () {
 PostMessage (WM_CLOSE);
}
```

The **AbortProc** is given the **APIENTRY** designation designating that it is a Win32 API style function. The external variable **userabort** is external so that the C style **AbortProc** message handler for the Abort Dialog can access it, preventing messages sent to a closed dialog. The **AbortProc** is a very simple function that must have access to the **HWND** of the Abort Dialog, here also external, **hprintdlg**.

Normal message processing loops invoke **GetMessage** and then **TranslateMessage** and **DispatchMessage**. However, all we wish to do is see if there is a message for us and then pass it along. The API function **PeekMessage** does just that—it examines the Windows message queue to see if there are any messages. The loop should continue as long as **userabort** is **false**, which indicates that the user has not yet pressed the Cancel button, and as long as the dialog is still active and not being destroyed and removed from the system. When a window is being removed, a **PM_REMOVE** message is sent. Therefore, the loop should continue as long as the **PM_REMOVE** message has not been sent.

Next, the Abort Dialog messages must be filtered out from all other application messages and processed. Hence, if the handle to the dialog box is not set to the Abort Dialog, pass the message along. And, if that message is not destined for the Abort Dialog, pass the message along. The Windows API function, **IsDialogMessage**, determines if the message is destined for the dialog, specified by the passed **HWND**, and if so, actually processes the dialog's message. Thus, the **AbortProc** appears as follows.

```
int APIENTRY  AbortProc(HDC, int) {
 MSG msg;
 while (!userabort && PeekMessage (&msg, NULL, 0, 0, PM_REMOVE)){
  if (!hprintdlg || !IsDialogMessage(hprintdlg, &msg)) {
   TranslateMessage(&msg);
   DispatchMessage(&msg);
  }
 }
 return !userabort;
}
```

Let's look at the **FrameWin** class to see how printing occurs. In the definition file, the user's selected font is kept in a **LOGFONT** structure, that is copied from the common Choose Font dialog. The user color selection is also used, although not when printing. In the implementation file, the constructor initializes these to no font and black. **OnPaint** acquires the paint DC and then invokes the **Render** function. Under the MFC, a **CPaintDC** must be constructed. In order for a single function to render the image on both display surfaces, the screen and the printer, that function must be passed a DC on which to render the data. All of the normal paint coding has been moved into **Render**: install any user font and color, display the text, draw the rectangle and restore all original objects back into the DC.

Next, examine the **CmFilePrinterSetup** function that responds to the File|Print Setup menu item. An instance of the Windows common print dialog is allocated on the stack. The first parameter is **TRUE** indicating Printer Setup is to be invoked. If **FALSE**, then Print is invoked. The flags include the following.

```
PD_ALLPAGES          - indicates all pages button is selected
PD_USEDEVMODECOPIES  - if the printer supports multiple copies,
                       enable the Copies control; if it does not,
                       disable it
PD_NOPAGENUMS        - disables the Pages button
PD_HIDEPRINTTOFILE   - hides the print to file option
PD_NOSELECTION       - disables the page selection controls
```

Consult the documentation for the numerous other lesser used Ids.

Here, **PD_USEDEVMODECOPIES** is used, letting Windows make the determination of whether or not to enable the Copies control based upon the specific printer chosen. Handling Printer Setup is then the simple matter of two lines of coding.

```
CPrintDialog printdlg (TRUE, PD_USEDEVMODECOPIES, this);
printdlg.DoModal ();
```

Unfortunately, handing File|Print is much more complex. Similar to Printer Setup, the first action is to allocate an automatic storage instance of the Windows printer common dialog, but passing **FALSE** this time.

```
CPrintDialog printdlg (FALSE, PD_USEDEVMODECOPIES, this);
```

Next, the initial pages for user selection are set. The member **m_pd** contains the common print dialog structure members that define the initial pages for user selection. Since only the screen is to be printed, all page limits are set to 1 as is the number of copies.

Next, the common print dialog is launched as normal with **DoModal**. If Cancel is selected, the print function is terminated. Notice that should the user select the setup button, Windows automatically changes to the Printer Setup dialog and then returns back to the Print dialog. If the user selects OK, then the printing process commences. Our member function **HandlePrinting** handles the entire printing process. Notice that if the process fails for any reason, I display a simple message box informing the user.

HandlePrinting performs the many sequences necessary to getting the file printed. First, it must initialize the external **userabort** flag and our own **printerror** flag which are used to signal any error in the printing process. Next, the printer DC must be acquired. Conveniently, the **CPrintDialog** member function **GetPrinterDC** returns the handle of the currently selected printer DC from the Windows common print dialog. A **CDC** object can be constructed on that **HDC** by encapsulating the real DC using the **Attach** member function.

```
CDC  *ptrprinterDC = new CDC;
ptrprinterDC->Attach (ptrprintdlg->GetPrinterDC ());
```

Next, an instance of our Abort Dialog box is constructed and its handle saved in the external **hprintdlg** field for use in the **AbortProc**. Then, our **AbortProc** function must be installed in the message processing loop. This is done by the **CDC** member function **SetAbortProc**.

```
if (ptrprinterDC->SetAbortProc (AbortProc) < 0) {
```

which takes a pointer to the function. The name of a function has the data type of a pointer to those instructions or a pointer to a function with that prototype. Should the process fail, clean up actions are done and the printing process aborted.

Windows requires a **DOCINFO** structure to control the printing process. The **DOCINFO** structure contains these members.

```
int     cbSize;        // size of the DOCINFO structure
LPCSTR lpszDocName;    // name of document to print - 32 chars
                       //  including the NULL
LPCSTR lpszOutput;     // name of file to print to - also 32 chars
LPCSTR lpszDatatype;   // specifies the type of data used to record
                       // the print job
DWORD  fwType;         // 0 or DI_APPBANDING if the application
                       // will use banding
```

We must create an instance and fill up its members as follows.

```
DOCINFO doc;
doc.cbSize = sizeof(DOCINFO);
doc.lpszDocName = "Printing the screen";
doc.lpszOutput = NULL;
doc.lpszDatatype = NULL; // new in Windows 95
doc.fwType = 0;          // new in Windows 95
```

The document name is used by Print Manager to identify this print job during the spooling process. Windows uses the last two fields to handle print banding.

Design Rule 50: A failure to set these last two fields, even though NULL, results in no printout!

Design Rule 51: Many of the newer structures begin with a member field that stores the size of the structure; in the DOCINFO structure, it is the cbSize member. When creating an instance of such a structure, always initialize the size member! Failure can yield application crashes.

In this example, I coded this.

```
doc.cbSize = sizeof(DOCINFO);
```

Note that in this case, the MFC actually fills in the size just in case you forget to do so; do not count on this action for all such structures!

Next, scaling values must be determined. The scale factor to be used represents the ratio of the actual client window size versus the printed page size in pixels. Here, I fill the **CSize clrect** with the client window size; similarly **pagesize** contains the dimensions of the printed page obtained from **GetDeviceCaps**.

```
CRect clrect;
GetClientRect(clrect);
CSize clsize = clrect.Size();
CSize pagesize (ptrprinterDC->GetDeviceCaps (HORZRES),
                ptrprinterDC->GetDeviceCaps (VERTRES));
```

Finally, the actual printing cycle can begin, following the C style Escape sequences: **StartDoc, StartPage, EndPage, EndDoc. StartDoc** is passed the **HDC** of the printer and a reference to the document structure for Print Manager. If all is OK, then **StartPage** is invoked for the sole page to be printed. Note that for multiple pages, a loop must be placed around the **StartPage/EndPage** functions. (See the next example program.)

Design Rule 52: When StartPage is executed, the printer DC is reset to default values.

Design Rule 53: Upon every entry to Render, the printer DC must be reset to the proper circumstances for this particular page, including brushes, pens, fonts, palettes, and most importantly scaling.

Notice that **Render** is surrounded by the scaling code. Because Windows resets the DC for each page, before we can **Render**, we must set the scale and restore the original values when the page is complete.

```
if (::StartDoc (ptrprinterDC->m_hDC, &doc) >0) {
 if (::StartPage (ptrprinterDC->m_hDC) >0) {
  oldmode  = ptrprinterDC->SetMapMode (MM_ISOTROPIC);
  oldwinext = ptrprinterDC->SetWindowExt (clsize);
  oldprintext = ptrprinterDC->SetViewportExt (pagesize);
  Render (ptrprinterDC);
  ptrprinterDC->SetWindowExt (oldwinext);
  ptrprinterDC->SetViewportExt (oldprintext);
  ptrprinterDC->SetMapMode (oldmode);
  if (::EndPage (ptrprinterDC->m_hDC) >=0)
   ::EndDoc (ptrprinterDC->m_hDC);
  else printerror = TRUE;
 }
 else printerror = TRUE;
}
else printerror = TRUE;
```

The scaling is done with the **MM_ANISOTROPIC** or **MM_ISOTROPIC** mode using the **CDC** member function **SetMapMode**.

```
int   ptrdc->SetMapMode (MM_ANISOTROPIC);
```

where the old mode is returned. Remember that all objects and settings in any DC must be reset to their original objects, the old mode is saved. Scaling in one (ISOTROPIC) or two (ANISOTROPIC) dimensions is done by setting a combination of window and viewport extents. In this case, I wish to have both dimensions properly scaled to the page resembles the screen. The window's extents or dimensions are set to the actual client screen's dimensions (the logical coordinates), while the viewport is set to the printer's page size (the device or physical coordinates).

```
oldwinext = ptrprinterDC->SetWindowExt (clsize);
oldprintext = ptrprinterDC->SetViewportExt (pagesize);
```

The window extent is then set using **SetWindowExt**, which returns the original window extent. The viewport to the printer is set using the **SetViewportExt** function, which also returns the old viewport extent. Both values must be saved for later restoration.

It is important to note that the window extent **must** be set before setting the viewport, because Windows must know about the window extent as it sets up the viewport extent. The scaling works as follows. Assume that you have the window rectangle is 300 pixels wide and the page is 2400 dots wide or 8 times larger. Therefore, when the GDI plots 1 pixel, it must plot 8 pixels on the paper. If the rectangle being displaying is ½ of the client area wide, or 150 pixels, then the page size would be 1200 pixels wide for it to be in proportion.

You should run the program as-is and then experiment. Comment out the mode and extent changes; then rerun the program to see the effect of scaling. Try resizing the window both small and large. What effect does this have if the printer is not scaled. Then adjust the mode to **MM_ISOTROPIC** and repeat the experiment. What effect does the mode have?

In Chapter 15 when the document-view is covered, the onscreen view has a member function of **OnDraw** that is called by both **OnPaint** and by **PrintPage** similar to the way the function **Render** is done in this example.

Figure 13.2 shows the common Printer Setup Dialog while Figure 13.3 shows the common Print Dialog.

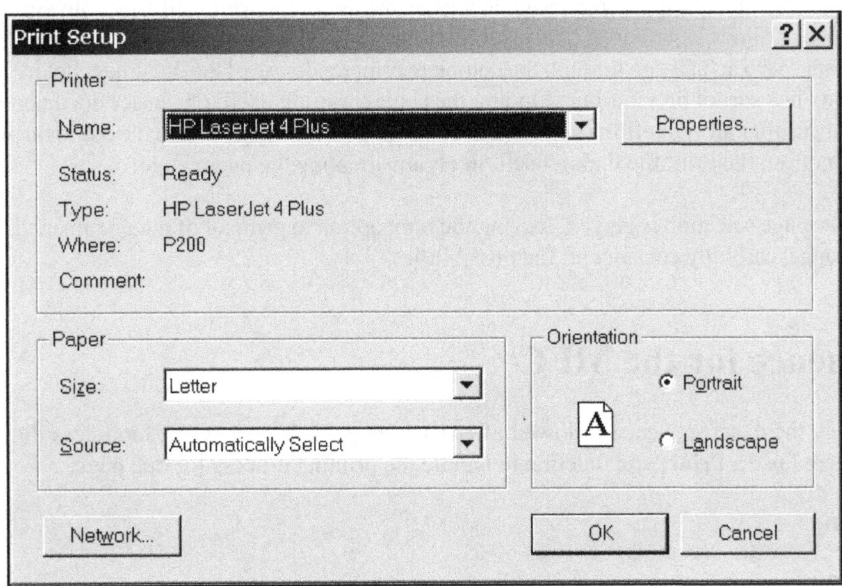

Figure 13.2 The Common Printer Setup Dialog

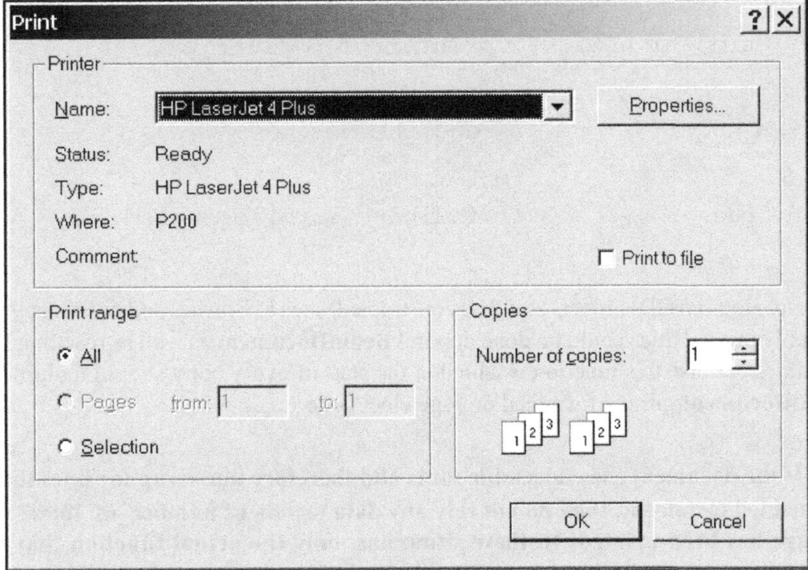

Figure 13.3 The Common Print Dialog

Modifying Data in the Print Dialog Box

CPrintDialog provides the means to alter the various values in the Print dialog and, when the user has finished making selections, to retrieve the user's choices. The Window common Print dialog is shown in Figure 13.3 The Common Print Dialog Box. These options should be set to reflect the document to be printed.

While this seemingly simple task should be an easy one to implement, in reality setting the correct page range can be so complex, it is often ignored. Why? First, consider the actual document. The initial total number of lines usually is easily determined as well as the known page width. But what is to be done with lines that are too wide for the current page width? Truncation is often a poor choice because of the loss of information. It is a better practice to just line wrap, which of course, adds lines which may impact the number of pages! Line wrapping would occur only when actually **rendering** that line to the printer, **long** after the dialog box is used. If user fonts are supported, line wrap can become a serious factor with larger font sizes.

Additionally, if a document contains user-forced page breaks by the use of the formfeed code, obviously the page total determined from the number of lines is wrong, if it is just based upon the number of lines. Often the only accurate method to determine the page range is to actually go through the complete print rendering of the document before presenting the user with the print dialog box in a sort of preview but skipping the actual printing itself. On larger documents, this can be time-consuming. And even then, after all your efforts to get the accurate page range displayed in the common print dialog box, the user can switch printers from the Print file dialog itself, likely invalidating the page range!

This is why so often the page selection is grayed, leaving the only option to print all of the document. Should you desire to implement the page range, carefully consider all the possibilities.

The Printing Sequence for the MFC

Now let's examine more closely the exact sequence followed after launching the Printer Abort modeless dialog box to actually print the document. Here I use a **PrintPage** function to handle the printing process for one page.

```
// BeginPrinting:
if (::StartDoc (ptrdc->m_hDC, &doc) >0) {
 // BeginDocument:
 while (not at the document end and !printerror) {
  if (::StartPage (ptrdc->m_hDC) >0) {
   ptrdc->SelectObject (ptrfont); // install font
   PrintPage ();                  // actually print the page
   if (::EndPage (ptrdc->m_hDC) <0) printerror = true;
  }
 }
 ::EndDoc (ptrdc->m_hDC);         // end the doc
 // EndDocument:
}
else printerror = true;           // indicate error occurred
// EndPrinting:
```

At point **BeginPrinting** any required GDI objects could be constructed, such as brushes and pens. They are deleted at point **EndPrinting**. Any once only printed titles could be done at point **BeginDocument** as well as resetting the starting page number and other needed values because this function is called at the start of every copy should multiple copies be selected by the user. At point **EndDocument**, print a formfeed or page eject code.

Design Rule 54: If the document uses selectable fonts and therefore line-wrap for lines that are too long or has imbedded formfeeds, then do not rely any data member "number_of_lines" to know when the last page has been printed. In these situations, only the actual function that is rendering the document, line by line, really knows when the end of the document is reached. It is better to have a bool member that the render function sets to true when the physical end is reached. The while loop would test this member to detect when the printing is finished.

Printing Directly Within the MFC's PrintPage

Thus far, our documents have been quite simple. If there was a font change, the new font is applied to the entire document. Now consider a more practical document. It should support various fonts on the screen any time via some kind of control codes indicating begin-font and end-font. Some provision must be present for bold and underlining (perhaps italics). Some scheme must be devised for printing both page numbers and headers at the top of the page. Provisions may be made for centering and so on. Soon, you'll have your own word processor or a Rich Text Edit document.

Or perhaps the image on the screen is not at all the way you want the image on the printed page. On the screen, you present data in various **CEdit** controls and so on. Yet on the printed page, another layout would better express the information. This is often true for mailing labels and printed invoices and reports. In these situations, the best method is to render each page directly within **PrintPage**, never invoking the screen **OnPaint** function.

However, when fonts are mentioned, one needs to exercise caution in the printing process. Some fonts cannot be rendered directly by the specific device. Often, to control exactly how the output appears, you must create your own special printer font, especially altering the character dimensions to fit the required scale.

Text Output Functions for Variable Width Fonts

Until now, we favor using fixed fonts because column and caret positioning are greatly simplified. But when printing, we must understand how to process variable width fonts. Let's review the text outputting functions as they apply toward handling the printer and introduce some new ones.

The most common function to display a string is the **TextOut** function.

```
dc.TextOut (xstart, ystart, string, length);
```

For null-terminated strings, the length may be omitted. The string is displayed beginning at the logical (x, y) coordinates given. The meaning of the (x, y) coordinates are modified by the use of the function **SetTextAlign**.

```
dc.SetTextAlign (flag);
```

The groups of flags consist of these.

```
TA_LEFT,        TA_RIGHT,    TA_CENTER
TA_BOTTOM,      TA_TOP,      TA_BASELINE
TA_NOUPDATECP,  TA_UPDATECP
```

When the update current position flag is enabled (**TA_UPDATECP**), the starting (x, y) values are ignored. Instead, the current position of the last **MoveTo** or **LineTo** function is used and the current position is reset. This represents an alternative method of printing successive fields. If **TA_RIGHT | TA_UPDATECP** is in force, then subsequent **TextOut** requests appear successively after each other.

Another method of solving the problem of creating columnar alignment is to use the **TabbedTextOut** function.

```
CSize dc.TabbedTextOut (x, y, string, length,
                        int numtabpositions,
                        int tabpositions[], int taborigin);
```

The function returns a **CSize** containing the resultant dimensions.

If the string has imbedded tabs ('\t'), then they are expanded in one of two ways based on the three tab parameters. The **tabpositions** array specifies each tab position in device units with **numtabpsoitions** showing the array bounds. Note that if both **numtabpositions** and **tabpositions** are 0, then all tabs are expanded to successive 8 times the average character width units. If **numtabpositions** is 1, all tabs are expanded **tabpositions[0]** apart. **taborigin** specifies the x logical units from which the tab expansion occurs. Most often it is the same value as the x coordinate of the starting point. The function is also modified by **SetTextAlign** values. Using this slightly more complex function, columnar alignment can also be achieved.

A higher-level display function is **DrawText**.

```
dc.DrawText (string, length, &rectangle, format);
```

If the length is -1, then the null-terminated length is used. The text is displayed in the rectangle (**CRect**) according to the format flags. Multiple lines can be displayed, using the carriage return line feed combination as the signal for a new line or using blanks between words. Special effect: if the flag is **DT_CALCRECT**, no text is displayed, rather the rectangle's width and height are determined such that the text would fix according to the other flags.

When the **format** is 0, Windows interprets the string as a series of lines and begins displaying at the upper left corner of the rectangle. When a carriage return <CR> is encountered, a new line is begun, spaced one character height below the previous line. Any characters that exceed the rectangle dimensions, either too long a line or too many lines, are clipped. **DT_LEFT**, **DT_RIGHT**, and **DT_CENTER** operate as expected. **DT_SINGLELINE** ignores <CR> codes. **DT_TOP**, **DT_BOTTOM**, **DT_VCENTER** also work as expected. Using **DT_WORDBREAK** specifies line breaks occur whenever a line exceeds the rectangle's width. Windows backs up and moves the offending words onto the next line, a line wrap, if you please. **DT_NOCLIP** draws without clipping. **DT_EXPANDTABS** expands tabs using a default of 8 characters.

Other necessary functions to properly display text include the following functions.

```
dc.SetTextColor (RGB (. . .)); // to set the text color
dc.SetBkMode (TRANSPARENT or OPAQUE);
dc.SetBkColor (RGB (. . .)); // the color to appear with OPAQUE
dc.SetTextCharacterExtra (extra spacing in logical units);
```

This last one converts the extra spacing in logical units into pixels and then adds that extra amount of spacing between each character to be displayed. Normal value is 0.

Perhaps the **most** useful function for processing variable width fonts is the **GetTextExtent** function.

```
CSize size = GetTextExtent (string, length);
```

This highly useful function calculates the total dimensions the string requires if it were to be displayed using the current font and DC setup. When working with variable pitched fonts, this function is a workhorse. In text entry situations, after a character is input and appended onto the line string, **GetTextExtent** returns the length which is used to position the caret at the correct position. In printing situations, the function is used to detect line wrap, as we will see in the next program.

Formatting Text

If you have created or chosen a font and selected it into the DC, and the average character dimensions have been determined, text formatting can begin. The formatting would include left justifying a string, right justifying a string (often called flush-right, in word processing), and proportional spacing or justifying both the left and right ends of the string and adding extra white space between the words of the string. When working with only one line strings, the process is simple. Assume that a string is to begin at coordinates (x, y) and that the margin locations are given by **xleft** and **xright**. First, will the line fit between x and the right margin?

```
int maxlinelen = xright - xleft;
CSize sz = dc.GetTextExtent (string);
if (sz > (xright-x) ) {
  // error too long, now what?
}
else // left justified
 dc.TextOut (x, y, string);
```

or

```
else // right justified
 dc.TextOut (xright - sz.width, y, string);
```

or

```
else // centered
 dc.TextOut (x+(xright -x -sz.width)/2, y, string);
```

Alternatively, assume that we are at row y and wish to display the string given no x offset into the line.

```
int maxlinelen = xright - xleft;
CSize sz = dc.GetTextExtent (string);
if (sz > (maxlinelen) ) {
  // error too long, now what?
}
else // left justified
 dc.TextOut (xleft, y, string);
```

or

```
else // right justified
 dc.TextOut (xright - sz.width, y, string);
```

or

```
else // centered
 dc.TextOut ((xleft+xright-sz.width)/2, y, string);
```

For proportional spacing or justifying both ends of the string, try this sequence.

```
dc.SetTextJustification (xright-xleft-sz.width, numblanks);
dc.TextOut (xleft, y, string);
dc.SetTextJustification (0, 0);
```

The tricky item is finding out the number of blanks in the line. And what about color? While colors should be allowed on the screen, the printed copy should be just black, unless the printer allows the use of color and you want to print in color.

When dealing with word processing, the basic unit of manipulation is the paragraph. When the user entry exceeds the right margin, the offending word is placed on the next line. When the font is changed, the paragraph may need to be reformed. Similarly the paragraph may need to be reformed when margins are adjusted or when text is inserted, and so on. Additional complications arise from user font requests within a document. A word processor should allow as many fonts as desired. A paragraph could potentially have several font changes, including point size, bold and underlining.

Creating a Program Editor with Print Support: Pgm13b

For our major application of this chapter, let's construct a program editor with full printing capabilities. Since **Pgm12a** already provides the **EditWin** Editor program, let's extend that program to also support printing.

The fonts that can be selected by the user should include printer-only fonts along with TrueType fonts. Figure 13.4 shows how the Choose Fonts dialog identifies printer-only fonts from TrueType fonts. Notice the two different small icons to the left of the font names. Remember that printer only fonts allow dot matrix printers to print at a much faster rate.

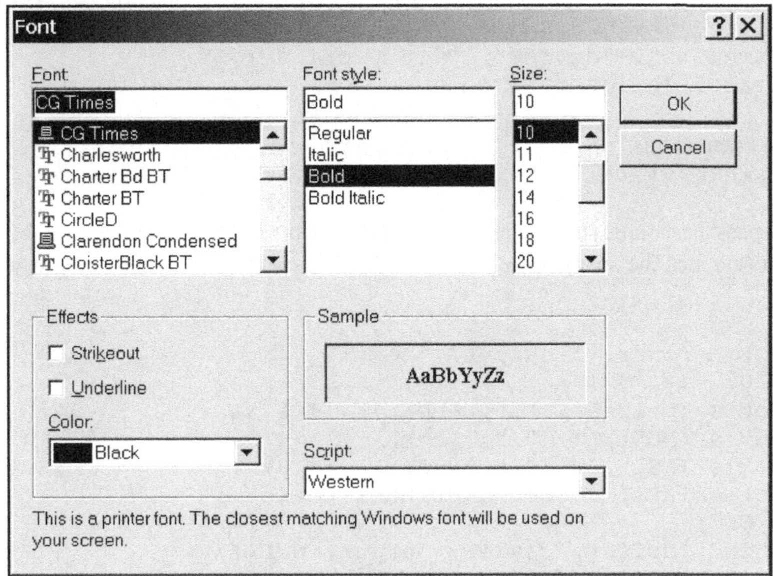

Figure 13.4 Choose Fonts Showing Printer Only Fonts and TrueType

Forced page breaks should be supported along with a title placed at the top of the first page. The title is the file name. Further, there should be margins at the top and bottom, avoiding the usual 66 lines per page mess. Additionally, with some fonts, even 80 character lines cannot be shown without clipping. Therefore, we provide any needed line wrapping whenever a line is too long for the given font. This approach to printing can be easily adapted to printing a spreadsheet, database reports, mailing labels and other similar "record" oriented files.

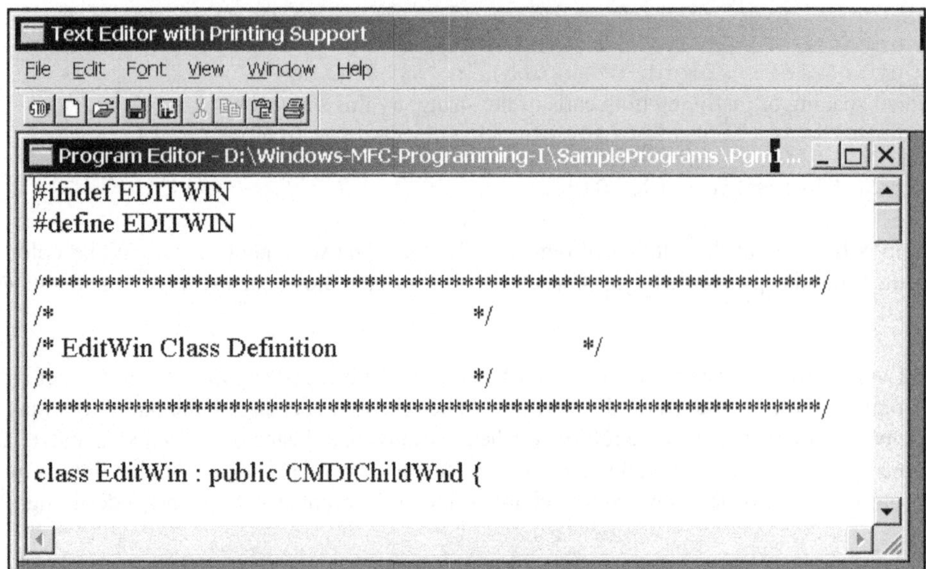

Figure 13.5 Pgm13b Editor with Printing Support

Figure 13.5 shows **Pgm13b** in operation after I have opened a file. Notice the effect of the variable width font. Blanks have a narrower width than other letters.

There are a few changes to the sequences in the **CmFontChange** function. Since we wish to allow printer-only and TrueType fonts, we must now pass a DC to the Choose Fonts common dialog so that the system can retrieve fonts supported by the indicated printer. The **CWinApp** class maintains the current selected printer. Additionally, Windows maintains the current default printer that the user has selected. The current printer is retrievable by using the function **GetProfileString**.

```
char   printer[80];
GetProfileString ("windows", "device", "...", printer,
                  sizeof (printer));
```

The string returned in **printer** on my system is this.

```
HP LaserJet 4 Plus,winspool,LPT1:
```

In order to create a printer dc, we must pass these three strings to the **CreateDC** function. The three strings can be extracted by using the C function **strtok** which searches the string for a delimiter—here a comma—and replacing it with a null terminator.

```
char          *device, *driver, * output, *next;
CDC* ptrprinterDC = 0;
if ( (device = strtok_s (printer, ",", &next)) != 0 &&
     (driver = strtok_s (NULL,    ",", &next)) != 0 &&
     (output = strtok_s (NULL,    ",", &next)) != 0) {
 // a default printer exists, so get a printer DC for it
 ptrprinterDC = new CDC;
 ptrprinterDC->CreateDC (driver, device, output, NULL);
}
```

Notice that the **CDC** pointer, **ptrprinterDC**, is initialized to 0. If there is no printer on the machine, then that pointer remains 0. Thus, we can construct the **CFontDialog** passing that pointer as the third parameter which is either 0 or an actual printer DC.

```
CFontDialog  dlg (ptrlogfont, CF_EFFECTS | CF_PRINTERFONTS |
                  CF_FORCEFONTEXIST, ptrprinterDC, this);
```

Also note that I used the **CF_PRINTERFONTS** flag as well.

Now when the Choose Fonts dialog box is executed, you can see many fonts in the listbox that have a little image of a printer to the left of the font name. These are the printer-only fonts. Those that do not have the printer icon are supported fonts that can be displayed graphically via a bitmap on the printer. The TrueType fonts have a "TT" icon before their names.

Notice that when a printer-only font is selected, a message appears below the Sample Example of that font. See

Figure 13.4 once again. Windows notifies you that it is doing a reasonable fit when attempting to render that font on the screen. Namely, the size is sufficiently increased so that you can read it. Remember most printer fonts if rendered true size would be unreadable on the screen. Once the font is selected, we then again send the **CEdit** window the **WM_SETFONT** message to immediately implement that font on the screen. As you select and try out the various printer only fonts, remember that most choices within the **same** family can be rendered **identical** on the screen. They are rendered correctly when sent to the printer.

The File|Print coding closely follows **Pgm13a** in many respects. We must install the Abort Dialog and run the Print Dialog—all are unchanged from the previous program. Let's examine the sequence required to handle the printing operation.

In **HandlePrinting**, the number of bytes currently in the **CEdit** control is retrieved and a global memory area allocated to receive the text via the **CWnd** function **GetWindowText**.

```
long filesize = ptreditwin->GetWindowTextLength ();
hbuffer = GlobalAlloc (GMEM_MOVEABLE, filesize);
ptrbuf = (char*) GlobalLock (hbuffer);
ptreditwin->GetWindowText (ptrbuf, filesize);
```

The total length is saved in **maxoff**, the maximum offset member variable, so that later when rendering, the end of the data can be detected. A report title is constructed from the file name.

```
maxoff = filesize;        // save filesize
GlobalUnlock (hbuffer); // unlock buffer
reporttitle = filename[0] == 0 ? "Untitled" : filename;
```

The two error flags are then cleared and the actual printer **HDC** constructed by the Print Dialog is borrowed for our printer **CDC**.

```
bool printerror = false;
userabort = false;
ptrdc = new CDC;
ptrdc->Attach (ptrprintdlg->GetPrinterDC ());
```

Then, the Abort Printing dialog and its message hook are installed just as was done in **Pgm13a**.

```
PrintingDlg  *ptrprintingdlg = new PrintingDlg ();
hprintdlg = ptrprintingdlg->m_hWnd;
if (ptrdc->SetAbortProc (AbortProc) < 0) {
 ptrprintingdlg->DestroyWindow ();
 delete ptrprintingdlg;
 delete ptrdc;
 GlobalFree (hbuffer);
 return false;
}
```

Next, the user chosen **LOGFONT** is copied so that it can be scaled, created, and installed. At this point, the average character dimensions on this printer DC can be determined.

```
LOGFONT  *ptrprtlogfont;
CFont    *ptroldfont;
if (ptrlogfont) {
 ptrprtlogfont = new LOGFONT;
 memcpy (ptrprtlogfont, ptrlogfont, sizeof(LOGFONT));
 if (ptrprtfont) delete ptrprtfont;
 ptrprtfont = new CFont ();
 HDC hdc = CreateDC ("DISPLAY",NULL,NULL,NULL);
 float xscale = ptrdc->GetDeviceCaps (LOGPIXELSX) /
                (float) GetDeviceCaps(hdc, LOGPIXELSX);
 float yscale = ptrdc->GetDeviceCaps (LOGPIXELSY) /
                (float) GetDeviceCaps(hdc, LOGPIXELSY);
 DeleteDC (hdc);

 // install scaled dimensions
 ptrprtlogfont->lfHeight =
                 (long) (ptrprtlogfont->lfHeight * yscale);
 ptrprtlogfont->lfWidth =
                 (long) (ptrprtlogfont->lfWidth * xscale);
 ptrprtfont->CreateFontIndirect (ptrprtlogfont);
```

```
  ptroldfont = ptrdc->SelectObject (ptrprtfont);
  delete ptrprtlogfont;
 }
 TEXTMETRIC tm;
 GetTextMetrics (ptrdc->m_hDC, &tm);
 avg_char_width  = tm.tmAveCharWidth;
 avg_char_height = tm.tmHeight + tm.tmExternalLeading;
 avg_caps_width  = (tm.tmPitchAndFamily & 1 ? 3 : 2) *
                    avg_char_width / 2;
```

From this information, the pagination data are calculated. These include the dot per line, characters per line, lines per page, and the theoretical number of pages to print. In this example, there is to be a heading and bottom margin. Depending upon the size of the page and the size of the user's font, one should make sure that at least one line can be displayed, wholly or partially.

```
dotsperline   = GetDeviceCaps (ptrdc->m_hDC, HORZRES);
int charsperline = dotsperline / avg_char_width;
linesperpage = GetDeviceCaps (ptrdc->m_hDC, VERTRES) /
               avg_char_height;
if (linesperpage < (TopLines + BotLines + 1) )
 linesperpage = 1 +BotLines +TopLines;
int numpages = (totallines + linesperpage
     - BotLines - TopLines - 1)/
    (linesperpage - BotLines - TopLines);
```

The number of pages can then be used to set the number of pages to print in the Print Dialog box.

Next, the **DOCINFO** structure is filled out which is to be given to the Print Manager.

```
DOCINFO doc;
doc.cbSize = sizeof(DOCINFO);
doc.lpszDocName = filename;
doc.lpszOutput = 0;
doc.lpszDatatype = 0;
doc.fwType = 0;
```

As the main printing loop begins, three key things are set. Since the printing process must go byte by byte through the data printing just what can fit on a line, the variable **offset** keeps track of where we are within the data. Because we do not know if there are page breaks or formfeed codes embedded within that data, the total lines cannot be used to determine when the printing process is done. Instead, a **bool**, **docdone**, will be set to **true** when we reach the end of the data. Also, the report title is going to be displayed only on the very first page.

```
offset = 0;
docdone = false;
showtitle = true;
```

The main printing loop is much the same as before, except that there may be many pages printed. When this loop is done, the various objects must be deleted just as in the previous program.

```
if (::StartDoc (ptrdc->m_hDC, &doc) >0) {
 while (offset < maxoff && !printerror && !docdone) {
  if (::StartPage (ptrdc->m_hDC) >0) {
   if (ptrprtfont)
    ptrdc->SelectObject (ptrprtfont);
   PrintPage ();
   if (::EndPage (ptrdc->m_hDC) <0) printerror = true;
  }
 }
 ::EndDoc (ptrdc->m_hDC);
}
else printerror = true;
```

All of the work is done in **PrintPage**. This includes printing headings, the amount of text that can fit on the page, any footnotes and page numbers. Allowance should be made for top and bottom margins. Some form of line counting should be employed, displaying text at **avg_char_height * line**. Blank lines are emulated by simply adding to **line** so that the next **TextOut** occurs at **avg_char_height * line**.

As you might expect, the logic for printing a page with many options can become involved. It must be able to handle imbedded formfeeds, user printer fonts, top and bottom margins, line wrapping, and place a title (the filename) on the very first line.

The **offset** member contains the offset from the beginning of the file of data to the current page. Thus, every time **PrintPage** is invoked and we lock down the global memory area for the file, we can adjust the pointer to where we were last at within the file. The member **docdone** is set to **true** when **PrintPage** detects the end of the data. This approach guarantees that all pages are printed. Remember that because of large point size fonts, line wrapping, and imbedded formfeed codes, an accurate count of the total pages to print cannot be determined without completely previewing the document performing all of the actions except actual printing.

We must provide the margins at the top and bottom. I used two defines for these: **TopLines** and **BotLines**, which are currently set to 4 and 2 respectively. I intend to display the title on line 2 of the four top lines only on the first page; on all other pages the four top lines are blank.

While you are examining the #defines, notice that there are defines for the three DOS codes for which we are scanning while printing a page: the formfeed or new page code, the carriage return code, and the line feed code. Normally, DOS generates a CR followed by a LF code. However, in some unusual cases, I have seen only the CR code with no LF.

```
#define  TopLines 4     // number of lines for top margin
#define  BotLines 2     // number of lines for bottom margin
#define  FF       0x0c  // formfeed - new page code
#define  CR       0x0d  // carriage return code
#define  LF       0x0a  // line feed code
```

All of the major activity of printing variable width fonts occurs in the **PrintPage** function. When it begins, the current line on which to display and that line's length stored in **dif**, are set to 0. The **ptrbuf** pointer is locked onto the global memory area containing the document. Since this may not be the first page, **offset** is added to **ptrbuf** to set **ptrbuf** to the first byte that we need to examine on this page.

Next, the initial title situation is handled. It is complicated by the fact that sometimes a formfeed is the first character in the file. We do not want to print the title and then do a page eject. Rather, if that is the situation—an initial formfeed—do the page eject, then, print the title on the next page. Thus, if we are to show the title and if the first character is the FF code, then the offset is incremented and the **bool ok** is set to **false**, preventing the main processing loop from executing. This causes control to leave the **PrintPage** routine and the API printing functions then does the form feed automatically as it goes to the next page.

On the other hand, when the first byte is not the FF code, the title is displayed on line 2, **showtitle** is set to **false** and **ok** is set to **true** to cause the actual main processing loop to be run. The line counter is incremented by the number of **TopLines** we want for the top margin.

```
void EditWin::PrintPage () {
 int  line = 0;             // current lines on the page
 int  dif;                  // current chars to print
 bool ok;                   // loop controller
 // get locked ptr to global buffer
 ptrbuf = (char*) GlobalLock (hbuffer);
 ptrbuf += offset;          // set ptrbuf to next char to process
 if (showtitle) {           // print doc title on first page
  if (*ptrbuf == FF) {      // formfeed is first code
   offset++;                // so skip over it
   ok = false;              // and do not print title
  }
  else {                    // no formfeed, so print title
   // display title line
   ptrdc->TextOut (0, avg_char_height * 2, reporttitle);
   showtitle = false;       // signal title has been printed
   ok = true;               // signal ok to continue this page
  }
 }
 else ok = true;          // show title done, so continue this page
 line += TopLines;        // leave TopLines blank on other pages
```

The main processing loop invokes **GetNextLine** to get the next line; it returns the length of that line or a special value indicating whether the EOF or end of data condition was found or that a formfeed was encountered.

If **dif** which contains the length of the line is above 0, the line is displayed and the line number is incremented.

If **dif** or a length of 0 is found, indicating only a CRLF or blank line was found, just the line number is incremented. Remember, that a line is displayed at a y location of **avg_char_height * line**.

If **dif** is -1, indicating EOF and no line at all, **docdone** is set to **true**, which is used to terminate the printing process. Here, the break terminates the loop, leaving **PrintPage**.

If **dif** is -2, indicating a formfeed was encountered and no line at all, then I check further to see if the next byte is EOF so we can avoid a needless double page eject. Anyway, the break ends the loop because of the formfeed.

Finally, the full page condition is checked. If we now have a full page, less the **BotLines**, I again check the next character for a formfeed to avoid double formfeeds and check for the EOF code. In any event, the break ends the loop again. If all is normal, **ptrbuf** is set to **ptrend**, ready for the next byte.

The member **ptrend** is set by **GetNextLine** and points to the next byte to process. Upon leaving, the original font is restored and the global memory unlocked.

```
 while (ok) {               // continue until full page or eof breaks
  dif = GetNextLine (); // get a line to display
  if (dif > 0)              // positive dif means chars to display
   // display line
   ptrdc->TextOut (0, avg_char_height * line++, ptrbuf, dif);
  else if (dif == 0)        // 0 dif means solitary <CR>, skip line
   line++;
  else if (dif == -1) { // -1 = eof and no line
   docdone = true;          // signal end of doc
   break;                   // and quit this page
  }
  else {             // here, dif == -2 meaning a newpage and no line
   if (*ptrend == 0)        // avoid double new page if next is eof
    docdone = true;
   break;                   // and quit this page
  }
  if (line >= linesperpage - BotLines) { // do we have full page?
   if (*ptrend == FF) offset++;           // avoid FF as next char
   else if (*ptrend == 0)           // avoid double FF at doc end
    docdone = true;
   break;
  }
  ptrbuf = ptrend;          // reset for start of next line
 }
 GlobalUnlock (hbuffer);// unlock file buffer
}
```

GetNextLine must parse the document handling the different circumstances. The logic is straightforward through the checking for EOF, formfeed, and CRLF. If the current byte is none of those, then the potential for line wrap must be examined.

```
int EditWin::GetNextLine () {
 CSize sz;
 long  dif = 0;
 ptrend = ptrbuf;

 while (true) {
  if (*ptrend == 0) {       // is this byte EOF?
   offset += dif;           // update offset
   if (dif == 0) dif = -1;// set EOF and no line
   break;                   // leave with dif set and ptrend ->'\0'
  }
  else if (*ptrend == FF){// is this byte a formfeed?
```

```
    if (dif > 0) {           // any preceding chars?
     offset += dif + 1;      // yes, so return those - update offset
     break;                // leave with dif set & ptrend -> FF byte
    }
    ptrend++;                // no, so point to next char
    dif = -2;                // and set newpage
    offset++;                // account for the ff code
    break;                   // and leave signaling FF with no lines
   }
   else if (*ptrend == CR){// is this byte a carriage return?
    ptrend++;                // point to next byte
    if (*ptrend == LF) {     // is next byte the line feed?
     offset += dif + 2;      // yes, update offset for both codes
     ptrend++;               // point to next byte after the LF
    }
    else {                   // next char is not the LF
     offset += dif +1;       // update offset allowing for the CR
    }
    break;             // leave with dif set and ptrend -> next char
   }
```

First, I assume that all is fine and increment both **ptrend** and **dif**. Then, the **GetTextExtent** function is invoked to figure out the total width of the line to this point.

```
   else {                    // this byte is valid
    ptrend++;                // point to next byte
    dif++;                   // add 1 to the total len of this line
    sz = ptrdc->GetTextExtent (ptrbuf, dif); // check for linewrap
    if (sz.cx > dotsperline) {// if line length exceeds page width
     ptrend--;               // attempt to back up a character
     dif--;                  // and remove 1 from total line length
     if (dif == 0){// avoid problem of even 1 char being too large
      ptrend++;              // force only 1 char to print
      dif = 1;               // and set dif to the 1 char
     }
     offset += dif;          // update offset
     break;            // leave with dif set and ptrend -> next char
    }
   }                   // here line len is ok, so go do another char
  }
 return dif;
}
```

Then, if the **sz.cx** length exceeds the dots per line, Windows would clip part or all of the last character. So we fake a CRLF by backing up one byte, which means decrementing **ptrend** and **dif**. However, I force at least one character to be printed in the case of huge fonts and tiny display areas. Note that the general philosophy was to return all good text up to the special code.

There is no escaping the fact that printing is complex. When we examine the document-view architecture in Chapter 15, some simplifications result.

Here is the complete coding for the **EditWin** class.

EditWin Class Definition

```
#pragma once

/***************************************************************/
/*                                                             */
/* EditWin Class Definition                                    */
/*                                                             */
/***************************************************************/

class EditWin : public CMDIChildWnd {
```

```
 /**********************************************************/
 /*                                                        */
 /* Class Data Members                                     */
 /*                                                        */
 /**********************************************************/
protected:
CEdit    editwin;        // the CEdit main window
CString  filename;       // full path file spec
LOGFONT* ptrLogFont;     // the user's chosen font, if any
// for printing only
CDC*    ptrdc;           // passed printer DC
int     linesPerPage;    // number of lines per page
int     dotsPerLine;     // number of printer dots per line
long    offset;          // current offset into file
long    maxoff;          // maximum offset into file
bool    docdone;         // true when at EOF
bool    showtitle;       // true at the start to print a title
CString reporttitle;     // header
HANDLE hbuffer;          // handle to global memory file buffer
char*   ptrbuf;          // locked ptr to file buffer
char*   ptrend;          // ptr to file buffer end line work area
int     totalLines;      // total lines at time of printing
CFont* ptrprtfont;
int     avgCapsWidth;  // avg capital letter width - printing
int     avgCharWidth;  // avg character width - printing
int     avgCharHeight; // avg character height - printing
 /**********************************************************/
 /*                                                        */
 /* Class Functions:                                       */
 /*                                                        */
 /**********************************************************/
public:
                 EditWin (CString& filename);  // constructor
                ~EditWin () {}                 // destructor
protected:
afx_msg int  OnCreate (LPCREATESTRUCT); // create CEdit & load
afx_msg void OnDestroy ();              // save file, delete font
afx_msg void OnClose ();                // save query
afx_msg void OnSetFocus(CWnd* pOldWnd); // give CEdit the focus
afx_msg void OnSize (UINT, int, int);   // reposition CEdit
// utility functions
void SaveCheck ();                    // query user - save file
void SaveFile ();                     // save the file
int  DisplayMsg (int, int, UINT);     // display message box
void SetNoFileErr (int, UINT);        // dsply error and no file
bool HandlePrinting (CPrintDialog*); // do the actual printing
void PrintPage ();                    // prints one page
int  GetNextLine ();                  // retrieve one line of text
                 // command processors
afx_msg void CmFilePrint ();          // print the file
afx_msg void CmFilePrinterSetup ();  // set up the printer
afx_msg void CmEnableHaveFile (CCmdUI*); // common menu enabler
afx_msg void CmFontChange ();       // get new user chosen font
afx_msg void CmFileSave ();         // save the file with same name
afx_msg void CmFileSaveAs ();       // save with new name
```

```
afx_msg void CmEditUndo ();        // undo last change
afx_msg void CmEditCut ();         // cut to clipboard
afx_msg void CmEditCopy ();        // copy to clipboard
afx_msg void CmEditPaste ();       // paste from the clipboard
afx_msg void OnRButtonDown (UINT, CPoint);  // pop up edit menu

             // command enablers
afx_msg void CmEnableEditUndo (CCmdUI*); // enable/disable Undo
afx_msg void CmEnableEditCut  (CCmdUI*); // enable/disable Cut
afx_msg void CmEnableEditCopy (CCmdUI*); // enable/disable Copy
afx_msg void CmEnableEditPaste (CCmdUI*);// enable/disable Paste

DECLARE_MESSAGE_MAP()
};
```

EditWin Class Implementation

```
#include "stdafx.h"
#include "FrameWin.h"
#include "EditWin.h"
#include "resource.h"
#include "EditWinRC.h"
#include "printdlg.h"

/***************************************************************/
/*                                                             */
/* Externals: the printing dialog and abort flag               */
/*                                                             */
/***************************************************************/

static HWND  hprintdlg;  // for the msg handler
bool         userabort;  // abort when true

/***************************************************************/
/*                                                             */
/* AbortProc: replacement msg handler for printing abort dialog*/
/*                                                             */
/***************************************************************/

// While printing, the Printing dialog box is displayed with a
// Cancel button. This routine replaces the normal message
// handling mechanism, until printing is done or the Cancel
// button is pressed.

int APIENTRY AbortProc (HDC, int) {
 MSG msg;
 while (!userabort && PeekMessage (&msg, NULL, 0, 0, PM_REMOVE)){
  if (!hprintdlg || !IsDialogMessage(hprintdlg, &msg)) {
   TranslateMessage(&msg);
   DispatchMessage(&msg);
  }
 }
 return !userabort;
}

/***************************************************************/
/*                                                             */
/* EditWin Messsage Map                                        */
/*                                                             */
/***************************************************************/

BEGIN_MESSAGE_MAP(EditWin, CMDIChildWnd)
 ON_WM_CREATE ()
```

```
 ON_WM_DESTROY ()
 ON_WM_CLOSE()
 ON_WM_SETFOCUS()
 ON_WM_SIZE()
 ON_WM_RBUTTONDOWN ()
 ON_COMMAND(CM_FILEPRINT,        CmFilePrint)
 ON_COMMAND(CM_FILEPRINTERSETUP, CmFilePrinterSetup)
 ON_UPDATE_COMMAND_UI(CM_FILEPRINT,     CmEnableHaveFile)
 ON_COMMAND(CM_FONTCHANGE,          CmFontChange)
 ON_COMMAND(CM_FILESAVE,            CmFileSave)
 ON_COMMAND(CM_FILESAVEAS,          CmFileSaveAs)
 ON_COMMAND(CM_EDITUNDO,            CmEditUndo)
 ON_COMMAND(CM_EDITCUT,             CmEditCut)
 ON_COMMAND(CM_EDITCOPY,            CmEditCopy)
 ON_COMMAND(CM_EDITPASTE,           CmEditPaste)
 ON_UPDATE_COMMAND_UI(CM_EDITUNDO, CmEnableEditUndo)
 ON_UPDATE_COMMAND_UI(CM_EDITCUT,  CmEnableEditCut)
 ON_UPDATE_COMMAND_UI(CM_EDITCOPY, CmEnableEditCopy)
 ON_UPDATE_COMMAND_UI(CM_EDITPASTE,CmEnableEditPaste)
END_MESSAGE_MAP()

/*************************************************************/
/*                                                           */
/* EditWin: Construct the window object - save file name     */
/*                                                           */
/*************************************************************/

EditWin::EditWin (CString& filenm) : CMDIChildWnd () {
 ptrLogFont = 0;     // no user font chosen as yet
 ptrprtfont = 0;
 filename = filenm; // save the filename
 hbuffer = 0;                          // set no file in memory
}

/*************************************************************/
/*                                                           */
/* OnDestroy: save file if modified & wanted, delete user font */
/*                                                           */
/*************************************************************/

void EditWin::OnDestroy () {
 if (editwin.GetSafeHwnd() && editwin.GetModify ())
  SaveCheck (); // save file if needed
 if (ptrLogFont) delete ptrLogFont;
 if (ptrprtfont) delete ptrprtfont;
 CMDIChildWnd::OnDestroy ();
}

/*************************************************************/
/*                                                           */
/* CmFontChange: choose font dialog - use current printer    */
/*                                                           */
/*************************************************************/

void EditWin::CmFontChange () {
 char printer[80];
 char *device, *driver, *output, *next;
 CDC* ptrprinterDC = 0;

 // get access to printer DC from the ini file installed printer
 GetProfileString ("windows", "device", "...", printer,
                   sizeof (printer));
 if ( (device = strtok_s (printer, ",", &next)) != 0 &&
      (driver = strtok_s (NULL,    ",", &next)) != 0 &&
```

```
      (output = strtok_s (NULL,    ",", &next)) != 0) {
  // a default printer exists, so get a printer DC for it
  ptrprinterDC = new CDC;
  ptrprinterDC->CreateDC (driver, device, output, NULL);
 }

 // construct the Choose Font dialog
 CFontDialog  dlg (ptrLogFont, CF_EFFECTS | CF_PRINTERFONTS |
                   CF_FORCEFONTEXIST, ptrprinterDC, this);
 if (dlg.DoModal () == IDOK) {     // get user font choice
  if (!ptrLogFont) {
   ptrLogFont = new LOGFONT;       // 1st time, create LOGFONT
  }
  // copy user choice of font into our LOGFONT instance
  memcpy (ptrLogFont, &(dlg.m_lf), sizeof (LOGFONT));
  // build the font and give it to the CEdit control
  HFONT hfont = ::CreateFontIndirect (ptrLogFont);
  editwin.SendMessage (WM_SETFONT, (WPARAM) hfont, 0);
  editwin.Invalidate ();
 }
 if (ptrprinterDC) delete ptrprinterDC;
}

/*************************************************************/
/*                                                           */
/* OnCreate: create the CEdit control - load in the file or  */
/*           set up an empty new file                        */
/*                                                           */
/*************************************************************/

int EditWin::OnCreate (LPCREATESTRUCT lpCS) {
 int retcd = CMDIChildWnd::OnCreate (lpCS); // create our window
 CRect rect;
 GetClientRect (&rect);
 // allocate a CEdit control as a client window
 if (!editwin.Create (WS_CHILD | WS_VISIBLE | ES_AUTOHSCROLL |
              ES_AUTOVSCROLL | ES_MULTILINE | ES_WANTRETURN |
              WS_VSCROLL | WS_HSCROLL, rect, this, EDITWINDOW)) {
  // if not able to build CEdit, display error
  DisplayMsg (IDS_MSG_ERROR, IDS_MSG_NOMEM, MB_OK);
  return -1;
 }

 // load a null file or load the real file into the CEdit control
 if (filename.GetLength() == 0) {
  editwin.SetWindowText (0);     // send new text to CEdit window
  editwin.SetModify (FALSE);     // set CEdit not modified yet
  editwin.EmptyUndoBuffer ();    // clear CEdit's undo buffer
  return retcd;
 }

 // attempt to open the file
 HANDLE hfile = CreateFile (filename, GENERIC_READ, 0, NULL,
                    OPEN_EXISTING, FILE_ATTRIBUTE_NORMAL, NULL);
 if (hfile == INVALID_HANDLE_VALUE) {
  // file create failed, so show error msg and install null file
  SetNoFileErr (IDS_MSG_FILEOPEN , MB_OK | MB_ICONSTOP);
  return -1;
 }

 // get file size and reset DOS offset back to the beginning
 DWORD filesize = SetFilePointer (hfile, 0L, NULL, FILE_END);
 SetFilePointer (hfile, 0L, NULL, FILE_BEGIN);

```

```
 // CEdit can handle upto 64K absolute maximum
 if (filesize > 65535L) {
  // show err and install null file
  SetNoFileErr (IDS_MSG_FILEBIG, MB_OK);
  CloseHandle (hfile);
  return -1;
 }

 // allocate a file input buffer - add one for NULL terminator
 // Note that any dynamic memory allocation method is ok to use
 HANDLE  hbuffer = GlobalAlloc (GMEM_MOVEABLE, filesize + 1);
 if (!hbuffer) {  // error, not enough memory for buffer
  // show err and install null file
  SetNoFileErr (IDS_MSG_NOMEM, MB_OK | MB_ICONSTOP);
  CloseHandle (hfile);
  return -1;
 }
 // get locked ptr to global buffer
 char *ptrbuf = (char*) GlobalLock (hbuffer);

 // input the whole file
 DWORD actsz;
 ReadFile (hfile, ptrbuf, filesize, &actsz, NULL);
 CloseHandle (hfile);

 if (actsz != filesize) { // check for input read error
  // show err and install null file
  SetNoFileErr (IDS_MSG_FILEREAD, MB_OK | MB_ICONSTOP);
  GlobalUnlock (hbuffer); // remove the global memory
  GlobalFree   (hbuffer);
  return -1;
 }

 // install the text file into the CEdit control
 ptrbuf [filesize] = 0;       // insert null terminator for CEdit
 editwin.SetWindowText (ptrbuf); // set CEdit to new text
 editwin.SetModify (FALSE);      // set CEdit to unmodified
 editwin.EmptyUndoBuffer ();     // clear CEdit's undo buffer
 GlobalUnlock (hbuffer);         // unlock file buffer
 GlobalFree   (hbuffer);         // and free global memory
 return retcd;
}

/******************************************************************/
/*                                                                */
/* SetNoFileErr: display file open error                          */
/*               and install null file in CEdit                   */
/*                                                                */
/******************************************************************/

void EditWin::SetNoFileErr (int id2, UINT flags) {
 DisplayMsg (IDS_MSG_ERROR, id2, flags); // display the error msg
 filename = "";                  // install untitled new file
 editwin.SetWindowText (0);      // send null text to CEdit window
 editwin.SetModify (FALSE);      // set CEdit not modified yet
 editwin.EmptyUndoBuffer ();     // clear CEdit's undo buffer
}

/******************************************************************/
/*                                                                */
/* OnSize: resize the CEdit client                                */
/*                                                                */
/******************************************************************/

```

```
void EditWin::OnSize (UINT, int width, int height) {
 if (editwin.GetSafeHwnd())
  editwin.MoveWindow (0, 0, width, height, TRUE);
}

/***************************************************************/
/*                                                             */
/* OnSetFocus: pass the focus on down to the child window      */
/*                                                             */
/***************************************************************/

void EditWin::OnSetFocus(CWnd*) {
 editwin.SetFocus();
}

/***************************************************************/
/*                                                             */
/* SaveCheck: query user about needed file save                */
/*                                                             */
/***************************************************************/

void EditWin::SaveCheck () {
 // based on user request and whether or not file has a name,
 // send ourselves the save messages
 if (DisplayMsg (IDS_MSG_QUERY, IDS_MSG_NOTSAVE,
                 MB_YESNO | MB_ICONQUESTION) == IDYES) {
  if (filename.GetLength() == 0)
      SendMessage (WM_COMMAND, CM_FILESAVEAS, 0L);
  else
      SendMessage (WM_COMMAND, CM_FILESAVE, 0L);
 }
}

/***************************************************************/
/*                                                             */
/* CmFileSave: save an existent file                           */
/*                                                             */
/***************************************************************/

void EditWin::CmFileSave () {
 // if no name, use SaveAs otherwise use SaveFile
 if (filename.GetLength()==0)
  SendMessage (WM_COMMAND, CM_FILESAVEAS, 0L);
 else SaveFile();
}

/***************************************************************/
/*                                                             */
/* SaveFile: write the file                                    */
/*                                                             */
/***************************************************************/

void EditWin::SaveFile () {
 // allocate a buffer based upon current size of text in CEdit
 long filesize = editwin.GetWindowTextLength ();
 HANDLE hbuffer = GlobalAlloc (GMEM_MOVEABLE, filesize);
 if (hbuffer==NULL) {   // error, not enough memory for buffer
  DisplayMsg (IDS_MSG_ERROR, IDS_MSG_NOMEM, MB_OK | MB_ICONSTOP);
  return;
 }
 char* buf = (char*) GlobalLock (hbuffer);

 // transfer the updated text from CEdit control into global buf
 editwin.GetWindowText (buf, filesize);
```

```

 // open the file, replacing any existing file
 HANDLE hfile = CreateFile (filename, GENERIC_WRITE, 0, NULL,
                    CREATE_ALWAYS, FILE_ATTRIBUTE_NORMAL, NULL);
 if (hfile == INVALID_HANDLE_VALUE) {
  DisplayMsg (IDS_MSG_ERROR,IDS_MSG_FILEERR, MB_OK| MB_ICONSTOP);
  GlobalUnlock (hbuffer);
  GlobalFree (hbuffer);
  return;
 }

 // write the whole file
 DWORD actsz;
 WriteFile (hfile, buf, filesize, &actsz, NULL);
 CloseHandle (hfile);     // close file and delete global memory
 GlobalUnlock (hbuffer);
 GlobalFree   (hbuffer);

 if (actsz != (DWORD) filesize) // if write fails, show error
  DisplayMsg (IDS_MSG_ERROR, IDS_MSG_FILEWRT, MB_OK|MB_ICONSTOP);
 else
  editwin.SetModify (FALSE);    // set CEdit to unmodified
}

/***************************************************************/
/*                                                             */
/* CmFileSaveAs: Save an existent file with a new name         */
/*                                                             */
/***************************************************************/

void EditWin::CmFileSaveAs () {
 CFileDialog filedlg (FALSE,    // use SaveAs dialog
                      "*.CPP", // default extension
                      "*.*",    // current file name
          OFN_HIDEREADONLY | OFN_OVERWRITEPROMPT | OFN_LONGNAMES,
          "All Files (*.*)|*.*|CPP Files (*.CPP)|*.CPP|C Files"
          " (*.C)|*.C|Header Files (*.H*)|*.H*||", this);
 // install current file name
 strcpy_s (filedlg.m_ofn.lpstrFile, MAX_PATH, filename);
 if (filedlg.DoModal () == IDOK) {  // user has chosen a file, so
  filename = filedlg.GetPathName ();// extract its filename
  SaveFile ();                      // save the file
  CString title;                    // construct window title
  title.LoadString (IDS_EDIT);
  title += filename;
  SetWindowText (title);            // install new title
 }
}

/***************************************************************/
/*                                                             */
/* OnRButtonDown: pop up edit menu as a floating menu          */
/*                                                             */
/***************************************************************/

void EditWin::OnRButtonDown (UINT, CPoint point) {
 CMenu *ptrmenu  = GetMenu ();        // point to main menu object
 CMenu *ptrpopup = ptrmenu->GetSubMenu (1); // edit pop up menu
 ClientToScreen (&point);
 ptrpopup->TrackPopupMenu (0, point.x, point.y, this, 0);
}

/***************************************************************/
/*                                                             */
```

```
/* OnClose:  query user if we can terminate                       */
/*                                                                */
/******************************************************************/

void EditWin::OnClose () {
 if (editwin.GetSafeHwnd() && editwin.GetModify ())
  SaveCheck (); //save file if needed
 if (((FrameWin*) GetParentFrame())->fastClose == FALSE) {
  if (DisplayMsg (IDS_MSG_QUERY, IDS_MSG_EDITQUIT,
                  MB_YESNO | MB_ICONQUESTION) == IDYES) {
   MDIDestroy ();
  }
 }
}

/******************************************************************/
/*                                                                */
/* DisplayMsg: displays error message and return user response */
/*                                                                */
/******************************************************************/

int EditWin::DisplayMsg (int id1, int id2, UINT flags) {
 CString msg1, msg2;
 msg1.LoadString (id1);
 msg2.LoadString (id2);
 return MessageBox (msg2, msg1, flags);
}

/******************************************************************/
/*                                                                */
/* CmFilePrint: print an existing file                            */
/*                                                                */
/******************************************************************/

void EditWin::CmFilePrint () {
 totalLines = editwin.GetLineCount ();  // get the total lines
 if (totalLines == 0) return;           // nothing to print, quit

 CPrintDialog printdlg (FALSE, PD_USEDEVMODECOPIES, this);

 // make a rough guess at the number of pages. You could go ahead
 // and create a default printerDC and select the current font
 // into it then determine the page size and the number of pages
 // here I approximate - but will print all the pages

 int numpages = totalLines / 50;

 printdlg.m_pd.nMinPage = 1;
 printdlg.m_pd.nMaxPage = (short) numpages;
 printdlg.m_pd.nFromPage = 1;
 printdlg.m_pd.nToPage = 1;
 printdlg.m_pd.nCopies = 1;

 // display print dialog box for user selections
 if (printdlg.DoModal () == IDCANCEL) return; // if cancel, quit

 // go handle the printing, displaying error msg if it fails
 if (!HandlePrinting (&printdlg))
  DisplayMsg (IDS_MSG_CANNOTPRT, IDS_ERR_PRINT,
              MB_OK | MB_ICONEXCLAMATION);
}

/******************************************************************/
/*                                                                */
```

```
/* HandlePrinting: print the document                              */
/*                                                                 */
/*****************************************************************/

#define  TopLines 4      // number of lines for top margin
#define  BotLines 2      // number of lines for bottom margin
#define  FF       0x0c  // formfeed - new page code
#define  CR       0x0d  // carriage return code
#define  LF       0x0a  // line feed code

/*****************************************************************/
/*                                                                 */
/* Prints all pages of a document                                  */
/*                                                                 */
/* Uses TopLines as a margin, printing a filename as the title */
/*      within thetop margin area on the first page only           */
/*                                                                 */
/* Recognizes FF codes:                                            */
/*  if FF is the first code, does FF and places the title on       */
/*  next page - if FF occurs exactly at the bottom of a page,      */
/*  it is ignored since the printer automatically ejects           */
/*                                                                 */
/* Handles linewrap on lines that exceed width based on font       */
/*         in use and the printer                                  */
/*                                                                 */
/*****************************************************************/

bool EditWin::HandlePrinting (CPrintDialog *ptrprintdlg) {
 // allocate a file buffer based upon current size in the CEdit
 long filesize = editwin.GetWindowTextLength ();
 hbuffer = GlobalAlloc (GMEM_MOVEABLE, filesize);
 if (!hbuffer) {    // error, not enough memory for buffer
  DisplayMsg (IDS_MSG_ERROR, IDS_MSG_NOMEM, MB_OK | MB_ICONSTOP);
  return false;
 }
 // get locked ptr to global buffer
 ptrbuf = (char*) GlobalLock (hbuffer);

 // transfer the updated text from CEdit control
 editwin.GetWindowText (ptrbuf, filesize);

 maxoff = filesize;      // save filesize
 GlobalUnlock (hbuffer); // unlock buffer

 // construct print title for system use: "filename"
 reporttitle = filename[0] == 0 ? "Untitled" : filename;

 // set clear all error flags
 bool printerror = false;
 userabort = false;

 // setup a printer DC from the print dialog's results
 ptrdc = new CDC;
 ptrdc->Attach (ptrprintdlg->GetPrinterDC ());

 // setup a printing cancel dialog box
 PrintingDlg  *ptrprintingdlg = new PrintingDlg ();
 // set the external hwnd for abort proc
 hprintdlg = ptrprintingdlg->m_hWnd;

 // attempt to install the abort procedure
 if (ptrdc->SetAbortProc (AbortProc) < 0) { // failed, so abort
  ptrprintingdlg->DestroyWindow (); // delete printing dialog box
  delete ptrprintingdlg;            // remove the dialog object
```

```
  delete ptrdc;
  GlobalFree (hbuffer);
  return false;
 }

 // load font and scale TrueType fonts
 LOGFONT  *ptrprtlogfont;          // printer version of user font
 CFont    *ptroldfont;             // place to save old font

 if (ptrLogFont) {                 // install any user font
  // copy the real LOGFONT because we will scale the font
  ptrprtlogfont = new LOGFONT;
  memcpy (ptrprtlogfont, ptrLogFont, sizeof(LOGFONT));
  // remove any existing CFont
  if (ptrprtfont) delete ptrprtfont;
  ptrprtfont = new CFont ();

  // get a screen DC for scaling
  HDC hdc = CreateDC ("DISPLAY",NULL,NULL,NULL);
  // calculate both x and y scale dimensions between the screen
  // and the printer
  float xscale = ptrdc->GetDeviceCaps (LOGPIXELSX) /
                 (float) GetDeviceCaps(hdc, LOGPIXELSX);
  float yscale = ptrdc->GetDeviceCaps (LOGPIXELSY) /
                 (float) GetDeviceCaps(hdc, LOGPIXELSY);
  DeleteDC (hdc);

  // install scaled dimensions
  ptrprtlogfont->lfHeight =
                       (long) (ptrprtlogfont->lfHeight * yscale);
  ptrprtlogfont->lfWidth =
                       (long) (ptrprtlogfont->lfWidth * xscale);
  // make the new CFont scaled for the printer dc
  ptrprtfont->CreateFontIndirect (ptrprtlogfont);
  ptroldfont = ptrdc->SelectObject (ptrprtfont);
  delete ptrprtlogfont;
 }

 // determine real character dims on the printer and total pages
 TEXTMETRIC tm;
 GetTextMetrics (ptrdc->m_hDC, &tm);

 // calculate average character parameters
 avgCharWidth  = tm.tmAveCharWidth;
 avgCharHeight = tm.tmHeight + tm.tmExternalLeading;
 avgCapsWidth  = (tm.tmPitchAndFamily & 1 ? 3 : 2) *
                      avgCharWidth / 2;

 // calculate pagination data
 dotsPerLine   = GetDeviceCaps (ptrdc->m_hDC, HORZRES);
 int charsPerLine = dotsPerLine / avgCharWidth;
 linesPerPage = GetDeviceCaps (ptrdc->m_hDC, VERTRES) /
                avgCharHeight;

 // if we are removing BotLines for a bottom margin,
 // we must account for printing at least 1 line
 if (linesPerPage < (TopLines + BotLines + 1) )
  // rounds up to nearest number of pages
  linesPerPage = 1 + BotLines + TopLines;

 // calc a theoretical number of pages to print
 int numPages = (totalLines + linesPerPage -BotLines-TopLines-1)/
                (linesPerPage - BotLines - TopLines);

```

```
 // setup the DOCINFO for Print Manager
 DOCINFO doc;                         // used by Windows for title
 doc.cbSize = sizeof(DOCINFO);        // install doc size
 doc.lpszDocName = filename;          // install filename
 doc.lpszOutput = 0;
 doc.lpszDatatype = 0;
 doc.fwType = 0;

 offset = 0;               // set to the beginning of the file
 docdone = false;          // will be set true when doc is done
 showtitle = true;         // indicate title yet to be printed

 // main document printing loop
 // if copies>1 are desired, wrap a copies loop around this loop
 if (::StartDoc (ptrdc->m_hDC, &doc) >0) { // start the document
  while (offset < maxoff && !printerror && !docdone) {
   if (::StartPage (ptrdc->m_hDC) >0) {     // set for begin page
    // note that Windows resets the DC each time
    if (ptrprtfont)
     ptrdc->SelectObject (ptrprtfont); // install font
    PrintPage ();                      // actually print the page
    if (::EndPage (ptrdc->m_hDC) <0) printerror = true;
   }
  }
 ::EndDoc (ptrdc->m_hDC);  // end the doc
 }
 else printerror = true;   // indicate printer error occurred

 if (!userabort) EnableWindow (TRUE); // restore main wnd action
 delete ptrdc;                        // clean up
 ptrprintingdlg->DestroyWindow ();    // remove printing dialog
 delete ptrprintingdlg;
 GlobalFree (hbuffer);                // remove the text buffer
 return !printerror && !userabort;    // return success code
}

/***************************************************************/
/*                                                             */
/* PrintPage: actually prints the page                         */
/*                                                             */
/***************************************************************/

void EditWin::PrintPage () {
 int  line = 0;            // current lines on the page
 int  dif;                 // current chars to print
 bool ok;                  // loop controller

 // get locked ptr to global buffer
 ptrbuf = (char*) GlobalLock (hbuffer);
 ptrbuf += offset;         // set ptrbuf to next char to process

 if (showtitle) {          // print doc title on first page
  if (*ptrbuf == FF) {     // formfeed is first code
   offset++;               // so skip over it
   ok = false;             // and do not print title
  }
  else {                   // no formfeed, so print title
   // display title line
   ptrdc->TextOut (0, avgCharHeight * 2, reporttitle);
   showtitle = false;      // signal title has been printed
   ok = true;              // signal ok to continue this page
  }
 }
 else ok = true;         // show title done, so continue this page
```

```
 line += TopLines;       // leave TopLines blank on other pages

 while (ok) {            // continue until full page or eof breaks
  dif = GetNextLine (); // get a line to display
  if (dif > 0)          // positive dif means chars to display
   // display line
   ptrdc->TextOut (0, avgCharHeight * line++, ptrbuf, dif);
  else if (dif == 0)    // 0 dif means solitary <CR>, skip line
   line++;
  else if (dif == -1) { // -1 = eof and no line
   docdone = true;      // signal end of doc
   break;               // and quit this page
  }
  else {         // here, dif == -2 meaning a newpage and no line
   if (*ptrend == 0)    // avoid double new page if next is eof
    docdone = true;
   break;               // and quit this page
  }
  if (line >= linesPerPage - BotLines) { // do we have full page?
   if (*ptrend == FF) offset++;          // avoid FF as next char
   else if (*ptrend == 0)          // avoid double FF at doc end
    docdone = true;
   break;
  }
  ptrbuf = ptrend;       // reset for start of next line
 }
 GlobalUnlock (hbuffer);// unlock file buffer
}

/*****************************************************************/
/*                                                               */
/* GetNextLine: returns the length of the next line              */
/* -1 = end of file - no line to print - ptrend->the '\0' byte */
/* -2 = new page - no line to print - ptrend->next byte          */
/*  0 = <CRLF> on line with no characters to print               */
/*            - ptrend-> next byte                               */
/*                                                               */
/* offset is updated for correct number of bytes analyzed        */
/* Formfeeds, <CRLF>, and linewrap are handled                   */
/*                                                               */
/*****************************************************************/

int EditWin::GetNextLine () {
 CSize sz;
 long  dif = 0;
 ptrend = ptrbuf;

 while (true) {
  if (*ptrend == 0) {      // is this byte EOF?
   offset += dif;          // update offset
   if (dif == 0) dif = -1;// set EOF and no line
   break;                  // leave with dif set and ptrend ->'\0'
  }
  else if (*ptrend == FF){// is this byte a formfeed?
   if (dif > 0) {          // any preceding chars?
    offset += dif + 1;     // yes, so return those - update offset
    break;               // leave with dif set & ptrend -> FF byte
   }
   ptrend++;               // no, so point to next char
   dif = -2;               // and set newpage
   offset++;               // account for the ff code
   break;                  // and leave signaling FF with no lines
  }
  else if (*ptrend == CR){// is this byte a carriage return?
```

```
   ptrend++;                // point to next byte
   if (*ptrend == LF) {     // is next byte the line feed?
    offset += dif + 2;      // yes, update offset for both codes
    ptrend++;               // point to next byte after the LF
   }
   else {                   // next char is not the LF
    offset += dif +1;       // update offset allowing for the CR
   }
   break;             // leave with dif set and ptrend -> next char
  }
  else {                    // this byte is valid
   ptrend++;                // point to next byte
   dif++;                   // add 1 to the total len of this line
   sz = ptrdc->GetTextExtent (ptrbuf, dif); // check for linewrap
   if (sz.cx > dotsPerLine) {// if line length exceeds page width
    ptrend--;               // attempt to back up a character
    dif--;                  // and remove 1 from total line length
    if (dif == 0){// avoid problem of even 1 char being too large
     ptrend++;              // force only 1 char to print
     dif = 1;               // and set dif to the 1 char
    }
    offset += dif;          // update offset
    break;            // leave with dif set and ptrend -> next char
   }
  }                   // here line len is ok, so go do another char
 }
 return dif;
}

/*************************************************************/
/*                                                           */
/* CmFilePrinterSetup: set up the printer parameters         */
/*                                                           */
/*************************************************************/

void EditWin::CmFilePrinterSetup () {
 CPrintDialog printdlg (TRUE, PD_USEDEVMODECOPIES, this);
 printdlg.DoModal ();
}

/*************************************************************/
/*                                                           */
/* CmEnableHaveFile: enabler for printing menu items         */
/*                                                           */
/*************************************************************/

void EditWin::CmEnableHaveFile (CCmdUI *ptrenabler) {
 ptrenabler->Enable (editwin.GetWindowTextLength () > 0 ? 1 : 0);
}

/*************************************************************/
/*                                                           */
/* CmEnableEditUndo: enables/disables edit undo menu item    */
/*                                                           */
/*************************************************************/

void EditWin::CmEnableEditUndo (CCmdUI *ptrenabler) {
 ptrenabler->Enable (editwin.CanUndo());
}

/*************************************************************/
/*                                                           */
/* CmEnableEditCut: enables/disables edit cut menu item      */
/*                                                           */
```

```
/***************************************************************/

void EditWin::CmEnableEditCut (CCmdUI *ptrenabler) {
 ptrenabler->Enable (editwin.GetSel()>0? 1: 0);
}

/***************************************************************/
/*                                                             */
/* CmEnableEditCopy: enables/disables edit copy menu item      */
/*                                                             */
/***************************************************************/

void EditWin::CmEnableEditCopy (CCmdUI *ptrenabler) {
 ptrenabler->Enable (editwin.GetSel()>0? 1: 0);
}

/***************************************************************/
/*                                                             */
/* CmEnableEditPaste: enables/disables edit paste menu item    */
/*                                                             */
/***************************************************************/

void EditWin::CmEnableEditPaste (CCmdUI *ptrenabler) {
 ptrenabler->Enable (IsClipboardFormatAvailable (CF_TEXT));
}

/***************************************************************/
/*                                                             */
/* CmEditCut: Remove text data and place on clipboard          */
/*                                                             */
/***************************************************************/

void EditWin::CmEditCut () {
 editwin.Cut (); // cut it to clipboard
}

/***************************************************************/
/*                                                             */
/* CmEditCopy: copy text to clipboard                          */
/*                                                             */
/***************************************************************/

void EditWin::CmEditCopy () {
 editwin.Copy (); // copy it to clipboard
}

/***************************************************************/
/*                                                             */
/* CmEditPaste: Paste text from the clipboard                  */
/*                                                             */
/***************************************************************/

void EditWin::CmEditPaste () {
 if (IsClipboardFormatAvailable (CF_TEXT))
  editwin.Paste (); // paste from clipboard
}

/***************************************************************/
/*                                                             */
/* CmEditUndo: Undo last change                                */
/*                                                             */
/***************************************************************/

void EditWin::CmEditUndo () {
```

```
editwin.Undo ();
}
```

Programming Problems

Problem Pgm13-1 Revised Acme Inventory with Printing Support

Revise program **Pgm12-1**, Acme Inventory, to support printing operations. Add File|Print Setup and File|Print menu options along with a tool bar button for File|Print.

When File|Print is chosen, print the report. The report contains a heading line such as Acme Inventory Report. Include a page number on each page. Include appropriate column headings. Each page should have the heading and column headings.

Use whatever font that the user has installed, if any.

If a mark up percentage, include the mark up percentage column. Also, include the mark up percentage value in the heading line. If no mark up is in effect on the screen, then do not include any mark up column.

Chapter 14 Sound, Splash Screens, Animation Effects and Animated Presentations

Sound

Sound generation is an extensive topic on which we could spend many chapters. Instead, only the minimal basics are covered so that you can at least play sound files as part of the application. In fact, fancier multimedia applications open with a splash screen and intro music. After you have studied this section and the next one on splash screens, I invite you to add in sound effects during the opening logos in **Pgm14b**.

Sounds can be played from the PC's tiny speaker or through sound cards, such as Sound Blaster and compatibles. Sound through the PC speaker is extremely limited not only in fidelity but also in notes. Only one note at a time can be sounded through the PC speaker. With sound cards, many voices or notes can be sounded simultaneously, creating chords. Rather than dwell on the obsolete PC speaker, I am assuming that you have a sound card and have installed the proper Windows sound drivers. You can verify that your sound system is functioning properly by using "Accessories—Multimedia—Media Player" to play the supplied Windows WAV short sound sequences.

Windows provides three methods of programming sound operations through the Multimedia API, MMSYSTEM, which provides a Media Control Interface, MCI. The MCI provides a very high level method to play back recorded sound files known as WAV or wave sound files via either **MessageBeep** or **sndPlaySound** functions.

For more control, the middle level consists of many MCI driver functions as command strings. For exacting, detailed control, the low-level MIDI API can be accessed. MCI can support MIDI devices, waveform, and CD devices.

A note has a specific pitch and duration. A series of notes, such as "Twinkle, Twinkle, Little Star," becomes a voice. A chord is made up of often three or more separate voices. Often several voices are required to emulate the sound quality of certain instruments so that the notes sound like an organ or regal. The PC speaker can only play one voice, while a sound card can play many, often 20 or so, yielding a quality HI-FI sound. In a WAV file, all of the voices have been merged into one combined sound. The resulting collected sound waves are recorded in one group or package. It is this packaged collection that is played back when one "plays" a WAV file.

The sound recording process consists of two parts: recording and playback. When recording, a microphone picks up the sounds to be recorded. The output of a microphone is an analog signal, fluctuating electric voltage, rather like sine waves. This analog signal is input to the A/D (Analog to Digital) Converter section of the sound card that periodically measures the voltage and digitizes that value either as a byte (8-bit sampling) or as a word (16-bit sampling). Obviously, the 8-bit sampling has a much narrower range of fluctuations. (0-255 versus 0-65535) The frequency that the incoming sound waves are sampled is known as the sampling rate, a variable quantity.

If one is recording voice only, voice sounds vary over a narrow range so that a low sampling rate of say 4kHz could be used. Music quality sounds, on the other hand, vary in frequency across the entire audible spectrum, requiring a high sampling rate to reproduce fidelity, say 44kHz. The music industry standard guideline is to use a sampling rate that is 2x the highest frequency in the mix. Thus, if full fidelity up to 20,000 hertz is required, the sampling rate is 44kHz.

The sampling rate affects disk storage. If you are sampling with 8-bit at 44kHz for excellent quality, one second of sound requires 44,000 bytes. If you are at 16-bit, 1 second requires 88,000 bytes. So you want to record a song that lasts for four minutes. Using 16-bit at 44kHz, you may need 21 megabytes! If you wish to be able to edit each instrument and adjust the final mix, as a sound recording engineer might do, assuming you need eight tracks or voices, you only need about 170M free disk space! If you get into the digital sound recording arena, be sure to have dedicated Gigabyte disk drives! On playback, the disk digital data is fed to the sound card's DAC, digital to audio converter, which produces a weak analog signal that is then amplified and sent to speakers.

Windows MCI then provides a layered approach. At the highest level, Sound Recorder and **sndPlaySound** create and play back wave files with minimal coding (1 line!). The MCI or string interface permits much more direct control over the entire operation. The coding of this is best encapsulated into C++ classes. And the low-level API permits total control with a maximal amount of user coding. There is an excellent MCI strings class design presented in William Roetzheim, Uncharted Windows Programming, SAMS, 1993.

In this chapter, I present only the highest level of the API, using the **sndPlaySound** function. The **sndPlaySound** function accepts the WAV file name and the play options flag.

```
sndPlaySound (filename, flags);
```

The commonly used flags include the following.

```
SND_SYNC    - returns after finishing play
SND_ASYNC   - start playing the file asynchronously and return to
              the application
SND_LOOP    - endlessly repeat the sound file
SND_NOSTOP  - if a sound is currently playing, return without
              playing
```

If you only want to hear the wave file, the flag would likely just be **SND_ASYNC**. This would allow your application to go on to other processing actions while the sound is playing in the background. If you use **SND_LOOP**, then, to terminate the endless playing loop, invoke **sndPlaySound** with NULL as the filename.

In order to utilize this function, two changes must be made. First, include the **mmsystem.h** header file. Second, link to the **winmm.lib** file by coding this library in the Object/Library Modules edit control of the General category of the Link tab of Project settings.

Pgm14a illustrates the endless loop style, playing the requested wave file for three seconds. Since some means for obtaining filenames is required, an Open File dialog box is used. Further, this sample has no visible main window. An application can be a dialog box only! Figure 14.1 shows **Pgm14a** in operation.

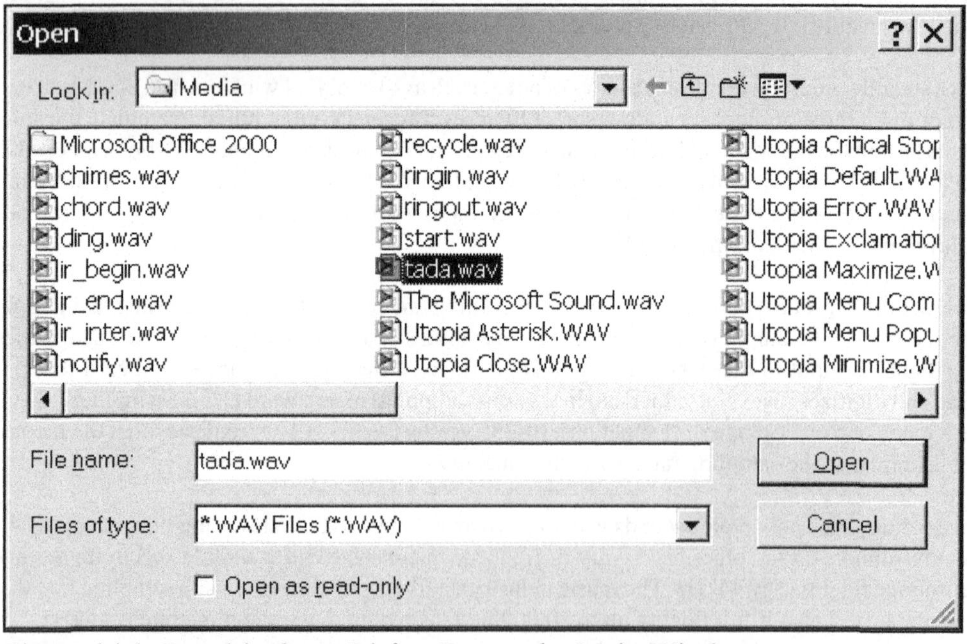

Figure 14.1 **Pgm14a** Open Dialog Box as the Main Window

Pgm14a: Playing WAV Files and Using a Dialog Box as the Main Window

Examine **Pgm14a**'s implementation. It is so short that all coding is contained within the **InitInstance** function. The first action is to construct a File Open dialog box to permit the user to select the desired wav file followed by setting our filename filter to *.wav.

```
CFileDialog filedlg (TRUE,      // use Open dialog
```

```
                        "*.WAV",   // default extension
                        "*.WAV",   // current file name
        OFN_FILEMUSTEXIST | OFN_PATHMUSTEXIST | OFN_LONGNAMES,
                        "*.WAV Files (*.WAV)||", NULL);
char filename[MAX_PATH] = "*.wav";
char filter[MAX_PATH] = "*.wav";
```

For convenience to the user, we should set the initial directory to the Windows Media folder which contains a lot of wav files. This is complicated a bit because the folder structure is different between Windows 95/98 and NT/Win2000 systems. In Windows 95/98 systems, the system folder is usually C:\Windows, while in the NT/Win2000 systems, the system folder is usually C:\WinNT\System32. The **GetSystemDirectory** function obtains the system folder.

```
char sysdir[_MAX_PATH];
GetSystemDirectory (sysdir, sizeof (sysdir));
```

At this point, the **sysdir** string contains typically either "c:\windows" or "c:\winnt\system32." One way to extract the system32 is to use the **_splitpath_s** function. This function splits a full file specification into four parts: the drive string, the path, the file name and the extension. There is a reverse function, **_makepath_s**, that takes the four partial strings and concatenates them into single string.

In this case, there is no extension expected. If this is an NT type system, then the file name string would contain system32.

```
char drive[_MAX_DRIVE];
char dir[_MAX_PATH];
char fn[_MAX_PATH];
char ext[_MAX_EXT];
_splitpath_s (sysdir, drive, _MAX_DRIVE,
              dir, _MAX_PATH, fn, _MAX_PATH, ext, _MAX_EXT);
```

Now, we can rebuild the path to the media folder location based upon whether or not the file name string contains "system32" or not.

```
CString path = drive;
path += dir;
if (_stricmp (fn, "system32") != 0) {
 path += fn;
 path += "//Media";
}
else path += "Media";
```

Finally, we can install initial Media folder in which to look for wav files into the dialog.

```
filedlg.m_ofn.lpstrInitialDir = path;
```

The main loop continues to process requests until the user selects any button other than OK. When a file is chosen, the sound is played for three seconds. The **GetTickCount** function tracks milliseconds. Thus, three seconds is 3,000 tick counts.

```
int retcd = IDOK;
while (retcd == IDOK) {
 // install *.wav for the filename
 strcpy_s (filename, sizeof(filename), filter);
 retcd = filedlg.DoModal (); // get user's file choice
 // if .wav selected, play the sound file for 3 seconds
 if (retcd == IDOK) {           // extract its filename
  strcpy_s (filename, sizeof(filename),
            filedlg.GetPathName ());
  // endless play of file
  sndPlaySound (filename, SND_ASYNC | SND_LOOP);
  beginticks = ticks = GetTickCount ();
  while (ticks < beginticks + 3000)
   ticks = GetTickCount ();         // delay 3 sec
  sndPlaySound (NULL, SND_ASYNC); // abruptly terminate play
 }
}
```

Finally, when the user chooses to cancel the dialog, the loop terminates. However, since we are in the middle of **InitInstance**, we need to terminate the application. If we terminate with **m_pMainWnd** not set to a valid window, an assertion results. Thus, install the dialog that was just terminated as the main window.

```
m_pMainWnd = &filedlg;
PostQuitMessage(0);     // terminate application
```

If you have recorded some music, you could install a continuous background play menu item along with a Halt Play menu item. When the play music item is selected, invoke the **sndPlaySound** in the continuous play mode. When the halt music option is selected, send the NULL file to terminate **sndPlaySound**. You could even use menu item replacement, like the Hide/Show tool box.

Here is the complete application class implementation.

Pgm14a.cpp Dialog Main Window that Plays Sound Files

```
#include "stdafx.h"
#include "pgm14a.h"
#include <mmsystem.h>    // the multimedia system

Pgm14a theApp;   // launch app

/***************************************************************/
/*                                                             */
/* InitInstance: runs File Open dialog box to play sounds      */
/*                                                             */
/***************************************************************/

BOOL  Pgm14a::InitInstance () {
 DWORD ticks, beginticks;       // for tick delay on endless play

 CFileDialog filedlg (TRUE,      // use Open dialog
                      "*.WAV",   // default extension
                      "*.WAV",   // current file name
           OFN_FILEMUSTEXIST | OFN_PATHMUSTEXIST | OFN_LONGNAMES,
           "*.WAV Files (*.WAV)||", NULL);    // no parent pointer
 char filename[MAX_PATH] = "*.wav"; // set for .WAV files
 char filter[MAX_PATH] = "*.wav";
 filedlg.m_ofn.lpstrFile = filename;
 // set the default dir by attempting to find the media folder
 char sysdir[_MAX_PATH];
 GetSystemDirectory (sysdir, sizeof (sysdir));
 // typically either c:\windows or c:\winnt\system32
 char drive[_MAX_DRIVE];
 char dir[_MAX_PATH];
 char fn[_MAX_PATH];
 char ext[_MAX_EXT];
 // split off the possible system32 folder
 _splitpath_s (sysdir, drive, _MAX_DRIVE, dir, _MAX_PATH, fn,
                _MAX_PATH, ext, _MAX_EXT);
 // rebuild the possible media folder location
 CString path = drive;
 path += dir;
 if (_stricmp (fn, "system32") != 0) {
  path += fn;
  path += "//Media";
 }
 else path += "Media";

 // install initial Media folder in which to look for .wav files
 filedlg.m_ofn.lpstrInitialDir = path;

 int retcd = IDOK;                  // prime the play sound loop
 while (retcd == IDOK) {
```

```
  // install *.wav for the filename
  strcpy_s (filename, sizeof(filename), filter);
  retcd = filedlg.DoModal ();    // get user's file choice

  // if .wav selected, play the sound file for 3 seconds
  if (retcd == IDOK) {           // extract its filename
   strcpy_s (filename, sizeof(filename), filedlg.GetPathName ());
   // endless play of file
   sndPlaySound (filename, SND_ASYNC | SND_LOOP);

   beginticks = ticks = GetTickCount (); // set start tick counts
   while (ticks < beginticks + 3000)
    ticks = GetTickCount ();          // delay 3 sec
   sndPlaySound (NULL, SND_ASYNC);    // abruptly terminate play
  }
 }
 // avoids assertion failure for NULL main win
 m_pMainWnd = &filedlg;
 PostQuitMessage(0);     // terminate application
 return TRUE;
}
```

Splash Screens

A splash screen is an initial bitmap that is displayed just at the moment an application is launched and before its main window is displayed. Whenever you click on the Developer Studio icon to launch the IDE, a small splash screen, the colorful logo image, appears in the center of the screen. A splash screen is often displayed when an application takes a rather long time to load and initialize itself. Its purpose it to give the user some idea that something is occurring or to display copyright information. Once the main window is set up, the main window display writes over the area where the bitmap was.

Under the MFC, the best point to insert the splash display is in the **CWindApp**'s **InitApplication** overridden function because this function is invoked only once per application and before **InitInstance** is called. Once the splash screen is displayed, the application continues with normal program initialization in **InitInstance**. The splash images are usually centered on the screen and are overlaid by the normal application window when it is finally displayed.

Figure 14.2 shows **Pgm14b** after it has displayed three splash images.

Pgm14b illustrates splash screens. I have designed a simple **ShowSplashScreen** function that can be inserted into any program to display the start up logo. The function requires only three parameters: an **hinstance**, the string name of the bitmap resource, and the number of seconds delay wanted. **ShowSplashScreen** loads the bitmap and then delays its return for the requested number of seconds. Why the delay? Our basic applications come up almost at once. Without a small delay, we'd never get the opportunity to view the splash; it'd be gone in a blink. The delay can be zero seconds, in which case **ShowSplashScreen** would return at once.

For the bitmaps, I have used three images representing fictitious company logos: **acme.bmp**, **builder.bmp**, and **candles.bmp**. The sample program uses the shell from **Pgm4a** that simply displayed a "Hello" screen.

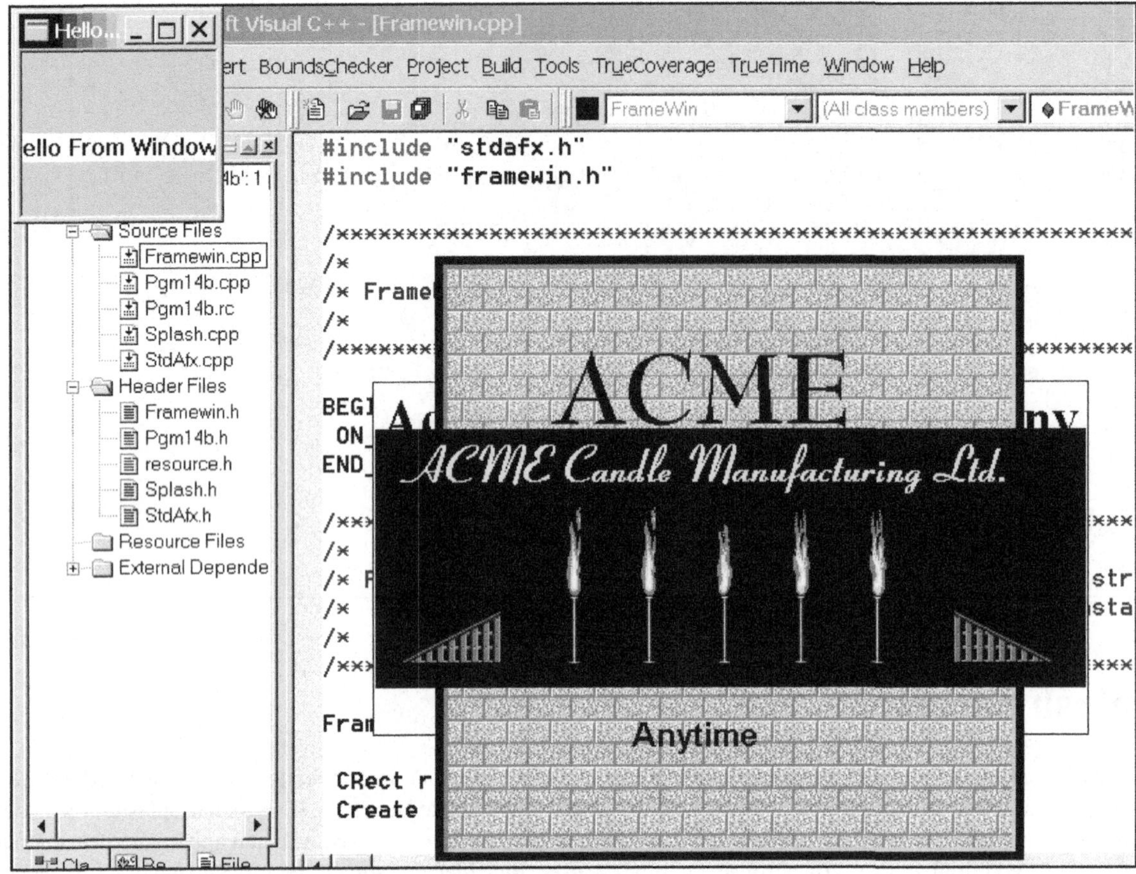

Figure 14.2 Pgm14b After Showing Three Splash Screens

The splash header file must be included to pick up the function prototype. Notice that **ShowSplashScreen** is **not** a class member function, rather a simple C function. Therefore, it can be invoked by nearly anyone. This means that if the program had to do a lengthy subsection switch later, another splash could be used. Here, it is invoked three times just for fun. The MFC **InitApplication** function returns **TRUE** if the application can continue launching.

```
BOOL  Pgm14CApp::InitApplication () {
 ShowSplashScreen (m_hInstance, 2, "IMAGE1");
 ShowSplashScreen (m_hInstance, 2, "IMAGE2");
 ShowSplashScreen (m_hInstance, 2, "IMAGE3");
 return TRUE;
 return CWinApp::InitApplication ();
}
```

These three bitmaps have been included into the resource file.

```
IMAGE1  BITMAP  "..\\bmps\\acme.bmp"
IMAGE2  BITMAP  "..\\bmps\\builder.bmp"
IMAGE3  BITMAP  "..\\bmps\\candles.bmp"
```

The header file **Splash.h** defines the function as follows.

```
void ShowSplashScreen (HINSTANCE hinst, int seconds, char* name);
```

The splash function is a C Style function to increase its flexibility. It can be invoked from many places as it only really requires the application's **hinstance**. It does not require any handles to windows. The basic method is to **BitBlt** from a DC containing the loaded bitmap onto a screen DC. Since the splash screen should appear on top of everything else that is on the whole screen, this DC is the "desktop" DC. Another DC is created that is compatible with this desktop DC and the bitmap inserted into the compatible DC. The **BitBlt** then transfers the bitmap from the compatible DC onto the desktop DC. Since we are dealing with C Style, the DCs are of data type **HDC**. A DC for the whole screen can be gotten by using a **CreateDC** using the name of the screen, "DISPLAY."

```
desktopdc = CreateDC ("DISPLAY", NULL, NULL, NULL);
```

The bitmap is loaded from the resource file using the argument string resource name.

```
hbitmap    = LoadBitmap (hinst, name);
```

Note that this is the only place where the application's **hinstance** is needed. You could redesign the splash function to accept a handle to the splash bitmap and remove the **hinstance** and the resource name. For centering and **BitBlt** purposes, I need the bitmap's dimensions. This is done by using the **GetObject** function to fill the **BITMAP** information structure.

```
GetObject (hbitmap, sizeof(bm), &bm);
```

The following calculates the (x, y) coordinates for the upper left corner of the bitmap so that it is centered on the screen.

```
int x = (GetSystemMetrics (SM_CXSCREEN)/2) - (bm.bmWidth/2);
int y = (GetSystemMetrics (SM_CYSCREEN)/2) - (bm.bmHeight/2);
```

Next, a compatible DC to the desktop is created and the bitmap inserted into it. However, the original bitmap contents of the compatible DC must be preserved so that the DC can be deleted. Remember that you cannot delete DCs with new objects currently selected in them—memory leaks. The handle of the old bitmap, **holdbitmap**, is used to deselect our splash bitmap before deleting the compatible DC.

```
hcompatdc = CreateCompatibleDC (desktopdc);
holdbitmap = (HBITMAP) SelectObject (hcompatdc, hbitmap);
```

Next, the bitmap is displayed.

```
BitBlt (desktopdc, x, y, bm.bmWidth, bm.bmHeight, hcompatdc,
        0, 0, SRCCOPY);
```

And the splash screen appears nicely centered on the whole screen, independent of the resolution in use.

However, you may notice that the color palette is wrong. One could improve the splash function by loading and realizing the proper color palette for the bitmap. The cleanup section is straight forward; delete all objects allocated. But remember to deselect objects first.

```
SelectObject (hcompatdc, holdbitmap);
DeleteDC (hcompatdc);
DeleteObject (hbitmap);
DeleteDC (desktopdc);
```

The final action is to delay the requested number of seconds. If the application really had some work to perform, it would have passed in zero seconds. Further, when the splash function returned, the application most likely would have replaced the arrow cursor with the hourglass wait cursor. Windows provides a function to detect large scale elapsed times. The unit of resolution is 1 millisecond, or a thousandth of a second. This is a large unit compared to the internal clock speed that is in nanoseconds. On the faster machines, this millisecond time may represent nearly ½ million instructions!

The Windows clock maintains a count of the total number of milliseconds that Windows has been up and running. In other words, the clock started from zero when the DOS command WIN was entered. The count is stored in a **DWORD** or **unsigned long** and the clock rolls over after some 49 hours of continuous operation. The time is retrieved by the Windows function **GetTickCount**. The following represents a simple method to delay the requested number of seconds without using a Windows built-in timer.

```
DWORD beginticks = GetTickCount ();
DWORD ticks = beginticks;
while (ticks < beginticks + 1000*seconds)
 ticks = GetTickCount ();
```

If zero seconds is passed, the while loop ends almost at once. When you run **Pgm14b** and watch the three splash images, realize that the next step would be the construction of your real company or program logo bitmap.

Splash.cpp - the Splash Screen Function

```
#include "stdafx.h"

```

```
/*****************************************************************/
/*                                                               */
/* ShowSplashScreen: displays start up screen for n seconds     */
/*                                                               */
/*****************************************************************/

void ShowSplashScreen (HINSTANCE hinst, int seconds, char *name){

 HDC     desktopdc;  // DC for whole screen
 HBITMAP hbitmap;    // handle for the bitmap of the splash .bmp
 BITMAP  bm;         // the actual splash bit map
 HDC     hcompatdc;  // compatible DC to hold the bitmap
 HBITMAP holdbitmap; // the original screen bitmap

 desktopdc = CreateDC ("DISPLAY", NULL, NULL, NULL);
 hbitmap   = LoadBitmap (hinst, name);
 GetObject (hbitmap, sizeof(bm), &bm);

 // calc the center pos of screen & back off to upper left corner
 int x = (GetSystemMetrics (SM_CXSCREEN)/2) - (bm.bmWidth/2);
 int y = (GetSystemMetrics (SM_CYSCREEN)/2) - (bm.bmHeight/2);

 hcompatdc = CreateCompatibleDC (desktopdc);

 //insert bitmap into the compatible dc, saving the original bmp
 holdbitmap = (HBITMAP) SelectObject (hcompatdc, hbitmap);

 // display the bitmap
 BitBlt (desktopdc, x, y, bm.bmWidth, bm.bmHeight, hcompatdc,
         0, 0, SRCCOPY);

 // clean up section
 SelectObject (hcompatdc, holdbitmap); // install original bitmap
 DeleteDC (hcompatdc);                 // remove compatible dc
 DeleteObject (hbitmap);               // remove splash bitmap
 DeleteDC (desktopdc);                 // remove screen dc

 // pause section
 // ticks are total milliseconds since Windows started
 DWORD beginticks = GetTickCount ();   // the beginning time
 DWORD ticks = beginticks;             // the current time

 // delay the requested number of seconds
 while (ticks < beginticks + 1000*seconds)
  ticks = GetTickCount ();
}
```

Animation

Many chapters could be spent on this topic, especially if you wish to write games! Animation may take several forms. Traditional cartoons use the painstaking cel animation or frame animation approach. Here the action sequence is broken down into frames that are presented or shown at about 20 to 30 frames per second, yielding a uniform motion. (See The Animation Studio, Walt Disney Computer Software, Burbank, CA, 1991.) If you are serious about game development, please take a close look at the new Microsoft Direct-X Games Development Kit.

The action of animation often requires the display of some foreground object over an existing background image. As the foreground object moves, the existing foreground image must be removed as the new image is shown. A way to keep screen flicker down while moving objects around the screen is to keep the amount of movement to one pixel in any direction. That is, move the foreground object in tiny steps.

The most straightforward approach to displaying graphical animation is to use XOR logic, plotting the previous image for removal and then plotting the new image. The drawback of this approach is flicker. A small amount of flicker is seen as the old image abruptly disappears and the new one appears. Keeping the amount of movement down to one pixel at a time greatly decreases the visual impact of the flicker effect.

If you have a video card that supports two or more graphics video pages (generally at least 2M on the video card is required for higher resolutions), then, while the user watches the current image, you draw the next scene on the other page and then do an "instantaneous" page swap. This approach is often used with the Direct-X gaming.

Modern game hardware introduces the concept of a **sprite**. A sprite is a small action object that moves about a background image. The background can consist of a series of sprite tiles. In this next program sample, I have created a flying saucer sprite. The saucer flies about the screen, bouncing off the sides of the screen.

Under Windows, an approach that works well is to **simulate** the video page switch by using an off-screen bitmap for drawing. While the user is viewing the current screen, in the memory DC, redraw the scene with the next position of the moving object and then **BitBlt** the altered portion onto the screen, avoiding the flicker. Obviously, one could and should create a fully functional Sprite Animation class system. However, because of space and time constraints, a simpler example illustrates the basic effect.

Figure 14.3 **Pgm14c** Animation Action - Saucer Moving Around the Earth

Pgm14c illustrates the basic principles of animation via both the XOR and the off-screen buffer approach. The sample program has been kept very simplistic so that the difference between the two methods can be readily observed. The animation is a flying saucer that circles the planet or "tank pong" with a saucer. (I have a penchant for the old Tank Pong arcade game.) Figure 14.3 shows **Pgm14c** in operation. The earth forms the background and the small flying saucer moves about the screen.

The program begins by using XOR logic to display the moving sprite ship. The user controls the speed by using the up or down arrows. A beep sounds to let the user to know when the slowest timer value (1 millisecond) has been reached. If the down arrow is pressed after that, then the program then switches over to a different approach to obtain even faster action. Again the up and down arrow can adjust the speed in this fast action scenario. When the absolute fastest speed is achieved, any further attempt to decrease the rate also sounds the beep. (The flying saucer appears then more like a ray gun!)

To switch over to the smooth move mode, the user can at any time press the right arrow key. The program resets back to using the timer with a 10-millisecond delay. Again, the speed is adjusted by the up and down arrows. When a decrease below the fastest possible timer is requested, the program again shifts into fast action that is similarly controlled by the user. The beep sounds as the change is made and sounds again whenever there is a request to go faster than the fastest possible speed. If the right arrow key is pressed again, the program switches back to using the XOR method.

The program requires minimal resources: two bitmaps. The earth bitmap serves as the background and is stored as a DIB in **Back.bmp**. **Saucer.bmp** is a small bitmap that was created with the Resource Editor and is supposed to represent a flying saucer. I load in the larger **Back.bmp** as a DIB but include the **Saucer.bmp** and its mask **Saucerm.bmp** as DDBs in the resource file. I chose this route because the sprites are very small while the background image is large and would make the exe file much larger if it was also included as a DDB.

XOR Images and Transparent Backgrounds

Before we begin to examine the application coding, let's discuss how the program operates and see the need for some new functions. The program begins using the fast XOR logic to paint the saucer. The cycle of action begins by drawing the saucer at position 1 by XORing the saucer's color bits with the background's color bits. The program pauses for the requisite time. When the time has elapsed, the ship is erased by redrawing the saucer at the original position 1 by again XORing the bits. The saucer is moved to position 2 and redrawn using XOR logic. Remember that doing two XOR operations on the same objects results in the original color returning.

```
background color          0 0 0 1
ship color                0 1 0 0 XOR
                          -------
new resultant color       0 1 0 1
ship color                0 1 0 0 XOR
                          -------
original background color 0 0 0 1
```

While quite fast, this XOR method has one major drawback—the resultant color is neither that of the ship nor that of the background. Thus, as the ship moves over the earth, the ship is rendered in **unusual** colors. Likewise, the continual direct updating of the screen causes the image to flicker. This XOR color effect is illustrated in the next figure, Figure 14.4.

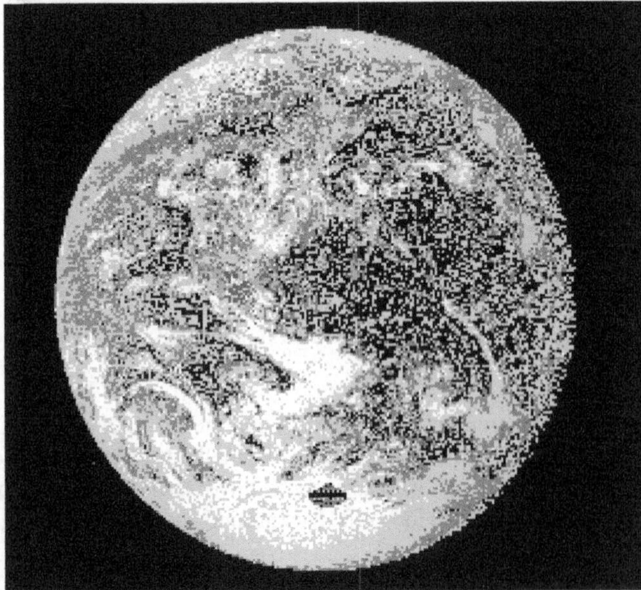

Figure 14.4 The XOR Image of the Saucer Image

By using a smooth move approach with an off-screen buffer, the flicker is removed. Smooth moving utilizes off-screen memory DCs to construct the final image that is then **BitBlt**ed once onto the screen.

I could have removed the XOR flicker by using a memory DC to construct the final images, but the objectionable resultant color problem made it seem hardly worth the effort.

AND-OR logic is combined in order to render the object's true colors onto the background image. The key to the whole operation is to have the saucer's background color become **transparent**. If you just **BitBlt** (**SRCCOPY**) the saucer's image onto the background, that area of the rectangular saucer bitmap, here black, overlays the background, here the earth yielding a completely useless result. Instead, we need to have the background image's colors replace the transparent pixels of the saucer image. How do you make the saucer's background color transparent over the earth's image? The transparent effect is accomplished by making all pixels that are to be transparent a specific color that is not used as a real color in the saucer image rendering.

In this case, I made the background around the saucer black; thus, black is in this case the transparent color. The process to render the ship requires two steps. First, we must make a "hole" in the background image where the actual pixels of the saucer image are to be seen. Second, we can then copy in only those saucer image pixels that are not transparent. In order to make the "hole," construct a copy of the saucer bitmap and make the black background white and make all colors of the saucer black; this becomes the **mask**. The monochrome **mask** with the white background and black ship image is then ANDed onto the background image, producing a "hole" in the background, silhouetting the ship. AND logic permits any background image colors to remain wherever there is white in the mask. But because the saucer proper is black, or color 0, AND logic results in a color 0 appearing, masking out the background image color.

```
                       pel 1    pel 2
background colors      0001     0001
ship mask              1111     0000   white & black pels ANDed SCRAND
                       ----     ----
resultant background 0001     0000
ship proper            0000     1100   black & yellow pels ORed SCRPAINT
                       ----     ----
final image result     0001     1100
```

Here pel 1 of the real background image which is going to be overlain by the background of the saucer's image retains the real background image's color. Pel 2 which is to become part of the actual saucer has its original background image's color removed and the saucer's color inserted.

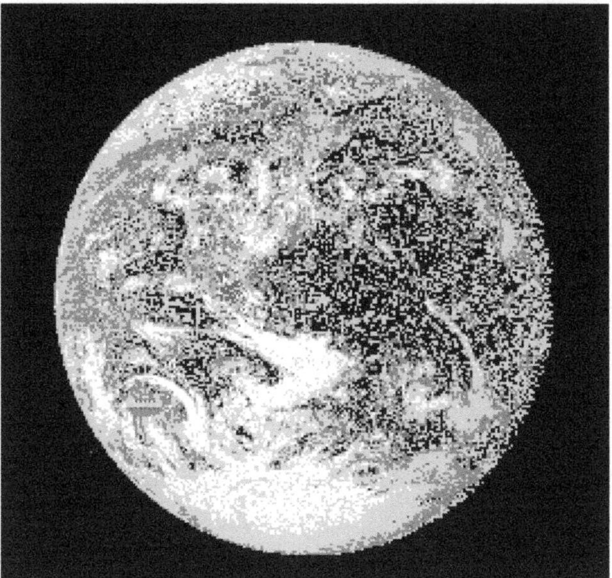

Figure 14.5 The Transparent Saucer Image

Thus, it is quite simple to overlay one background image with another image whose background becomes transparent. Paint the background of the overlaying image black; copy the image and paint the background white and change all colors to white; this becomes the mask. AND the mask onto the background image then OR the overlay image. Figure 14.5 shows what the transparent saucer looks like.

Creating Faster Action: Beyond Windows Timers

The sample program begins in the XOR mode using the Windows timer. When the timer goes off, the ship is moved one pixel in both the x and y direction for smooth animation. (You can experiment with the basic values of **dx** and **dy**, the incremental values, and observe the increasing jerkiness of the animation.) Since the timer has at best 1 millisecond response, only slow motion effects can be displayed. The program begins with a 10-millisecond delay.

The speed of the delay can be controlled by the user through an elementary user interface. By pressing the down arrow, the timing rate is decreased 1 millisecond. By pressing the up arrow, the rate is increased by 1 millisecond. As you will see when you run the program, using the timer is acceptable only for slower motion effects.

To gain a higher motion level or faster movement, the built-in timer is bypassed. The fastest possible motion for a specific image setup under Windows could be represented by the following loop.

```
while (TRUE) {
 get new position
 show at new position
}
```

Of course there is one fatal flaw in such an implementation; it is endless. Under Windows, it is even worse. In such a loop, all other Windows messages begin to pile up in the queue, since the routine never ends. The user may be quite frustrated since the only way to stop the program loop would be to use Ctl-Alt-Del and have Windows Task Manager abort the program.

This situation or a related one is actually often encountered in Windows programming. The program enters a long sequence that requires a good deal of time to accomplish. How can we avoid "locking up" the machine or "backlogging the message queue" while the work is being done? We need a method to yield some CPU time back to Windows and the user as well as a way to have the user halt operations. The **CWinApp** provides just such a function for us, **PumpMessage**. **PumpMessage** yields some processing time back to Windows and the MFC functions. Specifically, it checks the message queue and handles any messages in the queue before returning back to the caller.

While in our endless loop, we can insert this new function call.

```
while (TRUE) {
 get new position
 show at new position
 AfxGetApp()->PumpMessage();
}
```

Pgm14c: Timer and Fast Animation

Since the background is a large BMP file, a DIB, I once more re-use the **CDib** class from **Pgm09b**. Recall that this class handles the inputting of BMP files into a memory DIB structure. Once in memory, use **SetDIBits** to convert the DIB into a DDB for fast display.

The required resources are minimal; a window caption, the folder that contains the files, and the bmp files. Here is the relevant portion of the **Pgm14c.rc** file. From the string table, notice that there are two possible captions, one for XOR action and one for Smooth Move action.

```
/////////////////////////////////////////////////////////////////////////////
//
// Bitmap
//
IDB_SHIP                BITMAP  MOVEABLE PURE    "saucer.bmp"
IDB_SHIPMASK            BITMAP  MOVEABLE PURE    "saucerm.bmp"
/////////////////////////////////////////////////////////////////////////////
//
// String Table
//
```

```
STRINGTABLE DISCARDABLE
BEGIN
    IDS_MAINTITLE          "XOR Animation - Up/Down Arrow adjust speed - Right =>
Smooth Move"
    IDS_BACK                "back.bmp"
    IDS_MAINTITLE2         "XOR Animation - Up/Down Arrow adjust speed - Right =>
XOR Move"
END
```

Here is the **FrameWin** definition.

FrameWin.h Definition File

```
#pragma once

#include "CDib.h"

/*************************************************************/
/*                                                           */
/* FrameWin Class Definition: Animate Spaceship XOR style    */
/*                                                           */
/*************************************************************/

class FrameWin : public CFrameWnd {

 /************************************************************/
 /*                                                          */
 /* Data Members                                             */
 /*                                                          */
 /************************************************************/

protected:
bool        first;
CDib*       ptrdib;          // the dib for the bmp file background
HDC         hdc;             // handle to client dc compatible dc
CClientDC*  ptrclientdc;     // client dc for displaying action
CDC*        ptrbackmemdc;    // memory dc for drawing bkground
CDC*        ptrshipmemdc;    // memory dc for drawing ship
CDC*        ptrshipmaskmemdc;// memory dc for drawing shipmask
CDC*        ptrmovememdc;    // memory dc for drawing bkground
CBitmap*    ptrbackbitmap;   // bitmap of background
CBitmap*    ptrshipbitmap;   // bitmap of ship
CBitmap*    ptrmovebitmap;   // work bitmap for smooth move
CBitmap*    ptrshipmaskbitmap;// bitmap of ship in mask format

CRect       dimrect;         // dimensions of the space ship
CRect       shiprect;        // position of the space ship
int         dx, dy;          // amount to move the ship each time
int         rate;            // controls the speed rate of action
bool        usetimer;        // true when timer is being used
bool        smoothmove;      // true when smooth move is in effect
int         shipheight;      // ship bitmap dimensions
int         shipwidth;

bool      canclose; // when true we can close while in fast action

 /************************************************************/
 /*                                                          */
 /* Functions:                                               */
 /*                                                          */
 /************************************************************/

public:
               FrameWin ();        // constructor
afx_msg void OnPaint ();           // also handles fast move requests
```

```
virtual BOOL DestroyWindow (); // remove GDI objects

protected:
afx_msg int  OnCreate (LPCREATESTRUCT);// load bitmaps and memdcs
afx_msg void OnTimer (UINT);          //process slow move requests
afx_msg void OnSize (UINT, int, int);// set initial ship position
afx_msg void OnClose ();              // shut down

// the user interface = arrow keys
afx_msg void OnKeyDown (UINT, UINT, UINT);

        // helper functions
        void CheckDims ();    // moves ship and handles collisions
        void SmoothMove ();   // perform smooth movement of ship
        void XORMove ();      // perform XOR movement of ship
        void BuildBitmaps ();// load bitmaps and start the action
        void Render ();       // render the images
        void Fast ();         // display fastest possible action

DECLARE_MESSAGE_MAP()
};
```

The class definition defines several GDI member objects. The **ptrclientdc** provides access to the client window upon which the animation is seen. The animation uses a memory DC for the background bitmap and for the ship's bitmap. Additionally, the smooth move operation needs a scratch DC upon which to make needed changes, copying the alterations to the **ptrclientdc**. Each memory DC also must have a corresponding bitmap. To construct the memory DCs as compatible to the client DC, the **CreateCompatibleDC** function is required. The member **hdc** is used to contain this compatible DC for use in construction of the other three memory DCs. When the program is finished, the **hdc** can be deleted. Failure to do so results in a memory leak.

The current ship's location is contained in the **shiprect**. I assume that the center of the ship bitmap is the current position. To avoid having half of the ship going off the edge of the screen while the remainder is visible, the rectangle **dimrect** contains the altered dimensions of the screen. For example, if the upper left client area coordinate is 0 pixels and the ship is 20 pixels wide, then the **dimrect**'s upper left coordinate would be set to 10. To get the correct client area dimensions, **OnSize** is used.

The members **dx** and **dy** hold the current number of pixels to move the ship. Initially they are both one pixel for the smoothest animation. Whenever there is a collision with a border, the offending rate is negated, pong style. I have set these two variables to one pixel for the smoothest effect. You should alter these to larger values to really see the differences between the XOR and smooth move methods.

When **usetimer** is **true**, the Windows timer is in use; when **false**, our faster method is in use. When **smoothmove** is **true**, the final image is constructed in the move DC and the altered area is copied back onto the screen. Here is the implementation of the **FrameWin**.

FrameWin.cpp Implementation File

```
#include "stdafx.h"
#include "FrameWin.h"
#include "resource.h"
#include "Pgm14c.h"

/*****************************************************************/
/*                                                               */
/* Message Map                                                   */
/*                                                               */
/*****************************************************************/

BEGIN_MESSAGE_MAP(FrameWin, CFrameWnd)
 ON_WM_KEYDOWN()
```

```
 ON_WM_CREATE()
 ON_WM_SIZE ()
 ON_WM_TIMER()
 ON_WM_PAINT()
 ON_WM_CLOSE()
END_MESSAGE_MAP()

#define TIMERID      1  // normal action timer
#define TIMERCLOSEID 2  // close down while in fast action timer

/***************************************************************/
/*                                                             */
/* FrameWin: init all GDI objects                              */
/*                                                             */
/***************************************************************/

FrameWin::FrameWin () {
 ptrdib        = 0;
 ptrbackbitmap = 0;
 ptrmovebitmap = 0;
 ptrshipbitmap = 0;
 ptrbackmemdc  = 0;
 ptrshipmemdc  = 0;
 ptrshipmaskbitmap = 0;
 ptrshipmaskmemdc  = 0;

 rate          = 10;    // set for 10 millisec delay
 usetimer      = true;  // begin using timer
 smoothmove    = false; // begin using XOR logic
 first         = true;  // set no GDI setup yet
 shipheight    = 0;     // and no ship setup yet
 canclose      = true;  // indicate can close -not in fast action

 CString title;
 title.LoadString (IDS_MAINTITLE);
 Create (AfxRegisterWndClass (
             CS_VREDRAW | CS_HREDRAW,
             AfxGetApp()->LoadStandardCursor (IDC_ARROW),
             (HBRUSH) GetStockObject (LTGRAY_BRUSH),
             AfxGetApp()->LoadStandardIcon (IDI_APPLICATION)),
         title, WS_OVERLAPPEDWINDOW, CRect (0,0,640,480), 0, 0);
}

/***************************************************************/
/*                                                             */
/* OnCreate: build the memory dc and bitmap and drawing once   */
/*                                                             */
/***************************************************************/

int FrameWin::OnCreate (LPCREATESTRUCT lpCS) {
 if (CFrameWnd::OnCreate (lpCS) == -1) return -1;
 BuildBitmaps ();
 return 0;
}

/***************************************************************/
/*                                                             */
/* BuildBitmaps: loads, constructs bitmaps - starts timer      */
/*                                                             */
/***************************************************************/

void FrameWin::BuildBitmaps () {
 // create DCs for client, backgrnd, ship, and smooth move
 // construct the bitmaps of the background, smooth move work,
```

```
// and the flying saucer and the background dib from BACK.BMP
CRect r;
GetClientRect (&r);
CString filename;
CRect dibrect;
filename.LoadString (IDS_BACK);
// attempt to load the file into a dib
ptrdib = new CDib (filename);
if (!ptrdib) {
 MessageBox("Cannot load in BACK.BMP file",
            "Error In Construction", MB_OK);
 PostMessage (WM_QUIT);
}
// set up the dib size in a rectangle
dibrect.left = dibrect.top = 0;
dibrect.right = ptrdib->GetDibWidth();
dibrect.bottom = ptrdib->GetDibHeight();
CClientDC dc (this); // dc to copy

// copy to back memory set
ptrbackmemdc = new CDC;                    // the memory dc
ptrbackmemdc->CreateCompatibleDC (&dc);  // copy client dc
ptrbackbitmap = new CBitmap ();            // create bm for memdc
ptrbackbitmap->CreateCompatibleBitmap (&dc, dibrect.Width(),
                                            dibrect.Height());
// copy dib bits into bm
SetDIBits (ptrbackmemdc->m_hDC,
           (HBITMAP) (ptrbackbitmap->m_hObject), 0,
           dibrect.Height(), ptrdib->GetDibBitsAddr (),
           ptrdib->GetBitmapInfo (), DIB_RGB_COLORS);

// copy to smooth move memory set
ptrmovememdc = new CDC;
ptrmovememdc->CreateCompatibleDC (&dc);
ptrmovebitmap = new CBitmap ();            // create bm for memdc
ptrmovebitmap->CreateCompatibleBitmap (&dc, dibrect.Width(),
                                            dibrect.Height());
// copy dib bits into bm
SetDIBits (ptrmovememdc->m_hDC,
           (HBITMAP) (ptrmovebitmap->m_hObject), 0,
           dibrect.Height(), ptrdib->GetDibBitsAddr (),
           ptrdib->GetBitmapInfo (), DIB_RGB_COLORS);

// load in the ship memory set
ptrshipmemdc = new CDC;
ptrshipmemdc->CreateCompatibleDC (&dc);
ptrshipbitmap = new CBitmap ();
ptrshipbitmap->LoadBitmap (IDB_SHIP);
BITMAP bm;
::GetObject (ptrshipbitmap->m_hObject, sizeof(bm), &bm);
shipheight = bm.bmHeight;
shipwidth = bm.bmWidth;

// load in the ship mask memory set
ptrshipmaskmemdc = new CDC;
ptrshipmaskmemdc->CreateCompatibleDC (&dc);
ptrshipmaskbitmap = new CBitmap ();
ptrshipmaskbitmap->LoadBitmap (IDB_SHIPMASK);

// ship's position is measured from center of ship's bitmap,
// so adjust the real border of screen, dimrect, to account
// for the ship
dimrect.top    = shipheight / 2;
dimrect.bottom = r.bottom - shipheight / 2;
```

```
 dimrect.left   = shipwidth / 2;
 dimrect.right  = r.right - shipwidth / 2;

 // set ship to initial position
 // the location is actually centered at 110,110
 shiprect.top    = 100;
 shiprect.left   = 100;
 shiprect.bottom = shiprect.top + shipheight;
 shiprect.right  = shiprect.left + shipwidth;

 // set both incremental values to 1 pixel per move
 dx = dy = 1;

 ptrclientdc = new CClientDC (this);
 if (!ptrbackmemdc     || !ptrbackbitmap ||
     !ptrmovememdc     || !ptrmovebitmap ||
     !ptrshipmemdc     || !ptrshipbitmap ||
     !ptrshipmaskmemdc || !ptrshipmaskbitmap) {
  MessageBox("Cannot create MemoryDCs and Bitmaps",
             "Error In Construction", MB_OK);
  PostMessage (WM_QUIT);
 }

 // install background in back dc
 ptrbackmemdc->SelectObject (ptrbackbitmap);
 // install background in move dc
 ptrmovememdc->SelectObject (ptrmovebitmap);
 // install ship image in ship dc
 ptrshipmemdc->SelectObject (ptrshipbitmap);
 // install ship mask
 ptrshipmaskmemdc->SelectObject (ptrshipmaskbitmap);

 delete ptrdib;
 ptrdib = 0;

 // display ship at the starting point copy background to screen
 ptrclientdc->BitBlt (0, 0, r.right, r.bottom, ptrbackmemdc,
                      0, 0, SRCCOPY);

 // place ship on screen
 ptrclientdc->BitBlt(shiprect.left, shiprect.top, shiprect.right,
                 shiprect.bottom, ptrshipmemdc, 0, 0, SRCINVERT);

 // turn on timer for XOR action
 SetTimer (TIMERID, rate, NULL);
 first = false;
 return;
}

/**************************************************************/
/*                                                            */
/* DestroyWindow: remove all GDI Objects                      */
/*                                                            */
/**************************************************************/

BOOL        FrameWin::DestroyWindow () {
 // if timer still operating, kill it
 if (usetimer)      KillTimer (TIMERID);
 if (ptrdib)        delete ptrdib;
 if (ptrclientdc)   delete ptrclientdc;
 if (ptrmovememdc)  delete ptrmovememdc;
 if (ptrbackmemdc)  delete ptrbackmemdc;
 if (ptrbackbitmap) delete ptrbackbitmap;
 if (ptrmovebitmap) delete ptrmovebitmap;
```

```
 if (ptrshipbitmap) {
  ptrshipbitmap->DeleteObject ();
  delete ptrshipbitmap;
 }
 if (ptrshipmemdc)  delete ptrshipmemdc;
 if (ptrshipmaskbitmap) {
  ptrshipmaskbitmap->DeleteObject ();
  delete ptrshipmaskbitmap;
 }
 if (ptrshipmaskmemdc)  delete ptrshipmaskmemdc;
 return CFrameWnd::DestroyWindow ();
}

/**************************************************************/
/*                                                            */
/* OnSize: determine client rect size and adjust border endpts */
/*         and initially display the ship at its starting pos  */
/*                                                            */
/**************************************************************/

void FrameWin::OnSize (UINT, int cx, int cy) {
 // avoid if it is the first time
 if ((cx==0 && cy==0) || first) return;
 if (shipheight == 0) return; // avoid if not setup

// ship's position is measured from center of ship's bitmap, so
// adjust real border of screen, dimrect, to account for the ship
 dimrect.top    = shipheight / 2;
 dimrect.bottom = cy - shipheight / 2;
 dimrect.left   = shipwidth / 2;
 dimrect.right  = cx - shipwidth / 2;

 // here the window really has been resized, so start at
 // the beginning position - display ship at the starting point
 // copy background to screen
 ptrclientdc->BitBlt (0, 0, cx, cy, ptrbackmemdc, 0, 0, SRCCOPY);

 // place ship on screen
 ptrclientdc->BitBlt(shiprect.left, shiprect.top, shiprect.right,
                     shiprect.bottom, ptrshipmemdc, 0, 0, SRCINVERT);
}

/**************************************************************/
/*                                                            */
/* OnTimer: plot next position and show                       */
/*                                                            */
/**************************************************************/

void FrameWin::OnTimer (UINT id) {
 // if we are closing down during fast action,
 if (id == TIMERCLOSEID) {
  KillTimer (TIMERCLOSEID);  // kill the timer
  // indicate it is now safe to close down
  canclose = true;
  // and post another close down message
  PostMessage (WM_CLOSE, 0, 0);
  return;
 }

 // normal action timer event
 if (first) return;
 Invalidate (FALSE);
}

```

```

/***************************************************************/
/*                                                             */
/* XORMove: using XOR, move the ship one pixel                 */
/*                                                             */
/***************************************************************/

void FrameWin::XORMove () {
 // remove old ship
 ptrclientdc->BitBlt(shiprect.left, shiprect.top, shiprect.right,
                shiprect.bottom, ptrshipmemdc, 0, 0, SRCINVERT);
 // move ship to new position
 CheckDims ();
 // display ship at new position
 ptrclientdc->BitBlt(shiprect.left, shiprect.top, shiprect.right,
                shiprect.bottom, ptrshipmemdc, 0, 0, SRCINVERT);
}

/***************************************************************/
/*                                                             */
/* SmoothMove: move ship one pixel by off-screen drawing       */
/*                                                             */
/***************************************************************/

void FrameWin::SmoothMove () {
 // set offset of ship in backgrnd
 // replace the ship with the original background
 ptrmovememdc->BitBlt (shiprect.left, shiprect.top,
    shiprect.right, shiprect.bottom, ptrbackmemdc, shiprect.left,
    shiprect.top, SRCCOPY);

 // move the ship
 CheckDims ();

 // AND a hole in the move bm then OR in the new ship image
 ptrmovememdc->BitBlt(shiprect.left, shiprect.top,shiprect.right,
               shiprect.bottom, ptrshipmaskmemdc, 0, 0, SRCAND);
 ptrmovememdc->BitBlt(shiprect.left, shiprect.top,shiprect.right,
                shiprect.bottom, ptrshipmemdc, 0, 0, SRCPAINT);

 // calculate maximum possible affected area to replace on screen
 CRect newrect;
 newrect = shiprect;
 newrect.InflateRect (abs(dx), abs(dy));

 // set offset of affected area in move bitmap
 // copy affected area to screen
 ptrclientdc->BitBlt (newrect.left, newrect.top, newrect.right,
                      newrect.bottom, ptrmovememdc, newrect.left,
                      newrect.top, SRCCOPY);
}

/***************************************************************/
/*                                                             */
/* CheckDims: increments ship position by dx,dy                */
/*            check & handle collisions                        */
/*                                                             */
/***************************************************************/

void FrameWin::CheckDims () {
 // get new position by offsetting the rectangle by dx,dy values
 shiprect.OffsetRect (dx, dy);

 // check for collision with the top and bottom
```

```
 if (shiprect.top <= dimrect.top) { // hit top
  shiprect.top = dimrect.top;
  shiprect.bottom = shiprect.top + shipheight;
  dy = -dy; // reverse direction
 }
 else if (shiprect.bottom >= dimrect.bottom) { // hit bottom
  shiprect.bottom = dimrect.bottom;
  shiprect.top = shiprect.bottom - shipheight;
  dy = -dy; // reverse direction
 }

 // check for collisions with the left and right sides
 if (shiprect.left <= dimrect.left) { // hit left
  shiprect.left = dimrect.left;
  shiprect.right = shiprect.left + shipwidth;
  dx = -dx; // reverse direction
 }
 else if (shiprect.right >= dimrect.right) { // hit right
  shiprect.right = dimrect.right;
  shiprect.left = shiprect.right - shipwidth;
  dx = -dx; // reverse direction
 }
}

/*****************************************************************/
/*                                                               */
/* OnKeyDown: handle user requests for speed up/down and for    */
/*            switching between smooth move and xor versions    */
/*                                                               */
/*****************************************************************/

void FrameWin::OnKeyDown (UINT key, UINT, UINT) {
 if (first) return; // avoid operations before images are loaded

 if (key == VK_RIGHT) { // switch smooth/xor types
  if (usetimer) KillTimer (TIMERID); // kill any timer operating
  else usetimer = true;              // if not, set using a timer
  canclose = true;         // normal action, so can close anytime
  rate = 10;               // reset rate to initial starting value
  CString title;
  if (!smoothmove) {   // check for go into smooth move mode
   smoothmove = true;  // enable smooth move
   title.LoadString (IDS_MAINTITLE2);
   SetWindowText (title);
   // copy the ship's initial pos into the initial move bitmap
   ptrmovememdc->BitBlt (shiprect.left, shiprect.top,
                         shiprect.right, shiprect.bottom,
                         ptrshipmemdc, 0, 0, SRCPAINT);
   // copy the move image onto the screen
   ptrclientdc->BitBlt (shiprect.left, shiprect.top,
                        shiprect.right, shiprect.bottom,
             ptrmovememdc, shiprect.left, shiprect.top, SRCCOPY);
  }
  else { // switch to XOR move
   smoothmove = false; // enable smooth move
   title.LoadString (IDS_MAINTITLE);
   SetWindowText (title);
   // copy background to screen
   CRect r;
   GetClientRect (&r);
   ptrclientdc->BitBlt (0, 0, r.right, r.bottom, ptrbackmemdc,
                        0, 0, SRCCOPY);
   // place ship on screen
   ptrclientdc->BitBlt (shiprect.left, shiprect.top,
```

```
                          shiprect.right, shiprect.bottom,
                          ptrshipmemdc, 0, 0, SRCINVERT);
   }
   SetTimer (TIMERID, rate, NULL); // reactivate the timer
   return;
  }

  // process user speed up or slow down requests
  if (key == VK_UP)          // speed up
   if (usetimer) {           // and timer in effect
    KillTimer (TIMERID);     // remove old timer
    // install new timer with increased rate
    SetTimer (TIMERID, ++rate, NULL);
    canclose = true;         // normal action, so can close
   }
   else { // not using timer
    rate += 4000;            // increase delay by 4000
    canclose = false;        // now cannot close at once
   }

  else if (key == VK_DOWN) { // slow down
   if (usetimer) {           // and timer in effect
    rate--;                  // lower time
    if (rate == 0) {         // and if rate now hits 0,
     KillTimer (TIMERID);    // kill timer
     // warning so we know when fast action begins
     MessageBeep (0);
     rate = 500;             // fast loop rate
     usetimer = false;       // signal timer not in use
     canclose = false;       // fast action, so cannot close at once
     Fast ();
    }
    else {                   // slow down the timer
     KillTimer (TIMERID);    // remove old timer
     SetTimer (TIMERID, rate, NULL);  // install new timer
    }
   }
   else {                    // slow down and fast action in effect
    rate -= 4000;            // lower by 10
    if (rate<1) {            // do not let rate go below 1
     rate = 1;
     // sound warning so we know when going fastest
     MessageBeep (0);
    }
   }
  }
}

/*****************************************************************/
/*                                                               */
/* Render: draw the new images                                   */
/*                                                               */
/*****************************************************************/

void FrameWin::Render () {
 if (!smoothmove) XORMove (); // process new XOR position
 else SmoothMove ();          // process new smooth move
}

/*****************************************************************/
/*                                                               */
/* Fast: handle the fastest possible action                      */
/*                                                               */
/*****************************************************************/
```

```
void FrameWin::Fast () {
 DWORD x; // fields for the delay action
 int i;
 while (!usetimer) { // terminated by user keybd or mouse events
  // the small delay
  i = 0; x = 1;
  while (i<rate) {x *= 2; i++;}

  Invalidate (FALSE);           // display new images
  AfxGetApp()->PumpMessage (); // stall a brief bit of time
 }
}

/*******************************************************************/
/*                                                                 */
/* OnPaint: render the images                                      */
/*                                                                 */
/*******************************************************************/

void FrameWin::OnPaint () {
 CPaintDC dc (this);            // create a paint dc
 Render ();
}

/*******************************************************************/
/*                                                                 */
/* OnClose: gracefully shut down                                   */
/*                                                                 */
/*******************************************************************/

void FrameWin::OnClose () {
 if (usetimer)
  KillTimer (TIMERID);        // kill any user timer
 usetimer = true;
 // if coming from fast action Paint, give the system time to
 // finish the paint processing before closing down
 if (canclose)
  CFrameWnd::OnClose ();  // if it's safe to close, close
 else                      // if it's not, wait a moment
  SetTimer (TIMERCLOSEID, 100, NULL);
}
```

The **FrameWin** constructor sets all of the object pointers to zero and calls the **Create** function as usual. The initial situation uses the built-in timer with 10 milliseconds in XOR mode (**smoothmove** is **false**). Since the bitmaps have not been loaded yet, the **shipheight** is set to zero. The member **canclose** is used to help close the application down while it is in the fast move mode; when it is **true**, the application can shut down normally in response to **WM_CLOSE**.

All objects and any active timer are removed in **DestroyWindow**. **OnSize** is invoked several times as the application launches, once with zero dimensions and then, as the window is set up, with the correct dimensions. Since the bitmaps are not loaded until after the call to **OnCreate**'s base class, the size function returns if the dimensions are zero or if the ship height is still zero. Any other calls to **OnSize** represent resize operations while the action is ongoing. These must be handled by recalculating the overall **dimrect**, the action dimensions rectangle, and then **BitBlt**ing the background image and the saucer onto the resized client area.

As the window is coming up, the first action occurs in **OnCreate** which calls **BuildBitmaps** to load the images. **BuildBitmaps** is a rather long sequence. First, it loads the main background bitmap into an instance of **CDib** and initializes the **dibrect** rectangle to contain the DIB's dimensions. Next, a pair of memory DCs are created to hold the background image and the smooth move image—both of which must contain a copy of the background DIB. The image is copied using **SetDIBits**. The memory DC for the saucer is built and the saucer image is loaded. Notice that I stored the saucer as a DDB in the resource file because it is very small and to illustrate the differences between loading a DIB and a DDB. The saucer ship is actually two images—the saucer and its monochrome mask.

With the saucer image loaded and its size known, the **dimrect** or dimensions rectangle representing the actual range of motion can be calculated. The full window area cannot be used; the ship would appear to leave the screen before it "bounced" back. I reduce the dimensions rectangle from full client area by one-half of the height and width of the saucer. The ship's initial position is set in the **shiprect** rectangle and the amount to increment the (x, y) motion, **dx** and **dy**, are set to one pixel each. Notice that this gives the best motion effect. Try altering these to larger values and observe the "jerkier" motion.

If all has gone well, the four bitmaps are inserted into their respective memory DCs; the background **BitBlt**ed to the screen followed by the saucer at its initial position. Notice that the background **BitBlt** uses **SCRCOPY** while the saucer **BitBlt** uses **SRCINVERT**, which is the XOR mode. The timer is then set and the action commences. The **bool first** is used to track whether or not the images have yet been loaded so that other functions do not attempt to perform actions on nonexistent objects not yet loaded.

In **OnTimer**, ignoring for the moment the problem of fast action, when the timer goes off, the window is invalidated but the background is **not** repainted.

```
Invalidate (FALSE);
```

OnPaint does nothing more than call the **Render** helper function. **Render** calls either **XORMove** or **SmoothMove** to process the motion. Initially, XOR logic is used.

The **XORMove** procedure is quite simple. First, a **BitBlt** is used displaying the ship at the same location as before, using **SRCINVERT** or XOR; the ship disappears. Then, **CheckDims** moves the ship and checks for and processes any collisions with the window border. Finally, the ship is again **BitBlt**ed using XOR so that it appears at its new position.

CheckDims moves the ship. How? The **CRect shiprect** contains the position and size of the saucer. The increments, **dx** and **dy**, are added to all four rectangle members by using a **CRect** function, **OffsetRect**, which is a convenient method to add values to the rectangle's members. **Offset** adds the **dx** and **dy** values to all rectangle coordinates, effectively moving the center position. Next, collisions with the four screen edges are check for and handled by reversing direction.

For **SmoothMove**, the move DC and bitmap contain the ship at its current position. First, **BitBlt** with **SCRCOPY** copies the original background over that portion of the image occupied by the ship, removing the ship. **CheckDims** moves the ship, handling any collisions. **BitBlt** copies the ship onto the move DC and bitmap. Using the procedure described above, the ship mask is ANDed with the background, producing a black hole where the ship will be. Then, the ship is ORed onto the background, filling in the hole with the ship's colors. **SRCAND** is the ROP for AND while **SRCPAINT** is the ROP for an OR.

Since we do not necessarily know which direction the ship has moved, the onscreen rectangle is set up to be the size of the ship rectangle plus the absolute values of the **dx** and **dy** members. The **InflatedRect** function of the **CRect** class extends the bounds of the rectangle by adding/subtracting the x and y amounts from the current bounds. So **newrect** covers all possible movement directions. Lastly, a **BitBlt** copies the **newrect** area from the move DC onto the screen, producing the illusion of smooth movement.

The **OnKeyDown** user interface is the most complicated portion. If the right arrow is pressed, then a switch between the two modes is done. Any current timer must be halted. If no timer was in use, **usetimer** must be reset along with the rate to the initial speed of 10 milliseconds. For a switch to smooth move, the move DC can now be initialized by drawing the current ship's position on it and then copied onto the client DC or screen. Once the timer is set, smooth moving automatically commences. For a switch back to XOR moving, the entire background must be redrawn and the ship copied onto the screen.

When the up or down arrow is pressed, the timer must be slowed or speeded up. When no timer is in use, fast action, a different rate increment, is used. When the timer rate hits 0 milliseconds, then the program switches automatically into fast action mode by calling the helper function **Fast**.

Fast delays a very small amount before it calls Invalidate to force a redrawing of the image. Once the image is redrawn, the main message processing loop is checked for new messages. Should the user press on the right arrow key to switch modes, **usetime** is reset to **true** which ends this fast action loop.

```
while (!usetimer) { // terminated by user keybd or mouse events
  // the small delay
  i = 0; x = 1;
  while (i<rate) {x *= 2; i++;}
  Invalidate (FALSE);          // display new images
  AfxGetApp()->PumpMessage (); // stall a brief bit of time
}
```

When the fast action sequence is in effect (not the normal timer), we are in a very tight loop here. If the user attempts to terminate the application, we need a way to gracefully force the termination of this fast loop by setting **usetimer** back to **true** and give this **Fast** function a little time to return. To facilitate this, in **OnClose** check the **canclose bool**. If the fast action loop is in effect, then set up a new timer with a special id.

```
if (canclose)
  CFrameWnd::OnClose ();    // if it's safe to close, close
else                        // if it's not, wait a moment
  SetTimer (TIMERCLOSEID, 100, NULL);
```

Then, in **OnTimer**, reset **canclose** and re-post the quit message.

```
if (id == TIMERCLOSEID) {
  KillTimer (TIMERCLOSEID);   // kill the timer
  // indicate it is now safe to close down
  canclose = true;
  // and post another close down message
  PostMessage (WM_CLOSE, 0, 0);
  return;
}
```

This time, **OnClose** terminates the application.

Now go experiment with the **dx** and **dy** members; try a value of four pixels and see the effect on XOR and smooth move. Experiment with the two methods; while XOR requires less GDI, memory, and coding, the motion is jerkier. With the basics of animation understood, you should examine actual OOP implementations as given in the Bibliography.

Animated Presentations

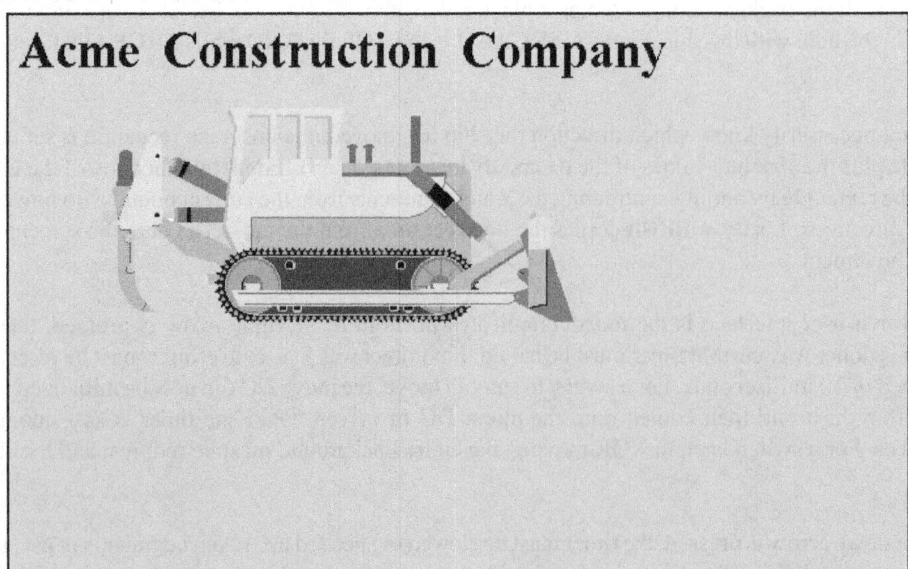

Figure 14.6 **Pgm14d**'s Initial Window Before Images Are Dropped-in

The principles of splash screens and animation can be combined into a form for animated business presentations. First, display the basic background image. Second, using a series of drop-in bitmap files, "smooth move" these bitmap overlays from their initial drop-in positions to their ending locations on the final image. Figure 14.6 shows the initial background image.

Figure 14.7 shows the final screen image in the main window after all of the eleven images have been dropped onto the background.

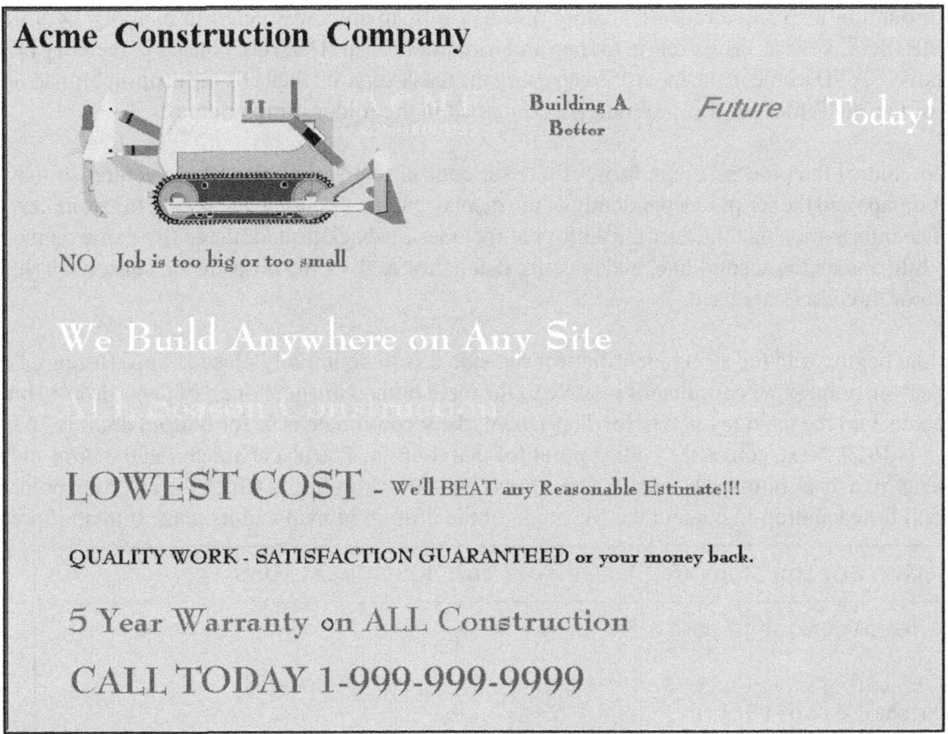

Figure 14.7 The Final Frame Window of **Pgm14d**

Notice that the frame window of this application as shown above in Figure 14.7 does not look like any other frame window in the text. This example also illustrates another type of window design that is useful not only in business presentation applications but also in writing games. Did you notice anything "unusual" about the main application window in Figure 14.7? Look again. There is no menu bar, title bar, control bar or status bar! The application main window occupies the entire screen. Gone are all of the normal window's controls. This application definitely does not fit the Windows look-and-feel which is just what might be desired in a game or animated business presentation. In such circumstances, unless otherwise overridden, Alt-F4 and the usual keyboard task switching still operate. It even overlays Windows task bar across the bottom of the screen.

The user interface is up to us to provide. Keystrokes, mouse clicks, and pop-up menus are used to create the user interface. In **Pgm14d**, both Alt-F4 and a right mouse button click terminate the application via the usual **OnClose** message box, while a left mouse click repeats the presentation.

Again, I have chosen DIBs that only use the standard Windows color palette. Therefore, once more, I have used Method 1 given in Chapter 9 for conversion of a DIB into a memory DC, avoiding the use of **CreateDIBitmap**. Its use, however, would speed up the slow display.

The animated drop-in bitmaps can be dropped into the main image from any of the four sides. If a bitmap is dropped in from the top, it "smooth moves" downward until reaching its predefined location in the final image. Once there, that bitmap is "permanently fixed" on the main bitmap image. Then, the cycle repeats for the next drop-in bitmap. If dropped in on the bottom, it moves up to its ending place. If dropped in on the right side, it moves leftward; if dropped in on the left, it moves rightward. Perhaps the two most useful motions for presentations are top-down and right-left. Once all of the drop-in bitmaps have been placed on the main image bitmap that bitmap becomes available to the main window's **OnPaint**, which in response to a **WM_PAINT** message, **BitBlt**s the final image onto the screen. If a left button click requests a repeat presentation, the main bitmap is replaced by the original background bitmap and the drop-in process continues.

One could add a couple of other details that I did not implement in **Pgm14d**. For real presentations, one could add a "pause before doing the next drop-in" interval to give the presenter say fifteen seconds to discuss the last drop-in. An option to manually control when the next drop-in starts would be useful.

The bitmap construction to smooth move the drop-in bitmaps follows the previous flying saucer example, **Pgm14c**. First, a main background bitmap and an identical smooth move bitmap are constructed in memory DCs from the same original DIB or BMP file. Likewise, each drop-in bitmap and its mask bitmap (DIB) are housed in memory DCs. Each time the drop-in is to "move," AND a hole in the move bitmap using the mask version; then OR the drop-in bitmap image's colors into the hole. (All of the BMP files for this program are contained in the folder **\bmps\demo**.)

In order to control the process, some form of a "user control text script" must be invented so that the user can construct both the bitmaps and the script independently of the display engine. Examine the listing for **Demo.txt** that controls this presentation. The information that the user must provide includes the background image file name on the first line, the number of drop-in bitmaps on the second line, and specific details for each of the drop-ins on subsequent lines. For each drop-in bitmap, two or three lines are used.

The first line begins with the string identifier for the side it is to be initially placed: Top, Bottom, Left, or Right. Next, comes the insertion point (x, y) coordinates relative to the main bitmap image. For all of these drop-in bitmaps, I have started them five pixels into the main image. So for Top-Down, the y coordinate is 5; for bottom up, it is 763; for left, x is 5 pixels; for right, x is 1019. Next, comes the ending point for that drop-in. The last character on the drop-in line is Y or N indicating the presence of a mask bitmap (Y) or not. This allows for static drop-ins, in which the insertion point is the ending point. The last line(s) for each drop-in contain the file name of the drop-in bitmap and its mask bitmap if present.

Demo.txt - the Script Control File for the Presentations

```
..\bmps\demo\demobkgd.bmp
11
Top 380 5 150 Y
..\bmps\demo\dropit0.bmp
..\bmps\demo\dropit0M.bmp
Top 530 5 150 Y
..\bmps\demo\dropit1.bmp
..\bmps\demo\dropit1M.bmp
Top 730 5 150 Y
..\bmps\demo\dropit2.bmp
..\bmps\demo\dropit2M.bmp
Top 880 5 150 Y
..\bmps\demo\dropit3.bmp
..\bmps\demo\dropit3M.bmp
Top 050 5 310 Y
..\bmps\demo\dropit4.bmp
..\bmps\demo\dropit4M.bmp
Bottom 35 763 310 Y
..\bmps\demo\dropit5.bmp
..\bmps\demo\dropit5M.bmp
Right 1019 380 40 Y
..\bmps\demo\dropit6.bmp
..\bmps\demo\dropit6M.bmp
Left 5 470 50 Y
..\bmps\demo\dropit7.bmp
..\bmps\demo\dropit7M.bmp
Right 1019 550 60 Y
..\bmps\demo\dropit8.bmp
..\bmps\demo\dropit8M.bmp
Left 5 610 50 Y
..\bmps\demo\dropit9.bmp
..\bmps\demo\dropit9M.bmp
Top 55 5 750 Y
..\bmps\demo\dropita.bmp
..\bmps\demo\dropitaM.bmp
```

So now we have an elementary presentation script that could be used for any presentation, not just this one. To actually input the variable data, I use the C++ **ifstream** because the extraction operator is most convenient to input these data. The variable number of sets of drop-in bitmap data is handled by dynamically allocating an array of **OBJECTS** structure that contains the definition data.

```
struct OBJECTS {
 char filenameobj[MAX_PATH];
 char filenamemask[MAX_PATH];
 CPoint insert;
 int    end;
 DropType type;
};
```

Provision is made for two filenames; if no mask file is present, its filename is a null string. The insertion coordinates are stored in a **CPoint** object. And the drop-in location is encapsulated into an **enum DropType** that is defined as follows.

```
enum DropType { TopDown, BottomUp, RightLeft, LeftRight };
```

Additionally, since the user is constructing the text file of directions, some bulletproofing should be done. I performed some basic error checking, but feel free to add much more.

The application design includes two main classes, **DisplayObject** and **Presentation**. **DisplayObject** encapsulates all of the actual bitmap operations including the initial loading, performing the smooth move drop-ins, and performing all **BitBlt** operations. The background, smooth move, and all drop-in sets are instances of the **DisplayObject** class. The instances of the move bitmap and all drop-in bitmaps are transitory and are kept only as long as needed to perform the actual animated sequence. The instance of the main background, which also holds the resultant image, is kept to service the main window's paint function. The **Presentation** class loads in the user's text script file and runs the presentation.

Although this presentation assumes a resolution of 1024x768, the size of the main image, smaller than full-screen main bitmaps can be used. I assume that smaller main images are going to be centered. Doing so adds a final coordinate adjustment when bliting the main window onto the screen.

What may not be clear is exactly how the drop-in process actually operates. If an image is dropped in from say five pixels from the top edge of the main window, only a tiny portion of the drop-in bitmap is visible. As it moves downward, more and more of the image becomes visible on the main image, until the entire drop-in bitmap is shown. From now on, the size of the drop-in window does not vary, rather only its position. Figure 14.8 shows these two situations using the variable names I assigned to them in the program.

When copying from the background image to the screen, the **screenoffset** point is used to offset the destination rectangle for the **BitBlt**. All other coordinates are relative to the start of the background bitmap. The lower left corner of the drop-in image is initially placed at **insertpt** at Position 1 in the figure and is to be moved until that point reaches the ending y coordinate indicated by the "X" in the figure. Initially, the **dropin** rectangle may be small; it may even be nonexistent if the drop-in point is not on the initial bitmap. As the image is moved downward, the **dropin** rectangle expands until the full size of the drop-in image is reached. In Position 2, the **dropin** rectangle is at its maximum size.

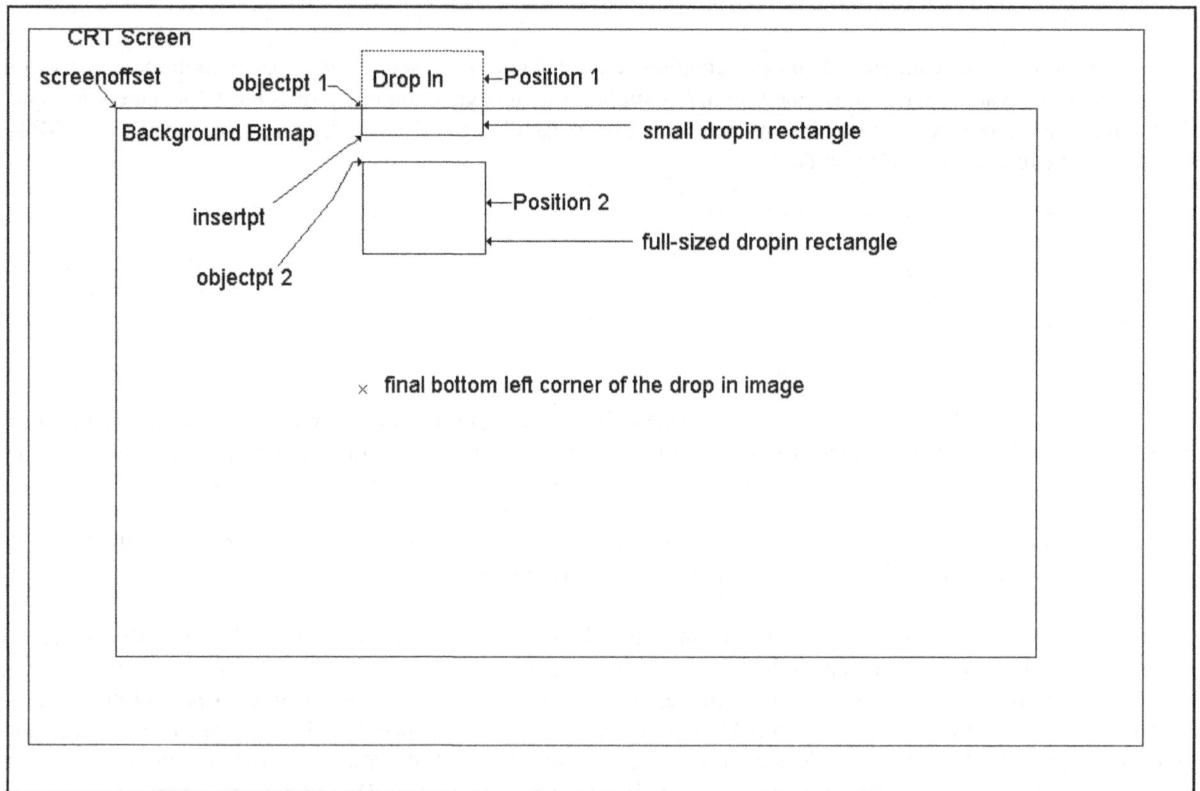

Figure 14.8 The Drop-in Top-Down Method

Notice that until the **dropin** rectangle becomes full-size, given by the dimensions of the drop-in bitmap, to move downward, only the **dropin** rectangle's **bottom** member is incremented. Upon reaching full-size, thereafter, both the **dropin** rectangle's **top** and **bottom** members are incremented. The **dropin** rectangle is used as the destination in **BitBlt** operations. The source point for the **BitBlt** functions is that point within the drop-in bitmap itself from which to copy pixels here called **objectpt**. **objectpt**'s x coordinate is fixed at the value of the **insertpt**'s x coordinate. Its y coordinate must be adjusted. Initially, **objectpt**'s y coordinate is the height of the drop-in bitmap less the **insertpt**'s y amount. As the image moves downward, the **objectpt**'s y coordinate must be decremented until it reaches zero when the **dropin** rectangle is now full-size. It thereafter remains at zero.

The Bottom-Up action is basically the reverse of the Top-Down. The sideways movements are done similarly, holding the y coordinate fixed at the insertion point while varying the x coordinates of the **objectpt** and **dropin** rectangle. Make a sketch similar to Figure 14.8 and satisfy yourself of the needed settings. With these preliminaries understood, let's examine the coding for **Pgm14d**.

Pgm14d: Presentations

The resource file includes the **OnClose** strings and a string that identifies the **demo.txt** script file name.

```
STRINGTABLE {
 IDS_DEMO,         "demo.txt"
 IDS_MSG_QUERY,    "Query?"
 IDS_MSG_QUIT,     "Do you want to quit the demo presentation?"
}
```

The application's **InitInstance** has one change. The frame window is maximized when it is first shown. **SW_SHOWMAXIMIZED**is passed to **ShowWindow**.

```
BOOL  Pgm14d::InitInstance () {
 FrameWin *ptrframe = new FrameWin ();
```

```
 m_pMainWnd = ptrframe;
 m_pMainWnd->ShowWindow (SW_SHOWMAXIMIZED);
 return TRUE;
}
```

This special **FrameWin** class does not appear significantly different from any other **FrameWin**. Look over the class definition. Notice there is a pointer to the current presentation object which is allocated in the constructor and used in the **OnPaint** function to perform the presentations and later for repainting the main window as needed. The **bool shown** controls whether a presentation is required or not. Initially, **shown** is set to **false** in the constructor. In **OnPaint**, whenever **shown** is **false**, the Presentation member function **Present** is invoked to carry out another action presentation.

FrameWin.h Definition

```
#pragma once

class DisplayObject; // forward references
class Presentation;

/***************************************************************/
/*                                                             */
/* FrameWin Class Definition                                   */
/*                                                             */
/***************************************************************/

class FrameWin : public CFrameWnd {

 /*************************************************************/
 /*                                                           */
 /* Class Data Members                                        */
 /*                                                           */
 /*************************************************************/

protected:

 bool          shown;      // false when presentation must be made
 Presentation* ptrpresent;// the presentation object

 /*************************************************************/
 /*                                                           */
 /* Class Functions:                                          */
 /*                                                           */
 /*************************************************************/

public:
             FrameWin ();     // make spcl window and presentobj
            ~FrameWin ();     // removes the presentation object
protected:

afx_msg void OnPaint ();      // requests the presentation
afx_msg void OnClose ();      // determines if app can quit yet
afx_msg void OnRButtonDown (UINT, CPoint); // quit the app
afx_msg void OnLButtonDown (UINT, CPoint); // show presentation

DECLARE_MESSAGE_MAP()
};
```

FrameWin.cpp Implementation

```
#include "stdafx.h"
#include "FrameWin.h"
#include "Present.h"
#include "resource.h"
```

```

/********************************************************************/
/*                                                                  */
/* FrameWin Message Map                                             */
/*                                                                  */
/********************************************************************/

BEGIN_MESSAGE_MAP(FrameWin, CFrameWnd)
 ON_WM_PAINT ()
 ON_WM_CREATE ()
 ON_WM_CLOSE ()
 ON_WM_RBUTTONDOWN ()
 ON_WM_LBUTTONDOWN ()
END_MESSAGE_MAP()

/********************************************************************/
/*                                                                  */
/* Framewin: Construct the window object                            */
/*                                                                  */
/********************************************************************/

FrameWin::FrameWin () : CFrameWnd () {
 DWORD style = WS_POPUP;
 // the following rect is an alternative to
 // ShowWindow (SM_SHOWMAXIMIZED)
 // and using rectDefault to get a full screen window
 CRect rect (0, 0, GetSystemMetrics (SM_CXSCREEN),
                   GetSystemMetrics (SM_CYSCREEN));

 Create (AfxRegisterWndClass (NULL,
               AfxGetApp()->LoadStandardCursor (IDC_ARROW),
               (HBRUSH) GetStockObject (LTGRAY_BRUSH),
               AfxGetApp()->LoadStandardIcon (IDI_APPLICATION)),
         0, style, rect, 0, 0);

 shown = false; // set presentation not yet shown
 // load this presentation
 ptrpresent = new Presentation (this, IDS_DEMO);
}

/********************************************************************/
/*                                                                  */
/* ~FrameWin: remove the presentation object                        */
/*                                                                  */
/********************************************************************/

FrameWin::~FrameWin () {
 if (ptrpresent) delete ptrpresent;
}

/********************************************************************/
/*                                                                  */
/* OnClose: determine if the app can be shut down                   */
/*                                                                  */
/********************************************************************/

void FrameWin::OnClose () {
 CString msg1;
 CString msg2;
 msg1.LoadString (IDS_MSG_QUERY);
 msg2.LoadString (IDS_MSG_QUIT);
 if (MessageBox (msg2, msg1, MB_YESNO | MB_ICONQUESTION) ==IDYES)
  CFrameWnd::OnClose ();
}
```

```
/*************************************************************/
/*                                                           */
/* OnRButtonDown: pop up edit menu as a floating menu        */
/*                                                           */
/*************************************************************/

void FrameWin::OnRButtonDown (UINT, CPoint) {
 PostMessage (WM_CLOSE);
}

/*************************************************************/
/*                                                           */
/* OnLButtonDown: request another presentation run           */
/*                                                           */
/*************************************************************/

void FrameWin::OnLButtonDown (UINT, CPoint) {
 shown = false; // set for repeat presentation
 Invalidate (); // force Paint to repeat the presentation
}

/*************************************************************/
/*                                                           */
/* OnPaint: displays presentations                           */
/*          or copies final image to screen                  */
/*                                                           */
/*************************************************************/

void FrameWin::OnPaint () {
 CPaintDC  dc(this);
 if (!shown) {
  ptrpresent->Present (dc);
  shown = true;
 }
 ptrpresent->Copy (dc);
}
```

Examine the constructor to see how this most unusual frame window is constructed. The keys to the unusual style lie in the parameters to the **Create** function. The window style is limited to only **WS_POPUP**. 0 or NULL is passed for the title, for the menu, and for the parent window.

The destructor removes the Presentation object. The buttons provide our rudimentary user interface. **OnRButtonDown** posts the **WM_CLOSE** message, while **OnLButtonDown** repeats the presentation. In **OnPaint** the status of **shown** controls whether or not the **Present** function is called. In all cases the screen repaint is done by the **BitBlt** of the final completed image via the Presentation class **Copy** function.

Here is the **Presentation** Class Definition.

```
Present.h Definition
```

```
#pragma once

class DisplayObject; // forward reference

/*************************************************************/
/*                                                           */
/* DropType: aids in identifying the four directions of motion */
/*                                                           */
/*************************************************************/

enum DropType { TopDown, BottomUp, RightLeft, LeftRight };
```

```

/******************************************************************/
/*                                                                */
/* OBJECTS: allocated as an array of the individual objects to */
/*          move specifying bmp and mask bmp files,              */
/*          insertion pt, end pt, and type                       */
/*                                                                */
/******************************************************************/

struct OBJECTS {
 char     filenameobj[MAX_PATH];
 char     filenamemask[MAX_PATH];
 CPoint   insert;
 int      end;
 DropType type;
};

/******************************************************************/
/*                                                                */
/* Presentation: Performs a graphic animated presentation        */
/*                                                                */
/******************************************************************/

class Presentation {

 /*****************************************************************/
 /*                                                               */
 /* Class Data:                                                   */
 /*                                                               */
 /*****************************************************************/

protected:

bool               isvalid;       // true when this is a valid object
OBJECTS*           objects;       // array of objects to utilize
int                numobjs;       // number of objects in the array
char               filename[MAX_PATH]; // filename of the main bmp

DisplayObject* ptrmain;           // holds final images
int                hmain;         // main bmp's height
int                wmain;         // main bmp's width
DisplayObject* ptrmove;           // smooth move copy of background

CRect              screenrect;    // the area on screen to BitBlt to
CPoint             screenoffset;  // screen offset of main bmp image
CRect              screendropin;  // the screen are to fill from main

                   // the current drop in object
DisplayObject* ptrobj;            // current object to drop in
int                hobject;       // current object's height
int                wobject;       // current object's width

CRect              dropin;        // main bmp area filled by an obj
CPoint             insertpt;      // insertion point of an object
DropType           type;          // DropType of this object
int                endat;         // ending coord for this dropin obj
CPoint             objectpt;      // offset of the object to dropin
                                  // incremental values
int                xnext;         // to get to next dropin pt
int                ynext;         // to get to next dropin pt

 /*****************************************************************/
 /*                                                               */
 /* Class Functions:                                              */
```

```
/*                                                              */
/****************************************************************/

public:

      Presentation (CWnd*, UINT); // make the presentation object
     ~Presentation ();            // removed allocate items
void  Present (CDC&);             // perform the presentation
void  Copy (CDC&);                // copy final image
bool  IsValid () {return isvalid;}// returns true when all is OK

protected:

void  DropInBitmap (CDC&); // does the actual drop in of this obj
void  AdjustDropInRects ();// adjusts for the next dropin spot
};
```

Look over the **Presentation** class definition. Since numerous bitmaps, memory DCs, and **CDib**s are going to be constructed, there are many opportunities for a GDI failure or for a "low on resources or memory" failure. Hence, an **isvalid bool** is set to **true** only if things go right. If there are any failures, it is set to **false**. By checking the **IsValid** function return, we can avoid using an improperly set up presentation.

The **filename** contains the name of the background bitmap which is copied into both the main and move memory DCs with each presentation. An **OBJECTS** structure defines a drop-in bitmap event and the member **objects** contains a dynamically allocated array of these **OBJECTS** structures. **numobjs** conveniently contains the number in the array. The **OBJECTS** structure contains the basic information input from the script file, including the pair of filenames for the image and its mask, the insertion point. For convenience in referencing the four locations that a bitmap may be dropped onto the screen, I defined a **DropType enum**.

```
enum DropType { TopDown, BottomUp, RightLeft, LeftRight };
struct OBJECTS {
 char filenameobj[MAX_PATH];
 char filenamemask[MAX_PATH];
 CPoint insert;
 int    end;
 DropType type;
};
```

The **DisplayObject** class encapsulates the memory DCs and the bitmaps and the actual bliting functions. The **ptrmain DisplayObject** instance is permanently kept once the action sequence is complete; it is used for later screen repaints if needed. For convenience, I store its bitmap's height and width.

The **ptrmove DisplayObject** instance is allocated at the start of each presentation and deleted when it is finished. Similarly, the **ptrobj DisplayObject** member and its corresponding **hobject** and **wobject** (height and width) hold the temporary allocation of each drop-in image and its dimensions while it is being "dropped in."

Since the final image in the main bitmap must be blited onto the screen and since it could be smaller than the full-screen dimensions, the member **screenrect** holds the current screen destination rectangle and **screenoffset** contains the upper left point of the main bitmap on the screen. The rectangle **screendropin** contains the current drop-in rectangle in screen coordinates. Note that if one has an image that is full screen to begin with, **screenoffset** contains the point (0, 0) and **screenrect** matches the screen dimensions.

The rectangle **dropin** coupled with **objectpt** plays a crucial role in the actual bliting operations. Again refer to Figure 14.8 for the details. Since I want one routine that can perform all four types of drop-in actions, I use the members **xnext** and **ynext** to hold the current increment values with which to expand the **dropin** rectangle. The members **type**, **endat**, and **insertpt** are copied values from the current **OBJECTS** structure and are included for convenience.

The member functions include the **Presentation** constructor that inputs the user's **demo.txt** presentation commands, verifying their validity to some small extent and storing them in the **OBJECTS** array. The destructor removes the main background bitmap **DisplayObject**.

The function **Present** actually runs the action sequence following the commands in the **OBJECTS** array. **Copy** provides a means of bliting the final resultant image to the screen as requested by the main window's **OnPaint** routine. **DropInBitmap** performs the actual movement of one object from its initial insertion point to its final destination. After each movement, **AdjustDropInRects** handles the calculations to determine the next drop-in position.

Present.cpp Implementation

```
#include "stdafx.h"
#include <fstream>
#include "DisplayObject.h"
#include "Present.h"
#include "resource.h"
using namespace std;
/**************************************************************/
/*                                                            */
/* Presentation: construct the presentation object            */
/*                                                            */
/**************************************************************/

Presentation::Presentation (CWnd *ptrparnt, UINT presentid) {
 objects = 0;      // the array of objects
 ptrmain = 0;      // the main final image bmp object
 isvalid = false; // assume bad, if all is OK reset to good

 int x, y;
 char mask;
 CString mainfile;
 char typ[10];

 // load in the filename that will define this presentation
 mainfile.LoadString (presentid);

 // construct an iostream to input the presentation definition
 ifstream is (mainfile);
 if (!is) {  // trap bad file - and abort
  ptrparnt->MessageBox (mainfile,
                    "Presentation Error - Bad Input File", MB_OK);
  return;
 }

 // stream in the presentation definition file
 is >> filename >> numobjs;      // bring in the main bmp filename
 // construct main image obj
 ptrmain = new DisplayObject (filename, 0);
 if (!ptrmain->IsValid ()) return; // abort if bad main image
 hmain = ptrmain->Height ();        // and set its dimensions
 wmain = ptrmain->Width  ();

 // allocate the OBJECTS array to store drop in object sets
 objects = new OBJECTS [numobjs];
 if (!objects) {                    // if out of memory, abort
  ptrparnt->MessageBox ("Out of Memory", "Presentation Error",
                        MB_OK);
  return;
 }

 // load in each object's definition
 for (int i=0; i<numobjs; i++) {
  // get the type and convert to DropType enum format
  is >> typ;
  if (_stricmp (typ, "Top") == 0)
   objects[i].type = TopDown;
  else if (_stricmp (typ, "Bottom") == 0)
   objects[i].type = BottomUp;
```

```
   else if (_stricmp (typ, "Right") == 0)
    objects[i].type = RightLeft;
   else if (_stricmp (typ, "Left") == 0)
    objects[i].type = LeftRight;
   else { // catch invalid Drop In Types
    ptrparnt->MessageBox (typ,
        "Presentation Error - Object's DropinType Invalid", MB_OK);
    return;
   }
   is >> x >> y; // construct the insertion point
   objects[i].insert = CPoint (x, y);
   // get the Y/N presence of a mask file
   is >> objects[i].end >> mask;
   is >> objects[i].filenameobj; // load object's filename
   // load its maskname if it is present
   if (toupper (mask) == 'Y')
    is >> objects[i].filenamemask;
   else
    objects[i].filenamemask[0] = 0;
  }
 is.close ();
 isvalid = true; // set successful construction
}

/***************************************************************/
/*                                                             */
/* ~Presentation: remove all objects                           */
/*                                                             */
/***************************************************************/

Presentation::~Presentation () {
 if (ptrmain) delete ptrmain;
 if (objects) free (objects);
}

/***************************************************************/
/*                                                             */
/* Copy: BitBlt a final image onto the screen when parent's    */
/*       OnPaint needs it                                      */
/*                                                             */
/***************************************************************/

void Presentation::Copy (CDC &screendc) {
 if (IsValid () && ptrmain && ptrmain->IsValid ()) {
  // copy main image to the screen
  ptrmain->Copy (screendc, screenrect, CPoint (0, 0));
 }
}

/***************************************************************/
/*                                                             */
/* Present: perform the actual presentation display            */
/*                                                             */
/***************************************************************/

void Presentation::Present (CDC &screendc) {
 CPoint pt (0, 0);
 if (!IsValid ()) return;  // avoid actions if not properly setup

 // construct a smooth move copy of the main background image
 ptrmove = new DisplayObject (filename, 0);
 if (!ptrmove || !ptrmove->IsValid ())
  return; // abort if bad move dc

```

```
// calculate the center position of screen and
// back off to upper left corner
screenoffset.x = GetSystemMetrics (SM_CXSCREEN)/2 - wmain/2;
screenoffset.y = GetSystemMetrics (SM_CYSCREEN)/2 - hmain/2;

// construct main on-screen full display rectangle and the
// rectangle for all of main bmp
screenrect.SetRect (screenoffset.x, screenoffset.y,
                    screenoffset.x + wmain, screenoffset.y + hmain);
CRect mainrect (0, 0, wmain, hmain);

// erase any previous showing of this presentation
// copy blank move bmp onto main canvas
ptrmove->Copy (ptrmain, mainrect, pt);
// copy main to the screen
ptrmain->Copy (screendc, screenrect, pt);

// drop each object into place
for (int i=0; i<numobjs; i++) {
 // construct next object to drop in
 ptrobj  = new DisplayObject (objects[i].filenameobj,
                              objects[i].filenamemask);
 if (!ptrobj || !ptrobj->IsValid ())
  continue; // bad one, skip it, try another
 hobject = ptrobj->Height (); // set its dimensions
 wobject = ptrobj->Width  ();
 // save its insertion point, end coord, and type
 insertpt= objects[i].insert;
 endat   = objects[i].end;
 type    = objects[i].type;

 // and go drop this object into place on main bmp
 DropInBitmap (screendc);
 delete ptrobj;
}
delete ptrmove;
}

/***************************************************************/
/*                                                             */
/* DropInBitmap: smooth moves a bitmap object onto the screen  */
/* and mainmemDC                                               */
/*                                                             */
/* when done, the main memory object now has the bitmap copied */
/* onto it so that when finally done, the main bitmap can be   */
/* kept and used as the completed presentation screen          */
/*                                                             */
/***************************************************************/

void Presentation::DropInBitmap (CDC &screenDC) {
 // always does a one pixel movement
 // construct first dropin rectangle which is the initial area
 // occupied on the move and main images - then set the
 // corresponding source point on the objects bmp
 // last set the incremental values to get to the next drop in pt
 switch (type) {
  case TopDown:    // top-down motion
   dropin.SetRect (insertpt.x, 0, insertpt.x + wobject,
                   insertpt.y);
   objectpt = CPoint (0, hobject - insertpt.y);
   xnext = 0;
   ynext = 1;
   break;

```

```
 case BottomUp:  // bottom-up motion
  dropin.SetRect (insertpt.x, insertpt.y, insertpt.x + wobject,
                  hmain);
  objectpt = CPoint (0,0);
  xnext = 0;
  ynext = -1;
  break;

 case RightLeft: // right to left motion
  dropin.SetRect (insertpt.x, insertpt.y, wmain,
                  insertpt.y + hobject);
  objectpt = CPoint (0,0);
  xnext = -1;
  ynext = 0;
  break;

 case LeftRight: // left to right motion
  dropin.SetRect (0, insertpt.y, insertpt.x,
                  insertpt.y + hobject);
  objectpt = CPoint (wobject - insertpt.x, 0);
  xnext = 1;
  ynext = 0;
  break;
};

// screendropin is screen dc's corresponding area to dropin
screendropin.SetRect (dropin.left   + screenoffset.x,
                      dropin.top    + screenoffset.y,
                      dropin.right  + screenoffset.x,
                      dropin.bottom + screenoffset.y);

// display drop in object at its initial position
// copy object to move
ptrobj->TransparentCopy (ptrmove, dropin, objectpt);
// copy move to screen
ptrmove->Copy (screenDC, screendropin, dropin.TopLeft());
// erase object from move
ptrmain->Copy (ptrmove, dropin, dropin.TopLeft ());

// based upon drop in type, move it to its final ending position
while (type == TopDown   ? dropin.bottom < endat :
       type == BottomUp  ? dropin.top    > endat :
       type == RightLeft ? dropin.left   > endat :
               dropin.left < endat) {
 AdjustDropInRects ();  // calc its next position
 // copy object to move dc
 ptrobj->TransparentCopy (ptrmove, dropin, objectpt);
 // remove from the screen the top piece from last image
 screendropin.top--;
 // and remove the bottom piece,then copy move to screen
 screendropin.bottom++;
 ptrmove->Copy (screenDC, screendropin,
               CPoint (dropin.left,dropin.top-1));
 // set screen coords back after the removal of the top & bottom
 screendropin.top++;
 screendropin.bottom--;
 // erase object from move
 ptrmain->Copy (ptrmove, dropin, dropin.TopLeft ());
}

// copy logo object final position to the main & work images,
// and to the screen
ptrobj->TransparentCopy (ptrmain, dropin, objectpt);
ptrobj->TransparentCopy (ptrmove, dropin, objectpt);
```

```
 ptrmove->Copy (screenDC, screendropin,
                CPoint (dropin.TopLeft ()));
}

/*************************************************************/
/*                                                           */
/* AdjustDropInRects: adjust all rects and pts for next move */
/*                                                           */
/*************************************************************/

void Presentation::AdjustDropInRects () {
 if (type < RightLeft) {
  // reached full object's dimensions yet?
  if (dropin.Height() < hobject) {
   if (type == TopDown) {  // if top-down motion
    // inc height, so move source obj's y up one more pel
    objectpt.y -= ynext;
    // expand the destination area down by one pixel
    dropin.bottom += ynext;
    // expand the screen area down by one pel
    screendropin.bottom += ynext;
   }
   else { // if bottom-up motion
    // inc height, so move destination area up one pel
    dropin.top += ynext;
    // and move screen area up one pel
    screendropin.top += ynext;
   }
  }
  else { // have hit full object height, so move whole area
   // dropin area down one pixel
   dropin.OffsetRect (xnext, ynext);
   // and move screen area down one pixel
   screendropin.OffsetRect (xnext, ynext);
  }
 }
 else {
  // reached full object dimensions yet?
  if (dropin.Width () < wobject) {
   if (type == RightLeft) { // no, so if right-left motion
    dropin.left += xnext;   // inc dropin width
    // and corresponding screen position
    screendropin.left += xnext;
   }
   else if (type == LeftRight) { // no, so if left-right motion
    objectpt.x -= xnext;  // expand object's source point one pel
    dropin.right += xnext;       // inc dropin width
    screendropin.right += xnext; // and screen width
   }
  }
  else { // have hit full object width, so move whole area
   // dropin area left/right one pixel
   dropin.OffsetRect (xnext, ynext);
   // and move screen area l/r one pixel
   screendropin.OffsetRect (xnext, ynext);
  }
 }
}
```

Now let us see how the user definition text file is inputted in the constructor. Note that the pointers **ptrmain** and **objects** are set to zero and **isvalid** set to **false**. Thus, if any failures occur, a return can be issued, leaving the **Present** instance in the invalid state. Only if all goes well are these reset to proper values. The filename of the user's commands is retrieved from the resource file. I then attempt to open an **ifstream** using that filename. If the stream cannot be constructed, I display an error message box and return.

I extract the background filename and the number of objects. Note that the filename cannot contain any blanks! I attempt to construct a **DisplayObject** using the background filename. By checking the **DisplayObject**'s **IsValid** function, I can tell if the action was successful. Again, if not, I return leaving **isvalid** still **false** so no other actions except destructors can be used.

```
is >> filename >> numobjs;
ptrmain = new DisplayObject (filename, 0, true);
if (!ptrmain->IsValid ()) return;
hmain = ptrmain->Height ();
wmain = ptrmain->Width  ();
```

Next, I allocate the array of **OBJECTS** which could fail.

```
objects = new OBJECTS [numobjs];
if (!objects) {
 ptrparnt->MessageBox ("Out of Memory",
                       "Presentation Error", MB_OK);
 return;
}
```

The final lengthy loop extracts each set of data for each of the drop-in requests. The only action that is not obvious is the conversion of the user type into the proper instance of the **DropType enum**. By using a **stricmp**, case insensitive compare, I can assign the **OBJECTS**'s type member the correct **DropType**. With the array loaded, I close the stream and finally set **isvalid** to **true**. Note that I have not checked for any positions that are illogical nor have I checked for the existence or validity of the drop-in bitmaps or mask bitmaps. If you wish to completely bulletproof at this point in the sequence, you can go ahead and attempt to instantiate each of the drop-in objects. Once allocated, check their **IsValid** functions and then delete the instance. If any return **false**, you can then not set **isvalid** to **true**. It is not necessary to delete the array nor the main **DisplayObject** at this point because the **Presentation** class destructor handles this.

```
for (int i=0; i<numobjs; i++) {
 is >> typ;
 if (stricmp (typ, "Top") == 0)
  objects[i].type = TopDown;
 else if (stricmp (typ, "Bottom") == 0)
  objects[i].type = BottomUp;
 else if (stricmp (typ, "Right") == 0)
  objects[i].type = RightLeft;
 else if (stricmp (typ, "Left") == 0)
  objects[i].type = LeftRight;
 ...
 is >> x >> y;
 objects[i].insert = CPoint (x, y);
 is >> objects[i].end >> mask;
 is >> objects[i].filenameobj;
 if (toupper (mask) == 'Y')
  is >> objects[i].filenamemask;
 else
  objects[i].filenamemask[0] = 0;
}
is.close ();
isvalid = true;
```

Now turn your attention to the **Copy** function which is invoked by the main window's **OnPaint** routine after a presentation is complete and when the screen needs to be repainted. Here the failsafe actions handle possible invalid conditions. First, I check the **Presentation** class for validity, then for the existence of the main **DisplayObject** and finally the main object's validity. Nothing is done if any are not valid.

```
if (IsValid () && ptrmain && ptrmain->IsValid ()) {
 ptrmain->Copy (screendc, screenrect, CPoint (0, 0));
}
```

The **Present** function runs the animation sequence. Look over its coding and the function that it calls, **AdjustDropInRects**. From the above discussions, the sequences should be understandable.

The **DisplayObject** class is fairly simple, encapsulating all of the GDI components required to display an image on some canvas.

```
DisplayObject.h Definition
```

```
#pragma once

/*******************************************************************/
/*                                                                 */
/* DisplayObject: class definition                                 */
/*                                                                 */
/*******************************************************************/

class DisplayObject {

 /*****************************************************************/
 /*                                                               */
 /* Class Data:                                                   */
 /*                                                               */
 /*****************************************************************/

protected:

CDC*        ptrobjdc;    // memory dc for the object's image
CDC*        ptrmaskdc;   // memory dc for the object's mask image
CBitmap*    ptrobjbm;    // object's bitmap
CBitmap*    ptrmaskbm;   // mask's bitmap
int         height;      // image's height
int         width;       // image's width
bool        hasmask;     // true when object has a mask
bool        isvalid;     // true when object is valid

 /*****************************************************************/
 /*                                                               */
 /* Class Functions:                                              */
 /*                                                               */
 /*****************************************************************/

public:

      DisplayObject (const char*, const char*);// make the object
     ~DisplayObject ();                         // removes allocations

bool  IsValid () {return isvalid;}     // returns true when all OK
int   Height ()  {return IsValid () ? height : 0;}
int   Width  ()  {return IsValid () ? width  : 0;}

// transparent copy functions where background color is invisible
void  TransparentCopy (CDC*, const CRect&, const CPoint&);
void  TransparentCopy (DisplayObject*, const CRect&,
                       const CPoint&);

// normal copy functions which place full image onto destination
void  Copy (CDC*, const CRect&, const CPoint&);
void  Copy (DisplayObject*, const CRect&, const CPoint&);
void  Copy (CDC&, const CRect&, const CPoint&);
};
```

The **DisplayObject** class encapsulates the construction and low level manipulations of the drop-in bitmaps and their masks, if present. A memory DC and its corresponding **CBitmap** are constructed for both the drop-in DIB and any mask DIB. If successful, the width and height of the drop-in bitmap are retrieved and saved in protected members, again for convenience. If all is successful, **isvalid** is set to **true**. The constructor provides for three cases. When constructing the main background **DisplayObject**, no mask file is present; the second filename is therefore zero. The assumption I have made is that all the bitmaps use the same color palette. The allocated objects are deleted in the class destructor.

There are two key member functions that are overloaded, servicing several combinations of bliting.

```
void  TransparentCopy (CDC*, CRect&, CPoint&);
void  TransparentCopy (DisplayObject*, CRect&, CPoint&);
void  Copy (CDC*, CRect&, CPoint&);
void  Copy (DisplayObject*, CRect&, CPoint&);
void  Copy (CDC&, CRect&, CPoint&);
```

TransparentCopy can copy an image onto either another **DisplayObject** or onto a memory DC. It first ANDs the mask bitmap and then ORs the drop-in bitmap, allowing the background of this object to become transparent. The **Copy** member copies this **DisplayObject** to another **DisplayObject**, a memory DC, or to a real DC. In this program, the "real" DC is the screen from the main window's **OnPaint** function.

DisplayObject.cpp Implementation

```
#include "stdafx.h"
#include "DisplayObject.h"
#include "CDib.h"
#include "resource.h"

/***************************************************************/
/*                                                             */
/* DisplayObject: construct the object(s) to be shown          */
/*                                                             */
/***************************************************************/

DisplayObject::DisplayObject (const char *filename,
                              const char *maskfilename) {
 isvalid    = false;      // initialize to unsuccessful,
 hasmask    = false;      // then if ok, these are reset
 ptrobjdc   = ptrmaskdc = 0;
 ptrobjbm   = ptrmaskbm = 0;

 if (!filename) return; // must have at least one filename

 CDib* ptrdib;
 CDC   dc;
 dc.CreateDC ("DISPLAY", NULL, NULL, NULL);
 try { // construct a DIB from file
  ptrdib = new CDib (filename);
  if (!ptrdib || !ptrdib->IsValid ()) {
   MessageBox (NULL, filename,
       "Present Display Object Error - bad main filename", MB_OK);
   return;
  }
  // install bitmap's dimensions
  height = ptrdib->GetDibHeight ();
  width  = ptrdib->GetDibWidth ();

  ptrobjdc = new CDC();                  // the memory dc
  ptrobjdc->CreateCompatibleDC (&dc); // copy client dc
  ptrobjbm = new CBitmap ();         // create the bitmap for memdc
  ptrobjbm->CreateCompatibleBitmap (&dc, width, height);
 }
 catch (CException* e) {
  MessageBox (NULL, filename,
       "Present Display Object Error - bad main filename", MB_OK);
  e->Delete ();
  return;
 }
 ptrobjdc->SelectObject (ptrobjbm);  // insert bitmap into memdc
```

```
// one time conversion of the DIB color bits
// to the compatible DC display
SetDIBits (ptrobjdc->m_hDC, HBITMAP (ptrobjbm->m_hObject), 0,
    height, ptrdib->GetDibBitsAddr (), ptrdib->GetBitmapInfo (),
    DIB_RGB_COLORS);
delete ptrdib;

if (maskfilename) {  // see if there is a mask .BMP file
 hasmask = true;     // set yes there is and load it
 try {               // construct a DIB from file
  ptrdib = new CDib (maskfilename);
  if (!ptrdib || !ptrdib->IsValid ()) {
   MessageBox (NULL, filename,
     "Present Display Object Error - bad mask filename", MB_OK);
   return;
  }

  ptrmaskdc  = new CDC();                  // the memory dc
  ptrmaskdc->CreateCompatibleDC (&dc);     // copy client dc
  ptrmaskbm = new CBitmap ();      // create the bitmap for memdc
  ptrmaskbm->CreateCompatibleBitmap (&dc, width, height);
  if (!ptrmaskdc || !ptrmaskbm) {
   MessageBox (NULL, maskfilename,
     "Present Display Object Error - bad mask filename", MB_OK);
   return;
  }
 }
 catch (CException* e) {
  MessageBox (NULL, maskfilename,
     "Present Display Object Error - bad main filename", MB_OK);
  e->Delete ();
  return;
 }

 ptrmaskdc->SelectObject (ptrmaskbm);// insert bitmap into memdc
 // one time conversion of the DIB color bits
 // to the compatible DC display
 SetDIBits (ptrmaskdc->m_hDC, HBITMAP (ptrmaskbm->m_hObject), 0,
    height, ptrdib->GetDibBitsAddr (), ptrdib->GetBitmapInfo (),
    DIB_RGB_COLORS);
 delete ptrdib;
}
isvalid = true;               // set this Display Object as valid
dc.DeleteDC ();
}

/***************************************************************/
/*                                                             */
/* ~DisplayObject: delete all GDI objects                      */
/*                                                             */
/***************************************************************/

DisplayObject::~DisplayObject () {
 if (ptrobjdc)    delete ptrobjdc;
 if (ptrmaskdc)   delete ptrmaskdc;
 if (ptrobjbm)    delete ptrobjbm;
 if (ptrmaskbm)   delete ptrmaskbm;
 isvalid  = false;
 ptrobjdc = ptrmaskdc = 0;
 ptrobjbm = ptrmaskbm = 0;
}

/***************************************************************/
/*                                                             */
```

```
/* TransparentCopy: use the mask to perform a transparent      */
/*                  background copy                            */
/*                                                             */
/***************************************************************/

void DisplayObject::TransparentCopy (CDC *ptrdest,
                     const CRect &dropin, const CPoint &srcpt) {
 if (!IsValid () || !hasmask) return;
 // use mask with AND operation to make a hole in the dest bitmap
 ptrdest->BitBlt (dropin.left, dropin.top, dropin.right,
            dropin.bottom, ptrmaskdc, srcpt.x, srcpt.y, SRCAND);
 // use main object image and PAINT over hole in the dest bitmap
 ptrdest->BitBlt (dropin.left, dropin.top, dropin.right,
          dropin.bottom, ptrobjdc,  srcpt.x, srcpt.y, SRCPAINT);
}

/***************************************************************/
/*                                                             */
/* TransparentCopy: use the mask to perform a transparent      */
/*         background copy Destination is another DisplayObject */
/*                                                             */
/***************************************************************/

void DisplayObject::TransparentCopy (DisplayObject *ptrdest,
                     const CRect &dropin, const CPoint &srcpt) {
 if (!IsValid () || !hasmask || !ptrdest->IsValid ()) return;
 // use mask with AND operation to make a hole in the dest bitmap
 ptrdest->ptrobjdc->BitBlt (dropin.left, dropin.top,
                           dropin.right, dropin.bottom,
                           ptrmaskdc, srcpt.x, srcpt.y, SRCAND);
 // use main object image and PAINT over hole in the dest bitmap
 ptrdest->ptrobjdc->BitBlt (dropin.left, dropin.top,
                           dropin.right, dropin.bottom,
                         ptrobjdc,  srcpt.x, srcpt.y, SRCPAINT);
}

/***************************************************************/
/*                                                             */
/* Copy: copy as is the actual display object onto the passed  */
/*         memory dc                                           */
/*                                                             */
/***************************************************************/

void DisplayObject::Copy (CDC *ptrdest, const CRect &dropin,
                         const CPoint &srcpt) {
 if (!IsValid ()) return;
 ptrdest->BitBlt (dropin.left, dropin.top, dropin.right,
            dropin.bottom, ptrobjdc, srcpt.x, srcpt.y, SRCCOPY);
}

/***************************************************************/
/*                                                             */
/* Copy: copy as is the actual display object onto another obj */
/*                                                             */
/***************************************************************/

void DisplayObject::Copy (DisplayObject *ptrdest,
                     const CRect &dropin, const CPoint &srcpt) {
 if (!IsValid () || !ptrdest->IsValid ()) return;
 ptrdest->ptrobjdc->BitBlt (dropin.left, dropin.top,
                           dropin.right, dropin.bottom,
                           ptrobjdc, srcpt.x, srcpt.y, SRCCOPY);
}
```

```
/**************************************************************/
/*                                                            */
/* Copy: copy as is the actual display object onto another CDC */
/*                                                            */
/**************************************************************/

void DisplayObject::Copy (CDC &destdc, const CRect &dropin,
                          const CPoint &srcpt) {
 if (!IsValid ()) return;
 destdc.BitBlt (dropin.left, dropin.top, dropin.right,
            dropin.bottom, ptrobjdc, srcpt.x, srcpt.y, SRCCOPY);
}
```

In the **DisplayObject** implementation, the coding to construct memory DCs closely parallels that of **Pgm09b**, loading the fancy DIBs. In the class constructor, to obtain a DC for the entire screen, use the **CDC** function **CreateDC** passing it the key string "DISPLAY" and NULL for all of the other parameters.

```
dc.CreateDC ("DISPLAY", NULL, NULL, NULL);
```

The **DisplayObject** constructor follows the same pattern as **Presentation** by setting all pointers to zero and **isvalid** to **false**. Only if all objects are successfully constructed is it reset to **true**. Since a large number of graphical objects are to be constructed, there is a fair chance that something could go wrong. So I wrapped this group in a **try-catch** block utilizing C++ Error Handling.

```
try { // construct a DIB from file
 ptrdib = new CDib (filename);
 if (!ptrdib || !ptrdib->IsValid ()) {
     ... display an error and return
 }
 height = ptrdib->GetDibHeight ();
 width  = ptrdib->GetDibWidth ();
 ptrobjdc = new CDC();                  // the memory dc
 ptrobjdc->CreateCompatibleDC (&dc); // copy client dc
 ptrobjbm = new CBitmap ();          // create the bitmap for memdc
 ptrobjbm->CreateCompatibleBitmap (&dc, width, height);
}
catch (CException* e) {
 MessageBox (NULL, filename,
     "Present Display Object Error - bad main filename", MB_OK);
 e->Delete ();
 return;
}
ptrobjdc->SelectObject (ptrobjbm);  // insert bitmap into memdc
SetDIBits (ptrobjdc->m_hDC, HBITMAP (ptrobjbm->m_hObject), 0,
    height, ptrdib->GetDibBitsAddr (), ptrdib->GetBitmapInfo (),
    DIB_RGB_COLORS);
delete ptrdib;
```

Rather than spell out exactly what exceptions for which I am looking in the **catch** statements, I catch the base class for all exceptions, **CException**. The next section discusses the various MFC **catch** possibilities. Next, the sequence is repeated for any mask image file.

The two **TransparentCopy** functions only differ in the destination object. Once more, the bliting occurs only if this **DisplayObject** is valid and the destination is valid; for transparent bliting, this object must have a mask.

```
if (!IsValid () || !hasmask) return;
ptrdest->BitBlt (dropin.left, dropin.top, dropin.right,
           dropin.bottom, ptrmaskdc, srcpt.x, srcpt.y, SRCAND);
ptrdest->BitBlt (dropin.left, dropin.top, dropin.right,
         dropin.bottom, ptrobjdc,  srcpt.x, srcpt.y, SRCPAINT);
```

Finally, the **Copy** functions, which only really differ in the destination object, perform a **SRCCOPY BitBlt** if the objects are valid.

```
ptrdest->ptrobjdc->BitBlt (dropin.left, dropin.top,
```

```
dropin.right, dropin.bottom, ptrobjdc, srcpt.x, srcpt.y,
SRCCOPY);
```

The try-catch and TRY-CATCH Logic for the MFC

Originally, the MFC used macros to handle runtime error trapping using **TRY**, **CATCH**, **AND_CATCH**, and **END_CATCH**. With Version 4.0, these have been replaced with the standard C++ **try** and **catch**.

The **try-catch** sequence catches the general **CException** class which is the base class for a number of possible MFC exceptions that could be thrown.

```
try {
 ...
}
catch (CException* e) {
 MessageBox ...
 e->Delete ();
 return;
}
```

Under the MFC, the base class is **CException** which can be used to catch all errors. The key exceptions thrown include these.

```
CMemoryException    - thrown if out of memory on an allocation
CFileException      - thrown if a file error occurs using the
                      CFile class
CArchiveException   - thrown if an error occurs during
                      serialization or archiving (see Chapter 15)
CResourceException - thrown if a resource allocation fails
CNotSupportedException - thrown if an action is not yet or
                      no longer supported
CUserException      - thrown under programmer defined
                      circumstances
```

A sequence that would catch specifically **CFile** errors and out of memory yet pick up any other errors could be this.

```
try {
 ...
}
catch (CFileException* e) {
 MessageBox ...
 // here e is not deleted and the error passed on up the
 //  line to another handler
 throw;
}
catch (CMemoryException* e) {
 MessageBox ...
 // here e is deleted and a new exception is thrown
 e->Delete ();
 throw new AnotherException;
}
catch (CException* e) {
 MessageBox ...
 // here e is deleted and the return says that we have
 // handled the exception
 e->Delete ();
 return;
}
```

You should also consider using the **ASSERT**, **TRACE** and **WARN** macros to assist in debugging. I have not done so in this book in order to keep the coding at a simpler level.

Looking over this example and after running it, I think that you can see many possibilities for similar coding. All manner of presentation screens can be handled. It can be extended to create scrolling marquis. If nothing else, the method of creating a non-Windows main window has its utility, especially in games and business applications.

Programming Problems

Pgm14-1—Acme Inventory Program Revised Again

Revise the Acme Inventory Program, **Pgm13-1** or an earlier version, to display a splash screen upon application startup. Create a reasonable splash image and show it for three seconds before continuing to launch the application.

Pgm14-2—Better Bagels Business Presentation Program

The Better Bagels Company wants a short animated presentation that can be run on laptops at conventions. Use **Pgm14d** as the presentation engine. You should not need to alter any of its coding, rather alter the contents of the **Demo.txt** file to specify your new presentation data.

Construct a background basic image with the company logo of your design in the upper left portion, similar to that of **Pgm14d**. Then design a series of drop-in bitmaps. You may use any of these jungles or others of your choosing.

Better Bagels Equals Better Business

A Better Bagel for Better Times

Have a Better Bagel Day!

When you have your jingles chosen, then use Paintbrush to make bitmap images of these jingles. Make sure you use a large font point size so the jingles are easily read on the screen. Then, copy each image and construct the black and white mask image.

Finally, write the script to load and use these; modify the **Demo.txt** file accordingly.

Chapter 15 The Document-View Architecture

Introduction

Consider a file of sales data consisting of pairs of year and sales amounts. Likely the data would be displayed in columnar form similar to a spreadsheet for ease in updating. However, management often prefers graphical presentations and, in this case, a bar chart would ideally illustrate the annual sales variations. How could this example be implemented?

The main window can display the columnar report with scroll bars as needed. A menu option or tool bar button could be added to display the bar chart graph in a child window. However, complexity enters when the user wishes **both** views on the screen simultaneously: window placement and movement, communication between the main and child windows become major problems. A far better implementation approach is to use the document-view architecture which supports multiple views.

The **document** may be thought of as a container for the data itself. It does not have an associated window for display purposes. The document class encapsulates the data, providing services to input and output the data along with prompting the user to save the data when it has been modified.

One or more **view** classes actually display the document's data on the screen and handle printing when requested. In this example, one view class could be written to display the data in columnar fashion, to handle scrolling as needed and to handle requests for updating the data. Realize that more than one instance of this view class can be on the screen simultaneously. For example, in one view, the user positions the file near the beginning of the data and in another view, positions the file near the end so that visual comparisons can be made. These multiple instances of the same view class are often positioned side-by-side. Additionally, another view class can be constructed to display the bar chart. Probably the user would like a small width columnar version on the left and the bar chart on the right occupying most of the screen real-estate.

Using a **Splitter Window** greatly simplifies the multiple views' window management. A splitter window can divide a window into multiple sections placing a user draggable divider border between the views. When the user drags the divider, the splitter window internally adjusts the size and placement of all the view windows with **no** effort on our part!

In this chapter, I illustrate how to implement the document-view architecture using two different view classes of the same document by using splitter windows. More details on the printing process are discussed and implemented, including **Print Preview**. We will see how the class libraries handle dynamic creation of documents and views in both an SDI and MDI implementation (Single Document Interface and Multiple Document Interface).

A powerful feature of any class is the ability to re-create itself from a data file at runtime; this is known as **Serialization.** Several approaches to the serialization process are discussed.

Lastly, the actual sales data is encapsulated into a **SalesData** object that is also capable of serializing itself. And a container class is used to maintain the array of sales objects.

Program **Pgm15a** is the SDI version and **Pgm15b** is the MDI version. Again you can see how easy it is to convert a properly designed application to the multiple document interface.

The Application Design

Suppose that our company is called the Acme Better Construction Company. Our task is to design a yearly sales application. Begin by examining the main screen of **Pgm15a** immediately after the application has been launched. Note that I have done nothing except launch the application — it has automatically loaded in the default document and constructed the complex display.

The title bar contains the actual file name, acme.dat, and the document title, ACME Sales Data. The tool bar buttons represent, from left to right, File|New, File|Open, File|Save, File|SaveAs, Add New Record, Update Selected Record, Delete Selected Record, Print, Print Preview, Choose Fonts, and Help-About. The left gray narrow window contains the columnar view with column headings displayed upon a raised rectangle. The large white window on the right is the plot view with a crude title that does not overlap the bars themselves. Across the bottom under each bar is the year of those sales. (No provision is made for a vertical scale.) Separating the two views is a thick border — the splitter window edge. If the user drags horizontally on this border, both windows resize together; they are coupled. Next, look over Figure 15.2 after I chose to open another much larger file.

Notice that the columnar view window now has scroll bars because the data ranges from 1935 through 1995. The plot view looks quite different. The plot operation must establish a uniform width for the bars and space between the bars. In Figure 15.1, the bars are constrained to a maximum width leaving a gap on the graph's right side. In Figure 15.2, in order to display the much larger number of bars, their thickness must be reduced. But if the bar's width becomes too narrow, the year's text cannot fit below the bar. One way around this is to display only the last two digits. On printouts, if the widths are still too small to show even the last two digits, merely construct a smaller font to squeeze the two digits into the width at hand.

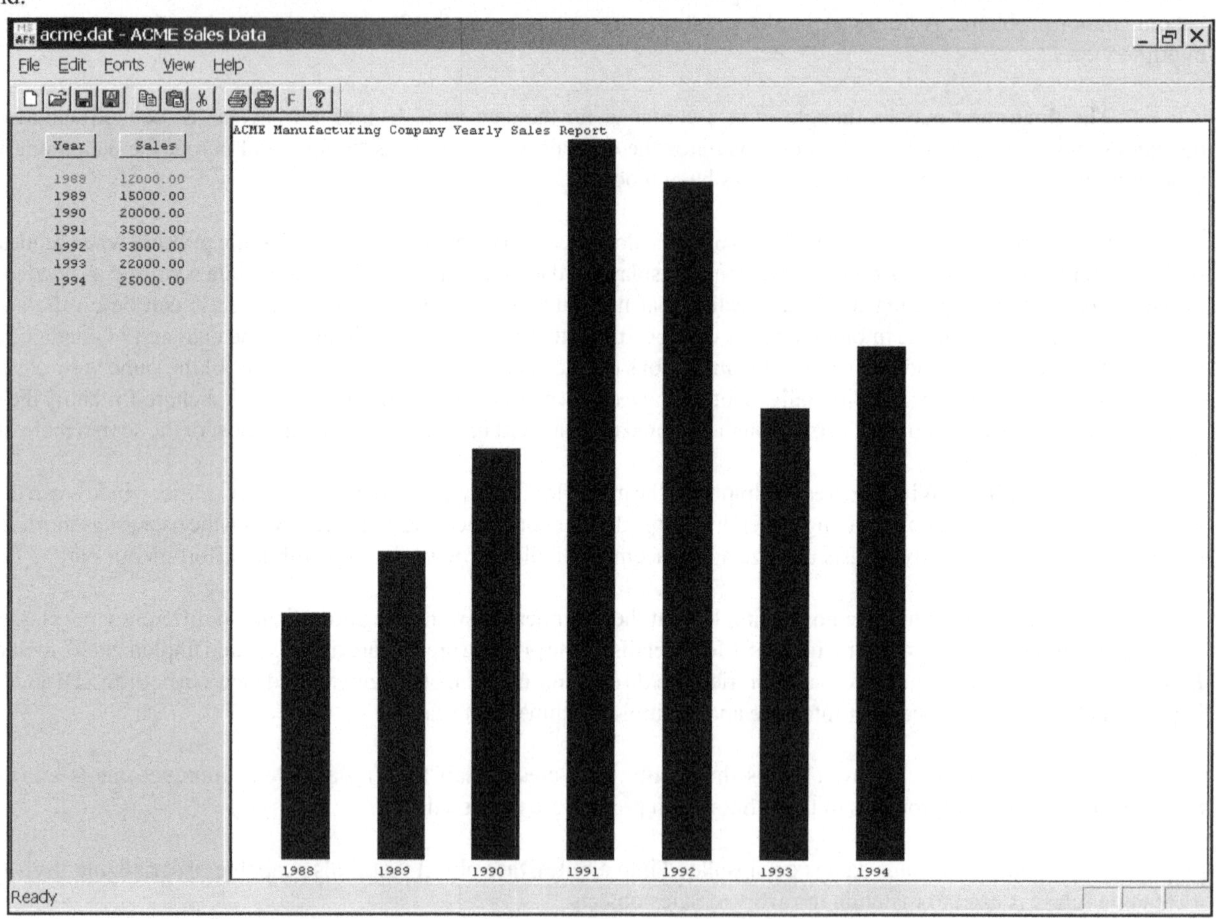

Figure 15.1 **Pgm15a** Upon Initial Launch Using acme.dat

Printing can be done normally (Portrait style) or Landscape style. The graphs are often shown in Landscape form. The application must be able to deal with the two different page layouts. The graph printout emulates the screen display; no user fonts are used. However, when printing the columnar report, the user can choose the font and point size to be used. Note that this user font is not used in the onscreen display which remains a small fixed font. When printing the columnar report, the company title is at the top of every page along with column headings above the data. On the last line of each page is a footer stating "Prepared by Broquard Consultants." Thus, you can see how to handle headings and footers and by emulation, setting left, right, top, and bottom margins.

Print|Preview is implemented as well. Figure 15.3 shows the preview window of the sales report while Figure 15.4 shows the corresponding bar chart preview window.

User fonts are implemented only for printing. In Figure 15.5, I chose a large font which thus extends the number of pages.

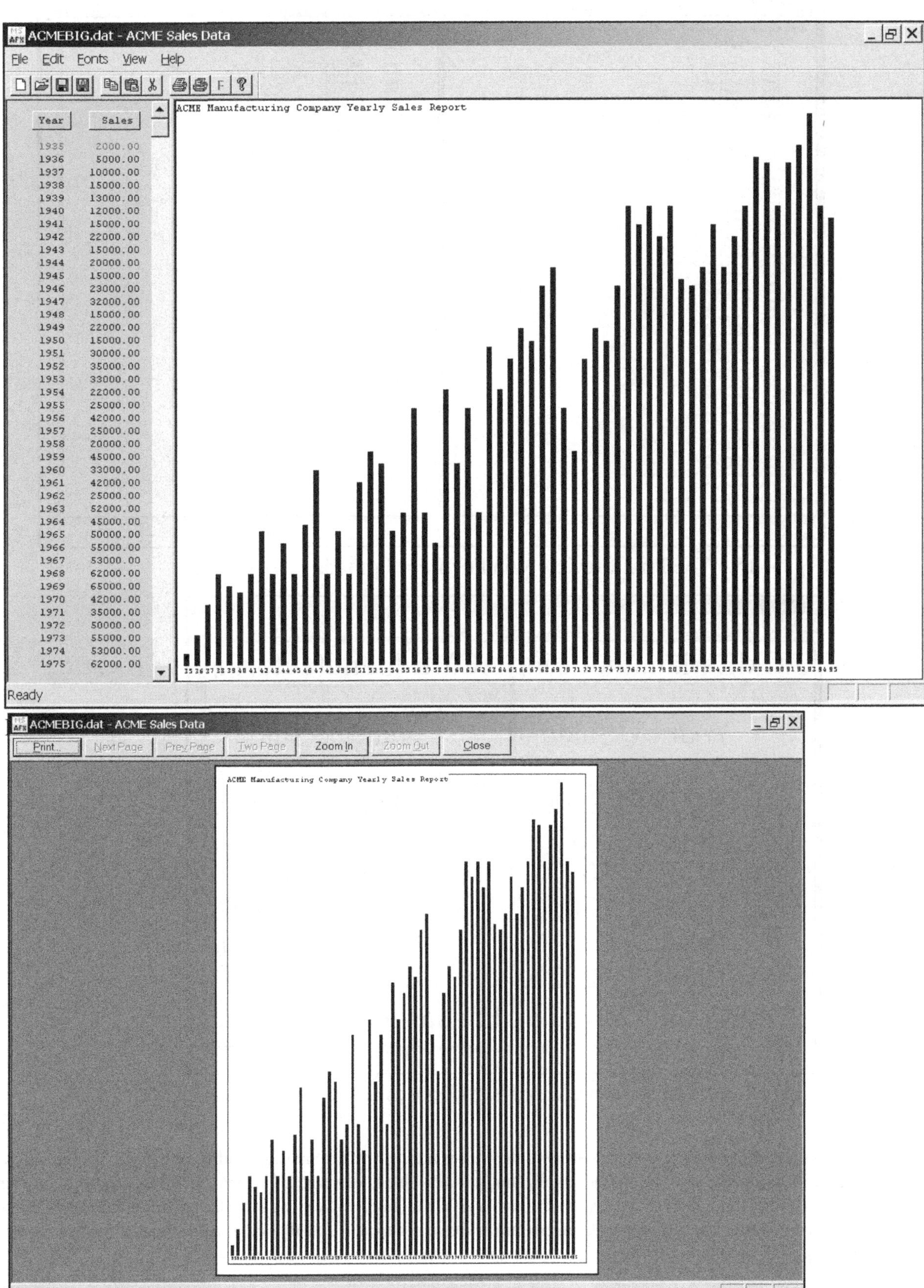

Figure 15.4 Print Preview of the Bar Chart View

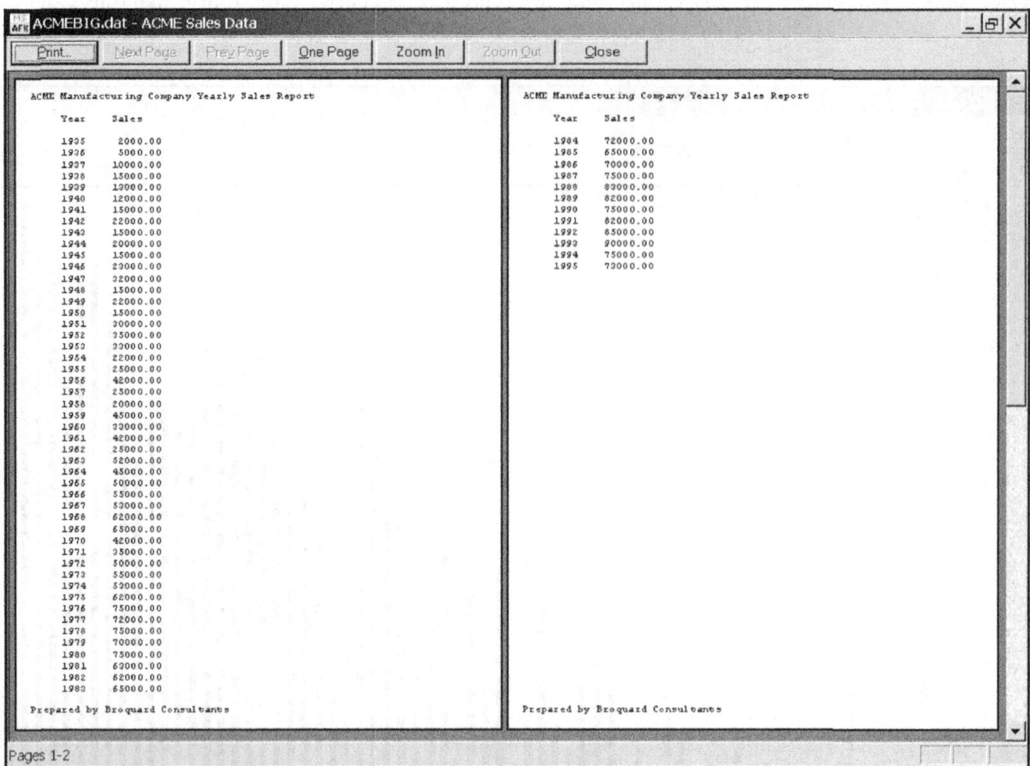

Figure 15.3 The Print Preview Window from **Pgm15a**

ACMEBIG.dat - ACME Sales Data

Print... Next Page Prev Page One Page Zoom In Zoom Out Close

ACME Manufacturin		ACME Manufacturin	
Year	Sales	Year	Sales
1935	2000.(	1941	15000.
1936	5000.(	1942	22000.
1937	10000.	1943	15000.
1938	15000.	1944	20000.
1939	13000.	1945	15000.
1940	12000.	1946	23000.
Prepared by Broqua		Prepared by Broqua	

Pages 1-2

Figure 15.5 Print Preview After User Chooses Large Point Font

The sales data files are in binary format; the year is a **long** and the sales, a **double**. When a class serializes itself to a file for later automatic restoration, the serialization process also adds some additional data fields to the binary stream, often the class name, for example, and a version number. If a container array class serializes itself, it appends the index of the next sales data object so that on input, the container knows where to store that data. Additionally, some runtime class information is added so that it can verify it is reading in its own data.

How does the binary file of data get built in the first place? Often the initial text data is input by a combination of reading a text file or real-time user data entry. To make this program more flexible, I provide two File Menu items for loading and saving the data to/from a DOS text file. Remember, normal operations input and output binary files. These two additional choices allow the creation of alternate text file versions. In the **Pgm15a** program folder are both a **.txt** and **.dat** file for the small data case (**acme.dat** and **acme.txt**) and for the larger file (**acmebig.dat** and **acmebig.txt**). Serialization and the MFC **CFile** class use binary format. The two File menu items load and save the data to and from a txt file.

The Document-View Implementation of Pgm15a

Designing a Serializeable SalesData Class

Ignoring the serialization process for a moment and keeping the complexity down, what would a class to encapsulate the sales data look like? We might begin with something like the following.

```
class SalesData {
public:
 long   year;   // year of sales
 double sales;  // sales
        SalesData ();
        SalesData (long, double);
};
```

With this simple beginning, let's examine the MFC serialization process. Under the MFC, for the environment to support dynamic class serialization, a class **must** be derived from the MFC class **CObject**. Nearly all of the MFC classes, like **CWnd** for example, are ultimately derived from **CObject**, which has a virtual function for serialization whose prototype is this.

```
virtual void Serialize (CArchive &);
```

For a class derived from **CObject** to read or write itself to permanent storage, it must override this function. The function can throw three runtime exceptions: **CMemoryException**, **CArchiveException**, and **CFileException**. Our overridden version handles reading or writing this class instance data to the file. However, the function is not passed a file directly, rather a reference to an instance of the **CArchive** class which encapsulates the file I/O and implements a binary file version of the insertion and extraction operators for our convenience.

Note that we do not create instances of **CArchive**, rather we use the reference that is passed to us by the MFC serialization system. Normally, our use of **CArchive** involves using one of its member functions and the two operators. The **CArchive** function **IsStoring** returns **TRUE** if the instance is to output itself; **FALSE** for input.

```
BOOL IsStoring ();
```

The **CArchive** class provides normal C++ stream insertion and extraction operators (<< and >>) which are used for the I/O to the binary file. The following data types can be streamed.

```
CObject, BYTE, WORD, LONG, DWORD, float, double
```

Notice that an **int** is **not** among the list! Assuming that our **SalesData** class is derived from **CObject**, the overridden **Serialize** function first calls the base class and then uses the extraction operators on the **long** and **double** as follows.

```
void SalesData::Serialize (CArchive &ar) {
 CObject::Serialize (ar);
 if (ar.IsStoring ()) ar << year << sales;
 else ar >> year >> sales;
}
```

Design Rule 55: **For a class to be able to use the MFC serialization process, the class must include the DECLARE_SERIAL macro and in its implementation file must include the IMPLEMENT_SERIAL macro.**

```
DECLARE_SERIAL (class name);
IMPLEMENT_SERIAL (class name, base class, UINT version number)
```

The version number is user-defined and is encoded into the stream. In this manner you can keep track of multiple revisions of your classes. The version number cannot be –1. For our **SalesData** class the coding is done this way.

```
DECLARE_SERIAL (SalesData);                 // in the header file
IMPLEMENT_SERIAL (SalesData, CObject, 0) // in the .cpp file
```

The **DECLARE_SERIAL/IMPLEMENT_SERIAL** macros implicitly include the **DECLARE_DYNAMIC/IMPLEMENT_DYNAMIC** macros which are used to make a class capable of accessing runtime class information.

Design Rule 56: For a class to be able to be serialized, it must have a constructor with no arguments, that is a default constructor.

Now you can see why the vast majority of the MFC class constructors take no arguments; they use **CObject** as their ultimate base class and are serializeable.

Combining all of these points, our **SalesData** class would now be as shown in the two files **SalesDat.h** and **SalesDat.cpp** shown below.

SalesData.h Definition

```
#pragma once

/***************************************************************/
/*                                                             */
/* SalesData & SalesDataArray: the sales data object and the   */
/*                             array of sales data             */
/*                                                             */
/***************************************************************/

class SalesData : public CObject {

DECLARE_SERIAL (SalesData);

 /***************************************************************/
 /*                                                             */
 /* Class Data:                                                 */
 /*                                                             */
 /***************************************************************/

public:

long      year;    // year of sales
double    sales;   // sales

 /***************************************************************/
 /*                                                             */
 /* Class Functions:                                            */
 /*                                                             */
 /***************************************************************/

public:
      SalesData ();              // constructor for serialization
      SalesData (long, double); // constructor
 void Serialize (CArchive&);     // handles I/O for sales data
};


/***************************************************************/
/*                                                             */
/* SalesDataArray: array container for sales data objects      */
/*                                                             */
/***************************************************************/

```

```
class SalesDataArray : public CObArray {

DECLARE_SERIAL (SalesDataArray);

 /***************************************************************/
 /*                                                             */
 /* Class Functions:                                            */
 /*                                                             */
 /***************************************************************/

public:
        SalesDataArray () {}     // constructor for serialization
};
```

```
SalesData.h Implementation
```

```
#include "stdafx.h"
#include "SalesData.h"

IMPLEMENT_SERIAL (SalesData, CObject, 0)
IMPLEMENT_SERIAL (SalesDataArray, CObArray, 0)

/***************************************************************/
/*                                                             */
/* SalesData: default constructor                              */
/*                                                             */
/***************************************************************/

SalesData::SalesData () {
 year  = 0;
 sales = 0;
}

/***************************************************************/
/*                                                             */
/* SalesData: constructor                                      */
/*                                                             */
/***************************************************************/

SalesData::SalesData (long yr, double sale) {
 year  = yr;
 sales = sale;
}

/***************************************************************/
/*                                                             */
/* Serialize: input or output a sales data object              */
/*                                                             */
/***************************************************************/

void SalesData::Serialize (CArchive &ar) {
 CObject::Serialize (ar);
 if (ar.IsStoring ())
  ar << year << sales;
 else
  ar >> year >> sales;
}
```

The next design factor is how does one store the array of **SalesData** objects? Using C style, one could code simply this.

```
SalesData sales_array[MAX_LIMIT];
```

However, the array would not be dynamic and would force us to keep track of the current number of objects in the array. Of course, you could add further functions to expand and contract the array as records are added and deleted. But there is a far simpler way—use an MFC object container. The MFC provides some container classes that are derived from **CObject**. For our use here, two key possibilities include these.

```
CObArray - supporting arrays of CObjects
CObList  - supporting ordered linked lists of Cobjects
```

Here, either class could be used. Since I am ignoring all interrelationships between sets of sales data, a simple array container works well. If you desire to maintain sorted lists, try using **InsertAt** or try changing to a **CObList**. Both array classes operate in a similar manner. They maintain an array of pointers to the **CObjects** themselves.

Thus, I define a container class, **SalesDataArray**, to hold all of our **SalesData** objects.

```
class SalesDataArray : public CObArray {
DECLARE_SERIAL (SalesDataArray);
public:
    SalesDataArray () {} // constructor for serialization
};
```

No other functions are necessary because the base class, **CObArray**, provides all the access methods needed. However, I must include the corresponding **IMPLEMENT_SERIAL** macro in an implementation file. Examine the **SalesDat h** and **cpp** files once more to see our container class definition.

The key member functions of **CObArray** include the following.

```
int      GetSize ();      // returns number of elements in the
                          // array
CObject* GetAt (int index); // returns the item at this index
                            // or 0 if the index is out of range
int      Add (CObject*); // adds new object, returns its index
void     InsertAt (int index, CObject*, int count);
                           // inserts count objs beginning at index
void     RemoveAll ();    // deletes all ptrs in the array
void     RemoveAt (int index, int count);
                           // removes count ptrs beginning at index
```

Note that both remove functions **only** delete the container's pointer to the objects. We must manually **delete** the actual objects. To use our new container class, in the appropriate class (derived from **CDocument**) define the array as follows.

```
SalesDataArray sales_array; // container for list of sales data
```

Notice that the typecast **(SalesData*)** is nearly always required when working with the container classes. To delete the contents of the sales array, code a sequence as follows.

```
if (sales_array.GetSize () ==0) return; // is already empty
for (i=sales_array.GetSize()-1; i>=0; i--) {
 SalesData* ptrdata = (SalesData*) sales_array.GetAt (i);
 if (ptrdata)
  delete ptrdata;
}
sales_array.RemoveAll ();
```

Next, to serialize the entire array of sales data, just invoke the **Serialize** base class function of **CObArray**. The container serializes itself inputting or outputting all objects it contains by invoking the **Serialize** function of each object in the array.

```
void      someclass::Serialize (CArchive &ar) {
 if (ar.IsStoring ()) {
  if (sales_array.GetSize () == 0) return; // none to save
  sales_array.Serialize (ar);
```

```
 }
 else sales_array.Serialize (ar);
}
```

One could display all sales objects by iterating through the array. Assuming that **ptrarray** contains the address of the sales array, one would code something like this.

```
SalesDataArray *ptrarray;
SalesData      *ptrdata;
for (int i=0; i<ptrarray->GetSize (); i++) {
 ptrdata = (SalesData*) ptrarray->GetAt (i);
 if (!ptrdata) continue;
 sprintf_s (msg, sizeof(msg), "%4ld", ptrdata->year);
 dc.TextOut (avg_char_width*5, avg_char_height*i, msg);
 sprintf_s (msg, sizeof(msg), "%8.2f", ptrdata->sales);
 dc.TextOut (avg_char_width*13, avg_char_height*i, msg);
}
```

Sometimes, serialization cannot be easily done by using the extraction operator. Suppose that a bitmap image file needed to be serialized as part of the document data. **CArchive** is derived from **CFile**. At any point, one can gain access to the underlying **CFile** object using **GetFile**.

```
CFile* GetFile () const;
```

However, if you are going to mix **CArchive** operations with direct **CFile** operations, call the **Flush** function before calling **GetFile** to ensure that the file buffer remains synchronized. For example, if **ar** is an instance of **CArchive**,

```
ar.Flush();
CFile* ptrfile = ar.GetFile ();
ptrfile->Read (...);
```

The archive class also supports **Read** and **Write** functions that are used to I/O blocks of data.

```
UINT Read  (void* lpBuf, UINT nMax) throw CFileException;
UINT Write(void* lpBuf, UINT nMax) throw CfileException;
```

Both are passed the address of the input or output area and the maximum number of characters to read or write. By using these functions, often the need to resort to dealing directly with the underlying **CFile** is obviated.

Finally, realize that you do not have to load a document using the built-in serialization method. In the document class that we will soon examine, you can I/O the document in any manner best suited to the data at hand. In this sample program, the sales data are easily encapsulated into a class that can be derived from **CObject** and thus easily stored into a serializeable array with minimal coding on our part.

Other MFC Container Classes

CPtrArray stores an array of void pointers which we examined in Chapter 8. The **CByteArray**, **CDWordArray**, **CStringArray**, **CUIntArray**, and **CWordArray** similarly store an array of **BYTE**, **DWORD**, **CString**, **UINT**, and **WORD** values. All operate similarly. Each of these is a growable array.

For efficiency, all have a **SetSize** function that can be called to specify the initial number of elements in the array and the number of elements to physically allocate when the array must be grown in size.

```
SetSize (int maxNumber, int growBy) throw CMemoryException;
```

Thus, if you knew that usually 1,000 items needed to be added to an array, then using the default values of 0 initial size and grow by a single element each time severely degrades processing speed. Instead, consider calling **SetSize** before you begin adding items.

```
CPtrArray array;
array.SetSize (1000, 100);
```

There are also some list container classes: **CObList**, **CStringList**, and **CPtrList**. All of these array and list classes along with **CObArray** are not template classes and thus have a simpler syntax to use than template classes. For further information, consult the online documentation.

The MFC Document-View Implementation

With these basic building blocks understood, let's proceed to see how to construct a document-view application. The basic idea is to divide the work load into four components.

The first component is a **CDocument** derived class whose purpose is to house the data perhaps within a container class instance, to provide facilities for its I/O often by serialization, and to support communications among the possible views.

The **CView** derived class (or one of the other view type classes) is the second component whose function is to display the document on the screen, to render it on the printer, and to display it in the Print Preview window. The MFC provides several different view classes from which we may derive our views. The basic view class is called **CView**. Other view classes include **CScrollView, CFormView, CRecordView** and **CEditView**. In the sample programs, I use the simplest case, **CView**, from which to derive the two view classes.

The third component is the frame window. A view class must have a container; a view is a client window, not a frame window. In the SDI implementation, a **CFrameWnd** derived class is used as the frame window. However, in the MDI implementation, a **CMDIChildWnd** acts as the frame window. The frame window handles the decorations, that is, the tool bars and status bar, and any menu, if present.

The fourth component is the application class with its several support classes, **CWinApp**. The application class is responsible for launching or dynamically allocating the needed instances of the document, view and frame windows for a specific **document type** that the application can handle. The document type is really the file extension of the actual data file. In **Pgm15a**, the document type is any **.dat** file. Okay, I admit that this is a very poor choice of file extension because it is not a unique file extension — **.dat** is an extremely common extension in widespread usage containing more than Acme Sales Data. However, the idea is that when a **.dat** file is dropped on an instance of **Pgm15a**, or one double clicks a **.dat** file, or one does a File|Open action, **Pgm15a** should respond and open that **.dat** file and show its sales data in both the sales scroll view and the bar chart plot view.

Notice one very crucial aspect. For a specific document, the application must launch a specific frame window instance with a specific tool bar and menu and icon, a specific document class and a specific view class. The **document template** classes store this relevant information. There are two of these classes: **CSingleDocTemplate** for SDI and **CMultiDocTemplate** for MDI. Each of these template instances supplies the requisite four items: the resource Id of the tool bar and menu, the frame window class, the document class, and the view class.

Thus, in **Pgm15a**, two SDI document templates must be created because there are two different views, the scroll view and the bar char plot view. The application class allocates these two document templates and stores them in a template array that is maintained by a helper class, **CDocManager** which maintains the array of document templates. When a document is opened, the doc manager looks through its array of document templates to find the best **matching** template. It does its matching based upon file extensions. Should the doc manager find two or more templates that match the indicated file extension, then the doc manager displays a rather simpleton dialog box asking the user to pick which template to use to open the file.

If you run **Pgm15a** and ask for File|New, since there are two possible templates that match, the doc manager shows its Choose View dialog. Figure 15.6 shows this dialog. Normally, one does not need to derive a new doc manager class. The most common reason for deriving a new doc manager class is to provide a better Choose Document dialog box.

Figure 15.6 The Doc Manager Choose Dialog

In my Hunter Image Collection Manager Database application available on the Internet, many different types of documents can be opened or created. Figure 15.7 shows the replacement dialog that my derived doc manager displays. (The current version is free and is available at http://www.broquard-ebooks.com and take the Hunter link.

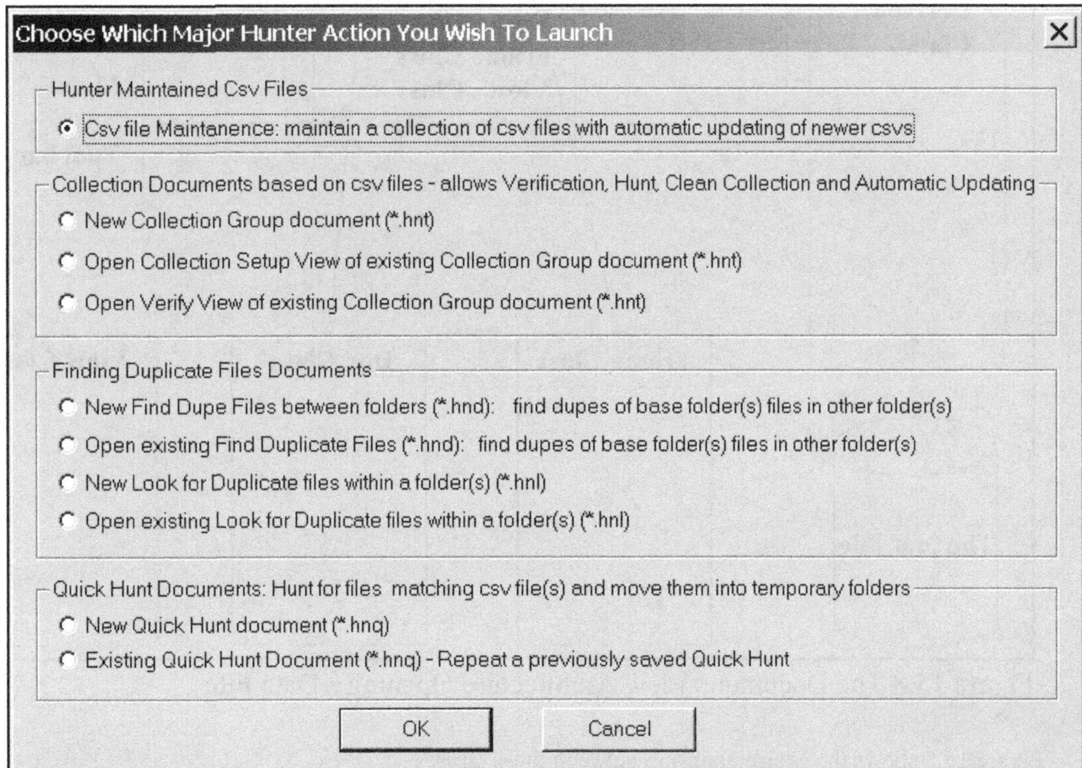

Figure 15.7 The Hunter Doc Manager Choose Document Dialog Box

After the document manager finds the right document template, the construction begins. An instance of the document class is created and the data in the file is loaded. The frame window is created loading in the required tool bar and main menu. Finally, the view class is created. The view is sent two notification messages as it is being created.

The first view notification message is handled by the function **OnInitialUpdate**. In this function, the view class can perform any needed initialization based upon the document's data. When the base class's **OnInitialUpdate** is called, it then sends the second notification message which is handled by the function **OnUpdate**.

OnUpdate is also called any time the document's data has changed so that the view can update its display of the data. When the base class's **OnUpdate** is called, it in turn calls **OnPaint** which calls **OnPrepareDC** followed by **OnDraw**.

The purpose of **OnPrepareDC** is to prepare the DC for drawing operations. Brushes, pens, fonts, and scaling are commonly installed in the passed **CDC** instance.

If the background needs to be erased, **OnEraseBkgnd** is called before **OnPaint** calls **OnDraw**. All actual window painting is then done in **OnDraw**. Please note that we never override a view's **OnPaint** function — we perform the actual painting in **OnDraw**, not **OnPaint**.

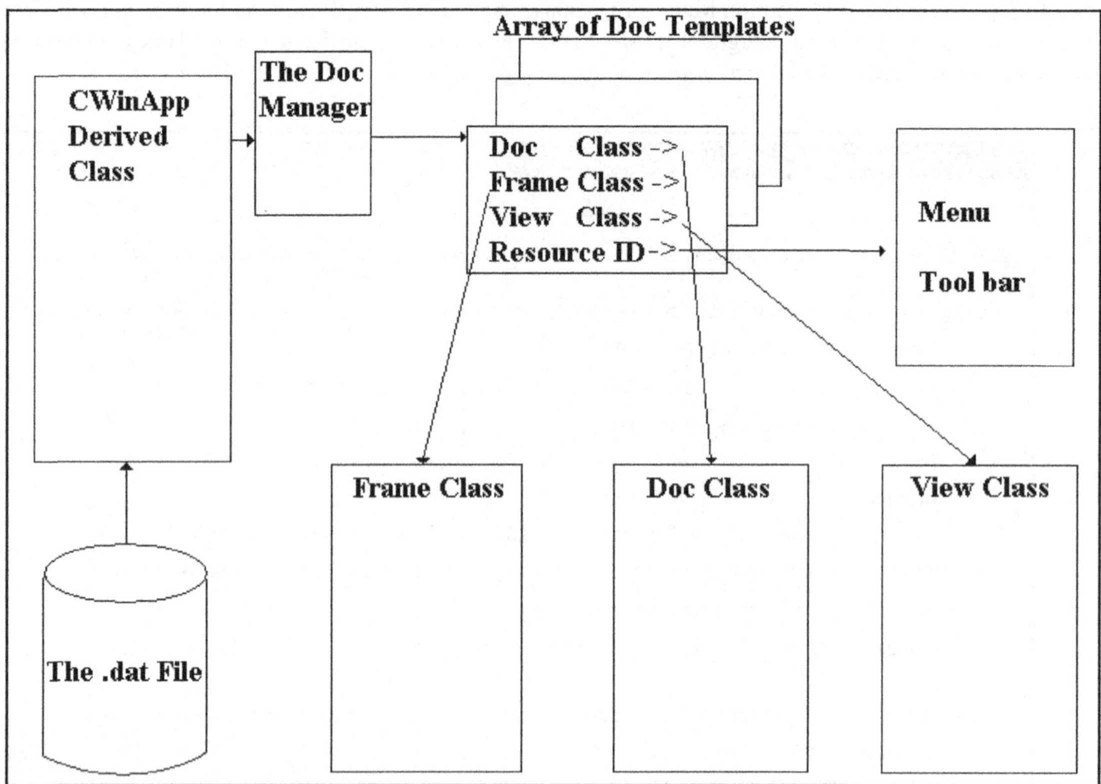

Figure 15.8 The Document-View Architecture Opening a Data File

Figure 15.8 shows the interrelationship between these classes.

Which class responds to the data update type of messages, such a Add, Update or Delete? There is no pat answer. It mostly depends upon how you wish to view the situation. Either the **CDocument** or **CView** derived class can launch the Add/Update/Delete data dialogs and modify the data.

One caution before you get too excited about the **CScrollView** class. While this class fully supports scrolling with virtually no effort on our part other than initially defining the total document size, it is limited in size (64K or 32,767 lines) under Windows 95/98/ME, just as the **CEdit** control is limited. Only under WinNT/2000 and XP can **CScrollView** support larger volumes of data.

Creating the Document-View Shell Application

When creating a document-view program, the best way to begin is to actually use the Application Wizard. In other words, we let the AppWizard create the shell files. Launch Visual Studio and choose File|New Project and select MFC Application and enter the new project name as usual. Next, a series of property pages is shown. On the first page shown in Figure 15.9, I chose Single Document.

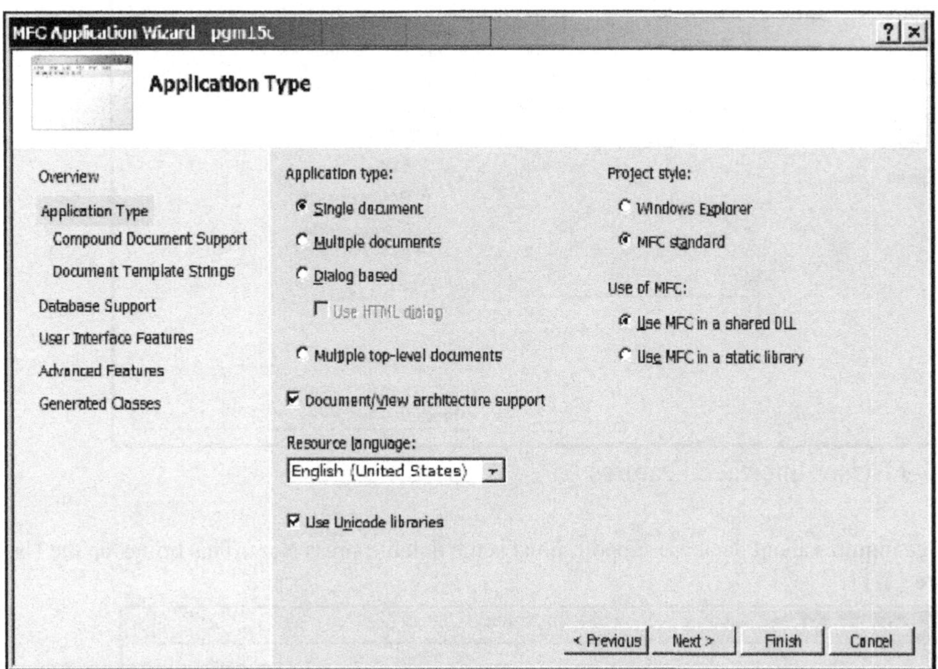

Figure 15.9 Application Wizard - Choose Single Document

When Next is pressed, the Page 2 inquires about what data base support you desire. Choose no data base support and press Next again. This page deals with the Document Template Strings. Suppose that we are making a Tester program that will read and save .tst files, for test. Here is where we specify the type of file our program handles. When a user double clicks a .tst file, Windows will launch our Tester program and have it open that file. Figure 15-10 shows this.

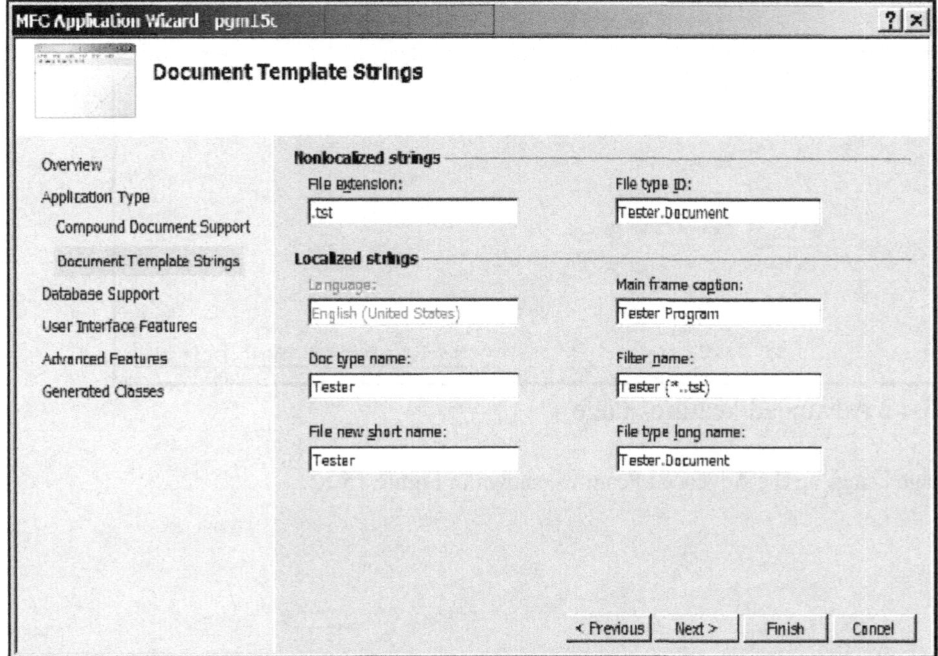

Figure 15-10 Entering the File Extension and Names the Program Handles

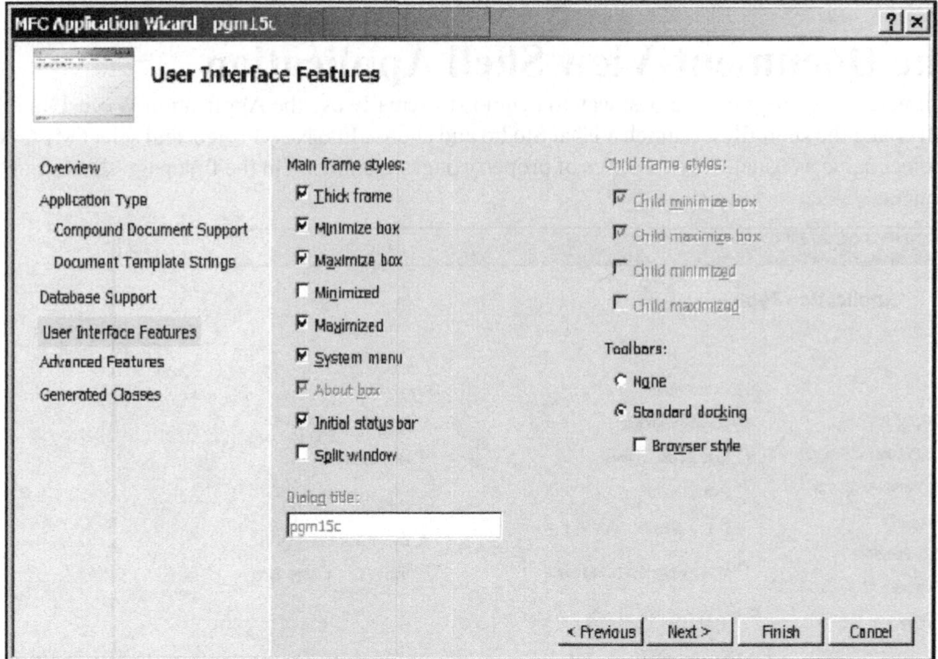

Figure 15-11 User Interface Features

The next page inquires about database support; none is the default; press Next. This brings up the User Interface page, shown in Figure 15-11.

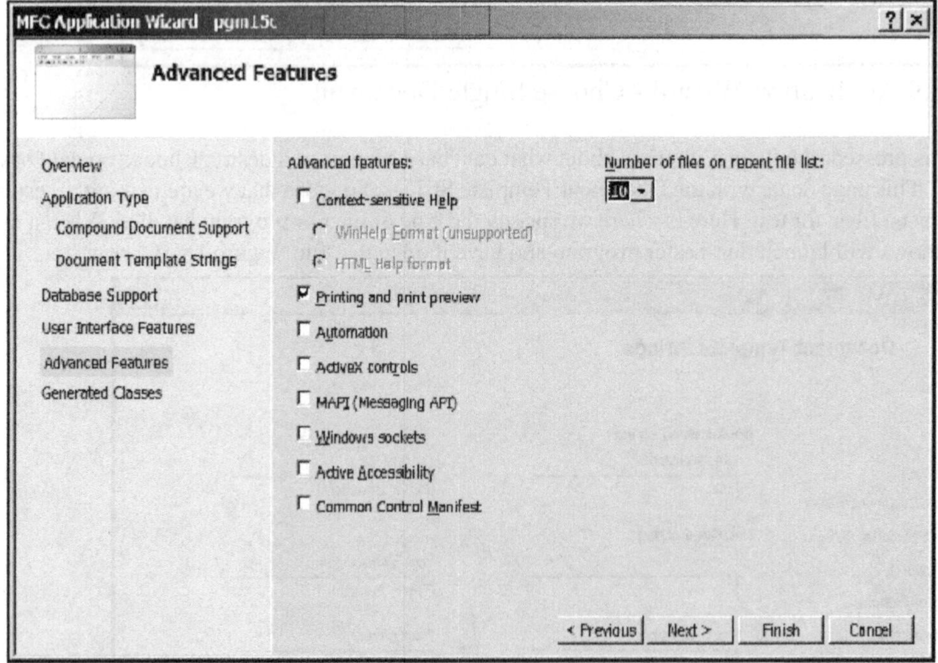

Figure 15-12 Advanced Features Page

The next page brings up the Advanced Features, shown in Figure 15.12.

Here we want to select Printing and Print Preview. Also you can set the number of files to be shown in the Most Recently Used portion of the program's File menu. The last page allows you to alter the generated class names and their files. When Finish is pressed, the Application Wizard builds the whole shell application which can be compiled and run, though it really does nothing functional as yet.

The AppWizard places the needed resources in a subfolder called **Res**. It also creates a **.rc2** file which is an auxiliary resource file which can contain non-editable user special resources.

The CDocument Derived Class for Pgm15a

The application's document class is derived from **CDocument** and is often quite small for simpler applications. As expected, there must be a default constructor that takes no arguments and a serializer function that uses the **CArchive** object to stream the document's data to or from the binary data file when the framework requests it.

If the class stores the data in container classes or in a form that is not destroyed automatically on the stack, then the member function **DeleteContents** must be overridden to specifically provide the coding necessary to remove the data objects. The framework and the **CDocument** base class handle all other details. In this application, however, methods to I/O a text form of the document are provided. Examine the document header file, **AcmeDoc.h**.

AcmeDoc Class Definition

```
#pragma once
#include "SalesData.h"

/***************************************************************/
/*                                                             */
/* AcmeDoc: Class Definition                                   */
/*                                                             */
/***************************************************************/

class AcmeDoc : public CDocument {

DECLARE_DYNCREATE (AcmeDoc)

public:

SalesDataArray sales_array;    // container for sales data objects

 /*************************************************************/
 /*                                                           */
 /* Class Functions:                                          */
 /*                                                           */
 /*************************************************************/

public:
     AcmeDoc () : CDocument () {};     // no parms if serializing
int  GetNumSales ();                   // gets number of sales data
void Serialize (CArchive&);            // I/O sales data
BOOL OnNewDocument ();                 // construct new document
BOOL OnOpenDocument (const char*);     // opens existing document
void DeleteContents ();                // removes SalesData objects
void LoadTextDocument (const char*); // load text file of data
void SaveTextDocument (const char*); // saves as a text file

afx_msg void OnFileTextLoad ();    // respond to menu Open As Text
afx_msg void OnFileTextSave ();    // respond to menu Save As Text

DECLARE_MESSAGE_MAP()
};
```

The document class defines our sales array as an instance of the **SalesDataArray** just discussed. The **DeleteContents** function deletes each **SalesData** object in the array container, then removes all of the container's pointers. Typically with document classes, the constructor does nothing. All of the action occurs in response to the framework's requests for opening a new or an existing document — the functions **OnNewDocument** and **OnOpenDocument**, both of which return non-zero values if the action is successful. The sole argument to the **OnOpenDocument** is the filename. Normally, these two functions do not need to be overridden, but I have here to show you the places where you can customize the loading of documents.

Since the document does not contain a member that holds the current number of sales objects, I include a user function, **GetNumSales** that the views may invoke to obtain the current number. The **OnFileTextLoad** and **OnFileTextSave** respond to the menu choices for document loading and saving in text format. Both functions use the common File Open Save dialogs to obtain the user's filename and then invoke either **LoadTextDocument** or **SaveTextDocument** to actually handle the I/O. Did you notice the new macro in the class header?

```
DECLARE_DYNCREATE (AcmeDoc)
```

The entire document-view system is launched dynamically at runtime. In other words, specific instances of the document and view classes are going to be constructed and streamed from disk. In fact, the user can drag the document file and drop it on the icon representing this application (**Pgm15a.exe**) and Windows launches this application instructing it to open the indicated document file! Try it; open Explorer or File Manager, drag **acme.dat** and drop it on the **Pgm15a.exe** file and watch the action.

Specifically this dynamic creation from disk can be done for objects derived from **CObject**, but the classes must notify the framework that they can be so created in order for the MFC to install proper coding to do so. This is done by using the following macros.

```
DECLARE_DYNCREATE (classname)
IMPLEMENT_DYNCREATE (classname, baseclassname)
```

There are three vital rules.

1. The declaration macro must be in the class definition in the header file.
2. The class must have a default constructor (one with no arguments).
3. The implement macro must appear in the class implementation file.

Examining the **AcmeDoc.cpp** implementation file, notice the first line after the #includes is the implement macro. Next comes the message map; the document class responds to the two special menu choices for loading and saving text files. The **GetNumSales** and **DeleteContents** contain the coding discussed above with the container class, **CObArray**. If you wish to customize the opening of documents process, override **OnNewDocument** and **OnOpenDocument**. First, invoke the base class and save the return code or else manually return **TRUE** or **FALSE**. Note that calling the base class of **OnOpenDocument** in turn attempts to call your document's **Serialize** function, if one is present. After the base class has done its actions, you can insert additional customization code. Additionally, you could alter the filename before passing it to **CDocument**'s **OnOpenDocument**.

Next, notice how simple the serialization coding really is. Based upon return value of the archive object's **IsStoring** function, invoke the serializer for **SalesDataArray** class, which, in turn, invokes the base class **CObArray**'s serializer which I/Os each object in the array by invoking our **SalesData**'s serializer which actually streams the **long** and **double** fields.

```
if (ar.IsStoring ()) { // binary save to a dat file
 if (sales_array.GetSize () == 0) return; // none to save
 sales_array.Serialize (ar); // invoke container's serializer
}
else // binary input from a dat file
 sales_array.Serialize (ar); // invoke container's serializer
```

When the user opts to load or save in text format, **OnFileTextLoad** and **OnFileTextSave** are invoked. Both use the common dialog box to get the user's choice of the filename, but there is one serious problem with the filenames. The documents are registered as having the **.dat** extension and text files should have the **.txt** extension. In the load function, after the user's filename is returned from the open dialog box and after the file is actually loaded into memory, the document's name and filename must be altered to the new file that was just loaded. The extension **.txt** must be stripped off and **.dat** installed. Then, the **CDocument** member function **SetPathName** can be invoked to install the new file and document name that appears in the title bar.

```
SetPathName (newfilename, TRUE);
```
where the **BOOL** indicates that this file is to be added to the most recently used listing on the File Menu.

The reverse must be done when saving a document to a text file. The current document name must have the .dat removed and .txt installed and the new filename passed into the Save dialog box as the initial file name. The document name can be retrieved using the function **GetPathName**.

```
CString*  GetPathName ();
```

With short filenames, the 8.3 DOS version, this is not a problem. However, with Windows's long filenames, the rules for filenames have changed. Specifically, blanks and periods can be part of the long filename. For example, one could have a silly filename like "Acme.Dat Main .DAT data file.DAT." Parsing long filenames becomes quite tricky.

A pair of Windows functions handles the parsing of these long filenames: **_splitpath_s** and **_makepath_s**. The **_splitpath_s** function takes a fully qualified path and splits it into four pieces: the drive string, the path string, the filename string, and the extension string. The **_makepath_s** function takes the four pieces and concatenates them into the full path name, i.e. the reverse of **_splitpath**_s. Here is how they are used when the user chooses the menu item to load in a text file. I have boldfaced the key lines. Notice that there are also some #defines for the maximum length each of these strings could be on a Windows platform.

```
void AcmeDoc::OnFileTextLoad () {
 CFileDialog filedlg (TRUE, "*.TXT", "*.TXT",
          OFN_FILEMUSTEXIST | OFN_PATHMUSTEXIST | OFN_LONGNAMES,
          "Text Files (*.TXT)|All Files (*.*)|*.*||", 0);
 if (filedlg.DoModal () == IDOK) {
  LoadTextDocument(filedlg.GetPathName ());
  char drive[_MAX_DRIVE];
  char dir[_MAX_PATH];
  char fn[_MAX_PATH];
  char ext[_MAX_EXT];
  char filename[_MAX_PATH];
  _splitpath_s (filedlg.GetPathName (), drive, _MAX_DRIVE, dir,
                _MAX_PATH, fn, _MAX_PATH, ext, _MAX_EXT);
  _makepath_s (filename, _MAX_PATH, drive, dir, fn, ".dat");
  // install the new document name
  CDocument::SetPathName (filename, TRUE);
  // cause all views to be updated with newdata
  UpdateAllViews (NULL, 0, NULL);
 }
}
```

The actual coding to load the document from a text file is very common coding. Just use an instance of an **ifstream** and extract sets of data. The initial call to **DeleteContents** is not obvious. It is done to ensure that any existing data that the document currently has is deleted. This is an important point.

Design Rule 57: In the SDI model, when subsequent documents are opened, the framework merely reuses the existing instances of the various classes. In the MDI model, each subsequent document is given its own separate instances of the classes.

Thus, we must call **DeleteContents** to remove any current data that may be in the document.

```
void AcmeDoc::LoadTextDocument (const char* filename) {
 DeleteContents ();
 long yr;                  // years
 double sls;               // sales
 SalesData *ptrdata;       // SalesData object to be add to array
 int i = 1;                // line counter in case of I/O error
 ifstream infile (filename);
...
 while (infile >> yr >> sls) {
  ptrdata = new SalesData (yr, sls); // allocate a new SalesData
  sales_array.Add (ptrdata);         // and add it to the array
```

```
  i++;
 }
...
```

Finally, there are several useful member functions of **CDocument** that are frequently used, especially by view classes which modify the document's data.

```
UpdateAllViews (CView* ptrsender, LPARAM hint, CObject *ptrhint);
BOOL IsModified ();
SetModifiedFlag (BOOL modified);
```

When a view modifies the document's data or the document itself modifies its data, it invokes the document's **UpdateAllViews** function which sends **OnUpdate** notification messages to all views that are associated with this document so that they can correctly display the altered values. Usually 0's are passed for the three arguments. However, for customization, a pointer to the view that has caused the change is passed along with user-defined **long** value and a user-defined pointer to the base **CObject** class of the changed data.

Additionally, the view that alters the document's data or the document itself **must** invoke the **SetModifiedFlag** document function. The **CDocument** class maintains a modified flag that is initially set to **FALSE**. When the document is to be destroyed, either by opening a new document or the frame window closing, the **CanCloseFrame** member function is called. If the data has been modified, the **CDocument** displays a message to the user and saves the data if so requested by the user. Typical coding in our view class that modifies the data would be as follows.

```
     ptrdocument->SetModifiedFlag (TRUE);
     ptrdocument->UpdateAllViews (NULL);
```

AcmeDoc Class Implementation

```
#include "stdafx.h"
#include <fstream>
using namespace std;
#include "AcmeDoc.h"
#include "resource.h"

IMPLEMENT_DYNCREATE(AcmeDoc, CDocument)

/***************************************************************/
/*                                                             */
/* AcmeDoc: Message Map                                        */
/*                                                             */
/***************************************************************/

BEGIN_MESSAGE_MAP(AcmeDoc, CDocument)
 ON_COMMAND(CM_FILE_LOAD_TEXT,   OnFileTextLoad)
 ON_COMMAND(CM_FILE_SAVE_TEXT,   OnFileTextSave)
END_MESSAGE_MAP()

/***************************************************************/
/*                                                             */
/* GetNumSales: returns the number of sales data objects       */
/*                                                             */
/***************************************************************/

int AcmeDoc::GetNumSales () {
 return sales_array.GetSize ();
}

/***************************************************************/
/*                                                             */
/* DeleteContents: remove the sales array of Sales objects     */
/*                                                             */
/***************************************************************/

```

```
void AcmeDoc::DeleteContents () {
 int i;
 if (sales_array.GetSize () ==0) return; // none to delete
 for (i=sales_array.GetSize()-1; i>=0; i--) {
  SalesData* ptrsales = (SalesData*) sales_array.GetAt (i);
  if (ptrsales) delete ptrsales;
 }
 sales_array.RemoveAll ();        // now empty the array container
}

/*************************************************************/
/*                                                           */
/* OnNewDocument: launch a new document                      */
/*                                                           */
/*************************************************************/

BOOL AcmeDoc::OnNewDocument () {
 if (!CDocument::OnNewDocument ()) return FALSE;
 return TRUE;
}

/*************************************************************/
/*                                                           */
/* OnOpenDocument: open existing document                    */
/*                                                           */
/*************************************************************/

BOOL AcmeDoc::OnOpenDocument (const char *filename) {
 BOOL retcd = CDocument::OnOpenDocument (filename);
 return retcd;
}

/*************************************************************/
/*                                                           */
/* Serialize: input or output the whole document             */
/*            - I/O binary data only                         */
/*                                                           */
/*************************************************************/

void AcmeDoc::Serialize (CArchive &ar) {
 if (ar.IsStoring ()) { // binary save to a dat file
  if (sales_array.GetSize () == 0) return; // none to save
  sales_array.Serialize (ar); // invoke container's serializer
 }
 else // binary input from a dat file
  sales_array.Serialize (ar); // invoke container's serializer
}

/*************************************************************/
/*                                                           */
/* LoadTextDocument: loads in a text document                */
/*                                                           */
/*************************************************************/

void AcmeDoc::LoadTextDocument (const char* filename) {
 // remove current document's sales array of SalesData objects
 DeleteContents ();

 long yr;                   // years
 double sls;                // sales
 SalesData *ptrdata;        // SalesData object to be add to array
 int i = 1;                 // line counter in case of I/O error

 ifstream infile (filename);
```

```
 if (!infile) {
  MessageBox (0, filename, "Error: cannot open file:",
              MB_ICONSTOP | MB_OK);
  return;
 }

 while (infile >> yr >> sls) {
  ptrdata = new SalesData (yr, sls); // allocate a new SalesData
  sales_array.Add (ptrdata);         // and add it to the array
  i++;
 }
 if (!infile.eof()) {
  char msg[80];
  wsprintf (msg, "Bad data on line %d", i);
  MessageBox (0, msg, "Error: bad data encountered",
              MB_ICONSTOP | MB_OK);
  return;
 }
 infile.close ();
}

/***************************************************************/
/*                                                             */
/* SaveTextDocument: saves this document as a text file        */
/*                                                             */
/***************************************************************/

void AcmeDoc::SaveTextDocument (const char* filename) {
 SalesData *ptrdata;
 ofstream outfile (filename);
 for (int i=0; i<sales_array.GetSize (); i++) {
  ptrdata = (SalesData*) sales_array.GetAt (i);
  if (!ptrdata) continue;
  outfile << ptrdata->year << " " << ptrdata->sales << "\n";
 }
}

/***************************************************************/
/*                                                             */
/* OnFileTextLoad: load a new document from a text file        */
/*                                                             */
/***************************************************************/

void AcmeDoc::OnFileTextLoad () {
 // get user's file choice by creating a new File Open Dialog Box
 CFileDialog filedlg (TRUE,    // use Open dialog
                      "*.TXT", // default extension
                      "*.TXT",   // current file name
           OFN_FILEMUSTEXIST | OFN_PATHMUSTEXIST | OFN_LONGNAMES,
           "Text Files (*.TXT)|All Files (*.*)|*.*||", 0);
 if (filedlg.DoModal () == IDOK) {  // user has chosen a file, so
  // go load in the text file
  LoadTextDocument(filedlg.GetPathName ());
  // now convert the filename into a proper document name by
  // removing the .TXT extension and substituting .DAT
  char drive[_MAX_DRIVE];
  char dir[_MAX_PATH];
  char fn[_MAX_PATH];
  char ext[_MAX_EXT];
  char filename[_MAX_PATH];
  _splitpath_s (filedlg.GetPathName (), drive, _MAX_DRIVE, dir,
                _MAX_PATH, fn, _MAX_PATH, ext, _MAX_EXT);
  _makepath_s (filename, _MAX_PATH, drive, dir, fn, ".dat");
  // install the new document name
```

```
   CDocument::SetPathName (filename, TRUE);
   // cause all views to be updated with newdata
   UpdateAllViews (NULL, 0, NULL);
  }
 }

/**************************************************************/
/*                                                            */
/* OnFileTextSave: save a new document to a text file         */
/*                                                            */
/**************************************************************/

void AcmeDoc::OnFileTextSave () {
 // get user's filename choice - make a File Save dialog
 CFileDialog filedlg (FALSE,     // use SaveAs dialog
                      "*.TXT", // default extension
                      "*.*",    // current file name
          OFN_HIDEREADONLY | OFN_OVERWRITEPROMPT | OFN_LONGNAMES,
                   "Text Files (*.TXT)|All Files (*.*)|*.*||",0);
 // converte the document name into a .TXT file name
 char drive[_MAX_DRIVE];
 char dir[_MAX_PATH];
 char fn[_MAX_PATH];
 char ext[_MAX_EXT];
 char filename[_MAX_PATH];
 _splitpath_s (filedlg.GetPathName (), drive, _MAX_DRIVE, dir,
               _MAX_PATH, fn, _MAX_PATH, ext, _MAX_EXT);
 _makepath_s (filename, _MAX_PATH, drive, dir, fn, ".txt");
 // and copy suggestion of filename into the dialog box
 strcpy_s (filedlg.m_ofn.lpstrFile, _MAX_PATH, filename);

 // invoke the Save dialog and get user's choice
 if (filedlg.DoModal () == IDOK) // if ok, save it with that name
  SaveTextDocument (filedlg.GetPathName ());
}
```

The Resource File for Pgm15a

Before we get into the complex coding of the view, let's examine the overall application setup and exactly how the document is installed in the framework. Begin by looking at the resource file and its header. There are several new items and many new identifiers. Since I am now using the MFC framework for most all of the default document-view implementation, I must use the AppWizard defined ID values so that the framework can invoke the correct member functions. To assist you in spotting which IDs are ours and which are the MFC internal IDs, I use the CM_ prefix for user-defined menu items. All those that begin with ID_ are the MFC internal IDs.

In the File pop-up menu File|Print Preview has been added to provide Print Preview support. Also note the special menu item "Recent File." Up to the last four data files that have been opened are inserted into the File menu at this point. The menu ID that corresponds to the most recently used file is **ID_FILE_MRU_FILE1**. Although there is only one menu item reserved, as you open other documents, the framework inserts up to four filenames here. If you select any of these, the current document is closed and the selected one opened — all without any special coding on our part! Of course, you are not limited to only four recently used files here in the menu, the number is controlled by In the application class implementation, merely include one line of coding to tell the framework to use this feature.

```
LoadStdProfileSettings (int number);
```

The number represents how many recently used files to show.

Finally, the identifier **IDR_MAINFRAME** is used to ID the **application icon**, the **main menu**, the **accelerator table** and a very special **string table** entry that defines the file extension that this application handles.

```
IDR_MAINFRAME "ACME Sales Data\n\nACME\nACME Files
```

```
(*.dat)\n.DAT\nACME\nACME Document"
```

This application string table entry is **vital** proper for document-view operations. It has a special syntax that defines seven separate strings; each one is separated by the newline code (\n). They are as follows.

```
string #  here coded            meaning
   1      ACME Sales Data\n     the application window caption
   2      \n                    constructs the doc name for file new
                                default is "Untitled"
   3      ACME\n                the file new name provides a type name
                                like "DataBase"
   4      ACME Files (*.dat)\n  filter name specifies a description
                                for the "List File of Type" combo box
   5      .DAT\n                file extension associated with this
                                document type
   6       ACME\n               if using the Registration Database,
                                provides the file type ID to be
                                registered so that Explorer/File Mgr
                                can automatically launch the app
   7       ACME Document        if using the Registration Database,
                                provides a meaningful name for
                                the registered files
```

If you are not going to register the document files with Windows, the last two strings can be omitted — numbers 6 and 7. Here, I register the **ACME.DAT** document with Windows the very first time that you run the application. After you have run **Pgm15a** one time, try launching the Explorer and double clicking on the **ACME.DAT** icon. The Windows registration database is searched for applications that can be launched to "view" this file. The extension **.dat** is a poor choice because many other commercial packages also use **.dat**. Specifically on my system, WordPerfect gets first crack at opening the **.dat** files.

Here are the key portions of the **Pgm15a.rc** file. Notice the extensive strings that have been generated by the MFC for the framework messages. If you do not like the existing framework message, feel free to modify its text string.

```
////////////////////////////////////////////////////////////////////////
// Icon
//
// Icon with lowest ID value placed first to ensure application icon
// remains consistent on all systems.
IDR_MAINFRAME            ICON    DISCARDABLE     "pgm15a.ico"
IDR_ACMETYPE             ICON    DISCARDABLE     "acmedoc.ico"
////////////////////////////////////////////////////////////////////////
// Bitmap
//
IDR_MAINFRAME            BITMAP  MOVEABLE PURE   "toolbar.bmp"
////////////////////////////////////////////////////////////////////////
/ Toolbar
//
IDR_MAINFRAME TOOLBAR DISCARDABLE  16, 15
BEGIN
    BUTTON      ID_FILE_NEW
    BUTTON      ID_FILE_OPEN
    BUTTON      ID_FILE_SAVE
      SEPARATOR
    BUTTON      ID_EDIT_CUT
    BUTTON      ID_EDIT_COPY
    BUTTON      ID_EDIT_PASTE
      SEPARATOR
    BUTTON      ID_FILE_PRINT
      SEPARATOR
    BUTTON      ID_APP_ABOUT
END
////////////////////////////////////////////////////////////////////////
// Menu
//
```

```
IDR_MAINFRAME MENU PRELOAD DISCARDABLE
BEGIN
    POPUP "&File"
    BEGIN
        MENUITEM "&New\tCtrl+N",                ID_FILE_NEW
        MENUITEM "&Open...\tCtrl+O",            ID_FILE_OPEN
        MENUITEM "&Save\tCtrl+S",               ID_FILE_SAVE
        MENUITEM "Save &As...",                 ID_FILE_SAVE_AS
        MENUITEM SEPARATOR
        MENUITEM "File &Load from .TXT",        CM_FILE_LOAD_TEXT
        MENUITEM "File Sa&ve to .TXT",          CM_FILE_SAVE_TEXT
        MENUITEM SEPARATOR
        MENUITEM "&Print...\tCtrl+P",           ID_FILE_PRINT
        MENUITEM "Print Pre&view",              ID_FILE_PRINT_PREVIEW
        MENUITEM "P&rint Setup...",             ID_FILE_PRINT_SETUP
        MENUITEM SEPARATOR
        MENUITEM "Recent File",             ID_FILE_MRU_FILE1, GRAYED
        MENUITEM SEPARATOR
        MENUITEM "E&xit",                       ID_APP_EXIT
    END
    POPUP "&Edit"
    BEGIN
        MENUITEM "&Add Record...",              CM_ADD
        MENUITEM "&Update Current Record",      CM_UPDATE
        MENUITEM "&Delete Current Record",      CM_DELETE
    END
    MENUITEM "&Fonts",                      CM_FONTS
    POPUP "&View"
    BEGIN
        MENUITEM "&Toolbar",                    ID_VIEW_TOOLBAR
        MENUITEM "&Status Bar",                 ID_VIEW_STATUS_BAR
    END
    POPUP "&Help"
    BEGIN
        MENUITEM "&About Pgm15a...",            ID_APP_ABOUT
    END
END
IDR_UPDT_DEL MENU DISCARDABLE
BEGIN
    POPUP "Choose"
    BEGIN
        MENUITEM "&Update the Current Record",  CM_UPDATE
        MENUITEM "&Delete the Current Record",  CM_DELETE
    END
END
IDD_ADD_UPDATE DIALOG DISCARDABLE  0, 0, 146, 77
STYLE DS_MODALFRAME | WS_POPUP | WS_VISIBLE | WS_CAPTION | WS_SYSMENU
CAPTION "Add New Sales Data"
FONT 8, "MS Sans Serif"
BEGIN
    EDITTEXT        IDC_EDIT_YEAR,12,22,40,14,ES_AUTOHSCROLL
    EDITTEXT        IDC_EDIT_SALES,69,22,62,14,ES_AUTOHSCROLL
    DEFPUSHBUTTON   "OK",IDOK,11,47,50,14
    PUSHBUTTON      "Cancel",IDCANCEL,78,46,50,14
    LTEXT           "Year",IDC_YEAR,12,11,37,7,NOT WS_GROUP
    LTEXT           "Sales",IDC_SALES,70,11,52,7,NOT WS_GROUP
END
/////////////////////////////////////////////////////////////////////////////
// String Table
//
STRINGTABLE PRELOAD DISCARDABLE
BEGIN
   IDR_MAINFRAME        "ACME Sales Data\n\nACME\nACME Files"
                        " (*.dat)\n.DAT\nACME\nACME Document"
```

```
AFX_IDS_APP_TITLE   "Pgm15a"
AFX_IDS_IDLEMESSAGE "Ready"
ID_INDICATOR_EXT    "EXT"
ID_INDICATOR_CAPS   "CAP"
ID_INDICATOR_NUM    "NUM"
ID_INDICATOR_SCRL   "SCRL"
ID_INDICATOR_OVR    "OVR"
ID_INDICATOR_REC    "REC"
ID_FILE_NEW        "Create a new sales document\nNew Sales Doc"
ID_FILE_OPEN       "Open an existing sales document\nOpen Existing"
ID_FILE_CLOSE      "Close the active sales document\nClose"
ID_FILE_SAVE       "Save the active sales document\nSave"
ID_FILE_SAVE_AS    "Save the active sales document with a new "
                   " name\nSave As"
ID_FILE_PAGE_SETUP "Change the printing options\nPage Setup"
ID_FILE_PRINT_SETUP    "Change the printer and printing "
                        " options\nPrint Setup"
ID_FILE_PRINT          "Print the active sales document\nPrint"
ID_FILE_PRINT_PREVIEW  "Display full pages\nPrint Preview"
ID_APP_ABOUT           "Display program information\nAbout"
ID_APP_EXIT            "Quit the application; prompt to save "
                       "sales documents\nExit"
ID_FILE_MRU_FILE1      "Open this sales document"
ID_FILE_MRU_FILE2      "Open this sales document"
ID_FILE_MRU_FILE3      "Open this sales document"
ID_FILE_MRU_FILE4      "Open this sales document"
ID_NEXT_PANE           "Switch to the next window pane\nNext Pane"
ID_PREV_PANE           "Switch back to the previous window "
                       " pane\nPrevious Pane"
ID_WINDOW_SPLIT        "Split the active window into panes\nSplit"
ID_EDIT_CLEAR          "Erase the selection\nErase"
ID_EDIT_CLEAR_ALL      "Erase everything\nErase All"
ID_EDIT_COPY           "Copy the selection and put it on the "
                       " Clipboard\nCopy"
ID_EDIT_CUT            "Cut the selection and put it on the "
                       " Clipboard\nCut"
ID_EDIT_FIND           "Find the specified text\nFind"
ID_EDIT_PASTE          "Insert Clipboard contents\nPaste"
ID_EDIT_REPEAT         "Repeat the last action\nRepeat"
ID_EDIT_REPLACE        "Replace specific text with different "
                       " text\nReplace"
ID_EDIT_SELECT_ALL     "Select the entire document\nSelect All"
ID_EDIT_UNDO           "Undo the last action\nUndo"
ID_EDIT_REDO           "Redo the previously undone action\nRedo"
ID_VIEW_TOOLBAR        "Show or hide the toolbar\nToggle ToolBar"
ID_VIEW_STATUS_BAR     "Show or hide the status bar\nToggle "
                       " StatusBar"
AFX_IDS_SCSIZE         "Change the window size"
AFX_IDS_SCMOVE         "Change the window position"
AFX_IDS_SCMINIMIZE     "Reduce the window to an icon"
AFX_IDS_SCMAXIMIZE     "Enlarge the window to full size"
AFX_IDS_SCNEXTWINDOW   "Switch to the next document window"
AFX_IDS_SCPREVWINDOW   "Switch to the previous document window"
AFX_IDS_SCCLOSE        "Close the active window and prompts to "
                       "save the documents"
AFX_IDS_SCRESTORE      "Restore the window to normal size"
AFX_IDS_SCTASKLIST     "Activate Task List"
AFX_IDS_PREVIEW_CLOSE  "Close print preview mode\nCancel Preview"
CM_FILE_LOAD_TEXT      "Load document from a text file\nLoad from"
                       " .TXT"
CM_FILE_SAVE_TEXT      "Save document to a .TXT file\nSave to "
                       ".TXT"
CM_FONTS               "Choose Fonts\nChoose Fonts"
CM_ADD                 "Add a new sales data record to the "
```

```
                        "end\nAdd Record"
   CM_UPDATE            "Update the current record\nUpdate Red Record"
   CM_DELETE            "Delete the current record\nDelete Red Record"
   IDS_MSG_QUIT         "Do you want to quit the application?"
   IDS_MSG_QUERY        "Query?"
   IDS_YEARS            "Year"
   IDS_SALES            "Sales"
   IDS_ACMETITLE        "ACME Manufacturing Company Yearly Sales Report"
   IDS_FOOTER           "Prepared by Broquard Consultants"
   IDS_CONFIRM1         "Confirm Deletion of the Current Record (in Red)"
   IDS_CONFIRM2         "Press Yes to confirm deletion"
END
```

The Application Class for Pgm15a

While no changes are required in the application class definition, the **InitInstance** and message map have numerous changes to support document-view. The **CWinApp** class handles launching documents as well as main windows. The base class handles the menu items File|New and File|Open as well as picking one of the most recently used files from the File menu. It also handles the File|Print and File|Preview operations. The base **CWinApp** class message map simply routes these menu requests on down to the base class handler functions.

With document-view, **InitInstance** is more complex. The first action defines a new instance of the SDI document-view template, **CSingleDocTemplate**. The template ties all of the parts together.

The first **UINT** is the ID for the main menu, icon, accelerator table and string resource for this document. The string resource, as we have just seen, contains vital information on the file names and types for this document.

The next trio defines the document class that is to be created, the main window that is to be launched to support the document, and the specific view class that is to be instantiated to display the document. Because there are two different view classes, two templates are needed.

```
CSingleDocTemplate *ptrdoctemplate1;
ptrdoctemplate1 = new CSingleDocTemplate (IDR_MAINFRAME,
                                  RUNTIME_CLASS (AcmeDoc),
                                  RUNTIME_CLASS (FrameWin),
                                  RUNTIME_CLASS (AcmeView));
CSingleDocTemplate *ptrdoctemplate2;
ptrdoctemplate2 = new CSingleDocTemplate (IDR_MAINFRAME,
                                  RUNTIME_CLASS (AcmeDoc),
                                  RUNTIME_CLASS (FrameWin),
                                  RUNTIME_CLASS (AcmeView));
AddDocTemplate (ptrdoctemplate1);
AddDocTemplate (ptrdoctemplate2);
```

The **RUNTIME_CLASS** identifies this class is using the C++ runtime type identification mechanism. That is, if a pointer or a reference to this class or any of their base classes is used, C++ can determine what the derived class actually is.

Next both templates are added to the **CWinApp** instance's document manager using the member function **AddDocTemplate** so that it can dynamically construct the document and views when requested by File|New and File|Open commands. This function takes a pointer to the SDI template instance.

By setting **m_nCmdShow** to maximized we guarantee that when a document is opened, the frame window occupies the full screen. This instruction is followed by a series of **CWinApp** member function calls designed to activate several key features. The functions **EnableShellOpen** and **RegisterShellFileTypes** combine to provide DDE support. Also, by invoking the frame window's **DragAcceptFiles** member function, the user can drop any of the **.dat** files on the **Pgm15a.exe** icon and Windows launches the application with that document. By invoking the **CWinApp** member function **LoadStdProfileSettings**, we activate the most recently used lists, making them fully functional, all handled by the framework. The number passed to the function determines how many recent files to include in the File pop-up menu.

```
m_nCmdShow = SW_SHOWMAXIMIZED;
EnableShellOpen ();          // enable DDE Execute open
RegisterShellFileTypes (); //register DAT types for DDE open
LoadStdProfileSettings (4);// activates 4 Most Recent File
if (m_lpCmdLine[0] == 0)    // no file given on the cmd line,
 OpenDocumentFile ("acme.dat"); // so use our default file
// or use: OnFileNew (); for a new file
else
 OpenDocumentFile (m_lpCmdLine); // open file on cmd line
m_pMainWnd->DragAcceptFiles (); // enable drag and drop open
```

If there is a filename on the command line, it is passed to the member function **OpenDocumentFile** to open the document file, launch the associated frame window and the views. On the other hand, if the command line is a null string, then you have your choice. Here, I chose to open the default small document, **ACME.DAT**. If you wish to present the user with an empty new document, use the function **OnFileNew** instead. These functions are the same ones that respond to the File menu commands handled by the **CWinApp** class default message map.

I took the liberty of setting the option for the main window to be maximized when it is created. This makes good sense because most of the screen area is to contain the bar chart.

Have you noticed any "missing" coding — coding that until now was in **InitInstance**? No instance of the **FrameWin**, main window class, is created! Instead, when the **CWinApp** opens or creates a new document, it examines the installed templates to see what main window class is to be dynamically constructed to support that document.

Pgm15a CWinApp Class Implementation

```
#include "stdafx.h"
#include "Pgm15a.h"
#include "FrameWin.h"
#include "AcmeDoc.h"
#include "AcmeView.h"
#include "AcmePlot.h"
#include "resource.h"

Pgm15a    theApp;   // launch app

/***************************************************************/
/*                                                             */
/* Pgm15a: message map                                         */
/*                                                             */
/***************************************************************/

BEGIN_MESSAGE_MAP(Pgm15a,           CWinApp)
 ON_COMMAND(ID_FILE_NEW,            CWinApp::OnFileNew)
 ON_COMMAND(ID_FILE_OPEN,           CWinApp::OnFileOpen)
 ON_COMMAND(ID_FILE_PRINT_SETUP, CWinApp::OnFilePrintSetup)
 ON_COMMAND(ID_APP_ABOUT,           OnHelpAbout)
END_MESSAGE_MAP()

/***************************************************************/
/*                                                             */
/* InitInstance: allocate instance of our frame main window    */
/*                                                             */
/***************************************************************/

BOOL Pgm15a::InitInstance () {

 // construct two document templates, one for each view
 CSingleDocTemplate *ptrdoctemplate1;
 ptrdoctemplate1 = new CSingleDocTemplate (IDR_MAINFRAME,
```

```
                                        RUNTIME_CLASS (AcmeDoc),
                                        RUNTIME_CLASS (FrameWin),
                                        RUNTIME_CLASS (AcmeView));

 CSingleDocTemplate *ptrdoctemplate2;
 ptrdoctemplate2 = new CSingleDocTemplate (IDR_MAINFRAME,
                                        RUNTIME_CLASS (AcmeDoc),
                                        RUNTIME_CLASS (FrameWin),
                                        RUNTIME_CLASS (AcmePlot));

 // install both templates
 AddDocTemplate (ptrdoctemplate1);
 AddDocTemplate (ptrdoctemplate2);

 m_nCmdShow = SW_SHOWMAXIMIZED;  // main window to be maximized

 EnableShellOpen ();            // enable DDE Execute open
 RegisterShellFileTypes ();     // register .DAT types for DDE open
 LoadStdProfileSettings (4);    // activates Most Recent File menu

 // determine which document file to open first
 if (m_lpCmdLine[0] == 0) // none on cmd line, so use default
  OpenDocumentFile ("acme.dat");
                          // or use: OnFileNew (); for a new file
 else OpenDocumentFile (m_lpCmdLine); // open file on cmd line

 if (m_pMainWnd->GetSafeHwnd())
  m_pMainWnd->DragAcceptFiles (); // enable drag and drop open
 return TRUE;
}

/*****************************************************************/
/*                                                               */
/* OnHelpAbout: shows who wrote this app                         */
/*                                                               */
/*****************************************************************/

void Pgm15a::OnHelpAbout () {
 // informational modal dialog
 CDialog aboutdlg ("IDD_ABOUT");
 aboutdlg.DoModal ();
}
```

The Frame Window Class: FrameWin

The main frame window class, **FrameWin** derived as usual from **CFrameWnd**, becomes very streamlined. However, since it is being dynamically created during the document open process, it must also use the **DECLARE_DYNCREATE** and **IMPLEMENT_DYNCREATE** macros. As expected, the frame window owns the tool bar and the status bar. It also owns the new object, the **CSplitterWnd** that manages the two views, side-by-side.

OnCreate as always constructs the tool bar and status bar. In many previous examples, there was no client window attached to the frame or else I launched a **CWnd** derived class to be the client window, such as the **DrawWin** or **ScrollWin**. To use a splitter window, the frame window's instance of the **CSplitterWnd** must be constructed instead of the normal default client window. This is why **OnCreateClient** is overridden. It is in **OnCreateClient** that I construct the splitter window telling it exactly what views I want and how they are to be initially positioned. If the user drags on the divider line, the pair of windows' widths can be adjusted as desired.

Although we have not had any need to override the function **PreCreateWindow** which is invoked at the beginning of the window creation process, now it can be used to set the **WNDCLASS** style flags to best support the document-view system.

```
FrameWin Class Definition
```

```
#pragma once
/***************************************************************/
/*                                                             */
/* FrameWin Class Definition                                   */
/*                                                             */
/***************************************************************/

class FrameWin : public CFrameWnd {

DECLARE_DYNCREATE (FrameWin)

 /*************************************************************/
 /*                                                           */
 /* Class Data:                                               */
 /*                                                           */
 /*************************************************************/

protected:

CToolBar      toolbar;     // the control bar
CStatusBar    statusbar;   // the status bar
CSplitterWnd  splitterwin; // our splitter window with two views

 /*************************************************************/
 /*                                                           */
 /* Class Functions:                                          */
 /*                                                           */
 /*************************************************************/

public:
              FrameWin () : CFrameWnd () {}

protected:
         BOOL PreCreateWindow(CREATESTRUCT&);// set wndclass style
afx_msg int  OnCreate(LPCREATESTRUCT); // make tool & status bars

         // make splitter windows
virtual BOOL OnCreateClient (LPCREATESTRUCT, CCreateContext*);

DECLARE_MESSAGE_MAP()
};
```

In **PreCreateWindow**, OR in the **FWS_ADDTOTITLE** style. This style flag tells the framework to append the document name to the main title automatically during File|New or File|Open or File|SaveAs operations. The coding to construct the tool and status bars has no changes for document-view. If you do not want this behavior, the filename being appended to the caption, then remove this flag from the style.

It is in the **OnCreateClient** that the splitter window construction takes place. Splitter windows come in two forms: static splitter windows and dynamic splitter windows. With static splitter windows, the number of panes (rows and columns of views) is determined at compile-time and cannot be altered at runtime. With dynamic splitter windows, the number of panes (rows and columns) is variable and is controlled at runtime by either the user or application events. In this first look at splitter windows, a static splitter window is used.

The first parameter, the **LPCREATESTRUCT** is not needed; however, the second, a pointer to the **CCreateContext** structure is. When this function is called, the structure has been filled with pointers to the document, the document template, the current frame, and a **CRuntimeClass** pointer to the new view to create. Our use is to simply pass this pointer onto the other member functions that require it.

The first step in the construction of a static splitter window is to invoke the **CreateStatic** function, saving its return code to later return back when the function ends.

```
BOOL retcd = splitterwin.CreateStatic (this, 1, 2);
```

The first **int** is the number of rows and the second **int** is the number of columns. Here I want one row of two columns. Thus, there are going to be two panes or two views side by side.

Next, the views that are to be in each pane must be created. The order of creation does not determine into which split window pane the view is placed. Rather, the first two parameters to **CreateView** determine the pane that is to be used. I want the narrow columnar scroll view to be in the left pane, so it is in row 0, column 0. However, the order of creation is important. The splitter window is the surrogate parent window for each view and therefore determines the dimensions or size of each view. The splitter window attempts to make the first view occupy the dimensions coded. Since these views are side by side, the height of both views ends up being the actual height of the client area, less any space occupied by the splitter window itself. However, the width of the views is constrained because they are side by side. If there is sufficient width available, the splitter creates the scroll view with the requested width, here 180 pixels. Then, all of the remaining width is given to the second pane containing the bar chart plot view.

```
retcd |= splitterwin.CreateView (0, 0, RUNTIME_CLASS (AcmeView),
                                 CSize (180, 100), ptrc);
retcd |= splitterwin.CreateView (0, 1, RUNTIME_CLASS (AcmePlot),
                                 CSize (100, 100), ptrc);
```

The first parameter is the row and the second is the column; both are zero-based. The third parameter is the view class to be created and installed in this pane, while the fourth parameter is a **CSize** indicating an initial width and height of the view. Here after some experimentation, I chose 180 pixels as the initial width of the normal view. When the splitter window is actually displayed, the views are resized to match the client area of the frame window, here maximized. Thus, the height of both views is going to be greatly increased to fill the large maximized window. However, the splitter window respects our initial width for the first window, allowing the last window to expand its width. It maintains the proportions between the windows.

If there were three side-by-side windows, then only the last rightmost window would be expanded; the other two would retain their initial widths, assuming that there was sufficient space.

The last parameter is the passed pointer to the **CCreateContext**. Note that I OR into the return code the return code from the **CreateView** function calls. I can then return one combined success or fail return code.

FrameWin Class Implementation

```
#include "stdafx.h"
#include "FrameWin.h"
#include "AcmeView.h"
#include "AcmePlot.h"
#include "resource.h"

IMPLEMENT_DYNCREATE(FrameWin, CFrameWnd)

// control bar buttons - IDs are command buttons
static UINT BASED_CODE buttons[] =
{
  // same order as in the bitmap 'toolbar.bmp'
  ID_FILE_NEW,
  ID_FILE_OPEN,
  ID_FILE_SAVE,
  ID_FILE_SAVE_AS,
  ID_SEPARATOR,
  CM_ADD,
  CM_UPDATE,
  CM_DELETE,
  ID_SEPARATOR,
  ID_FILE_PRINT,
  ID_FILE_PRINT_PREVIEW,
```

```
  CM_FONTS,
  ID_APP_ABOUT,
};

static UINT BASED_CODE indicators[] =
{
  ID_SEPARATOR,           // status line indicator
  ID_INDICATOR_CAPS,
  ID_INDICATOR_NUM,
  ID_INDICATOR_SCRL,
};

/***************************************************************/
/*                                                             */
/* FrameWin Message Map                                        */
/*                                                             */
/***************************************************************/

BEGIN_MESSAGE_MAP(FrameWin, CFrameWnd)
 ON_WM_CREATE ()
END_MESSAGE_MAP()

/***************************************************************/
/*                                                             */
/* PreCreateWindow: assign style options                       */
/*                                                             */
/***************************************************************/

BOOL FrameWin::PreCreateWindow(CREATESTRUCT& cs) {
 cs.style = WS_OVERLAPPED | WS_CAPTION | FWS_ADDTOTITLE
          | WS_THICKFRAME | WS_SYSMENU | WS_MINIMIZEBOX
          | WS_MAXIMIZEBOX | WS_MAXIMIZE;
 return CFrameWnd::PreCreateWindow(cs);
}

/***************************************************************/
/*                                                             */
/* OnCreate: construct status and control bars                 */
/*                                                             */
/***************************************************************/

int FrameWin::OnCreate (LPCREATESTRUCT lpCS) {
 if (CFrameWnd::OnCreate (lpCS) == 0)
  if (toolbar.Create (this) && toolbar.LoadBitmap (IDR_MAINFRAME)
      && toolbar.SetButtons (buttons,
                             sizeof(buttons) / sizeof(UINT)))
   if (statusbar.Create (this)
       && statusbar.SetIndicators (indicators,
                             sizeof(indicators) / sizeof(UINT)));
   else return -1;
  else return -1;
 else return -1;

 toolbar.EnableDocking (CBRS_ALIGN_ANY);
 EnableDocking (CBRS_ALIGN_ANY);
 DockControlBar (&toolbar);
 toolbar.SetBarStyle (
            toolbar.GetBarStyle() | CBRS_TOOLTIPS | CBRS_FLYBY);
 toolbar.SetWindowText ("Toolbar");
 return 0;
}

/***************************************************************/
/*                                                             */
```

```
/* OnCreateClient: construct splitter window static style      */
/*                                                              */
/***************************************************************/

BOOL FrameWin::OnCreateClient (LPCREATESTRUCT,
                               CCreateContext *ptrc) {
 // construct the basic splitter window
 BOOL retcd = splitterwin.CreateStatic (this, 1, 2);
 // construct two views side by side - same row with two columns
 // make a guess at the width needed by the first view
 // the AcmeView - 180 pels and then let the plot view have all
 // of the remaining window width - if short, user can adjust it
 retcd |= splitterwin.CreateView (0, 0, RUNTIME_CLASS (AcmeView),
                                  CSize (180, 100), ptrc);
 retcd |= splitterwin.CreateView (0, 1, RUNTIME_CLASS (AcmePlot),
                                  CSize (100, 100), ptrc);
 return retcd;
}
```

Splitter windows can also be dynamically created by menu item selection or by dragging a splitter box. In an SDI application, splitter windows can hold different views as done here or they can display multiple views of the same view class. Using multiple views from the same view class, one can position one view to the start of the data and position another view to the end for comparison purposes. When using the static splitter windows, the user can only drag the separation borders to alter their respective sizes. They cannot be unsplit or re split.

On the other hand, dynamic splitter windows and be unsplit and re split as the user chooses; menu items are usually added to facilitate these actions.

To construct dynamic splitter windows, alter the coding in the **OnCreateClient** function to use just the **Create** member function.

```
return splitterwin.Create (this, 2, 2, CSize (1,1), ptrc);
```

Then add a menu item "Split Window" giving it the ID of **ID_WINDOW_SPLIT**. The framework recognizes this ID to mean start the splitting process. The user can then adjust the bars to split the client area into a maximum of four panes, all showing the same view class, each of which can be scrolled to a different portion of the data.

The CView Classes AcmeView

Last come the lengthy **CView** derived classes. **AcmeView** displays the **SalesData** objects in a scrollable columnar view, while **AcmePlot** draws a bar chart graph. Let's begin with a walk through of the function sequences involved in launching a document's view.

Dynamically the framework allocates a new instance of the **CView** derived class. After invoking **OnCreate** as expected, this first time allocation sequence then invokes **OnInitialUpdate** to allow the new view to perform beginning actions, such as obtaining the number of sales data in the set of data. Then, shortly afterwards, the first **OnUpdate** message is sent. **OnUpdate** is called once during the view's launching and then later on whenever the document's data is altered in any way. The purpose of **OnUpdate** is to reacquire the document's data. Every time the document's **UpdateAllViews** is executed, it invokes each view window's **OnUpdate** function to permit that view instance to adapt itself to the changed data, typically reacquiring the current number of sets of sales data. The base class implementation of **OnUpdate** sends the paint message to actually get the new data displayed.

As the view window is resized to fit in the client area and in the splitter pane, **OnSize** is invoked followed by **OnPaint**.

OnPaint in a view class is quite different. First, the **OnPaint** function calls **OnPrepareDC** to permit us to get the paint DC setup properly with needed brushes, pens, fonts and scaling. Then, it calls **OnDraw** passing it the prepared DC. It is **OnDraw**'s responsibility to actually paint the screen.

When the user selects File|Print, the framework first calls **OnPreparePrinting** whose task it is to set the number of pages and other values that are to be shown in the print dialog box. If the user clicks the OK button, **OnBeginPrinting** is invoked starting the lengthy printing cycle. Here, one typically creates the printer font, sets up the printer DC, and determines pagination information, such as the number of pages to print and so on. We will examine the details in a later section. The **OnEndPrinting** function is called at the very end of the printing sequence so that we can perform any clean up actions, such as removing the printer font.

The framework then invokes **OnPrepareDC** followed by **OnPrint** for each page to be printed. **OnPrint** handles the page setup operations, such as printing headings, column headings, and footers. Once these are printed, **OnPrint** invokes **OnDraw** to render the body of the page. **OnPrepareDC** has the added responsibility of notifying the framework when the last page has been printed, at which point the framework then terminates the printing process by calling **OnEndPrinting**.

Did you notice the two dual-duty functions? **OnPrepareDC** and **OnDraw** are used to render the image both on the screen and on the printer!

OnPrepareDC generally installs the correct font for the device at hand, gets the average character dimensions, and if printing, determines when the last page has been printed.

OnDraw can be fairly ignorant of whether it is displaying on a screen DC or a printer DC. It just paints the text. However, you can override **OnPrint** and not invoke the base class which in turn invokes **OnDraw**, substituting instead your own function to render directly to the printer. However, Print|Preview is going to use this same sequence to render the sneak preview, passing a preview DC to this pair of functions. So if you use this dual duty combo, then you can implement Print Preview with no extra coding!

For our example, more complications enter because I wish to keep track of the current user-selected record so that it could be updated or deleted. (Add records are always placed at the end of the array; you could alter this and place the added data into year-sorted order if desired, use the **InsertAt** function instead of **Add**.) Notice that double clicking on a line of sales data not only selects that as the current record but immediately opens the Update Sales Data dialog on it. In addition, the view must be scrollable. I could have derived the class from the **CScrollView** class, however, I chose to use the more basic class **CView** for this first exposure to document-view. Thus, functions are needed to handle scrolling; they are basically the same functions that have been used throughout all of these examples.

Look over the **AcmeView** class member functions. Since this class is to be dynamically created, it must have a default constructor (no arguments); this time a destructor is required to delete the fonts used for the display and for printing.

OnDraw renders the screen display with fancy raised column headings or renders the body of a printed page.

```
void OnDraw (CDC *ptrdc);
```

As we implement the various functions, we constantly need a pointer to the document class. Hence, I define a utility routine, **GetDocument**, that returns a pointer to the document. The **CView** class maintains a pointer to the **CDocument** base class as well as a **GetDocument** function. My version of the function returns that pointer typecasted to an **AcmeDoc***. Similarly, I define a **SetupPrinterFont** that constructs a correctly scaled printer font based upon the user's font choice, if any. The prototypes for the usual printing functions of **CView** that are overridden are as follows.

```
BOOL  OnPreparePrinting (CPrintInfo*);
void  OnBeginPrinting (CDC*, CPrintInfo*);
void  OnEndPrinting (CDC*, CPrintInfo*);
void  OnPrepareDC (CDC*, CPrintInfo*);
void  OnPrint (CDC*, CPrintInfo*);
```

The **CPrintInfo** contains several key members.

```
m_bPreview           - a BOOL flag set by the framework indicating
                       that Print Preview is in effect
m_bContinuePrinting  - a BOOL - when TRUE continues the print loop
                       OnPrepareDC should set this to FALSE
                       after the last page has been printed
m_nCurPage           - the number of the current page to print
m_nNumPreviewPages   - indicates whether 1 or 2 pages are shown in
                       Preview window
m_rectDraw           - rectangle specifying the current usable
                       page area and can be used on OnPrint
```

OnInitialUpdate does not need to be coded in this application, however, I included it for your future reference. In **OnUpdate**, the scroll range is reset based upon the new number of sales data objects. In addition to the familiar **SetOurScrollRange** utility function to adjust the range and thumb position, **CalcCurrentSelection** maintains the integrity of the user's current record selection. **OnVScroll** responds to scroll bar messages, while **OnKeyDown** provides a keyboard scrolling interface. **OnSize** also must adjust the scroll bar range based upon the new size.

The user may select a specific set of data by clicking the left mouse button on its line. **OnLButtonDown** obtains the new user's current record selection. It is then displayed in a red font. Again, a double click opens the Update dialog using the selected set of sales data. **OnFont** responds to the menu item to choose fonts. Note that the fonts chosen are **not** going to be used on the screen. Rather, the fonts are used only for printing and Print Preview. Finally, **OnAdd**, **OnUpdate**, and **OnDelete** provide an elementary interface for altering the sales data.

Now examine the data members that coordinate all of this action. The first group of fields controls the onscreen aspects, such as the average character dimensions. The field **topline** contains the index of the **SalesData** object that appears at the top of the screen. **selrecnum** contains the index into the sales array of the current user selection, while **sellinenum** contains the corresponding line on which it is currently displayed in red.

The last group of fields is used during printing. **prlogfont** contains the user's font in a **LOGFONT** structure, while **ptrlogfont** points to the **scaled** version of that font. The pair of **CSize** objects, **clsize** and **pagesize**, contain the size values for viewport scaling during printing. Also, there is another set of character dimensions and current top line to service printing and print preview operations.

This is one common source of trouble for all programmers attempting to support print and print preview operations. Print Preview is often run as a separate thread. That is, when chosen, the framework launches it as a second executing thread, separate from the main application thread. The net result is that the preview operation ends up executing concurrently with the rest of the application. A collision of values can occur. For example, assume that we are using just a single set of character dimension variables. If we set the average character dimensions to the screen font and then launch the print preview operation, the preview operation then alters those character dimensions to match the preview operation's scaled font. But since the main application is also running, it then changes the character dimensions back to the screen. The result is that both windows can end up using incorrect values for these items held in common. The simplest way around this multitasking effect is to use separate sets of these critical values, the character dimensions and the current top line.

```
AcmeView Class Definition
```

```
#pragma once
#include "acmedoc.h" // access to the document

/**************************************************************/
/*                                                            */
/* AcmeView Class Definition                                  */
/*                                                            */
/**************************************************************/

class AcmeView : public CView {

DECLARE_DYNCREATE(AcmeView)

protected:

int avg_caps_width;    // average capital letter width
int avg_char_width;    // average character width
int avg_char_height;   // average character height
int height;            // window height
int width;             // window width
int topline;           // current top line for scrolling
int selrecnum;         // current record number selected in Red
int sellinenum;        // and its corresponding screen line number

int num_sales;         // current number of SalesData objects

int num_lines_per_page; // the number of lines per page
int max_vscroll_lines;  // maximum number of vert lines to scroll

                       // printing and preview fields
int prt_width;         // character dimensions on print or preview
int prt_height;
int prt_topline;       // top line when printing or preview
int prt_num_lines;     // number of lines per page
CRect    rect_print;   // working area of the printed page
int      footer_y;     // location of footer on a page
LOGFONT  prlogfont;    // printer version of user selected font
LOGFONT* ptrlogfont;   // scaled copy of the user font
CFont*   ptrfont;      // the display font in use
CFont*   ptrprfont;    // corresponding printer font in use scaled
CSize    clsize;       // the size of the screen for scaling
CSize    pagesize;     // the size of the printed page for scaling

 /*************************************************************/
 /*                                                           */
 /* Class Functions:                                          */
 /*                                                           */
 /*************************************************************/

public:
         AcmeView ();    // no parms required for serialization
        ~AcmeView ();    // removes any fonts
AcmeDoc* GetDocument (); // returns the doc associated with view
void     OnDraw (CDC*);  // displays a screen or printer page

protected:

BOOL OnPreparePrinting (CPrintInfo*);        // inits Print dialog
void OnBeginPrinting (CDC*, CPrintInfo*);    // save screen values
void OnEndPrinting (CDC*, CPrintInfo*);      // restore screen value
void SetupPrinterFont (CDC*, CPrintInfo*);// make a printer font

void OnPrepareDC (CDC*, CPrintInfo*);  // make font-get char dims
void OnPrint (CDC*, CPrintInfo*);      // print heading & footer
```

```
void OnInitialUpdate ();                  // initial settings
void OnUpdate (CView*, LPARAM, CObject*); // reset settings
void SetOurScrollRange ();                // reset scroll range
void CalcCurrentSelection ();             // maintains cur selection

afx_msg BOOL OnEraseBkgnd (CDC* pDC);  // paint bkground lt gray
afx_msg int  OnCreate (LPCREATESTRUCT);// make fixed font
afx_msg void OnKeyDown (UINT, UINT, UINT); // scroller interface
afx_msg void OnVScroll (UINT, UINT, CScrollBar*);// scroll screen
afx_msg void OnSize (UINT, int, int);  // reset scrolling range
afx_msg void OnLButtonDown (UINT, CPoint); // select a record
afx_msg void OnLButtonDblClk( UINT nFlags, CPoint point );// updt
afx_msg void OnRButtonDown (UINT, CPoint); // context menu
afx_msg void OnFonts ();                   // get new user font
afx_msg void OnAddSalesData ();            // adds new rec at end
afx_msg void OnUpdateSalesData ();         // updates current rec
afx_msg void OnDeleteSalesData ();         // deletes current rec

DECLARE_MESSAGE_MAP()
};
```

Notice that the class implements dynamic creation as expected. The constructor sets the initial user-selected record as the top line or index 0 and sets the pointer to the user fonts to 0. If the user does not select a font, I use a fixed font from the Courier New group and it is created in **OnCreate**. I used a height of 14 which is an arbitrary; it works well on my system in 1024x768 resolution. This font is the main display font. If the user does not select a printing font, this font is scaled to the printer.

In this example, **OnInitialUpdate** does not really need to be overridden since the constructor has already set these values and **OnUpdate** is invoked before the initial display occurs anyway. In **OnUpdate** the scroll range may need to be reset after obtaining the current number of sales objects.

Next let's look at the **OnPrepareDC** and **OnDraw** pair from the viewpoint of screen display **only**. When **OnPrepareDC** is invoked, the window is at last completely constructed with its final dimensions and, at this point, the average character dimensions are finally correct. After the current font is installed and character dimensions obtained, the scroll range can now be properly adjusted as required. The framework then passes the prepared DC onto **OnDraw** to paint the screen.

Since the document and the sales array are going to be referenced several times, **OnDraw** first makes a local copy of the pointer to the document and also a pointer to the sales array. The integer **line** is used in the **TextOut** functions to determine the y coordinate; it is initialized to the second line, 1, so that the column headings are not immediately touching the top border.

How can **OnDraw** detect whether or not this DC is the screen, the printer or the print preview window? The **CDC** member function **IsPrinting** returns **TRUE** if this is a printer DC.

```
BOOL IsPrinting ();
```

To avoid repetitious function calls, the **BOOL isprinting** is set to the **BOOL** returned from **IsPrinting**.

If the current DC is not a printer, then the column headings are drawn on a raised area. To construct a raised box, draw the top and left edges in white and the bottom and right edges in black. To create a depressed box, reverse these, drawing the top and left edges in black and the bottom and right in white.

Next, **OnDraw** must display the correct screenful of sales data objects. Recall that **topline** contains the index of the **SalesData** object to be displayed on the first line of this page. If the entire set of data can be displayed on one screen, then **topline** would always be 0. It is non-zero if the user has scrolled down. The number of lines that can fit on this DC is the lesser of the maximum number of lines that can potentially be on this screen and the number of remaining sales data objects, given by the **num_sales** minus **topline**. If **topline** is then added to this, the result is the index of the last sales object to be displayed this time. For convenience, these two values are stored in two temporary variables, **start** and **end.** The display loop begins by getting a pointer to the current **SalesData** object in the array.

```
start = topline;
end = min (num_sales - topline, num_lines_per_page) + topline;
for (int i=start; i<end; i++) {
 ptrdata = (SalesData*) ptrarray->GetAt (i);
 if (!ptrdata) continue;
```

Next, I handle the current record situation. The application must indicate which record being displayed is the current record (which could be updated or deleted by the user). I chose to display that record in red. The extra field, **sellinenum**, contains the line number of that selection (the value is kept in synch with the actual sales array index, **selrecnum**, in the **CalcCurrentSelection** function). Thus, if printing is not ongoing and the current line matches the selected line number, I insert a red pen; otherwise, the default black pen is used to display the data.

```
 if (!isprinting && line == sellinenum)
  ptrdc->SetTextColor (RGB (255,0,0));
 sprintf_s (msg, sizeof(msg), "%4ld", ptrdata->year);
 ptrdc->TextOut (char_width*5, char_height*line, msg);
 sprintf_s (msg, sizeof(msg), "%8.2f", ptrdata->sales);
 ptrdc->TextOut (char_width*13, char_height*line++,msg);
 if (!isprinting && line-1 == sellinenum)
  ptrdc->SetTextColor (RGB (0,0,0));
}
```

For the screen display, **num_lines_per_page** gets assigned in **SetOurScrollRange**, once the current pane in the splitter window's height and width are found.

```
GetClientRect (&rect);
height = rect.Height();
width  = rect.Width();
num_lines_per_page = height / avg_char_height
                   - (HEAD_LINE+HEAD_SPACE);
if (num_lines_per_page <1) num_lines_per_page = 1;
```

Next, the maximum number of lines to scroll is calculated. At this point, **topline** may need to be reset. Remember that the index of the topmost line must be less than the maximum number of lines to scroll or else you can scroll lots of blank lines as you reach near the end of the data.

```
 max_vscroll_lines = max (0, num_sales-num_lines_per_page);
 topline = min (topline, max_vscroll_lines);
 SetScrollRange (SB_VERT, 0, max_vscroll_lines, FALSE);
 SetScrollPos (SB_VERT, topline, TRUE);
}
```

Once the scrolling factors are adjusted, the effect, if any, on the user's current record selection must be examined. For example, if record 0 shown on the top line is the selected record and if the user scrolls down one line, the current record must be moved down one. This adjustment is done in **CalcCurrentSelection**. In order to simplify the **OnDraw**, which must know which line is the current selection to be shown in red, I maintain **sellinenum**, which is the screen line number of the selected record. This complicates the adjustment process. If the selected record is now less than **topline**, the user's choice has been scrolled off-screen; make the selection now be the top record. If the selected record is off the bottom of the screen, that is, greater than **topline** plus the number of lines per page, then force the selected record to be the last line on the screen.

```
int num_to_eof = num_sales - topline;
if (selrecnum < topline) {
 selrecnum = topline;
 sellinenum = HEAD_LINE + HEAD_SPACE;
}
else if (selrecnum >= topline + num_lines_per_page) {
 selrecnum = topline + num_lines_per_page;
 if (selrecnum >= num_sales) {
  selrecnum = num_sales -1;
  sellinenum = (selrecnum - topline)+ HEAD_LINE +HEAD_SPACE;
 }
 else sellinenum =HEAD_LINE +HEAD_SPACE +selrecnum -topline;
}
else sellinenum =(selrecnum-topline) +HEAD_LINE +HEAD_SPACE;
```

User selections are made by pressing the left mouse button on the desired line. In **OnLButtonDown**, hit testing is done to determine first which line is selected and then what record number or sales data object that line represents. You must avoid bogus selections.

```
// calculate the line number clicked upon
int line = point.y / avg_char_height -HEAD_LINE -HEAD_SPACE;
// select that line if it is within range
if (line < 0 || line > num_lines_per_page) return;
if (line <= num_sales - topline -1) {
 selrecnum = topline + line;
 sellinenum = line + HEAD_LINE + HEAD_SPACE;
 Invalidate ();
}
```

Most of the rest of the scrolling code is the same as in all previous examples. However, I made one slight alteration in the keyboard interface to accommodate user selection of the current record. Suppose that the current record is the top line and the user wishes to make the second line be the selected line. It is likely that the user may press the down arrow to do so. Hence, in **OnKeyDown** the up and down arrow key presses must consider this effect in addition to normal scrolling requests.

```
case VK_UP:
 if (selrecnum <= topline)
  SendMessage (WM_VSCROLL, SB_LINEUP, 0L);
 else {
  if (selrecnum -1 <0) break;
  selrecnum--;
  sellinenum--;
  Invalidate ();
 }
 break;
case VK_DOWN:
  if (selrecnum + 1 < num_sales) {
  selrecnum++;
  sellinenum++;
  Invalidate ();
 }
 SendMessage (WM_VSCROLL, SB_LINEDOWN, 0L); break;
```

Alterations to the document's data are done through functions **OnAdd**, **OnUpdate**, and **OnDelete** with the last two using the current record in red. In this example, since the dialogs are executed by the view class and the new or modified data gathered, I had the view class go ahead and directly update the data in the document's array. Assuming **ptrdata** is an instance of the **SalesData** class that is filled with the new data to be added, **OnAdd** then inserts the data into the document.

```
ptrarray->Add (ptrdata);
ptrdoc->SetModifiedFlag (TRUE);
ptrdoc->UpdateAllViews (NULL, 0, NULL);
```

The document's modified flag is set and all views are notified of the change so that they can repaint their screens. Personally, I would prefer that the document class actually handles all modifications to its data.

As you look over the complete coding below, ignore the Print and Print Preview sections. We will explore these next.

AcmeView Class Implementation

```
#include "stdafx.h"

#include "AcmeView.h"
#include "SalesData.h"    // access to SalesData object
#include "AddUpdateDlg.h" // access to add update dialog
#include "resource.h"     // access to resource IDs

IMPLEMENT_DYNCREATE(AcmeView, CView)

#define HEAD_LINE      1 // line number on which to display header
#define HEAD_SPACE     2 // number of blank lines after header
#define MAX_LINE_LEN 20 // max line width in characters
```

```

/*************************************************************/
/*                                                           */
/* AcmeView Message Map                                      */
/*                                                           */
/*************************************************************/

BEGIN_MESSAGE_MAP(AcmeView, CView)
 ON_WM_VSCROLL ()
 ON_WM_ERASEBKGND ()
 ON_WM_KEYDOWN ()
 ON_WM_LBUTTONDOWN ()
 ON_WM_LBUTTONDBLCLK ()
 ON_WM_RBUTTONDOWN ()
 ON_WM_SIZE ()
 ON_WM_CREATE ()
 ON_COMMAND(ID_FILE_PRINT,         CView::OnFilePrint)
 ON_COMMAND(ID_FILE_PRINT_PREVIEW, CView::OnFilePrintPreview)
 ON_COMMAND(CM_FONTS,              OnFonts)
 ON_COMMAND(CM_ADD,                OnAddSalesData)
 ON_COMMAND(CM_UPDATE,             OnUpdateSalesData)
 ON_COMMAND(CM_DELETE,             OnDeleteSalesData)
END_MESSAGE_MAP()

/*************************************************************/
/*                                                           */
/* AcmeView: Construct the view object                       */
/*                                                           */
/*************************************************************/

AcmeView::AcmeView () : CView () {
 topline = 0;      // sales array index of top line on the screen
 selrecnum = 0;    // sales array index of current selection
 sellinenum = HEAD_LINE + HEAD_SPACE; // current selection line
 ptrprfont = 0;    // set for no printer font as yet
 ptrlogfont = 0;
}

/*************************************************************/
/*                                                           */
/* OnCreate: build the window & make display font            */
/*                                                           */
/*************************************************************/

int AcmeView::OnCreate (LPCREATESTRUCT lpCS) {
 int retcd = CView::OnCreate (lpCS); // pass along to base class
 // make an initial Courier New font
 ptrfont = new CFont ();
 ptrfont->CreateFont (14, 0, 0, 0, FW_NORMAL, FALSE, FALSE,
             FALSE, ANSI_CHARSET, OUT_TT_PRECIS, CLIP_TT_ALWAYS,
             DEFAULT_QUALITY, DEFAULT_PITCH, "Courier New");
 return retcd;
}

/*************************************************************/
/*                                                           */
/* OnEraseBkgnd: patin background light gray                 */
/*                                                           */
/*************************************************************/

BOOL AcmeView::OnEraseBkgnd (CDC* pDC) {
 pDC->SelectStockObject (LTGRAY_BRUSH);
 CRect r;
 GetClientRect (&r);
```

```
 pDC->PatBlt (r.left, r.top, r.Width(), r.Height (), PATCOPY);
 return TRUE;
}

/***************************************************************/
/*                                                             */
/* ~AcmeView: remove all fonts that were used                 */
/*                                                             */
/***************************************************************/

AcmeView::~AcmeView () {
 if (ptrfont)
  delete ptrfont;
 if (ptrlogfont)
  delete ptrlogfont;
}

/***************************************************************/
/*                                                             */
/* GetDocument: retrieve a pointer to the main document        */
/*                                                             */
/***************************************************************/

AcmeDoc* AcmeView::GetDocument () {
 return (AcmeDoc*) m_pDocument;
}

/***************************************************************/
/*                                                             */
/* OnInitialUpdate: nothing to do initially, but coded so you  */
/*                  can see where to place items that must be  */
/*                  done before OnUpdate is called and painting*/
/*                                                             */
/***************************************************************/

void AcmeView::OnInitialUpdate () {
 CView::OnInitialUpdate (); // this calls OnUpdate next
}

/***************************************************************/
/*                                                             */
/* OnUpdate: reset num_sales, scroll range, current selection  */
/*                                                             */
/***************************************************************/

void AcmeView::OnUpdate (CView *ptrsender, LPARAM hint,
                         CObject *ptrdata) {
 // obtain the current number of entries in the sales array
 num_sales = GetDocument ()->GetNumSales ();
 // the next two lines are not needed here because in this case
 // I am letting OnPrepareDC determine tha avg character dims
 // and then call these two functions. If you already have
 // calculated the character dimensions, then these two
 // calls below set up the scrolling properly
 SetOurScrollRange ();     // set scroll range based on num recs
 CalcCurrentSelection (); // update current user selected record
 // base class then calls OnPaint which calls OnPrepareDC and
 // OnDraw, in that order
 CView::OnUpdate (ptrsender, hint, ptrdata);
}

/***************************************************************/
/*                                                             */
/* OnPrepareDC: setup printer or screen DC by                  */
```

```
/*                inserting the fixed font and mode               */
/*                                                                */
/******************************************************************/

void AcmeView::OnPrepareDC (CDC *ptrdc, CPrintInfo *ptrinfo) {
 CView::OnPrepareDC (ptrdc, ptrinfo); // let base class make DCs
 TEXTMETRIC  tm;

 if (ptrinfo) {                     // Printer or Preview this time
  // Option 1: use mode and extents
  ptrdc->SetMapMode (MM_ANISOTROPIC); // scaling on both axis
  ptrdc->SetWindowExt (clsize);       // window size to screen sz
  ptrdc->SetViewportExt (pagesize);   // viewport to printer page

  // Option 2: no mode and extents
  // use scaling factors in setup print font
  // so remove Option 1 above three lines
  ptrdc->SelectObject (ptrprfont);    // install printer font
  if (!ptrinfo->m_bPreview) {         // is printer this time
   ptrinfo->m_bContinuePrinting = TRUE;
  }
  else {
   // set continue printing flag for preview
   ptrinfo->m_bContinuePrinting = TRUE;
  }
 }
 else {                              // paint screen dc this time
  ptrdc->SelectObject (ptrfont);     // install fixed font
  ptrdc->GetTextMetrics (&tm);       // get the font information
  // calculate average character parameters
  avg_char_width  = tm.tmAveCharWidth;
  avg_char_height = tm.tmHeight + tm.tmExternalLeading;
  avg_caps_width  = (tm.tmPitchAndFamily & 1 ? 3 : 2) *
                    avg_char_width / 2;
  SetOurScrollRange ();   // set scroll bar range using real font
  CalcCurrentSelection ();// update current user selected record
 }
}

/******************************************************************/
/*                                                                */
/* OnDraw: display the document as a table on screen or printer*/
/*                                                                */
/******************************************************************/

void AcmeView::OnDraw (CDC *ptrdc) {
 char msg[80];
 AcmeDoc *ptrdoc = GetDocument ();   // acquire access to the doc
 SalesDataArray* ptrarray = &ptrdoc->sales_array;
 SalesData* ptrdata;                 // will point to SalesData
 int line = HEAD_LINE;               // the current line to show
 // get a flag that we can use to tell if we are printing or not
 BOOL isprinting = ptrdc->IsPrinting();
 ptrdc->SetBkMode (TRANSPARENT);  // set transparent display mode

 int start;     // these are the subscripts into the array to show
 int end;       // depending upon whether printing or on screen
 int char_height; // print or screen character dimensions
 int char_width;

 if (!isprinting) { // if on screen display, display column heads
  // set the starting and ending subscripts to show
  start = topline;
  end = min (num_sales - topline, num_lines_per_page) + topline;
```

```
   // set the screen character dimensions
   char_height = avg_char_height;
   char_width = avg_char_width;

   // display headings as raised areas above columns of data
   CString yrs, sls;
   yrs.LoadString (IDS_YEARS);
   sls.LoadString (IDS_SALES);
   ptrdc->SelectStockObject (WHITE_PEN);

   // draw years box and show "Year" in it
   CRect ryr (4*avg_char_width, line*avg_char_height-3,
              10*avg_char_width, (line+1)*avg_char_height+3);
   ptrdc->MoveTo (ryr.right, ryr.top);
   ptrdc->LineTo (ryr.left,  ryr.top);
   ptrdc->LineTo (ryr.left,  ryr.bottom);
   ptrdc->SelectStockObject (BLACK_PEN);
   ptrdc->LineTo (ryr.right, ryr.bottom);
   ptrdc->LineTo (ryr.right, ryr.top);
   ptrdc->TextOut (5*avg_char_width, avg_char_height, yrs);

   // draw sales box and show "Sales" in it
   CRect rsl (13*avg_char_width, line*avg_char_height-3,
              21*avg_char_width, (line+1)*avg_char_height+3);
   ptrdc->SelectStockObject (WHITE_PEN);
   ptrdc->MoveTo (rsl.right, rsl.top);
   ptrdc->LineTo (rsl.left,  rsl.top);
   ptrdc->LineTo (rsl.left,  rsl.bottom);
   ptrdc->SelectStockObject (BLACK_PEN);
   ptrdc->LineTo (rsl.right, rsl.bottom);
   ptrdc->LineTo (rsl.right, rsl.top);
   ptrdc->TextOut (15*avg_char_width, avg_char_height*line, sls);
  }
  else {
   // printing or preview - set the starting and ending subscripts
   start = prt_topline;
   end = min (num_sales - prt_topline, prt_num_lines)+prt_topline;
   char_height = prt_height;
   char_width = prt_width;
   line++;             // if printing add one line for readability
  }

  // display each sales entry whether or not going to the printer
  line += HEAD_SPACE;   // set line to first data line

  // for each line beginning at the top line offset in the array
  for (int i=start; i<end; i++) {
   // get a pointer to this SalesData object
   ptrdata = (SalesData*) ptrarray->GetAt (i);
   if (!ptrdata) continue;
   // if not printing & this is the selected record,
   // then use Red as the color
   if (!isprinting && line == sellinenum)
    ptrdc->SetTextColor (RGB (255,0,0));

   sprintf_s (msg, sizeof(msg), "%4ld", ptrdata->year);
   ptrdc->TextOut (char_width*5, char_height*line, msg);
   sprintf_s (msg, sizeof(msg), "%8.2f", ptrdata->sales);
   ptrdc->TextOut (char_width*13, char_height*line++,msg);

   // reselect black as the color if needed
   if (!isprinting && line-1 == sellinenum)
    ptrdc->SetTextColor (RGB (0,0,0));
  }
```

```
}

/********************************************************************/
/*                                                                  */
/* OnFonts: get the user's font choice for printing                 */
/*          note that this font is not for displaying on the CRT*/
/*                                                                  */
/********************************************************************/

void AcmeView::OnFonts () {
 char  printer[80];
 char *device, *driver, * output, *next;
 CDC* ptrprinterDC = 0;

 // get access to a printer DC from the default installed printer
 GetProfileString ("windows", "device", "...", printer, 80);
 if ( (device = strtok_s (printer, ",", &next)) != 0 &&
      (driver = strtok_s (NULL,    ",", &next)) != 0 &&
      (output = strtok_s (NULL,    ",", &next)) != 0) {
  // a default printer exists, so get a DC for it
  ptrprinterDC = new CDC;
  ptrprinterDC->CreateDC (driver, device, output, NULL);
 }

 // construct an instance of the Choose Fonts dialog
 CFontDialog dlg (ptrlogfont, CF_EFFECTS | CF_PRINTERFONTS |
                  CF_FORCEFONTEXIST, ptrprinterDC, this);
 if (dlg.DoModal () == IDOK) {     // get user font choice
  if (!ptrlogfont)
   ptrlogfont = new LOGFONT;       // 1st time, create LOGFONT
  memcpy (ptrlogfont, &(dlg.m_lf), sizeof (LOGFONT));
  // here notify user that chosen font is only used for printing
  MessageBox ("Use Print Preview to see results",
              "Font Chosen For Printing", MB_OK);
 }
 delete ptrprinterDC;
}

/********************************************************************/
/*                                                                  */
/* OnSize: gets window dims and sets new scroll bar range           */
/*                                                                  */
/********************************************************************/

void AcmeView::OnSize (UINT flags, int width, int height) {
 CView::OnSize    (flags, width, height);
 SetOurScrollRange ();        // reset scroll bars ranges
 CalcCurrentSelection ();     // recalc the current selected record
}

/********************************************************************/
/*                                                                  */
/* SetOurScrollRange: sets up the new scroll range                  */
/*                                                                  */
/********************************************************************/

void AcmeView::SetOurScrollRange () {
 CRect rect;
 GetClientRect (&rect);       // get the size of the client window
 height = rect.Height();      // calc and save current height
 width  = rect.Width();       // calc and save current width
 if (height == 0 || width == 0 || avg_char_height == 0) return;

 // calc the number of SalesData objects per page
```

```
 num_lines_per_page = height / avg_char_height -
                      (HEAD_LINE + HEAD_SPACE);
 if (num_lines_per_page <1)
  num_lines_per_page = 1; // force at least one
 // set max number of scrolling lines for the range to scroll
 max_vscroll_lines = max (0, num_sales - num_lines_per_page );
 // adjust current top of page index into the Sales array
 topline = min (topline, max_vscroll_lines);
 // then set the scroll range and current thumb bar position
 SetScrollRange (SB_VERT, 0, max_vscroll_lines, FALSE);
 SetScrollPos (SB_VERT, topline, TRUE);
}

/***************************************************************/
/*                                                             */
/* CalcCurrentSelection: set the current selection             */
/*                                                             */
/***************************************************************/

void AcmeView::CalcCurrentSelection () {
 if (selrecnum < topline) {// if selection is no longer on screen
  selrecnum = topline;      // reset cur selection to be top line
  // and set its screen line number
  sellinenum = HEAD_LINE + HEAD_SPACE;
 }
 else if (selrecnum >= topline + num_lines_per_page) {
  // here it's off screen so force cur sel to be last line
  selrecnum = topline + num_lines_per_page;
  // check if this goes off the end of the array
  if (selrecnum >= num_sales) {
   selrecnum = num_sales - 1;  // yes, so make last array item it
   sellinenum = (selrecnum - topline) + HEAD_LINE + HEAD_SPACE;
  }
  else
   sellinenum = HEAD_LINE + HEAD_SPACE + selrecnum - topline;
 }
 else
  sellinenum = (selrecnum - topline) + HEAD_LINE + HEAD_SPACE;
}

/***************************************************************/
/*                                                             */
/* OnLButtonDown: get current record selection under mouse ptr */
/*                                                             */
/***************************************************************/

void AcmeView::OnLButtonDown (UINT, CPoint point) {
 // calculate the line number clicked upon
 int line = point.y / avg_char_height - HEAD_LINE - HEAD_SPACE;
 // select that line if it is within range
 if (line < 0 || line > num_lines_per_page)
  return; // ignore because it is out of range
 // if it is in range, then select this line
 if (line <= num_sales - topline -1) {
  selrecnum = topline + line;
  sellinenum = line + HEAD_LINE + HEAD_SPACE;
  Invalidate (); // force a repaint to show it highlighted
 }
}

/***************************************************************/
/*                                                             */
/* OnLButtonDblClk: update or delete the current record        */
/*                                                             */
```

```
/*******************************************************************/

afx_msg void AcmeView::OnLButtonDblClk (UINT, CPoint) {
 OnUpdateSalesData ();
}

/*******************************************************************/
/*                                                                 */
/* OnRButtonDown: display update/delete menu                       */
/*                                                                 */
/*******************************************************************/

void AcmeView::OnRButtonDown (UINT, CPoint point) {
 CMenu menu;
 menu.LoadMenu (IDR_UPDT_DEL);
 CMenu* ptrpopup;
 ptrpopup = menu.GetSubMenu (0);
 ClientToScreen (&point);                 // convert coordinates
 ptrpopup->TrackPopupMenu (0, point.x, point.y, this, 0);
}

/*******************************************************************/
/*                                                                 */
/* OnKeyDown: provides a keyboard scroller interface               */
/*  and allows user to up/down arrow for current record select */
/*                                                                 */
/*******************************************************************/

void AcmeView::OnKeyDown (UINT key, UINT, UINT) {
 // check for and handle any possible keyboard scroll request
 switch (key) {

  case VK_UP:             // requests scroll up 1 line
   if (selrecnum <= topline)  // if cur rec is off screen, scroll
    SendMessage (WM_VSCROLL, SB_LINEUP, 0L);
   else {                 // cur record is on screen, so no scroll
    if (selrecnum -1 <0)
     break;               // quit if already at the top
    selrecnum--;          // back cur rec selection up by one line
    sellinenum--;
    Invalidate ();        // and force a repaint to show in red
   }
   break;

  case VK_DOWN:           // requests scroll down 1 line
   if (selrecnum + 1 < num_sales) { // can do down one line, so
    selrecnum++;          // set cur record selection down one line
    sellinenum++;
    Invalidate ();        // and force a repaint to show in red
   }
   SendMessage (WM_VSCROLL, SB_LINEDOWN, 0L); break;

  case VK_LEFT:  // requests scroll left 1 col
   SendMessage (WM_HSCROLL, SB_LINEUP, 0L); break;

  case VK_RIGHT: // requests scroll right 1 col
   SendMessage (WM_HSCROLL, SB_LINEDOWN, 0L); break;

  case VK_PRIOR: // request scroll 1 page up
   SendMessage (WM_VSCROLL, SB_PAGEUP, 0L); break;

  case VK_NEXT:  // request scroll 1 page down
   SendMessage (WM_VSCROLL, SB_PAGEDOWN, 0L); break;

```

```
  case VK_END:   // request goto the bottom
   SendMessage (WM_HSCROLL, SB_PAGEDOWN, 0L); break;

  case VK_HOME:  // request goto the top
   SendMessage (WM_HSCROLL, SB_PAGEUP, 0L);  break;
 }
}

/***************************************************************/
/*                                                             */
/* OnVScroll: scroll window vertically                         */
/*                                                             */
/***************************************************************/

void AcmeView::OnVScroll (UINT type, UINT pos,
                          CScrollBar *ptrsb) {
 int num_lines_to_scroll;
 switch (type) {

  case SB_LINEUP:     // scroll up 1 line
   num_lines_to_scroll = -1; break;

  case SB_LINEDOWN:   // scroll 1 line down
   num_lines_to_scroll = 1; break;

  case SB_PAGEUP:     // scroll 1 page up
   num_lines_to_scroll = min (-1, -num_lines_per_page); break;

  case SB_PAGEDOWN:   // scroll 1 page down
   num_lines_to_scroll = max (1, num_lines_per_page); break;

  case SB_THUMBTRACK: // follow thumb bar
   num_lines_to_scroll = pos - topline; break;

  default:
   num_lines_to_scroll = 0;
 }

 num_lines_to_scroll = max (-topline,
                       min (num_lines_to_scroll,
                            max_vscroll_lines - topline));

 if (num_lines_to_scroll !=0) {
  topline +=num_lines_to_scroll;         // add to top line index
  SetScrollPos (SB_VERT, topline, TRUE); // set new scroll pos
  CalcCurrentSelection (); // do any cur record select adjustment
  Invalidate ();           // force repaint to scroll lines
 }
 CView::OnVScroll (type, pos, ptrsb);
}

/***************************************************************/
/*                                                             */
/* OnAdd: add a new sales data record at the end of the set    */
/*                                                             */
/***************************************************************/

void AcmeView::OnAddSalesData () {

 SalesData* ptrdata = new SalesData; // transfer buffer for sales

 AddUpdateDlg add (ptrdata, false, this);
 if (add.DoModal () == IDOK) {
  AcmeDoc *ptrdoc = GetDocument ();  // get access to the doc
```

```
  SalesDataArray *ptrarray = &ptrdoc->sales_array;
  ptrarray->Add (ptrdata);     // add the new object to the array
  ptrdoc->SetModifiedFlag (TRUE);// tell doc it has been modified
  // tell document to update all views
  ptrdoc->UpdateAllViews (0, 0, 0);
 }
 else delete ptrdata;
}

/***************************************************************/
/*                                                             */
/* OnUpdate: alter the current record in red                   */
/*                                                             */
/***************************************************************/

void AcmeView::OnUpdateSalesData () {
 bool newdata = false;             // true when new data item
 AcmeDoc *ptrdoc = GetDocument (); // get access to the document
 // get access to the current record to be updated
 SalesData *ptrdata =
             (SalesData*) ptrdoc->sales_array.GetAt (selrecnum);
 if (!ptrdata) { // if it fails to get a record, make a new one
  ptrdata = new SalesData;
  newdata = true;
 }

 AddUpdateDlg update (ptrdata, true, this);
 if (update.DoModal () == IDOK) {
  if (newdata) ptrdoc->sales_array.Add (ptrdata);
  // tell document that it is modified
  ptrdoc->SetModifiedFlag (TRUE);
  // tell doc to update all views
  ptrdoc->UpdateAllViews (0, 0, 0);
 }
 else if (newdata) delete ptrdata;
}

/***************************************************************/
/*                                                             */
/* OnDelete: remove the current record in red                  */
/*                                                             */
/***************************************************************/

void      AcmeView::OnDeleteSalesData () {
 AcmeDoc *ptrdoc = GetDocument ();     // get access to document
 SalesDataArray *ptrarray = &ptrdoc->sales_array;
 // verify record is there
 if (ptrarray->GetSize () > selrecnum && selrecnum >= 0) {
  SalesData *ptrdata = (SalesData*) ptrarray->GetAt (selrecnum);
  // confirm the deletion request
  CString msg1, msg2;
  msg1.LoadString (IDS_CONFIRM1);
  msg2.LoadString (IDS_CONFIRM2);
  // user confirms, then delete this record
  if (MessageBox (msg2, msg1, MB_YESNO) == IDYES) {
   ptrarray->RemoveAt (selrecnum, 1);// remove ptr from array
   delete ptrdata;                   // delete the Sales object
   selrecnum--;                      // dec current record number
   ptrdoc->SetModifiedFlag (TRUE);   // tell doc it's changed
   ptrdoc->UpdateAllViews (0, 0, 0); // tell doc to update views
  }
 }
}
```

```
/**************************************************************/
/*                                                            */
/* OnPreparePrinting: set number of pages for Print dlg       */
/*                                                            */
/**************************************************************/

BOOL AcmeView::OnPreparePrinting (CPrintInfo *ptrinfo) {
 if (ptrinfo->m_bPreview) {
  // guess at the number of pages - will be reset OnBeginPrinting
  ptrinfo->m_nNumPreviewPages = 2;
  ptrinfo->SetMaxPage (2);
 }
 return CView::DoPreparePrinting (ptrinfo);
}

/**************************************************************/
/*                                                            */
/* OnBeginPrinting: save display values, install print values */
/*                  and the printer font                      */
/*                                                            */
/**************************************************************/

void AcmeView::OnBeginPrinting (CDC *ptrdc, CPrintInfo *ptrinfo){
 prt_topline = 0;                     // set for whole document
 SetupPrinterFont (ptrdc, ptrinfo);   // make up the printer font

 int pages = num_sales / prt_num_lines; // calc # pages to print
 if (num_sales % prt_num_lines > 0) pages++; // round up

 // set the number of preview pages to show
 ptrinfo->m_nNumPreviewPages = pages > 1 ? 2 : 1;
 // set max number of pages to print
 ptrinfo->SetMaxPage (pages);
}

/**************************************************************/
/*                                                            */
/* OnEndPrinting: ending printing cycles                      */
/*                                                            */
/**************************************************************/

void AcmeView::OnEndPrinting (CDC* /*ptrdc*/,
                              CPrintInfo* /*ptrinfo*/) {
 delete ptrprfont;                    // and remove the print font
}

/**************************************************************/
/*                                                            */
/* SetupPrinterFont: setup the printer font and get avgchardims*/
/*                                                            */
/**************************************************************/

void AcmeView::SetupPrinterFont (CDC *ptrdc, CPrintInfo*) {
 int savedc = ptrdc->SaveDC ();  // save the DC
 // load user's chosen font, if any, and scale TrueType fonts
 if (!ptrlogfont) {           // no user font, so use default font
  // extract the LOGFONT object for scaling
  ptrdc->SelectObject (ptrfont);
  ptrfont->GetObject (sizeof(LOGFONT), &prlogfont);
 }
 else prlogfont = *ptrlogfont;    // assign the user's font

 // Begin Option 1 coding - use mode and extents
 // set screen size to that of a full screen
```

```
CRect clrect (0, 0, GetSystemMetrics (SM_CXSCREEN),
                    GetSystemMetrics (SM_CYSCREEN));
// clsize holds the size of the screen for window extent
clsize = clrect.Size();
// set the printer page size for viewport extent
pagesize = CSize (ptrdc->GetDeviceCaps (HORZRES),
                  ptrdc->GetDeviceCaps (VERTRES));
// install mode and scaling effects
ptrdc->SetMapMode (MM_ANISOTROPIC);
ptrdc->SetWindowExt (clsize);
ptrdc->SetViewportExt (pagesize);
// end Option 1 coding
// begin Option 2 coding
/*
// get a screen DC for scaling
HDC hdc = CreateDC ("DISPLAY",NULL,NULL,NULL);
// calculate both x and y scale dimensions between the screen
// and the printer
float xscale = ptrdc->GetDeviceCaps (LOGPIXELSX) /
               (float) GetDeviceCaps(hdc, LOGPIXELSX);
float yscale = ptrdc->GetDeviceCaps (LOGPIXELSY) /
               (float) GetDeviceCaps(hdc, LOGPIXELSY);
// or scale by true size
CRect clrect (0, 0, GetSystemMetrics (SM_CXSCREEN),
                    GetSystemMetrics (SM_CYSCREEN));
CSize clsize = clrect.Size();
pagesize = CSize (ptrdc->GetDeviceCaps (HORZRES),
                  ptrdc->GetDeviceCaps (VERTRES));
float xx = pagesize.cx/(float)clsize.cx;
float yy = pagesize.cy/(float)clsize.cy;
DeleteDC (hdc);
// install scaled dimensions
// scale choice 1:
// prlogfont.lfHeight = (long) (prlogfont.lfHeight * yscale);
// prlogfont.lfWidth = (long) (prlogfont.lfWidth * xscale);
// scale choice 2:
prlogfont.lfHeight = (long) (prlogfont.lfHeight * yy);
prlogfont.lfWidth = (long) (prlogfont.lfWidth * xx);
*/
// end Option 2 coding
// construct the true printer font from the logfont and install
ptrprfont = new CFont ();
ptrprfont->CreateFontIndirect (&prlogfont);
ptrdc->SelectObject (ptrprfont);
TEXTMETRIC tm;
ptrdc->GetTextMetrics (&tm);         // get the font information
// calculate average character parameters
prt_width  = tm.tmAveCharWidth;
prt_height = tm.tmHeight + tm.tmExternalLeading;
 // calculate pagination data
CPoint pt (ptrdc->GetDeviceCaps (HORZRES),
           ptrdc->GetDeviceCaps (VERTRES));
ptrdc->DPtoLP (&pt);
// setup the full page area
rect_print.SetRect (0, 0, pt.x, pt.y);
```

```
  // calculate y location for the footer
 footer_y = rect_print.Height () - prt_height -1;
 // adjust the printer info drawing rectangle to exclude the
 // space occupied by the header and footer
 rect_print.top += 4*prt_height;
 rect_print.bottom -= prt_height + 1;
 // calc the number of data lines that fit on a printed page
 // inside the margins
 prt_num_lines = rect_print.Height () / prt_height;

 ptrdc->RestoreDC (savedc); // restore the DC
}

/***************************************************************/
/*                                                             */
/* OnPrint: handle headings and footers                        */
/*                                                             */
/***************************************************************/

void AcmeView::OnPrint (CDC *ptrdc, CPrintInfo *ptrinfo) {
 // print the title and column headings
 CString s;
 s.LoadString (IDS_ACMETITLE);
 ptrdc->TextOut (0, 0, s);
 s.Empty ();
 s.LoadString (IDS_YEARS);
 ptrdc->TextOut (prt_width*5, 2*prt_height, s);
 s.Empty ();
 s.LoadString (IDS_SALES);
 ptrdc->TextOut (prt_width*13, 2*prt_height, s);

 prt_topline = prt_num_lines * (ptrinfo->m_nCurPage - 1);

 // print the main SalesData objects
 CView::OnPrint (ptrdc, ptrinfo);

 // print the footers
 s.Empty ();
 s.LoadString (IDS_FOOTER);
 ptrdc->TextOut (0, footer_y, s);
}
```

The Printing and Print Preview Process of AcmeView

At last we come to the details of the printing process. First examine the font situation. In **OnCreate** a default screen font, 14-point Courier New fixed font, is constructed. If the user does not choose another font, then the **LOGFONT** structure of this font is extracted and used as the base for the printer font.

In **OnFonts**, since the font is going to be used for printing purposes only, we should include printer-only fonts along with the normal True-Type fonts. The **GetProfileString** function can be used to obtain information on the default printer. The string that is returned consists of three separate strings separated by commas. The **strtok** function is used to parse this long string into the three portions that define the printer. When the **strtok** function is passed a string for the first parameter, it begins searching for the first occurrence of the second parameter string in the first string, returning a pointer to the start of the first string occurrence. When **strtok** is called with 0 as the first parameter, it continues looking for that second string from where it left off on the previous call.

```
char  printer[80];
char *device, *driver, * output, *next;
CDC* ptrprinterDC = 0;
// get access to a printer DC from the default installed printer
```

```
GetProfileString ("windows", "device", "...", printer, 80);
if ( (device = strtok_s (printer, ",", &next)) != 0 &&
     (driver = strtok_s (NULL,    ",", &next)) != 0 &&
     (output = strtok_s (NULL,    ",", &next)) != 0) {
 // a default printer exists, so get a DC for it
 ptrprinterDC = new CDC;
 ptrprinterDC->CreateDC (driver, device, output, NULL);
}
```

Notice how the three strings are then passed to the **CreateDC** function to build a printer DC.

Then, this DC is passed to the constructor of **CFontDialog**.

```
CFontDialog dlg (ptrlogfont, CF_EFFECTS | CF_PRINTERFONTS |
                 CF_FORCEFONTEXIST, ptrprinterDC, this);
if (dlg.DoModal () == IDOK) {      // get user font choice
```

Should the user choose another font for printing, I allocate a new **LOGFONT** instance if there currently is none. In all cases, I copy the **LOGFONT** structure that defines the user's selected font from the dialog into our local copy. Since this font is only used for printing purposes, I display a reminder message box.

```
  if (!ptrlogfont)
   ptrlogfont = new LOGFONT;        // 1st time, create LOGFONT
  memcpy (ptrlogfont, &(dlg.m_lf), sizeof (LOGFONT));
  MessageBox ("Use Print Preview to see results",
              "Font Chosen For Printing", MB_OK);
}
delete ptrprinterDC;
```

So either way I have a **LOGFONT** ready for printing. It contains the default Courier New font or the user's choice. Now look over Chart 15.1 The Flow of Control During the Printing Process.

Chart 15.1 The Flow of Control During the Printing Process

File Print is Chosen by User

OnPreparePrinting (No printer DC as yet)

- Set the Print Dialog Box values, such as the number of pages
- **Base Class** -> displays Print Dialog box and get the user's choices such as Landscape
- here user's choices are available

OnBeginPrinting

- Save screen values for later restoration
- Set up printing values, such as beginning page number, current line
- Construct the printer font to be used

For each page to be printed

OnPrepareDC

- **Base Class** -> construct the DC
- Install the font
- Get character dimensions
- Set window & viewport extents and the mapping mode
- Determine if there are any more pages to be printed

OnPrint (only called if there is another page to be printed)

- Adjust main print rectangle, if desired to allow for headings, footers, and margins
- Prints headings, footers, and page numbers, as required
- Could install a clipping rectangle to force **OnDraw** to stay within margins
- **Base Class** -> calls **OnDraw**

OnDraw

- Paints one page
- If margins are desired, use the main print rectangle to assist **TextOut** positions

OnEndPrinting

- Restore screen settings and delete printer font

The printing functions are passed an instance of the **CPrintInfo** class whose members provide key information that is needed to handle printing operations. Some data members and functions include the following.

Data Members:

m_bPreview — Contains a flag indicating whether the document is being previewed.
m_bContinuePrinting — Contains a flag indicating whether the framework should continue the print loop.
m_nCurPage — Identifies the number of the page currently being printed.
m_nNumPreviewPages — Identifies the number of pages displayed in the preview window; either 1 or 2.
m_rectDraw — Specifies a rectangle defining the current usable page area.

Functions:

SetMinPage — Sets the number of the first page of the document.
SetMaxPage — Sets the number of the last page of the document.
GetMinPage — Returns the number of the first page of the document.
GetMaxPage — Returns the number of the last page of the document.
GetFromPage — Returns the number of the first page being printed.
GetToPage — Returns the number of the last page being printed.

In **OnPreparePrinting** the number of pages and potential page range values should be transferred into the Print Dialog box. The problem, of course, is that there is no printer DC as yet upon which to base page calculations. The expedient solution is to ignore the settings or install only "All Pages" as the user selectable options. If you wish a more complete handling, you must manually acquire the printer DC similar to the coding in **OnFonts**. For an accurate page count, you could perform a dummy run fake-printing all pages, handling line wrap. With the accurate page count, and therefore page number range, set the dialog values. The base class invocation actually invokes the Print Dialog. When the base class returns, the user selections are available, if needed.

In this program, since the number of pages that will be needed is unknown at this point, I just call the base class and will actually install the key information from the next function that is called, **OnBeginPrinting**.

However, if Print Preview has been selected, I make a few arbitrary settings.

```
if (ptrinfo->m_bPreview) {
 // guess at the number of pages - will be reset OnBeginPrinting
 ptrinfo->m_nNumPreviewPages = 2;
 ptrinfo->SetMaxPage (2);
}
```

In **OnBeginPrinting**, we really must determine the number of pages needed for this action. This cannot be done unless we have both a printer DC and a scaled printer font with its associated text metrics. Hence, I use a helper function, **SetupPrinterFont**, to handle these actions. And at this point, we must be very careful in our coding.

When Print Preview is chosen, the framework often launches the preview action in a separate parallel execution thread. This means that we cannot simple reuse all of the normal display variables, such as the current top line which controls the beginning line to be displayed on a specific page, the average new scaled character dimensions, and so on. Why? Before the Preview begins, all of these variables contain those that are required to display the current scrolled set of sales data on the screen with the screen character dimensions. When the preview is launched, if we go ahead and reset all of these variables to the new preview values, everything is now appropriate for the first preview page. However, because of the multithreading action, the original thread that launched the preview action now returns control back to the main message processing loop, which, in turn, determines that a screen repaint is needed because the preview window has overlain the main application window. **OnPaint** for the screen now is using these preview parameters and the screen display eventually is completely incorrect! If the screen actions in turn reset all of the variables to screen values, the ongoing preview window now begins to use the incorrect values as well and preview is trashed. Thus, the simplest solution is to use a separate set of preview variables.

Design Rule 58: When implementing Print Preview, maintain separate copies of the relevant pagination data, including character dimensions.

Hence, I set the printing top line to 0 and call my helper function **SetupPrinterFont** to build the scaled printing font and determine pagination information.

```
void AcmeView::OnBeginPrinting (CDC *ptrdc, CPrintInfo *ptrinfo){
 prt_topline = 0;                     // set for whole document
 SetupPrinterFont (ptrdc, ptrinfo);  // make up the printer font
```

Then, I calculate the number of pages to print or preview. However, don't forget that last partial page. Round the number of pages.

```
 int pages = num_sales / prt_num_lines; // calc # pages to print
 if (num_sales % prt_num_lines > 0) pages++; // round up
```

Now I set the actual number of Preview pages based upon the actual number of pages to view and the Print dialog's total number of pages to print or preview.

```
 ptrinfo->m_nNumPreviewPages = pages > 1 ? 2 : 1;
 ptrinfo->SetMaxPage (pages);
```

Notice there is no base class invocation required here; it does nothing.

SetupPrinterFont is rather lengthy and you have several ways to handle the scaling operations. Because we will be changing many DC aspects, it is simpler to use the **SaveDC** and **RestoreDC** functions than it is to save and restore each item that we change. The action begins by obtaining the **LOGFONT** in use. If the user has not yet chosen a font, I must extract one from the default Courier New font.

```
 int savedc = ptrdc->SaveDC ();  // save the DC
 if (!ptrlogfont) {           // no user font, so use default font
  ptrdc->SelectObject (ptrfont);
  ptrfont->GetObject (sizeof(LOGFONT), &prlogfont);
 }
 else prlogfont = *ptrlogfont;   // assign the user's font
```

Next, the font must be scaled. Scaling can be done several ways. The first method is to set the **MM_ANISOTROPIC** mode and set the window and viewport extents.

```
 // set screen size to that of a full screen
 CRect clrect (0, 0, GetSystemMetrics (SM_CXSCREEN),
                     GetSystemMetrics (SM_CYSCREEN));
 clsize = clrect.Size();
 // set the printer page size for viewport extent
 pagesize = CSize (ptrdc->GetDeviceCaps (HORZRES),
                   ptrdc->GetDeviceCaps (VERTRES));
 ptrdc->SetMapMode (MM_ANISOTROPIC);
 ptrdc->SetWindowExt (clsize);
 ptrdc->SetViewportExt (pagesize);
```

The second method is to scale the actual printing font. If you wish to use this Option 2, manually scaling the font size, the basic principle is to multiply the **LOGFONT**'s height and width by a proper scaling factor. Here, there are two ways of determining the desired scaling factor. One way is to get the logical pixels per inch of the screen and divide that by the logical pixels per inch of the printer. The other way is to divide the total full-screen number of pixels by the total number of pixels of the printed page. The difference is that the logical pixels per inch on the screen have been adjusted for better visibility and are slightly larger than a true point size.

```
 HDC hdc = CreateDC ("DISPLAY",NULL,NULL,NULL);
 // calculate both x and y scale dimensions between the screen and the printer
 float xscale = ptrdc->GetDeviceCaps (LOGPIXELSX) /
                (float) GetDeviceCaps(hdc, LOGPIXELSX);
 float yscale = ptrdc->GetDeviceCaps (LOGPIXELSY) /
                (float) GetDeviceCaps(hdc, LOGPIXELSY);
```

Alternatively once can scale by true size this way.

```
 CRect clrect (0, 0, GetSystemMetrics (SM_CXSCREEN),
                     GetSystemMetrics (SM_CYSCREEN));
 CSize clsize = clrect.Size();
 pagesize = CSize (ptrdc->GetDeviceCaps (HORZRES),
                   ptrdc->GetDeviceCaps (VERTRES));
 float xx = pagesize.cx/(float)clsize.cx;
 float yy = pagesize.cy/(float)clsize.cy;
 DeleteDC (hdc);
```

Next, these scaled dimensions must be installed into the actual **LOGFONT** members.

```
// scale choice 1:
 prlogfont.lfHeight = (long) (prlogfont.lfHeight * yscale);
 prlogfont.lfWidth = (long) (prlogfont.lfWidth * xscale);
```

or

```
// scale choice 2:
prlogfont.lfHeight = (long) (prlogfont.lfHeight * yy);
prlogfont.lfWidth = (long) (prlogfont.lfWidth * xx);
```

Next, with either Option 1 or 2 complete, we construct the true printer font from the **LOGFONT** and install it and acquire the text metrics. Again, notice that these values are stored in different class members.

```
ptrprfont = new CFont ();
ptrprfont->CreateFontIndirect (&prlogfont);
ptrdc->SelectObject (ptrprfont);
TEXTMETRIC tm;
ptrdc->GetTextMetrics (&tm);         // get the font information
prt_width  = tm.tmAveCharWidth;
prt_height = tm.tmHeight + tm.tmExternalLeading;
```

With the character dimensions known, we can now calculate pagination information. The **rect_print CRect** instance contains the total printable page size.

```
CPoint pt (ptrdc->GetDeviceCaps (HORZRES),
           ptrdc->GetDeviceCaps (VERTRES));
ptrdc->DPtoLP (&pt);
rect_print.SetRect (0, 0, pt.x, pt.y);
```

The **DPtoLP** function converts device coordinates into logical coordinates. Here, the DC is the printer. So we are converting the device total dimensions into logical dimensions. The logical dimensions are in pixels if we are still using the default **MM_TEXT** mode or they are in other units if **MM_ANISOTROPIC** mode is in effect. There is also a **LPtoDP** function that converts logical coordinates back into device coordinates.

Now using this logical size, we can layout pagination data. We must remove the space occupied by the headings and footer, which yields the actual available space for the sales data display.

```
footer_y = rect_print.Height () - prt_height -1;
rect_print.top += 4*prt_height;
rect_print.bottom -= prt_height + 1;
```

Finally, the number of data lines that can actually fit on a printed page is given by the following.

```
prt_num_lines = rect_print.Height () / prt_height;
ptrdc->RestoreDC (savedc); // restore the DC
```

Next the framework begins the printing process by repetitive calls to **OnPrepareDC** followed by **OnPrint**. Notice that **OnPrint** is only called **if OnPrepareDC** determines that there is another page to be printed.

In **OnPrepareDC** if this is either Print or Print Preview, then the setup actions depend upon which of the two methods we chose to use to scale the fonts. The framework saves the printer DC context, then calls **OnPrepareDC** and **OnPrint**, and then restores the DC. Thus, whatever alterations are made to the printer DC in **OnPrepareDC** remain in effect through the **OnPrint** process.

The changes made always include installing the printer font and setting the average character dimensions. However, there are two different methods you may use for printing that handle proper scaling of the font. Option 1 involves setting the mapping mode to **MM_ANISOTROPIC** and then setting the window and viewport extents to the size of the screen and the size of the printer page respectively. Here the mapping mode handles all scaling effects. Using this method, every time that **OnPrepareDC** is called for printing, the mode and extents must be reset. Option 2 involves manually scaling the **LOGFONT**'s height and width before the font is actually created and installed. Once multiplied by the scaling factor (often around a factor of 4 or 5) and created, the font only needs to be selected into the printer DC. No changes to the mapping mode or extents are made. Option 2 is perhaps a little faster in execution if only text is printed on a large number of pages. Option 1 also permits the occasional graphic bitmap or drawing to be correctly scaled as well.

```
if (ptrinfo) {                    // Printer or Preview this time
 // Option 1: use mode and extents
```

```
ptrdc->SetMapMode (MM_ANISOTROPIC); // scaling on both axis
ptrdc->SetWindowExt (clsize);       // window size to screen sz
ptrdc->SetViewportExt (pagesize);   // viewport to printer page
// Option 2: no mode and extents
// use scaling factors in setup print font
// so remove Option 1 above three lines
```

Next, here is where we determine whether or not there are additional pages to be printed or viewed. Notice that I always set **m_bContinuePrinting** to **TRUE**.

```
 ptrdc->SelectObject (ptrprfont);     // install printer font
 if (!ptrinfo->m_bPreview) {          // is printer this time
  ptrinfo->m_bContinuePrinting = TRUE;
 }
 else {
  // set continue printing flag for preview
  ptrinfo->m_bContinuePrinting = TRUE;
 }
}
```

Next, **OnPrint** is called by the framework. In **OnPrint** one can adjust for margins and print the headers and footer. Notice that the same **CString** object is used to load each heading and footer string. The **Empty** function can be called to delete all characters in a **CString** instance.

```
void AcmeView::OnPrint (CDC *ptrdc, CPrintInfo *ptrinfo) {
 CString s;
 s.LoadString (IDS_ACMETITLE);
 ptrdc->TextOut (0, 0, s);
 s.Empty ();
 s.LoadString (IDS_YEARS);
 ptrdc->TextOut (prt_width*5, 2*prt_height, s);
 s.Empty ();
 s.LoadString (IDS_SALES);
 ptrdc->TextOut (prt_width*13, 2*prt_height, s);
```

One crucial aspect handled in this function involves tracking which page we are on so that printing can be terminated when the end of the document is reached. The member **topline** is used when displaying on the screen. However, **prt_topline** is used when printing. Thus, after calling the base class to print this current page, we add the number of lines per page to **prt_topline**. The framework can then tell when the end of the document is reached.

```
 prt_topline = prt_num_lines * (ptrinfo->m_nCurPage - 1);
 CView::OnPrint (ptrdc, ptrinfo);
 // print the footers
 s.Empty ();
 s.LoadString (IDS_FOOTER);
 ptrdc->TextOut (0, footer_y, s);
```

If you desire margins, set up a rectangle with the extents allowed for **OnDraw** to use. Although not done here, you could install a clipping rectangle or region so that **OnDraw** could not draw outside the margins. If you desire margins, then you must make **OnDraw** aware of the available area. The passed **CPrintInfo** structure contains just such a member for this communication, **m_rectDraw**. In **OnPaint** adjust the rectangle to account for your margins and headings and footers. Then, let **OnDraw** use that information in its **TextOut** function calls.

OnEndPrinting just deletes the printer DC we have been using throughout the printing or preview process.

The AcmePlot View Class: Creating a Bar Chart

The plot view presents different challenges. Reexamine Figures 15.1 and 15.2 where the short file and the larger file are displayed on the screen. The static splitter window expands the width of the last view to the unused remainder of the frame window's client area so that there is the maximum space available to display a graph.

Design criteria must include how the width and uniform spacing between the bars are determined. Here, I divide the window's width by two times the number of sales objects +1 so that there can be both left and right margins. However, if there are only a few objects, monster widths would result. Thus, I then force the bar width to be less than the window's width divided by twenty pixels. To be robust, you should also decide what to do when there are too many bars for the given space. Here, I ignored that situation.

To see this effect, run the application and drag the splitter bar to the left, expanding the columnar view while shrinking the plot view and watch what happens. What impact does this design have on the implementation? It simplifies **OnDraw**. As long as the current width and height associated with the passed DC are used for the bar scaling, the drawing function does not need to know anything else. Specifically, this means that the mapping mode and window and viewport extents do not need to be used. Instead, the font can be scaled as indicated in Option 2 in **AcmeView**.

The corresponding year is displayed beneath each bar. When the bar's width becomes so narrow that there is not enough room to fit the four-digit year, I display only the last two digits. Should the bars become even smaller, then I attempt to create a smaller font to squeeze the two digits into the space.

Since no user fonts apply to the plot view and since there is no mechanism for user modifications to the data in this view, the class definition becomes much smaller with most member functions dealing with the printing process.

When you run the application, watch the tool bar buttons; when you click in the plot window, the font, add, update, and delete buttons become grayed. If you then click in the columnar view, they become active once more. This also dictates which view is printed when File|Print or Preview is chosen.

Examine the **AcmePlot** definition file; notice that it likewise must use the **DECLARE_DYNCREATE** and **IMPLEMENT_DYNCREATE** macros so that the framework can dynamically construct instances of the plot class. The member variables parallel those of the **AcmeView** class, storing the average character dimensions and the window's height and width with other save areas defined to save these screen values while printing. The usual printer members are present including the fonts for screen and printer displays and the copied screen's **LOGFONT** used for scaling during construction of the printer font.

AcmePlot Class Definition

```
#pragma once
#include "acmedoc.h" // access to the document

/***************************************************************/
/*                                                             */
/* AcmeView Class Definition                                   */
/*                                                             */
/***************************************************************/

class AcmeView : public CView {

DECLARE_DYNCREATE(AcmeView)

protected:

int avg_caps_width;    // average capital letter width
int avg_char_width;    // average character width
int avg_char_height;   // average character height
int height;            // window height
int width;             // window width
int topline;           // current top line for scrolling
```

```
int selrecnum;          // current record number selected in Red
int sellinenum;         // and its corresponding screen line number
int num_sales;          // current number of SalesData objects
int num_lines_per_page; // the number of lines per page
int max_vscroll_lines;  // maximum number of vert lines to scroll
                        // printing and preview fields
int prt_width;          // character dimensions on print or preview
int prt_height;
int prt_topline;        // top line when printing or preview
int prt_num_lines;      // number of lines per page
CRect    rect_print;    // working area of the printed page
int      footer_y;      // location of footer on a page
LOGFONT  prlogfont;     // printer version of user selected font
LOGFONT* ptrlogfont;    // scaled copy of the user font
CFont*   ptrfont;       // the display font in use
CFont*   ptrprfont;     // corresponding printer font in use scaled
CSize    clsize;        // the size of the screen for scaling
CSize    pagesize;      // the size of the printed page for scaling
 /*************************************************************/
 /*                                                           */
 /* Class Functions:                                          */
 /*                                                           */
 /*************************************************************/
public:
         AcmeView ();     // no parms required for serialization
        ~AcmeView ();     // removes any fonts
AcmeDoc* GetDocument (); // returns the doc associated with view
void     OnDraw (CDC*);  // displays a screen or printer page
protected:
BOOL OnPreparePrinting (CPrintInfo*);      // inits Print dialog
void OnBeginPrinting (CDC*, CPrintInfo*); // save screen values
void OnEndPrinting (CDC*, CPrintInfo*);    // restore screen value
void SetupPrinterFont (CDC*, CPrintInfo*);// make a printer font
void OnPrepareDC (CDC*, CPrintInfo*);  // make font-get char dims
void OnPrint (CDC*, CPrintInfo*);      // print heading & footer
void OnInitialUpdate ();               // initial settings
void OnUpdate (CView*, LPARAM, CObject*); // reset settings
void SetOurScrollRange ();             // reset scroll range
void CalcCurrentSelection ();          // maintains cur selection
afx_msg BOOL OnEraseBkgnd (CDC* pDC);  // paint bkground lt gray
afx_msg int  OnCreate (LPCREATESTRUCT);// make fixed font
afx_msg void OnKeyDown (UINT, UINT, UINT); // scroller interface
afx_msg void OnVScroll (UINT, UINT, CScrollBar*);// scroll screen
afx_msg void OnSize (UINT, int, int);  // reset scrolling range
afx_msg void OnLButtonDown (UINT, CPoint); // select a record
afx_msg void OnLButtonDblClk( UINT nFlags, CPoint point );// updt
afx_msg void OnRButtonDown (UINT, CPoint); // context menu
afx_msg void OnFonts ();                   // get new user font
afx_msg void OnAddSalesData ();            // adds new rec at end
afx_msg void OnUpdateSalesData ();         // updates current rec
afx_msg void OnDeleteSalesData ();         // deletes current rec
DECLARE_MESSAGE_MAP()
};
```

Much of the implementation of **AcmePlot** is similar to **AcmeView**. The constructor sets **ptrprfont** to 0. In **OnCreate** the sole display font is created just as it was in **AcmeView**. This font is deleted in the destructor. **GetDocument** returns a pointer to the actual document so that the sales array can be accessed. **OnInitialUpdate** and **OnUpdate** do not even need to be overridden; I included them so that you have a more complete framework for your modifications.

Most of the coding lies in the **OnPrepareDC** and **OnDraw** functions. Let's examine the screen display first and then the printing section. **OnPrepareDC** now becomes quite streamlined. Based on whether this is a printer or screen DC, it selects into the passed DC the correct font.

```
 ptrdc->SelectObject (ptrinfo ? ptrprfont : ptrfont);
```

It then acquires the average character dimensions that **OnDraw** is going to require.

The real work lies in **OnDraw**. After gaining local access to the document and to the sales array, based upon whether the function is printing or not, the local copy of the height and width (**h** and **w**) are set. This is a crucial action, because if all scaling is done based on the local height and width, the drawing becomes independent of the device characteristics.

```
 BOOL isprinting = ptrdc->IsPrinting();// get printing flag
 int h = isprinting ? print_height : height;
 int w = isprinting ? print_width : width;
```

Once these are set, I draw a black border around the entire graph, framing it nicely on the printed page.

```
 // draw an outline around the graph
 ptrdc->SelectStockObject (WHITE_BRUSH);
 ptrdc->SelectStockObject (BLACK_PEN);
 ptrdc->Rectangle (0, 0, w, h);
 ptrdc->SelectStockObject (BLACK_BRUSH);
```

Next, if there are no sales data to plot, I print the title and return. If there are data, the range of sales amounts must be determined to construct the vertical scale. Hence, a pass through all sales objects is made, storing the largest value.

```
 int spacing   = num_sales*2 + 1;
 double mx = ((SalesData*) ptrarray->GetAt (0))->sales;
 int i = 1;
 while (i < num_sales) {  // for all sales objects
  ptrdata = (SalesData*) ptrarray->GetAt (i);
  if (!ptrdata) continue;
  if (mx< ptrdata->sales)
   mx = ptrdata->sales;   // replace if it's bigger
  i++;
 }
```

Now the scaling factors can be determined. Note that the vertical pixels per sales dollar, **vpels_per_val**, must be a double. From the device height total pixels, I removed one character height for the year display across the bottom, and I removed 5 additional pixels to account for the top/bottom border line, another 2 for a one pixel gap between the edge of the bar and the border, plus one pixel gap above the year display. Similarly, the horizontal uniform spacing allows for both a left and right margin. The four accounts for the left/right border and one pixel gap. Again, I avoided monster width bars. You could at this point check for a zero width and force it to be at least a one pixel width.

```
 double vpels_per_val = (h - 5 - 2*avg_char_height) / mx;
 int    hpels_per_val = (w - 4) / spacing;
 if (hpels_per_val > w/20)
  hpels_per_val = w/20; // for few bars, avoid monster bar widths
```

Now the actual plotting of the bars can begin. It is convenient to fix the bottom coordinates — they do not vary from bar to bar — and calculate the height based on the current sales amount. Since the y-axis is positive downward, it looks as if I am plotting backwards.

```
 x = hpels_per_val + 2;        // set initial x pos of first value
 y = h - 3 - avg_char_height; // set bottom y pos of all values
 // now plot all sales bars
 for (i=0; i<num_sales; i++) {
  ptrdata = (SalesData*) ptrarray->GetAt (i);
  if (!ptrdata) continue;
  // get top y position
  yobj = y - (int)( vpels_per_val * ptrdata->sales);
```

```
 // plot this value
 ptrdc->Rectangle (x, yobj, x+hpels_per_val, y);
 // set x for next value
 x += 2*hpels_per_val;
}
```

Notice how easy it is to draw the bars once the scaling details are calculated. Next the title is printed across the top. Next comes the tricky part — displaying the years beneath the bars, an action that can be complicated by narrow bars. The new (x, y) position for the start of the year display is calculated, once more allowing for the single line border and a one pixel gap on all sides. The display action uses two local variables to help sort out the exact situation. If only the last two digits of the year are to be displayed, the **bool which** is set to **true**. Then if the bars are still too narrow, a tiny font is constructed and selected into the DC. The old font is saved in **ptrold**.

```
CString s;
s.LoadString (IDS_ACMETITLE);
ptrdc->TextOut (1, 1, s);
// print captions
x = hpels_per_val + 2;          // set x for first caption
y = h - avg_char_height -1;    // set y for all captions
// if bars are tiny, use last two digits of the year
// if that is still too big, try a smaller font size
CFont *ptrold = 0;            // non-NULL when using smaller font
bool which = false;           // true when using only 2 digits
if (avg_char_width*4 > hpels_per_val) {
 // is there room for whole year?
 if (avg_char_width*2 > hpels_per_val) {
  // is there room for 2 digits?
  CFont smallfont;
  // construct a smaller font based upon display or printer dims
  if (isprinting)
   smallfont.CreateFont ((int)(-8*savescale), 0, 0, 0,FW_NORMAL,
            FALSE, FALSE, FALSE, ANSI_CHARSET, OUT_TT_PRECIS,
            CLIP_TT_ALWAYS, DEFAULT_QUALITY, DEFAULT_PITCH,
            "Courier New");
  else
   smallfont.CreateFont (8, 0, 0, 0, FW_NORMAL, FALSE, FALSE,
            FALSE, ANSI_CHARSET, OUT_TT_PRECIS,
            CLIP_TT_ALWAYS, DEFAULT_QUALITY, DEFAULT_PITCH,
            "Courier New");
  ptrold = ptrdc->SelectObject (&smallfont);
  which = true;     // set using 2 digits only
 }
 else which = true; // set using 2 digits only
}
```

If the average character width times the four digits exceed the bar width (**hpels_per_value**), **which** is set to **true**. Additionally, if the character width times 2 digits exceeds the bar width, make a smaller font. At this point, one must know whether it is a printer font or screen font that must be made, because the printer font must be scaled properly. I arbitrarily chose a smaller font of height 8. As the new font is selected into the DC, the old font is saved in **ptrold** so that it can be reinstalled and the small font deleted. Remember do not delete GDI objects that are selected into an active DC. At last, iterate through the sale object's years and display them underneath the bars. What happens if the bar width is still too small for the small font? Overprinting of the year digits occurs.

```
// now display the year values
for (i=0; i<num_sales; i++) { // for each year
 ptrdata = (SalesData*) ptrarray->GetAt (i);
 if (!ptrdata) continue;
 // make a caption string
 wsprintf (msg, "%d", ptrdata->year);
 if (which)
  ptrdc->TextOut (x, y, &msg[2]);  // use 2 digits for caption
 else
```

```
  ptrdc->TextOut (x, y, msg);       // display full year caption
 x += 2*hpels_per_val;              // advance x for next caption
}
if (ptrold)
 ptrdc->SelectObject (ptrold);      // remove any small font
```

The **AcmePlot** printing process is much simpler than in **AcmeView** primarily because the printing requirements are stripped down to the basics. A few values must be saved and restored; the font created and destroyed as it was in **AcmeView**. **OnPrint** merely has to get the printed page dimensions and invoke the base class's **OnPrint** which in turn invoked **OnDraw** to perform the work Follow through the printing sequence. Notice that it is the same sequence used should Print Preview be selected.

AcmePlot Class Implementation

```
#include "stdafx.h"

#include "AcmeView.h"
#include "SalesData.h"     // access to SalesData object
#include "AddUpdateDlg.h" // access to add update dialog
#include "resource.h"      // access to resource IDs

IMPLEMENT_DYNCREATE(AcmeView, CView)

#define HEAD_LINE     1 // line number on which to display header
#define HEAD_SPACE    2 // number of blank lines after header
#define MAX_LINE_LEN 20 // max line width in characters

/*************************************************************/
/*                                                           */
/* AcmeView Message Map                                      */
/*                                                           */
/*************************************************************/

BEGIN_MESSAGE_MAP(AcmeView, CView)
 ON_WM_VSCROLL ()
 ON_WM_ERASEBKGND ()
 ON_WM_KEYDOWN ()
 ON_WM_LBUTTONDOWN ()
 ON_WM_LBUTTONDBLCLK ()
 ON_WM_RBUTTONDOWN ()
 ON_WM_SIZE ()
 ON_WM_CREATE ()
 ON_COMMAND(ID_FILE_PRINT,          CView::OnFilePrint)
 ON_COMMAND(ID_FILE_PRINT_PREVIEW, CView::OnFilePrintPreview)
 ON_COMMAND(CM_FONTS,               OnFonts)
 ON_COMMAND(CM_ADD,                 OnAddSalesData)
 ON_COMMAND(CM_UPDATE,              OnUpdateSalesData)
 ON_COMMAND(CM_DELETE,              OnDeleteSalesData)
END_MESSAGE_MAP()

/*************************************************************/
/*                                                           */
/* AcmeView: Construct the view object                      */
/*                                                           */
/*************************************************************/

AcmeView::AcmeView () : CView () {
 topline = 0;       // sales array index of top line on the screen
 selrecnum = 0;     // sales array index of current selection
 sellinenum = HEAD_LINE + HEAD_SPACE; // current selection line
 ptrprfont = 0;     // set for no printer font as yet
 ptrlogfont = 0;
}
```

```

/**************************************************************/
/*                                                            */
/* OnCreate: build the window & make display font             */
/*                                                            */
/**************************************************************/

int AcmeView::OnCreate (LPCREATESTRUCT lpCS) {
 int retcd = CView::OnCreate (lpCS); // pass along to base class
 // make an initial Courier New font
 ptrfont = new CFont ();
 ptrfont->CreateFont (14, 0, 0, 0, FW_NORMAL, FALSE, FALSE,
             FALSE, ANSI_CHARSET, OUT_TT_PRECIS, CLIP_TT_ALWAYS,
             DEFAULT_QUALITY, DEFAULT_PITCH, "Courier New");
 return retcd;
}

/**************************************************************/
/*                                                            */
/* OnEraseBkgnd: patin background light gray                  */
/*                                                            */
/**************************************************************/

BOOL AcmeView::OnEraseBkgnd (CDC* pDC) {
 pDC->SelectStockObject (LTGRAY_BRUSH);
 CRect r;
 GetClientRect (&r);
 pDC->PatBlt (r.left, r.top, r.Width(), r.Height (), PATCOPY);
 return TRUE;
}

/**************************************************************/
/*                                                            */
/* ~AcmeView: remove all fonts that were used                 */
/*                                                            */
/**************************************************************/

AcmeView::~AcmeView () {
 if (ptrfont)
  delete ptrfont;
 if (ptrlogfont)
  delete ptrlogfont;
}

/**************************************************************/
/*                                                            */
/* GetDocument: retrieve a pointer to the main document       */
/*                                                            */
/**************************************************************/

AcmeDoc* AcmeView::GetDocument () {
 return (AcmeDoc*) m_pDocument;
}

/**************************************************************/
/*                                                            */
/* OnInitialUpdate: nothing to do initially, but coded so you */
/*                  can see where to place items that must be */
/*                  done before OnUpdate is called and painting*/
/*                                                            */
/**************************************************************/

void AcmeView::OnInitialUpdate () {
 CView::OnInitialUpdate (); // this calls OnUpdate next
```

```
}

/*************************************************************/
/*                                                           */
/* OnUpdate: reset num_sales, scroll range, current selection */
/*                                                           */
/*************************************************************/

void AcmeView::OnUpdate (CView *ptrsender, LPARAM hint,
                         CObject *ptrdata) {
 // obtain the current number of entries in the sales array
 num_sales = GetDocument ()->GetNumSales ();
 // the next two lines are not needed here because in this case
 // I am letting OnPrepareDC determine tha avg character dims
 // and then call these two functions. If you already have
 // calculated the character dimensions, then these two
 // calls below set up the scrolling properly
 SetOurScrollRange ();     // set scroll range based on num recs
 CalcCurrentSelection (); // update current user selected record
 // base class then calls OnPaint which calls OnPrepareDC and
 // OnDraw, in that order
 CView::OnUpdate (ptrsender, hint, ptrdata);
}

/*************************************************************/
/*                                                           */
/* OnPrepareDC: setup printer or screen DC by                */
/*              inserting the fixed font and mode            */
/*                                                           */
/*************************************************************/

void AcmeView::OnPrepareDC (CDC *ptrdc, CPrintInfo *ptrinfo) {
 CView::OnPrepareDC (ptrdc, ptrinfo); // let base class make DCs
 TEXTMETRIC  tm;

 if (ptrinfo) {                      // Printer or Preview this time
  // Option 1: use mode and extents
  ptrdc->SetMapMode (MM_ANISOTROPIC); // scaling on both axis
  ptrdc->SetWindowExt (clsize);       // window size to screen sz
  ptrdc->SetViewportExt (pagesize);   // viewport to printer page

  // Option 2: no mode and extents
  // use scaling factors in setup print font
  // so remove Option 1 above three lines
  ptrdc->SelectObject (ptrprfont);    // install printer font
  if (!ptrinfo->m_bPreview) {         // is printer this time
   ptrinfo->m_bContinuePrinting = TRUE;
  }
  else {
   // set continue printing flag for preview
   ptrinfo->m_bContinuePrinting = TRUE;
  }
 }
 else {                              // paint screen dc this time
  ptrdc->SelectObject (ptrfont);     // install fixed font
  ptrdc->GetTextMetrics (&tm);       // get the font information
  // calculate average character parameters
  avg_char_width  = tm.tmAveCharWidth;
  avg_char_height = tm.tmHeight + tm.tmExternalLeading;
  avg_caps_width  = (tm.tmPitchAndFamily & 1 ? 3 : 2) *
                     avg_char_width / 2;
  SetOurScrollRange ();   // set scroll bar range using real font
  CalcCurrentSelection ();// update current user selected record
 }
```

```
}

/***********************************************************/
/*                                                         */
/* OnDraw: display the document as a table on screen or printer*/
/*                                                         */
/***********************************************************/

void AcmeView::OnDraw (CDC *ptrdc) {
 char msg[80];
 AcmeDoc *ptrdoc = GetDocument ();   // acquire access to the doc
 SalesDataArray* ptrarray = &ptrdoc->sales_array;
 SalesData* ptrdata;                 // will point to SalesData
 int line = HEAD_LINE;               // the current line to show
 // get a flag that we can use to tell if we are printing or not
 BOOL isprinting = ptrdc->IsPrinting();
 ptrdc->SetBkMode (TRANSPARENT);  // set transparent display mode

 int start;     // these are the subscripts into the array to show
 int end;       // depending upon whether printing or on screen
 int char_height; // print or screen character dimensions
 int char_width;

 if (!isprinting) { // if on screen display, display column heads
  // set the starting and ending subscripts to show
  start = topline;
  end = min (num_sales - topline, num_lines_per_page) + topline;
  // set the screen character dimensions
  char_height = avg_char_height;
  char_width = avg_char_width;

  // display headings as raised areas above columns of data
  CString yrs, sls;
  yrs.LoadString (IDS_YEARS);
  sls.LoadString (IDS_SALES);
  ptrdc->SelectStockObject (WHITE_PEN);

  // draw years box and show "Year" in it
  CRect ryr (4*avg_char_width, line*avg_char_height-3,
             10*avg_char_width, (line+1)*avg_char_height+3);
  ptrdc->MoveTo (ryr.right, ryr.top);
  ptrdc->LineTo (ryr.left,  ryr.top);
  ptrdc->LineTo (ryr.left,  ryr.bottom);
  ptrdc->SelectStockObject (BLACK_PEN);
  ptrdc->LineTo (ryr.right, ryr.bottom);
  ptrdc->LineTo (ryr.right, ryr.top);
  ptrdc->TextOut (5*avg_char_width, avg_char_height, yrs);

  // draw sales box and show "Sales" in it
  CRect rsl (13*avg_char_width, line*avg_char_height-3,
             21*avg_char_width, (line+1)*avg_char_height+3);
  ptrdc->SelectStockObject (WHITE_PEN);
  ptrdc->MoveTo (rsl.right, rsl.top);
  ptrdc->LineTo (rsl.left,  rsl.top);
  ptrdc->LineTo (rsl.left,  rsl.bottom);
  ptrdc->SelectStockObject (BLACK_PEN);
  ptrdc->LineTo (rsl.right, rsl.bottom);
  ptrdc->LineTo (rsl.right, rsl.top);
  ptrdc->TextOut (15*avg_char_width, avg_char_height*line, sls);
 }
 else {
  // printing or preview - set the starting and ending subscripts
  start = prt_topline;
  end = min (num_sales - prt_topline, prt_num_lines)+prt_topline;
```

```
  char_height = prt_height;
  char_width = prt_width;
  line++;              // if printing add one line for readability
 }

 // display each sales entry whether or not going to the printer
 line += HEAD_SPACE;  // set line to first data line

 // for each line beginning at the top line offset in the array
 for (int i=start; i<end; i++) {
  // get a pointer to this SalesData object
  ptrdata = (SalesData*) ptrarray->GetAt (i);
  if (!ptrdata) continue;
  // if not printing & this is the selected record,
  // then use Red as the color
  if (!isprinting && line == sellinenum)
   ptrdc->SetTextColor (RGB (255,0,0));

  sprintf_s (msg, sizeof(msg), "%4ld", ptrdata->year);
  ptrdc->TextOut (char_width*5, char_height*line, msg);
  sprintf_s (msg, sizeof(msg), "%8.2f", ptrdata->sales);
  ptrdc->TextOut (char_width*13, char_height*line++,msg);

  // reselect black as the color if needed
  if (!isprinting && line-1 == sellinenum)
   ptrdc->SetTextColor (RGB (0,0,0));
 }
}

/***************************************************************/
/*                                                             */
/* OnFonts: get the user's font choice for printing            */
/*          note that this font is not for displaying on the CRT*/
/*                                                             */
/***************************************************************/

void AcmeView::OnFonts () {
 char  printer[80];
 char *device, *driver, * output, *next;
 CDC* ptrprinterDC = 0;

 // get access to a printer DC from the default installed printer
 GetProfileString ("windows", "device", "...", printer, 80);
 if ( (device = strtok_s (printer, ",", &next)) != 0 &&
      (driver = strtok_s (NULL,    ",", &next)) != 0 &&
      (output = strtok_s (NULL,    ",", &next)) != 0) {
  // a default printer exists, so get a DC for it
  ptrprinterDC = new CDC;
  ptrprinterDC->CreateDC (driver, device, output, NULL);
 }

 // construct an instance of the Choose Fonts dialog
 CFontDialog dlg (ptrlogfont, CF_EFFECTS | CF_PRINTERFONTS |
                  CF_FORCEFONTEXIST, ptrprinterDC, this);
 if (dlg.DoModal () == IDOK) {      // get user font choice
  if (!ptrlogfont)
   ptrlogfont = new LOGFONT;        // 1st time, create LOGFONT
  memcpy (ptrlogfont, &(dlg.m_lf), sizeof (LOGFONT));
  // here notify user that chosen font is only used for printing
  MessageBox ("Use Print Preview to see results",
              "Font Chosen For Printing", MB_OK);
 }
 delete ptrprinterDC;
}
```

```

/**************************************************************/
/*                                                            */
/* OnSize: gets window dims and sets new scroll bar range     */
/*                                                            */
/**************************************************************/

void AcmeView::OnSize (UINT flags, int width, int height) {
 CView::OnSize    (flags, width, height);
 SetOurScrollRange ();      // reset scroll bars ranges
 CalcCurrentSelection ();   // recalc the current selected record
}

/**************************************************************/
/*                                                            */
/* SetOurScrollRange: sets up the new scroll range            */
/*                                                            */
/**************************************************************/

void AcmeView::SetOurScrollRange () {
 CRect rect;
 GetClientRect (&rect);     // get the size of the client window
 height = rect.Height();    // calc and save current height
 width  = rect.Width();     // calc and save current width
 if (height == 0 || width == 0 || avg_char_height == 0) return;

 // calc the number of SalesData objects per page
 num_lines_per_page = height / avg_char_height -
                      (HEAD_LINE + HEAD_SPACE);
 if (num_lines_per_page <1)
  num_lines_per_page = 1; // force at least one
 // set max number of scrolling lines for the range to scroll
 max_vscroll_lines = max (0, num_sales - num_lines_per_page );
 // adjust current top of page index into the Sales array
 topline = min (topline, max_vscroll_lines);
 // then set the scroll range and current thumb bar position
 SetScrollRange (SB_VERT, 0, max_vscroll_lines, FALSE);
 SetScrollPos (SB_VERT, topline, TRUE);
}

/**************************************************************/
/*                                                            */
/* CalcCurrentSelection: set the current selection            */
/*                                                            */
/**************************************************************/

void AcmeView::CalcCurrentSelection () {
 if (selrecnum < topline) {// if selection is no longer on screen
  selrecnum = topline;     // reset cur selection to be top line
  // and set its screen line number
  sellinenum = HEAD_LINE + HEAD_SPACE;
 }
 else if (selrecnum >= topline + num_lines_per_page) {
  // here it's off screen so force cur sel to be last line
  selrecnum = topline + num_lines_per_page;
  // check if this goes off the end of the array
  if (selrecnum >= num_sales) {
   selrecnum = num_sales - 1;  // yes, so make last array item it
   sellinenum = (selrecnum - topline) + HEAD_LINE + HEAD_SPACE;
  }
  else
   sellinenum = HEAD_LINE + HEAD_SPACE + selrecnum - topline;
 }
 else
```

```
  sellinenum = (selrecnum - topline) + HEAD_LINE + HEAD_SPACE;
}

/***************************************************************/
/*                                                             */
/* OnLButtonDown: get current record selection under mouse ptr */
/*                                                             */
/***************************************************************/

void AcmeView::OnLButtonDown (UINT, CPoint point) {
 // calculate the line number clicked upon
 int line = point.y / avg_char_height - HEAD_LINE - HEAD_SPACE;
 // select that line if it is within range
 if (line < 0 || line > num_lines_per_page)
  return; // ignore because it is out of range
 // if it is in range, then select this line
 if (line <= num_sales - topline -1) {
  selrecnum = topline + line;
  sellinenum = line + HEAD_LINE + HEAD_SPACE;
  Invalidate (); // force a repaint to show it highlighted
 }
}

/***************************************************************/
/*                                                             */
/* OnLButtonDblClk: update or delete the current record        */
/*                                                             */
/***************************************************************/

afx_msg void AcmeView::OnLButtonDblClk (UINT, CPoint) {
 OnUpdateSalesData ();
}

/***************************************************************/
/*                                                             */
/* OnRButtonDown: display update/delete menu                   */
/*                                                             */
/***************************************************************/

void AcmeView::OnRButtonDown (UINT, CPoint point) {
 CMenu menu;
 menu.LoadMenu (IDR_UPDT_DEL);
 CMenu* ptrpopup;
 ptrpopup = menu.GetSubMenu (0);
 ClientToScreen (&point);                 // convert coordinates
 ptrpopup->TrackPopupMenu (0, point.x, point.y, this, 0);
}

/***************************************************************/
/*                                                             */
/* OnKeyDown: provides a keyboard scroller interface           */
/*  and allows user to up/down arrow for current record select */
/*                                                             */
/***************************************************************/

void AcmeView::OnKeyDown (UINT key, UINT, UINT) {
 // check for and handle any possible keyboard scroll request
 switch (key) {

  case VK_UP:            // requests scroll up 1 line
   if (selrecnum <= topline)  // if cur rec is off screen, scroll
    SendMessage (WM_VSCROLL, SB_LINEUP, 0L);
   else {                // cur record is on screen, so no scroll
    if (selrecnum -1 <0)
```

```
      break;              // quit if already at the top
     selrecnum--;         // back cur rec selection up by one line
     sellinenum--;
     Invalidate ();       // and force a repaint to show in red
    }
    break;

  case VK_DOWN:           // requests scroll down 1 line
    if (selrecnum + 1 < num_sales) { // can do down one line, so
     selrecnum++;         // set cur record selection down one line
     sellinenum++;
     Invalidate ();       // and force a repaint to show in red
    }
    SendMessage (WM_VSCROLL, SB_LINEDOWN, 0L); break;

  case VK_LEFT:  // requests scroll left 1 col
    SendMessage (WM_HSCROLL, SB_LINEUP, 0L); break;

  case VK_RIGHT: // requests scroll right 1 col
    SendMessage (WM_HSCROLL, SB_LINEDOWN, 0L); break;

  case VK_PRIOR: // request scroll 1 page up
    SendMessage (WM_VSCROLL, SB_PAGEUP, 0L); break;

  case VK_NEXT:  // request scroll 1 page down
    SendMessage (WM_VSCROLL, SB_PAGEDOWN, 0L); break;

  case VK_END:   // request goto the bottom
    SendMessage (WM_HSCROLL, SB_PAGEDOWN, 0L); break;

  case VK_HOME:  // request goto the top
    SendMessage (WM_HSCROLL, SB_PAGEUP, 0L);  break;
 }
}

/*************************************************************/
/*                                                           */
/* OnVScroll: scroll window vertically                       */
/*                                                           */
/*************************************************************/

void AcmeView::OnVScroll (UINT type, UINT pos,
                          CScrollBar *ptrsb) {
 int num_lines_to_scroll;
 switch (type) {

  case SB_LINEUP:       // scroll up 1 line
    num_lines_to_scroll = -1; break;

  case SB_LINEDOWN:    // scroll 1 line down
    num_lines_to_scroll = 1; break;

  case SB_PAGEUP:      // scroll 1 page up
    num_lines_to_scroll = min (-1, -num_lines_per_page); break;

  case SB_PAGEDOWN:    // scroll 1 page down
    num_lines_to_scroll = max (1, num_lines_per_page); break;

  case SB_THUMBTRACK: // follow thumb bar
    num_lines_to_scroll = pos - topline; break;

  default:
    num_lines_to_scroll = 0;
 }
```

```

 num_lines_to_scroll = max (-topline,
                      min (num_lines_to_scroll,
                           max_vscroll_lines - topline));

 if (num_lines_to_scroll !=0) {
  topline +=num_lines_to_scroll;         // add to top line index
  SetScrollPos (SB_VERT, topline, TRUE); // set new scroll pos
  CalcCurrentSelection (); // do any cur record select adjustment
  Invalidate ();           // force repaint to scroll lines
 }
 CView::OnVScroll (type, pos, ptrsb);
}

/*************************************************************/
/*                                                           */
/* OnAdd: add a new sales data record at the end of the set  */
/*                                                           */
/*************************************************************/

void AcmeView::OnAddSalesData () {

 SalesData* ptrdata = new SalesData; // transfer buffer for sales

 AddUpdateDlg add (ptrdata, false, this);
 if (add.DoModal () == IDOK) {
  AcmeDoc *ptrdoc = GetDocument ();  // get access to the doc
  SalesDataArray *ptrarray = &ptrdoc->sales_array;
  ptrarray->Add (ptrdata);      // add the new object to the array
  ptrdoc->SetModifiedFlag (TRUE);// tell doc it has been modified
  // tell document to update all views
  ptrdoc->UpdateAllViews (0, 0, 0);
 }
 else delete ptrdata;
}

/*************************************************************/
/*                                                           */
/* OnUpdate: alter the current record in red                 */
/*                                                           */
/*************************************************************/

void AcmeView::OnUpdateSalesData () {
 bool newdata = false;              // true when new data item
 AcmeDoc *ptrdoc = GetDocument (); // get access to the document
 // get access to the current record to be updated
 SalesData *ptrdata =
            (SalesData*) ptrdoc->sales_array.GetAt (selrecnum);
 if (!ptrdata) { // if it fails to get a record, make a new one
  ptrdata = new SalesData;
  newdata = true;
 }

 AddUpdateDlg update (ptrdata, true, this);
 if (update.DoModal () == IDOK) {
  if (newdata) ptrdoc->sales_array.Add (ptrdata);
  // tell document that it is modified
  ptrdoc->SetModifiedFlag (TRUE);
  // tell doc to update all views
  ptrdoc->UpdateAllViews (0, 0, 0);
 }
 else if (newdata) delete ptrdata;
}

```

```
/***************************************************************/
/*                                                             */
/* OnDelete: remove the current record in red                  */
/*                                                             */
/***************************************************************/

void      AcmeView::OnDeleteSalesData () {
 AcmeDoc *ptrdoc = GetDocument ();      // get access to document
 SalesDataArray *ptrarray = &ptrdoc->sales_array;
 // verify record is there
 if (ptrarray->GetSize () > selrecnum && selrecnum >= 0) {
  SalesData *ptrdata = (SalesData*) ptrarray->GetAt (selrecnum);
  // confirm the deletion request
  CString msg1, msg2;
  msg1.LoadString (IDS_CONFIRM1);
  msg2.LoadString (IDS_CONFIRM2);
  // user confirms, then delete this record
  if (MessageBox (msg2, msg1, MB_YESNO) == IDYES) {
   ptrarray->RemoveAt (selrecnum, 1);// remove ptr from array
   delete ptrdata;                  // delete the Sales object
   selrecnum--;                     // dec current record number
   ptrdoc->SetModifiedFlag (TRUE);   // tell doc it's changed
   ptrdoc->UpdateAllViews (0, 0, 0); // tell doc to update views
  }
 }
}

/***************************************************************/
/*                                                             */
/* OnPreparePrinting: set number of pages for Print dlg        */
/*                                                             */
/***************************************************************/

BOOL AcmeView::OnPreparePrinting (CPrintInfo *ptrinfo) {
 if (ptrinfo->m_bPreview) {
  // guess at the number of pages - will be reset OnBeginPrinting
  ptrinfo->m_nNumPreviewPages = 2;
  ptrinfo->SetMaxPage (2);
 }
 return CView::DoPreparePrinting (ptrinfo);
}

/***************************************************************/
/*                                                             */
/* OnBeginPrinting: save display values, install print values  */
/*                  and the printer font                       */
/*                                                             */
/***************************************************************/

void AcmeView::OnBeginPrinting (CDC *ptrdc, CPrintInfo *ptrinfo){
 prt_topline = 0;                     // set for whole document
 SetupPrinterFont (ptrdc, ptrinfo);  // make up the printer font

 int pages = num_sales / prt_num_lines; // calc # pages to print
 if (num_sales % prt_num_lines > 0) pages++; // round up

 // set the number of preview pages to show
 ptrinfo->m_nNumPreviewPages = pages > 1 ? 2 : 1;
 // set max number of pages to print
 ptrinfo->SetMaxPage (pages);
}

/***************************************************************/
/*                                                             */
```

```
/* OnEndPrinting: ending printing cycles                        */
/*                                                              */
/****************************************************************/

void AcmeView::OnEndPrinting (CDC* /*ptrdc*/,
                              CPrintInfo* /*ptrinfo*/) {
 delete ptrprfont;                      // and remove the print font
}

/****************************************************************/
/*                                                              */
/* SetupPrinterFont: setup the printer font and get avgchardims*/
/*                                                              */
/****************************************************************/

void AcmeView::SetupPrinterFont (CDC *ptrdc, CPrintInfo*) {
 int savedc = ptrdc->SaveDC ();  // save the DC
 // load user's chosen font, if any, and scale TrueType fonts
 if (!ptrlogfont) {          // no user font, so use default font
  // extract the LOGFONT object for scaling
  ptrdc->SelectObject (ptrfont);
  ptrfont->GetObject (sizeof(LOGFONT), &prlogfont);
 }
 else prlogfont = *ptrlogfont;   // assign the user's font

 // Begin Option 1 coding - use mode and extents
 // set screen size to that of a full screen
 CRect clrect (0, 0, GetSystemMetrics (SM_CXSCREEN),
                     GetSystemMetrics (SM_CYSCREEN));
 // clsize holds the size of the screen for window extent
 clsize = clrect.Size();
 // set the printer page size for viewport extent
 pagesize = CSize (ptrdc->GetDeviceCaps (HORZRES),
                   ptrdc->GetDeviceCaps (VERTRES));

 // install mode and scaling effects
 ptrdc->SetMapMode (MM_ANISOTROPIC);
 ptrdc->SetWindowExt (clsize);
 ptrdc->SetViewportExt (pagesize);
 // end Option 1 coding

 // begin Option 2 coding
 /*
 // get a screen DC for scaling
 HDC hdc = CreateDC ("DISPLAY",NULL,NULL,NULL);
 // calculate both x and y scale dimensions between the screen
 // and the printer
 float xscale = ptrdc->GetDeviceCaps (LOGPIXELSX) /
                (float) GetDeviceCaps(hdc, LOGPIXELSX);
 float yscale = ptrdc->GetDeviceCaps (LOGPIXELSY) /
                (float) GetDeviceCaps(hdc, LOGPIXELSY);
 // or scale by true size
 CRect clrect (0, 0, GetSystemMetrics (SM_CXSCREEN),
                     GetSystemMetrics (SM_CYSCREEN));
 CSize clsize = clrect.Size();
 pagesize = CSize (ptrdc->GetDeviceCaps (HORZRES),
                   ptrdc->GetDeviceCaps (VERTRES));

 float xx = pagesize.cx/(float)clsize.cx;
 float yy = pagesize.cy/(float)clsize.cy;
 DeleteDC (hdc);

 // install scaled dimensions
 // scale choice 1:
```

```
// prlogfont.lfHeight = (long) (prlogfont.lfHeight * yscale);
// prlogfont.lfWidth = (long) (prlogfont.lfWidth * xscale);
// scale choice 2:
prlogfont.lfHeight = (long) (prlogfont.lfHeight * yy);
prlogfont.lfWidth = (long) (prlogfont.lfWidth * xx);
*/
// end Option 2 coding

// construct the true printer font from the logfont and install
ptrprfont = new CFont ();
ptrprfont->CreateFontIndirect (&prlogfont);
ptrdc->SelectObject (ptrprfont);

TEXTMETRIC tm;
ptrdc->GetTextMetrics (&tm);        // get the font information
// calculate average character parameters
prt_width  = tm.tmAveCharWidth;
prt_height = tm.tmHeight + tm.tmExternalLeading;

 // calculate pagination data
CPoint pt (ptrdc->GetDeviceCaps (HORZRES),
            ptrdc->GetDeviceCaps (VERTRES));
ptrdc->DPtoLP (&pt);

// setup the full page area
rect_print.SetRect (0, 0, pt.x, pt.y);

 // calculate y location for the footer
footer_y = rect_print.Height () - prt_height -1;
// adjust the printer info drawing rectangle to exclude the
// space occupied by the header and footer
rect_print.top += 4*prt_height;
rect_print.bottom -= prt_height + 1;
// calc the number of data lines that fit on a printed page
// inside the margins
prt_num_lines = rect_print.Height () / prt_height;

ptrdc->RestoreDC (savedc); // restore the DC
}

/**************************************************************/
/*                                                            */
/* OnPrint: handle headings and footers                       */
/*                                                            */
/**************************************************************/

void AcmeView::OnPrint (CDC *ptrdc, CPrintInfo *ptrinfo) {
 // print the title and column headings
 CString s;
 s.LoadString (IDS_ACMETITLE);
 ptrdc->TextOut (0, 0, s);
 s.Empty ();
 s.LoadString (IDS_YEARS);
 ptrdc->TextOut (prt_width*5, 2*prt_height, s);
 s.Empty ();
 s.LoadString (IDS_SALES);
 ptrdc->TextOut (prt_width*13, 2*prt_height, s);

 prt_topline = prt_num_lines * (ptrinfo->m_nCurPage - 1);

 // print the main SalesData objects
 CView::OnPrint (ptrdc, ptrinfo);

 // print the footers
```

```
 s.Empty ();
 s.LoadString (IDS_FOOTER);
 ptrdc->TextOut (0, footer_y, s);
}
```

Using the Multiple Document Interface (MDI): Pgm15b

The last step is to wrap the MDI around the document-view architecture so that multiple documents can be viewed simultaneously. In Figure 15.14, I have launched **Pgm15b**, opened the larger file, and tiled the two MDI child splitter windows. The user can easily compare documents in this manner. You may be pleased to know that no changes are required to any of the document-view files from **Pgm15a** to port them into MDI in **Pgm15b**!

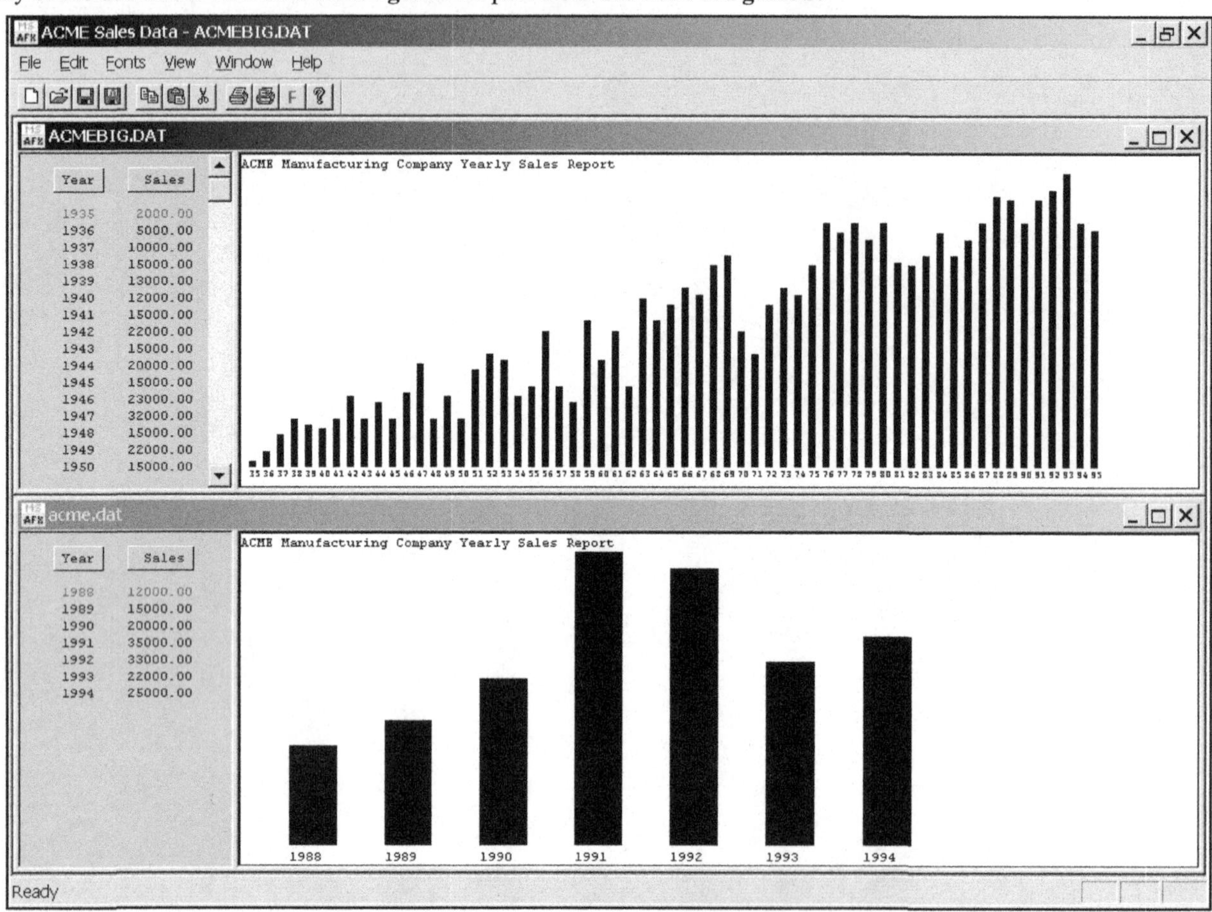

Figure 15.14 **Pgm15b** — the MDI Version with Two Child Views

All changes from SDI to MDI lie at the application and frame window level. The **Pgm15b** class changes occur in the **InitInstance** function which now launches an MDI frame with MDI documents. Specifically, the document templates are now instances of the **CMultiDocTemplate** class; one set is allocated for each view class on the document and then added as before. Then, an MDI frame window is allocated and launched. The other **CWinApp** function calls are the same as in the SDI example.

Pgm15b.cpp Application Class Implementation

```
#include "stdafx.h"
#include "Pgm15b.h"
#include "FrameWin.h"
#include "ChildWin.h"
#include "AcmeDoc.h"
#include "AcmeView.h"
#include "AcmePlot.h"
#include "resource.h"

Pgm15b   theApp;  // launch app

/******************************************************************/
```

```
/*                                                              */
/* Pgm15b: message map                                          */
/*                                                              */
/****************************************************************/

BEGIN_MESSAGE_MAP(Pgm15b,         CWinApp)
 ON_COMMAND(ID_FILE_NEW,          CWinApp::OnFileNew)
 ON_COMMAND(ID_FILE_OPEN,         CWinApp::OnFileOpen)
 ON_COMMAND(ID_FILE_PRINT_SETUP,  CWinApp::OnFilePrintSetup)
 ON_COMMAND(ID_APP_ABOUT,         OnHelpAbout)
END_MESSAGE_MAP()

/****************************************************************/
/*                                                              */
/* InitInstance: allocate instance of our frame main window     */
/*                                                              */
/****************************************************************/

BOOL Pgm15b::InitInstance () {

 // construct two document templates, one for each view
 CMultiDocTemplate *ptrdoctemplate1;
 ptrdoctemplate1 = new CMultiDocTemplate(IDR_MAINFRAME,
                                  RUNTIME_CLASS (AcmeDoc),
                                  RUNTIME_CLASS (ChildWin),
                                  RUNTIME_CLASS (AcmeView));
 CMultiDocTemplate *ptrdoctemplate2;
 ptrdoctemplate2 = new CMultiDocTemplate(IDR_MAINFRAME,
                                  RUNTIME_CLASS (AcmeDoc),
                                  RUNTIME_CLASS (ChildWin),
                                  RUNTIME_CLASS (AcmePlot));

 // install both templates
 AddDocTemplate (ptrdoctemplate1);
 AddDocTemplate (ptrdoctemplate2);

 m_nCmdShow = SW_SHOWMAXIMIZED;  // main window to be maximized

 EnableShellOpen ();           // enable DDE Execute open
 RegisterShellFileTypes ();    // register .DAT types for DDE open
 LoadStdProfileSettings (4);   // activates Most Recent File menu

 // create main MDI Frame window
 FrameWin* ptrframe = new FrameWin;
 if (!ptrframe->LoadFrame (IDR_MAINFRAME)) return FALSE;
 m_pMainWnd = ptrframe;

 // The main window has been initialized, so show and update it.
 ptrframe->ShowWindow (SW_SHOWMAXIMIZED);

 // determine which document file to open first
 if (m_lpCmdLine[0] == 0) // none on cmd line, so use default
  OpenDocumentFile ("acme.dat");
                          // or use: OnFileNew (); for a new file
 else OpenDocumentFile (m_lpCmdLine); // open file on cmd line

 if (m_pMainWnd->GetSafeHwnd())
  m_pMainWnd->DragAcceptFiles (); // enable drag and drop open
 return TRUE;
}

/****************************************************************/
/*                                                              */
```

```
/* OnHelpAbout: shows who wrote this app                           */
/*                                                                 */
/*******************************************************************/

void Pgm15b::OnHelpAbout () {
 // informational modal dialog
 CDialog aboutdlg ("IDD_ABOUT");
 aboutdlg.DoModal ();
}
```

Only a few changes are needed in the resource file. I added a few new strings to assist the MDI cascading and tiling operations.

```
ID_WINDOW_NEW         "Open another window for the active document\nNew Window"
ID_WINDOW_ARRANGE     "Arrange icons at the bottom of the window\nArrange Icons"
ID_WINDOW_CASCADE     "Arrange windows so they overlap\nCascade Windows"
ID_WINDOW_TILE_HORZ "Arrange windows as non-overlapping tiles\nTile Windows"
ID_WINDOW_TILE_VERT "Arrange windows as non-overlapping tiles\nTile Windows"
```

I added the MDI icon to be used for each child MDI window.

```
IDR_MDITYPE               ICON     DISCARDABLE      "mdidoc.ico"
```

I added the pop-up Window menu which handles MDI child windows.

```
    POPUP "&Window"
    BEGIN
        MENUITEM "&New Window",                     ID_WINDOW_NEW
        MENUITEM "&Cascade",                        ID_WINDOW_CASCADE
        MENUITEM "&Tile",                         ID_WINDOW_TILE_HORZ
        MENUITEM "&Arrange Icons",                  ID_WINDOW_ARRANGE
        MENUITEM "S&plit",                          ID_WINDOW_SPLIT
    END
```

Note that we do not need to insert any coding for these. With these ID_ identifiers, the framework automatically performs window maintenance for us.

The frame window is derived from **CMDIFrameWnd**. Its basic function is to construct and maintain the tool and status bars. All splitter window coding has been moved from the frame down to the MDI child windows.

FrameWin Class Definition

```
#pragma once

/*******************************************************************/
/*                                                                 */
/* FrameWin Class Definition                                       */
/*                                                                 */
/*******************************************************************/

class FrameWin : public CMDIFrameWnd {

DECLARE_DYNCREATE (FrameWin)

 /******************************************************************/
 /*                                                                */
 /* Class Data:                                                    */
 /*                                                                */
 /******************************************************************/

protected:

CToolBar      toolbar;     // the control bar
CStatusBar    statusbar;   // the status bar

```

```
/*************************************************************/
/*                                                           */
/* Class Functions:                                          */
/*                                                           */
/*************************************************************/

public:
              FrameWin () : CMDIFrameWnd () {}

protected:
         BOOL PreCreateWindow(CREATESTRUCT&);// set wndclass style
afx_msg int  OnCreate(LPCREATESTRUCT); // make tool & status bars

DECLARE_MESSAGE_MAP()
};
```

FrameWin Class Implementation

```
#include "stdafx.h"
#include "FrameWin.h"
#include "resource.h"

IMPLEMENT_DYNCREATE(FrameWin, CMDIFrameWnd)

// control bar buttons - IDs are command buttons
static UINT BASED_CODE buttons[] =
{
  // same order as in the bitmap 'toolbar.bmp'
  ID_FILE_NEW,
  ID_FILE_OPEN,
  ID_FILE_SAVE,
  ID_FILE_SAVE_AS,
  ID_SEPARATOR,
  CM_ADD,
  CM_UPDATE,
  CM_DELETE,
  ID_SEPARATOR,
  ID_FILE_PRINT,
  ID_FILE_PRINT_PREVIEW,
  CM_FONTS,
  ID_APP_ABOUT,
};

static UINT BASED_CODE indicators[] =
{
  ID_SEPARATOR,            // status line indicator
  ID_INDICATOR_CAPS,
  ID_INDICATOR_NUM,
  ID_INDICATOR_SCRL,
};

/*************************************************************/
/*                                                           */
/* FrameWin Message Map                                      */
/*                                                           */
/*************************************************************/

BEGIN_MESSAGE_MAP(FrameWin, CMDIFrameWnd)
 ON_WM_CREATE ()
END_MESSAGE_MAP()

/*************************************************************/
/*                                                           */
```

```
/* PreCreateWindow: assign style options                           */
/*                                                                 */
/*****************************************************************/

BOOL FrameWin::PreCreateWindow(CREATESTRUCT& cs) {
 cs.style = WS_OVERLAPPED | WS_CAPTION | FWS_ADDTOTITLE
          | WS_THICKFRAME | WS_SYSMENU | WS_MINIMIZEBOX
          | WS_MAXIMIZEBOX | WS_MAXIMIZE;
 return CMDIFrameWnd::PreCreateWindow(cs);
}

/*****************************************************************/
/*                                                                 */
/* OnCreate: construct status and control bars                     */
/*                                                                 */
/*****************************************************************/

int FrameWin::OnCreate (LPCREATESTRUCT lpCS) {
 if (CMDIFrameWnd::OnCreate (lpCS) == 0)
  if (toolbar.Create (this) && toolbar.LoadBitmap (IDR_MAINFRAME)
      && toolbar.SetButtons (buttons,
                             sizeof(buttons) / sizeof(UINT)))
   if (statusbar.Create (this)
       && statusbar.SetIndicators (indicators,
                             sizeof(indicators) / sizeof(UINT)));
   else return -1;
  else return -1;
 else return -1;

 toolbar.EnableDocking (CBRS_ALIGN_ANY);
 EnableDocking (CBRS_ALIGN_ANY);
 DockControlBar (&toolbar);
 toolbar.SetBarStyle (
            toolbar.GetBarStyle() | CBRS_TOOLTIPS | CBRS_FLYBY);
 toolbar.SetWindowText ("Toolbar");
 return 0;
}
```

The coding to create the splitter windows is moved into the **OnCreate** of the **ChildWin** MDI child class.

ChildWin Class Definition

```
#pragma once

/*****************************************************************/
/*                                                                 */
/* ChildWin Class Definition                                       */
/*                                                                 */
/*****************************************************************/

class ChildWin : public CMDIChildWnd {

DECLARE_DYNCREATE (ChildWin)

 /****************************************************************/
 /*                                                               */
 /* Class Data:                                                   */
 /*                                                               */
 /****************************************************************/

protected:

CSplitterWnd splitterwin; // our splitter window
```

```

/*************************************************************/
/*                                                           */
/* Class Functions:                                          */
/*                                                           */
/*************************************************************/

public:
            ChildWin () {}   // constructor

virtual BOOL PreCreateWindow(CREATESTRUCT&); // install style

// make the splitter windows with two views
virtual BOOL OnCreateClient(LPCREATESTRUCT, CCreateContext*);

DECLARE_MESSAGE_MAP()
};
```

ChildWin Class Implementation

```
#include "stdafx.h"

#include "ChildWin.h"
#include "AcmeView.h"
#include "AcmePlot.h"
#include "resource.h"

IMPLEMENT_DYNCREATE(ChildWin, CMDIChildWnd)

/*************************************************************/
/*                                                           */
/* ChildWin Message Map                                      */
/*                                                           */
/*************************************************************/

BEGIN_MESSAGE_MAP(ChildWin, CMDIChildWnd)
END_MESSAGE_MAP()

/*************************************************************/
/*                                                           */
/* OnCreateClient: construct client window                   */
/*                                                           */
/*************************************************************/

BOOL ChildWin::OnCreateClient (LPCREATESTRUCT,
                               CCreateContext* ptrc) {

 // construct the splitter window itself
 // by asking for two side by side views
 BOOL retcd = splitterwin.CreateStatic (this, 1, 2);

 // set AcmeView as left window - use width of 180 pixels
 retcd |= splitterwin.CreateView (0, 0, RUNTIME_CLASS (AcmeView),
                                  CSize (180, 100), ptrc);
 retcd |= splitterwin.CreateView (0, 1, RUNTIME_CLASS (AcmePlot),
                                  CSize (100, 100), ptrc);
 return retcd;
}

/*************************************************************/
/*                                                           */
/* PreCreateWindow: set the window style bits                */
/*                                                           */
```

```
/*****************************************************************/

BOOL ChildWin::PreCreateWindow (CREATESTRUCT& cs) {
 cs.style = WS_CHILD | WS_VISIBLE | WS_OVERLAPPED | WS_CAPTION
            | WS_SYSMENU | FWS_ADDTOTITLE | WS_THICKFRAME
            | WS_MINIMIZEBOX | WS_MAXIMIZEBOX | WS_MAXIMIZE;
 return CMDIChildWnd::PreCreateWindow(cs);
}
```

Thus, with minimal coding changes, we now can open multiple documents at the same time. Note that each time we open a new document file, the MDI framework launches a new instance of the document, child, and view classes. This is very different than SDI behavior which simply reuses the current document class instance.

Programming Problems

Pgm15-1 — Acme Inventory Program Final Revision

Revise the Acme Inventory Program, **Pgm14-1** or an earlier version, to use the document-view architecture.

Use the AppWizard to create a basic MDI shell program. Call the classes **AcmeSalesDoc** and **AcmeSalesView**.

Next, flesh out the **AcmeSalesDoc** by overriding **OnOpenDocument**. Create **CFile** instance using the passed filename and dynamically allocate new **InvMast** structure instances, reading in each instance, and adding that pointer to a **CPtrArray**. **OnSaveDocument** should output each instance in the array. **DeleteContents** should delete each instance and empty the array.

The **ChildWin** class should display the file name in the window caption.

Next, flesh out the **AcmeSalesView** by adding the normal display coding of each instance stored in the document's array. Make sure that there are column headings above the column headings and that the column headings do not scroll. Add in scrolling support. Add in font support.

Decide whether the document or view class is to handle the Add, Update, and Delete menu choices and implement them.

Upgrade the tool bar buttons and status bar to support the choices you desire, but at least the Add, Update, and Delete choices should be on the tool bar.

Then, add in the Mark up Percentage tool box into the **ChildWin** class. Respond to these choices in the view class.

Finally, add in all other support of features that you have in your previous program. Thoroughly test your program.

Congratulations. You have made it through basic Windows Programming!

What should you do next? Don't stop now. There's much more to learn about the MFC. Get my Windows MFC Programming II and III books, which will take you to the advanced MFC programming level!

Made in the USA
Las Vegas, NV
10 February 2024